SETTLEMENT, SOCIETY AND COGNITION IN HUMAN EVOLUTION

This volume provides a landscape narrative of early hominin evolution, linking conventional material and geographic aspects of the early archaeological record with wider and more elusive social, cognitive and symbolic landscapes. It seeks to move beyond a limiting notion of early hominin culture and behaviour as dictated solely by the environment to present the early hominin world as the outcome of a dynamic dialogue between the physical environment and its perception and habitation by active agents. This international group of contributors presents theoretically informed yet empirically based perspectives on hominin and human landscapes.

Fiona Coward is Lecturer in Archaeological Science at Bournemouth University. Her research has been published in a variety of journals including *Science*, the *Journal of Archaeological Science* and the *Cambridge Archaeological Journal*, as well as in several edited volumes including *The Cognitive Life of Things* (2010) and *The Sapient Mind* (2009). She has been associate editor for archaeology for the *Journal of the Royal Anthropological Institute* since September 2013.

Robert Hosfield is Associate Professor in Palaeolithic Archaeology at the Department of Archaeology, University of Reading. He has directed excavations in Britain and conducted fieldwork in Sudan. He is co-editor of *Quaternary History & Palaeolithic Archaeology in the Axe Valley at Broom* (2013). His work has also been published in the *Journal of Quaternary Science*, *Quaternary Science Reviews*, the *Journal of Archaeological Science* and the *Proceedings of the Prehistoric Society*.

Matt Pope is a Senior Research Fellow at the Institute of Archaeology, University College London. His doctoral research, supervised by Clive Gamble, focused on Lower Palaeolithic archaeology at Boxgrove. He has directed Palaeolithic excavations, including his current investigation of the Neanderthal site of La Cotte de St. Brelade, Jersey, and published on early human behaviour. He is a Fellow of the Society of Antiquaries and a council member of the Prehistoric Society.

Francis Wenban-Smith is Principal Research Fellow in the Department of Archaeology, University of Southampton. He has directed Palaeolithic investigations at numerous British sites including Swanscombe and Baker's Hole. He led Palaeolithic work for the High Speed 1 rail-link, leading to the monographs *The Ebbsfleet Elephant* and *Prehistoric Ebbsfleet*. He has published work in *Proceedings of the Prehistoric Society*, *Journal of Quaternary Science* and *Journal of Archaeological Science*, as well as many edited volumes.

Professor Clive Gamble: Trustee of the British Museum; Fellow of the British Academy; Fellow and former Vice President of the Society of Antiquaries; Fellow and former President of the Royal Anthropological Institute, and supervisor of more than 30 PhD students, many of whom are now Professors, Associate Professors, Senior Lecturers, Lecturers and Researchers of all levels across the UK and internationally.

SETTLEMENT, SOCIETY AND COGNITION IN HUMAN EVOLUTION

Landscapes in mind

FIONA COWARD

Bournemouth University

ROBERT HOSFIELD

University of Reading

MATT POPE

University College London

FRANCIS WENBAN-SMITH

University of Southampton

CAMBRIDGE
UNIVERSITY PRESS

CAMBRIDGE
UNIVERSITY PRESS

32 Avenue of the Americas, New York, NY 10013-2473, USA

Cambridge University Press is part of the University of Cambridge.

It furthers the University's mission by disseminating knowledge in the pursuit of
education, learning, and research at the highest international levels of excellence.

www.cambridge.org
Information on this title: www.cambridge.org/9781107026889

© Cambridge University Press 2015

First published 2015

Printed in the United States of America by Sheridan Books, Inc.

A catalog record for this publication is available from the British Library.

Library of Congress Cataloging in Publication Data
Settlement, society and cognition in human evolution : landscapes in mind / [edited by] Fiona Coward
(Royal Holloway University of London), Robert Hosfield (University of Reading), Matt Pope
(University College London), Francis Wenban-Smith (University of Southampton).
        pages   cm
Includes bibliographical references and index.
ISBN 978-1-107-02688-9 (Hardback)
1. Human evolution–Social aspects.   2. Human settlements–History–To 1500.   3. Cognition
and culture–History–To 1500.   4. Material culture–History–To 1500.   5. Prehistoric
peoples.   6. Antiquities, Prehistoric.   7. Paleolithic period.   8. Social archaeology.
9. Landscape archaeology.   I. Coward, Fiona Susan.   II. Hosfield, Robert.
III. Pope, Matthew (Archaeologist)   IV. Wenban-Smith, F. F. (Francis F.)
GN281.4.S48 2015
599.93′8–dc23   2014024992

ISBN 978-1-107-02688-9 Hardback

CONTENTS

FIGURES

TABLES

CONTRIBUTORS

Nick Ashton
Department of Prehistory and Europe, British Museum

Corrie C. Bakels
Faculty of Archaeology, Leiden University

Ofer Bar-Yosef
Department of Anthropology, Harvard University

James S. Brink
Florisbad Quaternary Research, National Museum, South Africa/Centre for Environmental Management, University of the Free State, South Africa

James Cole
University of Brighton

Robin Dunbar
Department of Experimental Psychology, University of Oxford

Paraskevi Elefanti
Ephoria of Palaeoanthropology and Speleology of Southern Greece, Athens

Sabine Gaudzinski-Windheuser
MONREPOS Archaeological Research Centre and Museum for Human Behavioural Evolution, Römisch-Germanisches Zentralmuseum, Germany

Chris Gosden
School of Archaeology, University of Oxford

John A. J. Gowlett
School of Archaeology, Classics and Egyptology, University of Liverpool

Matt Grove
School of Archaeology, Classics and Egyptology, University of Liverpool

Andy I. R. Herries
Australian Archaeomagnetism Laboratory, La Trobe University, and Geomagnetism Laboratory, School of Environmental Sciences, University of Liverpool

Sally Hoare
ACE, Department of Archaeology, Classics and Egyptology, University of Liverpool

Olaf Jöris
MONREPOS Archaeological Research Centre and Museum for Human Behavioural Evolution, Römisch-Germanisches Zentralmuseum, Germany

Sander E. van der Leeuw
School of Sustainability, Arizona State University and Sante Fe Institute

Gilbert Marshall
Wiener Laboratory, American School of Classical Studies, Athens

Steven Mithen
University of Reading

Margherita Mussi
Università di Roma "La Sapienza"

Isaya Onjala
National Museums of Kenya

Paul Pettitt
Department of Archaeology, University of Durham

Martin Porr
Archaeology/Centre for Rock-Art Research and Management, The University of Western Australia

Dwight W. Read
Department of Anthropology, University of California at Los Angeles

Wil Roebroeks
Institute of Prehistory, Leiden University

Stephen M. Rucina
Earth Science Department, National Museums of Kenya

Anthony Sinclair
School of Archaeology, Classics and Egyptology, University of Liverpool

Mark J. White
Department of Archaeology, Durham University

Rebecca Wragg Sykes
PACEA UMR-5199, Université Bordeaux 1

ACKNOWLEDGEMENTS

PORR, M.

This paper has profited from a large number of people over the years; none are responsible for the views expressed in this contribution. I was fortunate to be able to complete my Ph.D. under the supervision of Clive Gamble at Southampton University, and I profited very much from the vibrant research environment to which he contributed there. Most recently, I was fortunate to be able to work with three research students (honours) at the University of Western Australia: Samara Allen, Matthew Dix and Jessica Doyle. They have all provided invaluable bibliographical information, discussion and ideas that have enhanced this contribution.

GOWLETT, J. A. J., BRINK, J. S., HERRIES, A. I. R., HOARE, S., ONJALA, I. AND RUCINA, S. M.

Our thanks are owed to many others, including Derek Roe, the late Bill Bishop, Glynn Isaac and Pat Carter; to Willy Jones, Laura Basell, Fabienne Marret-Davies, Darren Curnoe, Robin Crompton, Stephen Lycett, Ginette Warr, Sian Davies, Mimi Hill and Natalie Uomini; as well as to colleagues in the Social Brain project – most notably Clive Gamble, and Robin Dunbar. JAJG is grateful for support from the British Academy Centenary Project, AHRC, and help and permissions from the President's Office and National Museums of Kenya, especially Emma Mbua. AIRH acknowledges the support of an Australian Research Fellowship linked to ARC Discovery Grant DP087760 and funding from UNSW Faculty of Medicine. We also thank especially Maura Butler and last, but most certainly not least, Jean-Claude (J.C.) Tubiana, recently departed and much missed.

SINCLAIR, A.

I would like to thank the participants at a workshop on lithic technology and skill at the University of Boulder, Colorado, in 2002, and the participants at the Skilled Production and Social Reproduction Workshop at the University of

Uppsala in 2003, for stimulating some of my early thinking on differential expertise contained within the paper. I would also like to thank two anonymous referees for their comments on an earlier draft of this paper alerting me both to new work in this area and considerably sharpening the thinking and language in this paper. All errors, of course, remain my own.

WRAGG SYKES, R.

I have been trying to write about Neanderthal birch pitch technology for a long time, and I have benefited from discussion with many people including Wil Roebroeks, Monica Knul, Rob Dinnis and especially Ana Jorge and Jeff Oliver who commented on several previous drafts. I also thank Alfred Pawlik for discussion over the past few years on the technology of birch pitch production, and especially for allowing me to include unpublished information about Inden-Altdorf. Thanks also to three anonymous commenters whose suggestions greatly improved this chapter.

I am very grateful to the editors for inviting me to contribute; my thinking on many topics in Palaeolithic archaeology has been shaped by Clive Gamble's boundary-pushing work, especially his inspiring teaching and supervision during my MA studies at Southampton. I hope that this chapter expresses the debt I owe and contributes something new at the same time. Any errors are my own.

ASHTON, N.

I would like to thank Simon Lewis for providing useful comments on the first draft of this paper and to Kathy MacDonald and an anonymous referee for further helpful suggestions. I also thank Simon Parfitt, Chris Stringer, Wil Roebroeks, Robin Dennell, Andreu Ollé and Marina Mosquera for fruitful discussions. I am also very grateful to Dave Horne for providing the present-day climate data for Figure 8.2 and to Craig Williams for producing Figure 8.1. Finally I would like to thank Clive Gamble for setting a research agenda over 25 years ago that has dominated much of my own and others research. This paper is a contribution to the *Pathways into Ancient Britain Project* funded by the Calleva Foundation.

ELEFANTI, V. AND MARSHALL, G.

We are grateful to the editors for their invitation to contribute to the volume as well as to Curtis Runnels, Panagiotis Karkanas and two anonymous reviewers for their valuable comments on earlier versions of the manuscript. The 'Prehistoric Stones of Greece' project was funded by an AHRC Resource Enhancement Grant and has also received a publication subvention grant by the Institute for Aegean Prehistory (INSTAP). Our biggest thanks however, are due to Clive who has been an enthusiastic and unfailing guide on our personal journey into the deepest human past and who taught us about the complexity of the – seemingly – unchanging Palaeolithic record.

ROEBROEKS, W. AND BAKELS, C.

We are grateful to our colleagues involved in the Neumark-Nord 2 project, especially to Wim Kuijper (Leiden). Richard Cosgrove (Melbourne) was instrumental in making the Tasmania evidence accessible, while Francis Wenban-Smith (Southampton) and three anonymous referees provided useful comments on an earlier draft of the paper. We thank Joanne Porck (Leiden) for her work on the figures. WR gratefully acknowledges support by the Humboldt Foundation, Germany.

BAR-YOSEF, O.

I thank the editors of this volume for inviting me to take part in a project honoring Clive Gamble for his contributions to world-wide prehistoric research. I thank the three anonymous reviewers who made substantial contributions for improving an earlier manuscript. I am grateful to Harvard China Fund, Asia Center and the American School of Prehistoric Research (Peabody Museum) Harvard University who funded my research in China. Without the cooperation of my Chinese colleagues Prof. Y. Wang, Prof. X. Xiaohong, Dr. T. Qu (School of Archaeology and Museology, Peking University), Prof. J. Xi (Director, Archaeological Museum of Shanxi), Dr. Y. Song (Shanxi University), Dr. D. Cohen and I. Patania (Boston University), I could not have written this paper. I thank Prof. D. Meltzer (Southern Methodist University) for his comments and careful editing of the manuscript. Needless to say, that all shortcomings are mine.

COLE, J.

This paper was based on my Ph.D. thesis supported by a full grant as part of the British Academy Centenary Project *'From Lucy to language: the archaeology of the social brain'* and I will be eternally grateful for the time, intellectual consideration and financial support graciously given by the project and its three directors, Clive Gamble, Robin Dunbar and John Gowlett. I would also like to thank Francis Wenban-Smith, Matt Pope, Rob Hosfield and Fiona Coward for inviting me to contribute to this Festschrift in honour of Clive Gamble; it truly is a privilege given all the advice and time that Clive has generously given me over the years. Special mention should also go to John McNabb and William Davies whose unceasing guidance through my thesis proved more valuable that I can possibly say. Finally my thanks to the three anonymous reviewers whose time, considerations, comments and suggestions were hugely appreciated and extremely helpful. Any errors that remain within this paper are entirely my own.

PETTITT, P.

It is a pleasure to contribute this paper to Clive's festschrift. The healthy scattering of references to his work should make clear his inspiration in this field alone; long may his agency continue to haunt me! Some of this work is based on research published in 2011, and many colleagues helped in that, and are acknowledged in Pettitt 2011a. Katherine Cronin kindly provided information about the death of Masya's daughter. I am grateful for the comments of three anonymous referees who helped improved the draft considerably.

GAUDZINSKI-WINDHEUSER, S. AND JÖRIS, O.

The present paper is based on research undertaken at the MONREPOS Archaeological Research Centre and Museum for Human Behavioural Evolution at Monrepos, Neuwied (Germany). At MONREPOS historical processes underlying the evolution of human behaviour are examined through the contextualised and interdisciplinary study of Pleistocene and early Holocene material remains, following a research strategy that constitutes the interface between chronology and chorology, adaptive strategies and social networks, providing the synergies necessary for understanding the process of becoming human. This research was first presented at a conference held in Vienna in 2008 celebrating the 100-year anniversary of the discovery of the Willendorf Venus ('From Willendorf to Gönnersdorf'). We are grateful to the organisers of the Vienna meeting who gave us the opportunity to present our studies. It is a huge honour and pleasure to have the opportunity to dedicate the outcome of this research to Clive, one of the great inspirational researchers who interpreted the rich body of Palaeolithic female depictions in terms of Palaeolithic societies. We very much hope that Clive will enjoy our contribution. We thank Francis Wenban-Smith and Matt Pope for inviting us to contribute to Clive's Festschrift. Thanks to Regina Hecht and Gabi Rutkowsky for their care and patience in the preparation of Figures 16.3–16.15. Thanks to Paul Pettitt for all his energy to improve our Denglish and for his many valuable comments. Finally our thanks go to Geoff Smith for final editing.

MITHEN, S.

I am most grateful to Fiona Coward, Francis Wenban-Smith, Rob Hosfield and Matt Pope for inviting me to contribute to this volume. Since 2004 research on the Mesolithic of western Scotland has been undertaken in collaboration with Anne Pirie and Karen Wicks. I am indebted to their contributions, especially from Anne regarding analysis of chipped stone and from Karen with regarding fieldwork and Bayesian chronological analysis. I am grateful to the anonymous reviews of an initial version of this contribution and to Sue Jones for helping with its preparation.

FOREWORD

> What Roman villa has such in situ evidence for behaviour? What Iron Age rubbish pit allows the archaeologist to construct the shortest of inferential chains concerning the role of hominid behaviour among the process of site formation? ... The preservation of landscapes with a comparably high spatial resolution is rare indeed outside the Lower Palaeolithic.
>
> (Gamble, C. 1996. 'Hominid Behaviour in the Middle Pleistocene: an English Perspective', in Gamble, C. and Lawson, A. J. (eds.) *The English Palaeolithic Reviewed*. Salisbury: Wessex Archaeology, pp. 61–71: 64)

This volume seeks to promote a social and ecological narrative of early hominin evolution, one which is theoretically informed yet empirically based and which links conventional material and geographic perspectives on the early archaeological record with the more elusive, social, cognitive and symbolic landscapes. All of the volume's contributors seek to move beyond limiting notions of early hominin culture and behaviour as imposed on, or dictated by, an external world. Instead, they present the early hominin world, and human evolution, as the outcome of a dynamic interaction between the 'external' landscape of habitat, physical environment and other animals and the 'internal landscape' of the perception and experience of the world.

Many of the chapters in this volume focus on the settlement and social relations of early hominins as intrinsic to their ecological situation in the physical world and the process of human evolution. Others explore how communal identities and cognitive landscapes become embedded in, and constructed through, the material environment, addressing the role of material objects and the physical landscape, not as a backdrop or vehicle for social relations and symbolic behaviour, but rather as active participants in the construction and evolution of society. All, however, demonstrate that any hard-and-fast distinction between these perspectives is neither inevitable nor, indeed, sustainable. Palaeolithic archaeology is the richer for combining these ultimately complementary and mutually reinforcing lines of evidence to create more than the sum of their parts.

An introductory chapter by Gosden reviews and critiques recent attempts at moving Palaeolithic studies closer to current social and cultural theory, and in addressing the big question of what it means to be human, provides an overview of many of the big themes of the volume: the nature of consciousness and intelligence; the importance of sociality and the embeddedness of humans in the world, as well as the role of material culture, technology and skill as modes of interacting with it.

ECOSYSTEMS, SETTLEMENT AND MIGRATION

This theme of the ecological situatedness of hominins and humans in the world is the starting – but certainly not the end – point for a number of contributions which focus first and foremost on the significance of ecological factors in the study of prehistoric societies, hominin evolution and the co-evolution of hominins and humans. However, each of these recognises the relevance of social factors as a driver for, rather than simply a by-product of, both physical evolution and cultural development. Dunbar and Grove explore the interplay between ecological and social factors in the evolution of cognition and behaviour, with specific reference to the socio-ecological context of fission-fusion in primate societies. They predict a series of thresholds in hominin cognitive evolution that can be evaluated against both the archaeological and fossil records of the Palaeolithic.

Gowlett and colleagues apply landscape and network perspectives to the major African Acheulean site of Kilombe. Combined with new work which has extended the site's archaeological timescales and landscapes, this chapter demonstrates how human activities can be mapped onto a framework comprised simultaneously of physical landscape, social constructs and cognitive routines.

At the other end of the Acheulean world, Ashton reviews the evidence for early human occupations of a diverse range of environments in northern Europe over 800 ka. Despite variations in climate and regional vegetation cover, he argues, hominins selected distinct ecological niches, predominantly in open grassland, close to a range of fresh-water habitats. However, these distinct niches are also argued to reflect pioneering populations who ultimately failed to successfully colonise northern latitudes until after 500 ka, when more sustained occupations may be the result of changes in technology, cognition or social structure, perhaps as part of a biological process of speciation.

The character of the more sustained post 500 ka occupation of northwest Europe is reviewed by Roebroeks and Bakels, whose contribution asks whether pre-sapiens hominins were capable of surviving in the forest environments that characterised European warm stages. New data from the Last Interglacial site of Neumark-Nord 2 is presented which suggests that not only were hominins able to survive in such habitats, but indeed that Neanderthals should perhaps be seen as active transformers of their surroundings, rather than passive pieces of 'forest furniture'. The impacts of challenging environments are also explored in the Balkans by Elefanti and Marshall, who discuss the contrasts between settlement in southeast Europe in the Middle and early Upper Palaeolithic and suggest that the region provided refugia during the cold phases of MIS 3 and 4 and thus became the possible origin for founder populations in subsequent warmer phases.

The nature of the post-500 ka settlement in northern Europe – specifically the British Isles – is explored further by White, who utilises recent sea-level reconstructions and sub-stage climatic cycles to explore the settlement patterns documented by the British archaeological record from this period. White argues that the piecemeal and broken record of settlement, abandonment and recolonisation is one of intermittent population renewal, driven largely by hominin responses to climatic change and sea-level fluctuations, and broadens out his focus from the physical landscape to investigate how the ecological processes of habitat and landscape change interdigitate with question of demography, social network and processes of cultural transmission and learning via the cultural patterning evident in in modes of handaxe manufacture and handaxe shape.

Technology, skill and learning

Such questions, focused around the socio-ecological context in which adaptations for technology, skill and learning are selected for is another significant theme that emerges from several other papers. Read and van der Leeuw's bold contribution takes a 'big picture' view of the issue, surveying the broad sweep of human socio-technological evolution from the Palaeolithic right the way through to the Industrial Revolution and indeed the present day. They argue that cognitive evolution itself is only explicable in terms of the relationship between the 'external' and 'internal' worlds, themselves experienced via socio-technological 'idea' systems. During human evolution these systems developed from individual engagements with the world into communal social systems of shared categorical relations, thus freeing us from the constraints of our own individual brains and resulting in the runaway social and technological innovation that has marked human (pre-)history.

Sinclair's contribution focuses in on the knowledge, know-how and embodied skills required to create such elaborate material cultures. He notes that to date such work has lacked an appreciation of the social support for the lifelong development of individuals' experience, but also that there is clear, albeit fragmentary, evidence for the identification of expertise in the Upper Palaeolithic. The question of the potential adaptive cost of complex cognition and the acquisition of knowledge and skill explored by Sinclair provides an interesting counterpoint to Grove and Dunbar's more ecologically-based take on a similar theme.

Wragg Sykes' contribution focuses in on a specific example of specialist Palaeolithic knowledge from Neanderthal society: that of composite technologies and the use of birch bark pitch as a hafting mastic, and the implications for Neanderthal cognition, memory and spatial and temporal perception of landscapes. Her focus on the ways in which micro-scale engagement with material culture can inform on the social and cognitive construction of wider landscapes echoes themes developed in Porr's contribution. Here the familiar Palaeolithic theme of hominin/human interaction with 'the environment' is given a relational and constructivist perspective more usually associated with the social archaeology of later prehistory, in order to investigate what such perspectives can add to our understandings of human evolution and early prehistoric hunter-gatherer society by extending our conceptualisation of 'social relations' beyond conspecifics to encompass other animal species.

Cole's contribution, meanwhile, ostensibly technological in focus, presents a new theoretical perspective exploring the potential links among hominin cognition, behavioural complexity and the development of language in terms of their significance for the production of material culture and its potential symbolising role in complex social interactions and hominin identity construction.

Identity and representation

These issues of the significance of technology as a potential means of construction of identity is also explored alongside more traditional Palaeolithic questions regarding the migration and colonisation of ecosystems by prehistoric hunter-gatherer groups by Bar Yosef, with reference to the little-known (at least in the West) Late Pleistocene foragers of China, Korea and Japan. Their 'micro-blade' industries provide a means of exploring the interaction between technological and ecological adaptations as a possible means of identifying and tracking the spread of specific groups, forming a complementary line of evidence to the genetic evidence for the migration of modern humans into East Asia, and to the palaeobotanical evidence for the emergence of cultivation in the China central plain.

The papers by Pettitt, Mussi and Gaudzinski-Windheuser and Jöris further develop the examination of the symbolising role played by material culture during social relations, and specifically the significance of overt symbolising practices, codes and behaviours. Although each tackles what could be rather over-familiar Palaeolithic topics such as Neanderthal burial and Palaeolithic female imagery, the papers investigate how interactions with others – living and dead – are part of the process of, and reflect the tensions between, the construction of individual and group identities and broader cultural repertoires. Incorporating ideas about the relationships between demographic factors, cultural transmission and social processes, Mussi and Gaudzinksi-Windheuser provide very different perspectives on the interpretation of human (particularly female) representations in Ice Age art of the European Upper Palaeolithic, Mussi proposes that subtle differences among the 'Venus' figurines provide evidence for the existence of formal rules of representation. However, misunderstandings during information transmission resulted in progressive distortion, resulting in the exaggerated anatomical features which characterise many of the 'Venuses'. In contrast, Gaudzinski-Windheuser and Jöris compare the stylistic, spatial and temporal characteristics of Mid Upper Palaeolithic and late Magdalenian figurines to suggest that the schematic style of the latest Upper Palaeolithic figurines represents an artistic reflection of changes in the social role of women during a period of rapid population expansion.

Finally, Mithen's concluding chapter compares and contrasts the two interpretative approaches all the contributions to this volume have sought to reconcile in their very different ways: the 'archaeology of settlement' (as derived from Binford's ethnoarchaeological work) and the 'archaeology of society', with reference to late Pleistocene/early Holocene lithic evidence from western Scotland.

CLIVE GAMBLE IN MIND: THE ECOLOGICAL, SOCIAL AND SYMBOLIC ROLE OF A PALAEOLITHIC RESEARCHER

As most readers will notice, the following contributions draw heavily from the pioneering work of a major figure in Palaeolithic archaeology: Professor Clive Gamble. In his research and teaching career to date Clive has reinvented the Palaeolithic with his typically lively and often radical work integrating 'traditional' geographical and ecological approaches to prehistory with an approach which foregrounds the social and cognitive aspects of Palaeolithic life. In doing so, he has fundamentally altered the ecosystem of Palaeolithic archaeology, and forced us all to adapt. The early, influential *The Palaeolithic Settlement of Europe* (Gamble 1986) and the typically provocative 'Man the Shoveler' (Gamble 1987), demonstrated how Palaeolithic archaeology could move beyond a sterile description of early European prehistory as a succession of lithic cultural traditions, where chimpanzees enter an environmentally driven conveyor belt at one end to emerge at the other as *Homo sapiens*, to an understanding of the interplay between the material archaeological record and the socio-ecology of hominins and early hunter-gatherers on a global scale. Subsequent work has widely traversed the landscape of Prehistoric discourse, ranging in scope from the social context of Upper Palaeolithic art to large-scale patterns and mechanisms of global colonisation, via some minor early digressions into Bronze Age Greece. Publication in 1999 of *The Palaeolithic Societies of Europe* exemplified wider archaeological concerns over the role of human agency and social interactions as drivers of the material record, and led the way in bringing the study of the Palaeolithic and early hominin societies into the mainstream archaeological fold, stressing the significance of both physical and social environments for human evolution. Since then, exploring the social underpinnings of hominin evolution and colonisation has formed a primary axis of Palaeolithic research, crossing over into anthropology, psychology and sociology to investigate the roots of hominin sociality and the social brain, for instance through the British Academy's Centenary Research Project *From Lucy to Language*.

However, the goal of this volume is not simply to celebrate Clive's previous work. The papers collected here are presented to act as a catalyst for distinctive and highly productive directions for new research into some key areas of hominin evolution, and new understanding of Palaeolithic societies across the globe and across the timespan of the Palaeolithic. In particular we hope that all of the papers stress an underlying theme of Clive's work, that research into the hunter-gatherers of the Palaeolithic and Mesolithic need not be limited to 'stomach-led' and 'brain-dead' models (Gamble 1999: 426). Instead the contributions to this volume seek to address the ways in which human social action and creativity are, and have always been, part and parcel of broader ecological patterns of adaptation to the world in which we live. This volume is offered in part as celebration of Clive's work, as a 'state-of-the-art' snapshot of work in the field of Palaeolithic archaeology and human evolution more generally, but also as a manifesto and call-to-arms to stimulate future research that will build on this to inspire future researchers to continue to push Palaeolithic research forward into new territory.

A PERSONAL NOTE

To paraphrase an un-named colleague of one of the editors: 'the Palaeolithic is much more interesting than when I used to teach it in the '80s'. Clive's inspirational research, teaching and leadership over the last four decades has been a huge factor in these changes, impacting upon academics, students, the wider public and, last but by no means least, funding bodies. Clive's hugely significant symbolic role in championing of the Palaeolithic through his involvement with such august institutions as the British Academy, the British Museum, the Royal Anthropological Institute, the REF panel and indeed Channel 5 has had a huge impact on the recognition and standing of all disciplines involved in Palaeolithic research. In addition, all the editors can attest to his significant social role in training, supporting and inspiring a new generation of Palaeolithic researchers.

We hope that Clive will recognise his own research in the roots of the papers presented here and not find too much evidence of 'dancing to the rhythms of the Pleistocene', and that his future will continue to bring us many new and thought-provoking contributions, perhaps on the wisdom of Arsenal buying Gareth Bale instead of Theo Walcott when pillaging Southampton's impressive youth setup, and ideally via Nevis and an occasional test match seat at Sabina Park.

Thank you

FIONA, ROB, MATT AND FRANCIS

CHAPTER I

WHAT USE IS THE PALAEOLITHIC IN PROMOTING NEW PREHISTORIC NARRATIVES?

CHRIS GOSDEN

Imagine a situation in which the world and the universe are as old as we know them to be, but in which people came into being in 4004 BC. Let us think for a minute about what implications such a scenario would have for our notions of the historical process. However people came to be (and we might have to invoke some form of divine intervention for such a sudden appearance), it is likely that people would be disengaged from the physical and causal processes of the rest of the universe. With our biological ties severed and the work of Darwin undone for the human realm, culture and human exceptionalism would inevitably loom large. Humans could not be seen as emerging through an evolutionary process in tandem with other organisms, nor would we be linked to the broader history of the universe through the operation of physical or chemical processes as normally understood. The radical discontinuity between people and everything else would require a special explanatory framework for humans. This might in turn lead to a division of knowledge, in some parts of the world at least, between those who study the social, cultural, philosophical, anthropological and historical aspects of people and those interested in the physical and biological worlds.

No reputable humanities scholar or social scientist believes that people are 6004 years old. But many act as if this were the case, so that the last few thousand years are when people became interestingly human, started farming for a living, dwelling in cities and commenced mass production and consumption. The rest is history: mass-consuming urbanites demonstrating culture at a level not glimpsed in any other species, the origins of which lie in a control of natural resources from which we are set apart. It is as if the Palaeolithic never happened.

NEW NARRATIVES FOR OLD PERIODS

I first properly got to know Clive in 1984 when we were both visitors at the Australian National University in Canberra. We drove out to Lake Mungo, which was described by the ranger there as 'an archaeological site the size of

Belgium'. Later Clive gave a seminar in the Department of Prehistory, Research School of Pacific Studies, known to people inside the department and outside as 'the piranha pool'. Seminars could be vicious and the department was particularly on the lookout for British visitors who might feel they were intellectually or socially superior. Clive, I know, was slightly nervous at this prospect, but predictably all went well, with Jack Golson, head of the department, describing it as the best seminar he had ever heard.

The basis of the seminar was the then in-press book *The Palaeolithic Settlement of Europe* (Gamble 1986). What impressed people was the tripartite synthesis of global hunter-gatherer studies, the new synthesis of the climatic and environmental data for the last 2 million years and a concerted attempt at archaeological analysis. It is interesting to look back at the reception of that book in the light of how Clive's thought has developed subsequently. The processualists claimed Clive as one of their own (see a representative review by L. Straus [1987]), and not just due to the Foreword by Lew Binford. The environmental framework in this book was strong, dividing Europe into nine cells on the basis of divisions by latitude and longitude, which allowed for the effects of temperature gradients on plants and animals to be felt. What complicated this framework were chapters 7 (Demography and Style) and 8 (Society, Sediments and Settlement), which together focused on the linkedness between individuals and groups into networks that covered huge areas of the continent, cutting across any ecological zones.

In many ways these two chapters became the starting point for the second incarnation of the book *The Palaeolithic Societies of Europe* (Gamble 1999). The one word change in the title belies a more fundamental shift in Clive's thought and the start of a sustained argument against teleological forms of prehistory writing. As is too well known to rehearse in any detail here, archaeology post-Childe has been structured around three revolutionary moments of the Neolithic, urbanism and industrialisation. These have never quite been joined by a fourth revolution concerning the emergence of fully modern humans and fully modern human behaviour. This very ancient modernity has never formed a convincing revolutionary moment because doubts exist over the basis for modernity (was it language, symbolism, a more joined up brain, better technology, body decoration and art?), doubts over chronology (did features picked out as modern come together too slowly to be a revolution?) and impact. The last issue has been raised most clearly and provocatively by Colin Renfrew through his idea of the Sapient Paradox (Renfrew 2004; Renfrew et al. 2009). To paraphrase somewhat, this paradox focused attention on this question: If humans became modern in the late Pleistocene, why did it take them so long to become fully human, through developing farming, sedentary ways of life and, eventually, a rich civil society with considerable productive power, social differences, art, writing and organised religion? These issues are laid out and critiqued much more effectively than I can in *Origins and Revolutions* (Gamble 2007), a book whose full impact has yet to be felt.

There are theoretical links between *Palaeolithic Societies* and *Origins and Revolutions*. In the former the individual is privileged, and this may be surprising to some, but Clive's emphasis was partly for empirical reasons – knapping episodes, butchery and the deposition of rubbish around a hearth can all be linked to skilled individuals performing social actions and create a mode of social reality as a result. This bottom–up view allows individuals to be combined into intimate (c. 5 people), effective (c. 20 people) and extended (100–400 people) networks. In the latter book the individual is still central but now more fully embodied, and this body helps gives rise to instruments and containers as extensions of and metaphors for the body. The body is more deeply relational, so that substances, be they stone, clay, wood or leather, are worked on by the skilled body, but also act back upon it, socialising it and skilling it in new ways. Relatedness between humans is part and parcel of relations with many other entities. Once one allows such a complexity of relations between humans and the world, then neat chains of cause and effect are jettisoned, along with clear direction to human prehistory. Change happens, but each significant change opens up a new space of possibility within which a range of directions can potentially be taken. Which direction is followed is momentarily under-determined. People may go from being mobile to sedentary, but the consequences of such a move are not always the same, nor is the move itself necessarily irreversible.

The argument is condensed into a key diagram (Gamble 2007, 9.1) and into this much complex argument is packed. The lack of a single direction is emphasised, except for a general shift from instruments to containers, and continuity over long periods is emphasised. Interestingly, Clive's argument overlaps in many ways with recent discussions of material engagement (Renfrew 2004, 2009) and entanglement (Hodder 2012). However, both these authors are in great agreement and both emphasise the post-Neolithic world, with the implicit assumption that humans are more deeply entangled or engaged once farming has laid the basis for a more materially complex form of life. A basic narrative structure has run through archaeology from at least Lubbock's *Pre-Historic Times* (1865) onwards. Post-processualism helped curb some of the emphases on progress and directionality, but much emphasis in post-processual thought has been on the world from the mid-Holocene onwards in Europe. Archaeology needs to expand its narrative structures to do justice to the full scope of prehistory over several million years, but also all those parts of the world in recent millennia which do not witness a straightforward transition to farming with its anticipated consequences. Huge swathes of Eurasia in the steppe and the forest regions, much of North America, most of the tropics, large areas of Africa and South America, and all of Australia do not fit easily into the farming-urbanism-industry teleology. Clive has been one of the most powerful voices arguing for a new, more open and varied narrative.

Clive's intellectual career has been unusual. Many move from young rebel to an established and dominant intellectual position. Binford in the 1980s found it very hard to be rebelled against once processualism had become a norm. Many of the 1980s rebels now constitute the archaeological mainstream. Clive's earliest major works were lauded by processualists as a most sophisticated expression of a global hunter–gatherer model applied systematically to a major set of Palaeolithic data. The exploration of art, style and human connections across ecological zones indicate the existence of a strand in Clive's thinking that would eventually lead to a stress on the senses, the emotions and the intelligent body. These are all aspects developed too by post-processualists (and by Colin Renfrew, whose own intellectual trajectory is intriguing). What differentiates Clive's position from that of many of the other major influences on the broader discipline is his vantage point from within Palaeolithic studies, requiring a more subversive stance towards the deep narratives of direction and increasing complexity. Archaeology is an odd discipline, the science of rubbish over the long term. We have not made enough of our oddness within the spectrum of the historical and social sciences. In insisting on a different view and through developing an intellectual framework that supports that view Clive's work is unusual and valuable. What follows is my small contribution towards an archaeology of oddness, drawing on Palaeolithic data, but unburdened by any great knowledge of it.

EVERYTHING IS IN MOTION

As I look out of the window, I can see rain falling from the sky, birds flying back and forth, various plants swaying in the wind. The mobile aspects of the scene are juxtaposed to the houses, fences and the earth itself which appear static. My view of what is mobile and what is not is an illusion (or function) of the nature of my perception, the timescales in which my organism and its movements (sensory, neural, etc.) mesh with those of the world. Either a smaller spatial scale or a longer time period would reveal different movements. Molecules are mobile and atoms are buzzing beyond my ken, so that the microprocesses (to us) of growth, chemical recombination and decay take place continually. Slow and lengthen the process of perception and it would become obvious that the houses have only been here some 130 years, together with their land divisions and gardens. At some point in the future all I can see will be replaced by other things which will have equal solidity and fixity to a human viewer.

Those philosophers of flux, Deleuze and Guattari (1987), developed new sets of terms to shake us out of our everyday view. 'The Body without Organs' (BwO) was one way of getting us to think about flows. At a series of different levels, from the sub-atomic, to the expansion of the universe after the Big Bang, the material world is in motion. We do not feel the universe expanding, the earth orbiting the sun, continental plates shifting or atoms recombining to form a new molecule, but all these things are happening now. Matter can be conceived of as existing at a series of strata of different temporal and spatial levels, where the word level only refers to scale and not to some area of more effective or ultimate cause. The BwO exists at each of these strata, being the most mobile manifestation of that stratum. So for what we would call life, the microbial level is volatile and motile, with much evolution taking place as cells or microbes combine, as Lynn Margulis (e.g., 1998) has shown. Evolution through cellular recombination, which embeds mitochondria into cells, has at least as much effect as that taking place through larger organisms. Nor is the boundary between the chemical and the biochemical totally distinct as entities like viruses show. However, it may be useful to distinguish the chemical and biochemical at their lowest scales of movement, which for the latter is the molecular and not microbial. In effect, such boundaries can be placed anywhere that seems helpful, rather than having any ultimate existence.

As well as movement in Deleuze and Guattari's world there is also (temporary) stasis, which they call territorialisations. The world takes on a temporary set of forms, bringing about particular modes of cause and effect. These can often appear solid and self-evident – like the houses and gardens out of my window – but such appearances depend on taking a single scale for granted. Just as a particularly convincing film or book will pull us into a time-space reality that makes temporary sense, so too do the temporal and spatial conventions we apply to the world (we should note here that Deleuze [1989] was amongst other things the philosopher of cinema). This is not to say that we make the world up, but that the universe is so vast that we can only attend to a tiny percentage of its properties, mistaking our modes of action, perceptions and tropes of explanation for reality more generally. We have a tendency to concentrate on territorialisations and not flows, maybe because a static picture is easier to discuss, analyse and grasp. But beneath each territorialisation is a flow, so that there are flows all the way down (and up).

For political theorists, a politics with materials left out or through some brute, inert materialism is just too human. Many of our most urgent problems derive from the pressing environmental problems mass consumption causes, so that to leave out the allure of objects or the broader processes of the planet as it responds to massed humanity is to have too partial a view of cause and effect. Causes are multiple and conditions deriving from people in the world are continually emergent through a series of complex, contradictory or concatenating forces. Jane Bennett identifies a strand of vitalism in western thought, deriving from (amongst others) Spinoza, Nietzsche, Darwin, Bergson and Deleuze (Bennett 2010: vii). For these varied thinkers not only life is alive, so that we should attribute as much liveliness as possible to matter-energy. Bennett follows them in recognising the vibrancy of matter and the power of material things to organise themselves. She uses the compelling example of the grid blackout across a large area of the northern United States and Canada in August 2003. Bennett feels that

> the electrical grid is better understood as a volatile mix of coal, sweat, electromagnetic fields, computer programs, electron streams, profit motives, heat, lifestyles, nuclear fuels, plastic, fantasies of mastery, static, legislation, water, economic theory, wire and wood.
>
> (Bennett 2010: 25)

Although the grid never rose 'to the level of an organism' (Bennett 2010: 24), it was a complex assemblage with its own unexpected properties. As automatic systems caused some power stations to shut down when parameters of heat and power loads were exceeded, the grid started to behave unpredictably, so that at one stage the electricity reversed its flow for reasons that even subsequent analysis struggled to reveal (Bennett 2010: 27–28). Such alarmingly emergent properties were due to no one element or aspect of the power system, but of many, often trivial, causes combining.

William Connolly is gripped too by the notion of emergent causality, where new conditions and properties emerge out of a series of influences. He acknowledges that linear or efficient causality is useful to explain situations that are stable or relatively simple (Connolly 2011: 171). However, in many more complex circumstances Connolly finds it useful to play with ideas of intersecting force fields, so that perturbations in ecological systems can feed through into market conditions, before restabilising in a novel form. 'Such complexity is endemic to an econo-political world bound to natural and cultural systems of multiple sorts ... sometimes, of course, a system expires, leaving simmering remains behind available for scavenging or colonisation by others at another time' (Connolly 2011: 172).

Such historical thoughts have been developed by Manuel De Landa (1997) using a philosophical approach to history directly inspired by Deleuze and Guattari. De Landa advocates not just a move away from Eurocentrism, but, more importantly, from anthropocentrism in which people are inevitably and always centre stage. He notes along the way how many disciplines have embraced history, so that physics now sees many processes involved in the expansion of the universe after the Big Bang as irreversible. In evolutionary biology too animals and plants seem to be 'piecemeal historical constructions, slow accumulations of adaptive traits cemented together via reproductive isolation' (De Landa 1997: 13). We are often guilty of category mistakes in fixing on the wrong units of change: 'Over the millennia, it is the flow of biomass through food webs, as well as the flow of genes through generations, that matters, not the bodies and species that emerge from these flows'

(De Landa 1997: 259). He also mixes up categories generally considered separate, so that the flow of information and the creation of languages, as temporary stabilisations of the norms of transmitting information, are considered alongside ecosystems, geological strata or the generation of urban forms. Such a mixing up of domains that have been radically separated provokes us to think about both the original categories (biology, economy, language, etc.) and their recombination to create new understandings of emergence (a term De Landa also plays with).

In mixing up what we have come to separate as nature on the one hand and culture on the other, obvious intellectual dangers occur. We are all well familiar with mechanical or biological explanations for cultural forms through environmental or genetic determinism. But equally in vivifying or humanising matter-energy we can fall into the trap of anthropomorphism, where matter-energy comes to seem exactly like life, or even like human life. The idea of the assemblage is useful in mixing everything up, but it still begs the question of what the links might be between information flows and genetic changes, for instance. Perhaps rather than deciding issues of complex causality in advance, we can try to establish empirically how complicated emergent systems might operate?

It *might* be clear now where I am taking my argument: the Palaeolithic is the period of flux, change and transformation, being both an aid and challenge to the ideas I have just been outlining. If notions of flux and occasional fixity work anywhere, they should do so in a period in which ice caps grew and retreated, new ecologies came into being and are then extinguished and humans change from being an African ape to a global species. In what follows, I shall address two questions very briefly – how can the ideas I have sketched here help in the understanding of very long-term histories? In what ways can we think about human diversity? I am very aware that Clive has tackled both these questions before me and with much greater knowledge of the period. Rather than completely re-invent the handaxe, I will draw on empirical evidence synthesised by Clive and on the broader patterns of thought he has developed.

THE MAMMOTH STEPPE

From around 2.5 million years ago, relatively minor changes in the earth's orbit, spin and tilt began to cause the climate to fluctuate between warm and cold periods, affected also by the influence of the Himalayas and Tibetan Plateau on global circulation systems (Gamble 1999: 99). This fluctuating climatic system provided the context for both hominin evolution and subsequent global expansion. The framework of late Pliocene and Pleistocene global climatic fluctuation is represented in continuous records of changing proportions of oxygen isotopes 16 and 18 in deep ocean sediments, known as marine isotope stages (MIS). Starting with MIS 1 in the present and stretching back through more than 100 cycles of cold and warm of varying lengths (Shackleton et al. 1991), the MIS framework now provides the climatic and ecological framework for Palaeolithic archaeology.

To gain some sense of variety at any one time and how this changes over time we can focus briefly on the cold stage MIS 12 (c. 480,000–425,000 years ago) in Eurasia, when large carnivores decline in number and a set of cold steppe ecosystems came into being with mammoths, woolly rhinos and reindeer as the most common large mammals – these ecosystems are now known by the shorthand of 'the mammoth steppe'.

> The mammoth steppe was an ecologically complex, medium-to-high-latitude suite of vegetation mosaics that produced a diverse fauna of grazing generalists. These mosaics depended primarily on the length of the growing seasons and these varied between regions … the mosaic of conditions … produced a structure whose "fabric" is compared to the weave in a plaid, rather than a striped, textile.
>
> (Gamble 1999: 111–112)

The mammoth steppe existed in cold periods for almost half a million years and with each warming the cold-loving plants and animals were driven to the tundra regions to the east and north, recolonising a huge swathe of Eurasia and Alaska with each downturn in temperature. An upswing of the temperature saw pulses of warm-loving ecosystems colonising from the south, with these ecosystems being erased again except for relatively small refugia as the ice sheets and tundra moved in from the north. Each iteration of the cold- and warm-loving ecosystems were broadly similar, but never quite the same; a series of complex variations on an already variegated theme. Both cold and warm adapted communities have no modern analogues, including the hominin communities that lived within them.

Not only did biotic communities fluctuate, but the surface of the earth was radically transformed. The ice sheets of MIS 12, for instance, pushed major river systems such as the Thames and the Seine to the south, close to their present positions: 'The same landscapes were also subjected to intense periglacial activity, with frost wedges, cryoturbation and mass wasting of sediments downslope' (Gamble 1999: 110). From this period on major depositions of loess occurred across Eurasia to become the focus, many millennia later, of intense agricultural systems from central Europe to China.

Gamble (1999: 107) calls MIS 12 'the hinge' partly because the evidence comes into new focus through extensive correlations of stratigraphy and fauna, in which small fast-evolving creatures like voles are key to understanding dates and temperatures. For a long period hominins were part of the warm adapted plant and animal communities. From around 500,000 years ago there was probably a thin, but even, distribution of hominins across all areas of Europe, apart from the northeast, making complex bifaces (handaxes) and flaked stone tools. These creatures were large, like the 1.8 m tall *Homo heidelbergensis*, and they lived in local groups without wide connections, as shown by the distances which raw material travel from their source (30–80 km). Against the background of the long cycle of climates and ecosystems, startling snapshots stand out, such as the knapping episodes which produced bifaces at the site of Boxgrove, near Chichester, southern England. Here blocks of stone can be fitted back together to show how knapping took place a few hundred metres from where the stone was procured, with the handaxes then being used to butcher animal carcasses on these tidal flats (Gamble 1999: 121). There was a strong investment in the emotional affective ties that bound the local group, with the symmetry of handaxes which is in excess of any demands of function, showing that there was a link between form and social relations: 'Hominids lead complex social lives with only minimum extension of co-presence beyond the gathering. The archaeological record across the eight occupied regions of Europe is very comparable' (Gamble 1999: 173).

As hominins spread across Europe half a million years ago, occupying a mosaic of ecosystems, it might seem that they existed in many natures, but with one culture. This is true to some degree as the thin spread of handaxes and flakes shows in assemblages with bones of local animals. Very subtle differences existed in the ways landscapes were created and used. As noted above, at Boxgrove knapping episodes can be reconstructed and in some instances bifaces are made, used and discarded all in the same place. But in others bifaces are removed from the vicinity, raising the question of where they were taken and finally deposited. Some places on the landscape may have been marked in memory, so that a waterhole at Boxgrove in Quarry 1/B had 'the richest density of cores and struck flakes but also a set of 321 bifaces, not all of them showing traces of being used' (Gamble 2007: 238). Some handaxes may have been made purely as forms of performance, demonstrating the skill of making but with no evidence of use along their cutting edges. Landscapes were being structured in subtle ways through memories of what had gone before in a particular spot. Localised acts of deposition form a pattern found wherever handaxes were used, although the exact modes of making and deposition may have varied in subtle ways between east Africa and Europe (Gamble 2007: 239). In a world of flux and becoming, subtle territorialisations were assayed – sets of connections with place, other species, stone and wood. The last substance is known from a number of middle Pleistocene locations, the most remarkable of which is Schöningen in eastern Germany where throwing and thrusting spears have been found, one of which may have had a hafting for a stone tool. Many were left to be preserved in peats while still in serviceable condition, raising the question of why, like handaxes they should have been deposited in that particular location and time. The tips of some spears were also made from the hard heartwood of spruce, showing a considerable appreciation for the variability and properties of materials (Gamble 1999: 135–136).

The evidence is sparse and difficult to interpret, and it is usually hard to know to which particular wiggle of the MIS climatic framework particular sites date. However, a picture is emerging of the long fluidity and occasional fixity of human becoming. The creatures we have been considering so far were not human in a biological and cultural sense. The early northwest European *Homo heidelbergensis* was probably part of a flow of genes and mutations linking African *Homo erectus* and the later European *Homo neanderthalensis*. None of these species led on to *Homo sapiens*, which emerged out of Africa after 100,000 years ago to eventually replace the Neanderthals (whether or not with any inter-breeding and hence genetic mixture is currently hotly debated; see Endicott et al. 2010; Stringer 2011a). Taxonomic methods attempt to fix the flows of genes into species, which is problematic in itself, especially given the paucity of physical remains for creatures like *Homo heidelbergensis*. The linking of these gene sequences to tools and sites is even trickier. There was a slow sedimentation of skills and abilities to join up time and space, but not in any progressive and irreversible manner. The flows of hominin genetic materials were not sufficient unto themselves, but linked to those of a great range of other species and we can see the bones of herbivore and carnivore animal species in sites across the European continent, hints as to the networks of relationships hominins had. By the Upper Palaeolithic it becomes obvious that some human groups, at least, had become entangled with reindeer, possibly following migratory herds, but similar close relationships may have been found with a range of species, the earlier of which are hardest to discern. Hominin society did not just include other co-specifics, but a range of other plants and creatures, with whom emotional relations were set up – certainly fear for some, possibly love or affection (if such terms are not too 'presentist' to be meaningful). Notions of animism are common to many human groups today, in which stones may seem active, or animals are humans in different bodily form. Who knows quite what notions of relationship, cause and effect would have existed half a million years ago, but we can be fairly sure that ideas and feelings about animals and plants would have been developed, communicated and contested in many ways, even without language as we have come to know it. On this last point an absolute division should not be seen between language and non-language, but instead we can see a spectrum of communication in which the making of a handaxe was a meaningful and communicative act, surrounded by gesture, forms of bodily comportment and some vocalisations, even though the nuances of the act could not be discussed using syntactic language.

The broader ecological situation of all our remote ancestors is only partly clear. We do not know with certainty whether hominins lived in Europe only in warm periods, or also in cold. Some of the oldest evidence in Britain and indeed in Europe, from Happisburgh, Norfolk over 800,000 years ago (Parfitt et al. 2010) appears to come from a period with boreal conditions equivalent to that found in southern Scandinavia today, raising questions about hominin survival in the deep winter if they did not have clothing, shelter or fire. However, the approach I am advocating here is not an ecological one, being also mineralogical, technological and cultural. We can say, following Gamble, that hominin abilities to be part of the world may have extended during the nine hundred millennia since their first appearance in northern Europe. From the relatively face-to-face social encounters at Boxgrove and before, there is evidence that materials for tools moved over much longer distances from the late Middle Palaeolithic onwards (Gamble 1999: Table 6.18) and by the Upper Palaeolithic movements of up to 200 km are common. In all cases of long distance movements, only small amounts of stone were moved, and these were used up in the process of making stone tools. There is also a shift from bifaces and flakes to blades (which are more than twice as long as they are wide). Blades have been interpreted in functional terms: they allow for longer cutting edges for the amount of stone used. Gamble has raised a different possibility following the work of Chapman (2000) on fragmentation. Greater numbers of blades allow for a proliferation of human social relations, as they can be given out and exchanged, but still retain a link back to the core from which they came and the maker. There is also the possibility of accumulation, as well as dispersal, allowing for diversifying strategies of identity creation (Gamble 2007: 190–193). Indeed, Gamble sees a shift over time in the balance between the drive to pull in or to give out: enchainment through gift giving or other forms of dispersal of materials gives way to a greater emphasis on accumulation. In material terms this is seen in a long shift through the Palaeolithic and into the Holocene from instruments, such as stone tools, to containers, like pots, baskets or houses (Gamble 2007: Chapter 7). Going along with this shift is another slow movement towards diversity in what we might call cultural forms and peoples relationship with the world more generally.

DIRECTION OR DIVERSITY?

Origins and Revolutions was a critique of a teleological, progressive and revolutionary view of human history generally and of the Holocene in particular, which renders the Palaeolithic as a long prelude after which the real action begins. The central direction of human history in this view is that from farming to cities to industry, as our ancestors progressively transform themselves into us. But viewed from the Palaeolithic, we can see a different slow shift without too many revolutionary moments and that is from similarity to diversity. The creation of diversity is in many ways the obverse of a single directional tendency to history: people develop their own ways of acting in and making sense of the world. Consider the multi-sited ethnography team transported back half a million years, with one member in southern England, another in

North Africa and a third in the east African Rift Valley. On gathering together after fieldwork and starting to write a comparative account of their three groups, subtle differences and judgements may have to be assayed concerning how handaxes were made, used and accumulated in various spots on the landscape, together, presumably, with a range of organic materials we can no longer see. There would undoubtedly have been differences in how hominins related to each other, the operation of memory in place making, the relationship with plants and animals and so on. However, these differences would have been of quite a reduced order compared with three studies in the same areas today, and in the present decisions would need to be made about whether urban or rural groups were looked at, agriculturalists or bankers, the young or the old and so on, such is the internal differentiation within any one area now.

Thinking Palaeolithically, there might be three broad periods in the diversification of human culture over the last 2.6 million years, the period over which hominins have a material culture that comes down to us. For a very long period, differences were relatively minor and from 2.6 million years ago down to roughly 30,000 years ago we need to retune the instruments we use to detect human difference to pick up fine nuances. Differentiation between areas was low, and it might also be that internal group distinctions, such as we would now call gender, class or status, were less marked or at least differently marked than those in the present. From 30,000 until about 500 years ago human groups differentiated massively. We are no longer comfortable with seeing people living in discrete cultures, as the boundaries are hard to draw and are generally porous, but over the earth generally one can see a huge field of differentiation in terms of languages, food, materials and customs, and also internal differences of age, class, gender and sexuality have grown up to provide a huge plethora of engagements in the world. Over the last five centuries difference has not been done away with through the forces of colonialism and capitalism, but has been re-ordered and massified through the growth of settler societies and then nations and the mass-production and consumption of material things, which has brought together novel communities of production and consumption. This last period is not relevant here, except for the fact that all our understandings of the world, including of the Palaeolithic, are shaped by it.

How do we account for these three periods, albeit ever so briefly? Let us go back to my initial consideration of emergent properties. Nothing is ever static as this wobbly planet revolves around the sun, with its continental plates moving, volcanoes erupting and ecosystems fluctuating as warm periods follow cold ones. There are periods of rapid change, such as at the end of the last glaciation and quite possibly the one we are living in now, interspersed with relative stability, such as the last 10,000 years, although even that has had its ups and downs. Hominins evolved as tool-using creatures in the long period of general instability which we call the Pleistocene. They created a series of worlds without modern analogies in either the ecosystems that existed or the hominin life forms. These creatures were highly adaptable, living in cool boreal climates some 900,000 years ago, as well as in warm Mediterranean climes. Their ability to make use of the emergent properties of the varying worlds of which they were part was somewhat limited by more recent standards. As Clive Gamble has shown us, hominins lived in relatively local areas with a range of engagements with plants and animals, wood, stone and so on, but also with a general similarity of lifestyle over large areas. We might call this a world of 'Many Natures and One Culture', although obviously such terms should not be seen as truly discrete one from the other.

After around 30,000 years ago, people become more a part of the worlds in which they live, shaping and being shaped by a great range of ecosystems. In a sense people become more a part of the emergence of the world. Distances over which materials were being moved are greater, as we have seen, clothing and personal ornament are in evidence, so that in Gamble's terms there is a greater range and depth of involvement with both instruments and, especially, containers. Connection with other living species may strengthen, with the closeness between people and reindeer being well known. In the Holocene we are used to thinking about such relationships in terms of cultivation or domestication. How far the former term can be used for the late Palaeolithic is a question for debate. Looked at globally, people are moving into a range of ecosystems, so that rainforests are being used in south east Asia and Papua New Guinea, with the human effects on the structure of the communities they encountered dating back to their earliest involvement. Rainforests and savannahs are not domesticated landscapes, but they do show mutual creation between the world and its human inhabitants not seen previously.

From recent ethnography we can see that people's intellectual traditions are shaped by notions of how they are a part of the world and it of them, so that we can only wonder how far back such notions date. Descola (1994) and Viveiros de Castro (1998) both draw from Amazonian ethnography to outline a world of animals considered to be persons, with their own cultural lives. Viveiros de Castro (1998) points out that whereas we see a world with a single nature but many cultures, Amerindians feel that nature is varied but that all beings have one culture which are all variants of that of the human culture. Ingold (2000) adds instances from circum-polar ethnographies to highlight worlds in which stones, trees or animals can be animate and intentional in ways parallel to the agency of people. Sahlins' (2011) recent restatement of the importance of kinship studies to anthropology draws many of these insights together around the importance of mutuality. All human beings are given identity through a multiplicity of meaningful relations, including those with entities of a variety of kinds that we might therefore consider 'people'. Here then is an historical ecology of an extended kind, where the notion of ecology includes a great range of relations. It is true to say such studies have hitherto looked little at history, and there is work here for archaeology to do (Gosden 2008). From the Upper Palaeolithic onwards a world of Many Natures and Many Cultures comes into being, with humans being enworlded (to use a phenomenological term slightly loosely) in a much deeper manner. Variety is everywhere: biological or geomorphological variety does not bring human variety into being in any straightforward manner, nor is the reverse true, but new forms of emergence emerge and these have shaped us and the planet deeply.

What Clive has given us is the intellectual and empirical means to think about the material basis of human identity over the very long durée. This is a considerable gift. The application of theories of materialism and culture to Palaeolithic data has brought the rather recalcitrant material of this long period into more intellectual contact with that of the Holocene, providing for a continuity of discussion and debate across the whole of human being. The impact that Clive has had has also been amplified through an extremely talented group of post-graduate students and post-doctoral researchers. Together they have created an emergent intellectual field, using the vast materials from the last 2.6 million years in novel and confronting ways. Temporal chauvinists that we are, no one has thought of questioning the usefulness of the Holocene to understandings of history and the present. The creation of nations, with their new and tricky identities, the rise of possessive individualism and a barrier between culture and nature in the west at least, makes the recent millennia untypical of most of what came before. Although the long, slow developments of the Palaeolithic are key to understanding the present interglacial, the reverse is not true, leading us to wonder: What use is the Holocene? Indeed, to return to my opening thought experiment, if we did still believe that humans were only 6000 years old, how could we frame modes of explanation that made any sense? It is the perspective provided by the Palaeolithic that Clive Gamble has insisted we take seriously, and such serious consideration is yet to really take hold in all areas of archaeology. We can be sure that Clive will push this debate in new directions, destabilising of old orthodoxies, indicating in the process a need for new archaeological narratives for all periods, irrespective of their antiquity.

CHAPTER 2

LOCAL OBJECTS, DISTANT SYMBOLS: FISSION-FUSION SOCIAL SYSTEMS AND THE EVOLUTION OF HUMAN COGNITION

MATT GROVE AND ROBIN DUNBAR

INTRODUCTION

Relative to other primates, modern humans live social lives of remarkable complexity, maintaining relationships with other individuals over entire life-spans and across continental divides. The spatio-temporal scales over which we interact define our society and highlight a marked break from other species. Nevertheless, there is clear evidence among some apes and monkeys of social systems that could be considered antecedent, or informative parallels, to our own. One such social system is characterised by the repeated division and aggregation of smaller groups into larger groups (termed 'fission-fusion': Kummer 1971). This apparently simple system is highly beneficial ecologically, yet leads to profound social and cognitive pressures. This paper will argue that these cognitive demands have played a considerable role in shaping the evolution of specific aspects of modern human cognition.

Gamble's (1993, 1996a, 1998a, 1999) network approach to Palaeolithic society, particularly as part of the British Academy's *Archaeology of the Social Brain* project, has facilitated the comparison of the social systems of extant primates, modern hunter-gatherers and archaeologically documented populations within a single framework. This links group size during prehistory to social complexity; social complexity as a whole is constrained by cognitive capacity, measured primarily by the relative size of the neocortex; and fission-fusion is an important signifier of social complexity, linking not only to a number of specific cognitive abilities but also to neocortical ratios in primates. We here combine Gamble's notion of the increasing scale of Palaeolithic life with a particular concern with the cognitive ramifications of stretching fission-fusion social organisation beyond the limits seen in extant primates. To this end, the following sections define and examine fission-fusion as a social system, survey work on the modern human fission-fusion system, introduce research on a number of cognitive abilities that may be tied specifically to this system, and discuss the evidence for those cognitive abilities (and for fission-fusion directly) in the archaeological record of the Palaeolithic.

WHAT IS FISSION-FUSION?

The term fission-fusion (henceforth FF) refers to a form of social organisation in which an overall group or 'community' splits periodically into subgroups. FF can be seen as one end of a continuum of group cohesiveness, with the other represented by social groups whose members are in close spatial proximity continually. FF social organisation is found in a diverse range of animals including bats, equids, cetaceans, social carnivores and elephants. Among primates, the two species of chimpanzees, seven species of spider monkeys, and at least four baboon species (including the drill and mandrill) show clear and consistent evidence of FF social dynamics, as do some howler monkeys and some macaque species. FF appears to be driven by the need to dynamically adjust group sizes to a fluctuating resource base, allowing individuals to balance the costs and benefits of group living by adjusting the sizes of the subgroups in which they gather. Where limiting resources are clumped, or when predation risk is high, larger aggregations are predicted to occur; when predation risk is low and resources are evenly distributed, smaller groups will be more efficient. Furthermore, the timescales over which these variables change may vary; predation risk may always be higher at night, whereas resource distribution and density may change according to a seasonal cycle. Once established, however, FF has social ramifications that go far beyond its presumed ecological function.

As studies of primate FF have become more numerous, a series of finer grained distinctions have been made among social systems at the low cohesion end of the grouping spectrum. Rodseth and colleagues (1991) distinguish between 'atomistic' FF, where the smallest unit is the individual, and 'molecular' FF, where the smallest unit is a subgroup, normally comprising a male, females, and their offspring (the 'one-male unit'). Atomistic systems are the most fluid in that even subgroups will be of different composition from day to day, whereas the subgroups in a molecular system are relatively stable. Kappeler and van Schaik (2002) offer a similar dichotomy, but regard atomistic groups as practising true fission-fusion, while molecular groups are referred to instead as operating in 'multilevel' societies. Chimpanzees are the quintessential atomistic system; there are several levels of grouping, with a series of subgroups of approximately five individuals forming a neighbourhood of around 15 (Thompson et al. 2007), who in turn form a community of 45–100 (see Lehmann et al. in press). Any given individual (with the exception of dependent young and occasional particular alliances) can encounter any other on any given day, with exchange of individuals between subgroups occurring routinely. Hamadryas baboons, on the other hand, are the classic example of a molecular or multilevel system, with four levels of grouping: several stable one-male units form a clan, several of which form a band. The key distinction is whether the lowest level groupings are stable or not.

The apparent dichotomy between atomistic and multilevel societies breaks down, however, when we come to examine FF dynamics in modern humans.

FISSION-FUSION IN MODERN HUMAN SOCIETIES

Rodseth and colleagues (1991) suggest that humans adopt a composite form of primate society, 'analogous to a chimpanzee community during the day and to a hamadryas band at night' (Rodseth et al. 1991: 239). The human combination of atomistic and molecular strategies makes us, in Kappeler and van Schaik's (2002) terms, both a fission-fusion and a multilevel society, and unique among primates, and yet is universal among humans. The multilevel aspect of human society has long been noted by hunter-gatherer ethnographers (e.g., Murdock 1949, 1969; Birdsell 1958, 1968), and by psychologists for modern sedentary societies (see Hill and Dunbar 2003; Zhou et al. 2005; Roberts 2010), suggesting that it is an ancient and important part of our evolutionary history.

While terms such as FF directly relate to the cohesiveness of the community, they do not comment directly on the actual spatial organisation of individuals at any particular level. Like hamadryas baboons, humans repeatedly aggregate at particular localities, with daily (or longer) forays radiating out from and returning to these localities (see, e.g., Lee 1968; Yellen 1977; Binford 1980). This pattern identifies us as central place foragers, a foraging mode prompted in other animals primarily by either the presence of altricial young or the need to fission and travel widely in search of food. Though all humans engage in some form of FF behaviour, the spatio-temporal extent of the fission phase can vary considerably: Binford (1978a, 1980) distinguishes between the relatively simple routines of 'foragers' and the more sophisticated radiating patterns of 'collectors', Washburn (1982) contrasts immediate and delayed return foragers, and Lieberman and Shea discuss circulating and radiating mobility patterns (1994). Perreault and Brantingham (2011) have recently characterised the forager-collector continuum in terms of the distance travelled (or the time elapsed) between visits to the same central place location: collectors return frequently to central places but reside there for longer durations, using wider foraging radii, while foragers return to central place locations only by chance at some later date and for a relatively short period of time, thus exploiting only a limited radius around it (Binford 1962; Grove 2009, 2010a).

Humans, then, are fission-fusion, multilevel, central place foragers. Though each of these aspects of social organisation can be found in numerous other animals, the combination of the three appears in no other living species. However, perhaps the most distinctive element of the human social adaptation is that our FF behaviour is expanded over far greater scales, both spatially and temporally, than that of any other animal; it is this 'release from proximity' (Rodseth et al. 1991: 240) that has become the focus of Gamble's (1998a, 1999,

2007) evolutionary scenario for the prehistoric development of human network structures. Mediated by the increasing use of artefacts as symbols and the linking of ever more distant locales within a social landscape created by the establishment of habitual paths and tracks, the gradual extension of social life is established throughout the Palaeolithic as local networks were incorporated into extended and ultimately global networks.

Larger group sizes, extended effective networks and, ultimately, extended 'social landscapes' require the storage of ever increasing quantities of information for longer and longer periods, and the transmission of that information over larger and larger distances. The handling of increasing quantities of information, whether iconic, indexical, or symbolic, can be expected to increase cognitive demands on individual hominins. The social brain hypothesis (Dunbar 1998a, 2003) has demonstrated the constraint imposed by executive cognitive capacity on group size; this constraint has been used to infer a progression of group sizes that is broadly in agreement with the scheme advocated by Gamble's (1998a, 1999) network approach. Furthermore, conclusions regarding the origins of language that form a central pillar of the SBH (Aiello and Dunbar 1993; Dunbar 1993, 2009) accord well with notions of an increasing requirement for information-handling over the course of human evolution. Building on the arguments of Gamble's network approach and employing the social brain framework in broad terms, the section below examines cognitive requirements that might be specific to FF rather than to increasing group size *per se*.

DISPLACEMENT

The concept of displacement identified by Hockett (1960, 1963) as one of the 'design features of human language' describes the fact that 'what is being communicated about can be removed, in time or space or both, from the setting in which the communication takes place' (Hockett 1960: 415) and is thus of particular relevance to the evolution of FF social systems and the 'release from proximity' in human societies. The uncoupling of relationships from spatial proximity is a direct social analogue of this process, and may therefore be equally demanding in cognitive terms; indeed, Rodseth and colleagues (1991: 240) go as far as to suggest that with this uncoupling 'social evolution as a human affair was launched upon its career'. Although there are possible examples of partial displacement in the vocalisations of baboons, gibbons and vervets (Altmann 1967; Hockett and Altmann 1968; Cheney and Seyfarth 1990), it seems that humans alone are capable of routine displacement both linguistically and socially. However, there is some evidence from chimpanzees and baboons that may contradict this.

For example, Washoe was able to use sign language to ask one of her handlers to get her an orange from the car (Lieberman 1984). The negotiations between hamadryas baboon males about the direction in which to forage during the day and which waterhole they should meet at may be another example of displacement (Sigg and Stolba 1981). Chimpanzees, being an atomistic FF society, do of course handle social displacement in the wild, though this takes place over a limited spatio-temporal scale relative to that of modern humans. If we assume that the evolution of hominin FF has involved the stretching of a chimpanzee-like fission-fusion template, the interesting question is whether linguistic and social displacement directly co-evolved. To put this another way, how far could the spatio-temporal range of a chimpanzee community be stretched before an alternative form of information transmission became necessary? The SBH suggests that beyond a certain group size language becomes essential due to the need for an efficient mechanism of social bond maintenance; the above argument further suggests that the frequency of inter-individual contact in chimpanzee communities could not be reduced any further without relations between individuals breaking down.

OBJECT PERMANENCE

A further ability required by animals living in FF societies is an understanding of object permanence: the ability to know that objects (or agents) continue to exist even though they are no longer apparent to the senses (Piaget 1952). Though the precise timing of object permanence development in children has been questioned, the sequence of acquisition is well established and is mirrored in apes, monkeys and some non-primate species (Gomez 2005). Potts (2004) has argued that the ability to track ephemeral and dispersed food sources among frugivorous primates would also have been beneficial in the social realm for FF species. Thus in solving the ecological problem of a variable and dispersed resource base, FF creates a new social problem. Potts (2004: 223) argues that in this way 'environmental and social factors would have reinforced each other in influencing the cognitive evolution in great apes'.

Hypotheses regarding the cognitive demands of ephemeral, dispersed food sources are of course a mainstay of research into primate cognitive evolution (e.g., Parker and Gibson 1977; Milton 1981), yet the recognition of the parallels between the ecological and social problems created by such a subsistence base constitutes a significant advance. It is necessarily the case that dispersed social relations are more demanding cognitively than their ecological analogue. All anthropoid primates are capable of tracking third-party relations, but in FF social systems it is not just the absence of certain conspecifics that individuals need to keep track of. In addition, 'animals need to recognize that the absence of a particular individual can affect the relative value of those that are present' (Barrett et al. 2003: 495). The need to adjust to a fluctuating social resource base and to negotiate a social world that is 'partially virtual, rather than purely physically instantiated' (ibid.) suggest that FF sociality demands considerable object permanence skill.

MENTAL TIME TRAVEL

A further cognitive ability potentially related to the evolution and extension of FF social systems is that of Mental Time Travel (henceforth MTT), defined as the reconstruction or simulation of both past and future events using episodic memory or personal memories of the past, rather than the abstract facts that comprise semantic memory (Suddendorf and Corballis 1997). Suddendorf and Corballis (1997, 2007) suggest that the substrates underlying episodic memory are also employed when we mentally construct potential events in the future, as persistent errors in episodic memory recall suggest that the past, like the future, is 'constructed' rather than simply recalled (see the long psychological literature on mental models: Johnson-Laird 1983). Both episodic memory (Tulving 1983) and MTT (Suddendorf and Corballis 1997) were originally conceived of as purely human abilities, yet it seems that some animals demonstrate elements of 'episodic-like' memory and foresight. Clayton and colleagues (2003) have suggested that the caching behaviours of scrub jays imply both episodic-like memory (required for retrieval of cached items) and foresight, as jays that are aware of others observing their caching activities will only later re-cache the observed items if they themselves have stolen from the caches of others in the past (Clayton and Dickinson 1998; Emery and Clayton 2001). Among primates, recent studies suggest that chimpanzees, bonobos and orang-utans are all capable of planning for future events via the understanding that tools may be useful in future situations (Mulcahy and Call 2006; Osvath and Osvath 2008), and chimpanzees and orang-utans are also able to trade an immediate gain for a subsequent, larger gain (Osvath and Osvath 2008).

The need for MTT in FF social systems – particularly those of modern humans – relates to the ability to mentally model future encounters with individuals with whom interactions are not continual. Like displacement, both episodic memory and MTT have been associated with linguistic capacities – a fact that has hampered their study in animals other than humans. Though Mulcahy and Call (2006) suggest that the precursor skills for MTT may have been present in the ancestor of all great apes, their studies were undertaken over relatively short periods of time. That apes such as bonobos can plan for activities that will take place up to 14 hours in the future may be perfectly in keeping with the scale of their own FF dynamics, but would not facilitate the kind of extensive spatio-temporal separation experienced routinely by modern humans. It is clear that, in expanding the scope of our social systems, humans have also placed extensive demands on the foresight elements of the MTT system. Barrett and colleagues (2003: 495) have even suggested that the core cognitive difference between humans and other apes might simply be 'the number of alternative future scenarios that can be managed and compared simultaneously'.

INHIBITION AND ANALOGY

A potential complexity of MTT involves the need to inhibit instinctive reactions while mentally simulating future events. The chimpanzees in Mulcahy and Call's (2006) experiments were able to inhibit the desire for an immediate, small gain in favour of securing large future gain, and study of inhibition in primates has recently suggested that this capacity might be better developed not in apes relative to monkeys but in FF societies relative to non-FF species (Amici and colleagues 2008). FF species were also significantly better than non-FF species at memory and withholding information tasks (Amici et al. 2009, 2010; see also Deaner et al. 2006), demonstrating not only inhibition and limited foresight but also an understanding of other animals' motivations and probable reactions to learning of the existence of the food. These researchers suggest that 'high levels of FF dynamics are associated with higher behavioural flexibility' (Amici et al. 2008: 1415), and argue that the large volumes of 'fragmented and varying social information' (Amici et al. 2010: 194) stored by FF primates may have led to a fundamental re-organisation of the way in which that information is accessed.

The substantial quantities of information that must be managed by FF primates about third-party social relationships occurring out of view may thus have led to the evolution of analogical reasoning as a way of reducing cognitive demands (Barrett et al. 2003; Potts 2004; Aureli et al. 2008; Amici et al. 2010). Though analogical reasoning is often considered a hallmark of human cognition primates are able to extract general relations between sets of stimuli and sets of responses, and the learning of such general relations is likely to be more economical than the individual mapping of many stimulus-response pairs (Whiten 1996; Call 2001). This understanding of the relations between relations – equivalent to the use of analogy – is not only easily applicable in the social sphere (Call 2001), but may have first arisen there (Barrett et al. 2003; Aureli et al. 2008). Barrett and colleagues (2003) have suggested that one explicitly analogical form of reasoning that would have particularly benefited animals in FF societies is the use of spatial descriptors to index temporal durations. The understanding of time as continuum, so important in MTT, is predicated upon the understanding of space as a similar continuum (Boroditsky 2000), a mapping evident not only in the use of linguistic analogies such as references to 'lengths' of time, but in experiments in which no linguistic stimuli or responses are required (Casasanto and Boroditsky 2008). The gradual stretching of the social landscape in both space and time would have been an obvious stimulus to the development of social parallels to the physical time/space analogy. Indeed, Barrett and colleagues go as far as to suggest that theory of mind itself may have developed as 'a specialized, socially-oriented form of analogical reasoning' based on the difficulties of managing dynamic social markets (Barrett et al. 2003: 496).

THE ARCHAEOLOGY OF FISSION-FUSION

The cognitive abilities highlighted above are more usually studied independently, yet it is immediately clear that similarities exist between them in terms of both observable behaviours and underlying processes. They are linked by the need for some ability to comprehend the flow of time, which some researchers have seen as the key to understanding the evolution of human cognition (e.g., Tulving 2002; Suddendorf et al. 2009). A search for archaeological evidence of an appreciation of the temporal in our ancestors will necessarily focus first on the question of whether activities leaving traces in the record reflect instances of foresight. Various such activities are discussed below, but the majority rely on lithics data, and while given the foregoing we can infer elements of foresight in the great ape clade as a whole, the archaeological record is essentially silent as to the pre-Oldowan development of these abilities in the earliest hominins prior to around 2.6 Ma.

From the very first appearance of Mode 1 technologies at sites such as Gona in Ethiopia (e.g., Semaw et al. 1997), archaeologists can begin to make inferences about levels of planning and foresight in hominin groups based on the complexity of the manufacture process and the extent to which raw materials and finished tools are transported around the landscape. Archaeological discussions of foresight as reflected in tool use frequently focus on 'curation' (*sensu* Binford 1979, 1989), and tend to assume there is little in the way of forward planning evidenced in the 'expedient' technology of the Oldowan. However, Hallos (2005: 157) notes that there is no contradiction in the idea of 'planning to be expedient'; there are cognitive implications of the earliest tool behaviours that move beyond the immediate ability to produce a useful cutting edge, Binford's (1979) checklist for identifying archaeological examples of curation in fact involves numerous subtleties such as raw material selection and differential discard as well as the actual transport of materials, and given great apes' abilities, it is hardly surprising that there are clear instances of curation in even the earliest archaeological localities. Evidence of both raw material selectivity (e.g. Braun et al. 2009; Goldman-Neuman and Hovers 2009) and the transport of tools over distances implying an organisation of space and time beyond that required for instant returns (e.g., Blumenschine et al. 2008) demonstrate that the behaviour of Oldowan hominins was more complex than suggested by the lithics alone.

The assumption that the transport of tools *per se* is a very basic form of planning for the future and, by extension, that tool transport distances will therefore at least loosely correlate with the spatio-temporal complexity of a society because movements between distant locales 'require the scheduling of larger blocks of time to accomplish' (Brantingham 2006: 440). Similarly, Gamble (1993, 1996a) has utilised the data of researchers such as Féblot-Agustins (1997) and Geneste (1988a, 1988b) to produce the first estimates of hominin home ranges from lithics datasets (Gamble and Steele 1999). This approach has proved particularly fruitful for the earlier Palaeolithic, when innovations in social organisation may have been equally if not more import-ant than more visible innovations in technology (Coward and Grove 2011).

The increase in the distance over which tools were transported, from around 10 km in the Oldowan to hundreds of kilometres in the Upper Palaeolithic, are the key archaeological elements Gamble uses to plot the emergence of the 'Social Landscape' (1993, 1996a, 1998a). However, it is clear that strategies of early lithic transport are just as important as the distances involved. It is also clear that FF groups must practise either periodic aggregation of the whole community (molecular) or regular, fluid exchange of individuals within sub-groups (atomistic), or there can be no overarching community to which all individuals or subgroups belong, and from which they receive the benefits of community membership (Rodseth et al. 1991). From an archaeological perspective, the important difference between the atomistic and molecular systems is that they lead to alternative spatial patterns of aggregation and dispersal and thus different signatures in the record. The maintenance of bonds in all but very modern FF societies depends on face-to-face contact, with the duration and geographic scope of intervening separations determining the scale of the system. Without periodic aggregation or the exchange of individ-uals between subgroups, such bonds cannot be maintained at all, and this poses a very serious problem for the 'release from proximity' in FF societies.

The simple fact is that a chimpanzee-like (atomistic) FF system could not be expanded into the type of system practised by modern human hunter-gatherers, because it lacks a central 'socio-spatial' focus to guarantee re-aggregation. Whilst chimpanzees do occasionally re-use particular localities, these are almost always directly linked to subsistence practices (e.g., an ant hill, a termite mound, or a tree root used as an anvil). Further, chimpanzees feed as they go, and sleep in a location determined largely by the location of their last meal of the day; humans and, by inference, some hominins, transport food to locales at which they gather *for the sake of aggregation*. The highly circum-scribed territories of chimpanzees thus ensure that the community maintains a degree of cohesion; without some kind of regularised aggregation locality an expanded chimpanzee-like community would simply fission permanently if stretched too far. We can conclude that existing chimpanzee communities endure at least partly because they have *not* undergone the release from proximity – they are both spatially and temporally limited in the scale of separations that occur between face-to-face meetings.

The localities at which hominins regularly met first entered archaeological parlance as Isaac's (1978) 'home bases', influenced directly by studies of modern African hunter-gatherers (e.g., papers in Lee and DeVore 1968) and supposed parallels in the excavations of Olduvai (Leakey 1971; Potts 1988) and Koobi Fora (Isaac 1997). Severe criticism of the concept (e.g. Binford 1981) had the unfortunate result that the essential importance of a spatial focus to evolving hominin social systems has been under-appreciated ever since. The existence of central places (to use the modified terminology; Isaac 1983ff) is a pre-requisite for the release from proximity, yet these places need not have been imbued with profound social meaning from the start. Many animals employ central places, and those that also practise molecular FF are of particular interest.

Classic molecular FF primates such as hamadryas baboons are constrained to gather at central places by the lack of resources such as suitable sleeping cliffs and (seasonally) the scarcity of water sources (Swedell et al. 2008; Schreier and Swedell 2009; Schreier and Grove 2010). It seems highly likely that early hominin aggregations would have occurred in response either to limiting resources or to the presence of locations particularly abundant in favoured resources. With the addition of raw materials for tool-making to the list of basic subsistence resources, and the likelihood that the first manufacture of stone tools related to greater meat consumption, a number of localities from lithic outcrops to waterholes to the locations of scavengeable carcasses could have emerged as localities for initially temporary aggregations. Gradually, some of these localities may have taken on explicitly social meanings as loci of bond maintenance, not just areas rich in key resources. Once such nodes are established in the landscape, the paths between them also come to be shared by numerous interacting groups now operating within wider communities (e.g., Gamble 1996a).

The structuring of the landscape can thus begin to emerge with limited cognitive capacities for the kind of time-dependent processing implied by problems such as displacement, object permanence, and mental time travel, yet it cannot be extended far beyond the basic primate template without development of these capacities. Most models of early hominin land use require some capacities for foresight that build on the basic idea of lithic transport as a reflection of planning for future action; many of these, in particular those of Binford (1984), Schick (1987), and Potts (1988), like Isaac (1978), are intended to explain the association of bones and stones in the early archaeological record, but each also shows how certain locations in the landscape come to be favoured over time due to the basic requirements of the foraging round. One of Binford's (1981, 1984) key criticisms of the home base model was that focal points, where they existed in the landscape, were determined largely by the local ecology rather than by social functions such as aggregation and food-sharing. It is undoubtedly the most parsimonious explanation that aggregations prompted by distributions of resources, such as Binford's (1984) 'magnet places' (e.g., shade trees, lithic outcrops and water sources) would naturally attract accumulations of cultural material, and were only later exapted for explicitly social purposes as over time 'hominins became less routed among places where nature had placed elements basic to life functions' (Binford 1984: 264), and localities repeatedly used by hominins were increasingly located to facilitate social exchange rather than to serve ecological necessity. This shift towards a more socially orientated use of the landscape would have required a greater level of planning and a more sophisticated spatio-temporal organisation as groups were able to fission for longer periods and to range over greater areas. Thus Binford's (1984) 'routed foraging' model can in fact be seen as evolutionarily antecedent to the development of Issac's home bases (1978). Similarly, the 'favoured places' of 'passive storage' resulting from persistent use of rich foraging areas as outlined by Schick (1987) can be seen as forerunners of the deliberate cache of stone suggested by Potts (1983, 1988) as an explanation for Oldowan localities at Olduvai Gorge whereby caches of tools and raw materials are spaced evenly in the landscape to reduce 'the energy expended in bringing stone artifacts and animal bones together' (Potts 1988: 272). Potts (1988: 281ff) explicitly addresses the extent of premeditation that would have been required for successful stone caching, noting that it necessitates as a minimum that hominins 'had a range of information about their environment' and could 'recall the distribution of resources' (Potts 1988: 281). Whilst such abilities are widespread throughout the animal world and do not require the kind of episodic memory often seen as instrumental to MTT, one could argue that the caching behaviour itself is indicative of at least the 'episodic-like' memory evidenced in modern corvids (e.g., Clayton et al. 2003). Furthermore, some archaeologists see the stone cache model as implying a mobility pattern towards the logistical end of the spectrum, a pattern demonstrated archaeologically only during the Upper Palaeolithic (e.g., Binford 1980, 1985; Straus 1986). It is clearly a behaviour that is quantitatively, if not qualitatively, different from the transport of tools by primates such as chimpanzees and capuchins, whose nut-cracking hammers are rarely transported more than a few hundred metres (e.g., Boesch and Boesch 1984; Ottoni and Izar 2008).

Nevertheless, the use of stone caches is still seen by most archaeologists as a pre-home-base phenomenon, and it is this later development that is key in facilitating Gamble's (1996a) transition from the local hominin network to the social landscape and the development of broad-scale FF. Potts (1988: 287) noted that 'the appearance of home bases involved changes in the spatial dimension of social life and feeding', but it is only through Gamble's (1996a, 1998a, 1999) network approach that the specific social benefits of this extended social milieu have become clear to archaeologists. The anchor provided by a home base is a pre-requisite for the release from proximity, but also provides a spatial focus for social exchange, whether of traditional commodities (hunted meat and gathered plant foods), or information. A predetermined aggregation location allows fissioning subgroups to spread over a wider area thus establishing vital knowledge of an extensive territory. The importance of such information in prehistoric societies was noted by Gamble (1980) as key to the emergence of the social landscape. Studies of extant hunter-gatherers have demonstrated that individuals travel far further than is required to meet immediate subsistence needs, with longer trips often explained as being specifically for the purpose of maintaining social bonds (e.g., Gamble 1983, 1993; Kelly 1995; Whallon 2006). The equitable bonds created between groups in this way act as insurance mechanisms providing access to neighbouring territories during periods of resource stress (Gamble 1983; Kelly 1995), necessarily requiring a long-term, risk sensitive view of subsistence management and considerable planning for future contingencies.

Gamble (1998a, 1999) argues that the social landscape may not have appeared until relatively late in human evolution, and the two thresholds he envisages accord well with archaeological evidence for the planning depth required to engage in extended fission-fusion sociality. An initial scaling-up is considered to coincide with the appearance of prepared-core technologies at around 300 ka (Gamble 1998a: 443). Not only does the Levallois mode of production itself demonstrate a degree of forward planning not seen in previous industries, but the distances raw materials are transported from this time onwards suggest a quantitative shift in the scale of landscape use (e.g., White and Pettitt 1995; Fernandes et al. 2008; Miller and Barton 2008) and imply an increase in the temporal cognition of early Neanderthals over their late European *H. heidelbergensis* ancestors. Prepared core technologies also become ubiquitous over a similar interval in the African MSA (e.g., Kuman 2001; McNabb 2001). Given the argument for independent evolution of prepared core techniques in the European Middle Palaeolithic (White and Ashton 2003), it is possible to suggest a geographically widespread threshold development at approximately 300 ka that depended on a greater capacity for planning depth in tool manufacture. However, recent analyses by Grove and colleagues (2012, based on data compiled by Binford 2001) based on group size increases and latitudinal gradients in population density suggest that higher levels of group fission would only have occurred in populations of Neanderthals, *H. sapiens* and, perhaps, a few late *H. heidelbergensis* groups in northern latitudes. A significant negative relationship between latitude and population density among hunter-gatherers, coupled with the finding of Dunbar (e.g., 1993; Aiello and Dunbar 1993) that group size has increased in line with neocortex size throughout the last three million years, mean that hominin migrations towards higher latitudes have involved ever larger groups living at ever lower population densities. Since energetic constraints prevent the exploitation of vast territories by cohesive groups (see, e.g.,

Chapman et al. 1995), groups are obliged to fission for foraging purposes. Thus we can argue that the social dynamics inferred for hominin populations from ~300 ka onwards demonstrate the need for advanced temporal cognition to facilitate ever-increasing periods of separation between individual subgroups.

A feature of the kind of multilevel societies in place by this time is that they lead to nested hierarchies composed of ever-larger tiers of social grouping (Dunbar 2003; Zhou et al. 2005; Grove 2010b, 2010c). Zhou et al. (2005), show recurrent groupings at approximately 5, 15, 50, and 150 individuals in both modern hunter-gatherer and sedentary western populations. Larger, periodic groupings occur at group sizes of approximately 500 and 1500 individuals (see also Hill and Dunbar 2003; Hamilton et al. 2007). Grove (2010b, 2011) has shown that later prehistoric monument distributions are consistent with this grouping pattern. However, it remains unclear exactly when in prehistory the 'outer' layers of 500 and 1500 were established. Whilst analyses of neocortex ratios in extant primates suggest a cognitive group size of approximately 150 for modern humans (Dunbar 1993; Aiello and Dunbar 1993), it is clear that something beyond encephalisation was required to establish the regional relations that typify modern hunter-gatherers (Grove and Coward 2008; Gamble 2010; Coward and Grove 2011). Gamble (1998a) and Dunbar (2009) have suggested that the 300 ka threshold would have been accompanied by at least a rudimentary form of language, which may have made possible the 500-strong 'megaband' as a standard element of hominin regional interaction.

The second threshold postulated by Gamble – the appearance of the social landscape itself – is dated to between 100 and 60 ka, and coincides with the establishment of the full, 1500-strong ethnolinguistic tribe and, by inference, the development of modern-like syntactical language. The fundamental shift here involves the 'stretching of social life beyond the practical limits set on co-presence interaction by time, the body and space' (Gamble 1998a: 440) into extended networks which are dependent upon the ability to view artefacts as symbols of 'distant persons who *in absentia* now determine the performance of social relationships' (Gamble 1999: 95). The equation of symbolic artefacts with extended networks, and the corollary that Palaeolithic societies lacking such networks would have been unable – or perhaps were never required – to produce such artefacts, hints at profound social developments during the latter stages of the MSA and in the Upper Palaeolithic of Europe. The notion that spatio-temporal 'distanciation' depends on the production of symbolic artefacts again implies that the flow of information is of paramount importance (Gamble 1980), and suggests that language, which is considered to have emerged during or before the 300 ka threshold, would have become a fully modern-like system of communication during the emergence of the social landscape. Modern externalists such as Clark and Chalmers (1998: 18) have argued that the appearance of behavioural modernity may have been scaffolded by a 'linguistically-enabled extension of cognition', yet the displacement that language implies is perhaps extended even further in both time and space by the use of artefacts, which can play precisely the role Clark and Chalmers envisage for language by allowing ideas to 'migrate between minds' (Mithen 2000a: 214). Given the distances artefacts were transported by the Late MSA and Upper Palaeolithic periods, such ideas could have migrated rapidly, and at continental scales.

Two examples of artefacts give an impression of the social landscape as established during the Upper Palaeolithic. The first is Vanhaeren and d'Errico's (2006) attempt to map the cultural geography of Aurignacian Europe using seriation and correspondence analyses of personal ornament types. These authors identify fifteen geographically distinct personal ornament 'sets' allied to geographical areas ranging from Greece in the south-east to Belgium in the north-west, arguing that they represent ethnolinguistic groupings akin to the tribes of modern hunter-gatherers. This finding appears to suggest a symbolism of exclusion among the first *H. sapiens* settlers of Europe, with personal ornaments reflecting regional identity and, by inference, establishing membership of an in-group to the exclusion of neighbouring tribes. Group signalling is certainly a common theme in studies of modern symbolic communication, yet Gamble's (1993, 1998a) approach suggests that exclusion would have been a feature of local groupings *prior* to the emergence of the social landscape and that, after this threshold, the release from proximity created an unbounded social sphere in which relations were built on the possibilities of inclusion.

The second example of widespread social and symbolic interaction comes from Gamble's (1982) work on the Gravettian 'Venus figurines', and shows how a single artefact form can in fact unite, rather than create boundaries between populations over vast areas. Gamble (1982: 99) argues that the appearance of a class of items such as the Venus figurines was 'a reflection of changing circumstances that required new means by which information could be transmitted and received'. The sheer scale of Venus figurine distribution – with very *similar* examples being found across almost the whole area surveyed by Vanhaeren and d'Errico (2006) for regional *differences* – suggests to Gamble (1982) that a limited set of stylistic rules governed figurine production, allowing socially distant groups to communicate with each other. The 'changing circumstances' could thus relate to an expansion in the scale of social interaction, with the negotiation of equitable relationships with distant groups providing advantages in terms of risk mitigation (Gamble 1993; Whallon 2006) and the need for a symbolic common currency. Social risk mitigation over large scales might have been of particular value during the increasingly harsh conditions of the Gravettian, whereas the relative climatic affluence of the Aurignacian could have encouraged the formation of neighbouring, but self-sufficient and perhaps competing populations. Alternatively, the two approaches could reflect contemporaneous phenomena. Gamble (1982) suggests that the use of common symbolic artefacts could cross-cut precisely the kinds of linguistic differences inferred by Vanhaeren and d'Errico (2006); whereas language is tribal, a common, simple symbolic currency such as the use of figurines could act as a truly extensive director of social intercourse.

CONCLUSIONS

The network approach to Palaeolithic society established by Gamble (1993, 1996a, 1998a, 1999) postulates a transformation of hominin society from a primate-like system, in which bonds are maintained through continual co-presence, into a distinctly human system in which relationships are maintained even in the absence of spatial proximity. This stretching of the human social system, involving the fission of subgroups for extended periods of time and the maintenance of equitable bonds with groups in distant geographical areas, brings a number of cognitive challenges. The social brain hypothesis has focused primarily on group size as an index of social complexity, yet in recent years this has been expanded to accommodate more fine-grained aspects of human social evolution such as the development of an ape-like fission-fusion pattern into the global web of networks visible among humans today. A combination of Gamble's network approach and the perspective on fission-fusion emerging from research into the social brain highlights a number of key cognitive attributes that would have facilitated the 'release from proximity' that is the hallmark of modern society. Looking into the archaeological record, clear signs of these cognitive attributes can be mapped chronologically as we trace the development of hominin societies towards modernity.

As Gamble has stressed time and again, the stones and bones of the Palaeolithic need not be silent on the subject of society. Beginning with the earliest evidence of raw materials and tools being transported around ancient environments, there is evidence for the kinds of cognitive abilities that would have accompanied the expansion of humans out of Africa and beyond. Displacement, object permanence, and mental time travel overlap in requiring the ability to hold objects (or agents) in mind when they are not physically present – a skill that would have developed in concert with the expanding spatio-temporal scope of hominin societies. From these initial skills more elaborate, humanlike abilities emerge, such as the capacity for analogical thought; the latter is seen particularly through the non-linguistic mappings of spatial extension onto temporal duration. As a potential demonstration of such analogical abilities, the appearance of symbolic artefacts is of particular importance to archaeologists. While evidence of trade and exchange are certainly valuable in establishing the scale of early hominin societies, it is at the point where artefacts begin to *stand for* distant places or people that a fully modern cognition emerges.

Gamble (1998a: 440) has argued that 'when artefacts become people, we have achieved that release from proximity which is our primate social heritage', yet this very social use of analogy is mediated by more than simply a spatio-temporal stretching of society. As is clear from the comparison of Aurignacian beads and Gravettian Venus figurines above, overlapping boundaries at multiple scales are established at various places in the landscape. These boundaries are traversed as groups disperse and aggregate, transforming the meanings of the artefacts they carry; it is this expanded fission-fusion process that requires 'the transformation in value from local to distant, from object to symbol' (Gamble 1999: 95). Thus material culture plays a far greater role in the evolution of hominin society than many archaeologists would acknowledge, not least as the medium of communication for the truly long-distance social exchange necessitated by expanded fission-fusion social systems. It is only when fission-fusion society reaches this uniquely human level of extension that 'the development of society through the elaboration of material culture is set in process' (Gamble 1982: 99).

CHAPTER 3

THE EXTENSION OF SOCIAL RELATIONS IN TIME AND SPACE DURING THE PALAEOLITHIC AND BEYOND

DWIGHT READ AND SANDER VAN DER LEEUW

INTRODUCTION

In recent work, culminating in the book *Origins and Revolutions*, Clive Gamble has suggested that we need to move away from a focus on the origin of individual, cognitive abilities of modern *Homo sapiens* towards the development of 'an external cognitive architecture by which hominins achieved social extension within local groups and a wider community' (Gamble 2010: 32). The shift in focus, he argues, is away from a rational to a relational explanation of behaviour (Gamble 2007); that is, from explanations that account for behaviour by criteria considering the individual in isolation to explanations framed around relations of individuals to both the material and the social domain.

Gamble argues that we need to work out the cognitive and emotional requirements necessary for individuals to operate simultaneously within a system of bounded groups and without through extended social relations that transcend local groups. He poses two questions. The first asks about 'the origins of group identity and ... social boundaries which are the building blocks of all subsequent archaeological periods from the Neolithic to the recent, more familiar past....', whereas the second, derived from insights regarding the social behaviour of primates, casts the process differently: 'Here it is how social relations were extended in time and space, which is at issue' (Gamble and Gittins 2004: 97). More recently and in the same vein he observes, 'Increasing brain and community size selected for mechanisms that both integrated and separated individuals in local groups' leading to 'ontological security, psychological continuity and the extension of the self to create the release from social proximity [i.e., non-human primate modes of social organisation based on face-to-face interaction]' (Gamble 2010: 36–37).

In these comments, Gamble has proposed a more encompassing view of the *context* in which modern human cognition became fully developed subsequent to the major advances in brain size associated with our current cognitive abilities. In his view, this context includes not only relationships among individuals, human groups and their environments (including artefacts), but, critically, also includes an expanded social field that developed over the same time period and which, he suggests, was actively involved in the evolution of our elaborated cognitive apparatus.

For those of us who have studied the close relationship between our ancestors' technological evolution and the evolution of human cognitive capacities, this is a timely observation. Archaeological data suggest that growth in the size of human groups composed of all individuals interacting on a regular basis is part of the long-term evolution of our species (Grove 2010c) and so increasing group size has been an integral component of our evolutionary history. We must thus link our ideas about the relationship between technological change and cognitive development with our ideas about societal change and explore the implications of both for the development of modern human cognition.

In this paper, we will provide tentative answers to Gamble's questions by considering the technological and the social domain as two areas that have individually, as well as jointly, positively affected the development of our cognitive capacity. To make this argument, we will incorporate empirical evidence from studies of primates, cognitive science, kinship, and ancient human technologies. But the core of our argument is a theoretical one – we ask at each step in our argument: What kind of 'tools for thought' did human beings require to obtain the desired artefact functionality in different domains and at different stages in their development, and how might they have acquired these?

During hominin evolutionary history, genetic transmission of biological information between generations was slowly but surely overtaken in importance by deliberate, social transmission of information *among members of the same generation and across generations*. That transition led humans to become the only species able to actively and purposefully organise its social as well as its material environment, a difference central to our understanding of human social systems (Read 1990).

The transition from biological to social transmission of information also implies the need to shift from a 'population perspective' of individual actions made in accordance with one's genetic disposition to an 'organisation perspective' in which cultural and social rules determine how people act collectively to organise themselves and the world around them (Lane et al. 2009; Leaf and Read 2012). The last point is critical, for if we only distinguish between the individual and population levels, then we cannot deal with the intervening levels of groups, networks, institutions and organisations that are framed through culture and shape our societies and behaviour as individuals.

For simplicity's sake, we will, in the remainder of this paper, consider hominin evolution as consisting of three phases: (a) the biological evolution of the cognitive capacities requisite for the florescence of stone tool technologies, (b) the evolutionary origin of cultural systems enabling the organisation of social groups no longer localised in space and time and (c) the emergence of increasingly complex forms of social organisations such as urban societies. We recognise that this distinction is, in part, artificial, as the phases of concern were not sequential but overlapping, with interaction among them. After describing changes that occurred in each of these phases, we will conclude with an outline of a general perspective on the relationship between the 'inside' and the 'outside' aspects of the human cognitive relationship with the external world identified by Gamble that can guide future ideas and research.

THE BIOLOGICAL PREREQUISITES FOR COGNITIVE DEVELOPMENT

We begin with a model of the brain's capacity to deal with information in an integrated manner through a neurological complex consisting of working memory coupled with short-term memory. We will refer to this complex as short-term working memory (hereafter STWM). In humans, working memory has been modelled by Alan Baddeley as consisting of a central executive system coupled to a phonological loop and a visuospatial sketchpad (the latter two are the short-term memory part of working memory in Baddeley's model) involved in 'a range of cognitive activities, such as reasoning, learning and comprehension' (Baddeley 2003: 829). Short-term memory refers to the ability to hold a small amount of information in an active, available state for a short period of time. Next, we need to identify measures of the size of short-term memory, the capacity part of STWM. The size of short-term memory affects the number of different sources, kinds or bits of information that can be held and processed together simultaneously in working memory when carrying out a particular train of thought or course of action.

There are different ways to reconstruct the change in the size of STWM during human evolution (Read and van der Leeuw 2008). One is by comparing the STWM of chimpanzees (the archetype for our closest common ancestor in the evolutionary tree that produced modern humans [Chapais 2008]) with that of modern humans. We consider the STWM of chimpanzees to be 2 ± 1, based on empirical observations such as that only 75% of the chimpanzees in a chimpanzee community (near the village of Bossou in Guinea, West Africa) are able to simultaneously manipulate three elements (an anvil, a nut and a hammerstone) in order to crack nuts for eating. Apparently, keeping as many as three items in mind simultaneously is difficult for them. Additional data on chimpanzee interaction with objects in a variety of contexts lead to the same conclusion (Read 2008).

In contrast to chimpanzees, experiments with different ways of calculating the human capacity to combine information sources point to an STWM of

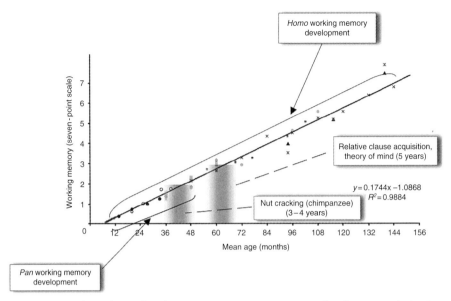

Figure 3.1: The relationship between cognitive capacity and infant growth in *Pan* and in *Homo sapiens*. The trend line is projected from the regression of time-delay response (Diamond and Doar, 1989) on infant age. Data are rescaled for each dataset to make the trend line pass through the mean of that dataset. Working memory scaled to STWM = 7 at 144 months. The 'fuzzy' vertical bars compare the age of nut cracking among chimpanzees with the age for relative clause acquisition and theory of mind conceptualisation in humans (Data sources are given in Read 2008: Figure 2. Reprinted from Read and van der Leeuw 2008 by permission of publisher).

7 ± 2 for modern humans (Miller 1956).[1] This difference in magnitude between chimpanzees and humans is consistent with assuming that the constant rate of increase in STWM from infancy until pubescence for humans (Read 2008) applies equally to chimpanzees but that chimpanzees reach pubescence about 3–4 years after birth, whereas modern humans do so around age 13–14 (see Figure 3.1). We assume, therefore, that the difference in age of pubescence is a proximal explanation for the difference in STWM capacity (cf. Read and van der Leeuw 2008: 1960).

We can correlate evolutionary increase in the size of STWM with increase in hominin encephalisation – the brain-to-body-weight ratio – during hominin evolution by assuming that STWM varies linearly with changes in encephalisation (see vertical axes in Figure 3.2) measured for each of the hominin phylogenetic groups. We can then relate the evolutionary pattern for changes in STWM and encephalisation to time-based changes in hominin conceptualisations involved in making stone tools, thereby establishing both the evolutionary pattern for change in STWM and its implications for changes in the complexity of conceptualisations involved in hominin production of stone tools.

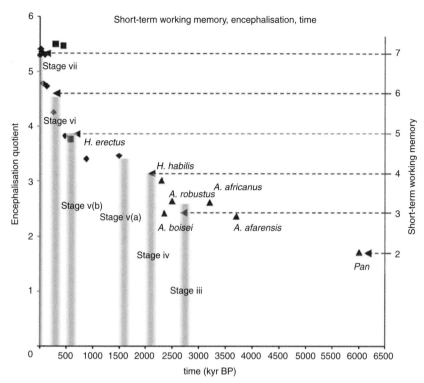

Figure 3.2: Graph of encephalisation quotient (EQ) estimates based on hominid fossils and *Pan* (Chimpanzees). Early hominid fossils have been identified by taxon. Each data point is the mean for hominid fossils at that time period. Height of the 'fuzzy' vertical bars is the hominid EQ corresponding to the data for the appearance of the stage represented by the fuzzy bar. Right vertical axis represents STWM. Data are adapted from the following: triangles, Epstein 2002; squares, Rightmire 2004; diamonds, Ruff et al. 1997. EQ= brain mass/$(11.22$ body mass$^{0.76})$, cf. Martin 1981 (Reprinted from Read and van der Leeuw 2008 by permission of publisher).

The time-based degree of encephalisation can be computed from measurements made on the skeletal remains of fossil hominins. We can relate the concepts invoked in the production of stone tools to the number of dimensions involved and thereby to the size of STWM required for the production of the kind of stone tools that exemplify each stage in hominin evolution (see Table 3.1). We can then graph all three measures simultaneously on a single graph (see Figure 3.2). As shown in Figure 3.2, change in encephalisation across the hominin phylogenetic groups corresponds to both a linear change in the size of STWM and regular change in the conceptualisations involved in stone tool technology during hominin evolution (cf. Read and van der Leeuw 2008: 164).

Figure 3.2 provides us with direct evidence for the way regular changes in STWM through time relate to changes in conceptualisations involved in artefact production. We may flesh out more fully evolutionary change in the

TABLE 3.1: *Evolution of stone tool manufacture from the earliest tools (stage 2, > 2.6 M. years ago; found in Lokalalei 1) to the complex blade technologies (stage 7, found in most parts of the world c. 50,000 BP). Columns 2–5 indicate the observations leading us to assume specific STWM capacities; column 8 (bold) indicates the stage's STWM capacity, and column 9 indicates the approximate age of the beginning of each stage. Column 10 refers to the relevant artifact categories documenting the stages. For a more extensive explanation, see Read & van der Leeuw 2008: 1961–1964.*

Stage	Concept	Action	Novelty	Dimensionality	Goal	Mode	STWM	Age BP	Example
1	Object attribute	Repetition possible	Functional attributes already present; can be enhanced	0	Use object		**1**		
1A	Relationship between objects	Repetition possible	Using more than one object to fulfill task	0	Combine objects		**2**		
2	Imposed attribute	Repetition possible	Object modified to fulfill task	0	Improve object		**2**	> 2.6 My	Lokalalei 1
3	Flaking	Repetition	Deliberate flaking, but without overall design	0: Incident angle < 90°	Shape flakes		**3**	2.6 My	Lokalalei 2C
4	Edge	Iteration: each flake controls the next	Débitage: flaking to create an edge on a core	1: Line of flakes creates partial boundary	Shape core	1	**4**	2.0 My	Oldowan chopper
5	Closed curve	Iteration: each flake controls the next	Débitage: flaking to create an edge and a surface	2: Edges as generative elements of surfaces	Shape biface from edge	2	**4-5**		
5A	Surface	Iteration: each flake controls the next	Façonnage: flaking used to make a shape	2: Surface intended elements, organized in relation to one another	Shape biface from surfaces	2	**5**	500 Ky	Biface handaxes
6	Surface	Algorithm: removal of flake prepares next	Control over location and angle of flaking to form surface	2: Surface of the flake brought under control but shape constraint	Serial production of tools	3	**6**	300 Ky	Levallois
7	Intersection of planes	Recursive application of algorithm	Prismatic blade technology; monotonous process	3: flake removal retains core shape – no more shape constraint	Serial production of tools	4	**7**	> 50 Ky	Blade technologies

level of cognitive development of our ancestral hominins by considering the sequence of changes in the conceptualisation required to eventually achieve the three-dimensional manufacture of stone tools mastered by our ancestors in the Upper Palaeolithic (cf. Figure 3.3 a–d; Pigeot 1991; van der Leeuw 2000).

The first formal stone tools are essentially cobbles from which a flake has been removed to create a sharp point (Figure 3.3a). Removing a flake (as opposed to simply chipping off a piece from the cobble in an uncontrolled manner) requires integration of three pieces of information: the future form to be produced, the movement of the hammerstone as it is used to strike the cobble, and the striking angle between the hammerstone and the cobble, which needs to be less than 90° to make the conchoidal fracture that will remove a flake without shattering the cobble. Making a flake that will be a tool with a sharp edge thus requires STWM = 3 to integrate these three dimensions. In the next stage, the flaking action is repeated sequentially along the cobble to form a cutting edge on the cobble. This requires control over the same three dimensions as well as a fourth one, namely the controlled sequence of flake removals through blows along a line. For this task, STWM = 4 (Figure 3.3b). Next, the edge is closed: the toolmaker goes all the way around the cobble or nodule until the last flake removal is adjacent to the first. By itself, this is not a completely new stage and we have assigned this STWM = 4.5. But once the closed loop is conceived topologically as defining a surface enclosed by an edge, the knapper has created two options: either to define a surface first by knapping an edge around it and then removing flakes from that enclosed surface, or to do the reverse – remove the flakes first from what will be the enclosed surface and then construct the edge. The conceptual reversibility and integration of the defined, enclosed surface in producing a tool shows that the knapper has now integrated five dimensions, and therefore that STWM ≥ 5 (Figure 3.3c).

The next stage extends sequentiality further, but in a more complex way that becomes the precursor for recursive use of an algorithm in the production of stone tools. In the so-called 'Levallois' technique (which is the algorithm), making one artefact serves, at the same time, as preparation for the next by dividing the nodule being worked conceptually into two parts separated along its edge. And finally, with the advent of blade technologies, the knapper works completely and recursively in three dimensions, preparing two surfaces at right angles, and then taking blades off the third, which is at right angles to both the others. At this stage, STWM needs to be around 6–7 (Figure 3.3d) and now the knappers are able not only to work a three-dimensional piece of stone, but also can conceive of it as three-dimensional and adapt their working techniques accordingly and in a recursive manner.[2]

Returning to the main argument, close observation of the tools and other traces of human existence available by 35,000 BP indicates that, after some

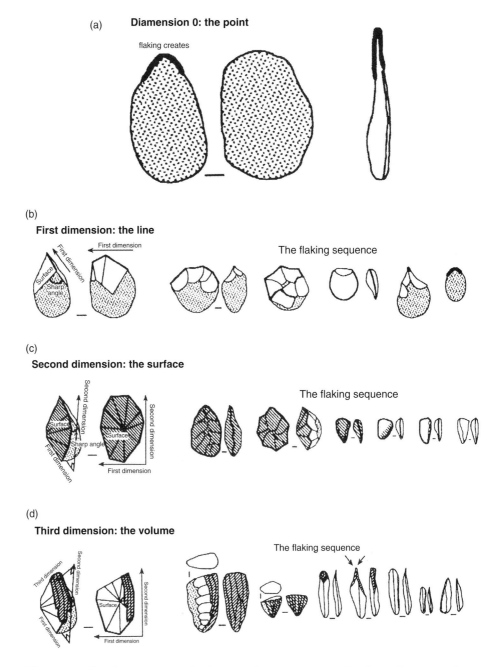

Figure 3.3: For humans to attain the capacity to conceive of a three-dimensional object (a pebble or stone tool) in three dimensions takes around 2 million years. (a) Taking a flake off at the tip of the pebble is an action in 0 dimensions, and takes STWM 3; (b) successively taking off several adjacent flakes creates a (1-dimensional) line, and requires STWM 4; (c) stretching the line until it meets itself defines a surface by drawing a line around it and represents STWM 4.5; distinguishing between that line and the surface it encloses implies fully working in two dimensions, and requires STWM 5; (c) preparing two sides in order to remove the flakes from the third side testifies to a three-dimensional conceptualisation of the pebble, and requires STWM 7 (after van der Leeuw 2000)

2,000,000 years of making stone tools, our ancestors had an STWM of 7 ±
2 and could (van der Leeuw 2000):

- Distinguish between reality and conception;
- Categorise based on similarities and differences;
- Engage in feed-back, feed-forward and time reversal in their thinking
  (e.g., mentally reverse an observed causal sequence in order to conclude
  from the result what kind of action could achieve it);
- Remember and represent sequences of actions, including control loops,
  and conceive of such sequences that could be inserted as alternatives in
  manufacturing sequences;
- Create basic hierarchies, such as point-line-surface-volume, or hierarchies
  of size or inclusion;
- Conceive of relationships between a whole and its constituent parts
  (including reversing these relationships);
- Maintain complex sequences of actions in the mind, such as between
  different stages of a production process;
- Represent an object in a reduced set of dimensions (e.g., life-like cave
  paintings).

As we will see below, a number of these cognitive and conceptual operations are a
necessary prerequisite to the development of the operations required for humans
to aggregate in larger groups. In particular, when forming larger groups and a
relational social field that is no longer bound by location (Gamble 2010), our
ancestors must also have been able to distinguish between reality and conception,
to categorise based on relations, to conceptualise reversal of relations (feed-back–
feed-forward), to create hierarchies and partonomies, and to represent phenomena using a subset of the total number of dimensions that are observed. All of these
capacities are fundamental to the development of socially more complex societies.

THE TRANSITION TOWARDS SOCIALLY MAINTAINED
ORGANISATION: PHASE ONE

In our hypothesis, this first phase of hominin evolution also selected for the
following cognitive capabilities that seem, in part, to have been acquired due
to selection arising from emerging tensions between group size and increasing
individuation on the one hand, and the need to keep the group socially
coherent on the other hand:

1. *Enculturation*, the process by which the cultural context into which a
   newborn is inducted teaches that individual the accepted norms and
   values of the group. Its introduction transfers the intergenerational
   transmission of information from the genetic (biological), and thus
   individual, realm to the cultural, and thus collective, realm.

Enculturation is not simply phenotype-to-phenotype trait transmission writ large, but refers to the lifelong process by which an individual conceptually becomes part of a community among whose members commonality of idea systems (i.e., culture) establish and provide collectively understood meanings of, and rules for, behaviour.

2. *Categorisation based on relations*, the creation of categorical descriptions that allow an individual to differentiate behaviour according to the *kind of relation* an individual has to an entity (including the material domain, in Gamble's argument) with which interaction will take place, rather than differentiating behaviour according to experience with the individual or object concerned, which limits the range of behaviours that can be anticipated prior to experience. This becomes particularly important because it enables encapsulation of information, hence reduces the information processing necessary to deal with larger groups while maintaining coherence of the group, thereby enabling the incorporation of more diverse behaviours into the community's repertoire.

3. *Development of cultural rule systems*, one of whose functionalities is enabling an individual to both generate and anticipate behaviours based on shared, conceptually framed systems of relations without depending on prior interaction (e.g., incorporation of cultural rules such as 'the enemy of my enemy is my friend'). The functionality of such systems depends upon them being shared by the members of the group, as this enables a consistent and predictable pattern of behaviour to emerge (Read 2012). Cultural kinship systems incorporate such rule systems. When group membership is based on cultural kin relatedness, as is the case with hunter-gatherer and other small-scale societies, the members of a group can easily determine who belongs to it, and who does not.

4. *A concomitant shift from individual to group functionality*. Whereas the transmission of information by genotypic or phenotypic means through gene transmission or imitation, respectively – referred to as dual inheritance – essentially serves the individual's fitness, the transmission by means of enculturation serves the fitness of the group and its chances of survival in competition with other groups. With elaboration of organisational structures increasingly incorporating differentiated behaviours, individual functionality is increasingly derived through group membership. The functionality derived from an idea system such as culturally defined kinship, for example, accrues to an individual only when that idea system is shared among group members. Moreover, the culturally defined and transmitted resources of the group, such as rule systems, can be modified to provide alternative functionalities. When different groups develop different rule systems, group competition can arise in the form of group selection driven by population density rather than by individual reproductive fitness (Read 1987).

THE TRANSITION TOWARDS SOCIALLY MAINTAINED ORGANISATION: PHASE TWO

This second phase progressively decoupled the emergent social systems from a genetic basis for social interaction, thereby, through a shift from face-to-face to relational forms of social organisation, overcoming a 'bottleneck' in maintaining the coherence of groups in the face of increased individuation that was not realised by chimpanzees or other primates (Read 2010b, 2012) and which was the foundation for our current large-scale and complex societies.[3] Which are the 'tools for thought' that these changes enabled? We argue, following Read (2012), that four essential biologically grounded characteristics of human cognition, acquired as part of Darwinian evolution and involved in the development of stone tool production, laid the basis for this non-Darwinian second phase of human evolution:

- A concept of 'self' – cognitive awareness of one's own existence and identity in contrast to that of others;
- A 'theory of mind' – the ability to attribute mental states to others, including the conceptualisation that other conspecifics may have different mental representations than oneself;
- The capacity to categorise relations between individuals, rather than just forming categories based on the characteristics of individuals;
- The capacity to reason recursively and thereby to form a composition of relations and generate new relations from existing relations.

Whereas chimpanzees have a theory of 'self', and there is some (debated) experimental evidence that they may have a limited 'theory of mind', the extent to which categorisation based on relations occurs among non-human primates is unknown, though clearly limited. The capacity for recursive reasoning seems to be completely absent among them, but is well documented in stone tool technology (Pigeot 1991; van der Leeuw 2000; Read and van der Leeuw 2008). Assuming these four capabilities allows us to outline the following derived cognitive capacities:

1. *Recursive composition of relations.* Applying recursive reasoning to relational categories such as kinship relations allows the construction of new relations (e.g., *grandmother* as *mother* of *mother*) and reciprocal relations (e.g., *mother* and *daughter*) *through the mind*, rather than from direct observation of behaviours. Once the new relation has been constructed in the mind, it can be applied to individuals. This also allows the formation of *reciprocal asymmetric* relations, for example *mother-daughter* versus *daughter-mother*.

The importance of such mental constructs lies chiefly in being able to *anticipate* (rather than merely observe) the probable (or at least potential) reaction of another individual to one's own actions, and thus to adapt one's behaviour accordingly. This provides a basis for *social interaction that is decoupled from any requirement of biological relations* among the individuals in question, as is the case with behaviours introduced through biological kin selection (Read et al. 2009; Read 2010b, 2012).

2. *Development of role systems.* Actual, rather than potential, social inter-action depends on actively engaging in reciprocal behaviours. Only if both parties in a potential reciprocal social relation engage in a behav-iour associated with that relation is the foundation laid for continued social interaction (Read 2010b, 2012). For this to happen, individuals must collectively recognise the kind of relation with which a behaviour is associated, which, in turn, depends on the degree of coordination among individuals – and thereby on the existence of a role system for those behaviours. For example, coordination in kinship systems is pos-sible because the system of kinship terms (1) is a computation system that allows the simple calculation of kin relations, (2) is a generative compu-tation system through which new kin relations may be computed, and (3) implies that reciprocity for all kin relations follows from reci-procity of the generating kin relations (Read 2007). In these, as in other kinds of systems, predictability is essential and made possible by having a commonly understood cultural computation system.

3. *Emergence of syntactically organised sets of relations.* An important aspect of the evolved system of rules is the distinction between the potential functionality of that system, based on the number of relations in the system, and its actual functionality, based on the number of coordinated individuals. The former is subject to transmission decay (Read et al. 2009), which will reduce the actual functionality of the system. When the relations are distinct and need to be individually learned (e.g., a pattern of genealogical relations making up a family tree), transmission decay is much higher than when the system is syntactically organised; i.e., when there is a set of rules and a small set of initial relations (a *generative syntax*) that suffice to generate the structure (a generative structure) for the whole set of relations, as it is just the generative syntax that needs to be transmitted (Read et al. 2009) and transmission errors can be detected as syntactically incorrect expressions.

Kinship terminologies are an example of a generative structure (the termin-ology) with an underlying generative syntax (the rules for generating new kin terms from a small set of primary kin terms) (Read 2001, 2007; Leaf and Read 2012). In the American/English kinship terminology, for example, interrelated kin terms can be generated from the English kin term *parent*, its reciprocal term, *child*, and a recursive generative rule of the form: 'If x and y are either generating kin terms or the outcome of this rule, then xy – the kin term product of the kin terms, x and y – is also a kin term'. (By the kin term product of the kin terms x and y is meant the kin term that speaker would use for alter 2 when speaker refers to alter 1 by the kin term y and alter 1 refers to alter 2 by the kin term x.) Thus for English speakers, the kin term product, xy, of the kin terms $y = uncle$ and $x = daughter$, is the kin term $xy = cousin$, for if speaker refers to him as *uncle* and he refers to her as *daughter*, then speaker knows to refer to her as *cousin. The capacity to develop such syntactic systems is another core cognitive function for a socially transmitted cultural system to emerge.*

We argue, following Leaf and Read (2012), that the cognitive abilities required to produce cave art show that the above cognitive operations were in place in human groups (but not Neanderthals) by sometime between 50,000 and 25,000 BP. These cognitive capacities allowed new forms of social organisation based on culturally constructed systems of kinship that freed social groups from dependence on face-to-face interaction for social cohesion. By the end of that period human groups were no longer limited in size by the 'biological bottleneck' of genetically-based social relations dependent on face-to-face interaction. Using systems of cultural kinship relations enabled redistribution of culturally kin-related individuals among social groups in accordance with resource fluctuations over which isolated groups had little control, enabling the shift from localised to widespread communities discussed by Gamble (2010) and also leading to greater population densities that gave such groups competitive advantage over other, still localised, groups (e.g., Neanderthal groups) (Read 1987; Leaf and Read 2012). In turn, increase in population density biased further change towards the development of widespread social networks that crosscut social groups as discussed by Gamble (2007). Changes like this tend to be uni-directional as reversion to previous forms of organisation requires reduction in population density (Read and LeBlanc 2003).

Because our ancestors had developed the cognitive ability to engage in more complex conceptualisations and mental representations involving both the material and social domains, as indicated by the evolutionary increase to an STWM of 7 ± 2, they were also able to deal with relatively complex challenges in virtually all domains without additional expansion of our cognitive abilities and developed culturally-based idea systems, such as kinship systems (Leaf and Read 2012), that enabled more complex interactions with the social and material domains, reflected in the evolution of more elaborate technologies, modes of food acquisition and forms of social organisation.

THE FIRST VILLAGES, AGRICULTURE AND HERDING: FOOD PROCUREMENT VERSUS FOOD PRODUCTION

In the next stage, the Mesolithic (c. 20,000 – 7,000 BP – precise dates vary by region), we observe an initially slow transition to a period of continued innovation (the Neolithic). The Mesolithic might be interpreted as the period in which the consequences of the human capacity to recursively and conceptually deal with seven or more dimensions simultaneously began to spread and change the lifestyle of many groups. In this period, for example, appears sedentation or, at least, territorialisation of certain groups in or near areas with high concentrations of specific foodstuffs (see, e.g., Newell and Constandse-Westerman 1986), while others continued a highly mobile, small-group hunter-gatherer subsistence strategy (see, e.g., Zvelebil 1986). By the term Neolithic we are referring to the following period in which sedentary and transhumant lifestyle based on cultivation and stockraising, respectively, dominated (see, e.g., Price 2000). From a cognitive point of view, it is difficult to distinguish, in general terms, between sedentism and transhumance during the transition away from highly mobile, small-group hunter-gatherer subsistence strategies because of the interplay between sedentary and transhumant strategies and the different patterns for this transition in different regions. We will therefore address them together here.

Some of the innovations that emerge in this period include:

1. *The introduction of ground stone objects,* completing the mastery of stoneworking at all scales from the micro- through the macroscopic. Control over the final shape is complete.

2. *The (conceptual) introduction of containers*[4] in wood, leather, stone and pottery. The manufacturing techniques involved vary, but all combine different innovations:

   - The introduction of *solids around a void*. This requires the conceptual separation of the surface of an object from its volume, and distinguishing between outside and inside surfaces, only possible with true three-dimensional conception of objects[5];

   - The *inversion of the sequence of manufacturing*, beginning with the smallest particles (clay platelets, fibers, hairs) and assembling them into larger two- or three-dimensional objects (cloth, baskets, coiled pottery);

   - *Correcting errors* by going back in a procedure, making the correction and proceeding again. This presumes that control loops link the past with the present and the future, and that *actions are conceived of as being reversible;*

   - Further *separation between different stages of production*. Grouping a large number of embedded control loops in stages reduces the information load at any one time, but small variations early on can have major consequences. Errors must easily be corrected.

3. *The introduction of conceptual tools to control the landscape.* This includes further transformation of the subsistence risks discussed above by shifting from a procurement to a production mode of obtaining food resources via horticulture, agriculture and herding techniques, which

makes the quantities of food resources obtained amenable to substantial increase through labour intensification. Hunter-gatherer groups that retained a resource procurement mode of obtaining food resources but with access to highly abundant resources amenable to intensive exploitation, such as salmon runs in northwestern North America or shell fish on the coast of southern California and of Florida, can also be included here.

The transformation from resource procurement to resource production is typified by:

- a mobile lifestyle with the breeding and herding of domesticated animals, or;
- the seasonal cultivation of wild plants as a principal subsistence strategy, or;
- settling in one place, building houses, clearing fields, and cultivating domesticated plants.

The domestication of different crops and animals in different parts of the world seems to imply that domestication is not a single 'technique', but this does not necessarily indicate independent invention for different reasons, as such developments may have been enabled by changes in the conceptualisation of space and time: in each case, resource production resulted in *long-term human investment in certain aspects of the environment*, which *channelled the adaptations of the people involved* and led to a more extended conceptualisation of space and time.

This required a *two-dimensional mental map of the landscape* and, in the case of houses and cultivation, the relational distinction between '*inside*' and '*outside*' – marked by the walls of a house or the perimeter of gardens or fields – as well as that between '*self*' and '*other*', acquired as part of the conceptualisation of kinship systems. Two-dimensional conceptualisation of space and the distinction between inside and outside are extended to objects larger than tools.

Temporally speaking, in the case of cultivation, clearance, planting or seeding are separated by several months – if not years – from harvesting a crop, and it takes years to build up a herd of sufficient size to ensure the survival of the group. Both involve stretching of temporal sequences and temporal separation of different parts of a 'production' sequence while still conceptualising the sequence as a whole.

In the absence of archaeological data, we must look to ethnography in order to understand the implications of these changes for people's perception of time and space. The Australian Aborigine use of 'song-lines' (Chatwin 1987; Molyneaux and Vitebsky 2000) is an example of mobile space-time perception. Songlines allow the traveller to find the way by matching a rote-learned song with the scenery that unfolds while travelling, allowing a person to be temporarily connected with a location or area in space, and thus to find his way or 'own' it. But as soon as the connection between the song and the landscape is broken, either by ceasing to sing the song, or by moving on in the landscape, the 'ownership' also ceases. The landscape neither can be interpreted without the song, nor does the song make sense without the landscape, because the song invokes time as an independent dimension to interpret space.

Frequent movement causes every trajectory to be observed and memorised from all directions. In many (semi-)sedentary cultures, however, spatial perception is encoded on a two-dimensional (mental) map (cf. Brody 2002). Settling down provides fixed points (settlements) around which spatial orientation is organised and provides the continuity of observation needed to unravel the respective roles of space and time in observed changes.[6] These advances opened up new domains for innovation, and particularly for innovations with long-range implications. Change in conceptions of what is possible itself generates action. Thus, beyond their functionality, tools conceptually 'contribute to the making of the universe of possibilities that make action itself' (Callon and Caliskan 2005: 18; quoted in Masys 2011: 9). Innovations relating to intensification of food production were part of the shift to sedentary societies and led to open-ended adaptations. These transformed the relationship between societies and their environments into a *reciprocal* one. As groups became more dependent upon food production methods for survival, they were less able to use mobility as a way to deal with environmentally induced risk and instead learned to *control environmentally induced risk* through *intervening in the environment* by: (1) *reducing or controlling the range of their dependencies on the environment*, (2) *simplifying (parts of) their environments (e.g., through clearing land of natural vegetation for growing food crops and through herd animals replacing wild animals as a protein source)* and (3) *spatial and technical diversification and specialisation (e.g., planting different crops in different environments)* (cf. van der Leeuw 2000). The necessary increase of *investment* in the environment anchored communities in their territory and led to building permanent dwellings. Differences in resource availability and know-how led to diversification and the intensification of relations between groups through trade. This drove societies to more complex solutions to the constraints of food production strategies such as modes of social organisation falling under the umbrella of tribal societies (here used as a descriptive term), which in turn, led to unexpected consequences accommodated by new systems of organisation. We attribute these changes to a new dynamic, in which *learning moved from the individual to the group,* as the dimensionality and information content of possible modes of adaptation increasingly exceeded the capability of individuals acting in isolation within groups, or of groups in isolation. This involved the emergence of the following feedback loop (van der Leeuw 2007):

Problem-solving structures knowledge → more knowledge increases the information-processing capacity → that in turn allows the cognition of new problems → creates new knowledge → knowledge creation involves more and more people in processing information → increases the size of the group involved and its degree of aggregation → creates more problems → increases need for problem-solving → problem-solving structures more knowledge ... etc.

The feedback loop enabled the continued accumulation of knowledge (information-processing capacity) and a concomitant increase in matter, energy and information flows through societies, thus the *growth of positively interacting and mutually reinforcing groups*. But group growth was constrained by the amount of information that could be communicated among the members of the group and among different groups. Miscommunication could lead to misunderstandings and conflicts, which would impair the cohesion of the communities involved. Communication stress provided the incentive for (a) *improvements in the means of communication* (e.g., by 'inventing' more precise concepts to communicate with [cf. van der Leeuw 1982]), and (b) *a reduction in the search time needed to find those that one needed to communicate with as the spatial scale for interacting groups increased* (e.g., through a more sedentary lifestyle, trade, etc.). In the process, more and more, the community rather than the individual, constituted the basis for handling risk and this required, at the individual level, increased investment in social skills and, at the community level, group investment in culturally defined social role systems such as the kinship roles defined through kinship terminologies, administrative roles defined through political systems, and so on.

THE FIRST TOWNS

The growth of the feedback system that drove societal growth and the conquest of the material world through innovation from the Neolithic on ultimately enabled the emergence of true 'world systems' such as the colonial empires of the early modern period (van der Leeuw 2007, 2010, 2012) or the current globalised world. The first step in this process is the emergence of towns.

From around 7000 BP, *communication using then current modalities became a major constraint, especially in the case of non-localised communication,* because of population, group and settlement growth. This stage saw a host of new innovations providing new modes of communication (writing and scribes), social regulation (administration, bureaucracies, laws), harnessing resources (mining) and exchange (over larger and larger distances).

As larger groups aggregated, the 'footprint' upon which they depended expanded exponentially, as did the effort required to transport materials. *Hence, access to energy emerged as a major constraint in the evolutionary expansion of societies* (cf. White 1959; Patzek and Tainter 2011). To deal with this, a core–periphery dynamic emerged, as *organisational capacity was generated in the towns and incorporated a wider and wider territory*, thereby increasing the energy and natural resources flowing towards expanding towns and cities. This made it possible to feed the ever-increasing number of individuals no longer directly tied to food production and who identified new needs, novel functions and categories, as well as new artefacts and challenges. This kept the system going by adding new organisation and information-processing capacity. Such feedback loops became the 'bootstrapping' drivers, creating larger and larger agglomerations and territories.[7]

Underpinning that dynamic is one that we know well in the modern world. Invention usually (and certainly in prehistoric and early historic times) involves individuals or small groups and a relatively small number of cognitively manipulated dimensions. When an invention draws the attention of larger numbers of people (found, for example, in towns), more uses are seen for it, ways to slightly improve it are identified, and so on. This may trigger a string of further innovations (an 'innovation cascade'), including new artefacts, new uses of existing artefacts, and new forms of behaviour and social and institutional organisations.[8]

EMPIRES

The above feedback loop systems ('flow structures') kept societies growing (albeit with ups and downs) until (from c. 2500 BC in the Old World, and c. 500 BC in the New). Single societies in the form of empires covered very large areas and concentrated large numbers of people at their centre, such as the Chinese, Achaemenid and Macedonian and Roman Empires in the Old World and the Maya, Zapotec and Inca Empires in the New World. *Throughout this period, means of communication and sources of energy remained the main constraints on further expansion and growth, and required new forms of technical and social organisation to circumvent.* Energy constraints were circumvented by harnessing animal energy (including slavery), wind power (for transportation in sailing vessels and for driving windmills), falling water (for mills) and so on. Means of communication expanded (e.g., 'highways' on land) and new technologies were introduced (better ships and navigation equipment on the sea). New systems of organisation, often grounded in over-arching religious ideologies, integrated previously discrete and opposing polities (e.g., the Zapotec Empire grew from three previously competing polities in the Oaxaca Valley, Mexico; e.g., Read and LeBlanc 2003: 76). All of these created and concentrated wealth that could be used to defray the costs of controlling potential and actual societal tensions (bureaucracies, armies, etc.).

Those constraints limited the extent of empires in space and time. Tainter (1988), for example, argues convincingly that it was only the energy (in the form of treasure) obtained by Rome through conquest of groups outside the Empire that made it possible for Rome to maintain its armies and bureaucracies. When expansion was no longer feasible and the Empire was thrown back upon recurrent (in essence solar) energy obtained through agriculture, it could no longer maintain the feedback loop. This reduced the advantages of being part of the Empire, causing groups to fall back on smaller, regional or local networks. Disaffection, or even dispersion of the population, followed.

CONCLUSION

Gamble's work places considerable importance on taking an integrated approach to changes taking place at both the individual level and at the societal and technological level. Rather than seeing these as separate domains where each affects the other as an external factor, he envisages a more encompassing approach in which we cannot understand what happens in one domain without taking into account the interconnections among these domains. Indeed, the development of our cognitive abilities can only reasonably be explained by focusing on the cognitive relationship itself – the relationship between the phenomena being perceived (the external world) and the perception derived from them (the internal projection of that world). Ideas similar to this have been advanced elsewhere, such as the recent interest in embodied cognition (e.g., Lakoff and Johnson 1999; Clark 2008; Rupert 2009; Shapiro 2011) in which cognition is not just seen as an aspect of mind but also of the body, and in more extreme form by Actor-Network theory (e.g. Callon 1986; Law 1992; Latour 2005), based on the idea that the social and material domains form a network that itself engenders action. However, integration between the former ('internal') and the later ('external') approach is essentially missing.

For Gamble, the evolutionary development of our cognitive abilities cannot be understood without also understanding our technological relations to the material world and our social relations, not only to the individuals making up the group in which we are located, but also to others connected to us through the conceptual relations and the idea systems we share with others (even without prior face-to-face interaction), expressed formally through kinship and other culturally defined role systems. Social and technological systems, expressed through organisation and production, are all interconnected through the idea systems we refer to as culture. It is the development of our cognitive abilities during Phase One of hominin evolution that eventually made possible the formation of the idea systems that underlie both the social and technological components of human adaptations.

From Phase One to Phase Two of human evolution we see elaboration of this by the development of our cognitive abilities, e.g. the increase in the capacity of working memory. These cognitive changes made technologies and human social systems as we know them possible (Leaf and Read 2012). The cognitive ability to mentally shift from face-to-face interaction as the basis of social interaction to social interaction based instead on a conceptual and mutually shared system of relations, such as a system of culturally constructed kinship relations, circumvented the 'cognitive constraint' (Read 2012: Figure 4.5) our hominid ancestors faced. They thereby opened the possibility for new forms of social organisation, no longer driven by individual traits and individual fitness, but by organisational systems through which functionality at the individual level is derived (Lane et al. 2009). The pattern of change we see in stone tools is not primarily, as Gamble points out, a historical record of technology seen in isolation, but a record of the way in which technology became cultural, in the sense of becoming a material expression of shared concepts and ideas about the relationships group members had to the material world, and thus part of the development of new forms of social and material organisation based on relations individuals have with each other (even in the absence of prior face-to-face interaction) as well as to the material world through technology. In brief, as discussed by Gamble, by the end of Phase One and going into Phase Two, the critical expansion of the field of relations, with its prior dependence on location severed, was in place as discussed by Gamble.

Once the basis for a new mode of social organisation, including technological systems defining the relationship of individuals and groups to the material world of artefacts, was in place, further change in the mode of adaptations (going from band to tribes, from temporary settlements to towns, and from acephalous to hierarchical systems [and sometimes the reverse]) has to be seen in the form of organisation and not at the level of individual traits, that is, as manifestations of changes in 'tools for thought' made possible by the cognitive changes that were already in place. Phase Two is a record of community-level changes with regard to idea systems and changes in concepts that made possible far-reaching innovations in interactions within and between the social and the material worlds. Increasingly, critical aspects of new adaptations centred on feedback loops involving groups and not just individuals (van der Leeuw 2007) and were dependent on changes in idea systems and not just traits of individuals, and thus change accelerates as groups develop idea systems that increase their ability to manipulate and modify the material world. For example, feedback loops that previously stabilised population size were diminished by new modes of adaptation that shielded women, in a local and immediate sense, from high fertility and its negative impact on the health of her family, thereby severing the negative feedback that had resulted in birth intervals maintaining a stable population size (Read 1998, 2010b). As a result, increase in population size became a driver for change in a way not seen in earlier, hunter-gatherer economies based on procurement rather than production of food resources. The long-term result has been the development of an increasingly global system dependent upon continued growth to maintain its economic well-being – a pattern that cannot continue indefinitely.

The pattern underlying that development is one in which the cognitive interaction between our perceptions (and hence values) and the material world has led us to favour material value creation over almost anything else to maintain the social dynamic. This has been facilitated by the industrial revolution, which essentially removed energy as a constraint in our societal dynamic. For some time, the acceleration of the innovation dynamic was kept in check by limitations in our information-processing capacity, as we were essentially reliant on our collective grey matter. However, the recent ICT revolution is now in the process of removing that check. As a result, (developed) societies now have a different relationship with our external world, in which the balance of power has shifted to the internal (cognised) world, enabling us to (a) create (given enough time) just about anything we want in the material world and (b) control many aspects of the natural (external) world. This concludes an evolution in which initially our human cognitive capability limited our interaction with the outside world via a phase in which the two enabled and constrained each other, to a situation in which our cognition in effect no longer limits our interaction with the external world. That shift in relationship has brought us to the point where, invoking innovation as the way to overcome the current sustainability crisis, we forget that it is unbridled innovation that got us into the present situation in the first place.

If we are to find ways to meet the challenges the current situation poses, much more research needs to be done on creativity, invention, and innovation as collective cognitive processes at the intersection between the individual, the group, and the material world, as Gamble proposes and as we have sketchily outlined here. Such research needs to overcome the reductionist bias of our current scientific tradition and to look at the emergence of phenomena (creations, inventions, innovations) and how they introduce new functionalities that society integrates by transforming itself (cf. van der Leeuw 2008; Lane et al. 2009; Westley et al. 2011). Only when we understand the process of invention and innovation can we hope to focus them in the domains where they are currently needed the most. We contribute this chapter in the hope that the study of innovation and change in archaeology will adopt Gamble's approach and that an improved knowledge of these phenomena over the long term will also stimulate the application of this approach to more recent times and to the present!

Notes

[1] Cowan (2000, 2005) has suggested a four-chunk limit for STWM when excluding supplementary memory storage mechanisms, but that 'a limited storage capacity can be divided ... among up to about six (or seven?) items using a rehearsal process to supplement the capacity-limited facility' (2005: 152). The latter appears to characterise the conditions for nut cracking by chimpanzees, hence the use of the 7-point scale for comparing the working memory capacity of humans with that of chimpanzees.

[2] The advantage of going from lower to higher dimensional technologies has generally been assumed to relate to increased efficiency (Leroi-Gourhan 1957). However, experimental evidence shows that the total cutting edge obtained per unit of raw material in Upper Palaeolithic blade technologies is, at best, only slightly greater when making blades rather than flakes (Tactikos 2003; Erin et al. 2008) and when the life cycle of an artefact is taken into account, more usable cutting edge is obtained with flakes than blades since flakes can be resharpened more often than blades (Erin et al. 2008). Gamble (2007) has suggested that we need to shift away from asking about the rationality of blade technology, which focuses on the individual and efficiency to consider how technology relates to a social context and points out that what is distinctive about blades is a technology that can repeatedly make blanks with the same form. We can extend his argument. The social importance of blade production lies in a shift from individually produced artefacts for individual use, to artefacts with a shared form across the members of a social group, hence artefacts became part of the cultural repertoire of that group and were imbued with cultural, thus shared, meaning. Prismatic blade technology, which lends itself to making standardised blanks, would have facilitated this change.

[3] As Gamble would put it, the 'bottleneck' is from our perspective in hindsight and assumes modern societies as the goal of societal change. Gamble (2007) has argued against an origin approach: from the perspective of hunter-gatherer groups there was no 'problem to be solved' and they were not laying the foundations for future change, but living and dying in their present time using means designed with their goals and interests in mind. It is only from our perspective that we, metaphorically, refer to what was put into place in the Upper Palaeolithic as a foundation for what was to come. We agree with the general thrust of his argument, though here we have reason to speak of an origin given the fact that it is only within the evolving hominin lineage (due to their expanded STWM) – that a radically new form of social organisation based on relations among individuals rather than face-to-face interaction came into play.

[4] Gamble (2007) considers containers to be ubiquitous throughout hominin evolution and even before, but he includes in his argument the relation of individuals to objects where, to use the anthropological distinction of etic (imposed) from emic (indigenous) concepts, the objects are containers from an etic perspective even if they are not containers from an emic perspective. We are concerned here with containers recognised emically by the folks concerned. Moreover, we are not concerned here with the occasional invention of such containers, but with containers as an innovation; that is, with their systematic acceptance as a widespread feature of everyday life in society. Hence, we would not be surprised to see an occasional discovery of containers earlier than this, but we do not expect these to be numerous.

[5] One craft in which the conceptual 'discovery' of the formation of such hollow shapes as containers may have occurred early on is leather working. In leather working, skins are removed from one kind of object where the skin already contains the animal, only to be transformed into another, differently shaped, containing object.

[6] Experimental results (Lachièze-Rey 2003) seem to confirm the existence of two modes of human spatial perception. The first links spatial markers in a sequential string just like the cause-and-effect strings that are a prerequisite for all human tool making. This kind

of spatial perception is at the root of the 'songlines' phenomenon. The second substitutes a second spatial dimension for the temporal one involved in such strings. That requires the substitution of a temporal sensation by a crosscutting spatial one at each and every point of the string, which means that each point on the trajectory must be observed from at least one crosscutting angle. That in turn presupposes a prolonged presence in an area, and crossing it in many different directions.

[7] Organisational structures such as matrilineal versus patrilineal forms of social organisation also affected the extent to which population agglomerations expanded. A strikingly different pattern occurred among patrilineal versus matrilineal societies, as population sizes expanded and administrative hierarchies became multi-level. Typically, patrilineal societies are constrained in the population size of settlements through settlement fission and only develop shallow administrative hierarchies, whereas matrilineal societies developed settlements with a much larger population size and greater depth of administrative hierarchies (Read 2010a).

[8] This is corroborated by the fact that when scaling a number of urban systems of different sizes against, respectively, metrics of population, energy and innovation, population scales linearly, energy sub-linearly and innovation capacity super-linearly (Bettencourt et al. 2006).

CHAPTER 4

BEYOND ANIMALITY AND HUMANITY. LANDSCAPE, METAPHOR AND IDENTITY IN THE EARLY UPPER PALAEOLITHIC OF CENTRAL EUROPE

MARTIN PORR

TOWARDS A NON-COLONIAL PALAEOLITHIC ARCHAEOLOGY – A PERSONAL INTRODUCTION

Over the last thirty years, Clive Gamble has made an important and impressive intellectual journey. During this time, his thinking about the Palaeolithic past has changed significantly and, one might even say, become more adventurous. In my view, C. S. Gamble is today the most important author to make serious and informed attempts to view the Palaeolithic beyond the most widely accepted framework for this period, behavioural ecology in a broad sense of the term. This framework assumes that the ultimate causes for anything that happened during the Palaeolithic are related to adaptations to environmental conditions and challenges. Looking at three major contributions that might be described as his most seminal and influential ones, *The Palaeolithic Settlement of Europe* (Gamble 1986), *The Palaeolithic Societies of Europe* (Gamble 1999) and *Origins and Revolutions* (Gamble 2007), I have gained the impression that these books reflect a growing dissatisfaction with such a narrow view of the Palaeolithic. While the first book is about the systematic relations between settlement patterns and the distribution of different forms of resources, the second book attempts to integrate the social dimension as an independent causal force. The third one takes on a topic that has virtually not been addressed in Palaeolithic contexts: the issue of identity.

It is not possible here to do justice to the importance and complexities of these contributions. I am not sure if Clive Gamble would agree with my reading of his work over the years, but for me it has always been of crucial importance that he has increasingly attempted to open up the study of the Palaeolithic to approaches and frameworks that traditionally are not used to analyse the actions and material expressions of humans who live a hunting and gathering life-style. The lives of Palaeolithic hunters and gatherers are traditionally described and analysed within frameworks that are borrowed from or inspired by evolutionary biology and related disciplines. Furthermore, Palaeolithic archaeologists and paleoanthropologists traditionally form an alliance with a particular strand in the anthropological study of hunting and gathering people, which also concentrates on behavioural ecological frameworks and explanations. Out of this alliance an image of the modern or ethnographic hunter-gatherer is created that is recursively strengthened by a vision of the deep Palaeolithic past. Both are seen as dominated and caused by material, ecological and environmental pressures and the constant fight by humans to overcome these challenges with better technologies and social strategies (Porr 2001).

Especially with *Origins and Revolutions*, Gamble (2007) has made a bold attempt to write a different version of the Palaeolithic past which is not purely governed by environmental and material pressures. In a certain sense, this attempt can be described as post-modern, because it breaks away from the modernist and materialist frameworks vehemently introduced into archaeology during the 1960s by the New Archaeology. However, I also want to draw attention to another aspect. This interpretative shift is also post-colonial because it represents a shift away from the dominant materialistic framework of interpretation in modern western society and science. This is a dimension that probably is not clear to archaeologists who work in Europe and prehistoric contexts and who have little exposure to indigenous people and their views.

In contrast, working in Australia has made me aware from a very early stage that some of the above-mentioned assumptions that govern the research designs in Palaeolithic archaeology are not shared by everybody. As a researcher one might be – sometimes violently – confronted with completely different interpretations of actions and material phenomena and also with the view that the theories and methods that are used by archaeologists are not only inappropriate but also offensive to indigenous people. One might argue that also people in western societies who are exposed to scientific procedures find these strange, intrusive and incomprehensible and that this can be 'corrected' by information and education. This is indeed an important component in every modern and responsible field research. However, despite the positive intentions that are usually guiding this approach, it also clearly shows the hierarchical structure of knowledge that is involved in these exchanges as well as the underlying assumptions about the hierarchy of causes influencing the hunter-gatherer's actions. Virtually all so-called research among hunting and gathering people has been conducted and still takes place in colonial or epicolonial contexts, in which a significant asymmetry in power exists, which affects the production and structure of knowledge that is generated.

I have mentioned elsewhere (Porr and Bell 2012: 11) that in major contributions which aspire to provide general explanations of hunter-gatherer behaviour (e.g. Kelly 1995; Binford 2001) actual statements by hunting and gathering people are usually missing. Within the behavioural ecological framework research is conducted in a formal way in which quantitative information is gathered according to standardised schemes, which will allow the statistical testing of hypotheses. The latter are developed with reference to assumptions about the most efficient use and management of different resources (e.g., energy, mating partners, time, etc.) and it is assumed that these elements have causal priority over other aspects within the hunter-gatherer life-world. This research design is a consequence of the a priori construction of the human hunter-gatherer as a being which has been shaped by evolutionary and selection forces to be able to act as an 'optimal forager' (in a broad sense of the term) and her or his actions need to be understood accordingly.

The problem here is not just methodological. It is clear that every research design has to define priorities and appropriate procedures that relate to the questions that should be examined and answered. The real problem that needs to be addressed is the underlying assumption that the human hunter-gatherer, today or during the Palaeolithic, is ultimately guided by certain core attributes that are central for explanations and other attributes that are assumed to be more peripheral and causally less relevant. The former are supposedly accessible through the formal and quantitative analysis of structured observations, while the latter can be ignored, because they are irrelevant for the 'real' explanation of people's actions and their material culture. It is somewhat ironic that this view in fact not only excludes a vast amount of expressions of human actions and material culture. It also excludes from analysis so-called expressions of symbolism and symbolic behaviour, which are supposedly the main characteristic that distinguish humans from other organisms and also provides the basis for the success of so-called 'behaviorally modern humans' (Porr 2011).

These observations do point to a very unfortunate state of affairs. Social anthropology and human evolutionary studies have over the last decades been constantly drifting apart until they have virtually reached a point where proponents of the respective fields have very little to say to each other (Gamble 1999: xix; Alden Smith et al. 2011; Kuper and Marks 2011). Palaeolithic archaeology has in this context firmly declared its allegiance and over the last fifty years the exploration of all aspects of the Palaeolithic has become dominated by approaches that stress evolutionary adaptation processes in a narrow sense of the term. Large areas of present-day anthropology that stress a dialogical and qualitative approach to research, self-reflexivity and non-mechanistic views of human actions and practices apparently have no relevance for modern reconstructions of the deep and not-so-deep past.

DEVELOPING RELATIONAL APPROACHES TO THE PALAEOLITHIC PAST

Since the acceptance of its antiquity in the 19th century, the study of Palaeolithic art has progressed through different well-known stages, which are still echoed in the current literature and popular culture. On a very general level, these stages are 'hunting magic', 'structuralism', 'ecology/information exchange' and 'shamanism'. It is not necessary here to recapitulate the individual problems connected to each of these approaches. I want to draw attention to the fact that each framework seeks to explain Palaeolithic art as an expression of something else and as an expression of a false understanding of reality. Perhaps most famously, 'hunting magic' was regarded as a reflection of sympathetic magic and therefore the mistaken view that similarities in appearance also point to similarities in causes and relationship. Leroi-Gourhan's (see, e.g., 1982) structuralistic interpretation of Palaeolithic art also assumed that Palaeolithic artists reproduced a pre-existing structure of meanings and imposed this onto the reality of the cave layout. In the behavioural-ecological interpretation, the art becomes a medium of information exchange about survival strategies (e.g., Jochim 1983; Mithen 1991); although it seems strange in this case that apparently adaptation did not favour a more efficient transmission strategy. The most recent perspective, the shamanism/neuropsychological model, takes into account different views of reality and experiences and sees figurative and abstract depictions and images as their reflections (Lewis-Williams and Dowson 1988). It is, however, hampered by a rather mechanistic view of the interpretation of supposedly universal neural phenomena (such as entoptics). All of the approaches mentioned assume that the people, who painted images on caves, carved or sculptured depictions were not aware of the 'real' functions of their art and their actions. These functions are, in contrast, accessible through scientific analysis, the application of relevant interpretative frameworks and can therefore be objectified.

The frameworks so far mentioned all present a romanticised version of the Palaeolithic past by implying that during this distant period everybody was following a clear and shared holistic ideology (in the wider sense of the term). Negotiations, conflicts and ambiguities are suspiciously absent. This overall tendency of Palaeolithic archaeology can be related to a vision of the human individual as ultimately passive. As I have explored with Clive Gamble elsewhere (Gamble and Porr 2005a), Palaeolithic archaeology tends to locate the causality of changes and phenomena in groups rather than individuals. The latter only become reflections of group and environmental dynamics; they do not have their own causal significance. All frameworks therefore represent an essentialist view of the human organism, because they all assume that individuals have internalised and are guided by the same attitudes, structural schemes or algorithms, which do determine their actions or behaviours. This view needs to be replaced by a vision of the human organism as active, socially situated, dynamic and constantly developing (Porr 2001, 2011; Gamble and Porr 2005a; Porr and Bell 2012). In short, and as Ingold (2011) most recently put it, it is necessary to view the human organism as alive.

The claim to view the human organism as alive in interpretative schemes might seem trivial or surprising. But, in fact, it has enormous implications. On a very fundamental level, this change in perspective does shift the focus of inquiry away from entities and their characteristics towards dynamic processes and relationships. Accepting the human organism as alive, constantly developing and growing, does also mean that it is not characterised by a specific essence or a collection of characteristics that is independent from its involvement in the world. The identity of the organism does not precede its existence. It is a product of the life history of the organism and its engagement with the world. While this does also sound like a trivial point, the current standard view of the human organism is overall very different. In most explanatory schemes that are used in Palaeolithic archaeology and which are based on behavioural-ecological considerations the human organism is mostly characterised by genetic factors that allow following certain algorithms to make the most efficient decisions during its life course. This perspective, however, creates the unusual result that the human organism is mostly defined by factors that indeed precede its existence as they are handed down through the generations as products of evolutionary adaptation and selection processes.

To challenge this view does not mean to challenge the importance of biological evolution, evolutionary processes in general and ecological factors. Challenging this perspective actually has to lead to giving dynamic and ecological factors a much more fundamental significance. Humans have to be seen as active organisms who are constantly engaged in relationships with their environments and together they undergo processes of dialectical growth and development. The living human organism is always bodily situated and is in constant exchange with its environment on numerous perceptual levels. 'Environment' here has to be understood in a very wide sense of the term and can include animals, other humans, the weather and so on. Because it cannot be assumed that human beings exist before these engagement begin, the relational perspective I suggest here also implies a focus on processes of social and individual learning. These processes do not simply add to the abilities and characteristics of the organism; they fundamentally create it. As the organism is always situated, knowledge also is situated and the product of situated and ongoing experience. It becomes consequently difficult to separate the organism from its environment – in its widest sense of the term – as both constantly create each other. However, the acquisition of so-called information within the world is not unproblematic. Learning does not equal information transfer between individuals. Every act of learning also is an act of interpretation. All forms of communication have to be viewed within such a framework. Equally, all human material expressions and artefacts, including so-called art objects, have to be viewed as such. In a sense, the human organism is constantly and fundamentally creating its own identity in continuous bodily interaction within its environment. The issue of identity is consequently not a side issue of Palaeolithic archaeology, but at the centre of any archaeological or anthropological inquiry (Gamble 2007).

BUILDING A PHENOMENOLOGICAL ECOLOGY OF
THE PALAEOLITHIC AND PALAEOLITHIC IMAGES

It is clear that developing a relational framework for understanding the Palaeolithic presents numerous methodological and epistemological challenges. Elsewhere, I have proposed the notion of a 'phenomenological ecology' (Porr 2010a) in this context and here I want to continue to discuss some of its implications. The idea of a phenomenological ecology relates to the fundamental interdependence of the active individual, its experiences and its continuous involvement with its environment. As I noted above, the notion of 'ecology' that I use here should not be confused with 'behavioural or evolutionary ecology', but rather has to be understood in the tradition of Gibson's 'ecological approach to visual perception' (Gibson 1979). It further incorporates important elements of Ingold's (2000) 'dwelling perspective' as well as Bird-David's insights into the ideologies of so-called hunting and gathering societies as well as her discussions of 'the giving environment' and 'animism' (Bird-David 1990, 1993, 1999). In the context of the latter term, however, it is important to note that these contributions also have their limits in that they themselves are in danger of falling into an essentialist trap and regarding 'animism' as a fixed ideology or world-view of 'hunting and gathering societies' (Porr and Bell 2012). Any inquiry rather has to concentrate on the dynamic processes and relationships that guide and influence the development of human organisms, not on the identification of seemingly stable or static concepts and schemes.

As animals play the central and most important role in Palaeolithic figurative representations, it is useful to briefly illustrate some of these issues in the context of human-animal relationships. Western thinking has traditionally viewed hunting and gathering people as living a 'short and brutish' life at the edge of extinction and in constant fear. While this vision certainly is no longer generally accepted, modern views within the evolutionary-ecological framework still emphasise issues of survival and subsistence and resource management as the essential characteristics of hunter-gatherer existence. Relationships with animals are in this context described as resource management problems in which the human hunter engages in a deadly confrontational game with the animal and both try to outwit each other. Even though these relationships are assumed to be a product of universal evolutionary processes it is interesting to note that hunting and gathering people themselves do perceive and conceptualise them very differently (Porr, 2010a: 148–150).

Bird-David (e.g., 1990, 1992, 1999) and Ingold (1992, 2000) have repeatedly drawn attention to the fact that so-called hunting and gathering people in fact perceive their environment in a giving and positive fashion, within a framework that emphasises sharing and mutual respect. Why is this case? Do these attitudes towards the environment in general and animals in particular represent a false understanding of reality and a denial of the 'real' (unforgiving) character of nature? These attitudes and views are in fact inseparably inter-twined with a particular being-in-the-world and experiences that relate to animals (and the environment as a whole) not from a perspective of attempted domination, but from a position of trust and equality (Ingold 2000: 61–76). As such, they are not wrong but accurate and rational reflections of reality and especially the ongoing relationships that characterise hunting and gathering existence. The anthropologist Hans Peter Duerr (1984) has described this as 'love for life as it is' (*Liebe zum Leben*) and Shepard (1998) has argued that living organisms provide the underlying guiding metaphor for these societies (while modern societies follow the metaphor of the machine, or, perhaps today the computer, to view themselves and the world). From a modern perspective, these observations have generally been dismissed as different forms of magical thinking or animism (Porr and Bell 2012). But what is actually reflected in these world-views is the ongoing, dynamic, interdependent and inseparable development of humans, animals, plants and the landscape. Animals and humans are not separate entities moving within a three-dimensional space in search for resources. Animals and humans constantly shape each other just as they constantly shape their environment. This is not some irrational and primitive world-view, but fundamental ecological think-ing. Animals, humans and the landscape do not have separate identities, but they are intertwined and develop in relation to each other and over the course of their lives.

It is important to recognise that the insight into these relationships are not acquired in abstract contexts or detached ways. The engagement with the environment is constant and specific, bodily and perceptually situated. You never ever encounter snow as such, but always encounter snow that is slightly different and never the same. Similarly, you never ever encounter a 'mammoth' as such; you always encounter individual mammoths that have their own histories and therefore their own identities and personalities. This is the basis for the sometimes dazzlingly complex linguistic categorisations by indigenous people that do not refer to an abstract system or structure, but are connected to real-life situations. With respect to animals, this translates into a personalisation of the encounter with the animal, because – like humans – every animal is different, has a particular identity and personality. This charac-teristic is enhanced by the being-in-the-world of hunting and gathering people, where the interaction with animals usually is not geared towards control, domination and transformation. It is, again, important to understand that this is not an essential feature of 'the hunting and gathering way of life' or a 'hunting and gathering world-view'. It is the product of a particular ongoing engagement between animals and humans, and this personalised and intense engagement can be found in other societies as well (for example, in the relationships between western people and their dogs).

Knowledge in indigenous societies is not regarded as abstract and context-independent, but always tied to people and places. In indigenous societies it is recognised that knowledge and its acquisition cannot be separated from living and growing in and moving through a particular environment. This is exactly the reason why in traditional cultures a careful social management exists to supply the right kind of knowledge to the right person at the right time. Growing and learning, as central elements of life, take a central role in traditional cultures. But learning is not simply the transfer of knowledge, but – because of the irreducible necessity of interpretation by every participant in every communication – takes the form of guided discovery and rediscovery. In indigenous Australian societies, young men were taken by close relatives on a 'grand tour' through the country so that they were able to experience and learn the Country. Australian indigenous people often express that their knowledge is 'in the land' or 'in Country' (Mowaljarlai and Malnic 1993). This is at first difficult to comprehend, but it becomes immediately understandable when it is recognised that this understanding is in fact a reflection of the insight that knowledge is not separated from being and growing in a particular environment. The land shapes the people through their continuous involvement with it and at the same time people shape the land. Knowledge becomes not something that is located in the heads and brains of people, but that is dispersed between bodies and country. Knowledge is in the land and the only way to learn about the land is to experience it, to walk it. There are no short-cuts here. Knowledge is bound to the growing and developing body, which is in turn inseparable from the landscape. Just as knowledge is dispersed and contained in the landscape, it is dispersed among members of society according to their age and gender, according to the fundamental parameters of the growth of the (human) organism. Maturity is not a value in itself, but respected, because it is a reflection of the bodily acquisition of knowledge over time through continuous involvement with the environment. These are the principal elements that need to be taken into account as I explore some mobiliary figurative representations in the Early and Mid Upper Palaeolithic of Central and Eastern Europe.

THE EARLY UPPER PALAEOLITHIC ART OF CENTRAL EUROPE

The Early Upper Palaeolithic of Central and Eastern Europe comprises the period of the so-called Aurignacian techno-complex. This complex is usually regarded as evidence for the migration of the first anatomically and behaviourally modern humans into Europe after 45,000 years BP. Technological elements that are associated with the Aurignacian, such as carinated scrapers and micro-blade technology, can be found over a large geographical area between Spain, the Levant and the Crimean Peninsula. Another element that has been put forward as particularly characteristic of this techno-complex is the intensified use of organic raw materials for the production of utilitarian tools, such as projectile points. The Aurignacian further sees the regular use of personal ornaments, either in the form of shells or animal teeth (see Floss and Rouquerol 2007 for overviews). Within such an enormous area of distribution, it is clear that Aurignacian material expressions are characterised by a complex dialectic between regional similarities and differences, which might be reflections of possible social groupings (Bar-Yosef and Zilhão 2006; see also, e.g., Zilhão and d'Errico 2003; Vanhaeren and d'Errico 2007). While the Aurignacian can be broadly linked to the moderately cold MIS 3, the following cooling of the climate after c. 28,000 BP and towards the Last Glacial Maximum sees the development of a number of regional interlinked Mid Upper Palaeolithic techno-complexes in Europe (e.g., Gravettian, Pavlovian, Périgordien supérieur, Streletskian, Kostenkian, etc.). Changes in material culture and its distribution seem to be related to changes in vegetation cover and the character of respective animal communities. Wide-ranging links across the continent from France to Russia seem to have connected communities much more closely than during the preceding period. Figurative and representational objects show more similarities between regions, pointing towards a greater degree in shared ideas and ideologies (Gamble 1986, 1991; Roebroeks et al. 1999). These different aspects of the archaeological evidence provide a wealth of information for the examination and contextualisation of processes of relational identity creation during this time. In the following I will take figurative representations – figurative 'art' – as the centre of my exploration, beginning with the Aurignacian mobiliary art from southwest Germany and will then proceed to explore some elements in the Mid Upper Palaeolithic of Central and Eastern Europe.

The Aurignacian is the time period in which in several contexts in Europe the first figurative representations can be observed. While there are isolated instances of figurative expressions during earlier periods, the Early Upper Palaeolithic record in Europe has yielded so far the earliest clear collections of figurative representations, including parietal images (Clottes 2003). With respect to mobiliary representations, most prominent are today the statuettes from the Swabian Jura Mountains in southwest Germany, which are dated to between c. 35,000 and 32,000 years ago (Hahn 1986; Conard 2003, 2009; Floss 2007; Figure 4.1). As I have argued elsewhere (Dowson and Porr 2001; Porr 2010a, 2010c), the figurines provide an unprecedented insight into a range of aspects that can be seen as reflections of the relational and situated construction of identity (Porr 2002). They further serve as a point of departure to examine further expressions of mobiliary art in contemporary and later contexts, in relation to processes of change and continuity.

The figurative representations during the Aurignacian are almost completely dominated by representations of large adult terrestrial animals. Felids and

Figure 4.1: Geißenklösterle (Germany): Fragmentary ivory statuette of a mammoth. The posture of the animal is neutral and symmetrical. No particular behaviours are depicted. Photo: P. Frankenstein, H. Zwietasch, copyright Landesmuseum Württemberg, Stuttgart. Reproduced with permission.

mammoths are best represented. Individual and clearly identifiable representations of human beings are missing altogether. An exception seems to be represented by the most recently discovered 'Venus' from Hohle Fels (Conard 2009). But even this statuette has been turned into an abstract representation through the removal of its head, which allowed it to be attached to an individual person or object. The figurative mobiliary art of southwest Germany is characterised by a tension between the individuality of the design and use of each object and the similarities that are visible in the design choices of the representation of different animal species. The latter relate to observable behavioural attributes of the animals, including social behaviours. This allows the construction of a core opposition between mammoths and lions who are separated by their social hierarchical and feeding behaviours, but are united by their overall dominance in the environment. During the Aurignacian, Pleistocene lions were the dominant predators that were most likely organised in harem systems, which were dominated by a single male individual (Kahlke 1994; Anton and Turner 2000; Figure 4.2). In contrast, there is solid evidence available that shows that Pleistocene mammoths – as dominant herbivores – were organised into herds around older female individuals (Haynes 1991; Maschenko et al. 2006; Lister and Bahn 2007). The statuettes consequently contain statements and reflections about gender and subsistence practices, but probably reflections of acceptable social behaviour as well.

Figure 4.2: Vogelherd (Germany): Isolated head of a lion with detailed facial feature. The erect ears show that an alert animal was depicted. Photo: P. Frankenstein, H. Zwietasch, copyright Landesmuseum Württemberg, Stuttgart. Reproduced with permission.

Although virtually no humans as such are depicted in the Aurignacian figurative art of southwest Germany, humans and human bodies are implicated in all of them. They are never absent in Palaeolithic art and archaeology, but are present in the empty spaces between the artifacts (Gamble and Porr 2005a); they are the producers, consumers, observers and interpreters. In the case of the Aurignacian mobiliary art, individual humans were also attached to the statuettes during their life-time as is attested by the presence of suspension holes and polish. The animal becomes a part of the human being, a part of his or her appearance. As the statuettes in part were also handled over a longer period of time, the statuettes were part of the everyday engagement of the human being with his or her environment in a direct, bodily and intimate way. The engagement with the values and views materialised in the statuettes continues beyond their production. The statuettes become an integral part of the creation of individual identity during the Aurignacian and they further-more reflect the relational creation of humans and animals during this time. The presence of therianthropic imagery, which fuses characteristics of human with feline bodies, further demonstrates that the boundary between these categories were seen as fluid (Piprani 2011).

As I have outlined above, this is not a reflection of a false belief, but recognition of a real relationship. Among the Maasai, the lion plays an important role in creating men and warriors, and the lion is seen as having human qualities and as a worthy human adversary. The lion is described simultaneously as a *shujaa* and *adui*, warrior and opponent (Lichtenfeld 2005: 36–37). Lions are seen as special creatures and admired with awe (ibid.: 54, 63). This tension is also recursively reflected in social roles and representations. The children, women and elders have shaved heads to differentiate themselves from prototypical wild beasts (such as lions), whereas the adult men (warriors) have long hair to signal their embodiment of the wild and nature (Arhem 1989: 10–11). They are expected to eat large quantities of meat and wear a distinctive dress made from lion mane; they also keep away from 'the cultural space of the homestead' when doing this just like the 'wild beasts' they represent (ibid.: 18). Similarly, lion manes are collected and

> worn proudly at the most significant celebration in the life of a warrior, the *Eunoto* ceremony. Once a warrior passes beyond into elderhood and considers the prospects of marrying, he will no longer be permitted to wear the headdress as it is only associated with the wild and promiscuous days of warriorhood.
>
> (Lichtenfeld 2005: 38)

Following the approach of a 'phenomenological ecology' it is not altogether surprising that for the Aurignacian mobiliary art of southwest Germany I have suggested elsewhere the existence of comparable interrelationships between social roles, metaphors and spatial segregation (Porr 2010a). Human beings and animals of course do inhabit the landscape and interact with it constantly. While it is very challenging to reconstruct Pleistocene environments in great detail, I suggested that two neighbouring cave sites in the Swabian Jura Mountains, the Vogelherd and Hohlenstein-Stadel, reflect the significance that was given to these sites by people during the Aurignacian in terms of social practices and values. The Vogelherd Cave near Ulm was the richest Aurignacian occupation site in the region (if not in Central Europe altogether) (Niven 2008). It contained substantial occupation evidence, which unfortunately cannot well be reconstructed anymore in great detail.

Already excavated in the 1930s, restudies of the remaining materials have recently emphasised the importance of this site (Niven 2007, 2008; Conard 2008; Conard et al. 2009). The Vogelherd is especially important because it yielded the first collection of Ice Age figurative objects in Central Europe (Riek 1934). The intensity and complexity of the artefactual material at this site is a reflection of its favourable location and structure. Elsewhere I have compared this site with a large tent that can be accessed through two or three entrances (Porr 2010a). It is well visible and situated above the valley floor with good views into almost all directions. The Vogelherd appears consequently as a place with an almost public character in the landscape and it was here that the largest collection of mobiliary art objects from the Aurignacian has been found.

These probably represent items of clothing or equipment that had the carved figurines attached. However, it was also among these statuettes that the fragments of a larger mammoth statuette have been found, which appears to be too big to be carried around by an individual person on a daily basis.

Because of the characteristics of the mammoth statuettes themselves as well as the social behavioural characteristics of these animals, I have argued that mammoths relate to metaphors of female reproduction and especially the protection of the domestic sphere. Consequently, the larger mammoth statuette, found at the centre of the Vogelherd, does not relate to a single human individual, but relates to the importance of the cave as a communal, public and domestic place. The use of an animal representation has to be seen not just as a reflection of the importance of mammoths for human subsistence and survival. It is a reflection of the interdependence of human and animal characteristics, and certainly has to be extended to similarities in social organisation and gender roles between humans and mammoths. Therefore, the mammoth placed into the centre of domestic life during the Aurignacian of southwest Germany also refers to the role of women in protecting and caring for the domestic sphere. This interpretation is further strengthened through the observation that apparently only adult or mature mammoths were depicted,

Figure 4.3: Hohlenstein-Stadel: The entry to the Stadel Cave is located only a few metres above the valley floor and is not visible from the Vogelherd. The Löwenmensch statuette was found in a deep section inside this cave and was intentionally deposited. Photo by the author.

Figure 4.4: Hohlenstein-Stadel (Germany): The large 'lion-man' statuette (Löwen-mensch) was carved from a complete section of a mammoth tusk. Photo: T. Stephan, copyright Ulmer Museum. Reproduced with permission.

which seems to refer to the importance of older female mammoths in leading and guiding the herds and of course to general processes of growth and experience of humans and animals alike.

The Vogelherd Cave with its emphasis on domestic and public activities can be contrasted with the Hohlenstein-Stadel Cave, which was occupied at the same time (the available evidence allows no chronological differentiation). The latter cave site is only a few hundred metres away from the Vogelherd and the two sites are not intervisible (Figure 4.3). The spatial structure of the two sites is different in that the Stadel Cave is only a few metres above the valley floor and presents a straight corridor into the limestone that can only be accessed from one side. It was in the deepest part of this cave that the extraordinary *Löwenmensch* (lion man) statuette was found in 1939 (Figure 4.4).

From an early stage it was recognised that this ivory statuette was not only too large for prolonged carrying (with an overall size of c. 30 cm); it was also seen as the only statuette in the collection that presented any evidence for an intentional placement.

Together with the overall interpretation of the meanings that were attached to the statuettes, a picture now emerges that not only humans and animals, such as mammoths and lions, were seen in close interdependence with each other, but also that these relationships were reflected in the landscape, in the meanings that were seen in and given to specific places in the environment. The two sites consequently stand in opposition to each other, but their proximity to each other nevertheless suggests that they formed elements within one socio-cultural system. This is of course also suggested by the overall collection of statuettes, which were attached to individual human beings and which contains mammoths and lions as well as a number of other representations that cannot be discussed here. There consequently emerges a complex picture of the individual as well as socially structured and negotiated creation of identity that not only recognises the interdependence of animals and humans, but also the role of the landscape and its features in these processes.

LIFE AND DEATH DURING THE MID UPPER PALAEOLITHIC IN CENTRAL AND EASTERN EUROPE

In 2009, in the Hohle Fels Cave an extraordinary ivory statuette was discovered in Aurignacian occupation layers. It depicts the shape of a mature and almost obese woman with broad hips and short arms and legs. The object has no head and was used as a pendant. Despite some clear differences that still need to be analysed comparatively in greater detail, it seems clear that this statuette extends some basic features of the so-called 'Venus' statuettes from the Gravettian period (c. 29,000–18,000 BP) into the Aurignacian (Conard 2009). As I have argued elsewhere (Porr 2010a), this statuette alone shows that it is necessary and promising to view Aurignacian and Gravettian cultural expressions within a developing continuity and not as two distinct phases within the European Upper Palaeolithic.

From 29,000 BP onwards and across Europe and Western Eurasia, the relative unity of the Aurignacian is transformed into a number of interrelated techno-complexes (e.g., Gravettian, Pavlovian, Périgordien supérieur, Streletskian, Kostenkian, etc.), which show especially in Central and Eastern Europe an increase in settlement size and intensity as well as an increased specialisation on the exploitation of mammoths (Gamble 1999; Roebroeks et al. 1999; Verpoorte 2009). This period is also characterised by increased aridity and cooler temperatures, leading eventually to the Last Glacial Maximum around 19,000 BP. It has long been recognised that these developments can be connected to the so-called 'mammoth steppe' (e.g., van Andel 2002; Haynes 2006), which allowed and facilitated the formation of larger social groupings within a rich and productive environment in which large herds of herbivores flourished across the plains of Eurasia.

With respect to figurative art, this period has mostly received attention because of the so-called 'Venus' statuettes (e.g., Soffer et al. 2000a; Jennett 2008). Despite the presence of some clear stylistic variation, the latter appear mostly to be representations of mature women and are recognisable from France across the whole continent into southern Russia. The overall similarities between these statuettes suggest interdependence and ongoing communication between social groups during this time, which reflects more extensive mobility patterns across the open environments of the mammoth steppe (see, e.g., Gamble 1986, 1991). It is noticeable that the focus of the distribution of the statuettes coincides roughly with the presence of this latter environmental zone, which is in turn related to the presence of intensely utilised settlement locations, for example, in Moravia or the Southern Russian Plain (Soffer 1985; Haynes 2006). It is not possible in this contribution to provide a detailed analysis of this complex category of material culture and it is acknowledged here that much more work has to be done on the analysis of variability, use and contexts. Therefore, only a few examples should be presented here that allow an insight into the metaphorical relationships that existed during this time and that were used by humans to reflect on their relationships with animals and their environment in general. As will become clearer below, they also throw light on issues related to views related to life histories and death.

All of the female statuettes were found in settlement contexts. They either occur near hearths or were buried in pits within habitation structures. The most impressive examples come from the Don River Valley, from Kostenki or Avdeevo, but also the so-called 'Venus of Willendorf' was found near a large hearth (Antl-Weiser 2008a). No statuettes have so far been discovered in burial contexts. Surprisingly little detailed work has so far been done on the archaeological contexts and associated materials, such as faunal remains, of the statuettes. However, it is noteworthy that in quite a few cases the statuettes have been buried with mammoth bones or remains. A little known but very interesting case is the ivory 'Venus' of Willendorf (II), which was found only a few metres away from the more famous stone statuette. While the latter can only be broadly associated with a hearth and a settlement layer, the former was intentionally deposited in a pit with mammoth bones and placed onto a mammoth jaw (Antl-Weiser 2008a: 130–133).

Another example is presented by the famous large and incomplete limestone statuette from Kostenki, discovered in 1988, which was buried in a large pit directly associated with mammoth remains, while the original excavator also noted that the pits discovered at this site were often covered with mammoth scapula (Praslov 1993: 165). At Avdeevo the pits were even arranged in a broadly circular fashion around the central hearths (Gvozdover 1995). A field of associations consequently emerges, within which the statuettes can be interpreted and which presents spatial contexts of human practices and relates these to animal metaphors. These were visible in the Aurignacian of southwest Germany in rudimentary form and with an emphasis on individual human beings. During the Mid Upper Palaeolithic the emphasis has shifted towards more permanent and larger settlement locations and structures. The 'Venus' statuettes are placed at the centre of human domestic activities and here they are regularly associated with mammoth bones. This placement mirrors the structure of mammoth social and behavioural organisation, where the herds are also guided by matriarchs that form the social centres of the groups.

In the literature, the 'Venus' statuettes have often been associated with the notion of fertility, even though clearly pregnant figures as well as children or young individuals are very rare in representations altogether. The significance of the fact that virtually only mature or older women are depicted has rarely been discussed. Knowledge is in traditional societies inseparably linked to age and bodily experience. As I mentioned above, there are no short-cuts and this applies both to animals and humans. The connection of the statuettes with mammoth remains relates to the similarities between humans and animals in this respect, but also recognises the interdependence between animals and humans in the mammoth steppe environment. Representations of felids are rare during this time and although they do occur, for instance at Dolní Vestonice (see examples in Wehrberger and Reinhardt 1994), they play no prominent role in the inner domestic sphere. Could this be a consequence of a division between life and death, where the habitation structures are rather dominated by reflections of protection and caring and are separated from aggressive imagery? These questions can only be addressed with further finds and analyses.

It has been mentioned above that the statuettes have not been found in the context of burials and therefore seem to be firmly attached to the realm of the living. However, the Mid Upper Palaeolithic has provided a large number of ceremonial burials (Formicola 2007) with numerous grave goods that allow a further exploration of the construction of identity within metaphorical relationships linking humans and animals. It can be observed that indeed the statuettes were broadly treated in a similar way. They both were formally buried in pits, often covered with red ochre and both were often associated with mammoth bones. Intriguingly, the latter is most prominent in the context of some exceptional cases from Austria and Moravia, geographically quite close to the Swabian Jura Mountains. In Moravia, both the multiple burials at Dolní Věstonice and Předmostí were

Figure 4.5: Krems-Wachtberg (Austria): A modified mammoth shoulder blade was used to cover and seal Burial 1. The burial and the skeletons of both individuals were excellently preserved. Photo and copyright Prehistoric Commission, Austrian Academy of Sciences. Reproduced with permission.

either intentionally associated or indeed covered with mammoth scapula (Trinkaus and Svoboda 2006; Svoboda 2008a: 22; Figure 4.7). More recently, an extraordinary burial of two infants was uncovered in Austria at the site of Krems-Wachtberg, which was also covered by a mammoth scapula that was resting on a section of a mammoth tusk (Einwögerer et al. 2006; Figures 4.5 and 4.6).

Mammoth bones provide here a link between contexts of life and death; and the uses of these remains strengthen the idea that this large herbivore was perceived as a symbol of protection and care. The significance of the mammoth is further attached to elements of life history developments in general and the importance of acquiring knowledge and experience, which is translated into social competence. The latter links human with animal society and allows inferences with respect to the importance of older or mature women in decision-making processes within the domestic realm. As I stated above, these configurations should not be perceived as expressions of a false understanding of reality. They are reflections of very real relationships between animals and humans, relations of interdependence, similarities and differences. In short, they are elements of the reflective relational and constant creation of the identity of both humans and animals during this time.

It is quite extraordinary that some of these elements discussed make an appearance in ethnographic sources from northern Eurasia. In this case, of course, the source of inspiration and reflection has not been living mammoths,

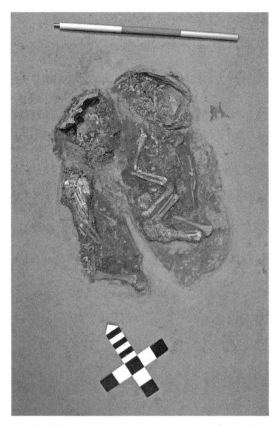

Figure 4.6: Krems-Wachtberg (Austria): Find situation of Burial 1 in the field. Two newborn infants had been buried in a pit embedded in red ochre. Photo and copyright Prehistoric Commission, Austrian Academy of Sciences. Reproduced with permission.

but rather the numerous bones and tusks that these animals have left in the landscape. In numerous myths and stories of Siberian peoples, the mammoth is seen as both an agent of creation and as a protector of the dead:

> According to the Evenki, the mammoth dug up earth with its tusks from the sea floor and tossed it in clumps to form the beginnings of the earth. Thus the earth, originally very small, grew large and capable of sustaining human life. To smooth the uneven surface of the earth, the mammoth called on a mythical snake, the *diabdar'a*. Where the snake slithered, rivers appeared; where the mammoth trod, lakes formed; and where the pieces of earth thrown from the bottom of the sea remained, mountains arose. In other myths the mammoth and the *diabdar'a* battled a mythological monster. This fight led to the topography of the earth as we know it today. [. . .] The Selkups believed that an immense and mighty animal lived under the ground, which they called the *koshar* (mammoth). It guarded the entry to the underworld, which was inhabited by dead people.
>
> (Serikov and Serikova 2005: 9)

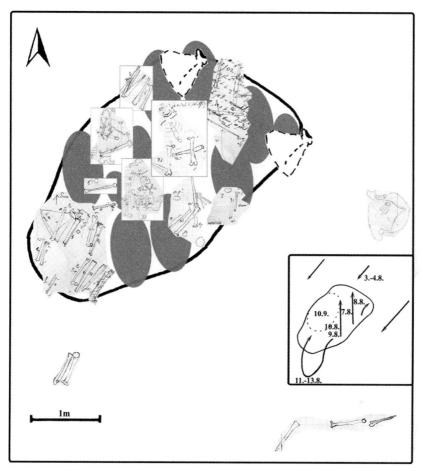

Figure 4.7: Předmostí (Czech Republic): Reconstruction of the mass burial area and its vicinity, based on original sketches. Missing bodies are hatched. On its northern side, two mammoth scapulae were placed, to the east a mammoth mandible was found (from Svoboda 2008: 22 reproduced with permission).

CONCLUSION

I am aware that a number of the thoughts expressed in this contribution can be regarded as speculative, especially when they have to be presented within the fairly restricted space of a book chapter. However, I do not only believe that Clive Gamble would appreciate some informed speculation with the aim to generate new views and hypotheses to understand and read the Palaeolithic record. I also think it is important to develop frameworks that allow exploring ways to approach the human deep past that are not solely inspired by western models of agency (Gershon 2011). I mentioned above that I found it recently very rewarding to be exposed to indigenous Australian world-views and philosophies in this context (Porr and Bell 2012). Australia is usually regarded as an exceptional case of cultural development with fairly limited value as a comparative case for understanding broader issues of human history (see, e.g., Barnard 1999). However, I am not advocating using Australian indigenous cultures as analogues for the interpretation of Eurasian (or any other) Palaeolithic evidence. I am rather arguing for a new phase of making inferences in Palaeolithic archaeology, in which material expressions are regarded as active, conscious and rational expressions of human engagement with their environments. With the few suggestions I made in this paper, I want to invite the reader to explore non-western and indigenous world-views with a more open mind and resist the attempt to interpret these solely within a western value and cost-benefit framework. The adherence to the latter not only produce a global human history that regards western modernity as its inevitable fulfilment; it also recursively leads towards an implicit disrespect for today's indigenous people and their world-views. Within a relational, fundamentally ecological and phenomenological framework, the wealth and richness of global human cultural diversity can provide ample inspirations for the reading of the Palaeolithic past.

CHAPTER 5

AT THE HEART OF THE AFRICAN
ACHEULEAN: THE PHYSICAL, SOCIAL
AND COGNITIVE LANDSCAPES OF KILOMBE

JOHN A. J. GOWLETT, JAMES S. BRINK, ANDY I. R.
HERRIES, SALLY HOARE, ISAYA
ONJALA AND STEPHEN M. RUCINA

INTRODUCTION – THE KILOMBE SITES AND THEIR PLACE
IN THE ACHEULEAN

Kilombe is one of a series of great Acheulean site complexes in eastern Africa. In this paper we use new evidence to reflect on how studies of its landscapes – geographical, ecological and sociocultural – have developed through a generation of studies. The first research in the 1970s was already influenced by a multi-disciplinary world – in East Africa, the geologists set 'frameworks' (Bishop 1972, 1978), and archaeologists worked to place their finds in stratigraphic, chronological and taphonomic contexts (Isaac 1977). The social lives of early humans were already a preoccupation (e.g., Washburn and DeVore 1961), and their use of large landscapes was already recognised. Even so, things have changed, and the social has moved to the centre. When Clive Gamble wrote in 1979 that the emphasis had shifted to 'resource exploitation, demography, settlement location, interaction and mating networks' (1979: 35), he was setting out an aspiration – one that is even now hard to realise for the Palaeolithic. At Kilombe, the old model of technology is familiar, but the opportunities for new approaches are conspicuously available, and this chapter will demonstrate how traditional in-depth archaeological and palaeoenvironmental study at even a single locale can provide insights crucial to tackling broader questions relating to hominin – landscape – material culture interactions.

Our renewed research since 2008 has aimed to develop a much fuller picture of Kilombe's various landscapes and their chronology. Not only are the opportunities on the ground vastly improved compared with a generation ago, but also there is a framework of social, cognitive, ecological and comparative studies which makes it far more feasible to develop a much broader picture. Our ability to date such sites has also improved in the last thirty odd years with improved instrumentation, a better understanding of regional faunal evolution and in some cases entirely new geochronological methods at our disposal.

THE KILOMBE BACKGROUND

The Acheulean site complex at Kilombe was found by the geologist W. B. Jones in 1972. Its exploration was first taken up by W. W. Bishop (1978) and one of the authors (Gowlett 1978), leading to the new research which we discuss. The sites lie on the western flank of the Kenya Rift Valley (Figure 5.1), about 6 km south of the Equator, and 40 km north-west of Nakuru. In this area there are no visible major rift faults. Instead the landscape is dominated by the Plio-Pleistocene Rift volcanoes of Londiani (c. 3010 m), and Kilombe (c. 2380 m), which sits at the side of Londiani extending further towards the Rift Valley floor (Figures 5.2 and 5.3). The main lines of drainage are the Molo and Rongai rivers, which rise on the Mau escarpment about 50 km to the south-west and flow past Kilombe northward towards

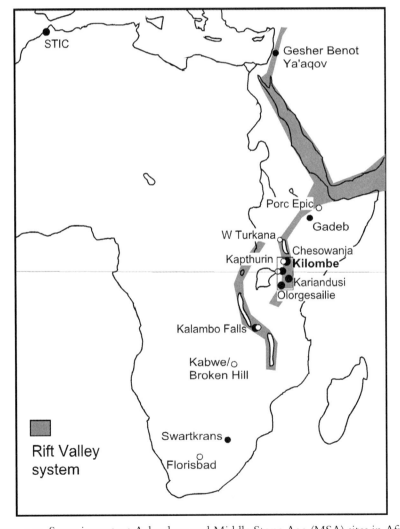

Figure 5.1: Some important Acheulean and Middle Stone Age (MSA) sites in Africa.

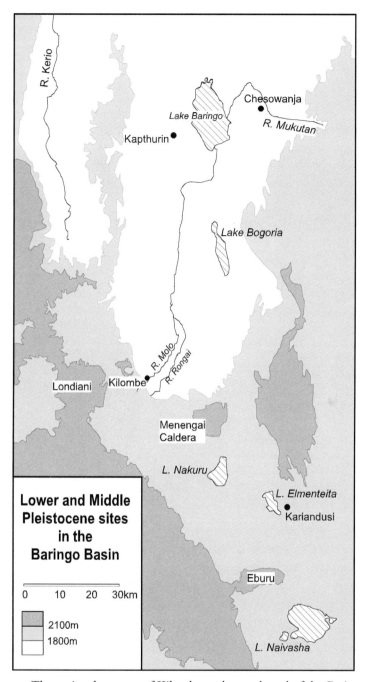

Figure 5.2: The regional context of Kilombe at the south end of the Baringo basin.

Lake Baringo, some 100 km away. Essentially this is a relatively old landscape – last lava flows at Kilombe have been dated to between 2.05–1.65 Ma (Jones 1975), and Kilombe volcano was probably already extinct before one and a half million years ago (we discuss below a lake that formed in the crater). There has been relatively little later faulting, and the depth of river valleys indicates their

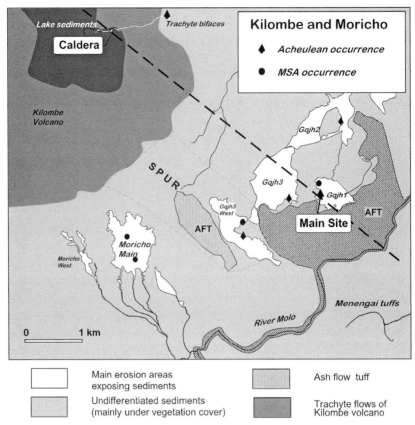

Figure 5.3: Kilombe – the site region showing the exposures of Kilombe and Moricho in relation to Kilombe mountain and the Molo valley. The white dotted line indicates the position of the landscape section shown in Figure 5.4, stretching from the Molo valley at the south-east to the crater lake at the north-west.

considerable age. At its southern end the Baringo basin is marked by the Menengai volcano, around 30 km south-east of the Kilombe sites, and visible from these. Menengai took shape about 200,000 years ago in its current form and was transformed again by a recent massive caldera explosion near the end of the Pleistocene (Leat 1984). It is probably the descendant of earlier active Pleistocene volcanoes (Jones 1985) and responsible for much of the deposition of pyroclastics in the area (Jones and Lippard 1979).

STRATIGRAPHY AND LOCALITIES

The original research at Kilombe concentrated largely on the main Acheulean site, which seemed exciting enough, with its extraordinary density of bifaces. At the time there was very limited time to move beyond Kilombe Main Site, although other small biface occurrences were found in the area. In dense bush it was a struggle to map the various outcrops and archaeological occurrences with theodolite, plane table and old air photograph cover. Now the regional perspective can be developed much more easily and fully through the (recent) ready availability of high-resolution satellite imagery.

The Kilombe Main Site (GqJh1) still provides one of the best local stratigraphies in the region. It was initially described by Bishop (1978) in an account which has largely stood the test of time, but which recent work has modified. The chief challenge was to understand a major break in the sequence, where a thick ashflow tuff was deposited over the landscape.

THE LOWER SEQUENCE AND MAIN SITE

At the base is trachyphonolite lava, dated to 1.70 ± 0.05 Ma (1.75–1.65 Ma) (Jones and Lippard 1979). This lava is extensive in the area, forming a low ridge stretching outwards from the base of the volcano towards the Molo River. Across the area it crops out at intervals, generally mantled to a depth of several metres by reddish-brown and brown clays which are its weathering products. The trachyphonolite formed an irregular surface, and its ridges appear to have constrained drainage, probably directing stream channels, and helping to cause some local ponding. The trachytes of Kilombe volcano and Londiani abut the trachyphonolite to the north. Although the stratigraphic relationship is not known, a K-Ar date on a trachyte flow of 1.90 ± 0.15 Ma (2.05–1.75 Ma) suggests that the two are potentially co-eval, especially given uncertainties in these older ages. The 'brown clays' of Bishop (1978), immediately overlying the trachyphonolite in the Main Site area, can actually be subdivided in three zones, a lower reddish-brown clay (RBC), overlain by a yellowish tuff (YT) that occurs in localised areas and an upper dark brown clay (DBC) (Figure 5.5). Fossils occur mainly at or near the contact between the two clays, which may represent an old landsurface onto which the yellowish tuff was deposited. A small amount of fauna came from the 'Brown Clays' of Main Site in the 1970s (Bishop 1978). Recent excavations recovered more fauna that came almost entirely from this old landsurface at or near the contact between the lower RBC and upper DBC. The fauna includes elephant, hippo and bovids (see p. 84–85). The top of the clays marks another major break, and coincides on the main site with the main artefact horizon, with its many bifaces. This is our first archaeological landscape.

This stratigraphy can be traced across several kilometres, but the main site (GqJh1) stands out because of the presence of a broad shallow depression, lower by about 1 m than the adjacent surfaces of the DBC. This depression must signal a local erosional event, following which the very large numbers of bifaces were deposited. Eventually the depression filled in with pale weathered tuffaceous material, which contains a few abraded artefacts, presumably washed in from the margins. This pale pumiceous tuff (PPT) seals in the handaxe layer throughout the main site. Hominins were still present: a further artefact horizon occurs in a lightly developed palaeosol at the top of PPT, about a metre above the main horizon. Although it remains well within Acheulean time, only flakes and flake tools have been found (Gowlett 1978).

THE THREE-BANDED TUFF COMPLEX

The next key event was a series of volcanic eruptions which blanketed the whole area with the 3-banded lapilli tuff (3BT), named for its distinctive profile, and traceable across several kilometres as an important marker horizon. This was a landscape-changing event. Bishop (1978) interpreted it as a primary airfall through standing water, and it appeared to map out a ponded area perhaps 2 km across. We can now trace it in an area extending approximately 3 × 2 kilometres, but its levels vary so considerably that the old explanation of a lake is no longer tenable. Rather, the tuff seems to have blanketed the catchment of small streams which ran off the eastern side of the ridge of trachyphonolite lavas, which projects south from Kilombe Mountain. Levels of the tuff can be seen to decline steeply from west to east, through as much as 100 m. The gradient is steeper than that found in the Molo River, which runs on a parallel course less than 2 km further south, and so cannot result from faulting, although minor faults may have occurred. These findings suggest the steep headwaters of local streams, which probably joined the Molo (or proto-Molo) within a few kilometres downstream. These local streams ran across an irregular surface of trachyphonolite lavas, coated with the clays which formed from their weathering. Recent erosion has re-exposed some of the channels which ran across the trachyphonolite surface.

The 3BT is somewhat degraded in parts of its westerly exposures, perhaps indicating erosion at its margins. In places, particularly to the east, its bands are slightly more separated, suggesting some significant difference in age between the eruptions, rather than the few hours that might have been envisaged. Dagley et al. (1978) showed in one of the first palaeomagnetic studies applied to the Acheulean that the 3BT recorded a reversed polarity, demonstrating an age older than the Brunhes-Matuyama boundary. This suggests the 3BT and Acheulean layers beneath it are older than 780,000 years based on the new dates for this boundary. Dagley et al. (1978) expressed caution in the interpretation of the results because the three samples taken were highly magnetised, possibly owing to a lightning strike. New palaeomagnetic sampling confirms the presence of reversed polarity throughout the 3BT in more than one location that argues against the strong remanence being a lightning strike. A single layer within the 3BT also recorded a normal polarity that may represent a short geomagnetic excursion, which would argue against the 3BT being a short event, however, more detailed sampling is needed to confirm the presence of such an event. In contrast the clay layers (RBC, DBC) below the handaxe layer record normal polarity. Based on the fauna from the site, which shows affinities with Olduvai Gorge Bed III-IV (see below), this normal polarity period is correlated to the Jaramillo Sub-Chron between 1.07 and 0.99 Ma (Herries et al. 2011; in prep.). As such, fauna can be dated to between 1.07 and 0.99 Ma, with the handaxe layer dating more broadly to some time between 1.07 and 0.78 Ma. PPT records reversed polarity towards its top and mixed polarity towards its base, which may suggest that the handaxe layer dates close to the reversal at the end of the Jaramillo SubChron at ~990,000 years old (Herries et al. 2011, in prep). Further work is still needed to identify the exact locations of the various polarity reversals within the sequence and constrain the ages of all the archaeological and fossil layers. The landscape of the late Lower Pleistocene is completed by new knowledge of a lake which occupied the Kilombe crater and is also older than 780,000 years based on a reversed polarity (and is under study by Herries SH; see below).

FARMHOUSE CLIFF AND THE ASHFLOW TUFF (AFT)

Recent investigations have confirmed that hominins were still present in the new landscapes overlying the 3BT. The sediments consist of a sequence of red-brown weathered pumiceous tuffs some 15 m thick (the Farmhouse cliff, and lateral equivalents), with sparse occurrences of handaxes at widely separated points. Most significant is the discovery in 2010 of a small biface site at GqJh3-West, with sufficient specimens to allow comparisons. These deposits are capped by an ashflow tuff some 7 m thick, a major feature of the landscape which Jones (1975; Jones and Lippard 1979) refers to the Lower Menengai tuffs (dated by K-Ar to c. 0.3 Ma). The ashflow tuff (AFT) indicates a major series of Middle Pleistocene eruptions which must have transformed the whole landscape. The Acheulean was still extant just before these major eruptions, as confirmed by a biface found in 2009 around one metre below the ashflow tuff, about 1500 m north-east of the main exposures.

The ashflow tuff (AFT) forms a prominent feature in the modern landscape, usually marking the top of cliffs along the southern edges of the Kilombe exposures (Bishop 1978), and also capping a scarp facing west towards Moricho. Jones and Lippard (1979) recognised the AFT as a Middle Pleistocene feature dated to a Menengai eruption at c. 300,000. Although Leat (1984) believed that the AFT can be linked with a more recent Menengai eruption (c. 30,000 ka), our work has confirmed an older age, as argued by Jones (1985). The AFT is widespread in the area north of the Molo River, and can be traced all the way from the side of the Molo River up to the top of the Kilombe Farmhouse cliff (Figures 5.4 and 5.5). It thus mantled a landscape in which the Molo river valley already existed. In high areas of topography overlying sediments have vanished, and the ashflow tuff itself has been eroded and in places breached, but elsewhere other sediments overlie it, indicating a long timescale of events consistent with Middle Pleistocene age.

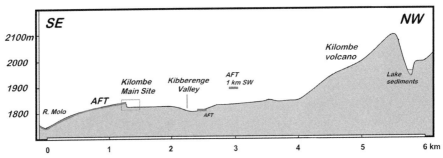

Figure 5.4: Kilombe – section of landscape and exposures along a line of 6 km from the River Molo to Kilombe crater (vertical scale x 4 horizontal). The position of the Kilombe main site is indicated by a box. Note at km 2.5–3 the very different heights of the ashflow tuff 1.3 km behind the section line and 200m on the observer's side of it. The drop of c. 100 m in 1.5 km, which cannot be explained by faulting, results from the gradient of the valley floor (sloping down towards observer).

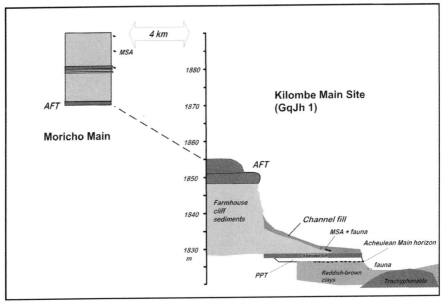

Figure 5.5: General section of Kilombe Main site (modified in the light of recent work after Bishop 1978, Gowlett 1994). On the main site Middle Stone Age artefacts and fauna are found in the basal fill of channels which formed following the erosional breach of the ashflow tuff. Units in stratigraphic sequence:

- Channel deposits cutting AFT, and containing MSA artefacts
- AFT – ash flow tuff
- Farmhouse Cliff – pumiceous tuffs
- 3-banded tuff
- PPT – pale pumiceous tuffs covering artefact horizon
- Main Acheulean artefact horizon
- Reddish brown clays including fauna
- Trachyphonolite lava

THE LATER SEDIMENTS

A further suite of impressive sediments representing the Middle and Upper Pleistocene extends widely along the southern flanks of Kilombe volcano, but was virtually unexplored until our recent research. Some 30 m thick, in places they have been eroded to form natural amphitheatres and huge gullies (Jennings 1971). In the sequence these sediments appear to be younger than the ashflow tuff. The AFT largely caps the trachyphonolite ridge which extends south from Kilombe Mountain, but in the areas to the west and to the east, it occurs at lower topographic levels, and appears to be blanketed by the later sediments. The extensive deposits consist of red sediments and further tuffs, visible especially in spectacular exposures at Moricho about 2 km west of Kilombe, and in huge gullies to the south-east of the mountain, towards the Rift Valley floor. These exposures, 20 to 30 m thick, include content of Middle Stone Age (MSA) and Later Stone Age (LSA) artefacts, mainly but not entirely made of obsidian. Typical long MSA points have been found in several areas, suggesting broad age limits of 50,000–250,000 years. Some are made of obsidian, others of fine-grained lava. In places there is also a microlithic component. Most of the red sediments have a characteristic layer-cake appearance, with alternations of paler tuffs and earthy sediments. At Moricho artefacts have been located low down in the sequence, just a few metres above the lowest tuffs. In the Kilombe catchment area (the Acheulean sites), this same series is represented by channels of streams which descended from high levels, cutting the older sediments. The channels are often floored with brown tuffaceous grits, and sometimes include other tuffs in their infilling. They were interpreted by Bishop (1978) as an integral part of the Farmhouse Cliff suite of pumiceous tuffs which immediately overlies the 3-banded tuff. They are however much later features, postdating the erosional breach of the ashflow tuff, and containing obsidian artefacts of the MSA. Fragmentary faunal remains have been found in the base of one such channel in the GqJh1 main site area. In 2011, a further MSA site was found at the western margin of Kilombe farm in the direction of Moricho, within one of the channel fills, in and around a yellowish tuff horizon (site GqJh3–200). It has produced numerous artefacts including long points. The artefacts are entirely fresh, sometimes with a thin calcareous coating. The points, made of obsidian, are visibly similar to those from Porc Epic in Ethiopia (Pleurdeau 2006). Broadly similar material was dated to c. 130,000 at Nasera and Mumba rockshelters in northern Tanzania (Mehlman 1991). From surface finds these levels had formerly been thought to belong to the LSA, but the discovery of typical MSA long points in situ would suggest an age of >50 ka for almost the entire sequence save superficial deposits. In total, then, the Kilombe sequence can be seen to preserve numbers of landscapes and sites from at least one million years ago up to very recent times.

REFLECTIONS ON THE NEW LANDSCAPES

In the new research since 2008 Kilombe Mountain has come to dominate the picture even more than previously. The original phase of research was able simply to treat the Acheulean sites as the key – lakeside – feature of an immediate local landscape, with just dimmest perceptions of what lay beyond. It was known that some handaxes were made of trachyte, probably from Kilombe mountain, and that a very few bifaces of obsidian came from much further away, so the handaxes in some way ghosted out a larger landscape, but in all other respects the research was site-centred by the constraints of resources. In short, there was a large Acheulean handaxe site holding centre stage within a framework chiefly known to geologists. On top was simply a hint of MSA or LSA activities in the form of scatters of obsidian artefacts.

Now the basic interpretation shifts from the idea of a lake to a secluded valley by the foot of the volcano and it can be seen that the Acheulean occurred regularly across the area, often at low density. It is preserved for us mainly in a valley descending eastwards from the trachyphonolite ridge (henceforth the Kibberenge Valley). The stream was less than 2 km away from the Molo River across the interfluve, but it may have run for several kilometres or more before finding its confluence with the river. Although the volcano was already extinct at least 1.5 Ma ago, it had shaped this local and regional drainage. The rivers Molo and Rongai, draining into the Baringo basin from the south-west, pass close by the mountain. The streams radiating from the west, south and east of the mountain make their way more or less directly into the Molo. Although the substrate of lavas became blanketed by 50 m or more of Lower, Middle and Upper Pleistocene sediments, we can now see that as both faulting and erosion of hard rocks have been limited, there has been a rare essential continuity in the landscape which hominins inhabited and exploited.

Several indicators now give us some picture of the local environment around 1 million years ago. The fauna comes almost entirely from the contact zone between the lower (RBC) and upper (DBC) brown clays at the north end of the main site, in the 4 m of sediments underlying the main artefact horizon. As no fauna has been observed at the same levels elsewhere, its local preservation suggests an area where the clays accumulated rapidly, but in two or more distinct phases, indicating periods of erosion or stillstands. Low ridges of trachyphonolite appear to have created a tendency for very local ponding, probably in a zone not much more than 100 m across, as indicated by the shallow depression in the brown clays, and the infilling with pale material. On the eastern side erosion had cut two (or possibly more) narrow exit channels in the rock. These may be the key to interpretation, as they could easily become blocked by vegetation or sediment choking.

Although bones are not prolific, several taxa are now known. Hippopotamus is most common, with elephant also present. There is a range of bovids, from giant buffalo down to gazelle-size. One piece of rodent microfauna has also been preserved. These remains are entirely consistent with the idea that the immediate environment was well-watered and, probably, swampy in places. The grey-green clays of the main site may indicate gleying and sandy runnels show the presence of ephemeral streams in the site area.

At about the level of the fauna a thin yellowish tuff (YT) occurs, which preserves root casts indicating the presence of grassy cover. Further evidence of a well-watered environment comes from the crater lake. The sediments were first reported by Jennings (1971) although McCall (1964) had been inclined to see them as a product of caldera formation rather than as lacustrine. We now know that lake sediments were deposited over a period, preserving thin laminations and occasional ripple marks through at least 10 m depth. They are overlain by very thick homogeneous tuff, and have reversed magnetic polarity, indicating an age >780,000 years and most likely <1.78 Ma based on the youngest age of lava flows from the volcano.

The presence of such water bodies could tally with the idea of Trauth et al. (2005) that there was a prolonged period of favourable climate in the late Lower Pleistocene, about a million years ago, and that numerous Acheulean sites are associated with this. As the idea of a sizeable lake associated with the 3BT can no longer be sustained, and as the exact age of the crater lake is not yet known, it is important to withstand any temptation to build such a link by 'assimilation'. The key factor in the environment was the presence of high mountains which attract more rainfall than lower regions in this part of the Rift. Although the later environments are less known to us, the same topographic factors would operate in influencing climate.

THE *LANGAGE* OF THE ARTEFACTS

The French term *langage* allows us to highlight how artefacts can speak to represent a world beyond themselves, pointing to a network of activities that for the early Palaeolithic is beyond the reach of any other category of evidence.

The Acheulean: Here clearly the dominant feature remains the extensive artefact horizon of the Kilombe main site, with hundreds of Acheulean bifaces exposed across a surface that runs for at least 200 m in different directions (Gowlett 1978, 1991, 1993, 2005; Figures 5.5 and 5.6). Apart from aspects of landscape, the Kilombe bifaces (Table 5.1) have offered the basis for various studies of cognitive capabilities, including the sense of proportion (Gowlett 1984, 2011, especially favoured ratios such as 0.61 or Golden Section [Boselie 1984]), the role of allometry (Crompton and Gowlett 1993) and investigations of the presence of traditions (Lycett and Gowlett 2008). In terms of site formation processes the essential point about Kilombe is that the favoured landscape was stable for some considerable time, and then rapidly covered in. Mary Leakey noted that, like Olduvai Bed I, the site is highly unusual in

TABLE 5.1: *Summary of key data, expressed as means and standard deviations. Correlation coefficients shown in the right-hand column are not discussed in text, and merely show that there is normally a very strong relationship between Length and Breadth.*

Site	N=	Length	Breadth	Thickness	B/L ratio	Correlation B & L
Kilombe	394	149 ± 31	90 ± 16	42 ± 10	0.61 ± 0.07	0.84
Kariandusi Upper Site (obsidian)	60	149 ± 31	79 ± 13	37 ± 7	0.64 ± 0.09	0.77
Kariandusi Lower Site (trachyte lava)	126	149 ± 31	94 ± 11	49 ± 9	0.58 ± 0.07	0.59
Kariandusi, All	186	152 ± 30	90 ± 14	45 ± 10	0.60 ± 0.08	0.77

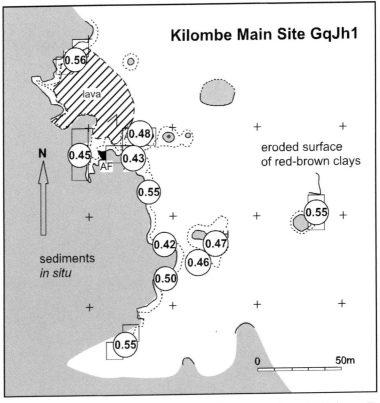

Figure 5.6: A plan of the main site. Note how the mean value of Thickness/Breadth in bifaces varies markedly from area to area.

TABLE 5.2: *Biface data from Kilombe EH and Kilombe GH illustrate differences in size and shape that can occur on the single surface.*

	Kilombe EH N= 106	Kilombe GH N = 54
Length	152 ± 30	135 ± 33
Breadth	94 ± 18	81 ± 15
Thickness	43 ± 10	45 ± 13
T/B	0.47 ± 0.12	0.55 ± 0.11
B/L	0.62 ± 0.07	0.61 ± 0.09
Weight	545 ± 265 g	412 ± 254 g

TABLE 5.3: *Supplementary data for the discriminant analysis.*

	Function 1	Function 2	Function 3
Eigenvalue	0.299	0.229	0.120
Variance accounted for	36.8%	28.1%	14.7%
Correlations			
Length	**0.750**	0.371	0.297
Breadth	0.652	0.267	0.264
Thickness	**0.747**	-0.157	-0.490
BA	0.293	**0.452**	0.361
BM	0.518	0.279	0.389
BB	0.525	0.229	0.173
PMB1	0.419	**0.584**	0.243
PMB2	0.550	0.440	**0.427**
TA	0.416	-0.235	**0.471**
TM	0.674	-0.137	0.212
TB	0.668	-0.365	-0.173

preserving artefacts on a clayey (rather than sandy or silty) surface (pers. comm.). The Kilombe complex thus provides a highly unusual – almost unique – opportunity to look at local variation within Acheulean bifaces on a single surface (Figure 5.6; Tables 5.2 and 5.3) – a local landscape (complexes such as the Somme or Boxgrove allow different comparisons of facies: Tuffreau et al. 1997; Pope et al. 2006). The stable facies shows that people were attracted by a prolonged conjunction of circumstances, including the presence nearby of a suitable raw material. This was abundant: the bifaces are chiefly made of the local trachyphonolite (about 93%). Artefacts are chemically weathered to a pale grey colour, but when broken through show the original near-black colour of the rock. It seems that boulders of fresh trachyphonolite were available nearby. They were knapped to produce large biface-flakes, some of which still preserve the boulder cortex on their dorsal surfaces, although the boulders themselves hardly appear on the site.

Almost all the remaining bifaces are made of trachyte, available from the flows of Kilombe volcano about 3 km away. This rock would not be transported to the main site area by local streams owing to drainage directions, so its presence indicates a fairly regular human movement from and to the volcano area. In 2011, two bifaces of trachyte were found by the mouth of the gorge which emerges on the east side of Kilombe volcano (Figure 5.3), confirming Acheulean presence on the trachyte flows (although these specimens are undated). Several obsidian bifaces have also been found on the main site. These must have been carried a much greater distance, but they are not from the sources used at the Kariandusi sites, 60 km to the south-east. At Gadeb, in Ethiopia, rare obsidian bifaces were similarly transported a long distance (Clark 1980).

The number of bifaces discarded across the surface can be calculated very roughly. In excavations mean densities vary from 4 per m^2 to 2 per m^2. There are indications that these are typical values over an area of c. 100 x 50 m as a minimum – which would give a value of c. 5000 m^2 multiplied by three (approximately) = 15,000. Arguably the total number is less important than the strong message of repeated return. If bifaces were 'cheap' in terms of raw material and effort and people kept returning to a 'favoured place', then even if just one task-group of six people visited the area three times a year discarding two bifaces each, that could create a discard of around 100 bifaces per three years or 1000 per 30 years, translating to some 10,000 bifaces in 300 years. Although some permutation of such repeated activity has to be anticipated to explain phenomena such as Kilombe, two features stand out about the surface:

1. the general similarity of the bifaces across the area
2. a contrasting variation of individual parameters, which vary far beyond random expectation, making the output distinctly characterisable area by area.

This local character suggests that bifaces were 'related' in groups of about twenty to sixty.

Cluster analysis has proved helpful for finding most similar bifaces. It is possible, for example, to consider all the areas, and to determine whether the nearest 'relative' to a biface is found close to it, or some way distant. A study using Wishart's density analysis found that to a considerable extent the most similar bifaces were grouped together in an area, or in adjacent areas (Gowlett 2005). This evidence hints at small groups working together on particular occasions, and sometimes the same individual hand may be involved a number of times (cf. Gamble and Porr 2005b).

We know the basic procedural parameters of the Acheulean far better than the uses to which the artefacts were put. Potts et al. (1999) demonstrate that the large biface concentrations at Olorgesailie are an extremely rare feature on the landscape, hugely outnumbered by low density artefact occurrences. The same holds true for the Kilombe area. It should be emphasised that the principal explanation cannot be taphonomic – at less than 2 km from their sources, the streams at Kilombe would have been simply unable to collect and spread out this quantity of material. The two main competing causes are that these are centres for butchery, or for the exploitation of plant resources. The first has the difficulty that so many carcasses would have to be brought to one place, the second that no plant resource has been identified that would lead to so many similar occurrences across such a large part of the Old World. A third possibility is that these may be working areas where bifaces were finished (or rejected) and where a variety of tasks took place. At Kilombe, Olorgesailie and elsewhere consistently small quantities of trimming flakes are found with the bifaces, indicating minor reworking, but not the principal stages of production.

One issue is whether variation is constrained in a local tradition. The small biface assemblage recently found above the 3-banded tuff – hence probably several thousand years younger than the main horizon – offers a valuable test. Does it (KW) fit within a single distinctive Kilombe tradition? It has similar length range, but includes unusually narrow or elongate specimens. Similar ones, however, are found in one small sub-assemblage of the main horizon, AS. Discriminant analysis (DA) is one means of plotting the Kilombe assemblages against other Acheulean sites (Figure 5.8). It underlines the generally distinctive nature of the Kilombe grouping, which keeps to its own 'site space', comfortably including the later KW assemblage, but it also emphasises a 'variable sameness' of the Acheulean, which allows far distant assemblages to be similar. Thus the heavyweight KZ strays into the zone of Cornelia (Brink et al. 2012) and Kalambo Falls Sangoan (B4) (Clark 2001), whereas EL tends towards the Kalambo Falls Acheulean (A6).

Notably, the Thickness/Breadth ratio varies enormously across the single surface. Contemporaneous local subassemblages vary from as little as 0.35 to about 0.56 in mean thickness, with differences significant at the 1% level. These differences emphasise that thickness/breadth can never be taken as an index of chronology, because it is a prime means of adjusting mass. In East Africa it is hazardous to see it as an index of refinement, but refinement does exist. Symmetry in bifaces is another issue of broad interest (e.g., Machin et al. 2007; Lycett 2008). Contrary to some thinking, handaxes with an advanced symmetry occur from at least one million years ago (cf. Figure 5.7). The patterns suggest that some of the small departures from symmetry are intentional symmetry-breaking probably linked with handedness in use.

Finally, Kilombe demonstrates along with other sites that early humans were capable of leaving a great deal of material on the landscape. Even if the repeated nature of activity is a partial explanation, we still see hominins

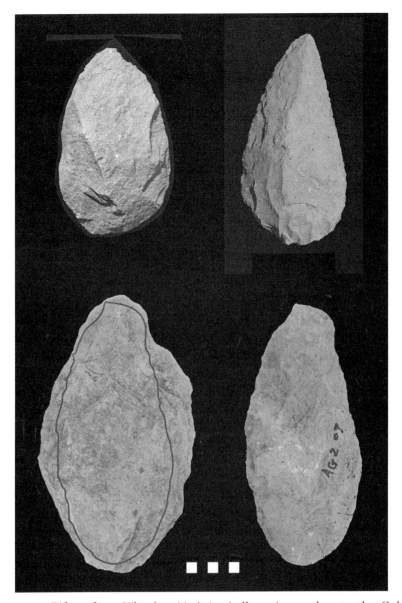

Figure 5.7: Bifaces from Kilombe: (a) A 'typical' specimen, close to the Golden Section ratio. Length 128 mm and breadth/length ratio 0.62; (b) A fine specimen showing slight asymmetry; (c and d), Examples of very long specimens. The massive specimen is unique on the site and illustrates the way in which the longest handaxes were made by striking of a very large flake, subsequently narrowed in trimming to give the shape of the more typical long specimen also shown.

'at home' on the landscape, and the notion that large sites come only with modern humans is not supported by the very visible evidence.

The Middle and Later Stone Age: The later exposures along the southern flank of Kilombe volcano contribute to sequence building, offering the opportunity

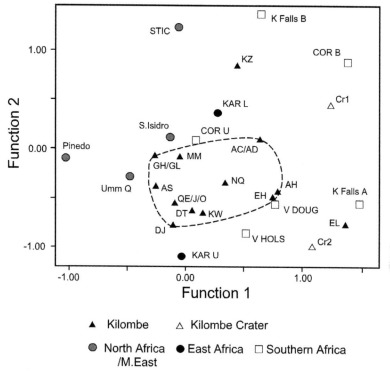

Figure 5.8: Discriminant analysis of bifaces: a plot of Function 1 and Function 2, based on selected sites from Africa and the Middle East using 11 variables. Most Kilombe biface assemblages are highly similar to one another, forming a tight cluster, but in this analysis one Main Site area (Z) groups more closely with heavy duty assemblages from distant sites. KW (Kilombe GqJh3 West), although above the 3-banded tuff, falls within the main group. These are examples of Acheulean 'variable sameness' extending through space and time. Other sites: CORB = Cornelia, basal; CORU = Cornelia Upper; VHOLS=Vaal Holsdam; VDOUG = Vaal, Douglas; Umm Q = Umm Qatafa; KFA=Kalambo Falls A6; KFB=Kalambo Falls B4; KAR U=Kariandusi Upper; KARL = Kariandusi lower site; STIC=Sidi Abderrahman. See Gowlett (2012), Lycett and Gowlett (2008) and Table 5.3 for further details.

to map out later landscapes in the same area, and to set them in their regional environmental context (Blome et al. 2012). They are currently less well known than the early levels, but have great potential because of the scale of the exposures. The scatters of MSA and LSA artefacts suggest a steady and widespread human use of the slopes on the south side of the volcano. At least in part this took place at the side of stream channels. They also show us clearly a new pattern of resource use, involving the use of imported raw materials. Some obsidian used in the region came from the Naivasha area around 100 km away (Merrick and Brown 1984), but there did remain some use of the local lavas, even for some long MSA points. Even so, the outline evidence is enough to show that hominins were operating on a new scale of network. Changes of technology may of course have helped this to operate: the small blanks of high quality raw material are far more transportable than the earlier handaxes.

This shift from the obvious larger tools to their smaller successors, parts of more sophisticated systems, is something that can be traced with a rare continuity in this region (Wendorf and Schild 1974; McBrearty and Brooks 2000; Basell 2008), as at Kapthurin to the north (McBrearty 1999; Tryon and McBrearty 2002, 2006; Tryon 2006; Johnson and McBrearty 2010) and at Prospect Farm and Olorgesailie to the south (Michels et al. 1983).

CONCLUSIONS: A VALLEY BY A VOLCANO

The exposures of Kilombe allow us to read a record of an early Pleistocene landscape at several levels, and to get first insights into equivalent later Middle and Upper Pleistocene occupations – all tucked away in the same Kibberenge valley.

At the base, the Kilombe main Acheulean complex gives a breadth of view which will be hard to match. In the full picture of the early Acheulean record it appears that such large handaxe concentrations are an anomaly, unusual on the landscape, as at Olorgesailie (Potts et al. 1999). Where they do occur, as at Kilombe, on close inspection they point to the existence of many minor sites and artefact scatters of different kinds. These make up a fuller landscape. They occur in different permutations in different site complexes. The great value of Kilombe for the Acheulean is that it preserves one huge pene-contemporaneous surface, and so allows intercomparisons of a kind that are very rarely possible. They show that variations within a site complex can be as great as those between them. Nevertheless, there is also a distinctive local Kilombe character, preserved and transmitted through its various assemblages.

Its artefacts allow particular insights into various practical and cognitive capacities, perhaps most of all the ability of early humans to carry out trans-formations of their material culture, varying the physical scale and form of the bifaces in a highly controlled way. This ability to transform, to have a sense of proportion, is an important underpinning for many later cultural developments. A wider perspective on Kilombe comes from the greater landscape – the outlying exposures, the crater lake and the finds of the higher levels. Together these offer a treasure trove of archaeological possibilities, with the possibility of assembling successive snapshots of a changing picture.

All together its evidence gives an impression of system and organisation in the hominins who settled there. They repeated similar activities many times, but also varied them. They had strong rules for their behaviour, but also subtle ones.

Working in from more general frameworks of human evolution and sociality we can say a good deal about the capacities of these early humans, almost certainly *Homo erectus*. Demonstrably they worked in sizeable groups, and conveyed information across those very accurately. They appear to have been 'mapped' to their environment strongly, in a local tradition. The artefacts and their settings give us some idea of the strength of communication flows. The ideas of the social brain also help to give some insight into the capabilities that we should expect (Gamble et al. 2011). They predict the existence of language at least 500,000 years ago (Dunbar 1998a), and anatomical evidence points in the same direction. How simple would that language be, and what could it achieve? We do not know, but the content and complexity of the Kilombe cultural package measures up with the idea that a large and detailed body of information was transmitted effectively.[1]

Note

[1] As of 2013 a series of Argon-Argon dates from Kilombe is being run by SUERC (Scottish Universities Environmental Research Centre) with the support of NERC. These will be published elsewhere. The dates do not fundamentally alter the stratigraphic or chronological outline given in the paper.

CHAPTER 6

ALL IN A DAY'S WORK? EARLY CONFLICTS IN EXPERTISE, LIFE HISTORY AND TIME MANAGEMENT

ANTHONY SINCLAIR

INTRODUCTION

Clive Gamble once suggested that if we wanted to look for the origins of the state we should start by looking at hunter-gatherer societies (Gamble 1985). Hunter-gatherers, Gamble argued, possess many of the complex features of states or urban societies listed in models of social evolution (for example: art, social stratification, organisation of labour, long-distance trade, externalised knowledge or writing). All they were missing was a commitment to permanency of residence. To explain the origins of the state, Gamble concluded, we needed to understand how the essential fission-fusion process might have been replaced by one of permanent residence with its concomitant outcomes (population increase, conflict resolution, maintenance of order, and so on) and state society forms of resolution.

If Gamble were writing this article today, however, he might also claim that ancient hunter-gatherer societies possessed another central feature of state societies: craft specialisation. In many models of state level development (i.e., Renfrew 1972), specialist goods and services become central to the achievement and maintenance of power by elites, who in turn supported craft specialists in their subsistence needs. Whilst some craft specialisation may lead to the mass production of similar items (see discussion in Wengrow 2008, and the example of obsidian blade mass production in Torrence 1986), in other instances it may lead to the production of restricted numbers of high quality craft goods. In both cases, however, we can imagine that becoming a craft specialist requires the acquisition of specific knowledge and skills, perhaps to an exceptional level, and the required freedom from subsistence tasks restricted such a development to after the origins of agriculture. Whilst Gamble did not highlight craft specialisation in his discussion, more recent research suggests that it was also in the context of a hunter-gatherer way of life that humans evolved the possibility for extensive investment in the learning of stocks of knowledge and the development of enhanced technical skills. So hunter-gatherer societies might also be the place to look for evidence for the development of expertise and specialisation.

In the first half of this paper I shall briefly review two distinct bodies of research that touch on the development of expertise, skills and knowledge; (i) studies of expert performance, innate talent and the development of expertise by individuals; and (ii) research into the evolved characteristics of human growth and life history. I shall emphasise two central findings. First, that the attainment of individual excellence in skilful activities always requires substantial time, deliberate practice and societal support (in many forms from subsistence provision of parents through to dedicated tuition). Second, if it was the transformation of human growth and life history, evolving during our time as hunters and gatherers, that facilitated the individual development of specialist knowledge and skill, then we might also look for the evidence of the first specialists in Palaeolithic societies. In the second half, I shall argue that there is sufficient evidence to suggest that a number of Palaeolithic individuals were experts in their 'craft'. This fact should not be surprising in itself. What should give a jolt to our thinking, however, is the commensurate social support needed for the achievement of such expertise, challenging our largely implicit assumptions of the nature of skill acquisition in hunter-gatherer society in the Palaeolithic. If it is human evolution, not sedentism or agriculture, that created the conditions in which individuals could become experts or craft specialists, why do we not more commonly discuss craft specialisation or the appearance of experts in the Palaeolithic? (See Milliken 1998 for a rare exception.) At the end, I shall also argue that the appearance of experts and specialists is not a revolutionary threshold, where once achieved there is no going back; expertise is scattered across time and place.

In this paper I shall focus on craft activities, specifically lithic manufacture, as a form of activity that is both open to expression of skill and knowledge and that can also be identified and analysed in the archaeological record. For the purposes of developing my argument I shall primarily use archaeological examples dating to the Upper Palaeolithic and produced by anatomically modern humans; the archaeological record from this latter period(s) of the Palaeolithic provides the most convincing evidence for the presence of individuals with specialist craft skills. Since the conditions for the development of these skills have evolved through time, there is no necessary reason why examples of advanced expertise might not be identified in earlier periods and in the actions of pre-modern or 'archaic' hominins if the necessary life history conditions were present. We should also not assume that such expertise was only achieved in lithic activities. Many, if not most, activities at this time required the practitioner to develop a body of specific knowledge and a suite of practical skills, which an individual might enhance over time; the arguments that I shall make below are equally applicable to these other activities. The central issue, however, is that the identification of expertise with its associated requirements requires us to open our investigations to comprehend the complexity and diversity of the social lives and organisation of Palaeolithic societies.

A NEW LANGUAGE FOR TECHNOLOGICAL ANALYSIS

Before proceeding we must clarify some terms that will be used later on. As noted above, specialists, such as craft specialists envisaged in the development of state societies, are individuals who are able to devote their working hours largely or perhaps even exclusively to performance within a single domain of activity: a specialism. They might be metalworkers, potters, scribes, religious officials and so forth. A specialism will often encompass individuals with different levels of knowledge and skill. At one end of a spectrum, specialists might be highly skilled individuals who can accomplish difficult skills or produce items of refinement beyond the level of others. I propose that these individuals should be recognised as having developed a high level of expertise. Expertise will vary amongst a population of such individuals; perhaps most commonly as a function of the time they have had to mature their skills. Within a population, the highest level of expertise is that possessed by experts. Expert in this sense is a strictly relative term; it does not make sense except in the context of a range of individual expertise. At the other end of the spectrum, however, specialists might also be individuals who, whilst also devoting their working hours largely or perhaps even exclusively to the performance of a single domain of activity, have no cause or reason to develop high levels of expertise. This may be because the production process has been separated into shorter and simply achieved constituent elements, as is common on a production line and described most famously in the eighteen stages in the making of a pin by Adam Smith. It may also be because the activity performed exists in a context in which there is no pressure to encourage the enhancement of expertise.

Specialists and/or specialisms, therefore, are defined by the time given to performance within a domain of activity. Expertise is the varying level of knowledge and practical skill developed and expressed in such an activity. An expert is someone who has developed very high and possibly exceptional levels of expertise in a domain. This language of experts, expertise and specialisms provides insights into aspects of ancient craft activity that align well with current approaches to the study of, for example, lithic technology.

When we consider the stone tools and associated debris that we find on sites and in landscapes we now think in terms of explicitly learned knowledge, practically acquired subconscious know-how, raw materials, implements and desired ends which come together in 'a moment of active engagement' through a socially situated individual at a moment in (evolutionary) time. The same complexity will also have been present in other crafts practised by hominins at this time such as textile technologies (Soffer et al. 2000a; Soffer, et al. 2000) or clothing technologies (Gilligan 2010), to name but two techno-logical activities, and activities in other domains such as subsistence activities. Palaeolithic life, as evidenced through its technology, was an intrinsically skilful activity developed and expressed through many lifetimes.

This 'moment of active engagement', however, also possesses another important time scale that is just as visible in the discrete moments that we detect, but which has been cumulatively structured on a different scale – the individual lifetime. Here we need to move from the reconstructed skilful activity of the moment to the acquisition of lifetime skill, or expertise, and its variable representation across populations. A growing number of experimental studies have reliably detected differences in skilled performance between knappers within a population that can be correlated with degree of prior experience in the domain of lithic reduction. Examples include differences in consistency of débitage dimensions (Williams and Andrefsky 2011), in the ability of individuals to control kinetic energy within any one striking blow so as to accommodate different weights of core and hammer stone (Bril et al. 2010, 2012), or to predict accurately the shapes of flakes that will be removed as an essential prerequisite for successful and predictable core reduction (Nonaka et al. 2010), or to change strategies of reduction (Roux et al. 1995). Archaeologically, it has been possible to identify skill difference between populations in, for example, the observable error rates in the reduction of microblade cores (Bleed 2008), and it has been suggested that certain elite individuals, such as 'big men', might support the differential development of skill for the purposes of self-aggrandisement (Olausson 2008).

EXPERT PERFORMANCE AND THE DEVELOPMENT OF EXPERTISE

Expert performance and expertise has become a focus of research in its own right with the publication of a number of syntheses (Anderson 1981; Bloom 1985; Chi et al. 1988; Ericsson and Smith 1991; Starkes and Allard 1993; Ericsson 1996; Starkes and Ericsson 2003), a dedicated journal (*High Ability Studies*), an academic handbook (Ericsson et al. 2006), and most recently a series of popular syntheses (Gladwell 2008; Coyle 2011; Syed 2011). This research is broad in scope, ranging from individual attributes and behaviours to the social context of learning and the control of experts. It debates the existence of innate talents and their potential for enhancement (Winner 1996; Howe et al. 1998; Sternberg 2003; Gagné 2004), the structuring and use of memory (Ericsson and Kintsch 1995; Richman and Gobet 1996), the necessity of practice (Ericsson et al. 1993), critical biographies of experts (Howe 1996), the social context of experts' support (Hunt 2006), and even the concept of professionalism (Evetts et al. 2006). Here I shall highlight the nature of experts' skills, the necessity for extensive and deliberate practice, the nature of tuition, and finally the need for both motivation and social encouragement in order to perform at an expert level. Each of these is suggested by the qualities that we can see in real examples of lithic technology and has implications for our understanding of the society in which such activities was present.

Before reviewing some of this literature, it is worth noting that the experts who form the individual subject matter of this research are more often than not engaged in domains of activity that might be considered either idiosyncratic (memory displays) or elite (musicianship, chess playing, professional sports). Whilst it is axiomatic within this literature that expert performance is possible in every domain of activity, we cannot ignore the fact that it has been a central feature of the capitalist system that the working life of individuals within many workplaces has been distanced from the natural rhythms of tasks (Thompson 1967) and progressively deskilled through the application of technological assistance to the extent that individuals are no longer at liberty to effectively develop or express their personal skills (Sennett 1998, 2009). It is, therefore, only in a few select domains that contemporary individuals can progress their expertise, be recognised and rewarded by the capitalist system for doing so, and be examined as case studies of expert performance. We should not assume that the domains of activity in which expert performance was possible would have been anything like so limited in the past. Indeed, surveys of cultures in contemporary Zimbabwe (Ngara and Porath 2004, 2007) reveal a broad range of domains of activity in which giftedness is recognised.

DEFINING EXPERTS

There are two basic understandings of expert in the research on expertise (Chi 2006). First, there is the 'eminent individual', like Albert Einstein or Thomas Edison perhaps, who is recognised as outstanding; we sometimes refer to these individuals as geniuses, and they are, by definition, exceptional and exceedingly rare and not amenable to comparative study. Second, there is the 'relative expert', whose ability is as good as experience and training might make it and who, when compared with others, exhibits the highest quality and consistency in their work. In the contemporary world, these are the individuals who have attained sufficient proficiency in their skills that they are now concert musicians, grandmasters in chess, international standard athletes and so forth. 'Relative experts' are the main focus of expert performance research and these are the type of expert who shall be referred to hereafter.

The significance of relativity in this definition is that it is about performance that can be measured rather than the identification of some rare or perhaps unique quality. Such qualities have proven to be difficult to identify in approaches focused on innate talent or giftedness (Ericsson et al. 2007), but performance can be evaluated against a proficiency scale such as academic qualifications, or to seniority and experience, or to specific domain-centred knowledge and associated performance tests. The expertise shown by an expert then exists in the form of reproducibly superior performance(s) (Ericsson et al. 2007). A scale derived from the levels of attainment in the crafts guilds (Figure 6.1) has been used to differentiate and label the relative performance of experts in practical activities (Chi 2006). Whilst the relative and progressive scale admits the possibility that every individual might reach expert status,

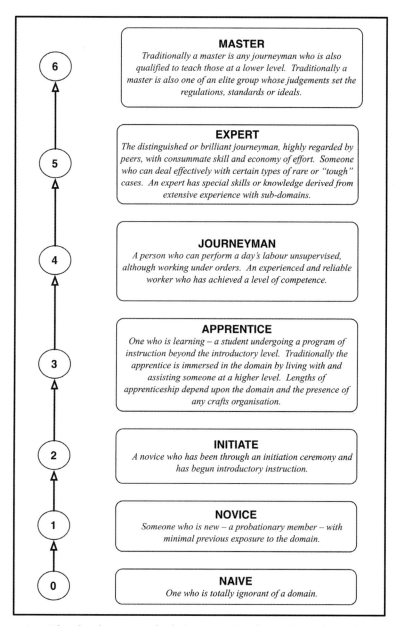

Figure 6.1: The development of relative expertise from Naïve through to Master (using definitions from Chi et al. 2006: table 2.1).

few individuals reach this level in reality. The numbers of experts within a population, compared with novices, apprentices and journeymen is small due to a number of factors such as natural interest, dedication to practice or the nature of social encouragement, discussed below.

Expert performance research (Chi 2006) has also identified common features in which experts excel and in which they also fall short (Table 6.1).

TABLE 6.1: *The ways in which experts excel and in which they fall short (modified after Chi 2006).*

Ways in which experts excel	Ways in which experts fall short
Generating the Best	Domain-Limited
Experts generate the best solutions, faster and more accurately than non-experts	*Experts excel in their domain of expertise, but rarely outside it.*
Detection and Recognition	Over-Confidence
Experts can detect features that novices cannot. They can perceive the deep-structure of a problem.	*Experts can miscalibrate their capabilities through being over-confident, although there are some domains where expertise is necessarily cautious and conservative.*
Qualitative Analyses	Glossing Over
Experts spend much time analysing a problem qualitatively, developing a problem representation by adding many domain-specific and general constraints to the problems in their domain of expertise	*Although experts may grasp the deep-structure of problems, they may also gloss over the surface and overlook details which they take to be less relevant to the problem at hand.*
Monitoring	Context-Dependence Within a Domain
Experts have more accurate self-monitoring skills in terms of their ability to detect errors and the status of their own comprehension, on the basis of the recognition of key domain-specific information.	*Due to their immersion within a domain, experts may rely on contextual cues for analysis that are not causally related to a problem. Without the contextual cues, expert judgement may be significantly impaired.*
Strategies	Inflexible
Experts choose more successful and appropriate strategies than novices. Experts possess better knowledge as to which strategies are better in any given situation, and also know which strategies have more frequently proved to be effective.	*Experts may have trouble adapting to problems that possess a deep structure that deviate from those 'acceptable' within a domain. Experts may also have problems recognising a deep-structure similar to that within their own expertise but presented within another domain.*
Opportunistic	Inaccurate Prediction and Judgement
Experts are opportunistic – making better use of whatever sources of information are available while solving problems, and in the use of resources.	*Experts can be inaccurate in the prediction of novice performance. This may be due to their inability to extrapolate from their own domain specific experience to that of novices.*
Cognitive Effort	Bias and Functional Fixedness
Experts can retrieve relevant domain knowledge and strategies with minimal cognitive effort. They can also execute skills with greater automaticity.	*Sometimes experts may have difficulty coming up with creative solutions to a problem since they become fixed on solutions that have proven to be effective within their domain.*

It is clear that experience and training provide experts with a carefully structured body of domain-specific knowledge that facilitates excellent judgement,
effective self-monitoring and the choice of the best strategies for tackling
problems. They also possess an ability to see beyond surface features and
recognise deep structures using cues and observed patterns. Experts can access

and make use of knowledge with less cognitive effort than others. Experts are usually domain-limited in their expertise, often overly confident and prone to miscalculate the difficulties encountered by non-experts. In an experimental study of experts as teachers, Hinds (1999) argued that the poor performance of experts as tutors stemmed from their inability to take on the perspectives of novices. Students can more directly take on feedback from peers, individuals closer in ability to themselves, than from experts.

Even though expert status is defined relatively, the number of experts within a population remains very small for any particular skill (Ericsson 1996). The road to attainment of expertise is a long one; individuals must be dedicated, persevering in their practice, and well supported both internally (through self-motivation) and externally (by family members, and social encouragement), if they are to realise expert performance rather than competence.

THE IMPORTANCE OF EXTENSIVE AND DELIBERATE PRACTICE

There are distinct and unresolved differences of opinion as to whether an expert is born with 'innate talent' for their domain of expertise, or whether he or she achieves a high level of expertise through dedication and perseverance alone (Ericsson et al. 1993; Ericsson and Charness 1994, 1995; Gardner 1995; Sloboda 1996; Winner 1996; Howe et al. 1998; Hunt 2006). Much of this literature has been written in the context of debates about the value of educational programmes for the identification and support of (exceptional) young children who are identified as 'gifted' through the possession of innate talents through the school system (Gagné 2004; Sternberg 2003). There is, however, no doubt that experts are not born fully skilled (Ericsson et al. 2007); the skills of any expert result from considerable experience and long periods of practice, beyond that necessary to achieve competence (Figure 6.2). Specifically there are no reliable examples of individuals who have attained expert status in the performance of a skilled activity without engaging in extensive practice under the guidance of proper tutors. It is practice that enables experts to perform consistently, to perceive the deep-structure of the task, to work according to well conceived strategies, and to work efficiently. It is also, possibly, this experience of extensive practice and the dedication given to their specific domain that makes experts less able to empathise with the problems faced by 'novices' and 'initiates', than perhaps 'journeymen' and 'apprentices'.

Published studies seem to indicate that there is a pattern in the age at which individuals attain the status of an expert (Ericsson et al. 1993; Charness et al. 1996; Simonton 1996) relating to the length of time that must be devoted to practice, and the degree of physical exertion involved. In 1899, Bryan and Harter stated that 10 years of experience was required to become a professional telegrapher (cited in Ericsson 2006a). Subsequently, a '10 year rule' or,

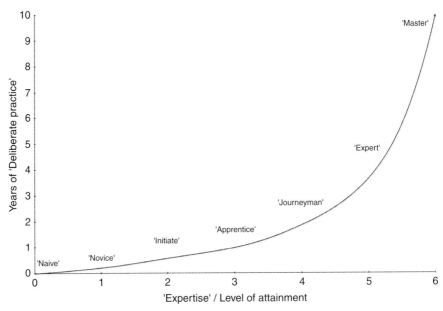

Figure 6.2: The relationship between years of practice and the development of level of expertise (following Ericsson 1996).

sometimes, '10,000 hours rule' (of practice) has been suggested as necessary for the attainment of expert status (Ericsson 1996). A similar length of time has been noted as necessary in order to become an expert in chess (Charness et al. 1996), or music (Sloboda 1996), as well as a range of sciences and arts (Ericsson et al. 1993). Ten years allows for the accumulation of thousands of hours of practice. Contemporary experts also record an increasing devotion to practice time as their career progresses.

In contrast to the impression given in the popular literature (Gladwell 2008; Coyle 2011; Sydel 2011), the '10,000 hour rule' is not fixed. Ericsson (2006b), for instance, has noted that the length of experience or practice needed for specific domains varies; some memory experts have achieved world-class levels of performance in 2 years; 6 years may be enough for certain, very tall, basketball players to make an impact; whilst elite musicians and authors may need more than 20 years. For vigorous activities, such as certain sports, expert performance is attained 5 to 10 years after the age at which individuals reach physical maturity; experts in sports are usually in their mid to late 20s. For activities which are not vigorous, such as chess or musicianship, expert levels of performance can be attained approximately 10 years after physical maturity (the late 20s and early 30s). Such variation is clearly a product of the balance between the increase in physical strength, the time taken to accumulate expert knowledge and practical know-how on the one hand and the onset of loss of physical strength and cognitive skills on the other, creating a window of peak performance in the human lifespan.

The length of time spent in practice by itself is not enough to ensure the attainment of excellence. Rather, it is the number of hours devoted to deliberate practice that counts. For Ericsson et al. (1993) deliberate practice is a highly structured activity, quite different from play. It is defined by an explicit goal towards improved performance. Thus specific tasks may be undertaken to overcome particular weaknesses. Moreover, whilst experts may perform with cognitive and energetic efficiency, this is not the case for those developing their skills. Practising individuals may spend just a few hours of practice a day according to their diaries, but, perhaps because of the nature of deliberate practice, these hours are physically and cognitively exhausting, with a consequent reduction in time that may be given to other activities (ibid.).

MOTIVATION, TUITION AND SOCIAL ENCOURAGEMENT AND SUPPORT

Howard Gardner (1995) asked why anyone should want to become an expert given the hard work and dedication required. He suggested that it was an affinity with the specific domain (an innate talent?) that facilitates the dedication. Another key factor, however, is the presence of appropriate tuition. For beginners, the very earliest experience of a specific domain may be playful, but very soon thereafter, a tutor or coach will be required if skills are to be developed properly (Bloom 1985). As the level of skill increases, so better tutors are needed, and these individuals are fewer and progressively harder to find. Only in the final stages of development might an individual surpass the need for a tutor and oversee their own development. (Sloboda 1996), in his study of the development of expertise in musicians, found that the motivation required to achieve expert status will often be external at the beginning – the support and encouragement of children by their parents and tutors. Self-motivation and self-direction come later from the drive to excel.

For Hunt (2006) there is an individual reward for motivation as well as certain fields of expertise which are socially encouraged and rewarded. We need to look beyond the individual and consider how societies value expertise: the differential rewards that drive an individual on to exceed the normal and achieve expert status. By way of illustration, he presents a series of examples which show that, within the United States today, certain experts, defined as those in the top salary quartile of a given population of domain specific practitioners, may be financially rewarded to three or more times the level of the average individual (ibid.: 34–37). In contemporary society, these experts are to be found within the fields of finance, law, medicine and dentistry, and not in education. Amongst certain hunter-gatherer societies, there are also indications that the practice of hunting provides rewards in terms of prestige and influence that would provide individual motivation and social encouragement to enhance one's expertise in this activity (Hawkes et al. 1993; Hawkes and Bliege-Bird 2002; Hawkes et al. 2010 and discussion below)

The temporal and financial costs of supporting the development of an expert place great burdens on a family, and it is often the case that families can offer such support to just one child (Bloom 1985). Given the time, dedication and support required in addition to any natural talent, it is reasonable to wonder how and why such an expensive pattern of behaviour developed amongst humans.

THE EXTENSION OF HUMAN LIFE HISTORY

Studies of life history have consistently noted a series of distinctive characteristics of human life history when compared with other primates (Charnov and Berrigan 1993; Gurven and Kaplan 2006, 2007; Hawkes et al. 1993, 1997, 1998; Leigh 1996, 2001, 2004; Leigh and Park 1998; Kaplan et al. 2000; Kaplan and Robson 2002; Robson and Kaplan 2003, 2006). They have shown, in simple terms, that human life expectancy and growth is much longer than other primates. Humans regularly live until their late 60s or even 70s, whilst chimpanzees die in the 40s. This is accompanied by a higher survival rate for human children through childhood and a lower rate of adult mortality after reaching maturity. Humans have a longer period of growth reaching their maximum size over a longer time, and physical maturity comes late. Connected to this longer growing period is the fact that dependency on parents and other relatives continues until much later in life, and the age of humans at first reproduction is considerably delayed. Finally, humans develop a significantly larger brain for their body size than do other primates.

A number of factors have been identified as potential causes for this distinctive pattern with a range of theories proposed to explain the human pattern (Leigh 2002). These include a proportionate scaling of the primate period of growth to match the scale of increase in human body size (the allometric model); an evolved balance between primate productivity, body size and the costs of investment in growing a large body (the adult mortality model); an evolved balance between rate of growth, predation risk and intra-group competition (the metabolic risk aversion model); slow physical growth to allow the growth of the expensive tissue of the large brain necessary for behavioural flexibility or the learning of a complex and copious body of information necessary for a productive adult life (the brain growth model); and an evolved balance between slow growth and learning, higher adult rates of productivity and trans-generational investment from parents and grandparents to children and grandchildren (the future investment model). The scale of the changes in human growth and life history, the range of factors which might play a part in the evolutionary process and the lack of certain data have made it difficult to discriminate clearly between any one of these models although detailed inter-specific study indicates that the scaling approach does not predict the period of the major growth spurts and their velocity which reveal a slow rate of physical growth in humans along with a later fast and quick spurt of sub-adult growth prior to physical maturity (ibid.).

On the basis of current evidence, Leigh (2002) has argued that the future investment model best accommodates the range of changes observed in human growth and life history. Two variants of the future investment model have been much debated in the hunter-gatherer and hominin evolutionary literature: the so-called 'grandmother hypothesis' on the one hand, and the so-called 'embodied capital hypothesis' on the other. This debate is important to the later arguments of this paper. The grandmother hypothesis argues that selection for increased longevity for females resulted from the increase in inclusive fitness brought about by the provisioning in both food and skills of grandchildren by post-menopausal females ('grandmothers') whose physical presence in the home provided the necessary childcare to allow prime-age adult females ('mothers') to be engaged in productive subsistence activities at some distance away that further supported the survival of their offspring (Hawkes et al. 1997, 1998). The embodied capital hypothesis (Kaplan et al. 2000; Robson and Kaplan 2003, 2006; Gurven and Kaplan 2006, 2007), however, argues that it was a particular expansion of the ecological niche of humans and their ancestors to become hunters of large mammals that drove life-history changes. Hunting large animals requires both high strength and high skill (defined as both cognitive knowledge and practical skills) and also requires a large body and a long period of time during which to learn the skills used (Figure 6.3). Hunting large mammals, therefore, selected both for the large human brain, as well as our long period of growth and extended dependency on parents and grandparents in which to learn the skills. Selection for a longer adult life then allowed the use of these hard won skills for a longer period of time to compensate (and more) for the time required to become proficient hunters. The long-term evolutionary reward was that success in this particular hunting niche allowed male hunters to become significantly more productive than other primates and enabled them to provision their female partners and offspring in a settled place increasing their chances of survival and successful reproduction, and thus the inclusive fitness of males.

A significant difference between these two models is that the grandmother hypothesis emphasises the contributions made by women, and the scale of these is determined by the freedom of time for subsistence offered by grand-mothers rather than the acquisition of knowledge and skill. The embodied capital hypothesis emphasises the contribution made by males, and proposes that the scale of this contribution is determined more by the acquisition of knowledge and skill in childhood rather than by the simple achievement of physical size. Both models recognise that there is a significant body of knowledge to be learned about the food resources exploited by males and

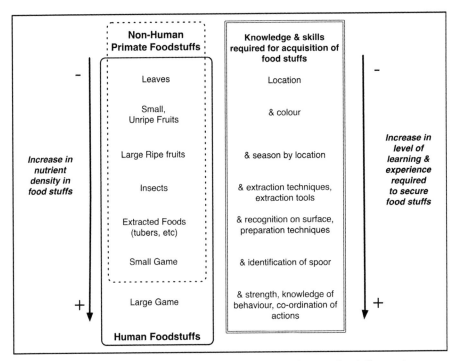

Figure 6.3: The unique subsistence niche of humans and exemplar skills requirements for the acquisition of different food stuffs (modified after Kaplan et al. 2000: figure 1).

females in hunter-gatherer societies, including the respective qualities of plant and animal foods, their seasonality, location, means of extraction and preparation. Some of this knowledge and physical skill can be directly compared to that required by primates; but proponents of the 'embodied capital model' argue that the skill demands of hunting large animals are unique to humans and are of a different order of magnitude (Figure 6.3). These skills include tracking; the identification of spoor; the estimation of the time, distance and direction of animal movements since the spoor was made; the estimation of the movements of wounded animals and possible competition from carnivores and scavengers; and so on (Liebenberg 1990). Such skills take much longer to acquire.

There is ethnographic evidence to support elements of both future investment models. Data on the life expectancy of a number of hunter-gatherer societies (including the Ache, !Kung, Hadza and Hiwi) indicate that the modal age of death is 68 (Kaplan et al. 2000), revealing the extended length of time during which both females and males might offer provision across the generations (Kaplan and Robson 2006). Data on the productive subsistence contributions made by adults shows that both males and females become net producers upon reaching adulthood and that they continue to be net producers until their late 50s (Robson and Kaplan 2003). Males reach their period of peak productivity some time after reaching physical maturity, although studies also indicate that there is significant variability in hunting success between individuals (ibid.).

THE ORIGINS OF EXCELLENCE AND CRAFT SPECIALISATION

It should be clear that there are a number of common threads in the three fields of research summarised above. Research into human life history has shown that, at one end of our lives, humans have evolved to live much longer than their reproductive years. So, whilst hunter-gatherers might only become net producers after reaching adult size, they can go on to make a significant net contribution for a long time thereafter. At the other end, humans have evolved to delay the onset of their first reproduction, remaining dependent on parental and grandparental support for a considerable number of years. The trans-generational support provided by parents and grandparents through the years of a dependent childhood, whatever its cause, facilitates development in the young of significant physical and cognitive skills that must be built up over time. This ties in neatly with studies of expert performance that stress the necessity for considerable cross-generational support, expert tuition and deliberate practice in order to become an expert, whether there is any such thing as innate talent or not. Practice takes time; individuals rarely become experts before they have reached physical maturity and often later. Indeed, we might even describe the embodied capital variant of the future investment model as an origins model for the development of (the original) expert performance – those of the large animal hunter. Finally, contemporary approaches to lithic technology have shown that stone tool knappers have, over time, acquired explicit stocks of knowledge (the proper sequences of flake removal for particular reduction processes, the qualities of raw material types and their locations, etc.), and gained extensive practical know-how as well as the physical techniques and appropriate muscles to be effective in application. The skills of the knapper are embodied over time. Using the language of Kaplan and others, one could describe the development of knapping skills as a form of embodied capital. Can Palaeolithic knapping skills, however, be examined as evidence of expert performance in the sense described in the research literature on expertise?

It is an unstated assumption within Palaeolithic archaeology that the knowledge and technological competence we observe in the archaeological record could be learned by all alive at the time. Whilst there are discussions about potentially effective divisions of labour on gender or age grounds, there are no claims made that certain individuals could not learn how to knap, hunt, sew and so on. Knowledge and skills were learned day-to-day, and element-by-element alongside the performance of daily life; such learning was driven by the need to practise. We also usually assume that Palaeolithic individuals were both multi-skilled and effectively skilled across a broad range of activities in which they would be engaged during their normal lives. This assumption also implies that Palaeolithic people were sufficiently skilled (or could each become sufficiently skilled) to produce the evidence that has been recovered (though see Soffer et al. 2000a; Soffer, Adovasio, Illingworth et al. 2000 in relation to textile skills).

The research literature on expertise does not challenge assumptions about the initial capabilities of individuals. It does, however, provide us with a mechanism for exploring whether sufficiency of skill and universality of learning occurred. The characteristics of expertise should indicate likely signatures of expert performance in the archaeological record (Table 6.2). Expert performance, as defined above, is relative, not unique; experts are at the far end of a continuum of human performance. Experts achieve excellence through long periods of deliberate practice – sometimes specifically directed to the mastery of particular elements of skill, with high levels of social support, including the availability of expert tuition. Expertise is valuable in a context in which the achievement of a particular skill is recognised and valued beyond experts or their immediate family.

EVIDENCE FOR RELATIVE EXCELLENCE

There are a number of classic, usually bifacial, examples of lithic technology that are accepted as exemplary of extreme skill in the Palaeolithic. These include the Solutrean laurel leaf points of south-western Europe, certain Palaeoindian bifacial points of North America, some microblade reduction strategies in Japan, and possibly the prismatic blade reduction evident on Magdalenian age sites in the Paris Basin. They stand out relative to other implements due to the elaboration of the bifacial reduction procedure evident, the thinness and associated fragility of the finished implements, the length of time and the difficulty inherent in their manufacture (as recognised by contemporary stone knappers) and the use of highly exotic materials (Sinclair 2000; Speth et al. 2010). This level of elaboration is not necessary to the utilitarian effectiveness of the implements themselves: it is possible that the elaborate manufacture evident in these implements is a costly means of signalling the value of the activities such as big-game hunting by men in the Palaeoindian case (ibid.) or possibly the importance of sharing large game animals or even the inherent qualities of the makers themselves (Sinclair 2000).

Despite the recognition of these elaborate items, detailed measurement of the range of variation, however, is rare. Bleed (2008) has shown, for example, that there are differences in the rate of error (an indicator of skill) evident in refitted microblade reduction episodes between the two sites of Araya and Kakuniyama in eastern Japan. In his original study of the Solutrean, Smith (1966, 1973), identified a number of different geographical variants of laurel leaf point shape, with differences visible in the elaboration of these pieces.

TABLE 6.2: *Possible archaeological signatures for the existence of expert performance in the Palaeolithic.*

Characteristics of Expert Performance	Possible Archaeological Signatures for Expert Performance in the Palaeolithic	Archaeological Examples cited in text
• Variation in levels of performance. • Evidence of expert performance	• Variation in observable levels of quality of practical performance (skill) including; • *frequency and form of errors* • *variability in the standardisation of shape and size* • Highly elaborated examples showing; • *evidence for considerable time in manufacture* • *evidence for considerable difficulty in manufacture*	Error Frequency *Japanese microblade reduction (Bleed 2008)* Variation in standardisation of form *Solutrean shouldered points (Geneste and Plisson 1990)* Highly elaborated examples showing time and difficulty in manufacture *Solutrean bifaces (Sinclair 1995, 2000)* *Scandinavian bifaces (Apel 2001, 2008)*
• Deliberate Practice	• Geographically separate areas for practice • Production not for use • Production beyond observable use • Repetition of particular stages of working	Areas for Practice of Manufacturing Skills *Magdalenian blades at Les Maîtreux (Aubry et al. 2008)* *Ceramic figurine firing at Dolní Věstonice (Bougard 2011, Gamble 1999)* Production not for use or beyond observable use *Magdalenian blades at Les Etiolles (Pigeot 1987, 2004)* Repetition of particular stages of working *Solutrean biface working at Les Maîtreux (Aubry et al. 2008)*
• Tuition	• Specific places for learning of skills • Proximity of knappers of different skills • Intervention in practice of knapping	Proximity of knappers of different skills *Magdalenian blades at Les Etiolles (Pigeot 1990)* *Solutrean lithic manufacture at Les Maîtreux (Almeida 2005)* Specific places for learning of skills *Les Etiolles (Pigeot 1990, 2004)*
• Social Support (incl. parental support) • Social value given to expertise	• Subsistence surplus • Specific places for learning of skills • Locations for social display of special knapping skills • Elaborated burials of experts	Locations for social display of special knapping skills *Magdalenian blades at Les Etiolles (Pigeot 1990)* *Scandinavian biface working (Apel 2008)*

So the laurel leaf points found at Volgu and in the surrounding area (Smith's type J) are significantly more elaborated than other variants, whilst experimental replication studies to replicate these points indicate that only a few modern knappers can achieve these forms (Aubry et al. 2008). Geneste and Plisson (1990) have detailed a range of elaboration in retouch for Solutrean shouldered points.

EVIDENCE FOR DELIBERATE PRACTICE AND TUITION

Evidence of the making of stone tools is commonly found as part of the normal residue on Palaeolithic sites, and sometimes we can identify places on sites that were distinct knapping areas. It is usually assumed that these areas are for the production of items destined for use. To confirm the existence of deliberate practice, we probably need to identify either an over-abundance in manufacture leaving 'finished' pieces unused, or the repeated performance of particular elements of the reduction process. The extensively refitted prismatic blade cores at Les Etiolles (Pigeot 1987a, 1987b, 1990) might be evidence of production beyond need, whilst the repeated performance of the middle stages of Solutrean laurel leaf manufacture at Les Maitreux might represent evidence for the practice of this stage of manufacture. At the site of Dolní Věstonice in Central Europe a large number of fragmented figurines made from local loess have been found. It has been suggested that this represents a form of pyrotechnic display in which there was deliberate intention to 'explode' figurines in a kiln (Gamble 1999). This same evidence, however, might also be interpreted as the waste from deliberate practice in the firing of ceramics, especially when considered in the context of the apparent standardisation of the figurines in form and dimension (Bougard 2011).

Perhaps the best-known evidence for tuition comes from the Magdalenian site of Les Etiolles in the Paris Basin. Here Pigeot has identified a single structure in which three distinctly different levels of skilled knappers can be identified, radiating concentrically out from a central hearth: highly skilled, less skilled and beginner level (Pigeot 1987a, 1987b, 1990). It is hard to imagine that there was not a transfer of information between the knappers of different levels of expertise in this context or that this concentric separation of skill is random.

EVIDENCE FOR THE DISPLAY OF EXPERTISE

Whilst we often see geographical separation of aspects of stone tool working in the Palaeolithic, we usually attribute this separation to utilitarian effectiveness: the embedding of procurement and testing or raw materials in other hunter-gatherer movements around the landscape, or the management of raw material procurement and transport costs (see Speth et al. 2011 for an extended

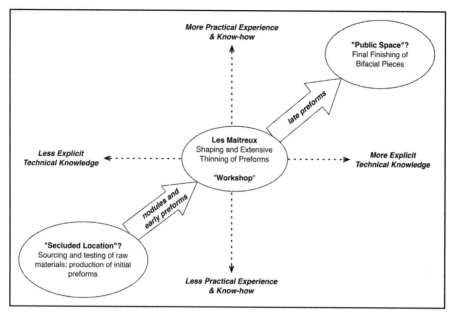

Figure 6.4: A possible model for the geographical separation of Solutrean biface reduction during the last glacial maximum according to the level of achievement in conscious technical knowledge and practical experience and know-how (modified after Apel 2008: figure 6 and Aubry et al. 2008: figure 2).

discussion of this in the Palaeoindian context). Some patterns, however, do not make easy sense in economic terms. At the Solutrean site of Les Maitreux Aubry and others have revealed a consistent pattern (Figure 6.4) in which basic rough outs are brought into the site and an extensive thinning process is performed on the site, but the final elaborate and visible surface retouching of the pieces is undertaken elsewhere (Aubry et al. 2008: figure 2). Economics might explain the first movement of action, but it is hard to think of a utilitarian reason for such consistent physical separation of thinning and surface finishing. Perhaps instead, the geographical isolation of the final surface finishing of the piece allows the expertise of the toolmaker to be highlighted and made public, in a similar way to the actions of bifacial dagger makers in the Scandinavian Neolithic (Apel 2001, 2008).

The examples noted above show that there is evidence, albeit fragmentary, for some of the characteristics of expert performance evident in the archaeology of the Upper Palaeolithic.

EXPERT PERFORMANCE THROUGH THE PALAEOLITHIC?

Both variants of the future investment models indicate that human life history, with its pattern of long-term trans-generational exchange, has developed in such a way as to allow children to delay their take-up of the full workload of adults. Certainly with the appearance of modern humans, therefore, we might infer that our children possessed the opportunity to develop their expertise in a supportive environment. It may be worth considering, however, whether the fragmentary nature of the Palaeolithic evidence cited above results from a lack of methodology and comparative data to aid the identification of expertise alone, or possibly a real reflection of fragmented opportunities to develop expertise in and beyond essential subsistence skills in the Palaeolithic. To answer this question we shall need to develop our methods of analysis and identify new sources of data on hunter-gatherer skills and the time pressures on lives in the context of the abruptly changing climatic conditions of the Palaeolithic.

At a methodological level, to prove the existence of experts, we need to be able to measure the range and frequency of expressed performance in skills on the one hand, and know how long it takes to achieve these skills on the other. For the former, we need techniques through which to evaluate the skill in individual pieces. An analysis of standardisation in the desired product (Torrence 1986) or of the error rates of certain types of reduction process (Bleed 2008) are possible approaches. Another approach would be to measure the investment of time in the production of individual pieces within assemblages. In this context it may not be insignificant that the examples of high skill in lithic implements which we currently recognise are often bifacial implements. Demonstrable excellence is an essential criterion in the everyday evaluation of expert quality (Sartwell 2003). In a world in which many, if not most, individuals could knap, bifacial technologies provide an opportunity in which an individual can demonstrate visibly a level of performance beyond the normal though size, symmetry and the thinness of reduction. There is a progressive difficulty in the task of bifacial thinning to the extent visible in the Solutrean (or later Scandinavian Neolithic). For the latter we need to acquire domain-specific data to compare with the studies of expert performance in other domains. A form of data that could be made available quite quickly is the biographic data generated by the structured interviews of current experts within a domain, similar to that acquired by expert studies (Simonton 1996; Sloboda 1996). These interviews would record such features as the ages at which individuals started, the length of practice time given to an activity, the nature of practice activities undertaken, the use of teachers, and when individuals think they reached expert levels of performance. We also need long-term experimental studies of lithic technology so that we can observe individual progress across a long period of time. In this way we might be able to go beyond the limits of short-term experiments into the problems faced by novices (Shelley 1990; Ferguson 2008; Geribas et al. 2010), or the ethnographic present of an observed community of makers (Stout 2002), to explore the nature of progress in technological skills in detail. These studies must necessarily run over years, not weeks; they will almost certainly require a concerted effort from the whole academic community to support them.

A recent debate about the nature and value of hunting skills in contemporary hunter-gatherer societies illustrates some of the missing ethnographic data that we need in order to understand the pressures of developing expertise. Hunter-gatherer anthropologists, as discussed above, have argued whether hunting is a necessary and difficult skill for hunter-gatherers, requiring considerable time to develop and leaving little time for other activities (Kaplan et al. 2000; Kaplan and Robson 2002), or whether it is a particular social strategy – a form of costly social signalling practised by a small number of men to communicate their 'better fitness' to mates, potential mates and other members of society (Hawkes et al. 1993; Hawkes and Bliege-Bird 2002; Hawkes et al. 2010). Blurton-Jones and Farlowe (2002) in an experimental examination of clearly defined subsistence-related tasks (shooting a target, digging for tubers, and preparing pegs and climbing trees (to collect honey)) performed by the Hadza show that there is no significant difference between individuals who have grown up and acquired these skills within the context of a practising hunter-gatherer society and individuals who spent time away at school and would therefore not have been engaged in these activities on a daily basis. They argue, therefore that subsistence skills are not difficult to learn. By way of contrast, Gurven et al. (2006) have shown that amongst the Tsimane Amerindians of the Bolivian Amazon, the effectiveness of individuals in a range of hunting related tasks (shooting targets, identifying prints, etc.) does not correlate with their physical growth. Lifetime data shows that peak productivity is achieved in the late 20s, almost 10 years after reaching physical maturity, and this rate of productivity is maintained for some time after physical strength declines. This is what should be expected if hunting skills were difficult and needed to be acquired over the longterm. The future contribution of hunting to the inclusive fitness of individuals is so great that the investment in these skills during youth is worth it.

The clear disagreement between these two studies stems from the fact that each uses data that is irreconcilable with the other. Blurton-Jones and Farlowe (2002) rely on data derived from singular performances of artificial and circumscribed activities. It is not obvious, for example, that successful performance in shooting a target with an arrow is comparable to that of hunting an animal. Gurven et al. (2006) use lifetime productivity data to infer task difficulty and the long-term development of expertise. We need data that examines the difficulties of tasks in authentic situations that follow individuals through a long time (perhaps a full life-time?).

This evidence also needs to accommodate the variable nature of hunting and gathering as activities within different environmental contexts. Since Binford (1980), we recognise that forms of hunting and gathering change according to latitude: plant foods are less abundant and large animals are more mobile in higher latitudes. Studies of lithic technology already stress the time pressure of high latitude hunting (Torrence 1983 and studies in

Torrence 1989). In the archaeological record of the Upper Palaeolithic we also recognise the existence of the targeting of migrating herds of animals such as reindeer as well as the use of forms of storage (Soffer 1989) of over-production for later consumption. These variations will bring different demands on knowledge, know-how and embodied skill. They may also provide different opportunities, or the lack of, for individuals to develop expertise in skills that we might observe in, for example, the manufacture of material items, and different possibilities for trans-generational support to facilitate individuals developing expertise in skills without an immediate calorific return.

For our purposes the various future investment models of human life history are not mutually exclusive; both allow for the development of skills by the young. Immediate time availability, lifetime performance and social value are distinguishing features of the debate between these models, drawing our attention to the conditions that affect the attainment of expertise. Whilst both of these future investment models presume that there is a useful return for the investment in subsistence skills (enhancement of individual productivity or the enhancement of social status), this was not necessarily the same for other skills during the Palaeolithic, especially in the context of competition for practice time between different skills. Put in the context of lithic technology, if there was little functional difference between the products of competent and expert knapping, the achievement of expertise as a stone toolmaker is likely to have been the outcome of a significant investment in practice beyond the level of an ordinarily competent knapper in which the majority of the time taken to achieve expert status involved an individual's self-investment in the context of a highly marginal rate of return (Figure 6.5) compared with individuals investing across a range of skills. In the constantly changing environments of the Upper Palaeolithic, it may have been a considerable individual, familial and societal risk to support the investment of such extra time in practice. This emphasises the social support that lies behind the attainment of expertise, as well as the necessity of some form of recognised value for these skills. It is possible, therefore, that whilst the attainment of expertise looks possible within the context of the life histories of modern hunter-gatherers, the same favourable conditions might not always have existed during the Palaeolithic.

A final necessary element of both future investment models is that adults beyond their normal reproductive years remain contributory members of society. This extends the 'payment period' on the investment made in skills in the young. Reliable data on human life expectancy is essential for an examination of this. The data currently published on the age at death of Neanderthal populations and the first anatomical moderns in the earlier part of the Upper Palaeolithic suggests that human life expectancy may have been too short for the existence of grandparents able to help support and provision the young, or perhaps to educate them in expert skills (Trinkaus 1995, 2010).

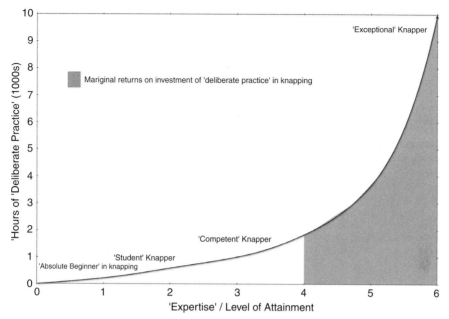

Figure 6.5: Marginal returns on investment in practice time for stone toolmakers (if competency in knapping can be achieved in a small number of years of practice, then excess practice beyond this moment represents a major investment against a potentially marginal return).

If this is true, then the challenges and risks of investment in craft expertise which we see clearly in the archaeological record must have been greater still.

FINAL COMMENTS

When Clive Gamble (1985) asked us to look for the origins of state societies in the hunter-gatherers of the Palaeolithic, he might not have had the origins of the development of expertise and craft specialism in mind. I have argued above, however, that there is every reason to look for our first experts within Palaeolithic societies, since the evolution of a particular form of life history in humans has created the broader context in which expertise can develop, at least on certain occasions. Moreover, there is also real archaeological evidence that can be interpreted coherently in terms of deliberate practice, tuition and expert performance. What is important about this search, however, is not the simple identification of experts or craft specialists per se, but rather the window which this search opens on questions about the complexities of social life and lifetime relationships in Palaeolithic society which have not been addressed in recent technological studies. In order to explain the attainment of these first examples of expertise, we must ask how the various forms of support (subsistence, time for practice, access to appropriate tuition) which expertise requires were made possible within a hunting and gathering context where populations change through processes of fission and fusion. Understanding these challenges is potentially revelatory in terms of our understanding of the social lives and lifetime strategies of Palaeolithic hominins.

We might end with the thought that hominins, through the use of material culture to signify forms of social identity (e.g., Vanhaeren and d'Errico 2006; Kuhn and Stiner 2007), were not just released from the proximity and pressures of local social relations (Gamble 1998a); this same material culture may have provided the focus for a complex elaboration of human social life centred on lifelong learning and the development of expertise.

CHAPTER 7

TO SEE A WORLD IN A HAFTED TOOL:
BIRCH PITCH COMPOSITE TECHNOLOGY,
COGNITION AND MEMORY IN NEANDERTHALS

R. M. WRAGG SYKES

INTRODUCTION

There has always been interest in the significance of certain prehistoric technologies as 'stageposts' in the evolution of human cognition (McBrearty and Brooks 2000; Ambrose 2001; Wadley 2001; d'Errico 2003; Wynn and Coolidge 2004; d'Errico et al. 2005; Zilhão 2007; Read and van der Leeuw 2008; Roebroeks and Villa 2011a; Brown et al. 2012; McBrearty 2012). Artefacts are central to this, as they are the surviving material expression of mental processes, and whilst not offering a PET scan of hominins' brains, they do permit informed inferences to be drawn about cognitive capacities in the deep past. Composite technology is one element lately receiving attention in terms of its implications for cognition (Rots and Van Peer 2006; Wadley et al. 2009; Wynn 2009; Wadley 2010; Lombard and Haidle 2012). Yet although featuring in syntheses of the archaeological record (e.g., d'Errico 2003: 193; Zilhão 2006: 191; Roebroeks and Villa 2011a and supporting materials) and included in comparison to the technological evolution of anatomically modern humans (Ambrose 2001, 2010; Wadley 2010: 117; Lombard and Haidle 2012: 255–256), Neanderthal composite technology has been not yet been examined as a complex tradition in its own right, despite the fact that it includes both the earliest known multi-component artefacts in the archaeological record, and the first truly synthetic material. The wider implications of this technology are explored here in terms of Neanderthal cognition, memory and perception of spatial and temporal landscapes.

COMPOSITE TECHNOLOGY AND BIRCH BARK PITCH
IN THE PALAEOLITHIC RECORD

Hafting is generally regarded as a significant innovation in technological evolution (Ambrose 2001, 2010; Read and van der Leeuw 2008; Wynn 2009: 9544; Wadley 2010; Lombard and Haidle 2012; McBrearty 2012). Before this, tools were only single units, however elaborate they might be individually (e.g., the late Lower/Early Middle Palaeolithic wooden throwing spears from Schöningen, Germany: Thieme 1997; Haidle 2010). Combining separate parts into one tool fundamentally changed the technological paradigm; this remarkable invention probably originated several times, in different regions, using different materials.

Composite tools are generally comprised of two or more elements: a haft acting as a handle, and an attached operational element, often a lithic artefact, but also bone or ivory. Hafting traditions of the Palaeolithic in general are not explored here, although there is evidence that composite tools were quite widespread (Shea 1988, 2006; Anderson-Gerfaud 1990; Boëda et al. 1996, 1998, 1999; Hardy et al. 2001; Mussi and Villa 2008; Villa et al. 2009, 2010; Rots 2013). The composite technology of the African Middle Stone Age (MSA) in particular has been investigated in detail (Lombard 2005, 2006; Wadley et al. 2009; Wadley 2010); however, the focus of this chapter is specifically the European Middle Palaeolithic hafting technology using birch bark pitch. There appears to be another contemporary hafting tradition utilising bitumen as an adhesive, demonstrated by residues on lithics from different Mousterian facies at the Syrian sites of Umm el Tlel and Hummal (Boëda et al. 1996, 1998). Recently, further residues were found on one artefact from a Mousterian level at Gura Cheii-Râşnov Cave, Romania (Cârciumaru et al. 2012). However bitumen is a naturally occurring substance and requires at most heating for softening, making its use less complex. As there is no evidence linking the two traditions, I will focus on birch pitch hafting in an attempt to refocus attention on the Neanderthals' development of this synthetic material, within their broader composite technology repertoire.

The very earliest composite technology probably comprised wedge hafts, involving only two elements. The famous Schöningen spear locality mentioned earlier (Thieme 1997) is now dated to late Marine Isotope Stage (MIS) 9 (c. 300 ka BP; Lang et al. 2012). Slightly below the spears stratigraphically, other wooden artefacts were found including three fir branches pointed and grooved ends, interpreted as wooden wedge hafts (Thieme 1999, 387). The Schöningen spears themselves clearly never had hafted lithic tips (Thieme 1997, 1999), suggesting that if hafting was practised here, it was primarily associated with processing tools rather than projectile weapons. Other broadly contemporary hafting evidence comes from Rots' (2013) functional analysis of lithics at Biache-St-Vaast, France: almost half the sample had been hafted (mostly wedge-type), and some had evidence for bindings.

The earliest firm European evidence of composite technology using adhesive – and the earliest example of hafting with adhesive in the archaeological record – comes from a fluvial context at Campitello, Bucine, Italy. The Levallois technology found here is a hallmark of the Middle Palaeolithic, and biostratigraphic and palaeomagnetic data indicate a Middle Pleistocene age (MIS 7–6). Three stone artefacts were recovered from sediments in

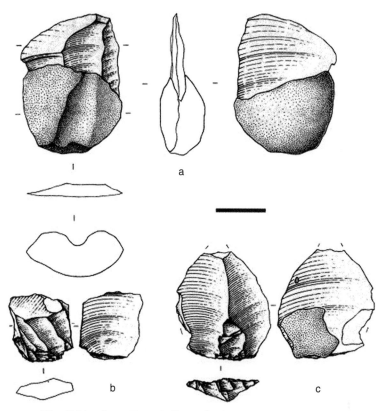

Figure 7.1: The lithics from Campitello, Italy (late MIS 7, early MIS 6 c. 200 Ka), showing one with its lower half encased in a lump of pitch, suggesting that this tool was intended to be used without an attached handle. Reprinted from Mazza et al. 2006 figure 2, with permission from Elsevier.

association with an *Elephas antiquus* individual (Mazza et al. 2006); two had adhering organic lumps chemically identified as birch bark pitch (Modugno et al. 2006). One bears partial pitch remnants, while the lower half of the other is encased by a large lump (Figure 7.1). There was no evidence for a handle (e.g., wooden remains or impressions), suggesting the tools were intended to be held directly in the hand.

Further evidence of birch pitch composite technology from the European Middle Palaeolithic comes from Königsaue, Germany. Originally excavated in the 1970s (Mania and Toepfer 1973), only in 2001 were two lumps of organic material chemically identified as birch pitch (Grunberg 2002; Koller et al. 2001). The pitch pieces came from two archaeological horizons of a lakeside occupation dating broadly to c. 85–74 ka BP (MIS 5a), much younger than Campitello. Both lumps had been hand-moulded into rounded shapes, with one bearing the imprints of a retouched lithic artefact and a wooden surface – direct hafting evidence – and the partial impression of a Neanderthal thumb (Figure 7.2).

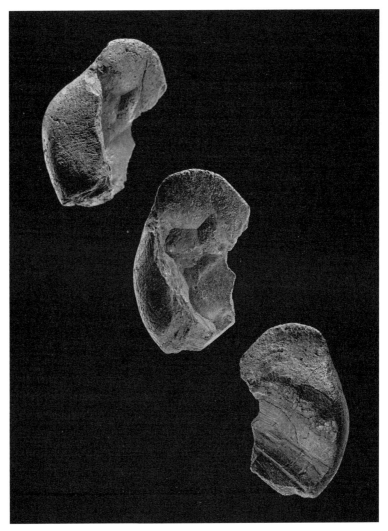

Figure 7.2: Piece of birch pitch from Königsaue, Germany, showing the impression of a retouched lithic artefacts and the print of a human thumb. On the other side is the impression of what was likely a wooden handle. Were the three elements, pitch, stone and wooden haft, all made by the individual who left the thumbprint? Copyright Landesamt für Denkmalpflege und Archaeologie Sachsen-Anhalt, Juraj Lipták

Recently another slightly older German site has yielded further evidence of the birch pitch tradition. Inden-Altdorf (Pawlik and Thissen 2011a, 2011b) is a concentration of c. 600 lithics from a river terrace sequence dated to c. 122–118 ka BP (MIS 5e). A total of 83 artefacts at this site had residue traces adhering to them, and most samples tested were birch pitch. The residues were in locations suggestive of haft placement, and on other areas of the artefacts, suggesting at least some were smeared accidentally. There is also evidence that pitch was applied in a liquid state to some tools which may have implications for its production method.

Further possible examples of Middle Palaeolithic birch bark pitch may come from Starosele, Crimea, where many artefacts were identified as having usewear and plant residues highly indicative of hafting. One retouched piece also has remnants of an 'amorphous black substance' adhering to it (Hardy et al. 2001: 10974). The precise context of this object is not clear, but the possible chronological range is c. 80–40 ka BP. Additionally, pieces of what were termed 'resin' were found in the Bockstein cave, Germany in the 1950s (Metzel quoted in Conard et al. 2012: 247). It is possible that other large Middle Palaeolithic assemblages may harbour residue traces and directed searches of existing collections could be fruitful.

TECHNOLOGY AND PRODUCTION OF NEANDERTHAL BIRCH BARK PITCH COMPOSITE TOOLS

Several authors have previously explored the technology and manufacture of composite tools. Rots (2003: figure 1) presents a chaîne opératoire for the technical steps needed for one scenario of hafting, while Haidle (2010) and Lombard and Haidle (2012) have examined the manufacture of composite objects from a cognitive perspective. Chaînes opératoires are mapped into detailed 'cognigrams' which track the required activity, thought and attention pathways involved in pursuing multiple distinct sub-goals within an overarching project. To understand the Middle Palaeolithic production and use of birch bark pitch, and to enable comparisons with other forms of composite technology (for example in the MSA), it is necessary to consider the manufacturing process in similar detail, based on evidence from the archaeological record. However, given the vagaries of preservation, and as for other authors, some common-sense inferences are also necessary.

Originally it was believed that the production of pitch from birch bark required dry distillation (intensive heating to produce a gas which is condensed into a liquid), leading to speculation as to how Neanderthals could have achieved this without technology to produce the necessary anoxic conditions (e.g., ceramic retorts, or sealed containers) (Koller et al. 2001; Grunberg 2002; Regert et al. 2003). However, recent experimental research has shown that birch pitch can be produced in simple covered pits (Pawlik 2004) or underneath stones inside a fire (Palmer 2007). It may even be possible through holding bark tightly wrapped around a stick inside the heart of a fire (Knul pers. comm. 2011), although others dispute the effectiveness of this method (Pawlik, pers. comm. 2011). In any case, the manufacture of pitch still requires pyrotechnic management to keep the fire between 340 and 400 degrees centigrade for the resins to transform chemically without burning (Koller et al. 2001; Grunberg 2002) and the whole process takes around 2 hours (Palmer 2007).

The characteristics of the pitch from Inden-Altdorf match those produced by experimental methods without fully anoxic conditions resulting in

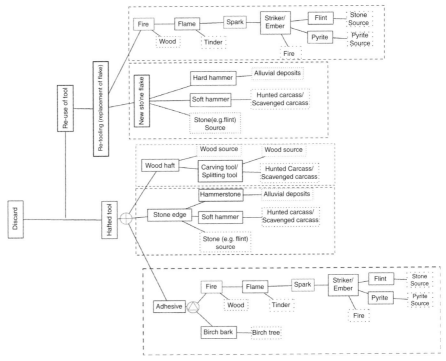

Figure 7.3: One possible chaîne opératoire for the production of a birch pitch hafted tool. The + symbol denotes an additive action, where the three elements are joined together. The triangle within a circle symbol denotes transmutation: the physical and chemical alteration of the bark into pitch. Different source materials and options are included to demonstrate the variability of choice in production, e.g., making fire from scratch using a striking kit, or taking an ember from another fire or a curated piece. A phase of re-heating and re-tooling is included to show the extended use-life potential of composite tools hafted with birch pitch. The chaîne opératoire can be read in conjunction with Table 7.1 where the cognitive stages and actions are outlined.

incomplete transformation and remnant plant materials (Pawlik 2004; Pawlik and Thissen 2011a, 2011b). However, one of the lithics had pitch filling hairline cracks in its surface, suggesting that at least some of the pitch was in a liquid state when applied, implying an extended even if partial transformation (Pawlik and Thissen 2011a: 1705). A pit containing birch pitch (not yet published) is claimed to have been preserved at Inden-Altdorf (Pawlik pers. comm. 2011), and a large sandstone block almost entirely coated in pitch could have been used to collect melted material within such a structure. This technique has successfully replicated experimentally, and certainly some form of container would be necessary if pitch was cooked extensively enough to liquefy. On the other hand it is clear from Campitello and Königsaue that birch pitch was also used in a more solid form, yet with enough plasticity to be moulded around stone tools and to preserve impressions.

Figure 7.3 portrays a chaîne opératoire for Middle Palaeolithic birch bark hafting. I have chosen to focus on the manufacture of a hafted processing tool rather than a projectile weapon because the best evidence from the archaeological record (from Campitello and Königsaue) thus far involves flake tools. Only Inden-Altdorf has some potential evidence for hafted projectiles. Although wood is employed for the handle in Figure 7.3, bone may have been used at Biache-St-Vaast (Rots 2013: 501), where there were also traces of binding materials – however, neither is included here because there is no clear link to birch pitch locales.

To promote standardisation and comparisons of composite technology, I have followed the approach of Haidle (2010; Haidle and Lombard 2012) in this chaîne opératoire; although an accompanying figurative cognigram is not included, a descriptive version is provided. The basic need motivating hafted tool production is identified here as a desire for protection for the hand and greater control during intense processing tasks, and/or more control over the angle of the operational edge of the tool (Wadley 2010). The chaîne opératoire traces the separate sub-tasks and phases of technological production of stone, wood and adhesive (pitch) to meet this overarching goal. Several assumptions have been made, and this is not presented as a definitive sequence of production. In particular, the following points should be noted:

a) not all material resources may have been available at the same spatial location, implying transportation;

b) some material resources or tools may already have been available. For example, appropriate stone tools for collecting the birch bark may have been to hand as part of a mobile toolkit or from previous stages of production, or the fire may already have been burning. Some of these possibilities for extending the chaîne opératoire are included;

c) the chaîne opératoire is represented here as a continuous process. However, different stages of production may have occurred embedded within other tasks, though still as part of a maintained overarching goal. For example, bark may have been collected when encountered during other activities. Additionally, more urgent tasks may have interrupted the process;

d) Multiple individuals may have been involved at different stages of production.

With these caveats, the chaîne opératoire in Figure 7.3 is formally described in Table 7.1 following Lombard and Haidle (2012).

The pitch thus produced could have been used immediately (if the stone tool and wooden handle were present), or the pitch could be collected and retained for future use after re-heating. One of the pieces from Königsaue must have been rolled up when in a soft state, and potentially was intended for later use. Further cycles of repair and re-tooling (replacement of the lithic element) are also possible with reheating and re-shaping of the pitch (Rots 2003). The actual time depth of the whole process is thus uncertain

TABLE 7.1: *Provides a formal description of the process of birch hafting outlined in the chaîne opératoire in Figure 17.3, following the approach of Lombard and Haidle 2012. The initial perceptions of needs are identified which motivate separate phases of activity, each including sets of actions that must be performed hierarchically. However, the initial phases of stone tool production, wood and bark collection may have been accomplished in a different order, or concurrently if multiple individuals were involved.*

Phase		Description
o	Perception of basic need	Carcass requiring intensive processing
oa	Perception of sub-problem	Hafted tool for protection of hand/control over angle of tool use
ob	Perception of partial problem 1	Stone tool needed
oc	Perception of partial problem 2	Wooden handle needed
od	Perception of partial problem 3	Adhesive needed
oe	Perception of partial problem 4	Fire needed
I	Produce stone tool	
	Action 1	Source stone: locate stone source/identify best stone source already known/search among collected stone
	Action 2	Source hammerstone: find alluvial deposits/collect hammerstone already possessed
	Action 3	Source soft hammer: find bone or antler in landscape/find bone or antler from existing material/collect soft hammer already possessed
	Action 4	Knap flake to be hafted, possibly including backing retouch or thinning for better adhesion
		Transport flake to location for hafting
II	Produce wooden handle	
	Action 5	Source wood: find tree suitable for handle/find fallen branch/search already collected wood
	Action 6	Process wood to required form for haft (may involve lesser or greater adjustments e.g. bark removal through to carving, and possibly extended drying phase if fresh wood)
	Action 7	Transport handle to location for hafting
III	Collect birch bark	
	Action 8	Source bark: retrieve previously collected bark/find birch trees
	Action 9	Collect fallen bark of suitable quality/remove bark with tool
	Action 10	Transport bark to location for pitch processing

TABLE 7.1: *(continued)*

Phase		Description
IV	Collect fire kit	
	Action 11	Source tinder, fuel
	Action 12	Source fire-starting tool: striking kit either already available or search for pyrite and flint/collect embers from another fire
	Produce birch pitch	
	Action 13	Build fire/Dig pit (requiring stone or other heavy-duty tool) and build fire
	Action 14	Source tool for placing bark in fire (sticks)/container or flat surface to collect pitch in pit
	Action 15	Place bark in fire/pit
	Action 16	Feed fire until correct heat is reached for bark transformation into pitch
	Action 17	Monitor fire/pitch if visible for length of time required to produce pitch
	Action 18	Retrieve pitch from fire to cool
V	Haft tool	
	Action 19	Bring together wooden handle, stone flake and pitch
	Action 20	Align the stone flake with the wooden handle for correct angle for intended functional application
	Action 21	Manipulate pitch into correct form, e.g., rolling in the hand
	Action 22	Apply pitch around the stone flake and handle or between them
	Action 23	Place hafted tool in safe area for pitch to dry and harden
VI	Satisfaction of need	Hafted tool has been created

and would be substantially altered by the availability of and spatial distance between material sources and the number of individuals involved. What might take a single individual several days working from scratch could be accomplished far more quickly using already available resources or in collaboration.

Perhaps the least realistic aspect of such a chaîne opératoire is its dislocation from the continuous tasks and events of Middle Palaeolithic life; hafting was one strand that had to be woven within the tapestry of other activities going on during daily life. In fact, as birch pitch can be saved for later use once it was produced, it could have been an ad-hoc endeavour, with birch bark collected as it was encountered, cooked later into pitch and only utilised for hafting once needed. Even so, the complete project comprised a complex series of steps involving diverse materials, tools and activities that could be spatially and temporally remote. The requirement for significant planning, time/energy commitments, multi-tasking and potentially active collaboration is clear, whether as a focused and discrete project, or one maintained within a broad mental schema of tasks and actions to be done as and when the opportunities arose.

TECHNOLOGICAL EVOLUTION AND COGNITION: THE COMPOSITE AND SYNTHETIC HORIZONS

The complexity of hafting as a technology comprising multiple streams of action and preparation converging to a focused production event has unsurprisingly led to its use as a marker of significant cognitive capacities (Ambrose 2001; Langley et al. 2008; Wadley et al. 2009; Wynn 2009; Wadley 2010; Lombard and Haidle 2012; McBrearty 2012; Brown et al. 2012), at least in early modern humans. However, although the Middle Palaeolithic production of birch pitch represents the earliest known manufacture of a synthetic material, and the oldest unequivocal example of a composite tool it, has not yet been explored in detail for Neanderthals (Ambrose 2010; Wadley 2010: 114; Lombard and Haidle 2012: 239, 255–256; although see Roebroeks and Villa 2011a: 5211).

Recent discussion of cognitive 'modernity' has focused on assessing technological evolution in the archaeological record for abilities identified in the cognitive sciences, including information processing capacity, attention, forward planning, symbolic/abstract thought and complex language. The role of the executive function of the frontal lobe and the capacity for working memory underlying this have been especially well explored (Wynn and Coolidge 2004, 2010; Coolidge and Wynn 2007, 2005; Read and van der Leeuw 2008; Wadley et al. 2009; Wynn 2009; Ambrose 2010; Haidle 2010; Wadley 2010; Welshon 2010; Lombard and Haidle 2012; McBrearty 2012). Working memory models, first proposed in the 1970s (Baddeley and Hitch 1974) have been enormously influential in cognitive studies. They posit a cognitive structure with different scales of processing and memory linking 'umbrella plans' (overall approaches to projects) and 'constellations of knowledge' (the physical and cognitive schemas for execution of tasks) through a 'central executive' to allow plans of action to be enacted (Wynn and Coolidge 2004). Working memory capacity controls the ability to focus and maintain attention on particular plans of action ('executive attention': Coolidge and Wynn 2005); short-term working memory (STWM) capacity measures the number of concepts/actions that can be synchronously held in mind.

Despite the potential composite technology offers for examining cognitive capacity, when Neanderthals have been explicitly considered within the working memory framework, the focus has been on Levallois (prepared core) lithic technology as the apogee of Middle Palaeolithic technological complexity. Read and van der Leeuw (2008: 1961) proposed seven stages of escalating conceptual complexity in the archaeological record based on the geometric and topological character of artefacts, noting an increase over time in required STWM capacity. Based on the Levallois technique, they limit the Middle Palaeolithic to a STWM of 6 (2008: 1963), and recognise STWM capacity of 7 – modern capacity – in Upper Palaeolithic prismatic blade reduction. Even then, they focus on lineal Levallois techniques and do not consider the recursive nature of recurrent Levallois (Scott 2010). Furthermore, despite initially noting that composite tools appear c. 300 ka BP, Read and van der Leeuw conclude that it is only after 25 ka BP that tools involving the assembly of elements (instead of their reduction) were introduced. They then argue that the first complex techniques involving spatially and temporally separate stages of production, requiring enhanced working memory to track – as well as the concept of reversible actions and therefore ability to link past, present and future – only appears with Neolithic pottery and metallurgy. I would argue instead that such complex technologies with reversible actions are present much earlier in the Middle Palaeolithic production of birch pitch, a plastic substance that can be re-modelled through re-heating, permitting the repair and recycling of hafted tools.

Wynn and Coolidge's influential work on working memory models and Neanderthal cognition (2004) has also focused primarily on Levallois, which they describe as a sequentially organised technology reflecting long-term working memory capacity equivalent to modern humans, based around the recall of 'expert memories' recreated through repetition to form 'constellations of knowledge' (Wynn 1993). But they see Neanderthals as limited to a 'very local and usually immediate' existence (cf. Gamble 1999: 242) because of a claimed lack of enhanced working memory (EWM) capacity necessary for long-range planning (Wynn and Coolidge 2004: 476). While they do discuss hafted artefacts as reliable tools requiring front-loading of time and energy for a future purpose and extended use-life (Bleed 1986), and thus evidence of temporally remote action and EWM, they only recognise this in Upper Palaeolithic hafted bone/antler points. Elsewhere they suggest that alloying metals and kiln-fired ceramics reflect the 'ability to bring together disparate materials from distantly separated sources' (Coolidge and Wynn 2005: 17), although the same could be said of composite technology.

Composite technology in the Middle Palaeolithic is discussed by Ambrose (2010) in his consideration of 'prospective memory' (ability to remember previously intended actions) and 'constructive memory' (ability to plan and imagine the future) as complementary models to working memory, which he claims is more about attentional capacity for current tasks or actions (see also Baddesley 2007). However, Ambrose only cites the bitumen hafting from Syria and does not mention the European birch pitch tradition.

Wadley (2010) gives a more detailed consideration of Neanderthal birch pitch hafting in relation to MSA composite technology, but while acknowledging the requirement for heat control involved in birch pitch manufacture, she regards MSA hafting as more cognitively complex than in the Middle Palaeolithic, pointing to the level of multi-tasking required in compound adhesive production: 'People were able simultaneously to talk, think, mix glue, maintain fire temperature, and mentally rotate stone tools', and some steps required 'abstraction, recursion and cognitive fluidity' (Wadley 2010: 117). However, I would argue that the only significant difference between MSA compound adhesives and Middle Palaeolithic production of birch pitch is the greater number of steps in the former, particularly grinding ochre. Neanderthal birch pitch hafting was not such an extended project, but it still required multi-tasking of multiple sequences of action, with certain steps requiring careful fire management, watching or checking the birch bark to ascertain its physical transformation into pitch, and the mental rotation of the lithic to ensure the correct edge would be hafted.

Wadley's other argument for greater cognitive complexity in MSA compound adhesive hafting is the artisan's comprehension that combining the material properties of ochre with acacia gum would provide a glue of appropriate consistency and strength (a process referred to as 'composition' by Lombard and Haidle 2012: 247). Yet I would suggest that the 'renovation' (Wadley 2010: 116) of acacia gum – a natural available adhesive – by adding ochre is not more cognitively complex than the Neanderthals' ability to conceptualise the process of physical transmutation of birch bark to pitch. Cooking bark at particular temperatures physically and irreversibly transforms it into a completely dissimilar substance, with markedly different material properties, a matter-state change even greater than that seen in MSA heat-treatment of stone (Brown et al. 2009). In fact, it might be argued that birch pitch hafting adds a further level of recursive complexity because unlike the MSA ochre-gum compound adhesives, birch pitch can be softened through re-heating and re-used, creating repeated iterations of adhesive applications.

Lombard and Haidle (2012) have mapped cognigrams and chaînes opératoires for compound adhesive manufacture within MSA bow and arrow technology (Lombard and Phillipson 2010; Lombard 2011; Brown et al. 2012), and suggest, contra Wadley, that the individual separate elements involved are no more complex cognitively than those in Neanderthal composite technology. They propose that the innovation of a complementary tool system, used symbiotically, is what distinguishes bow-and-arrow and other mechanical projectile technologies from composite technology per se (Lombard and Haidle 2012: 255).

It is clear that despite a great deal of recent discussion, Neanderthal composite technology has been to some extent overlooked in models of cognitive evolution which identify enhanced working memory and cognitive complexity primarily among early modern humans. Even more surprisingly, the manufacture of birch pitch itself has not been explored, despite its obvious potential for cognitive complexity. It can justifiably be described as the first crossing of the 'synthetic horizon' in the archaeological record, a concept generally ascribed to ceramic technology (Rice 1999), and thus deserves to be included more extensively in discussions of cognitive evolution and material culture.

SOCIAL TASKSCAPES OF BIRCH PITCH COMPOSITE TECHNOLOGY

The context of production and use of composite technology by Neanderthals is key to considering its functional, and beyond that, social roles. The Campitello artefacts (Mazza et al. 2006) were associated with the remains of an *Elephas antiquus* young adult. Deposition took place on a sandy gravel bar in a river channel within a large floodplain, surrounded by hilly country. Along with the skeletal remains, bioturbation in sediments indicates the locale was attractive to large fauna, but given the small size of the lithic assemblage (n = 3) Campitello could interpreted as a one-off butchery task-site, or simply a random loss.

Both of the other Middle Palaeolithic birch bark pitch sites, Königsaue and Inden-Altdorf, preserve greater contextual information to situate the manufacture and use of birch pitch hafted tools. At Königsaue (Mania and Toepfer 1973; Koller et al. 2001; Grunberg 2002), the two pitch pieces came from different archaeological horizons, A and B, separated by 20 to 30 cm and found along a c. 200-m stretch of the 12-km-long Achersleben palaeolake about 10 km north-east of the Harz Mountains, which rise to around 1200 m. The sediments containing the archaeology probably represent the Odderade interstadial of MIS 5a. The lakeshore was marshy, and the archaeological remains were in a partially wooded setting 50 m inland, with brush and grassy steppe areas further away. The lower horizon, Königsaue A, had a total of 1542 artefacts, while Königsaue B totalled almost 4200. Both assemblages utilised flint and some quartzite, but the tool forms present varied. A, including bifacial tools, such as keilmesser (bifacially backed knives), was attributed to the Micoquian, and B to the Mousterian (Mania and Toepfer 1973). Interestingly, the B-horizon assemblage included a stone point with ventral retouch on the base, which could be a modification for hafting (Villa et al. 2009: 854).

Despite typological and size differences, the two horizons are broadly technologically comparable, using similar core reduction methods – discoidal and some Levallois – and likely involved broadly similar activities of flake production, wood working and carcass processing (based on the presence of faunal remains). There is no evidence for in situ hafting; while there is a large amount of charcoal in the sediments of the B-horizon, this may have related to various other activities, and the pitch pieces at Königsaue may be waste from exhausted or broken hafted tools. One piece certainly had been part of a tool prior to deposition as shown by the wood and retouched lithic impression; the rolled/folded form of the other could suggest it may have been curated as part of a mobile tool-repair kit. Königsaue can therefore be interpreted as a re-tooling locale, where lumps of pitch manufactured elsewhere were re-heated to soften them and utilised to repair tools.

Inden-Altdorf, dated roughly 40,000 years older than Königsaue, is located some 400 km to the south-west (Pawlik and Thissen 2011a, 2011b). The archaeology is found within a preserved palaeosol on a terrace of the western Inde valley, bordering on the Pleistocene Maas River. The site is surrounded by an extensive floodplain enclosed to the west, south and east by highlands. Inden-Altdorf's suggested MIS 5 age is based primarily on stratigraphic and palaeobotanical evidence: Pinus and Picea were present, and the archaeological layers were positioned just beneath deposits correlated to a very brief cold and arid period c. 118 ka BP, known as the Late Eemian Aridity Pulse (Sirocko et al. 2005). The archaeological deposits were about 5 metres above the Pleistocene course of the Inde River and included activity within an eroded gully where flint cobbles were available. Shallow depressions probably caused by uprooted trees seem to be the focus of activity, with several possible fireplaces and pit features. The c. 600 lithics are typologically Micoquian like those from Königsaue A, and include a variety of retouched pieces, Levallois and blade cores and associated debitage.

Residue analysis identified 80 pieces with blackish staining, with several confirmed as birch pitch by SEM and EDX analysis. A mixture of artefact types had residues, including blades, flakes, retouched pieces and cores, suggesting that while some pieces were intentionally hafted, others may have become stained during pitch production (cf. the bitumen-stained core at Umm El Tlel, Böeda et al. 1998: 190). A program of usewear analysis on 136 lithics (including some unmodified flakes) found wear traces on 120 pieces. By correlating the residues with wear patterning interpreted as resulting from both hafting and use, the most commonly hafted tool type category was deemed to be projectiles. Other usewear results suggested a wide variety of materials were processed, including plants and wood, although these data should be treated with some caution as the site was not in primary context. Inden-Altdorf appears to have been less intensively occupied than Königsaue, and although similar general activities were enacted, there is little evidence of carcass processing. Instead the site could correspond to either pitch manufacturing if the 'pit' is a genuine feature, or perhaps another re-tooling locale.

This examination of the contexts of birch pitch hafted artefacts shows several things. First, all three locales were situated close to water: the river bar of Campitello, the lakeshore of Königsaue and the river bank of Inden-Altdorf. This may be a result of the type of taphonomic context (moist, low energy and aggradational) that is most likely to preserve substantial amounts of pitch, but it probably also reflects favoured locales of activity for Neanderthals due to the abundance of resources available. Second, there is no definite birch pitch 'site signature': activities seem to vary, as might be expected given that these three locales are in effect simply a grab sample of situations where researchers have identified pitch. The social context at Königsaue and Inden-Altdorf seems to be that of multi-activity sites: the relatively diverse lithic assemblages are suggestive of groups of people pursuing a variety of activities within quite spatially delimited locales, bounded by the lakeshore, forest and riverside. In contrast, Campitello could be evidence of a carcass processing locale, but given the limited number of bones and lithics, it is hard to be certain.

The question of cooperation in composite technology has also not been explored in recent discussions of the evolution of this technique and its cognitive implications. Was the individual that left a thumbprint on the pitch at Königsaue also the maker of the stone tool and wooden handle that similarly left impressions? A comparison can be drawn with megafaunal hunting, which is frequently cited as requiring collaboration and cooperation, with different individuals likely undertaking different roles (Roebroeks 2001; Coward and Gamble 2008: 1972; Rendu et al. 2011).

Gibson (1993) emphasised the fact that making a composite spear involves hierarchies of action and requires greater information processing than simpler tasks because a logical sequence must be constructed in advance, and the current and intended spatial relationships between different objects must be held in mind simultaneously (cf. Wadley's (2010) arguments for MSA cognitive complexity). Gibson also argues that the extended inputs involved require either substantial individual internalised knowledge and skills, or a shared knowledge base. Reynolds (1993) similarly makes a strong distinction between the solitary manufacture of tools by non-human primates (even if the contexts of use are relatively sociable) and the fundamentally coordinated, cooperative technological undertakings that are characteristic of humans (Cachel 2012).

Although the manufacture of a birch pitch tool could theoretically have been achieved by a single individual acting alone, various factors suggest this may not have occurred in reality. Studies have shown links between the locations of brain activity while maintaining attention on a primary project goal and concurrently considering secondary tasks, as well as in cooperative activities that involve collaboration with others, referred to as joint intentionality (Coolidge and Wynn 2005: 12; Sebanz and Knoblich 2008). Stout (2011: 1056) has noted that, in apes and modern human children, the ability to accurately imitate actions is constrained by the complexity of a task, particularly its degree of hierarchisation. The many spatially/temporally dislocated and obviously hierarchical steps required to make birch pitch hafted tools may not have been possible to remember and accomplish in a chimpanzee-type model where, in the absence of teaching, technology is effectively serially re-invented each generation (Tennie and Over 2012). Instead, birch pitch production and hafting as a technical project may have required collaborative activity within groups for the successful cultural transmission of such an extended set of skills and knowledge (Fay et al. 2000, 2008, 2010; Sterelny 2011; Ragir and Brooks 2012). The fact that it appears in the archaeological record in widely separated regions of Europe over more than a hundred thousand years could (assuming it was at least a locally surviving tradition in each case) suggest an increase in inter-group interaction and cultural exchange networks in the Middle Palaeolithic; something already suggested for Neanderthals based on greater distances of lithic raw material transfers indicating expansion of their landscape-scale activities (or even exchange), alongside regionally specific lithic traditions and personal ornamentation which could mediate such encounters (Wragg Sykes 2012).

As an extension of collaborative actions, Cachel (2012) notes that the social contexts of sharing and exchange underlie the division of labour in humans. Kuhn and Stiner (2006: 958) have argued against sexual division of labour in the Middle Palaeolithic, claiming that there is a 'low level of technological elaboration...' without 'complex, costly high investment artefacts'. Yet birch pitch composite tools are just such artefacts; their design renders them more specialised, creating the possibility for different individuals to contribute diverse skills to the various stages involved in procuring materials and manu-facturing the tools; furthermore, recent anatomical research is also hinting there may be sex-specific differences in the way Neanderthals performed repetitive tasks using their arms (Shaw et al. 2013). An additional interesting possibility is that, in ethnographic contexts, tool hafts are often passed down generations because of the effort involved in their production, creating a community inheritance of users as well as manufacturers (Rots and Williamson 2004).

MAKING TOOLS, MAKING WORLDS: MEANING, MEMORY AND MATERIALITY

The production of composite tools requires significant front-loading of time and energy (Bar-Yosef and Kuhn 1999); an organic haft can take several times longer to produce than a stone tool (Veil and Plisson 1990, cited in Villa et al. 2009: 851) and manufacturing adhesives such as birch pitch increase this even further. Composite technology must therefore offer significant benefits. Typical explanations for the development of composite tools focus on their mechanical effectiveness, particularly the way a haft allows greater application of force, control and protection of the hand during intense processing activities (Keeley 1984; Rots 2002, cited in Wadley 2010). Organic hafts are also more flexible than stone, absorbing more shock before breaking. As a tool-system, hafted artefacts increase reliability and maintainability (Bleed 1986; Bar-Yosef and Kuhn 1999) because in the event of failure an interchangeable lithic element can be easily repaired, therefore extending their life potential and offsetting the initial time and energy invested in their manufacture (Bousman 1993). Ethnographic survey and artefact design theory indicate that composite technology is especially likely to be part of the technical repertoire for groups for whom resource availability is spatially and/or temporally restricted (Bleed 1986; Bousman 1993; Torrence 1993). Neanderthals lived in high-risk environments: although overall environmental productivity varied, their prey was mobile, sometimes sparsely distributed and only available during limited time windows, making multi-part tools highly adaptive in the Middle Palaeolithic.

I would like to shift the focus away from economic output, and consider instead the how the technological and organisational development of birch pitch composite tools both stemmed from and affected Neanderthal social relations and lived experience (Gamble 1999, 2007; Coward and Gamble 2008). What new 'possibility spaces' (Kelly 2009) did the invention of birch pitch hafting open up? The lack of objects offering obvious routes for social analysis comparable to Upper Palaeolithic art has made consideration of Middle Palaeolithic social life difficult. Despite mounting evidence of potentially socially symbolic activities among Neanderthals such as collecting naturally-pierced shells (unrelated to subsistence) and mixing pigments from varied sources (Zilhão et al. 2010), the majority of their surviving material culture is not made up of obviously decorated or representational artefacts. I argue here that birch pitch composite technology was not simply a new technique for making more efficient tools, but was part of a reflexive and dynamic pattern of developing 'Neanderthalness'.

The suite of behaviours that appear with the Middle Palaeolithic include greater control and manipulation of lithic technology, the emergence of top trophic-level hunting of prime quality prey, and the expansion of scheduled activities across the landscape (Scott 2010). The manufacture of birch pitch composite tools should be added to this list, as objects which by their nature are made of parts from dispersed sources, therefore demonstrating significant evidence of planning and the extension of the taskscape across ever greater spatial and temporal scales. Yet birch pitch composite technology also created entirely new ways of interacting with this world, constructing a unique human cognitive niche (Blitzer and Huebner 2012).

A biographical approach to material culture acknowledges artefacts' capacity to accumulate histories: through their interactions with people and places, objects derive and become invested with significance (Wynn 1993; Gosden and Marshall 1999: 170). Through memory and imagination – closely related mental capacities – artefacts become nodes in a web of connections between places, social contexts and people (Ingold 1993). They are indexical (Rossano

2010a), referring to other things: the spatial and temporal relationships formed by the close attention their makers paid at each stage of manufacture made composite artefacts material indexes of multiple places and times with greater potential to accumulate meanings and associations than single objects such as handaxes, which, although subject to extended phases of use and even repair and recycling, were limited in their ability to embody connections because of their 'individual' biographies.

Fragmentation theory (Chapman 2000; Chapman and Gaydarska 2007) proposes that fragments of objects can serve for the whole, offering a means to 'enchain' relations between people, things and places, and that fragments brought together in accumulations become an aggregate of associations and relationships. Gamble (2007; Gamble and Gaudzinski 2005) has applied fragmentation theory to the Palaeolithic archaeological record, but although he mentions composite technology (Gamble 2007: 177, 188), it is not explored in detail. Yet it is clear that birch pitch tools are the first material hybrids, produced from the intentional accumulation of separate elements into larger wholes, their relations enchained throughout manufacture, use and discard.

Ecological theory has highlighted how changes in environments can act on organisms by inviting new interactions (Gibson 1979; Norman 1988). The same is true of human culture: new technologies and objects offer new ways of interacting with the world (Knoblich and Sebanz 2008; Kelly 2009) and can act as a cognitive scaffold in a cumulative process of skill acquisition (Jeffares 2012). Innovative cultural repertoires can themselves initiate novel cognitive organisation and faculties because actions effect change in the way information is processed (Greenfield 1984; Bavelier et al. 2010; Ragir and Brooks 2012), and because human tool use, even more so than in other primates, acts to alter embodied experience through changing neural bodily schemas (Longo and Serino 2012). The reflexive relationship between humans and material culture means artefacts can be seen as existing in 'the realm where brain, body, and culture conflate, mutually catalyzing and constituting one another', with tools possessing a transformative agency in relation to their creation and use (Malafouris 2012: 230; also 2008, 2010).

The archaeological record can be understood therefore as the testimony of people exploring new ways of being human both through and as a result of objects. Composite tools are by definition the sum of many parts, each element possessing a singular material nature, unique origin and context. As argued above, birch pitch hafted tools could well have been communally constituted artefacts, bringing together the invested information of many individuals, perhaps even inter-generationally via inherited tools (Rots and Williamson 2004). They therefore represent a new convention in organising information and action, encompassing the interaction and interconnectedness of their makers and users through time and space. This new type of object would have both stemmed from and acted to expand Neanderthal concepts of time and space through constructive memory (Ambrose 2010), thereby inflating their imaginary geographies (Coward and Gamble 2008). Making and using composite tools would have created the first maintained form of distributed cognition, a new ability to 'time-travel' both in memory and imagination.

The fundamental significance of hafted tools then is their nature as artefacts of connectedness: they expanded the scope for material biographies through their multi-component, genealogical nature. The dynamic, interdependent bond between people and their material culture meant that this was both a cause and an outcome of the new ways that Neanderthals were organising their relationships with each other. Expansion across ever-wider social landscapes, scheduled collaborative hunts (Rendu et al. 2011), regionally distinctive lithic traditions (Wragg Sykes 2012), mixing pigments (Zilhão et al. 2010) and the collection of ornamental shells and feathers (Zilhão et al. 2010; Peresani et al. 2011; Finlayson et al. 2012) are all further manifestations of the novel ways Neanderthals were expressing their increasingly complicated connections with each other.

New forms of objects are significant, but equally so are new forms of materiality itself. The production of birch bark pitch is the first appearance of a synthetic material in the archaeological record, and it too pushed the edges of human possibilities. Birch pitch represents a ramification of human informational organisation, through the invention of a substance with entirely novel material properties: a step as significant as composite technology, because a fundamental and non-reversible transformation of matter takes place. The significance of the manufacture of birch pitch was not as an accumulation with connotations beyond its components, but as a merging of the familiar into the mysterious: bark and fire became sticky black pitch, matter which could be moulded and re-moulded. Bringing about such a physical change must also have acted to forge new ideas and possibilities in the minds of Neanderthals. There are intriguing associations between the structures of the brain involved in performing hierarchical constructive actions, attention, memory and imagination, suggesting a possible reflexive relationship between the evolution of composite technology and syntactical language (Ambrose 2001, 2010). The physical processes of change and transformation embodied in the creation of birch pitch may have generated novel cognitive concepts of transmutation, metamorphosis and even transmogrification; perhaps also echoed in innovative forms of communication or even in the contemporary emergence of new ways of treating the dead (Defleur 1993; Pettitt 2002, 2011a: 78–138).

The advent of later synthetic technologies of ceramics and metallurgy has been explored in some detail, and although often focusing on origins and first appearances, some researchers have attempted to consider their wider cognitive or symbolic significance, for example the creation of 'artificial stone' in ceramic technology (Rice 1999: 3) and the radical physical transformation of a stone ore to a liquid and once again to a solid which can be moulded and reformed many times in metallurgy (Gosden 2008), a process which some have suggested acquired magical connotations in later pre-history (Budd and Taylor 1995). Yet this is precisely the succession of matter-state changes that occur in pitch manufacture: the materiality of pitch as a substance, created out of sight inside the fire – liquid then soft and warm in the hand, pungent smelling, with the strength to hold things together but the plasticity to be re-formed – was unique, as was the new class of artefacts it initiated. Although Neanderthals would have drawn on existing experience of the ability of fire to harden and change substances, the identification of novel material properties and repeated replication of the process would have created an entirely new skill, and, as with composite technology, a novel reference point for understanding material and cognitive possibilities. If the development of metallurgy created new ways of engaging with the material world (Gosden 2008), I would argue this is pre-saged by many tens of thousands of years in Middle Palaeolithic birch pitch hafting.

CONCLUSIONS

The Middle Palaeolithic invention of hafting using manufactured birch bark pitch represents a major increment in technological evolution. This technique necessitated the planning of actions formed of many steps that are spatially and temporally dissociated from one another. It also included the manufacture of the first synthetic substance, birch pitch, created following an irreversible chemical and physical transmutation producing new material properties. This Neanderthal technological practice should be recognised as equivalent in complexity to early modern human hafting traditions before the bow-and-arrow, involving multiple components and compound adhesive production, and implying similarly advanced cognitive capacities including enhanced working memory and attendant executive processing. The extended spatio-temporal dimensions intersected by the united elements and the production, use and repair of a hafted birch pitch tool illustrates the increasing scale of the Neanderthals' taskscape beyond the local, as seen in other aspects of Middle Palaeolithic behaviour. It was also the foundation for the first extension of the self across space and time, expanding memory and imagination through the relational potential of joined constituent pieces, well before any explicitly symbolic objects appear in the archaeological record.

    The inherently compound character of composite tools, their probable collaborative creation and subsequently extended biographies provided a novel form for the organisation of information – energetic and social – through the accumulation of historicised inputs from diverse sources and individuals. Hafted tools are therefore the material expression of new levels of communality and connectedness both within and between Neanderthal groups. As has been suggested for composite tools and complex language, the transmogrification of matter embodied in birch pitch manufacture could also have worked reflexively in generating concepts of mutability and meta-morphosis that bled into other areas of cognition. Fundamentally, birch pitch hafted tools were intersections where Neanderthals related to and engaged with landscapes and each other on an expanded scale; in a literal sense, perceiving their world within and through a hafted tool.

CHAPTER 8

ECOLOGICAL NICHES, TECHNOLOGICAL DEVELOPMENTS AND PHYSICAL ADAPTATIONS OF EARLY HUMANS IN EUROPE: THE HANDAXE-*HEIDELBERGENSIS* HYPOTHESIS

NICK ASHTON

INTRODUCTION

A major research debate over the past 25 years has been the environmental context of the early human occupation of northern Europe. The groundwork was laid and agendas set by Clive Gamble's seminal work 'The Palaeolithic Settlement of Europe' (1986) which provided a framework for describing the environmental background and understanding the challenges that various climates and habitats presented in six different zones organised east to west and north to south. The work was underwritten by two major premises; first, for the majority of time during the late Middle and Late Pleistocene, environments were characterised by cool, often steppic conditions, rather than the temperate forested peaks of interglacials or the cold troughs of cold, glacial maxima. Second, the distribution, availability and accessibility of usable biomass were higher in such intermediate environments than the two extremes of Pleistocene climate. Therefore humans during these periods were more likely to be better adapted to these intermediate conditions. This led to invigorating debates about human habitats (Gamble 1992a; Roebroeks et al. 1992; Mithen 1993a; Ashton 2002; Ashton and Lewis 2002; Parfitt et al. 2005, 2010; Ashton, Lewis et al. 2008; Ashton and Lewis 2012; Cohen et al. 2012; MacDonald et al. 2012) and was the keystone of projects such as EFCHED (The Environmental Factors in the Chronology of Human Evolution and Dispersal; www.nerc.ac.uk/research/programmes/efched/) and AHOB (the Ancient Human Occupation of Britain Project; Stringer 2005; Ashton et al. 2006, 2011). When Gamble first set the agenda (1986) one of the major difficulties of understanding the environmental context was the resolution of the environmental record and how directly that related to human occupation. The debates therefore led to improved methods of data collection and filtering of evidence that now provide a clearer indication of the range of human habitats.

Just as quality control has improved for the reconstruction of human habitats, a more rigorous approach has also been adopted for resolving questions about the earliest human occupation of Europe (Roebroeks and van Kolfschoten 1995). Distinctions between naturally modified and humanly manufactured tools have been heavily scrutinised, alongside problems over context and dating. At the same time there has been the discovery of a wide range of new sites in both southern and northern Europe with more robust dating (Carbonell et al. 1995, 2008; Dennell and Roebroeks 1996; Parfitt et al. 2005, 2010; Gibert et al. 2006; Arzarello et al. 2007). The result has been the construction of a chronological and archaeological framework that can be used to improve understanding of the early human occupation of Europe and of how favoured habitats may have changed through time.

This paper will review the sites from northern Europe ($> 45°$ N) that date to MIS 13 or earlier, and that, in most cases, contain a range of environmental proxies directly associated with archaeological evidence (Figure 8.1). This record will be compared with the source areas for human populations in southern Europe in an attempt to understand better the environmental conditions and technologies that were required to successfully colonise the North. The new site information from Early and early Middle Pleistocene sites will be compared against Gamble's original model of humans being best adapted to intermediate conditions. Beyond a regional study of the nature of human occupation, northern Europe also provides a unique area to study early human technological adaptation to higher latitudes. The evidence suggests that northwest Europe was the earliest region where humans survived in latitudes greater than 45 degrees north (Parfitt et al. 2005, 2010; Ashton and Lewis 2012) and possibly the first region to have more sustained occupation within these latitudes.

PRE–MIS 13 SITES IN NORTHERN EUROPE

Happisburgh Site 3 (HSB3), United Kingdom

HSB3 lies beneath cliffs formed of glacial sediments (Happisburgh Formation), which are now widely regarded as MIS 12 in age (Parfitt et al. 2010; Ashton, Parfitt et al. 2008; Preece et al. 2009; but see Lee et al. 2004, 2008 for MIS 16 attribution). Artefacts and associated environmental data come from a complex series of channels filled with fluvial gravels interdigitating with laminated silts and sands of estuarine origin, laid down by a large river. The lithology of the gravels suggests that HSB3 lay on a course of the proto-Thames. The dating of the site is based on reversed palaeomagnetism, biostratigraphy and lithostratigraphy, which in combination indicates an Early Pleistocene age between c. 0.78 and 1.0 Ma (Parfitt

Figure 8.1: Map of Europe showing locations mentioned in the text

et al. 2010; Preece and Parfitt 2012). The archaeology consists of over eighty primary context flint flakes, simple flake tools and a core. The sediments contain pollen, plant macrofossils, foraminifera, ostracods, beetles, molluscs and vertebrate remains, which indicate that humans were occupying Happisburgh during a period of cooling climate, within a grassland river valley close to its estuary, surrounded by conifer-dominated forest. Although summer temperature estimates are similar to present (16 to 18°C), winter temperatures appear to have been cooler with estimates of -3 to 0°C, compared with the present day average of 3°C. The combination of vegetation and climate suggest an environment similar to southern Scandinavia today.

Pakefield, United Kingdom

The site is exposed in coastal cliff sections to the south of Lowestoft (Parfitt et al. 2005). A channel that cuts into Early Pleistocene marine sediments is filled with interglacial fluvial, alluvial and estuarine deposits which underlie a sequence of glacial sands and clays. The age of the site is based on the mammalian biostratigraphy, specifically the presence of *Mimomys pusillus*. This species is thought to have become extinct by at least MIS 15. This, together with the normal polarity of the sediments, suggests an attribution to MIS 17 or possibly late MIS 19. The 32 artefacts from the interglacial sediments consist of flakes, flake tools and cores. The archaeology is directly associated with an array of biological evidence (pollen, plant macrofossils, foraminifera, ostracods, insects, molluscs and vertebrates) and climatic data from isotope analysis of soil carbonates. Overall, this evidence suggests that the human activity took place in a large river valley, close to its estuary, within a mosaic of open habitats of grassland, marsh, reedbeds and alder carr, but with deciduous forest on the higher ground. Summer temperatures were decidedly warmer than present and the site has been described as having a Mediterranean type climate with warm, dry summers and mild winters (Parfitt et al. 2005; Roebroeks 2005; Candy et al. 2006; Parfitt 2008).

Pont-de-Lavaud, France

On a high terrace of the River Creuse the site of Pont-de-Lavaud has produced over 8000 modified quartz pebbles, chunks and flakes which are argued to show 'clear evidence of human manufacture', although so far relatively few of the artefacts have been illustrated (Despriée et al. 2010: 347). They were found in coarse quartz gravels at the base of the fluvial sequence of Terrace D, which has been dated by ESR on quartz to ~1.1 Ma. Unfortunately there is no independent evidence of the age of the site. Pollen and phytoliths indicate deciduous forest in a warm, wet climate (Messager et al. 2011).

Lunery-Rosières, France

In the Cher Valley artefacts have been identified from a high terrace that has again been dated by ESR on quartz to 1.1 Ma (Despriée et al. 2010). The terrace deposits form the Rosières Sand Formation, which survives as several remnants along this stretch of the river. From one such remnant, 600 m to the north of the archaeological site, a mammalian faunal assemblage has been recovered and has been described as Early Pleistocene in age (Despriée et al. 2010). The lithic assemblage consists of around one hundred flakes and cores in flint, 'millstone' and silicified oolitic limestone. Unfortunately there is no environmental evidence associated with the assemblage.

La Noira and La Genetière, France

Two sites have been identified on a lower terrace of the Cher Valley, ~30 km apart at La Noira and La Genetière. Both have produced small assemblages, including handaxes made on flint, and in the case of La Noira also on 'millstone' slabs (Despriée et al. 2010). The only dating has again been ESR on quartz, which has provided an average age for the terrace of 690 ± 90 ka (Despriée et al. 2010). As with Lunery-Rosières there is no surviving environmental data.

MIS 13 SITES IN NORTHERN EUROPE

The selection of sites described below is limited to those directly associated with environmental evidence, while a better indication of the range of sites for this period is provided in the discussion. In addition, the sites listed are all of probable MIS 13 age, although in some cases alternative ages have been given.

Happisburgh Site 1 (HSB1), United Kingdom

Organic muds and silty clays, exposed on the foreshore 1 km to the south-east of HSB3, have yielded flint artefacts and bones and lie within a channel beneath Happisburgh Till (Ashton, Parfitt et al. 2008). The site has been attributed to a late Cromerian Complex age (probably MIS 13) based on the presence of *Arvicola cantiana* (Preece et al. 2009; although see Lee et al. 2004 and Field 2012, for possible earlier attributions). The recovery of surface artefacts together with the excavations by the *Ancient Human Ooccupation of Britain* project and the University of Leiden have produced an in situ assemblage of almost three hundred flakes, simple flake tools, cores and a single handaxe, with occasional refitting material. The archaeological evidence also comprises humanly altered bones of rhinoceros, roe deer and bovid, indicative of butchery by humans (Ashton, Parfitt et al. 2008). The combination of pollen, plant macroscopic remains, insects and vertebrates indicate marshlands on the edge of a slow-flowing river with heathland and coniferous forest beyond (Coope 2006; Ashton, Parfitt et al. 2008). From the beetle assemblage, estimates of average summer temperatures of 12 to 15°C and winters of −11 to −3°C suggest a distinctly cooler climate than Britain today.

High Lodge, United Kingdom

The main artefact-bearing sediments at High Lodge consist of clayey-silts laid down as overbank sediments of the Bytham River (Ashton et al. 1992), which were sub-glacially deformed and emplaced above younger glacial till

(Lewis 1992), but below glacio-fluvial sands and gravels. Both the till and glacio-fluvial sediments are attributed to the Anglian glaciation of MIS 12 age, implying that the clayey silts are MIS 13 or older. This date is supported by the recovery of a tooth from the extinct rhinoceros (Stuart 1992) attributed to the *Stephanorhinus hundsheimensis* group (Simon Parfitt pers. comm.; see Gibbard et al. 2008 for a later attribution). Over 1200 fresh flint artefacts were recovered from the clayey silts, consisting of flakes, scrapers, notches and cores, but no evidence of handaxe manufacture. However, handaxes were found in secondary context in the overlying glaciofluvial sands. Pollen and insects from the clayey silts indicate pools and marshland with vegetation dominated by pine, spruce, juniper and heathland plants (Hunt 1992). Average summer temperatures are estimated as between 15 and 16 °C and winters of − 4 to 1 °C (Coope 2006), suggesting a cooler climate than Britain today.

Boxgrove, United Kingdom

The extensive landscape exposed through excavations at Boxgrove consisted of freshwater pools and associated landsurfaces, situated within a semi-enclosed marine embayment beneath a marine-cut Chalk cliff. The artefact-bearing sediments of freshwater and lagoonal silts with overlying soil horizons have been attributed to a cooling climate at the end of MIS 13 (Roberts et al. 1994; Parfitt 1998; Roberts and Parfitt 1999a, 1999b). The rich assemblages consist of handaxes and in situ knapping scatters, with occasional cores and flake tools, directly associated with butchered animal remains. The environmental reconstruction has been based primarily on ostracods, foraminifera, molluscs and vertebrates, which together indicate a mosaic of grassland and freshwater pools, with developing scrub and woodland. The ostracods suggest temperature ranges of 14 to 20°C for July and − 4 to 4°C for January (Holmes et al. 2010). Study of the vertebrates (Parfitt 1999) and herpetofauna (Holman 1999) supports the interpretation of a relatively cool climate. Further groups of refitting artefacts were recovered from overlying slope deposits, where even colder conditions might be indicated perhaps during an interstadial sub-stage (McPhail 1999).

Miesenheim I, Germany

The excavations at Miesenheim revealed a sequence of Rhine alluvial sediments containing a lithic assemblage in association with a rich vertebrate fauna (Turner, E. 2000a). Dating by ^{40}Ar/^{39}Ar of pumice in sediments that overlie the archaeological horizons gave an age of 464 ± 4 ka, suggesting that the site can be attributed to MIS 13. The human activity is represented by a small lithic assemblage consisting of cores and flakes predominantly on quartz, while the skeletal composition of the mammalian fauna suggest the probable exploitation of roe deer, red deer and horse. Although the sparse pollen shows a dominance of birch and pine, this is thought to be due to differential preservation. Together, the molluscs and vertebrates suggest areas of open water with marshlands on the floodplain of a large river with open deciduous woodland nearby during an interglacial climate (Turner 2000b).

DISCUSSION

The sites outlined above display diversity in the human habitat from a 'Mediterranean' type environment at Pakefield, to distinctly cooler climates with coniferous forest at both Happisburgh sites, High Lodge and Boxgrove, while a fully temperate climate with deciduous woodland is suggested at Miesenheim. Although there is climatic variation, most sites were situated in open river valleys, the exception being Boxgrove, which was adjacent to freshwater springs and pools in grasslands on the coastal plain. The record so far suggests that from 800 ka humans were coping occasionally with living in northern latitudes, at times with temperatures cooler than present. The low number of sites and the small size of the assemblages suggest sporadic occupation. It seems that this pattern is not a reflection of poor preservation of primary context sites, as a similar record can be seen in the terraces of large rivers of a similar age, such as the Rhine, Somme, Seine, Thames and Solent (Wymer 1988; Bridgland et al. 2006, Antoine et al. 2010; Ashton and Hosfield 2010). In all these rivers there is a lack of firm evidence for artefacts in terraces older than MIS 13. One river system that might provide an exception is the Bytham. Here the sites of Maidscross Hill, Brandon Fields and Rampart Fields have yielded handaxes in the second terrace (Bridgland et al. 1995; Ashton and Lewis 2005). The first terrace is MIS 13 in age, which suggests that the artefacts in the second terrace are older and possibly date to MIS 15.

In contrast, by 500 ka there is an increase in the number of sites and the size of many of the assemblages, particularly in Britain. To the four sites of HSB1, High Lodge, Boxgrove and Meisenheim can be added sites such as Warren Hill (Bridgland et al. 1995; though see also Gibbard et al. 2009), Waverley Wood (Keen et al. 2006), Highlands Farm (Wymer 1988), Valdoe (Pope et al. 2009) and Kent's Cavern (Cook and Jacobi 1999). In northern France and Germany the record is still poor, although the sites of Karlich G (Bosinski 1995) and probably Abbeville can be added (Antoine et al. 2010). The increase in the number of sites and the large size of the assemblages suggests that humans were successfully adapting in a more sustained way to these environments.

Environments of source areas in southern Europe

In order to understand better the early occupation of northern Europe, the first question that should be asked is: what sort of environments were humans already adapted to in the Early Pleistocene landscapes of southern Europe?

Kahlke et al. (2011) argue that the essential ingredient to human colonisation of southern Europe was the diversity of open and woodland habitats that emerged during the Early Pleistocene caused by the shift to a 41 ka climatic cycle, which broke the permanence of the earlier, widespread forests. In a similar vein Leroy et al. (2011) suggest that as Early Pleistocene humans were adapted to grassland environments, they would have expanded into Europe during the more open landscapes of early interglacial episodes. They further suggest that the expansion would have been into areas with winter temperatures of between 0 and 6°C and with average monthly precipitation of between 30 and 60 mm. Although there is little direct evidence to support this interpretation, the idea that humans inhabited more open landscapes is broadly supported by the archaeological evidence. They also argue for discontinuous occupation during the Early Pleistocene, an idea further discussed by Dennell et al. (2011). This suggestion is extended into the early Middle Pleistocene by MacDonald et al. (2012) and supported by evidence from Atapuerca (Ollé et al. 2013). The implication is that human populations may only have survived during milder interglacial conditions.

Although the overall sequence of environmental change is beginning to be understood for southern Europe and particularly the Iberian peninsula (Agusti et al. 2009; MacDonald et al. 2012), trying to relate archaeological sites to specific environments is more difficult due to problems of correlation and the variations in habitat within a region. Reconstructions so far are largely reliant on the interpretation of the vertebrate assemblages and, on occasion, the floral record. For Dmanisi, Georgia, at c. 1.8 Ma a Mediterranean type climate is suggested, with a combination of open, steppe and forest environments (Gabunia et al. 2000; Messager et al. 2011). Although the site today sits at c. 900 m, it may have been considerably lower in the past due to tectonic uplift (Mitchell and Westaway 1999), suggesting that past winter temperatures would have been warmer. Equally, the expansion of the Caspian Sea at this time, perhaps to within 60 km of the site, may also have ameliorated winter temperatures (Gabunia et al. 2000).

Similar open environments and some forest are also indicated for the Orce sites, Spain, at c. 1.5 Ma (Martinez-Navarro et al. 1997; Oms et al. 2000; Scott et al. 2007), while more open, arid conditions are suggested for Pirro Nord, Italy, at c. 1.6 Ma (Arzarello et al. 2007). The evidence from the Atapuerca sites of Sima del Elefante and Gran Dolina reflects few changes through the Early and Middle Pleistocene sequences from c. 1.2 Ma and indicates a mosaic of coniferous and deciduous woodland with grassland in a slightly moister, warmer climate than present (Rodríguez et al. 2011; Blain et al. 2008, 2009). With the possible exception of Dmanisi, during the Early Pleistocene in southern Europe humans appear to have inhabited open landscapes with some woodland in similar climates to these areas today.

If the past climates of the southern European sites were similar to those of the present day, as suggested above, then modern climatic data can be used to compare with the temperature estimates for sites such as HSB3. It should be noted that if occupation in the southern European sites continued through downturns in climate, then the present-day values reflect the optimal situation for these sites and may at times overestimate past temperature values. This data is compared in Figure 8.2 (a, b) alongside estimates for HSB3. For HSB3 the January and July temperature estimates have been used to find a modern analogue (in this case Stockholm in southern Sweden) and then derive the monthly temperature curve. It is clear that although most of the South European sites may have had slightly warmer winters (Atapuerca, Monte Poggiolo and Lunery-Rosière) than HSB3, humans were still coping with comparatively cold conditions. What the average temperatures do not reveal of course, are the ranges, which in the case of Atapuerca for example frequently encompass temperatures below freezing. Although the caves at Atapuerca would have provided obvious buffering against the cold, all the other locations are open-air. The estimates shown for Dmanisi are similar to those of HSB3. However, these figures are probably under-estimates due to changes in palaeogeography and tectonic uplift in the southern Caucasus (see above). The implication from most of the sites in southern Europe is that unless climates were significantly warmer than present, then humans were already adapted to coping with relatively cold winters during the Early Pleistocene.

Strategies for coping with winter cold

If early humans were coping with winter cold in both northern and southern Europe during the Early Pleistocene, how was this achieved? Theoretically, one strategy could have been seasonal migration (MacDonald et al. 2012). To make any appreciable difference in winter temperatures, this would have required migration to areas on the Mediterranean, south-western French or Iberian Atlantic coasts. In the case of HSB3, this would have meant treks of at least 800 km to the south or for Atapuerca 120 km to the north. Certainly in the case of Happisburgh, the distances would have had significant costs in time and energy and imply detailed knowledge of the areas to be traversed for foraging. However, as a new behaviour that is unknown in other primates, it is really the implications for changes in social organisation, or ways of coping with dependents such as infants that make this strategy implausible. It is also likely that early hominins developed an increased period of infant dependency compared with other primates (Aiello and Key 2002; Burkart et al. 2009) compounding the difficulties of long seasonal migrations while carrying young. Such strategies would also have implications for group cooperation, particularly in acquiring food for extra energy demands.

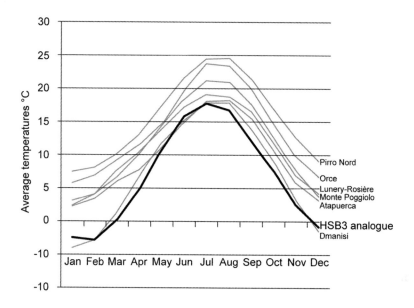

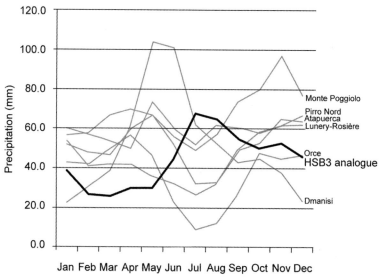

Figure 8.2a and 8.2b: Average monthly temperatures and preciptation for major European Lower Pleistocene site locations using modern data. For Happisburgh Site 3 a modern day analogue (Stockholm) has been selected based on beetle MCR January and July temperature estimates (see text). Data source: WorldClim interpolated climate dataset version 1.3, representing the period 1950–2000 (Hijmans et al. 2005).

An alternative strategy would have been to buffer against the cold by the use of effective clothing and shelter, but for which there is little evidence. The earliest claims for shelters in Europe date to the late Middle Pleistocene, but even here the evidence is disputed. At Terra Amata, France, shelters were claimed on the basis of post-holes (de Lumley 1969). However, the vertical displacement of the sediments indicated by refitting has cast doubt on this interpretation (Villa 1982; Kolen 1999). At Bilzingsleben, Germany, 'paved' areas of cobbles were associated with charcoal scatters, bones and stone tools and interpreted as shelters (Mania 1995), although a recent study has suggested that the associations are a product of taphonomic reworking (Beck et al. 2007). More direct evidence for the use of hides has been suggested from the horse butchery site 13II-4 at Schöningen, where cut-mark patterns and the lack of cordal vertebrae point to their careful removal and use elsewhere, presumably for clothing or shelter (Voormolen 2008a). A key element of hide use would have been hunting or prime-scavenging to ensure that the hides had not been torn apart by other carnivores. The sites of High Lodge at c. 500 ka and Hoxne at c. 360 ka, both of which had relatively cool climates, may provide evidence for hide-use and processing through the unusually high percentage of scrapers (Ashton et al. 1992; Ashton, Lewis et al. 2008). Although there is no direct evidence from these sites of their use in this task, later sites certainly suggest that scrapers were involved in hide-processing (Anderson-Gerfaud, 1990; Kuhn and Stiner, 2006). By contrast, there appears to be a paucity of such tools before 500 ka (e.g., Ollé et al. 2013; Parfitt et al. 2005, 2010).

The controlled use of fire also seems to make a late appearance in Europe, probably during the late Middle Pleistocene (Roebroeks and Villa 2011a). There are several claims for the earlier use of fire outside Europe (e.g., Gowlett et al. 1981; Brain and Sillen 1988), with the most convincing being from Gesher Benot Ya'aqov in Israel at just under 800 ka (Alperson-Afil 2008). The evidence is largely based on the differential spatial patterning between burnt and unburnt microartefacts from several successive horizons, indicating what they describe as 'phantom hearths'. However, from Europe the earliest record is from Beeches Pit at about 400 ka with a succession of clear hearths associated with burnt and unburnt artefacts (Preece et al. 2006). As Roebroeks and Villa (2011a) point out, the absence of hearths at sites such as Boxgrove at 500 ka where evidence should survive, suggests the late introduction of this technology, at least to Europe.

If early humans lacked the technologies to cope with winter cold, then they must have become physically adapted to survive in these environments, as also suggested by Wenban-Smith (2007: 62). Neanderthal adaptations included fore-shortened extremities, lower relative surface areas and may also have involved seasonally elevated basal metabolic rates with increased energy requirements (Steegman et al. 2002; Leonard and Snodgrass 2009). However, even with Neanderthal adaptation to cooler climates it is clear from several studies that their evident cold-adapted physiology would still have required technology to assist in maintaining body warmth without significant body hair (Sorenson and Leonard 2001; Aiello and Wheeler 2003; White 2006a; Chu 2009). The most detailed studies on hominin loss of body hair suggested that this was an early adaptation that developed in response to bipedalism in open equatorial regions (Wheeler 1984, 1991, 1992). The studies argued that bipedalism reduced exposure of the body and heat-loading and lessened the need for hair as protection from solar radiation. The loss of body hair enabled more effective cooling through sweat evaporation and, in temperatures less than 37 °C, conductive heat loss. Replacement of fluids would have been critical to the cooling system, but the modelling suggested that drinking water requirements for hairless bipedals would have been reduced in open savannah environments, with typical maximum daytime temperatures of 29–35°C. Importantly, the adaptation may also have allowed higher activity levels.

Although this research makes a good case for the loss of body hair as a daytime thermoregulatory advantage in open savannahs, it is less clear how early hominins would have coped in maintaining body heat at night (Amaral 1996). Equally, the loss of body hair would probably have been a distinct disadvantage for colonising areas with more seasonal temperature ranges, such as Europe. The question must remain open therefore as to whether the first humans in Europe still retained significant body hair or even redeveloped it to cope with the colder winters. The alternative hypothesis that body hair was lost as a result of the introduction of clothing (Glass 1966) could be developed further to suggest that this occurred much later than previously envisaged, and was an integral part of the more sustained colonisation of northern latitudes, such as Europe after 500 ka.

Only one other primate managed to cope with the climates of northern Europe during the Pleistocene, namely the macaque (*Macaca sylvanus*). Their Middle Pleistocene distribution is remarkably similar to that of humans and they occur at sites such as West Runton, Swanscombe and Hoxne (Delson 1974, 1980). Their environmental tolerances would appear to be similar to those of humans and perhaps study of how body hair affects the thermoregulation of macaques in northern environments today might inform us about how body hair might have enabled early humans to cope with winter cold in Europe.

Strategies for coping with shorter growing seasons

Winter cold was not the only problem to the occupation of Europe. Of perhaps far more significance to northern Europe was the shorter or less productive growing season, compared with southern Europe. Figure 8.2(a,b) can be used to compare the various sites with the number of months with average temperatures below the arbitrary figure of 5°C. This temperature is set as a threshold below which plant growth would have been minimal. Figure 8.2(a,b) indicates that using present-day estimates HSB3 and perhaps Dmanisi would have had longer fallow periods in winter. Other sites suggest longer growing seasons, although at Orcé the productivity of the growing season would have been offset by several summer months with low precipitation. More detailed ecological modelling would throw more light on comparisons between the different site locations.

It is likely that shorter growing seasons would have led to an increased reliance on animal resources (cf. Cordain et al. 2000), which in turn would suggest more proficient hunting or scavenging and the effective social cooperation that these tasks required. Year-round plant resources that would have been available and provided important carbohydrates were the various roots and tubers, in most cases requiring technology in the form of digging sticks to unearth (O'Connell et al. 1999). A greater problem would have been the need to process many of the tubers to make them edible or remove toxins through cooking or soaking. Even some of those that can be eaten raw (e.g., *Conopodium majus* or 'pignuts') would have needed local knowledge to find them before the leaf-growth in late spring (Hardy 2007). Others, such as *Typha latifola* (bulrush), would have been easier to recognise above ground.

For the inhabitants of HSB3 and Pakefield marine resources, such as collectible shellfish, would also have been available during winter months, and this might have been a key part of their survival strategy. The idea that coastal areas were the favoured habitat for the earliest humans in northern Europe has been suggested by Cohen et al. (2012). They argue that there was comparatively little variation in the range of habitats encountered along the Atlantic seaboard, and the coastline would have provided a natural link between south-western and north-western Europe.

Exploiting these coastal environments would have enabled early humans to avoid the difficulties of surviving in coniferous forest with few edible plants, and more dispersed game (Kelly 1983; Kelly and Todd 1988; Goebel 1999). Although these environments were less extreme than the boreal forests of Asia and North America, there would have been similar problems in obtaining usable food resources. More recent hunter-gatherer groups only successfully occupied sub-arctic boreal forests after c. 11,000 ka. This was achieved through innovative strategies, such as clearance of forest by fire to counter the problems of dispersed herds, or introducing new technologies such as fish-weirs to provide alternative foods (Goebel 1999; Sayles and Mulrennan 2010). It is highly unlikely that these strategies were used in the Lower Palaeolithic, and that survival at the edges of the boreal zone was only achieved, as at Happisburgh, by exploitation of a very specific grassland valley close to the coast.

The handaxe-heidelbergensis *hypothesis*

As argued above the North European record suggests differences in the scale of human colonisation before and after c. 600–500 ka, which has also been noted by Roebroeks (2006). There are other possible differences in the nature of the records of northern Europe before and after this time. The earliest sites would appear to lack handaxes, consisting of simple flakes, flake tools and cores, with the first robust evidence for handaxes being c. 600 ka. Although there are handaxe sites with earlier age estimates, such as La Noira and La Genetière in central France (690 ± 90 ka; Despriée et al. 2010) and Notachirico in Italy (640 ± 40 ka; Lefevre et al. 2010) their error bars could potentially make them as young as 600 ka.

There also seem to be other technological distinctions that seem to emerge from the end of the early Middle Pleistocene or beginning of the late Middle Pleistocene. There is a growing body of evidence to suggest advances in the use of fire, shelter or clothing from this time. The beginnings of hide use could reflect differences in scavenging and hunting; being first to the kill would have been an imperative for the recovery of undamaged hides. Therefore the evidence for hunting at Boxgrove at 500 ka (Roberts and Parfitt 1999a) also indicates prime access to hides and their potential use. However, the biggest difference may have been in the hominins themselves, with the evidence from Atapuerca suggesting that *Homo antecessor* is the most likely candidate for producing the assemblages prior to 600 ka and *Homo heidelbergensis* for sites dating from 600 ka (Wagner et al. 2010; Stringer 2011b; 2012; Ollé et al. 2013).

Therefore a model can be constructed around this data. The earliest coloniser of southern Europe was by the smaller-brained *H. antecessor* who deployed a simple flake-based technology, lacked the technologies of thermal buffering through hide acquisition and controlled use of fire, relying instead on functional body hair. They were perhaps successful scavengers rather than hunters, as suggested by the evidence from TE9 at Sima del Elefante at Atapuerca (Ollé et al. 2013). The brief incursions into northern Europe prior to c. 600 ka might be regarded as pioneering phases, which succeeded for short periods until climate cooled. It would seem that the earliest pioneers found it difficult to cope with the cyclical changes in climate and the successive depopulation or extinction and subsequent recolonisation required (Hublin and Roebroeks 2009; Dennell et al. 2011; Roebroeks et al. 2011).

By contrast, the larger-brained *H. heidelbergensis* first arrived in Europe at the end of the early Middle Pleistocene (Wagner et al. 2010; Stringer 2011b; 2012; Ollé et al. 2013). They quickly colonised both southern and north-western regions as fully fledged hunters, with the technological advantages of having effective clothing, shelters and the use of fire, and equipped with the ultimate butchery tool, the handaxe. These innovations were a technological and social package; handaxes were the essential ready-made tool to accompany the hunter, just as hunting was essential for the acquisition of intact hides.

As the first curated tool, handaxes reflect a more logistical use of the landscape, as exemplified at sites like Boxgrove (Roberts and Parfitt 1999a) where hominins were able to structure their own environment through patterns of handaxe use and discard that affected and helped map future actions within that landscape (Pope and Roberts 2005). As part of that structured landscape there would have been the first visible signs of a home-base in the form of shelters and fire. It is also likely that changes in methods of meat acquisition from scavenging to hunting would have had implications for extended territories through pursuit of game (Gamble and Steele 1999; Pope and Roberts 2005).

This package of innovations would have had huge implications for the social structure of these groups and changes in the way the groups and individuals negotiated their world. Hunting would have required a greater degree of cooperation (Roebroeks 2001), but also a change in power relationships being a very visible demonstration of prowess (Porr 2005). Pursuit of game would have led to a greater distinction between meat-winners and those unable to participate due to tending of young (Pope and Roberts 2005). Learning and acquiring new skills, such as handaxe manufacture, would have had costs in terms of time and generated new relationships between tutor and tutee, or between skilled and less skilled. The material culture of hearths, shelters, clothing and handaxes would have also led to a greater sense of ownership and consequently greater pressure on relationships. However, these material possessions, particularly handaxes, would also have been a visible expression of these intra-group relationships embodying both group and individual identity (Gamble 1999; White 1998a, this volume; Kohn and Mithen 1999; Porr 2005) and could almost be regarded as the social bond that allowed early hominins to negotiate their world in a new way.

CONCLUSIONS

Review of the evidence from Early and early Middle Pleistocene sites in northern Europe suggests that humans were able to cope in a range of climatic conditions from c. 800 ka with favoured habitats tending to be open river valleys, often near the coast. Investigation of probable source areas for these populations in southern Europe, suggests that early hominins were already adapted to coping with relatively cool winter temperatures. The lack of evidence for hide or fire-use suggests alternative means of coping with the cold. Seasonal migration seems an unlikely strategy for these populations, which certainly from northern Europe would have entailed long distances, but more importantly would have necessitated big changes in social structure. A more likely means of coping with the cold was the retention or re-development of functional body hair. A greater challenge for coping with northern latitudes may have been the shorter growing season and the probable increased dependence on meat and therefore improved methods of scavenging or hunting. Coastal areas, such as at HSB3 and Pakefield, would have had the benefit of collectable shellfish to help survival through winter months.

The striking contrast in the number of sites and size of assemblages from before and after 600 ka is matched by differences in technology and possibly hominin type. A model is proposed that suggests occupation of northern Europe largely failed prior to 600 ka, but that new strategies and technologies such as hunting, the processing and use of hides, the control of fire, together with new tools such as handaxes, enabled a more persistent occupation of northern latitudes, probably by *Homo heidelbergensis*. This package of innovations may imply a different use of the landscape and a more visual perception of the home-base with important implications for group size and social structure. Critical to the negotiation of the new relationships between individuals, groups and their landscape, may have been the handaxe as a means of expressing ownership and identity.

CHAPTER 9

'DANCING TO THE RHYTHMS OF THE BIOTIDAL ZONE': SETTLEMENT HISTORY AND CULTURE HISTORY IN MIDDLE PLEISTOCENE BRITAIN

MARK J. WHITE

INTRODUCTION

It has become almost axiomatic that the Middle Pleistocene of Britain (encompassing the Lower and Early Middle Palaeolithic) contains a much denser record of hominin activity than the Late Pleistocene (comprising the Late Middle and Upper Palaeolithic). The difference in the number of sites, findspots and artefacts between these two periods is at least an order of magnitude, a pattern evident since the late nineteenth century when John Evans (1872, 1897) devoted some 150 pages to the 'Drift Period' but only 50 or so to the 'Cave Period'. Today the gulf is even wider. Several factors conspire to create this pattern: the much longer duration of the Middle Pleistocene (~375 kyrs from MIS 13–MIS 6 compared with ~120 kyrs from MIS 5e to MIS 2), terrace height and accessibility, collection opportunities/biases and artefact visibility, but there is also a real sense that humans just did not visit Britain for much of the Late Pleistocene, and when they did it was in small numbers (Gamble 1986, 1987; Ashton and Lewis 2002; Pettitt 2008; Lewis et al. 2011; Pettitt and White 2012).

This relative abundance has made the Lower Palaeolithic a fertile battle-ground for equally fertile archaeological imaginations. Debates concerning the status of the Clactonian, the significance of handaxe variation and the apparent absence of cultural patterns have simmered for decades (e.g., Roe 1981; Wymer 1985, 1999; McNabb 1992, 1996, 2007; Ashton et al. 1992, 1998, 2005; Ashton, Bowen et al. 1994; Ashton and McNabb 1994; Ashton, McNabb et al. 1994; McPherron 1994, 1996; White 1996, 1998a, 1998b, 2000a; White and Schreve 2000; Wenban-Smith et al. 2000; Wenban-Smith 2004; Pope 2004; Pettitt and White 2012). This paper will not rehearse these, but will provide a new framework for understanding the settlement and cultural history of the British Lower Palaeolithic, building on previous work undertaken with Danielle Schreve. It proceeds from three key premises:

1. The Lower Palaeolithic settlement history of Britain can be understood in terms of fluctuating climatic and geographical conditions, leading to a series of more-or-less predictable colonisation, settlement and extinction events.

2. Throughout the Middle Pleistocene, Britain formed a population sink, an area where regular abandonment and/or extirpation necessitated the constant influx of people originating from elsewhere. Even during occupation populations probably reproduced below replacement levels, thus requiring 'topping-up' from outside (Dennell et al. 2011).

3. These two principles, coupled with a maturing understanding of the chronology of the British Palaeolithic, hold the key to understanding genuine cultural patterning now emerging from the British Lower Palaeolithic record.

Anybody familiar with my previous work may be somewhat surprised by the conclusions offered here.

BARRIERS AND CORRIDORS: KEEPING HOMININS INSIDE AND OUTSIDE OF BRITAIN

The rhythm of Pleistocene glacials and interglacials had a major impact on the occupation of northern Europe. The hostile conditions of full glacials, in particular, placed considerable adaptive strain on hominin societies (Gamble 1986, 1987, 1995). Understanding the specific settlement history of Britain, however, relies equally on the accompanying climatically driven sea-level fluctuations, which following the breach of the Dover Strait caused Britain to alternate between an island and a peninsula of Europe. The timing of this breach is therefore paramount.

During the Early Pleistocene and early Middle Pleistocene, the Weald-Artois Ridge connected Britain to continental Europe (Funnell 1995, 1996; papers in Preece 1995). Evidence from Happisburgh III (MIS 25 or 21), Pakefield (MIS 19 or 17) and MIS 13 archaeological occurrences at Boxgrove, High Lodge and Waverley Wood demonstrate that hominins successfully made this crossing, as and when climatic conditions matched their adaptive and social requirements (Ashton et al. 1992; Gamble 1995; Parfitt 1999; Parfitt et al. 2005, 2010; Roberts and Parfitt 1999a; Keen et al. 2006). However, the breaching of the Dover Strait and formation of the Channel River ('Fleuve Manche') created a significant barrier to movement and meant Britain became totally isolated from Europe during high sea-level stands.

The catastrophic overflowing of an ice-dammed lake (bounded by the coalescent Fennoscandian and British ice sheets to the north, the Weald-Artois ridge to the south and fed by the Rhine-Mass, Schedlt and Thames systems) first incised a channel through the land bridge during MIS 12

(Smith 1985, 1989; Gibbard 1988, 1995; Gupta et al. 2007; Busschers et al. 2008; Toucanne et al. 2009). A second ice-dammed lake, formed behind a weaker bedrock or moraine barrier in the southern North Sea basin, may also have broken with immediate and catastrophic effect during the Saalian (MIS 8 or MIS 6; Gibbard 2007; Gupta et al. 2007). This second mega-flood was argued to have greatly enlarged the Dover Strait and resulted in a combined Thames-Rhine system carrying half the drainage of western Europe into the Atlantic via the Channel River (Gibbard 2007).

Studies of the Pleistocene Channel River activity using mass accumulation rates and X-ray fluorescence of marine sediments indicate that the Dover Strait was open from MIS12 (Toucanne et al. 2009). Terrigenous inputs into the Armorican margin off the Bay of Biscay dating to MIS 10, 8 and 6 further suggest the Channel River connected the southern North Sea basin with the Atlantic during these periods. However, significantly lower Channel River activity during MIS 10 and 8 than during MIS 6 and 2 could indicate a gradual increase in the size of the Dover Strait, although ice sheet and fluvial dynamics in the North Sea may have had a greater control on discharge. Critically, the seasonal imprint of fluvial discharges indicated by laminated facies did not support large sediment input c. 160–150 ka BP, as required by Gupta et al.'s Saalian megaflood scenario. Instead a succession of Channel River discharges from c. 350 ka onwards may have produced the features they documented in the English Channel (Toucanne et al. 2009).

The formation of the Dover Strait was thus polycyclic, with one or more episodes of catastrophic overspill, erosion during marine transgressions and fluvial dissection during low sea-level stands, but overall the evidence suggests that the Strait was a significant feature from MIS 12 onwards. Thus, while early Middle Pleistocene hominins could potentially have entered Britain at any time, a significant water barrier may have kept Middle Pleistocene interglacial residents in and potential colonists out. The current limiting depths (i.e., the shallowest parts) of the Channel and North Sea basins are −50 m OD and −40 m OD, respectively (Keen 1995), and sea levels above these depths today isolate Britain from Europe. Reconstructing the bathymetry of the Channel and North Sea basins during the Middle Pleistocene, though, is complicated by a number of long- and short-term tectonic and depositional factors, including the cyclical accumulation and (catastrophic) erosion of sediments, progressive down-warping of the North Sea basin, general uplift in response to erosion, glacio-isostacy and hydro-isostacy and uplift of c. 30–40 m in the Channel (Lagarde et al. 2003). Ashton et al.'s 2011 model assumes gradual subsidence of the North Sea basin (Busschers et al. 2008) from a high stand of 0 m OD during MIS 11 to a low stand of −40 m OD today. The North Sea basin has certainly undergone net progressive down-warping (e.g., Koii et al. 1998; Busschers et al. 2008), but this was punctuated rather than gradual, varying cyclically in response to the processes mentioned above. Moreover, the depth of 0 m OD suggested for MIS 11 ignores the North Sea basin's recovery from the imprint of the MIS 12 ice sheet and a pro-glacial lake about four times the size of Wales (cf. Gibbard 2007: Figure 2). Furthermore, sedimentological and biological evidence for marine conditions around the coast of Britain from Cornwall to Essex during MIS 11, MIS 9 and MIS 7 demonstrate high sea levels in the North Sea and Channel basins during these periods (Table 9.1 and Figure 9.1), indicating that the depths of the relevant basins did not preclude isolation.

SEA-LEVEL RECONSTRUCTIONS

Figure 9.2 shows five different reconstructions of sea levels for the past 500 kyr. All clearly show that global sea levels exceeded modern limiting depths during each interglacial and approached modern levels several times in each cycle. Assuming a limiting depth of just −10m, or indeed gradual subsidence, makes little difference – Britain would have been isolated during parts of each interglacial, perhaps just for shorter periods – and at the human scale water depth of just a metre or so would surely have prevented humans from wading tens of kilometres across the North Sea.

Reconstructions by Waelbroek et al. (2002), Cutler et al. (2003) and Siddall et al. (2003) show a rapid peak in sea levels and probable isolation during early MIS 11, with reconnection to Europe during later sub-stages and the cooling limb. Shackleton's (2000) data, however, indicates two high sea-level stands in MIS 11, an initial peak (possibly subsuming the earlier parts of MIS 11c) and a later peak (possibly parts of MIS 11a), separated by a prolonged episode of low sea levels. The latter perhaps represents the re-establishment of a terrestrial link between the Thames and the Rhine which allowed the dispersal of the freshwater 'Rhenish' molluscan suite into Britain during Hoxnian pollen zone HoIIc of MIS 11c (cf. Kerney 1971; Meijer and Preece 1995).

The absence of southern elements in MIS 11 marine molluscan faunas around the North Sea might indicate that the Strait was still closed at this time (Meijer and Preece 1995), although this pattern is similar to modern distributions (ibid; Figure 9.2). Furthermore the delayed arrival of the Rhenish Suite, not complete until HoIIc, might reflect a time lag in immigration from distant refugia, or alternatively an initially inundated and then dry southern North Sea basin. Glacio-isostatic depression of the crust of north-west Europe after the extensive MIS 12 glaciation could have led to the sea flooding in before the crust could recover during the Hoxnian (White and Schreve 2000; cf. Kukla and Cílek 1996). If sufficient to disconnect Britain from continental Europe, later uplift combined with a global reduction in sea levels would then have re-connected Britain to continental Europe around the end of HoII, allowing the incursion of the Rhenish Suite.

TABLE 9.1: *Evidence for marine conditions around the southern and south-eastern coasts of Britain during MIS 11, MIS 9 and MIS 7 (summarised from White and Schreve 2000).*

Site	Tentative Age	Evidence for High Sea Level	Reference
Boxgrove and Norton Farm, West Sussex	MIS 13 and MIS 7	Differences in ostracods and foraminifera suggestive of different marine conditions	Bates et al. 1998
Aldinbourne Raised Beach	?MIS 11	Exotic pebbles suggestive of new source area to earlier deposits	Bates et al. 1998
Swanscombe, Kent: Barnfield Pit, Lower Loam	MIS 11 (Ho IIb)	Marine stenohaline fish	Irving 1996
Clacton-on-Sea, Essex: Holiday Camp Site	MIS 11 (Ho I-II)	Smelt Tooth Saline tolerant ostracods	Bridgland et al. 1999
East Hyde, Essex	MIS 11 (Ho III)	Marine molluscs and ostracods	Roe and Preece 1995; Roe 1999
Marks Tey, Essex	MIS 11	Brackish water ostracods	Turner, cited in Ventris 1996
Ingress Vale, Kent: Dierdens Pit	MIS 11 (Ho III, equivalent of Middle Gravels at Barnfield Pit)	Bottle-nosed dolphin (*Tursiops truncatus*) Brackish molluscs	Sutcliffe 1964; Kerney 1971
Cudmore Grove, Essex	MIS 9 (P.A.Z. II)	Molluscs, ostracods and diatoms	Roe 1994; Roe et al. 2009
Purfleet, Essex: Greenland Pit laminated silty-clay	Early MIS 9	Possible inter-tidal sediments, brackish ostracod (*Cyprideis torosa*)	Hollin 1977; Schreve et al. 2002
Globe Pit, Little Thurrock, Essex	MIS 9	Possible inter-tidal sediments	Hollin 1977
Barling, Essex	MIS 9 (P.A.Z II)	Brackish ostracod (*C. torosa*)	Bridgland et al. 2001
Nar Valley	MIS 9 (P.A.Z. IIc)	Lithological, palynological and molluscan evidence for a marine transgression	Ventris 1996
Aveley, Essex: Lower brickearths	MIS 7	Brackish ostracods and molluscs	Sutcliffe 1995; Holyoak 1983

TABLE 9.1: *(continued)*

Site	Tentative Age	Evidence for High Sea Level	Reference
Lion Pit Tramway Cutting, West Thurrock, Essex	MIS 7	Laminated sediments attributed to inter-tidal or estuarine conditions	Hollin 1977
Sussex Coastal Plain: Norton-Brighton Raised Beach, Sussex	MIS 7–6	Beach deposits	Bates et al. 1997; Bates 1998
Sussex Coastal Plain: Black Rock	MIS 7	Beach deposits	Davies 1984
Selsey, West Sussex	MIS 7	Sedimentological evidence for a marine transgression	West and Sparks 1960
Portland Bill, Dorset	MIS 7	Beach deposits	Davies and Keen 1985
Berry Head, Torbay, Devon	MIS 7	Sea cave deposits	Proctor and Smart 1991

The sea-level evidence for MIS 9 is more complex. Four of the reconstructions in Figure 9.2 suggest high sea-level stands during MIS 9e, 9c and 9a. In contrast, all five have sea levels sufficiently low to connect Britain to Europe in MIS 9b, but only two datasets (Shackleton 2000 and Siddall et al. 2003) suggest very low sea levels in MIS 9d. Lea et al.'s reconstruction (2003) suggests a very long period of insularity MIS 9e–MIS 9c, followed by reduced sea levels and peninsularity until the beginning of MIS 7. Terrestrial corroboration of these estimates is difficult because of the small number of well-dated sites from this stage.

All five reconstructions predict high sea levels during all three warm peaks of MIS 7. Depths of c. −10m OD during 7e, c. −5m OD during 7c and −11m OD during 7a (Waelbroeck et al. 2002) do not quite reach modern levels but largely agree with estimates from corals and geochemical data on submerged speleothems from Argentorola Cave, Italy (Gallup et al. 1994; Bard et al. 1996, 2000), although more recent work here has indicated that sea level in MIS 7a was actually much lower, probably no more than −18m OD (Dutton et al. 2009a, 2009b). Similarly, Shackleton's (2000) $\delta^{18}O$ data project generally lower sea levels for all MIS 7 warm peaks, although estimates from planktonic Mg/Ca and $\delta^{18}O$ (Lea et al. 2002) suggest that MIS 7e and MIS 7a possibly exceeded both modern and MIS 5e peaks. For the cold sub-stages of MIS 7d and MIS 7b, most estimates produced the expected reduction in sea levels, but while Waelbroeck et al.'s results show that during

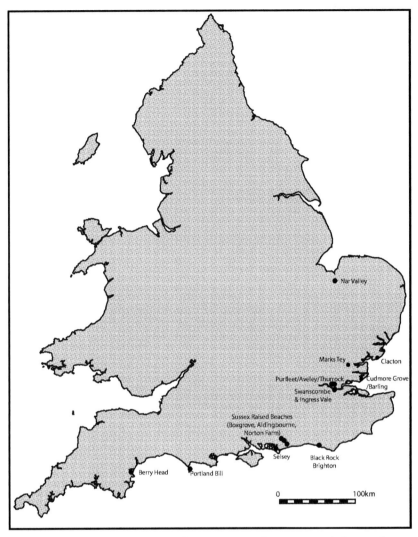

Figure 9.1: Sites yielding evidence for marine conditions around the southern and southeastern coasts of Britain during MIS 11, MIS 9 and MIS 7.

MIS 7d relative sea level plummeted to c. −85m OD, MIS 7b showed fell only to c. −25m OD, some 35 m higher than Shackleton's data suggests. Interestingly, the Italian speleothem data, Shackleton's δ18O reconstructions, Red Sea salinity (Siddall et al. 2003) and coral dating (Thompson and Goldstein 2005) all show a period of high relative sea level (around − 19m OD) during the early part of MIS 6 (MIS 6.5). The Norton-Brighton Raised Beach might provide terrestrial evidence for this event (Bates et al. 1997). So, despite inconsistent and contradictory reconstructions, Britain would have been an island during the warmer phases of MIS 7 (and possibly early MIS 6), and a peninsula during periods of depressed sea levels in MIS 8 and MIS 7d, but possibly not MIS 7b.

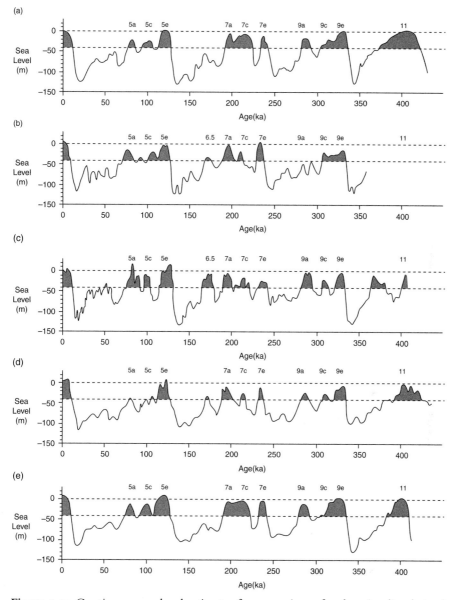

Figure 9.2: Continuous sea-level estimates from a variety of authors/studies derived from the benthonic isotope record and other sea-level indicators, with periods during which Britain was an island. Top dashed line: modern sea level. Lower dashed line: −40m below modern sea level, above which Britain is assumed to become an island (island periods are thus those marked in grey). A) Waelbroek et al. 2002, based on North Atlantic and equatorial Pacific benthonic isotopic record; B) Lea et al. 2002, based on foraminiferal Mg/Ca and planktonic oxygen isotopes; C) Shackleton 2000, based on oxygen isotope data from equatorial Pacific (V19–30) and Vostock air oxygen isotope ratio; D) Siddall et al. 2003, based on Red Sea salinity and oxygen isotope record; E) Cutler et al. 2003, based on scaled data from benthic isotope record of core V19–30.

A REVISED MODEL FOR HOMININ COLONISATION, ABANDONMENT AND RESIDENCY

Figure 9.3 shows a modified version of White and Schreve's (2000) three-phase framework for modelling the late Middle Pleistocene human settlement of Britain, which attempts to take into account isotopic sub-stage variation (see also Pettitt and White 2012).

Phase 1: *Cooling limb peninsula – residency and colonisation*

Increases in global ice volume and sea-level reductions during isotopic cooling transitions connected Britain to Europe, facilitating movement and occupation across the modern English Channel and North Sea basins ('the plains of Doggerland'). Cool but 'intermediate' conditions (Gamble 1986, 1987; Roebroeks et al. 1992) provided ideal mosaic habitats for human settlement,

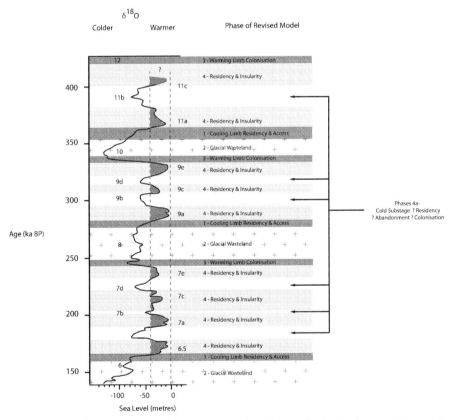

Figure 9.3: Schematic diagram showing tentative phases of colonisation, isolation and abandonment during marine isotope sub-stages from MIS 12 to MIS 6.
Illustrative isotopic curve and sea-level data derived from Shackleton 2000 and Waelbroeck et al. 2003. For description of the occupational phases see text.

with rich floral and faunal resources. During such periods transfers of animals and technologies from Europe are expected.

Phase 2: Glacial peninsula – human wasteland

As conditions worsened towards the glacial maximum, ice sheets on the British mainland and North Sea basin – and polar desert for hundreds of kilometres beyond – rendered Britain totally inhospitable to hominins and most animal and plant life. Abandonment and local extinction is expected.

Phase 3: Warming transition peninsula – recolonisation

During the warming limbs of each major cycle, deglaciation, climatic ameli-oration and the re-establishment of animal and plant communities provided renewed opportunities for hominin occupation. Low sea levels maintained terrestrial conditions in the North Sea and Channel basins for several millennia during MIS 5e; isolation occurred within ~3000 years (Shackleton 1987), sufficient time for humans to re-colonise from cold stage refugia (cf. Dennell et al. 2011 and see discussion below).

Phase 4: Interglacial island – residency and isolation

Rising interglacial (and warm sub-stage) sea levels cut Britain off from Europe, locking existing hominins in and keeping continental populations out. Local extinction and perturbations in ecology, societies and technology caused profound effects on archaeological signatures during this phase.

Sub-phase 4a: stadial peninsula:

A number of the sea-level reconstructions discussed above reveal that during cold sub-stages global sea levels were sufficiently reduced to temporarily re-connect Britain to Europe, and it remains to be seen if hominins abandoned Britain, became locally extinct or remained resident (despite sub-optimal conditions) until increased sea levels into warm sub-stages isolated Britain from the continent once more. If Britain was abandoned during stadials, the archaeological record suggests that recolonisation took place before each subsequent warm sub-stage.

SINKS AND SOURCES; ARKS AND LIFEBOATS

The model above suggests that Pleistocene hominins in Britain lived under conditions that rarely allowed stable long-term adaptations, a pattern also true of much of Europe (Dennell et al. 2011). Dispersal was the rule, and settlement was infrequent and intermittent; hominins were, it seems, 'dancing to the rhythms of the Pleistocene' (Gamble 1999: 125). Britain and large swathes of Northern Europe were probably human wastelands for more than 50% of Middle Pleistocene time, and even further south local extinction and possibly relocation was still frequent (Hublin and Roebroeks 2009; Dennell et al. 2011; Roebroeks et al. 2011). The Pleistocene peopling of Britain must be characterised as a pattern of 'expansion and contraction, abandonment and recolonisation, integration and isolation' (Dennell et al. 2011).

These temporal and geographic discontinuities suggest that hominin populations probably consisted of a few core groups and a number of peripheral ones, with survival of the core only in a few refugia (Dennell et al. 2011), where life persisted with relatively little change despite major climatic and environmental change elsewhere (Vrba 1988). In contrast, in the 'biotidal zone' different biomes replaced each other over Pleistocene time (Vrba 1988; Gamble 2009). Britain, of course, lies within the biotidal zone.

It is critical to emphasise that Pleistocene refugia served as 'lifeboats' for European hominins (saving only those who happened to be in the right place at the right time), not arks or sanctuaries that saved everyone; when the going got tough most groups faced regional extinction, not a southern exodus (Hublin and Roebroeks 2009; Dennell et al. 2011). The warmer climes of southern Europe – particularly Iberia, the Balkans and Italy – are the most likely refugia, although some cryptic refugia may also have existed north of the Alps (Dennell et al. 2011).

Such refugia preserved source populations for re-colonisation, although the record is too partial to determine whether even these areas were continuously occupied; different refugia may have operated at different times based on the intensity and local effects of climatic cycles and evolving survivorship traits (e.g., enhanced fire use and cooperative hunting) over time. Indeed, the early occupation of Iberia appears to be concentrated in warmer phases, perhaps suggesting that core populations during the most severe events were actually situated further east, maybe in Western Asia (Agustí et al. 2009, 2010; Dennell et al. 2011). If populations in southern refugia did occasionally become extinct, Europe would have become uninhabited, emphasising that Europe was never a closed system, but subject to immigration from outside its modern political boundaries, particularly western Asia (Dennell et al. 2011).

During challenging climatic conditions hominin populations across Europe may have fallen to levels that would today put them on the endangered list. Estimates suggest that populations in the refugia may have numbered 1500–2500 individuals, with perhaps only 60–100 surviving in more northerly cryptic refugia (Dennell et al. 2011). Such astonishingly low population densities further imply very small social and mating networks in which inbreeding was almost inevitable and extinction, recolonisation, integration and re-combination were the only manner in which Eurasian populations could maintain genetic viability (ibid.). The timing and pattern of movement out of refugia during phases of climatic amelioration would have been highly variable, with major geographical features such as the Alps and Pyrenees perhaps acting as permeable barriers (see, e.g., Hewitt 1999's discussion of patterns of post-glacial expansion in three non-human species in Dennell et al. 2011). The key is that the re-colonisation of Britain may have originated in a varied combination of distal and proximal sources, each perhaps contributing a different cultural flavour to the mix and also helping to explain why *Homo heidelbergensis* is such an ill-defined heterogeneous species (Dennell et al. 2011). If this species formed an anagenetic line to Neanderthals (Stringer and Hublin 1999), the evolutionary path was unstructured and contingent on the caprice of time and chance, not predictable, directional or linear (Dennell et al. 2011).

Whatever happened in the refugia, it is clear that Britain formed a 'sink' area that needed to be filled by people originating from elsewhere; even during periods of occupation populations may have been reproducing below replacement levels and thus continuously 'topped-up' from outside, although why they should come to Britain is unclear. The British Lower Palaeolithic (and equally that of much of northern Europe) is thus a long record of abandonment and colonisation, and a very short record of residency.

TOWARDS A SETTLEMENT HISTORY OF MIDDLE
PLEISTOCENE BRITAIN

Britain was connected to continental Europe throughout MIS 15 and MIS 13, with few major obstacles to hominin colonisation. Pre-Anglian (MIS12) Lower Palaeolithic occupation, though not in doubt (e.g., Wymer 1988), is limited to just 26 sites and findspots (Hosfield 2011) and only a handful of these can be regarded as securely dated (e.g., Waverley Wood, Boxgrove, High Lodge and Happisburgh I). Evidence for occupation during MIS 15 is remarkably poor (only the disputed archaeology at Westbury-sub-Mendip [Cook 1999; White 2000b] attests to human presence, unless one agrees with Westaway [2009a, 2009b, 2011] that Happisburgh III and Pakefield represent MIS 15e and not MIS 25/21 and 19/17 [Parfitt et al. 2005, 2010]).

The environmental records from the MIS 13 sites mentioned above all suggest occupation towards the end of the interglacial, when cool continental conditions prevailed (Ashton et al. 1992; Shotton et al. 1993; Roberts and Parfitt 1999a; Ashton, Parfitt et al. 2008). There is currently no evidence that hominins were present during the earlier climatic optima, suggesting that each represents a relatively brief pulse of occupation, perhaps the final terminus of the 'wave' of European colonisation c. 600–500 ka BP (cf. Roebroeks 2006). The number of sites and quantity of artefacts found within MIS 13–12 deposits do not suggest dense populations at this time (though see Ashton and Lewis 2002)

Evidence that hominins persisted into the early Anglian is found in Unit 8 of the Eartham Formation at Boxgrove (Roberts 1999), associated with a warmer interstadial. Human presence deep into MIS 12 has also been proposed on the basis of refitting artefacts from the 'head' gravel of unit 11, where evidence of short-lived soil formation shows a slight amelioration in climate (Roberts 1999). Whether these refits actually attest to mid-Anglian occupation or are in fact material moved en masse from interglacial deposits on the downland block and incorporated more or less intact into the cold climate gravels remains unclear (Roberts 1999: 384). The former certainly agrees with Wymer's (1968) belief that artefacts in the Anglian 'Caversham Ancient Channel' of the Middle Thames show that hominins returned to England during an MIS 12 inter-stadial.

The record from MIS 11 is far richer with numerous fluvial artefact accumulations within the fluvial archive, as well as several well-preserved primary context sites (see Wymer 1999). Figure 9.3 shows the modified White and Schreve phases plotted against isotopic and sea-level reconstructions based on Shackleton's (2000) data (this dataset, one of many, is used here for heuristic purposes). Much of MIS 11 would have been ideal for hominin settlement, with a generally warm climate, prolonged terrestrial links (at the end of MIS 12 and the middle of MIS 11 according to this reconstruction) interspersed with periods of insularity.

The archaeological record confirms that hominins were present more or less throughout this period, with Late MIS 12/early MIS 11 presence, during pollen zones Ian, HoI and IIa at the Lower Gravels at Swanscombe, and Golf Course Site at Clacton (Conway et al. 1996; Singer et al. 1973; Ashton, Lewis et al. 2008; but see McNabb 2007). Hominins were present in the later Phase I and Phase II deposits at Swanscombe (Lower Loam, Lower Middle Gravel, Upper Middle Gravel) during pollen zones HoIIb to HoIII, and at Beeches Pit during HoIII-IV. According to Ashton, Lewis et al. (2008), these classic sequences – along with the lacustrine deposits at the Hoxnian stratotype at Hoxne – represent only the first sub-stage of the MIS 11 interglacial (MIS 11c). Terrestrial sequences belonging to MIS 11b and MIS 11a might therefore occur in the Phase III deposits at Swanscombe and Beds B-A at Hoxne (Ashton, Lewis et al. 2008). Primary context artefacts are found in the Upper Loams at the former (and its local correlates at Wansunt Pit, for example; White et al. 1995) and in the Lower and Upper Industries of Beds B1 and A2 in the latter (Ashton, Lewis et al. 2008), meaning hominins were present during both warm sub-stages. Thus, several extensive phases of access and occupation have left a very rich record (cf. Ashton and Lewis 2002).

Evidence of human occupation in the MIS 9 archive is equally rich – the Lynch Hill Terrace of the Middle Thames alone boasts over 192 sites and findspots, with some 'supersites' such as Furze Platt yielding astonishing quantities of artefacts (Wymer 1968, 1988, 1996, 1999; Cranshaw 1983;

Bridgland 1994). The equivalent terraces of the Solent also contain large quantities of artefacts (Hosfield 1999; Ashton and Hosfield 2009). Human populations may have been at their greatest during this period, although much of the evidence is derived and only four 'flagship' sites can be identified for this period amongst the many 'dredgers' (Gamble 1996b) – Wolvercote Channel; Stoke Newington; Little Thurrock and Purfleet. The relative paucity of decent sites and the recent recognition of MIS 9 within the terrestrial record mean that, unlike MIS 11, little can as yet be said about its settlement history. Only the pits at Purfleet preserve a long sequence through the interglacial, the evidence here suggesting that hominins were active on three occasions during the beginning, middle and end of the interglacial, each time using a different technological repertoire (White 2000a; Schreve et al. 2002). If, as Figure 9.2 suggests, Britain was isolated from Europe on three occasions this is exactly what one would expect from the intra-stage model of colonisation, residency and extinction, with developments on Britain representing both in situ cultural evolution and contact and mixing with continental hominin populations.

Evidence for occupation during MIS 7 is remarkably poor. Ashton and Lewis (2002) argued this is because populations were small and only present during terminal MIS8 and early MIS 7, after which prolonged isolation from Europe meant that following local extinction or major crashes populations could not be replaced. White et al. (2006) disputed this, arguing that major changes in technology (the emergence of Levallois), the fashion in which that technology was used in the landscape, and changing raw material availability over time could account for the apparent paucity. The uncertain age of many MIS 7 sites – largely dependent on a mammalian biostratigraphical scheme constructed on the sequence at Aveley and somewhat at odds with other sites and environmental proxies (see Schreve 2001a, 2001b; Candy and Schreve 2007 vs. Parfitt 1998; Pettitt and White 2012) – make it difficult to precisely place humans within MIS 7. Artefacts from both the top and bottom of the Aveley sequence do suggest some human presence throughout MIS 7 and Britain was almost certainly reconnected to Europe for part of MIS 7d (long enough for the introduction of a suite of new mammals: White and Schreve 2000), and possibly also during MIS 7b. Thus MIS 7 was not vastly different from earlier interglacials. A major dating program, and better dating of the controversial Crayford material (Kennard 1944; White et al. 2006; Scott 2010), would clarify the situation.

A NEW CULTURAL HISTORY FOR MIDDLE PLEISTOCENE BRITAIN

Archaeologists have long believed that lithic assemblage variation among small and socially isolated hominin groups should show regional and/or chrono-logical patterning, or different local 'traditions' that evolved through time. As stated above, for much of the twentieth century, the Lower Palaeolithic of

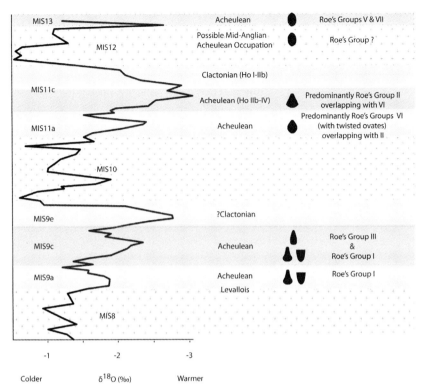

Figure 9.4: Summary diagram showing chronological distribution of Acheulean, Levallois and Clactonian industries from MIS 13 to MIS 8, with suggested position of Roe's handaxe sub-groups.

Britain was dominated by two such culture-history debates – the meaning of differences between handaxe versus non-handaxe ('Clactonian') assemblages, and of difference in handaxe shapes within handaxe assemblages (Acheulean variability).

I have argued elsewhere (White 2000a; White and Schreve 2000) that the Clactonian can be explained by initial (Phase 3) colonisation by groups of humans who did not habitually make handaxes, during late MIS 12/early MIS 11, and perhaps during Late MIS 10/early MIS 9 (Figure 9.4). These peoples probably spread via the non-handaxe zone of central Europe, and one must now re-consider the possibility that they represented a different hominin species, perhaps originating in Asia (cf. Warren 1923; Dennell et al. 2010, 2011). Later in MIS 11 these peoples were replaced by handaxe-making hominins from refugia further south, who gained access to Britain during periods of low sea level. Although such opinions have until recently been unpopular, in the light of new species from Spain, Siberia and Indonesia (Bermúdez de Castro et al. 1997; Brown et al. 2004; Reich et al. 2010) to contend that Europe or indeed any other region of the old world was occupied by a single species for c. 500,000 years is problematic.

Here, however, I am mostly concerned with the question of handaxe variation. Significant morphological variation exists in handaxes both within and between Acheulean assemblages (cf. Roe 1968a), and while most handaxe assemblages show a modal form, it has not previously been possible to firmly correlate variability in either time or space (although see Wenban Smith 2004), largely because of poor and incomplete dating (Roe 1968a, 1981). As a result, recent work has emphasised the role of reduction or raw materials in biasing assemblages (McPherron 1994, 1996; White 1998b). Recent advances in dating and correlating Pleistocene deposits, however, provide tentative hints that temporal variation may exist, but at a different scale of analysis.

In developing the raw material driven explanation, I noted that extra-somatic factors could not explain some characteristics, (White 1996, 1998a, 1998b), including the use and frequency of tranchet removals, the unique burin-type removals on pointed handaxes at Whitlingham, Norfolk and twisted ovate handaxes. The latter are most frequent in late MIS 11 assemblages and were offered as an example of endemic cultural variation occurring at a time when Britain was isolated from Europe (White 1998a). Twisted edges played no obvious functional role, but later work at Foxhall Road (White and Plunkett 2004) showed that only some individuals made this form, hinting at the possibility that individuals within a group adopted their own 'hand' or style of handaxe as an expression of identity (cf. Gamble 1998b, 1999). The prevalence of such traits within an assemblage might therefore relate to the frequency with which these individuals made handaxes or the role that these individuals played within a group. If the style developed by juveniles depended more upon their role model(s) than collective ideals, then choice of model was probably predicated on interpersonal relationships and social identities. The frequency of different forms within a group would therefore drift (cf. Isaac 1972) according to the players involved, the social and ecological context within which they acted and the time over which the assemblage accumulated. Usually assemblages are dominated by a modal form which, whatever one chooses to call it, thus stems from a community of shared practice predicated on social relationships, in other words – culture.

The regional spread of such characteristics might depend on inter-group networks or the size of a group's local operational area (White and Pettitt 2011). In a sink region such as Britain, they are equally likely to relate to characteristics introduced and spread by colonising groups dispersing into empty or sparsely populated landscapes. Therefore, any chronological pattern-ing will not just look disjointed because of the poor temporal resolution and broken nature of the data, it will actually be disjointed because it records the ebb and flow of different groups over time.

Two problems have prevented the detection of significant patterns in the data – chronological control, and the scale of most recent analyses, which have largely operated according to the gross measures of Roe's pointed versus ovate handaxe classes and traditions. The first has gradually been overcome by the major advances in our dating of Lower Palaeolithic sites over the past thirty years (e.g. Bridgland 1994; Schreve 1997, 2001). The second merely requires a re-orientation in the scale of enquiry.

Table 9.2 shows the new picture that emerges when moving from Roe's groups to his sub-groups, alongside recent age-correlations based on biostratigraphy, lithostratigraphy and absolute dating. Sites without decent date estimates have been omitted, as they contribute nothing. The intermediate group (Roe's Group IV) has also been removed because the mixed nature of these assemblages largely stems from a lack of stratigraphical or taphonomic integrity.

Table 9.2 and Figure 9.4 show that Group I sites all belong to MIS 10/9/8. The presence of handaxes and absence of a strong Levallois element suggests the artefacts at least probably belong to the middle half of the cycle. These sites contain ficrons – probably a deliberately constructed form expressing the maker's identity, and cleavers, reflecting resharpening practices widespread at this time (White 2006b). Group III (Wolvercote), also dates to MIS 9, and re-sharpening practices in a raw material poor region may also be responsible for the shape of the handaxes there (Ashton 2001). So, two practices, a selection for shape and a technological act of rejuvenation, pertained during this occupation event. It is also noteworthy that Acheulean sites attributed to MIS 9 have much higher proportions of scrapers than those from MIS 11 (see Roe 1868b), possibly reflecting greater frequencies of hide working or the development of more effective clothing.

Group II is dominated by squat, broad-pointed handaxes with a strong ovate element and, like the pointed-ovate dominated Group VI, dates to MIS 11. There is no simple division between MIS 11c, MIS 11b or MIS 11a, supporting the idea that although specific forms may have been socially preferred, others were culturally resonant in different raw material contexts, humans having more than one relevant style in their repertoire (White and Plunkett 2004; Catt et al. 1978). Nevertheless most of the Group VI sites (and Hitchin from Group II), contain high proportions of twisted ovates, while group II sites show the highest proportions of twisted tips. Recent work at Hoxne (Ashton, Lewis et al. 2008) suggests many sites with high percentages of twisted ovate handaxes (Hoxne; Wansunt Pit; Bowman's Lodge; Swanscombe Upper Loams) might belong to MIS 11a, perhaps supporting the contention that this form was an endemic development within an isolated island population; it was apparently not common in MIS 11 assemblages in neighbouring European countries (White 1998a). However, the frequent occurrence of twisted ovates at Elveden (?MIS 11c) perhaps shows the form was already present in Britain earlier during MIS 11.

That said, the re-dating of Hoxne to MIS 11a means that many of our previous biostratigraphical correlations might need revisiting, as similar floral and faunal sequences from MIS 11c and MIS 11a may have been

TABLE 9.2: *British Handaxe Traditions according to Derek Roe (1968a) with inferred ages. Sites in parenthesis added after White 1996, 1998a; White and Plunkett 2004. Age attributions based on Preece 1990; Bridgland et al. 1990; Ashton et al. 1992, 2005, 2008a; Bridgland 1994, 1996 and personal communication; Boreham and Gibbard 1995; White et al. 1995; Schreve 1997, 2001a; Roberts and Parfitt 1999; Wymer 1999; Green et al. 2004; White and Plunkett 2004; Wenban Smith 2004; Lundberg and McFarlane 2007; Hosfield 2011.*

| ← | Pointed Tradition | → | → | Ovate Tradition | → |
Group I (with cleavers)	Group II (with ovates)	Group III (plano-convex)	Group V (crude, narrow)	Group VI (more pointed)	Group VII (less pointed)
MIS 9–8	**MIS 11**	**MIS 9**	**MIS 13–15**	**MIS 11**	**MIS 13**
Furze Platt	Swanscombe MG	Wolvercote	Fordwich	Elveden	High Lodge
Bakers Farm	Chadwell St Mary		Farnham terrace A	Bowman's Lodge	Warren Hill Fresh
Cuxton	(Hoxne UI)		Warren Hill worn	Swanscombe UL	Corfe Mullen
Stoke Newington	Dovercourt		(Kent's Cavern Breccia)	(Wansunt)	(Boxgrove)
	Hitchin			(Foxhall Road Grey Clays)	
				(Hoxne LI)	
	(Foxhall Road Red Gravel)			**MIS 12–13**	
				Caversham	
				Highlands Farm	
				Middle Palaeolithic	
				Shide, Pan Farm	
				Oldbury	

171

conflated, as was once the case for MIS 11 and MIS 9 sequences (e.g., Roe et al. 2009). Oldbury and Pan Farm are Middle Palaeolithic and, while they show that forms recur throughout Pleistocene time, do not contradict the temporal pattern in Lower Palaeolithic forms. Roe's summary diagrams (1968a: 57, 60) show that in terms of modal shape, these assemblages were always outliers.

Group V and Group VII both date to pre-Anglian interglacials. Group VII, best exemplified at Boxgrove and High Lodge, is dominated by very well-made 'rounded' ovate forms, Group V by the crude metrical 'ovates' from Fordwich and Farnham Terrace A. In situ technological evolution in Britain is unlikely to have created the contrast between these two groups; I believe that the difference in shape and technology are adequately explained by differences in raw material packages. The character of the putative mid-Anglian occupation handaxes remains enigmatic. The two sites assigned here in Table 9.2 are both part of the Caversham Ancient Channel (Wymer 1968, 1999) but have been assigned to Groups VI and VII respectively. The Caversham assemblage could not really be considered 'a closed industry from a single site' (Roe 1968: 70), while the Highlands Farm material may similarly have been incorporated into the Ancient Channel from earlier deposits. We are still looking for a convincing signature of any mid-Anglian occupation.

Although the assemblages within each of these groups represent the actions of untold individuals over hundreds or thousands of years (or generations), the patterns should actually come as little surprise. The conservatism of the Acheulean demonstrates that the technological systems of Middle Pleistocene humans were strongly rule-bound. Variation in handaxe shape reflects constant modification to a basic formula but always within socially acceptable parameters and radical change is absent; inventiveness (the ability to be creative within the technology at hand) rather than innovation (those technological leaps to totally novel systems; Nowell and White 2010). Rejecting the notion that cognitive deficiencies are the explanation (e.g. Binford 1989; Mithen 1996; Klein 1999), one must conclude that within archaic human societies the power of individual agents to express themselves through technology may have been strong, but their power to actually change the overarching structure of the Acheulean was limited (Hopkinson and White 2005).

Such a major transformation was not achieved until c. MIS 9–8, with the emergence of Levallois technology. Precocious occurrences across the Old World from at least 1 million years ago suggest this was immanent within the Acheulean (White and Ashton 2003; White et al. 2011). Whether the occurrence of an unrefined form at Botany Pit Purfleet demonstrates that Levallois actually evolved in situ in different parts of Europe, or was, like different forms of handaxe and non-handaxe assemblages, introduced to Britain by a wave of new colonists, is now open to question.

CONCLUSIONS

The British Lower Palaeolithic represents a piecemeal record of settlement and abandonment tracing the ebb and flow of hominin populations from various parts of Europe. At certain scales the data show patterns pertaining to the cultural repertoires of these different groups, and despite conclusions of the past 20–30 years, handaxe shape was culturally resonant among Palaeolithic humans. Certain forms were a template for action among different groups; maybe predicated on interpersonal relationships building a shared group ideal. Using handaxes as a means to identify source populations in Europe is still some way off, however, as the necessary temporal correlations do not yet exist. As a final word, I would like to remind some of my colleagues in the wider field of Quaternary science that this is not a dating framework, but a pattern in the archaeological record that depends on independent chronological controls.

CHAPTER 10

'FOREST FURNITURE' OR 'FOREST MANAGERS'? ON NEANDERTHAL PRESENCE IN LAST INTERGLACIAL ENVIRONMENTS

WIL ROEBROEKS AND CORRIE C. BAKELS

INTRODUCTION

This paper is an 'exercise in speculation' (Gamble 1987). It starts from a debate that lasted about two decades and dealt with an at first sight very simple question: were Neanderthals present in north-western Europe during the Last Interglacial, when major parts of the European landscapes would have been covered with broad-leaved forests? After all, densely forested environments do pose challenges to hunter-gatherers, to the degree that some suggest that not even modern foragers are well suited to forested environments (Bailey et al. 1989). Like modern day temperate and tropical forests, Pleistocene interglacial deciduous forests in western Eurasia were characterised by a high primary biomass and a high primary production. Most of this richness consisted of trees, woody tissue not easily accessible for hungry hominins. Usable plant foods, such as nuts and other large seeds, were relatively expensive to process and mostly available during short periods of time only. Hence, animals must have constituted the critical food source, especially in winter. In contrast to the open mammoth steppe environments (Guthrie 1990), herbivore mass in forested environments was significantly lower, and medium-sized and larger mammals were more dispersed, with large prey animals rare and more difficult to find. Intercepting animals would have needed higher investments in retrieving information on their whereabouts and in terms of other search costs. On top of that, the largest species that roamed these forested environments, such as straight-tusked elephant and rhinoceros, had long life spans and low reproduction rates, which would have made sustained hunting of them a risky strategy. The first hominins to successfully deal with the challenges of Europe's forested environments were, in Gamble's (1986) view, the modern human hunter-gatherers of the Mesolithic, in the earlier phases of the current interglacial, the Holocene.

However, now, two decades later, we have good evidence that Last Interglacial Neanderthals as well as earlier hominins thrived in forested environments of the European Pleistocene, at least from MIS 11 onward (Preece et al. 2007; Roebroeks 2007). How did they do that? In this paper, we suggest that Neanderthals were not just passive 'users' of Pleistocene landscapes; instead they may have been moulding their landscapes, possibly to a degree not unlike that documented for more recent prehistoric hunter-gatherers. Before developing that suggestion we will give a short review of the background to the debate mentioned above, that is, an overview of the ecological problems at stake as well as a short overview of the data for the association of Neanderthals with wooded environments. Next we will move to a discussion of the ways hunter-gatherers manage their (wooded) natural environment, as exemplified in the ethnographic (and later archaeological) record from various parts of the world. That overview will be put to use in the next section, which deals with the various possibilities of how Neanderthals may have dealt with forested environments. We will argue there that the use of fire may have been an important tool for dealing with such settings.

BACKGROUND

In the 1980s and early 1990s Neanderthals, inferred to have made no contribution to modern human ancestry at all, were seen by many as very different from modern humans in most aspects of their behaviour (Stringer and Gamble 1993). In the domain of subsistence scavenging was considered an important way of obtaining animal resources for Neanderthals. Given their limited hunting capacities, 'Man the Shoveler' (Gamble 1987) would have preferred areas with high animal biomass and its resulting predictable natural mortalities, avoiding the challenging forested environments of the Pleistocene interglacials. Starting from such considerations and extrapolating the absence of traces of hominin occupation of Britain during the Last Interglacial, Gamble (1987, 1986, 1999) developed a model for the structure of the environments preferred by Neanderthals. In this view these consisted of the more open type of environments, in between the 'glacial' and 'interglacial' extremes of the Pleistocene cycles. The lower availability of large animals in forested environments and their low predictability reduced the chances of encountering an animal, 'either dead or alive' (Gamble 1999: 230), to a dietary threshold that Neanderthals could not deal with: 'Let me make it clear: they never lived in those 8% forests' (Gamble 1992a: 569).

Alternatively, Roebroeks et al. (1992) argued that the archaeological record did indicate that Neanderthals were present in the interglacial environments of the Last Interglacial, the Eemian, in Europe. In their view, the apparent rarity of Neanderthal traces in interglacial deposits was the result of various factors, including the short duration of the interglacials and large scale taphonomic processes as well as research-historical factors (Roebroeks et al. 1992; Roebroeks and Speleers 2002). The discovery of a full-interglacial Eemian site at Caours in the Somme valley, in northern France, ended the specific debate on how to read the distribution patterns of Last Interglacial (Eemian) sites

(Antoine et al. 2006). In this debate, some had by then retreated to a focus on the absence of traces in western, 'oceanic' Europe, explaining the – by then accepted – presence of Eemian sites in central Europe by the inferred more open 'mosaic' character of interglacial environments there (Ashton 2002). The excavations at Caours have yielded various archaeological find levels in Eemian fluvial deposits, associated with a fauna of full interglacial character, including *Dama dama*, *Capreolus capreolus*, the forest rhino *Stephanorhinus kirchbergensis* and *Sus scrofa*. Plant remains fossilised in tufa also testify to the full interglacial character of this Middle Palaeolithic site (Antoine et al. 2006). At Neumark-Nord 2 (Germany), we are able to assign the Neanderthal presence to specific pollen zones of an early part of the Eemian interglacial (see below, and Sier et al. 2010). With the recent discoveries at the site of Caours and the rich evidence from Neumark-Nord 2 (Sier et al. 2010), the presence of Neanderthals in Eemian forested conditions in western and central parts of Europe is now well established.

That is: with the exception of Britain, where still no archaeological sites can be attributed to the Last Interglacial. A comparison between MIS 7 and Last Interglacial sites (Lewis et al. 2011) supports previous interpretations that hominins were absent or scarce in Britain during the Last Interglacial. If we take this interpretation at face value and compare the British absence to the presence of Neanderthals in western Europe during fully forested, temperate conditions, following Lewis et al. (2011), factors at stake may be the insularity of Britain during the Last Interglacial, possibly together with low population levels in north-west Europe, an area that was often at the fringe of the Neanderthal distribution (Hublin and Roebroeks 2009; Roebroeks et al. 2011). It needs to be stressed though that even for Britain one still cannot rule out a taphonomical explanation for the Last Interglacial absence thus far: as discussed by Turner, C. (2000), the British Last Interglacial deposits are often fluvial, representing the infills of floodplain cut-off lakes, and hence cover only very restricted intervals of interglacial time. This is in contrast to the more complete interglacial coverage recorded in basins of glacial origin which yielded most of the central European sites (Roebroeks et al. 1992; see also Lewis et al. 2011).

Moving beyond the Eemian, recent years have also witnessed the accumulation of evidence that pre-modern hominins were able to survive in full interglacial environments before the Last Interglacial. For example, the rich paleo-environmental evidence from the English Hoxnian (MIS 11?) site at Beeches pit is associated with primary context flint artefacts which show that hominins were present from the beginning of the interglacial phase, through the height of it and persisted into the ensuing cold phase (Preece et al. 2007).

Gamble's insistence on the challenging character of forested environments for hunter-gatherers still stands: 'The effect of the forest was to reduce the predictability and biomass of the mosaics to a point where the expectation for hominids of encountering an animal resource, either dead or alive, declined to a threshold where dietary requirements could not be met without some form of intensification of effort' (Gamble 1999: 230). 'This intensification is a feature of the archaeological record of the Mesolithic where populations of northern Europe coped with a much reduced animal biomass and a succession of forest environments' (ibid.: 434). Now that we know that Neanderthals were also able to cope with (some of) these challenges, how did they actually do this?

SURVIVING THE FORESTS

One way to deal with the lower predictability and biomass in forested environments and the resulting higher search costs is by manipulating the environment to improve the predictability of prey animals as well as of plant food resources. The ethnographic record contains many examples of such types of search cost-reducing landscape management, for instance from Australia and Tasmania. When the first Europeans arrived in Tasmania, they were struck by the park-like landscapes they encountered in this 'uttermost end of the earth' (Gamble 1992b). John Glover (1836) fossilised some of these open landscapes in his early nineteenth-century paintings, commenting that '...It is possible almost every where, to drive a carriage as readily as in a Gentleman's Park in England' (Figure 10.1). As described by Gammage (2008), some did exactly that, with a certain David Collins declaring on oath in 1812: '...the forest land...is very open. To give an idea of the open country, the first intercourse we had by land from Hobart's Town to Launceston [authors' comment: a distance of about 200 km], a loaded cart was drawn without the

Figure 10.1: John Glover (1767–1849), Mill's Plain, 1836. Copyright Tasmanian Museum and Art Gallery, Hobart. Reproduced with permission.

necessity of felling a tree ... In general a very rich pasturage; it is a fine, beautiful picturesque country as can be' (quoted in Gammage 2008: 243).

Tasmanian Aboriginal burning kept the land open, and many of the open hills of Glover's paintings are covered in dense forests now. Some of the early nineteenth century explorers of Australia and Tasmania knew that Aboriginals fired the country to attract game, but it was only in the 1960s that the systematic way in which they used fire as a tool to continuously modify their surroundings came to be studied. Rhys Jones aptly coined the term 'fire-stick farming' for the practices of creating more complex vegetation mosaics by systematic and repeated burning (Jones 1969). It is still debated whether Australian Aboriginals intended the results of this firing, but there is little doubt that fire helped to manage the presence of resources by increasing the local availability and predictability of game as well as plant species, making mosaics of fresh grass to concentrate feed, and trees or old grass to shelter game and hunters. There is also debate over the scale of influence of Aboriginal burning in Australia. A simple caricature of the debate asks how the 'biological furniture' of the landscape was influenced by Aboriginal burning, if at all. Some see these effects as very marginal and Aboriginals as part of the Australian biological furniture, whereas others assume that they were actively rearranging the biological furniture with their burning practices (Bowman 1998). A recent study concludes that in the long term, Aboriginals were not using fire very frequently and very extensively in the landscape, but much more selectively around their campsites and where it worked for resources, hence on a more local scale (Mooney et al. 2011).

There exists a wide range of ethnographic sources from other parts of the world showing that woodland, bush and grassland burning was a practice carried out by many foragers, with a wide variety of benefits, mostly focused on creating favourable habitats for the foraging and the hunting of small and big game (see Daniau et al. 2010; Rolland 2004). The signal from the North American record is nicely illustrated by this quote from Pyne's *Fire in America:*

> ...the modification of the American continent by fire at the hands of Asian immigrants [now called American Indians, Native Americans, or First Nations/People] was the result of repeated, controlled, surface burns on a cycle of one to three years ... So extensive were the cumulative effects of these modifications that it may be said that the general consequence of the Indian occupation of the New World was to replace forested land with grassland or savannah, or, where the forest persisted, to open it up and free it from underbrush. Most of the impenetrable woods encountered by explorers were in bogs or swamps from which fire was excluded; naturally drained landscape was nearly everywhere burned. Conversely, almost wherever the European went, forests followed. The Great American Forest may be more a product of settlement than a victim of it.
>
> (Pyne 1982: 79–80)

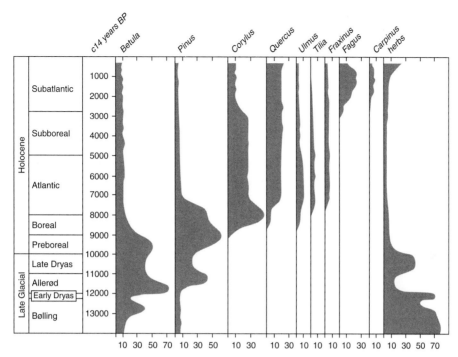

Figure 10.2: A generalised Late Pleistocene and Holocene pollen diagram of the Netherlands, after Van Zeist (1970). Tall deciduous trees like oak (*Quercus*), elm (*Ulmus*), lime (*Tilia*), ash (*Fraxinus*), beech (*Fagus*) and hornbeam (*Carpinus*) gain dominance after hazel (*Corylus*).

Notwithstanding the importance of these firing practices, both the exact role of the use of fire as a tool in landscape management as well as the intentional character of that use are difficult to study, even with recent and sub-recent hunter-gatherers, as shown by the current debate in Australia. It is obviously significantly more difficult to make explicit statements about the (intentional character of) use of fire in the prehistoric past. Nevertheless, such statements have been and are being made, especially relating to activities of Early and Mid-Holocene hunter-gatherers.

Palaeoenvironmental proxies retrieved from Mesolithic sites, in particular pollen and charcoal, have led a number of scientists to suggest that these foragers manipulated their surroundings to a considerable extent by the use of fire (for instance Smith 1970; Simmons and Innes 1987). These Mesolithic hunter-gatherers lived in a period when woodland gradually replaced the open 'Mammoth Steppe'--type vegetation of the end of the Last Glacial. At first the forests consisted of relatively open pine woods, but the climax vegetation to follow was a thermophilous deciduous forest, generally supposed to be characterised by a closed canopy, with not much of a herb vegetation growing underneath. However, before this climax was reached large parts of Europe were covered by hazel woods (*Corylus*) (Figure 10.2).

The prevalent explanation is that hazel arrived earlier than other deciduous trees from the refugia where they survived the Last Glacial Maximum and therefore could cover large areas before being supplanted by taller trees – however, it is remarkable that the period of hazel dominance lasted so long. At present hazel occurs mostly as an understorey and forest-edge shrub in deciduous forests and the one-time existence of hazel woods is still puzzling. Hazel stands are essentially a sub-climax vegetation type, that is, they represent a vegetational stage in which development into a true climax is inhibited. One of the explanations of the seemingly protracted hazel period points to the role of Mesolithic hunter-gatherers: by manipulating their environment through cutting and ringing, but especially by burning, these people would have created (and/or maintained) open spaces for their game animals to graze. By strategically positioning these 'pastures' in the landscape they would have reduced their hunting search costs. An extra bonus would have consisted in the larger amount of hazelnuts to be gathered (Holst 2010). Mason (2000) has discussed the possible role of fire in managing other potential plant food resources that are thus far not considered in detail, such as acorns, the fruits of oaks. This hypothesis has its roots in the frequent co-occurrence of Mesolithic sites with charcoal and charred hazelnuts. Indeed, hazel is very fire resistant and hazel stands may have been created and maintained by a regular use of fire. The detection of fire specific relationships in the palaeoenvironmental record is difficult though. Hence, the idea of humanly maintained hazel woods interspersed by open spaces is not a generally accepted one. Clark et al. (1989), for instance, wrote with regard to the Northern Alpine forelands that the hypothesis of maintenance by fire of hazel scrubland is not supported by charcoal data. Tinner and Lotter (2001: 551) state that '. . . on the basis of our data we conclude that the early Holocene high abundance of *C. avellana* [hazel] in Europe was climatically caused'. More recently, Finsinger et al. (2006) drew attention to the fact that in the Southern Alpine forelands the Holocene expansion of deciduous trees like elm, oak and lime is not preceded but followed by a hazel period. Hazel arrived and expanded much later than elsewhere. Pollen diagrams combined with charcoal particle counting show that high percentages of hazel due to the opening up of the landscape are accompanied by relatively high amounts of charcoal; the authors demonstrate that the expansion of hazel was favoured by a combination of high seasonality, summer droughts and frequent fires, which helped hazel to out-compete trees like oak.

The influence of fire is remarkable. Finsinger et al. (2006) ascribe these fires to natural causes, not to hunter-gatherer activities. Why? Their argument is that a similar pattern, mixed deciduous forest followed by hazel wood, is also observed during previous interglacials; it is a natural sequence – the implicit assumption being that for those earlier periods a hominin impact on vegetation can be excluded. But is this assumption correct? For instance where Neanderthals are concerned?

NEANDERTHALS IN THE FOREST

Zagwijn (1989) has described the Eemian vegetation of large parts of western and central Europe as a broad-leaved forest. That is, obviously, the large picture. Zooming in, open areas would have been discernible, for example, along wide river valleys, as open patches within forested landscapes as the result of natural fires, of droughts, storms and the activities of the large mammals which roamed Last Interglacial environments. The Eemian climate was oceanic far into central Europe, probably because the Eemian Sea had invaded many coastal lowlands and occupied the entire Baltic basin. This connected the North Sea, with the White Sea and the Arctic Ocean (Zagwijn 1989), and as a result, the forest succession during the Eemian was uniform over large parts of the continent and the vegetational gradient very gradual. And Neanderthals were present in these environments, both in western and in central Europe. Zooarchaeological studies have shown that Neanderthals subsisted in these environments as efficient and flexible hunters mostly preying on medium-sized to large mammals (Gaudzinski-Windheuser and Niven 2009; Gaudzinski-Windheuser and Roebroeks 2011). Neanderthals primarily relied on meat and fat from larger mammals for their daily subsistence, and isotopic studies reinforce this picture (Richards 2007). In the middle latitudes, the proteins consumed by Neanderthals were overwhelmingly of animal origin during cold periods as well as during the last interglacial (Bocherens et al. 1999). Neanderthals therefore appear to be highly carnivorous, occupying a high trophic position focused on the consumption of medium- and large-bodied terrestrial herbivores, probably already from the middle part of the Middle Pleistocene onward (Roebroeks 2001; Voormolen 2008b). Nutritional ecology studies however indicate that Neanderthals could not have survived on terrestrial animal products alone. Apart from the problem of protein poisoning, under-consumption of carbohydrates and micronutrients also could have constituted a major health issue. Obtaining a greater diversity of essential nutrients could only be achieved by consuming a greater diversity of food types, outside of the 'large mammal' spectrum, such as plant foods. As suggested by Hockett (2011) though, consumption of a diversity of animal types (such as fish, birds and shellfish) could have acted as a substitute for specific micronutrients found in specific plant foods. Small game stood at least occasionally on the Neanderthal menu, including tortoises, rabbits and birds, as documented from some sites on the southern edge of their range, for instance at Bolomor Cave in Spain (Blasco 2006, 2008; Blasco and Fernández Peris 2009; Hardy and Moncel 2011). There is also some rare evidence for the consumption of birds from northern sites, such as from Salzgitter-Lebenstedt in Germany. We also know that Neanderthals did consume (unknown) amounts of plant foods, through a series of studies documenting such consumption over the whole geographic range of the Neanderthal lineage, such as from Shanidar in Iraq up to Spy in Belgium (Henry et al. 2011).

Given their accomplishment in hunting large (and often dangerous) mammals with simple tools (Dusseldorp 2009), it is probable that Neanderthals invested significantly in their knowledge of animal behaviour. Predicting the whereabouts of animals is obviously likely to be more difficult than that of plant foods (Kelly 1995: 97–98). Where diet is relatively narrow, as is argued to be the case for Neanderthals (Stiner et al. 2000; Richards et al. 2001), search costs (the costs incurred while searching for the preferred prey animals) represent a large proportion of the costs of foraging (Roebroeks and Verpoorte 2009). In this context, an increased ability to predict the whereabouts of animals would have been a key way to reduce foraging costs (Kelly 1995). Neanderthal investment in detailed knowledge of animal behaviour and other clues to the whereabouts and predictability of prey could have taken the form of learning or social transmission of a body of knowledge to juveniles and the acquisition or sharing of up-to-date information among adults. In this context, efficient communication between individual hunters, and between adults and juveniles, would have been valuable. Unfortunately, such behaviour is difficult to detect in the archaeological record (Roebroeks and Verpoorte 2009).

Another way to reduce search costs could have consisted of using technology to make the presence of prey animals more predictable, and possibly even to increase their numbers – as with modern hunter-gatherers, fire could have been an important tool to achieve this. There now exists good evidence of the use of fire by Neanderthals (Roebroeks and Villa 2011a), even though there is no consensus about important details of the character of that usage, including the production of fire by Neanderthals (Roebroeks and Villa 2011b; Sandgathe et al. 2011). We can observe that Neanderthals used fire in a wide range of settings, over at least 250,000 years, and for a variety of purposes, which included the preparation of food and the usage of fire as a tool to produce new materials. Especially the finds of pitches, produced out of birch bark, chronologically scattered over more than 100,000 years, make it difficult to envisage that Neanderthals developed a hafting technology which involved complicated ways of producing pitches using fire as a tool without the know-how to produce fire itself (Roebroeks and Villa 2011b). There is some evidence of cooking a variety of local plant foods from the site of Shanidar in Iraq, suggestive of a dietary adaptation based on the use of fire (Henry et al. 2011) as well as of the importance of plant foods.

In the domain of the possible use of fire for landscape management, Daniau et al. (2010) recently addressed the question whether Palaeolithic communities, both Neanderthals and modern humans, modified natural biomass burning variability during MIS 3 and 2 in Europe. They were particularly interested whether modern human populations colonising Europe may have introduced fire as an ecosystem tool. If extensive fire use for ecosystem management was indeed a component of the modern human package, one would expect to find major disturbances in the signal of fire proxies associated with and following the colonisation of Eurasia by modern humans. In their study of micro-charcoal particles from two deep sea cores off Iberia and France, spanning the period c. 70–10 ka, they did not recover any sign that Upper Palaeolithic humans made any difference. They concluded that either Neanderthals and modern humans did not affect the natural fire regime, or they did so in comparable ways.

A CASE STUDY: NEUMARK-NORD 2

In recent years we have been involved in the multi-disciplinary study of a Last Interglacial Middle Palaeolithic site in East Germany. The site, Neumark-Nord 2, yields some tantalising evidence for a causal relationship between the presence of fire proxies, changes in the natural environment and the ubiqui-tous presence of traces of Neanderthal activities (Sier et al. 2010). The site is located approximately 35 km west of Leipzig, Germany (Figure 10.3).

This area of the Geisel Valley contains a series of Middle and Late Pleisto-cene sedimentary basins, rich with faunal remains and Palaeolithic artefacts. The basins, formed by isostatic movements induced by lignite diapirism (Eissman 2002; Mania and Mania 2008), include the sites of Neumark-Nord 1 (Mania et al. 1990; Mania and Mania 2008) and Neumark-Nord 3 (Laurat and Brühl 2006). Extensive excavations were carried out at Neumark-Nord 2 between 2004 and 2008. An excavated area of c. 500 m^2 yielded c. 20,000 Middle Palaeolithic flint artefacts and c. 120,000 faunal remains, dominated by

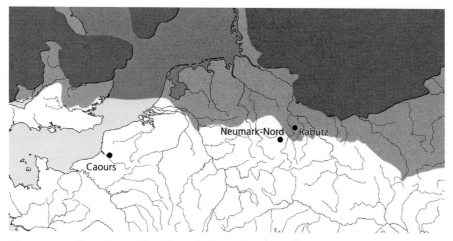

Figure 10.3: Location of Last Interglacial archaeological sites mentioned in the text. Light grey = the distribution of the Late Saalian (MIS 6) glaciers; Dark grey = the Weichselian (MIS 2) ice extension.

warm-temperate species (Sier et al. 2010). Multi-disciplinary studies of the Neumark-Nord 2 basin infill produced detailed climatic and chronological proxy records, which have shown that the archaeological find level NN2/2 preserved in the basin dates to the early part of the Last Interglacial. The age of the interglacial succession is constrained by the underlying diamicton, a till of Late Saalian/Drenthe age and by the overlying Weichselian deposits. Amino acid racemisation analysis of *Bithynia tentaculata opercula* (Penkman, in Sier et al. 2010) suggests that the interglacial deposits are contemporaneous with those at the Eemian localities near Amersfoort and Amsterdam, the Netherlands (e.g., Zagwijn 1961; Cleveringa et al. 2000; van Leeuwen et al. 2000). Thermoluminescence (TL) dating of five heated flint artefacts from the interglacial find levels yielded a weighted mean age of 126 ± 6 ka (Richter in Sier et al. 2010). Study of the basin infill also yielded a high-resolution record of the palaeomagnetic Blake-event (Sier et al. 2010).

Sedimentological and soil micromorphological studies indicate a gradual infilling of the basin with fine-grained calcareous silts, a near continuous process with very little evidence of soil formation during periods of non-deposition (Sier et al. 2010). Pollen is well preserved and demonstrates an interglacial succession that is typical for the Eemian interglacial in northern Europe: the succession starts with Pollen Zone I and ends with Zone VI/VII (*sensu* Menke and Tynni 1984) at the top of the sections. This further constrains the duration of deposition represented in these deposits (Sier et al. 2010), with the small basin most likely reflecting strictly local vegetation. This high sedimentation rate, and subsequent lack of soil formation and bioturbation, in addition to favourable local taphonomic conditions, has resulted in a well-stratified, well-preserved assemblage of mostly anthropogenically modified faunal remains.

Flint artefacts and (in general humanly modified) well-preserved faunal remains are present through the major part of the basin's infill, with the bulk of the material present in the fine-grained sediments dating to the earlier part of the dominance of *Corylus* (Figure 10.4). Studies of the site formation processes which created the horizontal and vertical distribution patterns of the finds are in their infancy yet. Over the (maximum) 2000 years of hominin presence there, the water body was prone to temporary drying out, leading to repeated expansion and contraction of the water body and shifting of the location of the shore zones. Primary flint knapping scatters have not been documented, even though knapping took place at the location; this suggests that some (limited) lateral displacement of the finds may have occurred.

The zooarchaeological record of the find bearing deposits at Neumark-Nord 2 is dominated by large mammals, bovids (*Bos primigenius* and/or *Bison priscus*), horse (*Equus* sp.) and medium-sized cervids (*Cervus elaphus* and *Dama dama*) but also includes other warm-temperate species such as straight-tusked elephant (*Elephas antiquus*), bear (*Ursus* sp.), boar (*Sus scrofa*), small carnivores

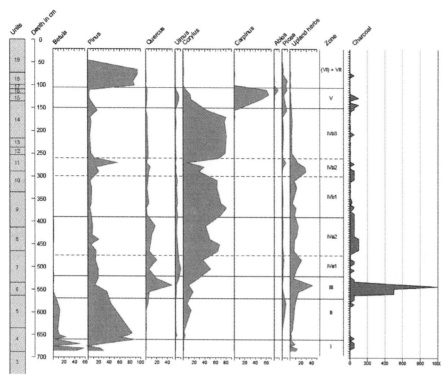

Figure 10.4: Pollen percentage curve (selected taxa) for the last interglacial sequence at Neumark-Nord 2. Pollen zones after Menke and Tynni (1984). The charcoal peak in Pollen Zone III coincides with the beginning of Neanderthal presence, with the bulk of the material present in unit 8. Artefacts occur up to the middle part of pollen zone IVb3 (unit 14). Charcoal expressed in number of particles per 5 litres of sediment (see Sier *et al.* 2011 for a detailed description of the sequence and the lithological units).

and pond tortoise (*Emys orbicularis*). Bones show abundant traces of butchery and marrow extraction, indications that they are related to Neanderthal subsistence activities there. The numerous flint artefacts found are the by-product of various simple ways of producing cores and flakes, with simple notches, denticulates and scrapers forming major tool categories.

The contemporary pollen record at the site evokes a relatively open land-scape during the deposition of the first metres of silt, as witnessed by the presence of a luxuriant herb vegetation during pollen zones III-IVb2 (Figure 10.4, upland herbs curve). Either trees were scarce close to the pool with forested areas at some distance, or trees or clumps of trees were standing individually or growing in groves nearby. A light mixed deciduous wood was replaced by a light hazel growth but the herbs remained (zones IVa2–IVb2). Later on the hazel woods became dense, to be followed by an equally dense hornbeam forest (Bakels, in Sier et al. 2010; Bakels, in press).

A detailed study of the charcoal present in the infill of the Neumark Nord 2 basin (Kuijper, in press) shows that charcoal particles are present all through the interglacial sequence (Figure 10.4). The particles retrieved by Kuijper are generally small (<5 mm), and not abraded, suggesting that they were not subjected to any significant movement. They show a very noticeable peak at the beginning of the Neanderthal presence at the site, with ten times the amount of charcoal of any other peak in the sequence. A potentially more important observation is that the charcoal peak and the beginning of a strong Neanderthal presence at the site also coincide with the first rise in the upland herbs curve. Kuijper (in press) was also able to retrieve charred plant remains from the main archaeological layer: fragments of hazelnut shell, kernels of sloe plum and acorns. Hazelnuts and acorns, the latter after being roasted or leached, are even potential staple foods. The Neumark-Nord 2 finds are not the only instance of charred plants in the region. Exposures of contemporaneous (Last Interglacial) find levels at the neighbouring site of Rabutz (Figure 10.4), studied before and during World War I, also yielded charred hazelnuts (Toepfer 1958; Weber 1920). The fruits are indicative of non-closed-canopy conditions. Hazelnuts and sloe plums grow on shrubs along forest edges and oak trees bear most acorns when not standing in a dense forest. Of course, the findings do not constitute direct solid evidence for the dietary use of these plants by Neanderthals. But it is a possibility.

It is tempting to compare the Neumark-Nord 2 data with the Holocene data of Europe and especially those obtained in the Southern forelands of the Alps. Finsinger et al. (2006) dismissed the idea that hazel might have benefited from fire set by Mesolithic people with the argument that comparable sequences are observed in previous interglacials. But we may turn this argument around. What if Neanderthals manipulated their environment through fire? What if the landscape around the Neumark-Nord 2 pool was not only kept open for a long stretch of time by climatic factors and/or by the trampling, eating and bulldozering activities of large herbivores, but also by hominins and their fires?

The former presence of fire around the Neumark-Nord 2 pool can be inferred from the heated flints recovered during excavations as well as from the charred bone and plant remains and the charcoal fragments. Do these traces of fire reflect natural fires or Neanderthal campfires, or possibly even vegetation actively burnt down by Neanderthals? At the very least the fact that the beginning of the hominin presence around the pool coincides with the charcoal maximum, as well as with the first rise of the upland herbs, indicates that the charcoal particles are not simply relatable to a few Neanderthal camp fires. The fires that produced (some of) the charcoal probably influenced the local vegetation, which is suggestive of a causal relationship between burning, hominin presence and an increase in the upland herb curve – even though the character of that burning remains elusive.

Fire could have been a tool in hunting activities around the pool. Animals probably visited the pool to drink. Fire could have increased the attraction of the pool to animals (and hence: their predictability in the landscape), as a result of repeated burning of the area surrounding the pool creating attractive pasture grounds for larger mammals. This was certainly an easy strategy for keen wildlife observers who were routinely using, if not producing, fire. If the data had been obtained from a Holocene site, they would, at least by some, be taken as tantalising evidence for hunter-gatherer landscape management.

DISCUSSION AND CONCLUSIONS

Our speculative scenario implies a shift from seeing Neanderthals as part of the biological 'furniture' to their possible role as movers of the furniture. This should not be so surprising, as all animals move the furniture by modifying their environments in a process that is called 'niche construction' (Laland et al. 2000). These modifications vary in their effect on the environments, with some vertebrates constructing artefacts in the process of moulding: these include burrow systems with underground passages, interconnected chambers and multiple entrances or the well-known landscape engineering works of beavers (Coles 2006). Many animals alter their landscapes to suit their needs, from the small leaf-cutter ants up to the elephants, which create their own waterholes and enlarge them while bathing and carrying away copious amounts of mud on their bodies.

Our reading of the Neumark-Nord 2 evidence suggests that Neanderthals may have manipulated the vegetation around the pool by means of fire. We are not suggesting that in general a vegetation succession with a hazel period following the expansion of taller deciduous forest indicates landscape management, whether in the Holocene or in earlier interglacials. It is more plausible to attribute the late arrival of hazel at sites like Neumark-Nord 2, to natural causes. The patchy vegetation of hazel scrub and open space overgrown with herbs as seen in the first half of the hazel period at this site could be attributed to the attractiveness of the pool for large animals such as straight-tusked elephants coming there to drink, combined with the fact that Neumark-Nord 2 is situated in the rain shadow of the Harz mountains. The aridity, the wildfires which go with drought, and a concentration of large browsers and grazers may have been the main cause of the relatively open landscape with hazel. This herbivore-filled kind of landscape must have been very attractive to hunter-gatherers. Nevertheless, it is only one step further to postulate that their fires may have occasionally created bush fires which supplemented the natural fires and in this way they may have influenced their environment. Why not take still one step further and support the idea that intentional landscape burning was practised by Neanderthals on a local scale? Intentions do not fossilise though. However, the significant rise in the upland herbs curve which coincides with the strong charcoal peak and the first signs of a Neanderthal presence is at least very suggestive of such a scenario.

Independent of this specific speculative exercise, the context of the debate of Neanderthals dealing with the challenges of forested environments has changed significantly over the last two decades. The view that Neanderthals were simply a part of the landscape furniture, essentially having no effect on the land, the wildlife and the ecosystems at large, has proven to be incorrect. They were hunter-gatherers equipped with a simple yet efficient technology who had been around in Europe for a few hundreds of thousands of years already, and were present in a wide range of environments. We have also come to appreciate that they had some powerful ecosystem engineering technologies at their disposal: hunting weapons, fire and, importantly, the knowledge to put these to good use. In the Levant there are multiple lines of evidence that Neanderthals even over-hunted some mammal species around Kebara Cave, Israel (Speth 2004; Speth and Clark 2006). In the domain of their tool kits, even current-day experimental archaeologists are still struggling to reproduce the birch bark pitch Neanderthals were able to extract, at least 200,000 years ago and which they used to haft their stone tools (Mazza et al. 2006; Palmer 2007; Roebroeks and Villa 2011a).

The emphasis in this paper was on highlighting a possible role of fire in Neanderthal landscape engineering. While this role is not visible in the palaeoenvironmental record on regional scale, we think that on a local scale there now exists some tantalising evidence, reported here for Neumark-Nord 2. On a local scale fire may have helped in concentrating game animals around specific locations in the landscape, in attracting game and in increasing the yield of the natural vegetation's plant food resources.

We hope to have shown that this speculative exercise has some heuristic value, and that it will be taken in the same vein as many of Gamble's eye opening papers which served as heuristic devices for new types of research. We occasionally need to move beyond what is clearly observable, or we might run the risk of missing the forest for the trees. Seeing Neanderthals and other early hominins as potential landscape managers will force us to look differently at the dichotomy of 'natural' versus 'humanly modified' landscapes, and to insert a fresh perspective on landscapes in our mind.

CHAPTER 11

LATE PLEISTOCENE HOMININ ADAPTATIONS IN GREECE

PARASKEVI ELEFANTI AND GILBERT MARSHALL

INTRODUCTION

The aim of this paper is to take a region-wide look at variation in the distribution of Palaeolithic sites in Greece as a basis for tackling broader questions about hominin perception and use of landscapes and how this changed over time. This research is founded on the results of the *Prehistoric Stones of Greece* project (SOG), which set out to collate and standardise information from field surveys and excavations and to present their results for others to use. The focus of the project was chipped stone, in particular from the Palaeolithic, Mesolithic and Neolithic (Elefanti et al. 2010). The sources used include published and grey literature and we are very grateful to the large numbers of individuals and institutions who allowed us to access this primary information. All of the data presented in this paper is based on our database, which can be accessed from the Archaeology Data Service at the University of York in the United Kingdom.

Greece is one of the most intensively surveyed locations anywhere, if not *the* most. The use of field survey as a tool for locating sites and documenting landscapes took off in the late 1970s (Alcock and Cherry 2004). The result was major growth in all types of surveys, mostly Bronze Age and Classical, but also those focusing on the Palaeolithic and Mesolithic (Elefanti et al. forthcoming). These followed on from a small number of influential projects begun in the 1960s, along the Pineios River in Thessaly (Milojcic et al. 1965), Ellis in the western Peloponnese (Chavaillon et al. 1969), Epirus and western Macedonia (Dakaris et al. 1964) and the Ionian islands (Sordinas 1969).

In this paper we focus on sites in which Palaeolithic material has been reported, comprising 471 of the total 720 sites so far in the SOG archive. The remaining 249 have Mesolithic and/or Neolithic and later material. Of these 471 sites, most (441) were identified during just 37 field survey projects. All have reported chipped stone artefacts and in a small number of cases human skeletal remains, definitely or possibly attributed to the Palaeolithic.

Our aim is to take a country-wide look at the distribution and nature of the Palaeolithic in Greece, from its beginnings until the end of the Pleistocene. We focus on all categories of sites, from in situ to surface scatters, and use this larger dataset to investigate changes in the spatial distribution of settlement. This is set against the evidence for changing environmental and climatic conditions, while mindful of imbalances in research intensity across the country and the difficulties in combining data from different types of sites, periods and history of investigation.

DATA SOURCES AND METHODS OF PRESENTATION

Our dataset is derived from both published and unpublished sources, with the site as the basic unit of reference. This is any location where material has been collected, and range from major in situ, to isolated stray finds and material in reworked contexts. Evaluating data from such a broad range of locations is difficult, with biases of recovery, preservation and presentation. These are common issues of concern when dealing with surface material (Alcock et al. 1994: 138). All the sites in this study have reported chipped stone, fauna and in a few cases human remains and other objects. The dataset includes only those sites for which we were able to obtain accurate grid coordinates using maps, photographs, descriptions and site visits.

For comparative purposes we have divided Greece into four regions: north, east, south and west (Figure 11.1). These broadly follow existing regional boundaries, but are orientated north-to-south along the Pindos Mountains, along the Gulf of Corinth and across from Epirus to the Aegean in the north.

THE GREEK PALAEOLITHIC

The SOG dataset contains information about 471 sites with Palaeolithic material (Figure 11.2, Table 11.1). Most were in the west (53.8%), east (20%) and south (19.8%), with relatively few from the north (3.2%). Counts from western, eastern and northern Greece include near-shore island sites which were probably connected to the mainland during much of the Middle and Upper Palaeolithic. There were also sites on four offshore central and northern Aegean islands (0.9%), two probably connected to mainland Turkey during the later Palaeolithic, and eleven (2.3%) reported from the southern Aegean islands of Crete and Gavdos.

Most sites (418, 88.7%) were open-air, of which seven have been excavated, four in the west in Epirus and on the Aegean islands of Lesvos, Limnos and Kythnos (Figure 11.1). Most (229, 55%) open-air sites were at low elevation located below 200 m, with 63 (15%) between 200–599 m, and 126 (30%) above 600 m. Based on published accounts, we estimate that 148 of open-air sites are probably more or less in situ, 167 reworked through fluvial or slope processes,

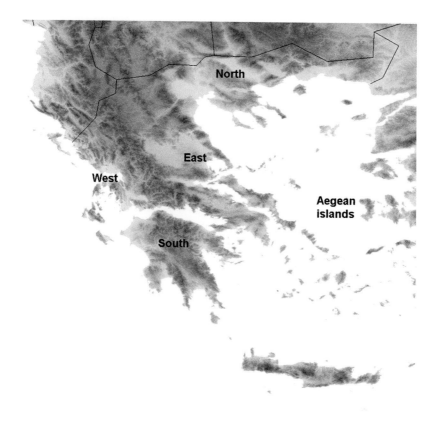

Figure 11.1: The regions of Greece, north, south, east and west.

and 103 are of unknown derivation and probably stray finds. Caves and rockshelters (hereafter referred to as caves) were much less common (53, 11.3%), of which 30 have been excavated. The majority are in the limestone regions of southern (21, 39.6%) and western Greece (21, 39.6%), with fewer (8, 15.1%) in the east and the north (3, 5.7%) (Table 11.1). Most caves (31, 59%) were located below 200 m (includes Theopetra and Ulbricht caves), with 12 (23%) between 200–599 m (8 in the west), and 10 (19%) above 600 m (all in the west). We estimate that twelve caves were probably major residential sites, although biased towards those which have been excavated.

Most artefact assemblages were small. Counts were collated for 343 Palaeo-lithic sites for which information was available, as category 3 (<20 pieces), 2 (20–100 pieces), and 1 (>100 pieces) (*sensu* Bailey et al. 1997). Category 3 sites were the most common (237, 69.1%), and were the only ones from northern Greece (Table 11.2). Category 1 and 2 sites were most common in the south (52 in total, 59%), west (45, 28.1%) and east (9, 10.8%), though admittedly these results are biased towards the largest surface-collected and excavated sites for which more comprehensive artefact counts are available.

TABLE 11.1: *Number of recorded Palaeolithic cave and open-air sites (n=471)*

Region	Open-air		Caves (and rockshelters)		Total	
	N	%	N	%	N	%
North	13	2.9	3	5.7	**16**	**3.2**
South	72	17.3	21	39.6	**93**	**19.8**
East	86	20.6	8	15.1	**94**	**20.0**
West	232	55.6	21	39.6	**253**	**53.8**
Offshore Aegean islands	4	1.0	–	–	**4**	**0.9**
South Aegean islands (Crete and Gavdos)	11	2.6	–	–	**11**	**2.3**
Total	**418**	**88.7**	**53**	**11.3**	**471**	

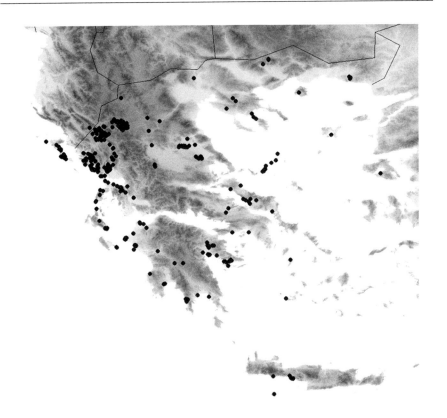

Figure 11.2: Reported Palaeolithic sites (n=471).

Plotted against elevation (Figure 11.3), all three size categories were common below 200 m. They were rare above this point and absent above 1000 m, although with the probable exception of the high elevation sites in the Grevena district (Efstratiou et al. 2006), for which counts are unavailable. Category 3 sites were common at all elevations, with 63% (149)

TABLE 11.2: *Numbers of reported artefacts per site; category 3 (<20 pieces), 2 (20–100 pieces), 1 (>100 pieces) (sensu Bailey et al. 1997).*

Size category	I		2		3		Total	
Region	**N**	**%**	**N**	**%**	**N**	**%**	**N**	**%**
North	–	–	–	–	3	1.3	**3**	**0.9**
South	21	50	31	48.4	36	15.2	**88**	**25.7**
East	4	9.5	5	7.8	83	35	**92**	**26.8**
West	17	40.5	28	43.8	115	48.5	**160**	**46.6**
Total	**42**		**64**		**237**		**343**	

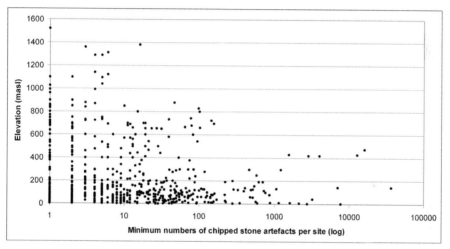

Figure 11.3: Absolute numbers (log) of artefacts per site (n = 343) plotted against elevation.

below 200 m. Larger categories 1 and 2 sites were mostly below 200 m (90, 85%), apart from the cluster of five excavated caves, four in Epirus and one in Thessaly between 300–500 m.

THE LOWER, MIDDLE AND UPPER PALAEOLITHIC

In this section we look in more detail at those sites with material attributed to either/and the Lower, Middle or Upper Palaeolithic (Table 11.3). A total of 292 sites had material or dates attributed to one or more these phases, with 403 attributed contexts; 36 Lower, 242 Middle and 125 Upper Palaeolithic. The larger number of contexts reflect multiple-phase use at some sites.

The Lower Palaeolithic

Sites definitely or possibly associated with the Lower Palaeolithic have been reported at 36 locations (Table 11.3; Figure 11.4). They fall within three basic

TABLE 11.3: *Palaeolithic sites (n = 292) with material or contexts (n = 403) attributed to specific periods, Lower, Middle or Upper. The larger number is due to multiple phases at many sites, mostly Middle and Upper Palaeolithic. The remaining 179 sites were attributed to the Palaeolithic generally.*

Region	Lower Palaeolithic (n=36)		Middle Palaeolithic (n=242)		Upper Palaeolithic (n=125)		Total	
	Open-air	Caves	Open-air	Caves	Open-air	Caves	N	%
North	6	1	11	1	1	1	21	5.2
South	1	–	56	7	44	16	124	30.8
East	8	–	57	2	15	5	87	21.6
West	8	–	101	3	29	11	152	37.7
Offshore Aegean islands	2	–	–	–	2	–	4	1
South Aegean islands (Crete and Gavdos)	10	–	4	–	1	–	15	3.7
Total	35	1	229	13	92	33	403	

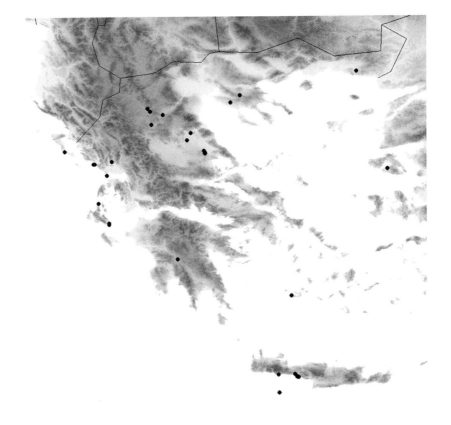

Figure 11.4: Reported definite and possible Lower Palaeolithic sites (n=36).

categories; those with human remains (2), with bifaces (21), and those with flake-based industries from geologically early contexts (13). It must be emphasised that the Lower Palaeolithic in Greece has only recently gained in prominence and many of the sites recorded are less than certain. Furthermore, not all sites have been explicitly linked with the Lower Palaeolithic. Our justification for their inclusion is based on shared morphology of the artefacts and the context in which they were found. Sites were distributed across northern Greece, along with isolated finds in the Peloponnese, and on the islands of Kephallonia, Corfu, Melos, Crete and Gavdos. The majority (27) are below 200 m above sea level, with seven between 200–599 m, and two at c. 800 m.

Sites with human skeletal remains include the Petralona Cave in central Macedonia (Harvati 2009), dated to between 150 and 250/350 ka (Grün 1996; Harvati et al. 2009), and a single tooth from pre-interglacial contexts at Megalopoli in the Peloponnese bracketed to between c. 950–300 ka (Tourloukis and Karkanas 2012: 2).

Definite and possible Lower Palaeolithic bifacial artefacts have been reported from at least twenty open-air sites. The most secure is Kokkinopilos in Epirus, dated to between 200–250 ka, with a small number of complete or fragmentary pointed handaxes of Acheulian type, all probably made of local chert (Dakaris et al. 1964; Runnels and van Andel 1993; Tourloukis and Karkanas 2012). There are the two stray surface finds made from volcanic raw materials from the Palaeokastro area (Dakaris et al. 1964) and possibly nearby Siatista in western Macedonia (Tourloukis and Karkanas 2012). Two small bifaces were picked up during surface survey at Ayios Thomas and Ormos Odysseus in western Epirus (Runnels and van Andel 2003), while in Thrace a small biface was reported at Krovili 10 (Ammerman et al. 1999). Bifacial artefacts have been reported from Kephallonia at Findspot 13:2–3, Nea Skala, and possibly Fiscardo (Cübuk 1976; Randsborg 2002). Bifaces made of banded rhyolite have been reported from Triadon Bay on Melos (Cheledonio 2001), and other sites on the island (Cherry 1982). Recent work on Lesvos in the northern Aegean has produced bifaces from fluvial contexts (Galanidou et al. 2013). Bifaces have also been reported from the island of Gavdos (Kopaka and Matzanas 2009), and on Crete at findspots located on the south coast close to the Preveli Gorge (Strasser et al. 2010, 2011), and at Loutro (Mortensen 2008). Some of the former findspots have been dated by sediment maturity and raised beach terraces, to older than 130 ka (Strasser et al. 2010, 2011) (Table 11.4).

Flake-based industries from early contexts have been reported from thirteen locations. They include Alonaki in Epirus (Runnels and van Andel 2003), Korissia on Corfu (Darlas et al. 2007) and the Aliakmonas River in western Macedonia (Harvati et al. 2008). The site of Rodia in Thessaly, along with six locations near Megalo Monastiri, produced similar material (Runnels and van

TABLE 11.4: *Directly dated and attributed Lower Palaeolithic sites (n = 5).*

Site	Chronology	References
Kokkinopilos	200–250 ka (OSL and sediment maturity)	Runnels and van Andel 1993; Tourloukis and Karkanas 2012
Megalopolis	300–950 ka (ESR and Matuyama-Brunhes polarity reversal)	Tourloukis and Karkanas 2012, and references therein
Rodia	200–400 ka (U/Th)	Runnels and van Andel 1993, and references therein
Petralona Cave	150–250/350 ka (ESR)	Grün 1996; Harvati et al. 2009
Preveli Gorge, Crete	>72–110 ka (sediment maturity and estimated high stand dates)	Strasser et al. 2010, 2011

Andel 1993). Two further possible early sites with flake cores and/or chopper tools include Doumbia and Ayios Charalambos in central Macedonia (Runnels et al. Langadas survey unpublished report). Rodia is thought to date to between 200–400 ka (Runnels and van Andel 1993, although see Tourloukis and Karkanas (2012: 5).

The Middle Palaeolithic

Middle Palaeolithic artefacts were reported at 242 sites (Table 11.3), the best represented of all three periods. They were common in western mainland Greece and on the Ionian islands of Corfu, Kephallonia and Zakynthos (n=103). The Peloponnese had 66 sites, most from clusters in the Argolid, Mani, and Ellis region (Figure 11.5). Eastern Greece had 59 sites, including concentrations along the Pineios River and on the Aegean islands of Evia and the Northern Sporades. Northern Greece had just twelve sites, with small clusters in Chalkidiki (Smagas 2007), the Langadas area (Runnels et al. Langadas survey unpublished report), and in Thrace in the Rhodope area (Ammerman et al. 1999). Mousterian artefacts have been reported from Maroulas on Kythnos, though probably a later introduction as raw material during the Mesolithic (Sampson et al. 2010: 50, 67, plate XI 6, 7), and possibly Gavdos (Kopaka and Matzanas 2009) and Crete (Strasser et al. 2010: 184). Most sites (179) were located below 200 m above sea level, with 38 between 200–599 m, and 25 above 600 m, the highest at around 1800 m in the Grevena district. There were 13 (5.4%) caves with reported Middle Palaeolithic, and 229 (94.6%) open-air sites. Skeletal remains have been recovered from four caves, three in the Mani in the southern Peloponnese (Kalamakia, Apidima and Lakonis), and Theopetra in Thessaly.

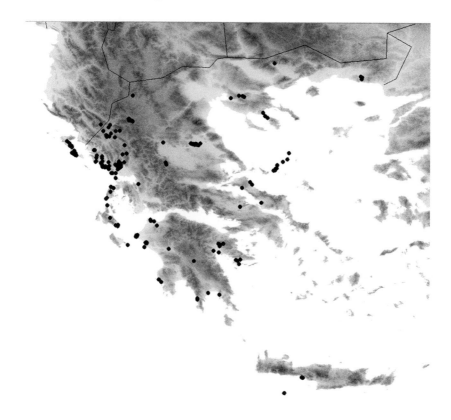

Figure 11.5: Reported Middle Palaeolithic sites (n=242).

Dated Middle Palaeolithic contexts fall within two chronological blocks, during the penultimate interglacial from MIS 5e or slightly before, and then the earlier half of MIS 3 (Table 11.5). Thermoluminescence estimates from Theopetra Cave of 124 ka and 129 ka (Valladas et al. 2007), have tripled the original radiocarbon chronology, which previously bracketed the Middle Palaeolithic to between 50 and 30 ka BP (Kyparissi-Apostolika 2000). Recent radiocarbon dates have produced similar young estimates compared to the TL, suggesting increasing contamination of charcoal samples with depth (Facorellis et al. 2013).

Provisional dates from Lakonis from the underlying sterile beach (<c. 128 ka BP) (Elefanti et al. 2008), and Kalamakia caves (<109±14–13 ka BP) (Darlas and de Lumley 1999) suggest a similar early chronology, with use of the sites after the c. +5m MIS 5e high stand which flushed both sites and formation of beach rock (Harvati et al. 2011; Kopp et al. 2009). Erosion at nearby Apidima during the same high stand led to exposure of two Neanderthal crania, suggesting an earlier date for the skulls between c. 400–105 ka and probably closer to the latter (Rondoyanni et al. 1995; Harvati et al. 2010, 2011). New as yet unpublished TL estimates from Klisoura also point to use from c. MIS 5e

TABLE 11.5: *Dated Middle Palaeolithic sites (n = 5)*

Site	¹⁴C BP	¹⁴C CalPal 2007 HULU (alternative method)	References
Theopetra Cave (Unit II4)	–	129±13 ka (TL, 7 sample mean)	Valladas et al. 2007
Theopetra Cave (Unit II2)		124±16 ka (TL, 2 sample mean)	
Lakonis Cave 1	–	<c. 128 ka (provisional OSL on underlying sterile beach)	Elefanti et al. 2008
Kalamakia (Unit II)	–	109±14–13 ka (Uranium disequilibrium on shell) 95±6 ka (Uranium disequilibrium on calcite covering underlying sterile beach)	Darlas and de Lumley 1999, 296
Asprochaliko (Layer 18)	–	102±14 ka (TL) 96±11 ka (TL)	Huxtable et al. 1992; Gowlett and Carter 1997, 445
Theopetra (Layer II11)	–	57±6 ka II11 (TL)	Valladas et al. 2007
Klissoura Cave 1 (Layer V)	40,100±740 –	43,841±764 >40 ka BP (CI)	Kuhn et al. 2010; Lowe et al. 2012
Lakonis Cave 1 (Unit Ib)	43,335±1800 43,150±1790	46,740±1920 46,560±1890	Panagopoulou et al. 2002–2004;
Lakonis Cave 1 (Unit Ia)	39,640±1000 45,500±2330 42,800±1700 38,240±1160	43,490±770 48,060±2560 46,190±1750 42,600±720	Elefanti et al. 2008
Kalamakia (top of Unit IV)	>40,000	–	Darlas 2007

(Karkanas pers. comm. 2013), while basal layer 18 at Asprochaliko produced a mean TL estimate of 98.5±12 ka BP, along with temperate fauna (Huxtable et al. 1992; Gowlet and Carter 1997: 445).

The second block of dates from four cave and rockshelter sites document the final phase and end of the Middle Palaeolithic. At Klissoura, Uluzzian Layer V is sealed by CI tephra dated to c. 40 ka BP (Lowe et al. 2012: 13535), and confirmed by new radiocarbon dates of c. 40 ka cal BP from Dentalium beads from the top of the layer (Karkarnas pers. comm. 2013). The lower part of Layer V where it overlies Mousterian Layer VI, has unpublished OSL estimates of c. 45 ka BP (Zacharias pers. comm. 2012). Radiocarbon dates from Layer VI of c. 44.5 ka cal BP suggest an end for the Mousterian in Greece, although the contact between Layers V and VI is complex with erosion and possibly hiatus

(Kuhn 2010: 41). At Franchthi, the early Upper Palaeolithic Aurignacian Layer Q is rich in CI tephra dated to c. 40 ka cal BP (Lowe et al. 2012). Underlying Layer P is undiagnostic and does not appear to contain an Uluzzian component. All that can be said is that the end of the Mousterian at Franchthi occurred before around 40 ka BP. At Lakonis, final Middle Palaeolithic (Unit Ib) and possible Initial Upper (Unit Ia) have produced indistinguishable age estimates of between 48–42.6 ka cal BP, with an average of 45.5 ka cal BP, while analysis of samples from both units produced no CI tephra (Panagapoulou pers. comm. 2012). All that can be said is that the Mousterian at Lakonis ended some time after c. 45.5 ka cal BP and before c. 40 ka BP. At Kalamakia, charcoal from the top of Mousterian Unit IV produced an AMS date (uncalibrated) of >40 ka BP (Darlas 2007). The cave lacks an Upper Palaeolithic component as it had become inaccessible by that stage.

The Upper Palaeolithic

Upper Palaeolithic artefacts were reported at 125 sites (Table 11.3; Figure 11.6). They were best represented in the Peloponnese with 63 sites, most close to the coast with clusters in the Argolid, the Mani and Ellis

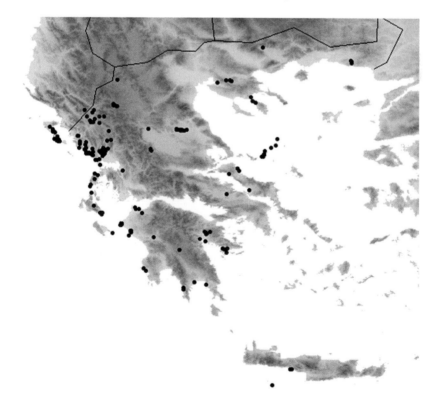

Figure 11.6: Reported Upper Palaeolithic sites (n=125).

regions. In western Greece there were forty reported sites, mainly Epirus and the Ionian island of Corfu, while Kephallonia and Zakynthos appear poor in terms of Upper Palaeolithic, in contrast to the Middle. Sixteen sites were reported from eastern mainland Greece and the Aegean islands of Evia and the Northern Sporades. Just two sites were located in northern Greece, mainland Gorgopi (EPSNG unpublished report), and the ochre mine on the near shore island of Thasos (Koukouli-Chrysanthaki and Weisgerber 1996). Other island sites include Ouriakos and other findspots on Limnos (Efstratiou and Kiriakou 2012: 55–62). Possible Upper Palaeolithic material has also been reported from Gavdos in the southern Aegean. Most Upper Palaeolithic sites (91, 72.8%) were located below 200m above sea level, with 22 (17.6%) between 200–599 m, and 12 (9.6%) above 600 m, the highest at around 1800 m in the Grevena highlands. Thirty-three caves (26.4%) have been reported and 92 (73.6%) open-air sites. Modern human skeletal remains have been found in six excavated caves, mostly as scatters of isolated pieces, as at Klithi, Franchthi, Theopetra and Klissoura, but with more complete remains at Apidima (cave C), and Kephalari (Marshall in prep.).

THE AURIGNACIAN (C. 40–35 KA CAL BP)

Aurignacian dates and material is present at 19 sites, 4 dated caves, and 15 surface scatters with artefacts (nosed and carinated cores and/or scrapers) (Figure 11.7; Table 11.6).

Aurignacian Layer Q at Franchthi is rich in CI tephra (c. 40 kyr) (Douka et al. 2011; Lowe et al. 2012). At Klisoura, Layers IV, IIIe-g are dated to between 37.5–35 ka cal BP (Kuhn et al. 2010; Stiner et al. 2010), a couple of millennia later than at Franchthi. An earlier date from Layer IIIe-g (39, 141±1869 cal BP) was based on conventional counts and has a wide error margin and appeared to be out of sequence (Kuhn et al. 2010: 40). However in the light of the dates from Franchthi and the position of the CI at both sites, this date may need to be reconsidered. The third cave is Kolominitsa in the Peloponnese dated to c. 36 ka cal BP (Darlas and Psathi 2008). The fourth is Kastritsa in Epirus, where basal Stratum 9 produced a small collection of artefacts thought to be comparable to early Aurignacian lithic phases I and II from Franchthi, including a carinated scraper of possible Aurignacian type (Galanidou 1997: 502). Recent dates of 28.5 ka cal BP (Adam 2007 and references therein) appear too young, perhaps the result of mixing. Two major undated open-air sites with Aurignacian artefacts include Spilaio in Epirus (Runnels et al. 2003) and Eleochori in the Peloponnese (Darlas 1999). Fourteen smaller surface scatters have produced artefacts attributed to the Aurignacian, specifically carinated cores/scrapers.

TABLE 11.6: *Dated Aurignacian sites (n = 4).*

Site	^{14}C BP	^{14}C CalPal 2007 HULU	References
Franchthi Cave	34,980±220	40,330–38,810	Douka et al. 2011,
Stratum Q	33,250±420	38,890–36,816	1142
Stratum R	30,580±160	35,070–34,520	
lower	29,780±160	34,580–33,400	
	32,110±200	36,650–35,300	
Klissoura	32,400±600	36,920±980	Kuhn et al. 2010, 38
Cave 1	31,150±480	35,232±506	
Layer IV	34,700±1,600	39,141±1,869	
IIIa-g	31,630±250	35,548±472	
Kolominitsa	33,870±550	39,168±1,272	Darlas and Psathi
Cave			2008
(Layers 3–8)			
Kastritsa Cave	23,880±100	28,755±388	Adam 2007, 146;
(Stratum 9)	23,840±240	28,746±430	Galanidou 1997, 502

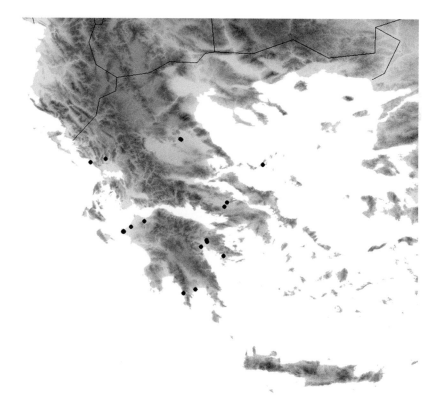

Figure 11.7: Dated Aurignacian sites and those attributed based on the presence of carinated pieces (n=19).

THE GRAVETTIAN (C. 30–23 KA CAL BP)

The Gravettian is present at 13 sites, 12 caves, 4 dated and 1 open-air scatter with artefacts including shouldered pieces and Gravettian points (Figure 11.8, Table 11.7).

Klissoura Layer III is dated to c. 30–28 ka cal BP (Kuhn et al. 2010: 38; Stiner et al. 2010: 312). Others include Franchthi Layers R and S1, between c. 27.5–24 ka cal BP (Stiner and Munro 2011), Asprochaliko Layer 10 at >30 ka cal BP, and Kastritsa at between c. 27–23 ka cal BP (Adam 2007). Undated caves with Gravettian artefacts include Grava on Corfu (*ibid*), Seidi in Boeotia (Kourtessi-Philippaki 1986), Skoini 3 and 4, Kolominitsa and Tripsana in the Mani (Darlas and Psathi 2008). A single shouldered point and bladelet core were reported by the Nikopolis Palaeolithic Survey from surface scatter Eli (SS92–19) in Epirus (Unpublished project notebook #5: 90). Theopetra Cave in Thessaly was previously attributed to the Gravettian on the basis of radiocarbon dates from Unit II11 of around 30 ka cal BP (Adam 2007: 146; Karkanas 2001), though with a largely undiagnostic

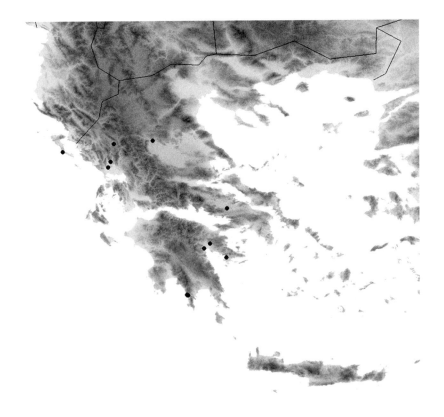

Figure 11.8: Dated Gravettian sites and those attributed based on the presence of shouldered pieces and Gravettian points (n=13).

TABLE II.7: *Dated Gravettian sites (n = 4)*

Site	^{14}C BP	^{14}C CalPal 2007 HULU	References
Franchthi Cave	22,330±350	26,906±661	Stiner and Munro
Layer R (upper), S1	21,480±1,270	25,818±1,601	2011
Klissoura Cave 1	23,000±540	27,566±690	Kuhn et al. 2010
(Layer III')			
Kastritsa Cave	22,230±210	26,843±597	Adam 2007
(Stratum 5 and 3)	19,660±160	23,460±370	
Asprochaliko	>26,100±900	>30,818±817	Adam 2007
Cave (Layer 10)			

assemblage. Thermoluminescence estimates from this unit have produced dates of 57±6 ka BP, which suggest that the radiocarbon determinations are too early (Valladas et al. 2007).

THE EPIGRAVETTIAN (C. 20–12 KA CAL BP)

There are 16 Epigravettian sites, 8 dated caves and 1 open-air, along with 5 undated caves and 2 undated open-air, attributed on the basis of backed pieces (Figure 11.9, Table 11.8).

The earliest dates are from Klithi and Megalakkos in Epirus, from around 20 ka cal BP, and from nearby Boila from 17.5 ka cal BP. Kastritsa is reoccupied again c. 16.5 ka cal BP after a hiatus which appears to have spanned the LGM, along with Klissoura c. 17.5 ka cal BP, and Franchthi slightly later at c. 15 ka cal BP. Other dated caves include Sarakeno in Boetia c. 13 ka cal BP, and Schisto Cave 1 in Attica at c. 15 ka BP (obsidian hydration) (Laskaris et al. 2011), along with the open-air site of Maroulas on Kythnos c. 13.5 ka cal BP (Facorellis et al. 2010). Five undated caves include Klissoura 4 and 7 (Koumouzelis et al. 2004), Zaimis and Ulbrich (Galanidou 2003) and possibly Kephalari (Marshall in prep). We take the end of the Upper Palaeolithic to be the beginning of the Holocene at 11.7 ka BP (Walker et al. 2009). This excludes some of the later dates from Maroulas, and the sites of Cyclope Cave on Youra (Laskaris et al. 2011 and reference therein), and the Old Klithonia Bridge (c. 11 ka BP) open-air site in Epirus (Gowlett et al. 1997).

DISCUSSION

Greece has a long history of Palaeolithic research, with excavations steadily increasing from the 1920s. Field survey developed in parallel, applying many of the techniques used in projects targeting later periods, though it would be fair to say that these had much more of a predictive element to them, informed by

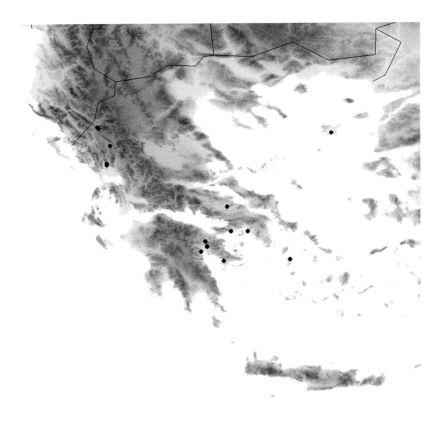

Figure 11.9: Dated Epigravettian sites and those attributed based on the presence of backed pieces (n=16).

previous discoveries and instinct. Well over 90% of known Palaeolithic and Mesolithic sites in Greece were discovered during field surveys. There are still major gaps in spatial and temporal coverage and a number of recent projects have begun to tackle this issue by targeting apparently empty areas (Elefanti et al. forthcoming). More of these types of surveys are needed, particularly in eastern and northern Greece, where – so far – it would appear as though evidence for the Palaeolithic is rare. The 'Prehistoric Stones of Greece' set out to collate in a standardised way, information about the Palaeolithic in Greece, using information provided by surface scatters and the small number of major excavated sites. The site is our basic unit of measure, defined as any location in which one or more artefacts or in rare cases human remains were reported.

Our dataset currently includes 471 sites distributed broadly across mainland Greece and the islands of the Ionian and Aegean, but with a significance asymmetry in their frequency. The largest regional concentration of Palaeolithic sites (253, 54%) was in the west in Epirus and the near-shore islands of the Ionian. Southern and eastern Greece was also well represented although with less than half the number of sites in each (93 and 94 respectively). Northern

TABLE 11.8: *Dated Epigravettian sites (n = 9).*

Site	^{14}C BP	^{14}C CalPal 2007 HULU (alternative method)	References
Franchthi Cave (Lithic Phases IV–VI)	12,540±180 10,260±110	14,832±412 12,055±286	Perlès 1999
Klissoura Cave 1 (Layers IIa, b, d)	14,280±90	17,475±257	Kuhn et al. 2010
Sarakeno Cave Unit 6/ Trench A	11,910±60	13,810±153	Sampson et al. 2011
Klithi Rockshelter	17,000±400 10,420±150	20,352±590 12,282±267	Gowlett et al. 1997
Megalakkos Rockshelter	15,410±210 16,100±160	18,515±364 19,245±276	Gowlett et al. 1997
Kastritsa Cave (Stratum 1, Layer 2)	13,400±210	16,293±487	Adam 2007
Boila Rockshelter (Units Ib–III)	14,310±100 10,190±90	17,493±259 11,877±316	Kotjabopoulou 2001
Schisto Cave 1 (Layer 4)	–	14,539±1,280 (obsidian SIMS-SS)	Laskaris et al. 2011
Maroulas (Layer 5)	11,370±110	13,277±156	Facorellis et al. 2010
Ouriakos	10,390±45	12,322±175	Efstratiou et al. 2013

Greece was comparatively poorly represented with just a handful (16) of sites. This east-west and north-south asymmetry was also apparent amongst those sites attributed separately to either/and the Lower, Middle or Upper Palaeolithic. In addition to the frequency of sites, there were also large regional differences in the number of artefacts reported, although with some exceptions such as the Pineios River and bearing in mind the many factors which may influence collection strategy during field survey. Just over half of all Palaeolithic sites in our dataset were located below 200 m, including almost all of the larger caves and shelters, though with exceptions including the cluster of sites in the Vikos Gorge in Epirus, and probably the open-air sites in the Grevena highlands.

The majority of Palaeolithic sites (418) are open-air, or just under 90% of all those recorded. Seven have been excavated to any extent, four in Epirus and one each on the Aegean islands of Lesvos, Limnos and Kythnos. Despite this relatively large number of recorded open-air sites, we estimate that approximately 35% can be considered broadly in situ, with 40% reworked and 25% stray finds and of unknown origin. There is also the issue of repeatedly surveyed locations and the duplication of findspots. The implications of these factors need to be considered when comparing open-air site distributions.

In contrast, caves represent fixed points in the landscape, more protected from processes of aggregation or dispersal. Fifty-three caves with Palaeolithic material have been recorded (11.3% of all sites in Greece), of which 30 have been excavated. They are located predominately in the limestone regions of southern and western Greece, with small numbers in the east and very few in the north. Around a third have been defined as Palaeolithic generally, the remaining two-thirds attributed to either/and the Lower, Middle or Upper. Like open-air sites, almost two-thirds of caves are located below 200 m, with declining frequencies at higher elevations and most of these were in the west in Epirus (18 out of 22). Of the 53 caves recorded, at least 12 appear to have been major residential hubs, although this is biased towards the excavated sites for which more information is available.

There are major gaps in spatial and temporal coverage, particularly in eastern and northern Greece where – so far – the Palaeolithic appears to be rare. The question is, do these apparently empty areas reflect a lack of investigation, preservation or a real absence of sites?

Regional differences in survey coverage may account for much of the observed difference. Most Palaeolithic sites were reported during a small number of field survey projects and these were more common in western and southern Greece (21), compared with the east and north (12). Moreover, surveys in former regions were typically larger in scale and duration and many were staffed by Palaeolithic specialists. This imbalance in survey frequency and intensity is strongly correlated with the numbers of sites in the four regions, with 346 in the west and south and 110 in the east and north.

But this cannot be the whole story as when surveys are carried out, material is usually found. Another possible reason for the asymmetry in sites may be differences in geology and geomorphology, mainly between the limestone dominated regions of southern and western Greece, compared with the east and north where major drainage systems dominate the landscape. Here, much of the evidence is likely to be deeply buried and only accessible under specific conditions, such as along the Pineios River in Thessaly where Middle Palaeolithic artefacts and fauna have been reported. Similar material may be present along other major river systems in central and eastern Macedonia as well as Thrace in northern Greece.

Another possibility is that the imbalance reflects real differential use of the landscape during the Palaeolithic, and that this resulted in fewer sites and smaller assemblages east of the Pindus Mountains and the northern part of the country. Pollen analysis from lake deposits at Tenaghi Philippon in eastern Macedonia, Kopais in Boeotia and Ioannina in Epirus, suggests that eastern and northern Greece would have been relatively drier during the last glacial, due to the rain shadow effect of the Pindus Mountains (Tzedakis et al. 2004). Phytolith evidence from Theopetra Cave in Thessaly, to the east of the Pindus, also points to generally cooler and drier conditions from the last interglacial onwards, with sporadic broad leaf vegetation and declines in those species indicative of wetter conditions (Tsartsidou et al. forthcoming). Wood charcoal from Theopetra points to a similar cool and dry trend, with open parkland vegetation and probably gallery forest along rivers (Ntinou and Kyparissi-Apostolika 2008).

However, despite these dryer conditions, there was sufficient rainfall to supply the major river systems which drain east and south into the Aegean, and these supported plant, animal and human communities, for example along the Pineios River. It may be that in eastern and northern Greece, communities were tethered along river systems, whereas in the west and possibly the south, wetter conditions and the rugged and dissected landscape would have supported more widely spread refugial plant, animal and human communities. This would result in different archaeological signatures; widely dispersed in the west and south and concentrated in the east and north, which has implications for preservation and discovery.

Whether the rain shadow effect was present in the south is unclear. The Pindus extend down into the central part of the Peloponnesian peninsula, and it may be that a similar west to east fall-off in precipitation occurred. In her phytolith study from Klissoura Cave 1, Albert (2010) highlights the presence of C4 grasses in late glacial levels, which suggest major changes in the climate, with expansion of open steppic landscapes and the disappearance of most trees. Charcoal studies from Klissoura also support this interpretation, with the identification of *Prunus amygdalus/spinosa,* which grows in relatively arid and more open environments (Ntinou 2010). We suggest that the asymmetry amongst sites is a combination of all of these factors; fewer surveys of lower intensity and scale in eastern and northern Greece, reduced potential for preservation and discovery due to major alluvial systems, and lower population density due to the dryer conditions, probably tethered along rivers.

The **Lower Palaeolithic** is poorly represented with just 36 attributed findspots, most of which should be treated with caution. The most secure findspots include the skull from the Petralona Cave in central Macedonia and the tooth from Megalopolis in the Peloponnese. Biface findspots at Kokkinopilos in Epirus, Rodafnidia on Lesvos and probably the stray find from Palaeokastro and Siatista in western Macedonia are technologically typical of the Lower Palaeolithic, although their exact provenance is uncertain. Quartz artefacts with Acheulian affinities have recently been reported from Crete, found on terraces with a relative age of more than 110 ka. Bifaces have also been reported from the nearby island of Gavdos. Other biface findspots include six surface scatters, two in Epirus and one in Thrace, three on the Ionian island of Kephallonia and one on the Aegean island of Melos. Other potential early findspots include 13 flake dominated non-bifacial assemblages in geologically early contexts from Epirus, Thessaly and central Macedonia close to the Petralona early hominin site. These flake-based industries made from chert, quartz and volcanic rocks are predominantly located on or within fluvial sequences, some possibly broadly in situ.

The patchy distribution of Lower Palaeolithic findspots is puzzling, particularly in contrast to the density of those attributed to the Middle. Tourloukis and Karkanas (2012) have suggested a number of possible explanations, including erosion and sedimentation due to extreme rainfall regimes, steep slope processes and changes in tectonics around the early Middle Pleistocene which led to the inversion of many of the major basins. It is also now known that much of what is now the Aegean Sea was sub-aerially exposed during the Pleistocene. With lower sea levels during much of MIS 12–8, beginning from at least c. 500 ka and probably much earlier, more than half of the northern Aegean would have been dry land (Lykousis 2009; Tourloukis and Karkanas 2012). This potential low-lying landscape of lakes, rivers, marshes and rapidly evolving coastlines would have been of high ecological value (*sensu* Bailey et al. 2008), and especially as a buffer against continental glacial conditions at higher elevations further inland. Such an area could also have served as a key bridge for migration into western Europe by early hominins (Muttoni et al. 2010), or models such as that proposed by Dennell (2010) in which western Asia functioned as a 'source region' feeding migration pulses into western Europe.

Another possible explanation for the apparent low visibility of the Lower Palaeolithic is the relative absence of good quality large raw materials, in contrast to areas of western Europe where they occur as reworked river gravels and within in situ chalk deposits. Although chert is common in Greece, it mostly occurs as small to medium sized nodules and slabs within hard limestone and is often heavily shattered by tectonics. Other fine-grained materials such as radiolarite and chalcedonies also occur mostly as small nodules and slabs. Those less commonly associated with biface manufacture, at least in the European context, such as quartz and various types of volcanic rock appear to be used as well. Although difficult to quantify, the general picture is of a lack of raw materials of sufficient size to make typical Acheulian handaxes from, though this would be an interesting model to test with further research.

All of these processes; reworking, burial and drowning along with a lack of suitable raw materials could have combined to reduce the visibility of the Lower Palaeolithic in Greece. If this was the case then it would imply that Greece was on the path of early hominin migration into Europe, rather than on the periphery as suggested by the current meagre material record. In this context, secure island sites such as Rodafnidia on Lesvos are important, although discoveries further south would arguably be more significant. Those from Crete perhaps, although the island would always have required open-water seafaring, even when much of the northern Aegean basin was dry land. The Cycladic islands would be promising areas for targeted investigation as these would have marked to the southern extent of the sub-aerially exposed Aegean basin, potentially providing a bridge from western Asia to central southern Europe (Muttoni et al. 2010; Tourloukis and Karkanas 2012: 12).

Middle Palaeolithic material has been recorded at 242 sites, which compared to the Lower, represents a major step change in archaeological visibility. How to interpret this is open to question, on the one hand pointing to the destruction of a previously much richer record, or on the other that region was sparsely occupied. To some extent we may be over emphasising the differences between the two periods by lumping the evidence from each. All of the early dated Middle Palaeolithic sites − so far − are in caves and thus protected. Most of the open sites remain undated and it is unclear where the majority of these would fall, early or late. It may be that the small number of early dated cave sites represent the remnant of a more extensive record, destroyed in the same way as the Lower Palaeolithic, with surface scatters late and therefore relatively less affected having only passed through one glacial-interglacial cycle. Why caves in Greece lack a Lower Palaeolithic component is perhaps the more interesting question, possibly just a reflection of the small sample of early dated inland sites including Klissoura, Asprochaliko and Theopetra, all of which appear to be first occupied during the penultimate interglacial. Similarly dated coastal cave sites in the southern Peloponnese, Kalamakia, Lakonis and possibly Apidima, may have had earlier material, however this would have been removed during the MIS 5e high stand.

The Middle Palaeolithic was the best represented of all three periods, with sites in a range of environments from coastal lowlands and river valleys, to mid-elevation basins and mountain ridges (Papagianni 2009: 129–130). Most of the sites are open-air (229) and we estimate that around a third of these are probably broadly in situ, the rest reworked, stray finds or of unknown derivation. Caves were in use during the Middle Palaeolithic (13), the majority of those so far identified, located in the limestone regions of western and southern Greece. A total of six, four in the Peloponnese and one each in Epirus and Thessaly, were clearly important residential sites, intensively used during the Palaeolithic and into the Mesolithic and later periods. A recent study of bone fragments at Kalamakia Cave identified a minimum of eight Neanderthal individuals of different age and gender (Harvati et al. 2013), perhaps pointing to a residential system with consumers and providers at the site, rather than logistically organised special purpose with hunters only. Although many faunal studies await publication, preliminary reports from Lakonis, Kalamakia and Klisoura point to sites located within a mosaic of habitats and resources, with hunting of large and medium-sized ungulates, and occasionally smaller animals such as tortoises.

The evidence so far is for only limited scales of mobility. Volcanic raw materials in use at Kalamakia were being collected and carried between 20–25 km from sources at Krokeai, close to the site of Lakonis (Darlas 2007).

At Lakonis, wear traces on a Neanderthal tooth suggest that the individual lived in a more wooded environment than that predicted for the site. This is supported by the strontium isotope results from the same tooth, which suggest that the individual spent his formative years in an area dominated by volcanic bedrock rather than limestone, possibly 20 km away at the Krokeai sources (Richards et al. 2008).

The earliest radiometrically dated or attributed Middle Palaeolithic sites or contexts coalesce around MIS 5e or slightly before. The sites are of two basic types, those (3) located along the coast in the southern Peloponnese, and those (3) from further inland in the Peloponnese, Thessaly and Epirus. The Middle Palaeolithic appears to have ended somewhere between 45 and 40 ka, probably closer to the earlier part of the range, with the appearance of the Aurignacian at around 40 ka. The intervening period is complex, with Uluzzian arched backed and splintered pieces at Klissoura Cave I (Layer V) and Kephalari Cave (Layer F). At Klissoura, this layer is capped by CI tephra and confirmed by new radiocarbon dates at c. 40 ka BP (Lowe et al. 2012). Kephalari is as yet undated, but has artefacts of the same type as Klissoura (Marshall forthcoming). Similarities with sites in Italy suggests a link with those in Greece (Kaczanowska et al. 2010), although with other potential points of origin for these transitional industries to the east (Mellars 2011; Moroni et al. 2013; but see also Douka et al. 2013). Despite considerable controversy, it is likely that the makers of the Uluzzian were modern humans (Benazzi et al. 2011). Elsewhere in the Peloponnese, the complex nature of the period is highlighted by the possible transitional phase at Lakonis, though without an obvious Uluzzian component (Panagopoulou et al. 2002–2004; Elefanti et al. 2008) and no CI tephra.

Upper Palaeolithic has been recorded at 125 locations, including 33 caves and 92 open-air sites. Overall they were half as frequent as those with Middle Palaeolithic material, which considering that the Upper Palaeolithic was less than half as long, may suggest continuity rather than decline. In broad terms, the Upper Palaeolithic was similar to the Middle in terms of the asymmetry of sites in the four regions, with most in the south and west, some in the east and very few in the north. Possible reasons have been suggested for this; a lack of survey coverage, poor preservation or a real lack of sites.

Comparison of the four regions in terms of absolute numbers of sites as well as proportions per period, pointed to decline in the east and north, continuity in the west and significant increase in the south. In fact the absolute numbers in the south remained constant between the Middle and Upper Palaeolithic (63 and 60 respectively), but with decline in the West by a factor of around 2.5, with 3.5 in the East and 6 in the North. If we equate the numbers of reported sites with population density, we suggest that there was continuity in the west, decline in the east and north and significant increase in the south.

Caves increased from just over 5% (n=13) of all Middle Palaeolithic sites, to more than 25% (n=33) of those with Upper. Regionally the increase was most marked in the west, with almost four times the number of Upper Palaeolithic caves, many in use for the first time, along with continued occupation of most of those used during the Middle Palaeolithic. In the south, the increase was slightly less, although still approximately between two and three times, of which two-thirds were probably in use for the first time, while almost all Middle Palaeolithic caves continued in use. In the east and north the picture was of continuity and decline in cave use during the Upper Palaeolithic, reflecting as well the overall reduction in sites generally in these two regions. All 13 Middle Palaeolithic caves were located close to or below 200 m (here we include those overlooking landscapes below 200 m). Twenty-four of the 33 caves with Upper Palaeolithic were located below 200 m. The remaining nine were at mid-to-upper (200–599 m) elevations (>600 m), all in Epirus.

We suggest there is evidence for increased use of caves during the Upper Palaeolithic (although see Bailey et al. (1997). In Epirus most of the increase was amongst mid-to-upper elevation caves (shelters) in the Vikos Gorge. In the Peloponnese, the number of caves more than doubled, along with continuity amongst those occupied during the Middle Palaeolithic. Apart from Epirus there was no evidence for change in elevation of caves from the Middle to Upper Palaeolithic, in general and apart from Epirus, reflecting continued occupation of areas close to the coast.

The Aurignacian in Greece begins at about 40 ka, during a warmer and wetter phase within MIS 3 as indicated by the fauna at Klissoura (Starkovich and Stiner 2010) and Franchthi caves (Stiner and Munro 2011). So far, the earliest dating evidence for the Aurignacian comes from Franchthi (Douka et al. 2011), and a couple of millennia later at Klissoura. A total of 19 sites have been attributed to the period, four caves and 15 open-air, mainly located in western and southern Greece. Some were in use earlier during the Middle Palaeolithic and transitional phases, Klissoura, Kephalari and possibly Franchthi. They indicate that the beginning of the Early Aurignacian in Greece is comparable with that from the rest of Europe (Douka et al. 2011: 1146), and therefore that Greece was not peripheral to modern human dispersal into the continent. Sites in Greece were part of a wider distribution of Aurignacian in the southern Balkans, including others such as Temnata and Bacho Kiro in Bulgaria (Kozlowski and Otte 2000; Jöris and Street 2008), in Albania (Runnels et al. 2009) and the Bosphorous region of Turkey (Runnels and Özdoğan 2001).

A total of 13 sites with Gravettian have been recorded, twelve caves (four dated) and one open-air scatter. Dates from Klissoura, Franchthi, Kastritsa and Asprochaliko point to the beginning of the Gravettian from around 30–28 ka cal BP, with the most recent dates so far from Kastritsa c. 23 ka cal BP. This was followed by hiatus in the use of Klissoura, Franchthi, Kastritsa spanning the

LGM, before being reoccupied from the onset of postglacial conditions during the Epigravettian (Stiner et al. 2010; Perlès 1999). The clusters of recorded Gravettian sites in Epirus and the Peloponnese may suggest population concentration, perhaps due to more favourable conditions (Tzedakis et al. 2004; Bailey and Gamble 1990). In contrast to western and central Europe north of the major mountain ranges, where there appears to have been an expansion of sites during the Gravettian, in Greece as in the rest of Mediterranean southern Europe, the opposite appears to have been the case (van Andel et al. 2003: 48).

Deteriorating environmental conditions led to pressure to expand the diet breadth. Faunal studies from Kastritsa (Kotjabopoulou 2001), Franchthi (Stiner and Munro 2011) and Klissoura (Starkovich and Stiner 2010) point to hunting of medium to large ungulates along with a range of smaller species and many of low nutritional value such as hare and tortoise. During this period we also see an increase in symbolic objects, pierced deer canines, shells and other bone and antler objects at sites such as Kastritsa (Kotjabopoulou and Adam 2004), Klissoura and Kephalari (Stiner pers. comm. 2012).

We have recorded 17 sites with Epigravettian, including 8 dated caves and 1 dated open-air site, along with 5 undated caves, and 2 undated open-air surface scatters. The onset of postglacial conditions led to a rise in sea levels and the loss of much of the coastal plain, along with the development of mixed forest-steppe (Ntinou 2010). This – along with possible increase in population – had a different impact in each region. In western Greece there appears to have been an expansion into novel areas such as the uplands of Epirus, at sites such as Klithi and Megalakkos in the Vikos Gorge. Increased vegetation attracted caprines (Bailey 1997), with selective hunting of these animals perhaps in response to the rapidly reducing coastal plains (Gamble 1997). In other areas there is continued evidence for an expansion in diet breadth, with the inclusion of smaller species at Klissoura and Franchthi (Stiner and Munro 2011; Starkovitch 2012), and the wider use of coastal and marine resources. Rising sea levels would have led to an increasingly complex and dynamic coastline, with lagoons, marshes and estuaries. The evidence for fishing at Franchthi and obsidian from Melos (Perlès 1999) points to increasing use of marine environments. Sites on Limnos (Efstratiou and Kiriakou 2012) and Kythnos (Sampson et al. 2010), point to open water seafaring, a trend which continues into the Mesolithic on more distant islands such as Ikaria and Crete. There may also be evidence for recolonisation of inland and upland areas, with possible final Upper Palaeolithic or early Mesolithic sites in the Grevena highlands (Efstratiou et al. 2006).

CONCLUSIONS

Far from being *terra incognito*, the Palaeolithic of Greece is now well established with increasing numbers of sites, dates and specialist studies. Our review of the Palaeolithic is based on information from about half of all sites recorded in the

Prehistoric Stones of Greece project dataset. The aim has been to attempt to move beyond excavated cave sites to include surface scatters, in order to take a wider regional look at presence or absence through time and space. Our review focuses on the most general of patterns, consistent with the types of information provided by surface scatters. We are aware of the major difficulties involved in using this type of material; however we believe that it can provide a useful region wide snapshot of settlement and to highlight areas of potential interest for future research into broader questions relating to how hominins thought about and used landscapes, and the ramifications of these patterns of use for hominin cognition and evolution.

CHAPTER 12

IN SEARCH OF GROUP IDENTITY – LATE
PLEISTOCENE FORAGERS
IN NORTHERN CHINA

OFER BAR-YOSEF

INTRODUCTION

Research into prehistoric times raises questions that are constantly on our
minds and expressed in the papers or books we publish. In conducting the
analysis of archaeological data – whether collected by us or by others, during
the past century or in recent years – we make efforts to understand the minds
of prehistoric people, their social relationships, economies and conceptualisations of their symbolic world, as embedded in the preserved elements. This is
what I wanted to do when I became interested in microblade assemblages in
China, and learned about their geographic distribution and chronology and
the social prehistory in north-east Asia (Figure 12.1), and the implications of
this for the colonisation of the Americas (e.g., Nelson 1937; Brantingham et al.
2004; Kuzmin et al. 2007 and papers therein).

The most common operations in Chinese Palaeolithic studies are surveys
which record surface sites, with or without a grid, and sometimes with the use
of augers to identify hidden layers, or drilling for obtaining deeper samples.
Natural or artificial cuts create exposures which are often important sources of
information, leading to the uncovering of sites older than those found on the
surface, whether in the central plain or the higher altitudes (e.g. Brantingham
and Gao 2006; Madsen et al. 2006; School of Archaeology and Museology and the
Zhengzhou Institute of Archaeology 2011). The buried sites facilitate investigation
of past landscapes and illuminate the processes which formed the current ones.

Excavations provide much more detailed information, but have their own
limits (Shizitan Archaeological Team 2002). In the past, recording was done by
spits, and assemblages from different layers or horizons were often later
combined into one. Palaeolithic excavations in the last fifteen years or even
earlier exposed large surfaces which were recorded by piece plotting. Stratigraphies are often described as 'cultural layers' that may incorporate sterile
levels as well occupational horizons.

However, my optimism in studying the Chinese Palaeolithic was challenged
when I recognised the 'darker side' of archaeological terminology: namely the

214

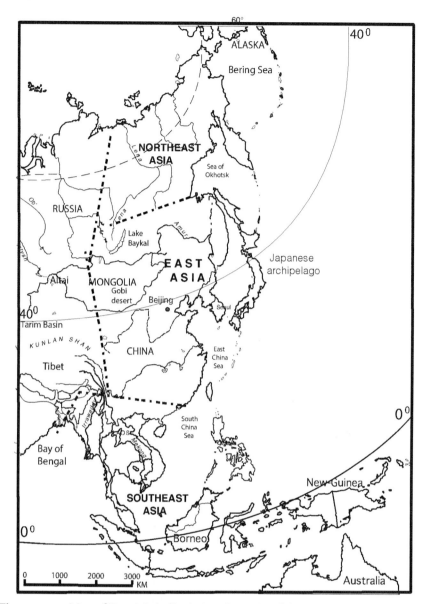

Figure 12.1: Map of East Asia indicating a schematic subdivision into north-east Asia and south-east Asia including political boundaries.

differences that emerge when studying Chinese Palaeolithic stone artefacts and pottery fragments – which date back to c. 20/19,000 years ago (Wu et al. 2012) – using our own Western classification systems. I feel that we should strive to develop a more comprehensive terminology based on clearer definitions, taking into account the diversity of core reduction strategies as well as the morphological classifications of stone tools. This will allow us to see more clearly the cultural differences and regional variants across the vast geography of Eurasia.

Whether using a 'processual' or 'post-processual' approach, or a mixture of both (my personal preference), and without denying 'culture-history' – of a population, a community or just a few individuals – we continue to make progress in our archaeological knowledge. We recognise the mounting difficulties that face us in organising all the available information into a coherent picture, static or dynamic, diachronic or synchronic, of past foragers' behaviour. The on-site activities of individuals are more easily traced. The results of away-from-camp activities are recorded in brought-in materials retrieved from excavations of the living areas. The challenge we face is to integrate the entire range of foragers' activities within a regional process of cultural evolution. In addition, the products of cultural transmission or evidence for acculturation are not easy to decipher in almost any region of Eurasia but particularly in China. We should remember that Chinese archaeology began to carry out large-scale field operations, laboratory analyses and publications later than in most western Eurasian countries, though the pace of such research has definitely accelerated in the last two decades.

An additional obstacle to a better academic understanding of variability across Eurasia is that we, 'the archaeologists' (a term that incorporates all of those investigating the past), publish the results of our research in different languages and journals, many of which – but not all – can be obtained through the internet. However, I sometimes wonder whether when we employ English as the language of science, like Latin or Arabic in Medieval times, the terminologies we use to discuss material culture carries the same meaning right the way across the continent.

While I do not intend to provide a full set of international comparisons between Western and Chinese definitions, I recently became cognizant that the Palaeolithic sequence and its subdivisions known so well from Africa and western Eurasia, cannot be directly applied in East Asia (e.g., Dennell 2009; Bar-Yosef and Wang 2012) but requires additional explanation in relation to the basic terms employed by local archaeologists. Moreover, Chinese scholars who study the Palaeolithic routinely use their own language and, in spite of some training in western Europe or North America, not surprisingly these researchers have their own, constantly evolving, terminologies. Therefore, in order to make this contribution worthwhile I will need to start by presenting a short description of those terms employed in Chinese archaeology which are directly related to the subject of this paper. Hence, the following section will serve as an introduction to different modes of description of the different archaeological components of the so-called 'microblade industries' – the main subject of this paper – based on a much fuller review of the available evidence (Qu et al. 2013), including my personal experience. This may highlight some of the difficulties encountered in deciphering the complex social processes and genetic changes which took place during the Upper Pleistocene in East Asia. However, it should not deter us from making a preliminary effort to identify

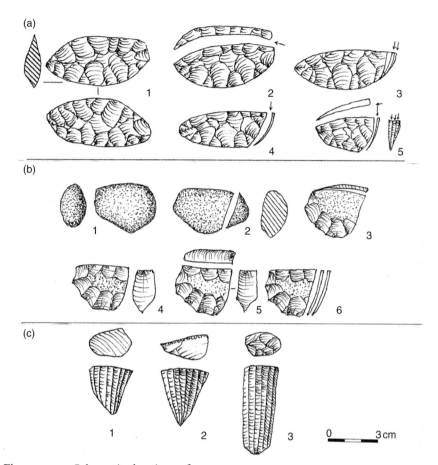

Figure 12.2: Schematic drawings of core types:
A) The production of a wedge-shaped core from a bifacial foliate: 1) First form. 2) Removal of ski spall. 3–4) Removal of bladelets. 5) Renewed platform and continued reduction.
B) The production of a boat-shaped core shaped from a small nodule covered with cortex: 1) Original nodule; 2–3) Removals of the first several flakes create a platform, a face and a keel. 4.-5) Reshaping the platform. 6) Removal of bladelets.
C) 1–2) The production of conical and semi-conical cores; 3) 'Pencil-shaped' core.

those groups of foragers that survived in the region, expanded across north-eastern Asia and eventually crossed to North America. It may also provide information concerning particular knapping techniques used in the production of microliths, probably invented by local Palaeolithic hunter-gatherers in East Asia. In China, these techniques persisted from the Late Pleistocene through the first several millennia of the Holocene. Thus to benefit the readers who are not familiar with these industries, I will first describe them and stress their differences from those of Western Eurasia, and then discuss the possible identity of the makers of these microblade assemblages (Tong 1979, figure 1; Figures 12.2 and 12.3), which were also retrieved in sites dated to the Neolithic and even Bronze Age farming communities.

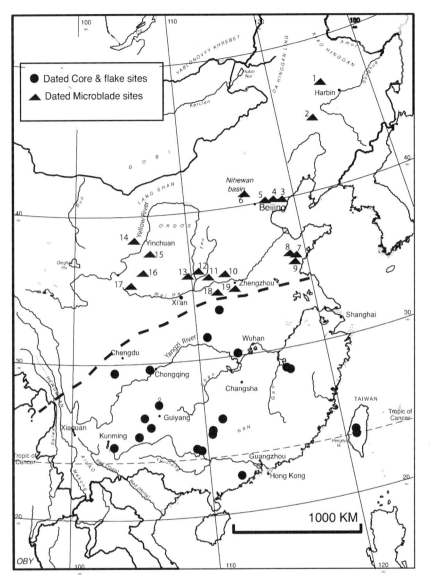

Figure 12.3: Recorded and mostly dated microblade sites (modified after Qu et al. 2013): 1) Daxingtun; 2) Dabusu; 3) Tingsijian; 4) Donghuishan; 5) Mengjiaquan; 6) Nihewan (cluster of sites); 7) Qingfengling; 8) Fenghuangli; 9) Wanghailou; 10) Xiachuan (cluster of sites, but presence of microblades refers to the upper layer); 11) Xueguan; 12) Shizitan (cluster of several sites) 13) Longwangchan (microblades); 14) Pigeon Mountain (microblades); 15) Shuidonggo (one context with microblades); 16) ZL05; 17) Dadiwan (microblades below the Neolithic layer); 18) Dagang (microblades below Neolithic); 19) Lijiagou (microblades below Neolithic). Note the continuous presence of 'core and flake' assemblages in south China.

BASIC DEFINITIONS OF MICROBLADE CORES FROM LOCAL AND WESTERN PERSPECTIVES

Microliths, small objects made of stone, have been known since the end of the nineteenth century. They were called 'Mesolithic' industries, and their relative chronological position was located between the Palaeolithic and Neolithic periods. However, further research during the first half of the twentieth century in Europe, North Africa and western Asia discovered that microliths – in particular backed bladelets and even geometric forms as triangle and trapeze-rectangles – were made during the Upper Palaeolithic or the period known as the Epi-Palaeolithic, mainly since the Late Glacial Maximum (LGM) (c. 24–18 ka cal BP).

The need for commonly accepted descriptions of lithics became a necessity as the study of prehistory advanced. Several classification systems were adopted in western Eurasia and North Africa based on replications (e.g., Sonneville-Bordes and Perrot 1953; Bordes 1961; Tixier 1963). Tixier defines artefacts known as blades (*lames*) as differing dimensionally from bladelets (*lamelles*) based on their actual width. Relying on his experience as an archaeologist in North Africa and as an avid flint knapper, Tixier defined 'bladelets' metrically, as blanks of blades up to c. 12 mm width. When modified by various types of retouch (inverse, semi-abrupt, abrupt and bi-polar) they are called 'microliths', and their maximum width is up to c. 9 mm. Length – in all cases – has no metrical limits. When retouched bladelets or small flakes are shaped into geometric forms they are called 'geometric microliths', with forms such as rectangle, trapeze, triangle and lunate (or 'crescent'). In sum, most researchers who study microlithic industries in Western Eurasia employ both the morphological and a metrically-based classification (e.g., Elston and Kuhn 2002 and papers therein).

In contrast, Chinese microblades are defined as bladelets up to 60 mm long and generally less than 10 mm wide, including rare retouched examples (Chen [C.] 1984, 2007; Chen and Wang 1989; Lu 1998; Keates 2007; Figure 12.2). Thus, the western subtypes of retouched and backed bladelets or well-shaped geometric microliths are not found in most of the Chinese sites. Hence, the term 'microblade industries' implies only the presence of bladelets, and not retouched microliths or geometric forms.

While Chinese microblades are visually similar to any other blades or bladelets, several operational sequences differentiate the reduction methods used to produce the two. Detachment of blades from prismatic and/or opposed platform cores can be done in two ways: direct and indirect percussion. The first technique describes the situation where the knapper holds the core in his hand or places it on his lap while sitting and hits it with a soft hammer. The alternative option is to use a punch while the core is held between the arches of the feet.

Microblade production can be done by direct and indirect percussion, as well as by pressure flaking, as exemplified in replication studies (e.g., Flenniken 1987; Inizan 1991, 2002; Inizan et al. 1992, 1999; Inizan and Lechevalier 1994; Zhao 2011). However, this requires the selection of good quality raw material, such as obsidian or heated siliceous toolstone, and the use of wooden braces to hold the core. Thus the change from one system to another demands additional technical knowledge.

The Chinese microlithic components of the 'microblade' assemblages were produced from flint, chalcedony and obsidian, to mention just a few of the crystalline rocks used. Most assemblages, as recorded in archaeological reports, are often enriched with a flake component. These could be the results of core preparation (biface shaping, as described below), as well as products of a 'core and flake industry' (recently also referred to as 'flake and shatter'; Barton et al. 2007), which are often made from different raw materials such as quartz and quartzite (Bettinger et al. 2007; Zhang et al. 2010). Larger pieces – such as scrapers – are also present alongside microliths, as comparable microlithic assemblages in Africa and Eurasia demonstrate. However, the distinctive Chinese well-shaped bladelets are thin, elongated and generally unretouched (e.g., Morlan 1967) as mentioned above.

In most of the reported assemblages in China the production system or operational sequence (chaîne opératoire) is described solely by the typological designation of the cores. Very few experimental studies were made in China, the most recent one being by Zhao (2011). By comparison, research on microblade assemblages in Japan is relatively advanced because many more Palaeolithic archaeologists are investigating various sites. Japanese reports are based on painstaking refitting and the descriptions of the detailed reduction sequences are often published in English (e.g., Kobayashi 1970; Kato and Tsurumaru 1980; Bleed 2001, 2002; Sato and Tsutsumi 2007). Given that good quality raw material – sometimes heat-treated flint or chalcedony – was manipulated for detaching these delicate bladelet blanks by direct, indirect percussion or pressure flaking, most studies focused on the classification of the cores and not on their products. The main core types described in American and Russian studies (e.g., Morlan 1970) were labelled as 'wedge-shaped', 'boat shaped', 'conical', 'funnel-shaped', 'semi-circular' and 'pencil shaped' (Figures 12.2a–12.2c), according to the way the objects are viewed when drawn by being placed on paper in such a way as to simulate the knapper's view, with the platform 'up'. In comparison, the western concept is 'reversed', with the platform at the lower part and the tip of the blades 'up', and thus do not correspond to the real detachment direction of the drawn cores. Another example of cultural difference in naming the items is that the 'pencil-shaped' core is known as a 'bullet core' in western Asia, reflecting the political situation common in the Near East rather than the knapper's view.

To aid readers' understanding of core types in China, they are described fully below (Figure 12.2):

1. 'Wedge-shaped' cores, produced by a technique known in Japan as the Yubetsu method, were prepared like relatively thin bifaces (Figure 12.2a). The elongated platform was formed by the removal of a crested blade along one of the edges of the biface, sometimes called a 'ski spall' (Flenniken 1987). Another blow then detached one of the edges, thus preparing it for the systematic removal of bladelets. Renewal of the platforms was done by producing a 'core tablet' or by carefully retouching and reshaping the platform. If the platform preparation removal ended being oblique and not parallel to the other edge of the object, it may appear to some scholars as a new core type (e.g., Chen 2007). Finally, unused 'bifacial cores' could result in a difference classification. A 'biface' abandoned before being shaped as a core would be called a 'tool', such as a 'spear head'.

2. 'Boat-shaped' cores differ from 'wedge-shaped' cores but their manufacture is essentially based on the same operational sequence (Figure 12.2b). Often the 'boat-shaped' core was prepared from a piece of tabular flint where cortex was preserved on both faces. A striking platform was created first, and the shaping of the two faces of the core followed. In addition, trimming the base of the core resulted in the formation of a keel that stopped the removal of bladelets as in the 'wedge-shaped' cores. The same operational sequence was successfully used with a thick flake for making a 'boat-shaped' core. The basic 'wedge-shape form' was obtained by trimming one edge bifacially and forming a platform that departs from the flake old striking platform. The shape of the core resembles a boat, with the bladelets being removed from one end (Chen 2007). A similar core reduction strategy was recorded in western Eurasia, where 'carinated cores' (Belfer-Cohen and Grosman 2007) recall the preparation of 'boat-shaped' cores. The striking platform was the first step, followed by the detachment of bladelets that were stopped by the notched keel, thus keeping the blanks from having a curved profile. Due to the French tradition that viewed the 'carinated cores' as a tool (*rabot*, 'push plane') belonging to the Aurignacian toolkit, these cores are drawn with the bifacial keel at the top and in a side view showing platform in vertical position. Once the keel is turned upside down, they look like 'wedge-shaped' or 'boat-shaped' cores.

3. 'Conical, semi-conical and funnel-shaped' cores are morphologically similar to each other and were shaped by a similar operational sequence (Figure 12.2c), similar to those referred to as 'pyramidal cores' in western Asia. They are similar to the common 'prismatic core' in that the core was either hand-held or enclosed within two wooden braces.

The detachment was done either by direct percussion or by indirect percussion using a punch. It seems that these three types with similar conical shapes are best classified in the same general category, but nevertheless recognising the options represented by their differences – in part relating to variability among the raw materials employed, as well as different skill level among individual knappers.

4. The pressure flaked cores known as 'pencil shaped' (Figure 12.2c[3]) and their final appearance with parallel edges almost to the distal tip is clear testimony – as shown experimentally – that the bladelets were obtained by pressure, either in a hand-held position or with a punch pushed by the chest (e.g., Inizan et al. 1992; Inizan and Lechevalier 1994; Inizan 2002). As already mentioned by Flenniken (1987), pressure flaking is more time consuming than direct or indirect percussion – due to the need for heat treatment among other reasons – but the advantage of the products is that the bladelets (or spalls) are long, straight and possess a uniform cutting edge.

In a cross-continental review, Kajiwara (2008) demonstrated that similar reduction techniques were recorded across most of Asia. Once the assemblages are placed within a well-established chronological scheme, it becomes possible to address questions concerning the origins of the microblade industries and the learning systems, transmission and acculturation of north-eastern Asia. In adding these social aspects, we can perhaps draw from the detailed Japanese studies, which may help us identify certain cultural entities within the Chinese world.

A BIRD'S-EYE VIEW: THE MICROBLADE INDUSTRIES IN EAST ASIA

A search for the origins of these assemblages should begin with the early part of the Upper Pleistocene, when hunter-gatherers occupying East and north-east Asia produced their usable stone artefacts using techniques such 'core and flake' and traditional Levallois and non-Levallois methods (e.g., Brantingham et al. 2001; Derevianko 2009; Bar-Yosef and Wang 2012). In the Altai Mountains, to the east of the Baikal Lake and southward into Mongolia, the Middle Palaeolithic industries fall squarely within the world of the Mousterian, as known from western Eurasia. Similar Mousterian contexts were exposed in Jinsitai cave in Jilin, next to Inner Mongolia province (Wang et al. 2010). The presence of Neanderthals – bearers of Mousterian assemblages in the Altai – may explain the finds from several caves (Derevianko 2011 and references therein). At the same time, however, the recently discovered unknown population of the 'Denisovans' in this area indicates that another population was present in East Asia. Whether the latter were the makers of the similar Middle Palaeolithic stone tools is not yet clear. We know that both

Neanderthals and archaic modern humans in the Levant used slightly different, though comparable, Levallois methods for tool making. Will this be the case in the East Asian Middle Palaeolithic? This question will probably keep us busy for years to come.

The Upper Palaeolithic assemblages in the Altai, Mongolia and eastern Siberia include blade industries similar to those of western Eurasia (e.g., Derevianko 2011 and references therein; Kuzmin et al. 2007 and references therein). It should be noted that this blade industry is also present in western China in Shuidenggou (Ningxia), next to the Yellow River (e.g., Ningxia 2003; Pei et al. 2012). Further away, in north-east China, several blade assemblages made of obsidian with burins and end scarpers were found in eastern Jilin province, near the border of North Korea (e.g., Chen et al. 2006), thus supporting the presumed route into the Korean peninsula (Bae 2010), from where the bearers of the blade industries apparently continued towards the Japanese archipelago. Apparently the same route was taken later by the makers of the microblade industries, which most scholars view as emerging technologically from the previous blade industries common in the Altai and north-western China (e.g., Kuzmin et al. 2007 and papers therein). Available 14C dates for a few of the Chinese microblade assemblages are grouped in Table 12.1 and indicate an earliest manifestation of these around 28–26 ka cal BP (Qu et al. 2013).

It should be also noted that in some areas of Korea handaxes and 'core and flake' assemblages persisted (Bae 2010). A somewhat similar situation was recorded in north and central China (Wang 2005; Chen 2007), where according to the available dates (see Qu et al. 2013 for additional lists of radiocarbon dates) contemporary 'core and flake' and microblade assemblages indicate that at least two different tool-making operational sequences (or two different populations?) were in use from around 28/27 ka cal BP through c. 20/18 ka cal BP (Figure 12.3). This persistent contemporaneity of these two or three knapping techniques is intriguing, as each required teaching and learning within a social group or an entity (a clan? a tribe?). The knowledge of microblade manufacture was not adopted instantly by other groups, as indicated by the example from Shandong Province (e.g., Chen 2007). It is hard to believe that every individual in each band of foragers mastered the making of these thin bladelets. The amount of practice required to master the skill of detaching these fine bladelets from small cores (2–3 cm long) –especially by pressure – is likely to have been significant and the number of skilled individuals was probably limited to perhaps one or two per band.

Limits to technical transmission (e.g., language? taboo on passing along knowledge?) or adherence to cultural traditions in making stone tools were in place during the Late and Terminal Pleistocene and, possibly, during the early Holocene. The production of microblades expanded rapidly during the post Late Glacial Maximum (Terminal Pleistocene), which raises the

TABLE 12.1: *Radiometric dates of Late UP*

Site	Layer/Context	Lab No.	Date (Uncal. BP)	Cal. BP (68%)	Material	Dating Technique	Reference
Longwangchan, Shaanxi	Layer4 (loc.1)	BA06005	21,405±75	25189–25854	Ch	[14]C	Zhang et al. 2011
Longwangchan, Shaanxi	Layer4 (loc.1)	BA06006	20,915±70	24683–25232	Ch	[14]C	Zhang et al. 2011
Longwangchan, Shaanxi	Layer4 (loc.1)	BA06009	20,995±70	24771–25498	Ch	[14]C	Zhang et al. 2011
Longwangchan, Shaanxi	Layer4 (loc.1)	BA091131	20,710±60	24489–24931	Ch	[14]C	Zhang et al. 2011
Longwangchan, Shaanxi	Layer5 (loc.1)	BA06008	21,920±80	25963–26673	Ch	[14]C	Zhang et al. 2011
Longwangchan, Shaanxi	Layer5 (loc.1)	BA06007	21,740±115	25455–26531	Ch	[14]C	Zhang et al. 2011
Longwangchan, Shaanxi	Layer5 (loc.1)	BA091132	22,105±50	26185–26870	Ch	[14]C	Zhang et al. 2011
Longwangchan, Shaanxi	Layer5 (loc.1)	BA091133	22,200±75	26260–27353	Ch	[14]C	Zhang et al. 2011
Longwangchan, Shaanxi	Layer6 (loc.1)	BA091129	24,145±55	28551–29303	Ch	[14]C	Zhang et al. 2011
Longwangchan, Shaanxi	Layer6 (loc.1)	BA091130	22,230±55	26288–27395	Ch	[14]C	Zhang et al. 2011
Longwangchan, Shaanxi	Layer4 (loc.1)	L1387	26,300±1200		Sediment	OSL	Zhang et al. 2011
Longwangchan, Shaanxi	Layer4 (loc.1)	L1388	30,400±1200		Sediment	OSL	Zhang et al. 2011
Longwangchan, Shaanxi	Layer4 (loc.1)	L1389	32,600±2000		Sediment	OSL	Zhang et al. 2011

TABLE 12.1: *(continued)*

Site	Layer/Context	Lab No.	Date (Uncal. BP)	Cal. BP (68%)	Material	Dating Technique	Reference
Longwangchan, Shaanxi	Layer5 (loc.1)	L1390	28,700±1100		Sediment	OSL	Zhang et al. 2011
Longwangchan, Shaanxi	Layer5 (loc.1)	L1391	29,800±1300		Sediment	OSL	Zhang et al. 2011
Longwangchan, Shaanxi	Layer5 (loc.1)	L1392	30,100±1000		Sediment	OSL	Zhang et al. 2011
Longwangchan, Shaanxi	Layer5 (loc.1)	L1393	27,700±1200		Sediment	OSL	Zhang et al. 2011
Longwangchan, Shaanxi	Layer5 (loc.1)	L1394	27,900±1300		Sediment	OSL	Zhang et al. 2011
Longwangchan, Shaanxi	Layer6 (loc.1)	L1395	27,800±1200		Sediment	OSL	Zhang et al. 2011
Longwangchan, Shaanxi	Layer6 (loc.1)	L1396	26,500±1100		Sediment	OSL	Zhang et al. 2011
Longwangchan, Shaanxi	Layer6 (loc.1)	L1397	27,800±1000		Sediment	OSL	Zhang et al. 2011
Longwangchan, Shaanxi	Layer6 (loc.1)	L1398	34,700±1200		Sediment	OSL	Zhang et al. 2011
Longwangchan, Shaanxi	Layer6 (loc.1)	L1399	39,900±3600		Sediment	OSL	Zhang et al. 2011
Longwangchan, Shaanxi	Layer6 (loc.1)	L1400	44,300±2400		Sediment	OSL	Zhang et al. 2011
Longwangchan, Shaanxi	Layer6 (loc.1)	L1401	41,600±1600		sediment	OSL	Zhang et al. 2011

TABLE 12.1: *(continued)*

Site	Layer/Context	Lab No.	Date (Uncal. BP)	Cal. BP (68%)	Material	Dating Technique	Reference
Heilongtan, Shandong	T307(2B)	ZK-2129	21,820±520	25347-27051	Ch	^{14}C	Barton et al. 2007
ZL05, Gansu	?	Beta 197632	21,180±100	24995-25685	Ch	^{14}C	Barton et al. 2007
ZL05, Gansu	?	Beta 197633	20,220±90	23885-24449	Ch	^{14}C	Barton et al. 2007
ZL05, Gansu	?	CAMS95088	18,920±520	21934-23311	Ch	^{14}C	
ZL05, Gansu	?	Beta 197631	16,750±70	19685-20272	Ch	^{14}C	Barton et al. 2007
TX04, Ningxia	?	CAMS94204	16,460±45	19478-20067	Ch	^{14}C	
PY03, Ningxia	?	CAMS94203	18,350±70	21688-22323	Ch	^{14}C	
PY04, Ningxia	?	CAMS94202	10,670±40	12622-12730	Ch	^{14}C	Barton et al. 2007
Xiachuan (loc. 1), Shanxi	I T8(2)	ZK-0417	23,224±1000	26490-29124	Ch	^{14}C	
Xiachuan (loc. 1), Shanxi	I T2-6(2)	ZK-0384	21,090±1000	24042-26668	Ch	^{14}C	
Xiachuan (loc.2), Shanxi	?	ZK393	20,115±600	23311-24738	Ch	^{14}C	
Xiachuan (Loc.SWP)	?	ZK634	19,046±600	22004-23554	Ch	^{14}C	Chen and Wang 1989
Xiachuan (loc. 1), Shanxi	IV T101-103(2)	ZK-0497	18,040±480	20937-22274	mud Ch	^{14}C	
Xiachuan (loc. 1), Shanxi	III T1-2(2)	ZK-0494	17,860±480	20716-22125	mud Ch	^{14}C	
Xiachuan (loc. 1), Shanxi	I T1(2)	ZK-0385	15,936±900	18208-20262	Ch	^{14}C	Chen and Wang 1989
Xiachuan (Loc.SWP)	?	ZK762	13,507±300	15811-16915	Ch	^{14}C	Chen and Wang 1989

Site	Layer/Context	Lab No.	Date (Uncal. BP)	Cal. BP (68%)	Material	Dating Technique	Reference
Erdaoliang, Hebei	?	?	18,085±235	21348–22214	bone	^{14}C	Xie et al. 2006
Xibaimaying, Hebei	?	?	18,000±1000		teeth	U-series	Xie et al. 2006
SDG1	top. Layer 3	?	17,250±210	20329–21074	bone	^{14}C	Ningxia 2003
SDG1	top. Layer 3	PV-0331	16,760±210	19647–20337	bone	^{14}C	Ningxia 2003
Mengjiaquan, Hebei	?	?	17,005±205	19914–20762	?	^{14}C	
Xibaimaying, Hebei	?	?	15,000±1000		teeth	U-series	Xie et al. 2006
Yujiagou, Hebei	boundary Layer5&6	?	12,200±1000		quartz sand	TL	
Yujiagou, Hebei	Layer3b middle	?	11,100±900		quartz sand	TL	
Yujiagou, Hebei	Layer3a	?	11,700		potsherd	TL	
Shizitan, Shanxi	?	BA93191	14,305±160	17217–17768	bone	^{14}C	
Shizitan, Shanxi	?	BA93189	13,935±250	16782–17503	BB	^{14}C	
Shizitan, Shanxi	?	BA93188	13,207±220	15634–16608	BB	^{14}C	
Shizitan, Shanxi	?	BA93187	12,303±190	14064–14932	BB	^{14}C	
Shizitan, Shanxi	?	BA93190	11,166±110	12909–13209	bone	^{14}C	
Shizitan, Shanxi	?	BA93186	10,194±540	11039–12533	BB	^{14}C	
Xueguan, Shanxi	?	BK81016	13,170±150	15659–16536	Ch	^{14}C	
Ma'anshan, Hebei	?	?	13,080±120	15562–16409	ch(hearth)	^{14}C	Xie et al. 2006
Hutouliang 73101, Hebei	?	PV-0156	11,000±210	12768–13152	bone	^{14}C	
Xiaonanhai, Henan	upper Layer	ZK-0170	12,710±220	14643–15604	bone	^{14}C	
Xiaonanhai, Henan	D1TB(3):(2) (3)		10,690±500	11693–13025	bone	^{14}C	
Daxingtun, Heilongjiang	T1(1)	PV-0369	11,470±150	13180–13544	bone	^{14}C	

TABLE 12.1: *(continued)*

Site	Layer/Context	Lab No.	Date (Uncal. BP)	Cal. BP (68%)	Material	Dating Technique	Reference
Zhalainuoer, IM	?	PV0015	11,440±230	13099–13578	Ch	[14]C	
Zhalainuoer, IM	?	PV0171	11,330±130	13080–13401	Ch	[14]C	
Pigeon Mtn, Ningxia	Stratum G	Beta097242	12,710±70	14793–15415	Ch	[14]C	
Pigeon Mtn, Ningxia	Strata F	Beta086731	11,620±70	13373–13646	Ch	[14]C	
Pigeon Mtn, Ningxia	Stratum E	Beta097241	10,230±50	11808–12099	Ch	[14]C	
Pigeon Mtn, Ningxia	Stratum D	Beta094119	10,120±60	11517–11927	Ch	[14]C	
Pigeon Mtn, Ningxia	Stratum D	Beta086732	10,060±60	11425–11791	Ch	[14]C	

question of whether this skill was characteristic of a specific population that either increased in size or gradually incorporated other groups of foragers.

The following sections – although focused on the current situation in China – benefit from in-depth research conducted in Siberia, Korea, the Japanese archipelago and western North America, from Alaska to California, although the list of references represents only a small selection of a vast literature (e.g., Nelson 1937; Kobayashi 1970; Yi and Clark 1985; Flenniken 1987; West 1996 and papers there in; Lu 1998; Seong 1998; Bleed 2001, 2002, 2008; Elston and Kuhn 2002 and papers therein; Goebel et al. 2003; Kuzmin *at al.* 2007 and papers therein; Nakazawa 2005; Pantukhina 2007; Bae 2010; Elston et al. 2011 and references therein).

SETTLEMENT PATTERNS AND FUNCTION OF THE MICROBLADES

The distribution of microblade sites across the different landscapes of northern China varies (Figure 12.3). Most sites or small stations are situated along creeks, river valleys or lake margins (e.g., Tong 1979; Lu 1998), a pattern which becomes obvious when sites are plotted on a map. However, we assume that the search for adequate raw materials also resulted in camps in hilly areas, along river valleys and some grassland areas (Tong 1979, figure 1; Figure 12.3). Among these 'ribbon-type' clusters of sites, those along the Nen River (between Heilongjiang Province and Inner Mongolia, northern China), the cluster of the Shizitan sites in Shanxi province (along the Qinshui River, a tributary of the Yellow River: Shizitan Archaeological Team 2002; Shi and Song 2010), and the cluster of Xiachuan (in the Fuyihe river valley in the Xiachuan basin; e.g., Wang et al. 1978; Tang 2000) merit specific mention, as does the cluster in Houtoliang, in the Nihewan basin, where nine localities are spread over 10 km (Xie et al. 2006). Each of these clusters comprise roughly a dozen localities and sometimes more – for example, along the Nen River in the North – and several of these were re-occupied more than once.

The spread of dates collected from the published reports range from several millennia prior to the LGM until after the onset of the Holocene. A few examples include: Longwangshan, that lasted c. 25.5–20 ka cal BP (Zhang et al. 2011); Xiachuan, where the early layers are from c. 25 ka through 22 ka and then two isolated dates of c. 19 ka and 16 ka cal BP (Lu 2010); and Shizitan, where the cluster of sites persisted from c. 24–10 ka cal BP (Shizitan Archaeological Team 2010). Smaller occupations include Shuidonggou 12 (layer 11) 13.0 ka cal BP (Pei et al. 2012) and Dadiwan, after 13.0 ka cal BP (Bettinger et al. 2010). At Nihewan, basin sites are dated from ca. 21.0 ka cal BP through to 11.6–10.0 ka (Xie et al. 2006; Zhang et al. 2010 and references therein). Early Holocene sites with microblades – such as Donghulin (west of Beijing) dates to c. 11,500–9,400 cal BP (Zhao et al. 2006) whilst the Lijiagou site (south of the Yellow River) dates to c. 10.5 – 10.3 ka cal BP

(Y. Wang, pers. comm.). Evidence for later use of microblades at Holocene sites is also known from Chinese reports but the details and the discussion concerning cultural continuity are beyond the scope of this paper.

The various assemblages of Longwangchan (Institute of Archaeology [CASS] and Shaanxi Institute of Archaeology 2007; Zhang et al. 2011) on the bank of a tributary of the Yellow River, produced a rich core and flake industry with low frequencies of microblades, many obtained by pressure flaking, and a few grinding stones. Until recently, given the similarity in microblade technology at all the sites, there was a tendency to assign them to one local culture and sometimes to group all the assemblages from the different layers of a particular site into one collection. Hence the available reports rarely provide the details of each assemblage, and therefore, it is not easy to identify changes in the toolkits that may have started c. 28/26 ka cal BP in China and slightly later in Korea and Japan.

A brief survey of the Japanese literature indicates two phenomena. First, procurement of obsidian from its sources required transport or transmission between groups over distances of 10–250 km (Sano 2007; Sato and Tsutsumi 2007). Two strategies regarding the siliceous rocks were identified: one was based on the transportation of nodules (such as pebbles with partially removed cortex); the second saw fully prepared cores and some of their products brought onto sites (Sano 2007).

Second, linking the geographic distribution of the sites in the archipelago and variability in techniques for the production of microblades (ten different ones were described) may in the future allow the identification of the prehistoric territories of local foragers. An additional opportunity concerns the typological changes through time that are also available in the Korean records, such as the appearance of tanged points (e.g., Seong 1998, 2007; Sato and Tsutsumi 2007; Bae 2010). Returning to North China, retouched points resembling arrowheads – as well as tanged points – were also found in Xiachuan and Xueguan. The possible range of dates for the appearance of these Terminal Pleistocene types is around 13–12 ka cal BP. An additional new type within the sequence of microblade assemblages is the hafted adze found in Houtoliang (Zhang et al. 2010). Therefore, there are possibly other sources of evidence for establishing a more detailed culture history of this period in northern China.

It is commonly accepted that microblades – either with plain edges or retouched edges – were employed as elements of composite tools and hafted in wood, bone or antler handles and shafts. There are at least three Chinese archaeological examples of hafted, unretouched bladelets (Figure 12.4). The earliest was found in Donghulin (Major Archaeological Discoveries of 2005 [2006]); one uncovered at a Neolithic site at Xinglonggwa (Inner Mongolia, c. 8000 cal BP); and two in YuangYangChi, a context considered as Late Neolithic (c. 4000 BP; see Tong 1979, figure 5; Lu 1998). In all

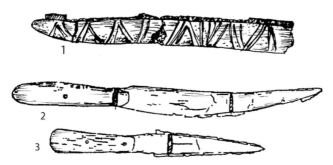

Figure 12.4: Hafted microblade fragments in bone handles from Donghulin (1–2; redrawn after major archaeological discoveries of 2005) and Yuanyouanchi (3; redrawn after Tong 1979: figure 4).

examples bladelets were inserted in one or two sides of a bone haft, apparently to serve as knives (Tong 1979; Lu 1998) and to be used as antler armatures (Elston et al. 2011).

Given the presence of many microblade assemblages in regions dominated by cold climates, often dated to the LGM and the ensuing millennia (Elston and Brantingham 2002; Goebel 2002; Elston et al. 2011), the bladelets were interpreted as parts of projectiles which marked the intensification of hunting of deer, antelope, bison and horse. However, the functional interpretation of microblades is still problematic because of a lack of microwear and edge damage studies. In addition, the only known hafted bladelets, as indicated above, were used as knives or daggers. Hence, viewing the microblades as an adaptation to particularly harsh environments raises additional issues. For example, why are these tool types considered more efficient in these conditions? (e.g., Kuzmin 2007).

The small size of cores and their products meant that they were easily portable elements with a high degree of maintainability, and their organic hafts would have been resilient in cold climate –important in a region with patchy resources, requiring a high degree of mobility. Pressure flaking was probably in use from the emergence of this industry and undoubtedly since the LGM, indicating the presence of skilled knappers.

A pattern of frequent residential moves or short-time hunting stations seems to fit the archaeological evidence of numerous small sites that generally produced small numbers of microblades along with a flake industry (see Ikawa-Smith 2007 for some general calculations). In addition to the amount of work needed for the production of such composite tools, this suggests that these foragers invested in making clothing and possibly tents.

Radiocarbon chronologies, as available today, indicate that the origin of the set of techniques incorporated under this generalised term is likely to have been somewhere between the Altai Mountains and the Yellow River (e.g., Chen and Wang 1989; Keates 2007; Kuzmin 2007; Bae 2010). Dispersal of this new techniques from west to east occurred along several routes, forming a pattern something akin to a 'braided stream'. It crossed into the northern Japanese archipelago into Hokkaido and, in the South, through the Korean peninsula and into Kiyushu. In China, the geographic spread was towards the East – south of the Yellow River – reaching the Shandong/Jiangsu border and, towards the south-west, arriving in northern Sichuan and also moving through Qinghai into Tibet (Madsen et al. 2006; Brantingham and Gao 2006: figure 2). Most of those more distant sites date to the final millennia of the Pleistocene and early millennia of the Holocene. Another path led from eastern Siberia into Alaska and, later, further south along the north-west coast of North America (although no further South than around the present region of the Pacific North-West) and persisted from c. 11.5 ka through 7.5 ka cal BP and possibly later (Ackerman 2007; Magne and Fedje 2007).

DISCUSSION: A STEP FORWARD IN INTERPRETATION

The relatively fast spread of microblade industries occurred especially during the LGM, when worsening environmental conditions forced many – but not all – groups of foragers to move away from the Loess Plateau (Bettinger et al. 2007, 2010). Some decided to stay, as indicated by LGM-dated microblades sites present in the area. These climatic triggers and the resultant environmental conditions could have been a force which motivated other groups to cross from Korea to Japan. In addition, the current genetic evidence suggests that modern humans, who generally arrived in East Asia through the southern route, also made their way from the North, perhaps from the Altai mountains into mainland China and from there further East into Korea and Japan (e.g., Bar-Yosef and Belfer-Cohen 2013 and references therein).

If this explanation is correct then the identity of the microblade industries' bearers is resolved. The Upper Palaeolithic population of western Eurasia registered faster migration rates than previous populations such as the Neanderthals and the Denisovans. Their spread across most of this vast region during the MIS3 was responsible for adding blades and microblade toolkits to the traditional 'core and flake' industries (Kuzmin 2007). If further research and dating can demonstrate that these groups of foragers emerged from a core area around the Altai Mountains, this may explain the earlier dates observed in the middle basin of the Yellow River. These groups of hunter-gathers had the prior knowledge that in addition to toolstones suitable for making knives and scrapers (such as quartz and quartzite) they could exploit flint, chalcedony and chert to make microliths. Several groups, who arrived earlier in obsidian-rich areas, could have been among the antecedents of the makers of microblades. Indeed, once the invention of these various techniques had occurred or been adopted by several different groups, the making of microliths – by pressure flaking, direct and indirect percussion – could have been distributed among other populations in East Asia through cultural transmission.

In summary, this paper set out to find the social groups who made the microliths in northern China, but it seems that the available evidence is too scanty and lacks the detail required to delineate territories of Late Pleistocene foragers. Instead, I end with a review of the current state of knowledge and the discussions reflected in some of the literature. Hence, this paper is another contribution to reconstructing cultural history, but one from which a major point can be drawn: too often prehistorians attribute cultural changes – as primarily recognised in the sequences of lithic industries – to climatic causes. There is no such correlation in East Asia, as the Chinese evidence indicates. Instead, the making of microblades here began during the comfortable conditions of MIS3, and not as a reaction to depleting sources during the LGM.

CHAPTER 13

HANDAXE SYMMETRY IN THE LOWER AND MIDDLE PALAEOLITHIC: IMPLICATIONS FOR THE ACHEULEAN GAZE

JAMES COLE

INTRODUCTION

Over two hundred years have passed since the first recorded discovery of a handaxe was noted by Frere (1800), and over a hundred and fifty years since the great antiquity of these artefacts was fully recognised (Gamble and Kruszynski 2009). Yet to a large extent the exact function of this artefact within the context of Lower and Middle Palaeolithic hominin societies, potentially spanning at least three distinct hominin species (McNabb 2013), remains a largely unresolved and speculative issue within Palaeolithic research. Similarly, the offered interpretations surrounding the Acheulean handaxe range from practical tools relating to butchery, mechanisms of sexual selection, aesthetic markers, cultural mediators and objects used to negotiate the landscapes and socialscapes of the Acheulean world (Wynn 1995; Gamble 1998b; Saragusti et al. 1998; White 1998a; Kohn and Mithen 1999; McPherron 2000; McNabb et al. 2004; Wenban-Smith 2004; Hopkinson and White 2005; Porr 2005; Pope et al. 2006; Machin et al. 2007 – to name but a few examples).

Why has the handaxe formed such a locus of debate? The answer lies in the notion that the handaxe is seen to represent the first tools shaped through deliberate attention to form (Wynn 1979, 2004; Iovita and McPherron 2011) corresponding to a significant shift in behaviour and cognition from the non-handaxe industries such as the Oldowan and Clactonian (Wynn 1981; White 2000a; McNabb 2013). Due to the poor preservation of organic artefacts from such deep antiquity, the main focus for Pleistocene hominin behaviour must lie with stone tools, where tool production reflects varying degrees of planning, problem solving, perceptual-motor coordination and sociality (Stout and Chaminade 2009). In particular, attention to handaxe form is perceived to be related to a behavioural standardisation in artefact morphology associated with agreed cultural practice within hominin societies (Ronen 1982; Mellars 1989, 1991; Saragusti et al. 1998; Kohn and Mithen 1999; McNabb et al. 2004; Wenban-Smith 2004; Monnier 2006; Stout and Chaminade 2009) – although see Chase (1991) for discussions against. The argument defending this position is as follows: the higher the degree of standardisation and deliberate imposition of shape and form within handaxe morphology, the higher the influence social learning plays on the formation of lithic tools (McNabb et al. 2004; Monnier 2006). Standardisation in artefact morphology is seen to represent a desired end product in accordance with socially defined or accepted parameters which in turn are the consequence of mental categories which may be representative in nature (Monnier 2006). The presence of symmetry within biface morphology is often seen to represent the epitome of the standardised handaxe, present throughout Acheulean assemblages and increasing significantly in occurrence through the Acheulean as time progresses (Saragusti et al. 1998; Hodgson 2009). Therefore, one of the key research questions regarding handaxes are whether they were purely functional in design, or whether they were imbued with significant cultural meaning expressed through the presence of symmetry and representing a clear attention to standardised form. As such discussions of handaxe symmetry have implications that go far beyond the physical or cognitive demands reflected through chaînes opératoire or façonnage, but are crucial to our understanding / identification of when material culture began to play an active role in mediating hominin social relationships through an agreed cultural norm.

This paper seeks to make a contribution to the continuing handaxe debate by presenting an analysis of bifaces, encompassing some 1838 artefacts from the British Palaeolithic record. The main focus of this paper will be to elucidate a number of key assumptions held within the wider academic community in regards to the presence of symmetrical form within handaxe morphology:

- Acheulean handaxes are often made to a symmetrical mental template.
- Symmetrical handaxes are present in large quantities throughout Acheulean assemblages.
- The presence of symmetrical handaxes within Acheulean assemblages increases through time as a marker of increasing hominin cognitive ability.

Versions of the three statements given above appear time and again throughout the literature on handaxes however there are very little published by which these statements are substantiated. I emphasise at this point that this paper questions the presence of symmetry within Pleistocene biface assemblages. In principle I do not have a problem with the interpretations of the symmetrical biface and its role in social communications if such patterns as described above genuinely exist. The data presented here should therefore engage and facilitate debate amongst researchers interested in hominin behaviour and cognition.

SEMIOSIS, LANGUAGE AND MATERIAL CULTURE

The active use of material culture within social mediation can also be linked to questions of language development (Davidson and Noble 1989; Wynn 1991; Stout and Chaminade 2012). Furthermore, it is widely accepted that language lies in the domain of human communication, while animal communications, including vocalisations, remain entirely distinct (Deacon 1997; Origgi and Sperber 2000; Dunbar 2004; Barbieri 2010). The main reasons for this lie with the different capabilities for semiosis (activity based on signs) between animals and humans. There can be little doubt that animals have the capability for semiosis as they receive signals from the world, process those signals and instigate an appropriate reaction (Kull 2009; Barbieri 2010). However, there is a noticeable difference in the ability for sign creation, reading and interpretation between animals and humans that must be clarified before continuing. Peirce (1906) identified three types of signs in the world, an icon, index and symbol. Wynn (1995), Deacon (1997) and Barbieri (2010) provide useful synopses of Peirce's original definitions where icons are associated with a similarity between a sign and an object, indexes are associated with a physical or temporal connection between sign and object and symbols are associated with a socially agreed conventional link between a sign and object.

In order to clarify how an icon, index and symbol work, I offer the following: the similarity inherent within an icon translates into resemblance identification or pattern recognition (Barbieri 2010), for example, a picture of a leaping stag warns motorists to be cautious of deer crossing the road (Wynn 1995). When something is an index, it is causally linked to, or associated with, something else in space and time (Deacon 1997), for example, a macaque alarm call will indicate the presence of danger when danger is sighted by one individual (Coss et al. 2007). The causal link being that macaque alarm calls are only used to signify danger, thereby creating an indexical link between the sounding of an alarm call and the presence of danger. A symbol is denoted when there is a social convention that establishes or agrees an arbitrary relationship linking one thing to another (Deacon 1997) such as an ampersand (&) being a logogram for the word 'and'. Essentially, symbols allow arbitrary associations between one thing and another (Barbieri 2010), where meaning is only recognised or achieved through the social conventions that construct and interpret the association.

The relevance of the three types of sign is in the degree of clarity it allows in defining the types of communication experienced by animals and humans. As exemplified by Deacon (1997) animal communications are based on icons and indexes, whilst human communications – in the form of language (both visual and verbal) – are based not only on icons and indexes, but also on the systematic and extensive use of arbitrary symbols (Origgi and Sperber 2000; Barbieri 2010). If this argument is accepted, then there must be a stage in the evolutionary development of the human species where hominins moved from communications centred around icons and indexes, into communications incorporating symbols and the emergence of a language system. It is the recognition of this seminal moment within the archaeological record where material culture begins to mediate social relationships through the use of assigned symbols that forms a central component to this paper.

LANGUAGE, COGNITION AND THE 'SOCIAL BRAIN HYPOTHESIS'

In order for language to develop, the ability for symbolic thought must be incorporated into the hominin cognitive repertoire. The capability to conceive of the symbolic is intrinsically linked to the ability to perceive a notion of the abstract (Deacon 1997). Identifying the presence of, and ability for, abstract thought in our hominin ancestors from the Palaeolithic record has been a longstanding question in Palaeolithic research (Wynn 1991, 1995; Carruthers and Chamberlain 2000; Barham 2002; Gamble 2007; Pettitt 2011a). One hypothesis in particular has provided a useful heuristic for archaeologists to investigate and assess hominin cognitive potential in relation to the development of abstract thought and language: the 'Social Brain Hypothesis' (SBH) (Dunbar 1998a, 2003). The SBH is essentially a biological model relating to hominin brain encephalisation where increasing group size and the subsequent complex social pressures required to maintain group cohesion selected for increasing brain size. Within hominin encephalisation there is one area of the brain that has increased in size at a faster rate than any other brain component and that is the neocortex – a part of the brain of marked relevance to the SBH because it governs reasoning and consciousness, stores memories, and organises social relationships (Dunbar 1998a). Therefore, the SBH suggests that the larger the neocortex, the greater the ability of the animal to maintain social cohesion within larger groups.

A number of studies have recently corroborated the idea that among primates, relative brain size and manifestations of social complexity such as group size are directly related (Kudo and Dunbar 2001; Reader and Laland 2002; Byrne and Corp 2004; Lindenfors 2005). The SBH does not reject other models of brain evolution (Gibson 1986; Faulk 1990; Aiello and Wheeler 1995; Henneberg 1998), but rather incorporates the ideas that biology and physiology contributed to encephalisation whilst social factors inspired the overall process. The social solutions to ecological problems (through increased group size) drove the intensification of social cohesion, and subsequently provided the selection pressure for large brain evolution (Dunbar 2003; Dunbar and Shultz 2007).

The SBH offers a further constructive heuristic in regard to assessing the cognitive ability of different hominin species by relating predicted group and brain size, to orders of intentionality and a theory of mind. Crucial to the discussion on language and the aptitude for the abstract concept is that a theory of mind marks the beginning step in the development of abstract thought and symbolic construction. A theory of mind may be defined as the ability to comprehend the mental state of one's own mind, and the mental state of the mind of another; but to also recognise that the mental state of another's mind may differ from the mental state of one's own. In regard to the development of language, it is important to note that in order to achieve an understanding of language (visual or verbal), a theory of mind is an essential component (Dunbar 1998b, 2007; Origgi and Sperber 2000).

In terms of cognitive significance, a theory of mind may be related to a hierarchy of intentional states termed orders of intentionality: the concept of intentionality comes from notions of philosophy of mind and essentially relates to belief states epitomised through words such as intend, suppose, imagine, think, and know (Premack and Woodruff 1978; Dunbar 2007). Crucially, notions of intentionality describe self-reflective mental states, or mental states experienced when we reflect upon the contents of our minds (Dunbar 2007). The importance of this in cognitive terms is that intentional mental states form a recursive hierarchy – Ben *intends* that Matthew *supposes* John to *imagine* Tim *thinks* that William *knows* (italics represent the orders of intentionality), and this hierarchical scale is commonly identified as levels or orders of intentionality (Premack and Woodruff 1978). First-order intentionality represents one mental state (Ben intends), second-order represents two mental states (Matthew supposes John to imagine) and so on, with the above example representing fifth-order intentionality. The orders of intentionality and a theory of mind have been directly correlated, with a theory of mind requiring an individual to imagine the content of two minds, their own and that of someone else. Therefore a theory of mind is equivalent to a second-order of intentionality (Dunbar 2003) – Matthew supposes John to imagine.

Through such an ordinal scale, a great deal of cognitive and social complexity can be imparted even if only a small number of different belief/ mental states are linked together (Premack and Woodruff 1978). Modern humans may operate at an upper limit of six orders (occasionally higher) of intentionality, although fifth-order intentionality is the average functional limit that we moderns tend to achieve (Dunbar 2004: 47) and as such I shall examine the behavioural and material archaeological record accordingly.

Based on current evidence, it would appear that it is only humans that have a confirmed incontrovertible theory of mind. Great apes, elephants and dolphins have been studied in theory of mind experiments and are said to posses mirror self-recognition, a phenomenon associated to an expression of self-recognition and self-awareness linked to a theory of mind/second-order intentionality (Povinelli et al. 1997; Reiss and Marino 2001; Plotnik et al. 2006). However, there have been claims that there is little direct empirical evidence to support the idea that mirror self-recognition (and a host of other behaviours such as imitation and pretend play) are developmental foundations to a theory of mind (De Veer and Van Den Bos 1999; Nielsen and Dissanayake 2004) and some doubt if non-human primates and other animals truly aspire to a theory of mind due to the difficulties in non-biased testing (Tomasello and Call 1997; Heyes 1998).

When asking the question of whether non-human primates (or Proboscidea, Delphinidae and Platanistoidea) have a theory of mind, the answer is not a simple yes or no. Based on laboratory experiments where chimpanzees and children are subjected to similar belief state tests, chimpanzees would appear to have a broad understanding of the goals, intentions, perceptions and knowledge of others, and they would appear to understand how these psychological states work together to produce intentional action, so in a wide, open sense, some would claim that chimpanzees have a theory of mind (Tomasello and Call 2008). However, it would appear that if great apes do possess a theory of mind, they do not appear to do it very well and only as a best-case scenario (Dunbar 2007), which may be explained in a number of ways. First, chimpanzees do not seem to be able to correctly understand false belief states and cannot therefore be said to possess a fully human-like belief-desire psyche (Tomasello and Call 2008). Second, the chimpanzees may not understand the purpose of the tasks they are being asked to perform, which calls into question the validity of any behavioural results that mimic theory of mind actually representing a true understanding of a theory of mind (ibid.).

There are some real concerns that the chimpanzees on which the majority of theory of mind/belief state experiments are conducted upon are mostly trained, hand-reared, or captive chimpanzees with extensive human contact (Davidson and Noble 1989). In order to truly assess the cognitive capabilities of our closest living hominid cousins and other intelligent animals, wild populations should remain the focus of these studies. An excellent recent example of such research is Crockford et al. (2012) where the authors have demonstrated through alarm call experiments that wild chimpanzees seem to recognise the knowledge and ignorance states of other members of their group. Although Crockford et al. do not directly relate such behaviour to a theory of mind, there are certainly some very interesting and clear implications arising from the study that could do with some further investigation that may well change the emphasis of the proceeding and following paragraphs in the future.

At present, in my opinion, it is only the hominin clade that has truly managed to break through the second-order intentionality boundary and attain a conscious theory of mind. Without a theory of mind, the ability for abstract thought and symbolic construction must remain elusive, and therefore a lack of a theory of mind must formulate part of the explanation for why animal communications are iconic and indexical rather than symbolic. Based on this reasoning, I view a theory of mind as a critical factor of the human condition, essential to the cognitive separation of primate versus hominin evolution, whilst orders of intentionality are used as an ordinal scale of cognitive complexity in relation to the hominin archaeological record.

If it is accepted that a theory of mind or second-order of intentionality is an essential prerequisite for the development of language, then it stands to reason that the capacity for language must have arisen after the theory of mind/second-order of intentionality threshold was breached in antiquity. Dunbar has related the orders of intentionality to the brain sizes of primates and

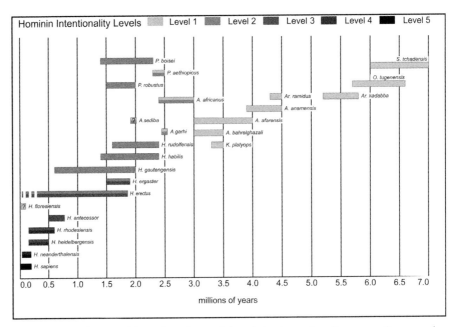

Figure 13.1: Summarising the view of hominin intentionality according to the Social Brain Hypothesis. The hominin phylogeny is a diagrammatic representation based on timelines, not cladistics. Figure 1 modified after Carlson et al. 2011; Dunbar 2007; Grove *pers. comm.*

interpolated them into the hominin fossil record based on correlations between frontal lobe volumes, group size and 'achievable levels of intentionality' as a predictive exercise in estimating hominin cognition levels (Dunbar 1992, 2004, 2007) (Figure 13.1).

From Figure 13.1 it can be seen that it is only with the advent of *Homo* (and possibly the late *Paranthropines*) where a second-order of intentionality is predicted to have been achieved by our hominin ancestors. However, it is unlikely that a fully developed ability for grammatical language emerged in hominin cognition at the same time as a theory of mind was realised. Rather, as I will expand upon below, I propose that a developed ability for language based on symbolic interaction not only requires a second-order of intentionality but may only be truly attainable with third-order intentionality as a minimum. Furthermore, as I argue below, I would suggest that it is only with a fifth order of intentionality that a full comprehension of the symbolic abstract occurs and subsequently grammatical language or speech develops as a selective advantage to allow the expression of the said symbolic abstract – defined here as a conceptual or metaphysical ideology made significant only through social and cultural constructions (Deacon 1997). Such a complex notion can only be explained to an external individual or group in such a way as to facilitate equal understanding through grammatical language. Non-verbal visual display utilising the body or material culture is simply not expressive or plastic enough to convey the full meaning of a totally abstract notion such as, for example, the supernatural.

Although there are many criticisms of the SBH (for example – Barrett et al. 2007; de Ruiter et al. 2011), this paper shall focus on one particular aspect. The SBH cognitive predictions have never been tested against the archaeological/ behavioural record. Dunbar (2007) argues that there is no real need for the SBH to be corroborated against the archaeological record because the SBH explicitly deals with the mental processes that underlie social behaviour rather than on the overt behaviour itself or aspects of cognition that focus on instrumental skills like tool making. The tools in effect become a 'red herring' as the mindsets that lie at the core of the SBH are unlikely to leave a visible trace in the fossil record that archaeologists may relate to the tools themselves (Dunbar 2007). However, there have been extensive archaeological studies identifying material culture as an active participant in maintaining and structuring social relations (Gamble 1999, 2007; Gosden and Marshall 1999; Ingold 2007; Barham 2010), supported through ethnographic studies illustrating that tools lie at the heart of mediating social relations, beliefs and social practices (Killick 2004). Even if it is often unclear which hominin species definitively produced different tool types, the act of tool making and material culture creation is intrinsically a social act when related to problem-solving and learning, however this was achieved – that is, through imitation, observation or demonstration (Stout 2002; Bamforth and Finlay 2008; Barham 2010). Additionally, in regard to primates, there are some interesting studies which underline the importance of social environments in the retention of learnt skills and innovation in tool making (van Schaik and Pradham 2003). Therefore, if tool making is correctly placed within the socialscape of their creation, and Palaeolithic tools are examined with this in mind, there can be little doubt that tools have great potential to inform on the behavioural and achieved cognitive complexities of their hominin creators, and in this paper I will outline my attempt to use orders of intentionality as a heuristic in relating degrees of hominin cognition to the archaeological record through constructs of identity.

THE IDENTITY MODEL

From an archaeological perspective, discourse on the nature of hominin evolution in regard to the development of material culture as a conscious mechanism of communication must also be related to discussions on hominin cognitive ability and methods of gauging that ability from the behavioural record (Wynn 1979, 1981, 1985; Stout 2002; Stout and Chaminade 2009). The identity model (a summary is offered here, see Cole 2011, 2012, in press for greater detail), proposes a theoretical framework that allows an assessment of the cognitive ability of ancient hominins through concepts of identity, linked to visual display, material culture and its role in hominin social

Orders of Intentionality				
1st - 2nd order	2nd order	3rd - 4th order		5th order

Categories of Identity

Internal Identity: Self is conscious of an awareness of own self. The awareness of *own* self formings a bridge between 1st and 2nd order intentionality.	**External Identity:** Self is conscious of their own mind, and that Other has a mind of their own. Subsequently, Self is also aware that Other may hold an opinion of Self other than that encapsulated within Self's internal identity.	**Intex Identity:** Is the identity that Self desires Other(s) to buy into. ***Perpetuated Intex:** Using material culture / behaviour to broadcast the intex.	**Collective Identity:** Self's belief in a commonality of understanding of the whole group	**Abstract Identity:** An ideational component to Collective identity. **Perpetuated Abstract:** Using material culture / behaviour to broadcast the Abstract Identity.

Fictitious Example

Xi *believes* he is a good hunter. This is a 1st to 2nd order of intentionality because Xi is aware of his own identity (a good hunter), rather than Xi just being aware.	Xi *hopes* that O'wa *believes* that Xi is a good hunter.	Xi *hopes* the group *accepts* O'wa's *belief* that Xi is an *exceptionally cunning hunter.* * Xi brings food to O'wa and re-enacts(falsely) his bravery and exceptional cunning in his hunt of a buffalo	Xi *expects* the group to *believe* that O'wa *considers* that Xi's *intex* is true. O'wa re-enacts Xi's kill for the group to convince the group of Xi's hunting prowess	Xi *intends* O'wa to *think* that the Ancesters *desire* the group to *accept* Xi's *belief* in his own intex. Xi achieves this by telling O'wa (using language) that the Ancestors have given Xi extraordinary prowess as a hunter

Potential archaeological predictions for perpetuated index / abstract**	• Social communication is centred around visual display, gesture and vocalisations. The body and material culture begin to play a more pronounced role in identity perpetuation broadcast on a context independent and individual by individual basis. • If assemblages have a definite biasv toward 'true' symmetry or contain artefacts of 'extraordinary design' (e.g. giant handaxes) then it may be that such artefacts have an implication beyond the purely functional and may hold some limited social significance. Ochre use for visual display purposes (such as limited body adornment) may be placed here as well. • Social communication is centred around visual display, gesture and grammatical language. The body's boundaries are now fully extended through material culture on an individual and group basis with material culture adopting a functional and symbolic role in identity perpetuation. • Material culture with a purely non-utilitarian design enters the archaeological (for example beads) art and figurines.

Figure 13.2. Illustrating the basic definitions of the categories of identity present within the identity model and an illustrative example as to how the identity model relates to the orders of intentionality. Modified after (Cole, in press figures 2 and 3). ** Archaeological predictions based on Cole 2011: table 4.3; Cole 2012: table 4).

communication. In contrast to the more traditional filter of brain size, the identity model represents a theoretical perspective allowing archaeologists to correlate the Palaeolithic record to the cognitive potential of hominin species based on notions of the self and others, linked into mechanisms of identity construction and perpetuation. The model sets out a minimum of seven categories of identity, each of which builds on, is informed by and informs the previous. Furthermore, each category of identity requires a certain minimum level of cognitive complexity on the part of the hominin. This minimum cognitive potential is measured through the orders of intentionality. Figure 13.2 below illustrates the essential basic definitions of the identity model and how they relate to the orders of intentionality.

From Figure 13.2 it can be seen that the key points of interest archaeo-logically speaking are the perpetuated intex (intex being an abbreviation derived from 'internal to external') and perpetuated abstract. Perpetuated intex deals with the deliberate manipulation of how the other views the external identity of the self in relation to the self's intex identity, or in other words, the way an individual desires to be seen by others – exemplified by Eliot's (1974: 4) J. Alfred Prufrock preparing 'a face to meet the faces that you meet'. In this respect there is some degree of similarity with Wiessner's (1983: 258) notion of assertive style defined as a formal variation in material culture which is personally based and which carries information supporting individual identity. Perpetuated intex at the third- to fourth-order intention-ality bracket involves symbolic broadcasting on an individual-to-individual basis, and on a larger individual to group basis. The use of the body and material culture within this third to fourth-order intentionality context relates to physical body manipulations such as gesture or visual displays, in which material culture is symbolically involved in structuring social interactions, tacking between individuals and the group (Gamble 1998b). The body and material culture become the context and the engine for the effective broadcast of perpetuated intex. In order for the manipulation of the perpetuated intex to carry meaning across to the other from the self, the self must be sure that the other will correctly interpret the intended meaning. In this instance, culture – as a function of collective identity – would be the framework that ensures standardised meaning, agreed social convention and commonality of understanding is present.

Abstract identity and perpetuated abstract deal with the deliberate creation and dissemination of an ideology. In many respects there is a clear affinity to the idea of emblemic style as described by Wiessner (1983: 257) where there is a prescribed adaptation in material culture with a distinct referent transmitting a clear message to a defined target population about conscious affiliation or identity, for example, a flag. I would suggest that a fifth-order intentionality is the minimum cognitive requirement not only to conceive of an abstract notion such as an ideology or emblemic style, but also to successfully commu-nicate the abstract and arbitrary nature of such an identity to an other individ-ual(s) through perpetuated abstract. Perpetuated abstract then becomes the mechanism through which the abstract identity is broadcast and should be closely linked to the appearance of grammatical language, as that is the only form of communication flexible enough to get the abstract arbitrary notions of abstract identity across to another individual(s) without misinterpretation or confusion. Visual display alone, in this instance, is simply not plastic enough to fulfil this role without some sort of additional explanation. Archaeological evidence for a perpetuated abstract could be linked to indicators for grammat-ical language such as art, figurines or ornamentation (for example, Conard 2003; d'Errico et al. 2005) where it is the physical expression of arbitrary abstract notions through speech, art, ornamentation and figurines which constitute the perpetuated abstract.

The crucial point to take away here is that once grammatical language markers enter the archaeological record, fifth-order intentionality must have been reached by the hominin creating the marker, although at the time of writing, such signatures are only related incontrovertibly to anatomically modern humans. This paper aims to identify the appearance of perpetuated intex within the archaeological record. When were artefacts first consciously incorporated into systems of social communication and visual display within a culturally meaningful context?

SITES AND METHODOLOGY

The eight sites and assemblages discussed here focus on the British Lower to Middle Palaeolithic. Such a regional study was thought to be a useful comparative analysis, as Britain represents the very edge of the hominin world for *Homo heidelbergensis* and *Homo neanderthalensis* – the typical hominin species associated with the sites mentioned here. As these hominins existed the edge of the hominin world, it is thought that if there was a genuine species level of cognition and behavioural practice – such as regularly making symmetrical handaxes as markers for social signalling – then such an important social practice/behaviour should clearly manifest itself as the hominins explore the landscape at the very limits of their geography. The sites and assemblages examined within this study span a range of dates from Marine Isotope Stage (MIS) 13 to 3, allowing the investigation of evolving patterns of hominin behaviour through time (Table 13.1).

TABLE 13.1: *The total number of handaxes examined from each site arranged in chronological order. MIS = Marine Isotope Stage. For the site of Cuxton numbers relate to the Tester Collection.*

Site	MIS stage	Handaxe Count	Date Reference
High Lodge	13	15	Ashton et al. 1992
Warren Hill	13	548	Hosfield 2011
Elveden	11	44	Ashton et al. 2005
Hoxne Upper Industry	11	24	Ashton et al. 2008
Broom Pits	9–8	912	Hosfield and Chambers 2009
Cuxton	8–7	186	Wenban-Smith et al. 2007
Pontnewydd Cave	7	58	Aldhouse-Green 1998
Lynford	4–3	51	Boismier et al. 2012
Total	–	**1838**	–

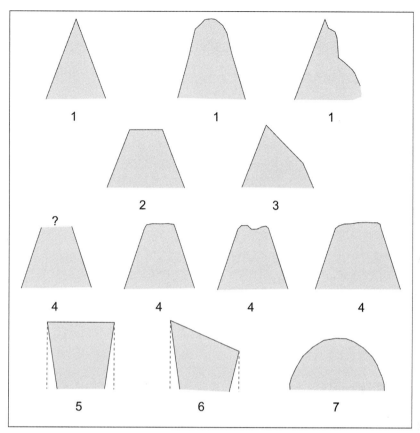

Figure 13.3: Illustrating the seven categories of tip classification: 1, markedly convergent; 2, convergent with a squared-off tip at right angles or nearly so; 3, convergent with an oblique tip; 4, convergent with a generalised tip; 5, wide (parallel) or divergent; 6, wide or divergent with an oblique tip; 7, wide with a very convex tip. Illustration and category description modified after McNabb and Beaumont 2011: figure 1.3.1; McNabb et al. 2004: figure 3.

A comprehensive study of the handaxes – and where appropriate their accompanying assemblages including flakes, flake tools and cores – including primary and secondary working analysis and raw material considerations can be found elsewhere (Cole 2011). As stated above, the case study presented here focuses principally on the degree of imposition of symmetry on handaxes.

The method of analysis for handaxes follows the methodology described in McNabb et al. (2004) and McNabb and Sinclair (2009). As part of this methodology, tip shape is examined and classified according to McNabb et al. (2004), where the top third of the artefact is considered the tip and assigned to one of seven potential categories illustrated in Figure 13.3.

By classifying handaxe tip shape through such a schema it should be possible to ascertain what tip shapes were being produced, allowing a comparison on an intra- and inter-assemblage basis. This in turn will allow researchers

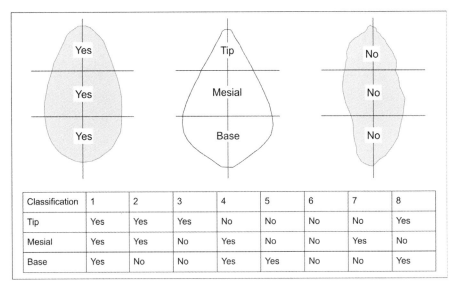

Classification	1	2	3	4	5	6	7	8
Tip	Yes	Yes	Yes	No	No	No	No	Yes
Mesial	Yes	Yes	No	Yes	No	No	Yes	No
Base	Yes	No	No	Yes	Yes	No	No	Yes

Figure 13.4: Illustrating handaxe symmetry and schema for recording. The grey hand-axe outlines represent real examples from the Warren Hill assemblage stored at Frank's House, The British Museum. Image adapted after McNabb et al. 2004: figure 5.

to determine whether there are any preferences (or not), for particular tip shapes, which may reveal any broad preferences for handaxe shape present in the sample.

Given that the level of symmetry analysis is looking for general trends within the dataset, the methodology for investigating symmetry as laid out by McNabb et al. (2004) and McNabb and Sinclair (2009) is sufficient for this task. Although there have been criticisms of this methodology (Machin and Mithen 2004; Underhill 2007), they have mostly focused upon the subjectivity of the system of analysis in regards to the fine-grained data scrutiny required for studying biface symmetry within tightly constrained time periods, and the desire for a metric quantification of symmetry. However, McNabb and Sinclair raises a cogent point when stating: 'if symmetry was important to the original knappers, appreciation by eye would have been the method through which they judged the results of their handiwork. A simple eyeball test of symmetry does therefore reflect this process' (2009: 87) and be more than sufficient to highlight a broad behavioural trend in the data should such a pattern present itself. Furthermore, although observer bias between more than one individual is acknowledged by McNabb (pers. comm.) and Underhill (2007), single observer consistency is high for the data presented for this discussion (Cole 2011).

Within this methodology, symmetry is determined by dividing the artefact into three equal sections along the long axis on both faces (Figure 13.4). Each horizontal third of the artefact is 'mentally folded over' to determine whether the edge outlines are symmetrical around the line of the long axis and a simple 'yes' or 'no' score recorded. The artefact is then categorised by the three scores (for the tip, medial and base) and assigned to a symmetry category based on the eight possible combinations of scores.

A further category was identified in McNabb et al. (2004: 658): parallel distinctive features along the margin – where there are visually distinct features located in parallel along opposite edges of the artefact, such as notches or trimmed concavities. Where appropriate this is shown within the results presented below.

Using such a methodology to assess the imposition of symmetry upon handaxes, researchers are able to compare the degree of symmetry and similarity in handaxe tip shape both within and between assemblages. Such a comparison a test of the long-held assumption that symmetry within handaxe manufacture becomes more marked over time (Saragusti et al. 1998), indicating that handaxes became increasingly important in mediating hominin social behaviour (for example Kohn and Mithen 1999).

RESULTS

Table 13.2 below assesses the regularity of imposed form through symmetry and tip shape upon the handaxes over time as per Table 13.1 (above), and illustrates that, in contrast to widely held beliefs (Ambrose 2001), completely symmetrical handaxes (those classed in the 'yes, yes, yes' category) do not seem to have held a strong degree of significance for the knappers within any of the assemblages examined for this discussion. Knappers were clearly capable of producing fully symmetrical handaxes; however, the frequency of occurrence within each assemblage through time remained at a consistently low level (less than 8% of any assemblage). This in turn would indicate that the imposition of perfect or true symmetry on handaxe form (the question of near symmetry categories are explored further below) was not a particularly important factor in handaxe manufacture. Furthermore, the degree of fully symmetrical handaxes for each assemblage does not appear to follow a clear chronological patterning. Rather, they seem to fluctuate randomly from 0% to a maximum of 7.8% of the assemblage across the whole dataset (Table 13.2). The only site that may possibly show an increase in the presence of symmetry comes from the Neanderthal site of Lynford (Boismier et al. 2012) with an absolute symmetry total of 7.8% (Table 13.2). However this still represents a relatively small percentage of the overall assemblage and is only 1% more than the site of Warren Hill at 6.8% total symmetry. Therefore, although there can be said to be a small increase in symmetry at Lynford in comparison to the other sites examined in Table 13.2, it is unlikely to constitute a significant behavioural/ cognitive change through time as described so often in the literature (for example, Saragusti et al. 1998; Ambrose 2001)

TABLE 13.2: *The broadly chronological relationship between sites and the variability of handaxe tip shape, and symmetry present therein.*

Site	Tip shape	Symmetry by Eye								Pdf[a]	Total
		yes, yes, yes	yes, yes, no	yes, no, no	no, yes, yes	no, no, yes	no, no, no	no, yes, no	yes, no, yes		
High Lodge N =15	Markedly convergent	.0%	6.7%	6.7%	6.7%	.0%	.0%	.0%	.0%	.0%	**20.0%**
	Convergent with oblique tip	.0%	.0%	.0%	.0%	.0%	6.7%	.0%	.0%	.0%	**6.7%**
	Convergent with generalised tip	.0%	.0%	13.3%	20.0%		26.7%	.0%	.0%	.0%	**60.0%**
	Wide or divergent	.0%	.0%	.0%	.0%	.0%	6.7%	.0%	.0%	.0%	**6.7%**
	Wide or divergent with oblique bit	.0%	.0%	.0%	6.7%	.0%	.0%	.0%	.0%	.0%	**6.7%**
	Total	**.0%**	**6.7%**	**20.0%**	**33.3%**	**.0%**	**40.0%**	**.0%**	**.0%**	**.0%**	**100.0%**
Warren Hill N = 548	Markedly convergent	.9%	2.2%	1.8%	.5%	.9%	4.4%	.7%	.9%	.2%	**12.6%**
	Convergent with square tip	.5%	1.1%	.5%	.4%	.5%	3.3%	.0%	.2%	.0%	**6.6%**
	Convergent with oblique tip	.0%	.0%	.2%	1.5%	.9%	4.2%	.5%	.0%	.0%	**7.3%**
	Convergent with generalised tip	3.5%	4.0%	3.8%	3.8%	4.0%	22.1%	1.6%	1.5%	.2%	**44.5%**
	Wide or divergent	.9%	.4%	1.1%	.9%	.9%	4.4%	.4%	.0%	.0%	**8.9%**
	Wide with convex tip	.9%	2.7%	2.6%	.9%	.7%	11.3%	.5%	.2%	.2%	**20.1%**
	Total	**6.8%**	**10.4%**	**10.0%**	**8.0%**	**8.0%**	**49.6%**	**3.8%**	**2.7%**	**.6%**	**100.0%**
Elveden N = 44	Markedly convergent	2.3%	.0%	4.5%	2.3%	.0%	9.1%	.0%	.0%	.0%	**18.2%**
	Convergent with square tip	.0%	.0%	.0%	.0%	.0%	4.5%	.0%	.0%	.0%	**4.5%**
	Convergent with oblique tip	.0%	.0%	.0%	.0%	2.3%	2.3%	.0%	.0%	.0%	**4.5%**

Sites	Tip shape	Symmetry by Eye								Pdf[a]	Total
		yes, yes, yes	yes, yes, no	yes, no, no	no, yes, yes	no, no, yes	no, no, no	no, yes, no	yes, no, yes		
	Convergent with generalised tip	.0%	2.3%	9.1%	6.8%	4.5%	36.4%	.0%	4.5%	.0%	63.6%
	Wide with convex tip	.0%	.0%	2.3%	.0%	.0%	2.3%	.0%	.0%	.0%	4.5%
	Profoundly asymmetrical	.0%	.0%	.0%	.0%	.0%	4.5%	.0%	.0%	.0%	4.5%
	Total	**2.3%**	**2.3%**	**15.9%**	**9.1%**	**6.8%**	**59.1%**	**.0%**	**4.5%**	**.0%**	**100.0%**
Hoxne Upper Industry N = 24	Markedly convergent	.0%	12.5%	8.3%	.0%	4.2%	25.0%	4.2%	.0%	.0%	54.2%
	Convergent with square tip	.0%	.0%	4.2%	4.2%	.0%	4.2%	.0%	.0%	.0%	12.5%
	Convergent with oblique tip	.0%	.0%	.0%	4.2%	4.2%		.0%	.0%	.0%	8.4%
	Convergent with generalised tip	.0%	.0%	.0%	.0%	.0%	4.2%	.0%	.0%	.0%	4.2%
	Wide or divergent	.0%	.0%	.0%	.0%	.0%	8.3%	.0%	.0%	.0%	8.3%
	Wide with convex tip	.0%	.0%	.0%	.0%	.0%	12.5%	.0%	.0%	.0%	12.5%
	Total	**.0%**	**12.5%**	**12.5%**	**8.4%**	**8.4%**	**54.2%**	**4.2%**	**.0%**	**.0%**	**100.0%**

Pdf[a]: Parallel distinctive features

Sites	Tip shape	Symmetry by Eye								Pdf[a]	Total
		yes, yes, yes	yes, yes, no	yes, no, no	no, yes, yes	no, no, yes	no, no, no	no, yes, no	yes, no, yes		
Broom Pits N = 912	Markedly convergent	2.3%	2.9%	3.0%	.8%	.5%	5.3%	.2%	.3%	.0%	15.2%
	Convergent with square tip	.4%	.3%	.5%	.7%	.7%	3.9%	.4%	.1%	.0%	7.1%
	Convergent with oblique tip	.0%	.0%	.1%	.8%	.7%	7.0%	.4%	.0%	.0%	9.0%
	Convergent with generalised tip	1.2%	2.2%	5.0%	4.2%	3.4%	33.9%	1.1%	1.6%	.0%	52.6%
	Wide or divergent	.0%	.4%	.3%	.5%	.0%	1.6%	.1%	.0%	.0%	3.1%

(continued)

TABLE 13.2: *(continued)*

Sites	Tip shape	Symmetry by Eye									
	Wide or divergent with oblique bit	.0%	.0%	.0%	.1%	.0%	1.0%	.2%	.0%	.0%	1.3%
	Wide with convex tip	.3%	.4%	1.2%	.7%	.3%	6.5%	.5%	.2%	.0%	10.2%
	Profoundly asymmetrical	.0%	.0%	.0%	.3%	.1%	1.0%	.0%	.0%	.0%	1.4%
	Total	**4.3%**	**6.3%**	**10.2%**	**8.0%**	**5.7%**	**60.2%**	**3.1%**	**2.3%**	**.0%**	**100.0%**
Pontnewy-dd Cave N = 58	Markedly convergent	1.7%	.0%	1.7%	.0%	.0%	8.6%	.0%	.0%	.0%	**12.1%**
	Convergent with square tip	.0%	.0%	3.4%	.0%	.0%	5.2%	.0%	.0%	.0%	**8.6%**
	Convergent with oblique tip	.0%	.0%	.0%	.0%	.0%	3.4%	.0%	.0%	.0%	**3.4%**
	Convergent with generalised tip	.0%	3.4%	10.3%	3.4%	.0%	46.6%	.0%	.0%	.0%	63.8%
	Wide or divergent	.0%	.0%	3.4%	.0%	.0%	3.4%	.0%	.0%	.0%	**6.9%**
	Wide with convex tip	.0%	.0%	.0%	.0%	.0%	3.4%	.0%	.0%	.0%	**3.4%**
	Profoundly asymmetrical	.0%	.0%	.0%	.0%	.0%	1.7%	.0%	.0%	.0%	**1.7%**
	Total	**1.7%**	**3.4%**	**19.0%**	**3.4%**	**.0%**	**72.4%**	**.0%**	**.0%**	**.0%**	**100.0%**
Cuxton N = 186	Markedly convergent	1.6%	3.2%	3.2%	.5%	.0%	8.1%	.0%	.5%	.0%	**17.2%**
	Convergent with square tip	.0%	.5%	.5%	.0%	.0%	3.2%	.0%	.0%	.0%	**4.3%**
	Convergent with oblique tip	.0%	.0%	.0%	.0%	.0%	4.3%	.5%	.0%	.0%	**4.8%**
	Convergent with generalised tip	.5%	1.1%	11.8%	.0%	1.6%	41.4%	1.1%	.5%	.0%	58.1%
	Wide or divergent	.0%	.0%	.0%	.0%	.0%	2.7%	.0%	.0%	.0%	**2.7%**
	Wide or divergent with oblique bit	.0%	.0%	.0%	.0%	.0%	1.6%	.0%	.0%	.0%	**1.6%**
	Wide with convex tip	.5%	.5%	1.6%	.0%	.0%	5.9%	.5%	.0%	.0%	**9.1%**

Lynford
N = 51

Profoundly asymmetrical	.0%	.0%	.0%	.0%	.0%	2.2%	.0%	.0%	.0%	2.2%
Total	**2.7%**	**5.4%**	**17.2%**	**.5%**	**1.6%**	**69.4%**	**2.2%**	**1.1%**	**.0%**	**100.0%**
Markedly convergent	2.0%	3.9%	.0%	5.9%	2.0%	9.8%	2.0%	2.0%	.0%	27.5%
Convergent with square tip	.0%	2.0%	.0%	2.0%	.0%	.0%	.0%	.0%	.0%	3.9%
Convergent with oblique tip	.0%	.0%	.0%	.0%	.0%	5.9%	.0%	.0%	.0%	5.9%
Convergent with generalised tip	5.9%	2.0%	5.9%	5.9%	5.9%	21.6%	5.9%	2.0%	.0%	54.9%
Wide or divergent	.0%	.0%	.0%	.0%	.0%	3.9%	.0%	.0%	.0%	3.9%
Wide with convex tip	.0%	.0%	.0%	.0%	.0%	2.0%	.0%	.0%	.0%	2.0%
Profoundly asymmetrical	.0%	.0%	.0%	.0%	.0%	2.0%	.0%	.0%	.0%	2.0%
Total	**7.8%**	**7.8%**	**5.9%**	**13.7%**	**7.8%**	**45.1%**	**7.8%**	**4.0%**	**.0%**	**100.0%**

Pdf.: Parallel distinctive features

TABLE 13.3: *The relationship between site and tips with a symmetrical element. Symmetry categories correspond to those seen in Table 13.2 and the McNabb et al. (2004) methodology described above.*

Symmetry by Eye

		yes, yes, yes	yes, yes, no	yes, no, no	yes, no, yes	**% of TA**
High Lodge N = 4 TA N = 15	Tips with a symmetrical element	.0%	6.7%	20.0%	.0%	**26.7%**
Warren Hill N = 164 TA N = 548	Tips with a symmetrical element	6.8%	10.4%	10.0%	2.7%	**29.9%**
Elveden N = 11 TA N = 44	Tips with a symmetrical element	2.3%	2.3%	15.9%	4.5%	**25.0%**
Hoxne Upper Industry N = 6 TA N = 24	Tips with a symmetrical element	.0%	12.5%	12.5%	.0%	**25.0%**
Broom Pits N = 210 TA N = 912	Tips with a symmetrical element	4.3%	6.3%	10.2%	2.3%	**23.1%**
Pontnewydd Cave N = 14 TA N = 58	Tips with a symmetrical element	1.7%	3.4%	19.0%	.0%	**24.1%**
Cuxton N = 49 TA N = 186	Tips with a symmetrical element	2.7%	5.4%	17.2%	1.1%	**26.4%**
Lynford N = 13 TA N = 51	Tips with a symmetrical element	7.8%	7.8%	5.9%	3.9%	**25.4%**
TA = Total Handaxe Assemblage						

In regards to the tip shape aspect to handaxe morphology, Table 13.2 shows that the most frequent tip form falls within the 'convergent with a generalised tip' category. From Figure 13.3, it is clear this is a highly variable morphology, suggesting that apart from a broad preference for a convergent tip, there is little evidence in this dataset for a preferred tip.

In order to establish whether near symmetry may have been a significant factor in handaxe morphology, Table 13.3 shows the percentage of each assemblage that contained handaxes with any symmetrical characteristic to their tip form. As can be seen, when tips with a symmetrical component are combined together, symmetry in tip form does seem to compose a significantly higher proportion of each assemblage (almost 25% as an average across the

TABLE 13.4: *The relationship between site, tips with a convergent element and symmetry.*

Symmetry by Eye

		yes, yes, yes	yes, yes, no	yes, no, no	yes, no, yes	% of TA
High Lodge N = 4 TA N = 15	Tips with a convergent element	.0%	6.7%	20.0%	.0%	**26.7%**
Warren Hill N = 116 TA N = 548	Tips with a convergent element	4.9%	7.3%	6.3%	2.6%	**21.1%**
Elveden N = 10 TA N = 44	Tips with a convergent element	2.3%	2.3%	13.6%	4.5%	**22.7%**
Hoxne Upper Industry N = 6 TA N = 24	Tips with a convergent element	.0%	12.5%	12.5%	.0%	**25.0%**
Broom Pits N = 183 TA N = 912	Tips with a convergent element	3.9%	5.4%	8.6%	2.0%	**19.9%**
Pontnewydd Cave N = 12 TA N = 58	Tips with a convergent element	1.7%	3.4%	15.4%	.0%	**20.5%**
Cuxton N = 44 TA N = 186	Tips with a convergent element	2.1%	4.8%	15.5%	1.0%	**23.4%**
Lynford N = 13 TA N = 51	Tips with a convergent element	7.8%	7.8%	5.9%	3.9%	**25.4%**
TA = Total Handaxe Assemblage						

dataset). However, as in Table 13.2, symmetry in tip form does not follow any clear patterns of distribution or chronological trends, making up between 16.7% to 38.1% of assemblages.

In order to test whether the presence of tips with a symmetrical aspect represents a genuine intent to produce symmetry, the relationship between handaxes with a convergent element to their tip shape versus handaxes with a symmetrical element to their form was assessed. Results are shown in Table 13.4.

Tables 13.3 and 13.4 show that the overwhelming bulk of handaxes that display a symmetrical element to their tip also appear to have a corresponding convergent component to tip morphology. This would suggest that the majority of tip symmetry present with the assemblages studied may actually be a product of the extra knapping required to construct a convergent tip, rather than a deliberately intended outcome. This result would support the original conclusion drawn from Table 13.2 that symmetry of any kind (full or near) does not seem to play a dominant role in handaxe production from any site or time period presented here.

DISCUSSION

As has been previously stated, conventional belief dictates that the imposition of symmetrical form upon handaxes was an important component of handaxe production and significantly increased in occurrence through time as greater degrees of social meaning and cultural communications were associated with handaxe production (Saragusti et al. 1998; Kohn and Mithen 1999; Ambrose 2001; Foley and Gamble 2009; Hodgson 2009). This in turn, according to the identity model, would have suggested that the Acheulean and Middle Palaeolithic hominins were capable of and practising a minimum of a third- to fourth-order of intentionality through intex perpetuation within a collective identity.

However, from the data presented here, it would appear that symmetry plays a relatively minor role in handaxe production (less than 8% of any assemblage). Moreover, symmetry does not significantly increase in presence through time, and where present appears to be randomly distributed. Furthermore, all assemblages tended to demonstrate a wide range of tip shapes, suggesting that that there was no real preference on a cultural level for particular handaxe morphologies beyond a broad preference for general convergence, where the tip is only broadly convergent in shape with no consistent final form.

Therefore, it would seem that the handaxes in this dataset do not correspond to a model for the imposition of symmetry, nor is there an expression of preference for particular tip shape morphology. Rather, the data seem to resemble the 'mental constructs' of Ashton and McNabb (1994), where the shape of the handaxe was a fluid idea in the mind of the knapper depending on individual ability, raw material constraints, function, time, place and circumstance. The variety of tip shapes present within the dataset indicates that the hominins were certainly attending to a range of potential handaxe morphologies and McNabb et al. (2004) and Cole (2011) show that there may be potential indications for some degree of normalised pattern in handaxe shaping or secondary working. However, this may relate to McNabb et al.'s (2004) notion of 'conceptual standardisation' based on 'individualised memic constructs' – where the notion of the handaxe was socially generated and sustained within a group; however, the final form was not determined through strong social imposition or strong social learning. Rather the data presented here and in McNabb et al. (2004) may suggest that handaxe morphology was rather the result of 'creating and manipulating chains of sequentially related routine actions' (McNabb et al. 2004: 667), rather than to a strong, culturally mediated reduction strategy.

If it is accepted that a lack of symmetry represents an absence of intex perpetuation (no use of handaxes in culturally mediated social signals) and therefore, potentially, that their makers lacked third-order intentionality (as per the identity model), the question arises as to what the cognitive potential of the hominins involved may have been. Returning to the concept of a theory of mind and orders of intentionality stated above, I proposed that a theory of mind marks a necessary step in the development of abstract thought and symbolic construction through the conscious conception of a mind that is separate and distinct to one's own. Similarly, I would suggest that McNabb et al.'s (2004) notion of 'conceptual standardisation' in handaxe form would also indicate an ability to conceive of a fluid abstract tool form in the mind's eye and to impose that form onto a handaxe blank through a series of related routine actions. This in turn could imply that the hominin handaxe knappers had a theory of mind or second-order intentionality – at a minimum – in order to be able to form a mental construct or a notion of conceptual standardisation (as examples of abstract thought). If so, why did they apparently not (based on the data presented here, and in Cole (2011) take that extra cognitive leap and utilise handaxes within social signalling?

One possibility may be that the lack of full standardisation or symmetry in handaxe manufacture may indicate that the hominin knappers imitating their contemporaries never quite realised what it was that their contemporaries were envisaging in relation to handaxe form. This in turn may suggest that the hominins were fixed within a second-order of intentionality/theory of mind, locked into the so-called Acheulean gaze (Foley and Gamble 2009) of attending to handaxe form imposition, without realising the full potential of such a gaze to consciously off-load social communications and culturally meaningful symbols onto the material culture with which they interacted, a conclusion which may have some neurological support based on the recent work and conclusions of Stout and Chaminade (2012).

Alternatively, perhaps the application of notions of symmetry and standardisation, as understood by modern researchers, to artefacts made by non-modern human species may be an inappropriate way in which to examine the Palaeolithic record or the brains/minds of our hominin ancestors (Chase 1991). Perhaps researchers should re-address the degree to which we associate standardisation with agreed cultural practice, and, rather than trying to pigeon-hole hominin behaviour in a way which is not apparent in or necessarily appropriate for the archaeological record, and embrace instead the diverse artefact morphology and potential complexity of Palaeolithic lithic assemblages.

CONCLUSION

From the results presented briefly above and in more detail in Cole (2011), it is clear that, contrary to widely held belief, symmetry as a marker of culturally mediated artefact manufacture in handaxe production does not seem to increase over time, or indeed to relate to overall handaxe form. This may suggest that symmetry was not a significant factor in handaxe production for the hominins represented by the dataset, and that the majority of handaxes examined may not have been incorporated within systems of social communication as has often been presumed (Ronen 1982; Mellars 1989, 1991; Kohn and Mithen 1999; Ambrose 2001; Foley and Gamble 2009).

It is thus clear that the potential role of handaxes as markers of hominin behaviour and cognitive ability often measured against the degree of standardisation present in artefact form or assemblage typology must be reassessed in light of the results presented above (and Cole 2011). Perhaps hominins of the Lower and Middle Palaeolithic did not view standardisation or the imposition of symmetry on tool form in the same way that modern humans do. Indeed it may be unfair of us to assume that symmetry or standardisation in artefact production should play a significant role in hominin social signalling when we are dealing with non-human species whose views of the world and their position in it would be drastically different from our own.

The evidence offered here may indicate that on a broad behavioural level, the hominins involved were limited to a second-order of intentionality and a notion of an internal and external identity bound to iconic and indexical sign reading and signalling. However, this observation is based on the apparent absence of evidence pertaining to a notion of perpetuated intex/symbolic sign propagation (through the lack of symmetry or significant standardisation in tool form) and formulated on only one artefact type: handaxes. The question of organic artefacts and their role in hominin behaviour from this deep period of antiquity may perhaps forever elude us, but their evidence is likely to be a crucial one in bearing out our behavioural assumptions of hominin species based on one medium of artefact manufacture.

Furthermore, the presence of giant handaxes within a small sample of Acheulean assemblages (for example, Wenban-Smith 2004) throws up the intriguing prospect of the ways in which individual artefacts within assemblages may carry more social weight than their counterparts, although it should be noted that the exact role of the so-called giant handaxes and their role within wider Acheulean assemblages is still unclear and in need of further work. Similarly, the question of specific variants such as the twisted ovates known from MIS 11 (White 1998b) or the handaxe pairs from Boxgrove and Foxhall Road (White and Plunkett 2004; Hopkinson and White 2005; Pope et al. 2006) also offer up intriguing implications for handaxe use in social signals. Perhaps what we are seeing with such individual extraordinary artefacts are localised independent innovations where hominins on the boarder of third-order

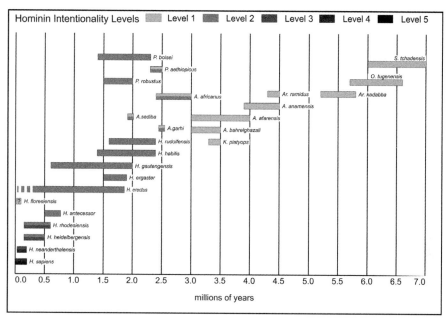

Figure 13.5: Summarising the view of hominin intentionality according to the application of the identity model to the archaeological record.

intentionality make a specific link with material culture and its potential symbolic role within mediating social relationships which, for whatever reasons, are not taken up at the broader species level of behaviour. Whatever the longevity of such individual innovations, it seems that, from a broad species level behavioural view offered here, the majority of handaxes remained within the functional, rather than the social, sphere. In addition the significant behavioural and cognitive implications of prepared core technologies and composite tools and the first ochre use appearing c. 300,000 years ago have been written about elsewhere and perhaps offer a more reliably archaeological marker for the presence of a third-order cognisance (Barham 2010; Cole 2011).

By examining the archaeological record through the heuristic of the identity model, I have suggested that the predictions of the SBH, in terms of hominin cognitive abilities did not quite match the behavioural evidence of the archaeological record if taken at the species level discussed here (see Cole 2011 for a more detailed review). As such, perhaps the SBH predictions of hominin cognition (Figure 13.1) should acknowledge the apparent realised behavioural marker for cognition as shown in Figure 13.5. Thus, it may be that the SBH predicts the potential cognitive ability of ancient hominin species whilst the archaeology, through the filter of the identity model, illustrates the realised cognitive ability, and the two are not necessarily mutually exclusive. Therefore it would appear that cognitive potential must be in place before it can be realised, which in turn suggests that physiological changes must occur before behavioural ones.

CHAPTER 14

LANDSCAPES OF THE DEAD: THE EVOLUTION OF HUMAN MORTUARY ACTIVITY FROM BODY TO PLACE IN PALAEOLITHIC EUROPE

PAUL PETTITT

> Burial provides an extreme case of a detaching ritual. . .the evidence for Neanderthal burial had the sense of *adieu* rather than an *au revoir*. The latter might be expected with a true detaching ritual since it implies meeting again in some other context.
>
> (Gamble 1999: 404)

INTRODUCTION: HOW THE DEAD ONCE LIVED

Human interactions with the dead constitute some of the most profound human characteristics which can be identified in the archaeological record. Some of the most ambitious and archaeologically recognisable constructions of prehistory served to contain the dead and project their continuing agency among the living, and if not for the refusal of the dead to retreat entirely from the societies they departed archaeologists would be denied of the lumps and bumps in the landscape that are so rewarding to excavate. Monuments and tombs, however, form merely a readily identifiable aspect of a vast range of mortuary activity; they appeared very late in the archaeological record; they were not afforded to everyone, and in many places even today the physical remains of the dead simply disappear, exposed to vultures, consumed in fire and floated down rivers. From an evolutionary perspective what we do with the dead is surface detail; the real evolutionary value lies in the assumptions which underlie any belief that minds persist and effect social agency beyond physical death.

Such assumptions almost certainly arose during the course of the Palaeolithic; the elaborate burials and 'art' of the European Upper Palaeolithic may be confidently interpreted as reflecting *some kind* of symbolic systems and cosmo-logical beliefs, even if their specific meaning will never be known to us. But how far can one push back the recognition that hominins believed in the persistence and agency of the dead? Palaeoanthropologists are concerned with understanding the cognitive abilities and behaviour of humans in evolutionary context, and from a burgeoning literature amassed over the last two decades, 'symbolism' (defined here as something which stands for (and communicates the concept of) something else) has emerged as the main – perhaps the only – characteristic separating modern, highly encephalised hominins (*Homo sapiens* and possibly *Homo neanderthalensis*) from others (e.g., Mellars 1991, 1995; McBrearty and Brooks 2000; Wadley 2001; Henshilwood and Marean 2003; d'Errico 2003; d'Errico et al. 2003). Such debate has concentrated on more obvious indicators of symbolism: pigments and art. But what are the dead if they are not symbols? Symbols of lives once lived, of past attachments and the ultimate detachment, their accumulated social baggage and agency maintained through material acts, group memory and commemoration?

Echoes of the Palaeolithic dead still linger on the river banks, lake edges and caves frequented by the subjects of our study and haunt the pages of academic publications which, ostensibly, focus on the living, or how the dead once lived. There are, in fact, many places in the world where the dead still linger, and it is not just archaeologists who are concerned with them. Many people, from most societies past and present, believe in the continued existence and agency of the dead; from the collective memories and superstitions of the past to the entertainments of the present day, the dead form powerful symbols in the lives of even the most sceptical of people. Given the ubiquity of the dead, it is surprising that few archaeologists have considered hominin interactions with the dead in long-term evolutionary context. 'Burial' is trotted out in increasingly outmoded 'checklists' of 'modern human behaviour' which fail to comprehend the nuanced cognitive and behavioural evolution of *Homo* or, indeed, the genuine cognitive ramifications of sticking a body in a shallow pit. Mortuary activity is not seen as one of the 'headline changes' of hominin evolution (Gamble 2010: 17), but studying it is a potentially powerful route into the elucidation of cognitive and symbolic evolution independent of the current emphasis on pigments, personal ornamentation and figurative and non-figurative art, and thus may provide a new perspective on our understanding of the emergence of the symbolic hominin. The elaborate burials and circulation of human remains in Mid Upper Palaeolithic Europe, particularly given the rich floruit of art in the period (Gamble 1982), may be confidently interpreted as deriving from supernatural underpinnings, but what about beforehand? Gamble (1999) is one of the very few Palaeolithic archaeologists who have recognised the social and evolutionary importance of mortuary activities in the Palaeolithic record, forwarding the notion of detachments (as a counterpart of social attachments) as an inherently social activity.

Individual agency and the agency (and particularly symbolism) of material culture have been well debated in Palaeolithic archaeology (e.g., papers in Gamble and Porr 2005, Henshilwood and d'Errico 2011 and others cited above). Here I wish to examine instead the evolution of hominin interactions with the dead, and specifically, when *places* and *landscapes* became associated

with and thus imbued with the symbolism of, the dead. When did these
locales cue certain behaviours, in this case associated with death and memory
(*sensu* Coward and Gamble 2008)? It may be safely argued that some aspects
of the Initial and Early Upper Palaeolithic record – whoever made it –
represent cosmological beliefs in which spirits and the dead were integral parts
(e.g., Tattersall 1998); therefore, I will focus on pre *Homo sapiens* hominins
and on the European record (as it forms the best archaeological record for such
pre-modern humans, at least in terms of mortuary activity). I shall argue that a
persistent association of the dead with specific locales can be observed for the
Neanderthals.

COGNITION, SYMBOLS AND THE EVOLUTION OF
SUPERSTITIOUS BELIEF

One of the most remarkable examples of the imagination of *Homo sapiens* is the
way we interact with entities other than fellow humans (Coward and Gamble
2008). Such interactions are facilitated through our ability to anthropomorph-
ise the thoughts of animals and to believe that once-living humans persist in
some form and continue to possess a degree of cultural agency *post mortem*.
Such 'moderately counter-intuitive' creations of our minds are given understandable form, meaning and power in the world (Atran and Norenzayan
2004), leading to some surprisingly complex and persistent belief systems
which might appear to be maladaptive. As Bloch (2009: 187) has asked;
'how could a sensible animal like modern *Homo sapiens,* equipped by natural
selection with efficient core knowledge – that is, knowledge well-suited for
dealing with the world as it is – hold such ridiculous ideas as these: there are
ghosts that go through walls; there exist omniscients; and there are deceased
people active after death?' The numerous ways in which belief in the
supernatural may increase evolutionary fitness have been detailed elsewhere
(see, for example, Atran and Norenzayan 2004; Boyer 2008; Rossano 2010b),
but it is clear why hominoid and hominin groups should be under selection for
such beliefs. Emotionally powerful existential anxieties such as those provoked
by death are a major motivation for religious belief; supernatural agents may
therefore be invoked to ease death anxiety (Atran 2002; Atran and Norenzayan
2004), making death a primary focus of religious speculation and ritual action
(Dickson 1990: 93). While Insoll (2004: 67) has cautioned that this should not
be seen as the sole purpose of religion, archaeologists have had a 'sometimes
obsessional focus upon the archaeology of death' (ibid.: 33).

The moderately counter-intuitive creations of our minds explain why in
most human societies there is no hard and fast intellectual distinction between
the natural and supernatural (Bloch 2009). Individual agency might originate
within humans, animals, non-organic items or those of a non-biological
nature, and in the case of the former, death is not conceived of as an abrupt

end of the individual but a transformation from one state to another, usually resulting in an increase in the power of their agency as the biological world is transcended (Huntington and Metcalf 1979; Ingold 2000: 93). Such beliefs are common to all known religions past and present; 'every religion assumes entities such as ghosts, angels, ancestor spirits, and so on. These often have mental lives (desires, beliefs, goals), but no physical form. In addition, most, if not all, religions posit an afterlife, and the purposeful creation of the universe, including humans and other animals' (Bloom 2007: 148). Transformational links of the body with the wider landscape are common to ways of thinking often simplified as 'animism' and 'totemism' (Insoll 2011b). Thus death, like the surfaces of decorated caves, links the biological and supernatural worlds in complex and varied ways. Archaeologically recognisable mortuary ritual should therefore form a heuristic link between the observable world and the underlying supernatural rationale that underpins it, much as we assume that figurative and non-figurative marks on a cave wall are somehow a heuristic for cosmological beliefs.

Echoes of the supernatural are ubiquitous in the present and the ethnohistorical past, and it seems likely the supernatural has been part of the belief systems of *Homo sapiens* since at least the earlier Upper Palaeolithic (see Germonpré and Hämäläinen 2007 for a specific example). Cognitive scientists researching the origins of religion appear to agree that hominins became cognitively predisposed towards the belief that minds could survive beyond physical death relatively early on (see references in Pettitt 2011c) and were hypersensitive towards reading meaning in natural patterning; this combination makes it natural for hominins 'to believe in gods and spirits, in an afterlife, and in the divine creation of the universe' (Bloom 2007: 150). But exactly when did hominins reach the cognitive stage at which such a dualism arose?

Pre-existing social rituals may provide a point of origin for the development and elaboration of supernatural beliefs. Incorporating supernatural elements would intensify rituals' meaning and agency, making them 'more effective, more dramatic, and just more fun' (Rossano 2010b: 118). For a more specific explanation of the elaboration of counter-intuitive imaginary notion one can turn to children. Gamble (2007: 228–230) has stressed the need to investigate the growing environment of children – the 'childscape' – and Bloom (2007: 149) noted that children universally accept the notion of the persistence of an individual's social agency after death, suggesting that the notion that the mind is separable from the body is natural, whereas specific religious explanations for what happens to the mind/soul are learned later. To Rossano (ibid.: 117) increasing social complexity will select for more imaginative children as they grow into more socially skilled adults; thus it is likely that childhood imaginations would become exapted for use in the wider ritual sphere. Bloch (2009) has provided an explicit example of the adaptive strength of the imaginative capacity in the origins of cognitively modern *Homo sapiens,* emphasising the interconnectedness between the 'transcendental social' – social structures comprised of established roles and groups wherein essentialised groups exist and can live in the imagination – and religion, which in this context may be taken to include concepts of the supernatural. A first step towards such societies of the mind would be the acknowledgement of the supernatural, and it is reasonable to assume that supernatural beliefs would further evolve alongside the evolution of a symbolic capacity.

It is quite easy to understand how the most obvious phenomena may have given rise to specific elements of supernatural belief. The disorientation and danger of night, for example, is associated with supernatural beings and transformation in many small-scale societies (Galinier et al. 2010). Places where deaths have occurred, dangers have been experienced or to which deceased individuals had close ties are often associated with ancestors, although such associations are complex, and no broad ethnographic generalisations can be made (Insoll 2011a). Such simple associations presumably have very deep evolutionary roots which may be elaborated as hominin cognition and social organisation developed, reaching a major watershed when the hominin brain became the human mind (Gamble 2010). Thus a starting point, firmly established in evolutionary anthropology and the cognitive study of religion, is that the hominin mind is *predisposed* to imaginary belief and thus religious expression (e.g., Barrett 2011; Bloom 2007; Boyer 2008; Atran 2002; Atran and Norenzayan 2004; Rossano 2010b).

Palaeoanthropology, I suggest, can make a significant contribution to this field; only hominin fossils and Palaeolithic archaeology will reveal whether religion 'emerged' only with *Homo sapiens* either as part of the process of becoming cognitively modern (the 'concurrence hypothesis'); as behavioural changes after this evolution (the 'adaptation hypothesis'), or whether it predated *Homo sapiens* (the 'Pre-human religious hypothesis') (see Barrett 2010 for discussion and critique of these hypotheses). I suggest below that a reading of the specific record of mortuary activity lends support to the pre-human religion hypothesis.

TASKSCAPES, BODIES AND THE EVOLUTION OF HOMININ MORTUARY ACTIVITY

As it is the body which experiences the world and the body which ultimately dies, it is no surprise that the origins of hominin mortuary activity must be sought among inter-individual activities which required no particular locational backdrop; these could occur ad hoc and face to face wherever hominoid and hominin groups were located. Bodies are biologically given and culturally created, and through them we interact as material projects within the world (Gamble 2007), as complex arrays of inter-related activities or *taskscapes* (Ingold 1993). Our own cognisance of our bodily lifecycles provides us with the notion of mortality and provides a timescale for our inevitable movement towards death (Gosden 1994: 80), and visual and audible rhythms encountered constantly constitute the taskscapes through which our bodies move (Gamble and Roebroeks 1999b: 9). Death pervades the taskscape. To hunter-gatherers the death of resources critical for survival shape their lives, and thus responses to the dead must occupy a central role in the constitution of their taskscapes. Intellectual curiosity and interaction with dead bodies (which I have termed *morbidity* – see below) and the evolution of mortuary activity must, therefore, be seen as integral to the wider taskscape. In life, bodies, like places, can be given increasingly nuanced meanings by being 'accessorised' with symbolic material culture (e.g., Pettitt 2011b), which may also represent beliefs about supernatural agency (White 1997).

Although the body may bridge the gap between biology and culture (Gamble 2007), belief in the agency of the dead may have arisen from the interaction of two distinct cognitive systems; one which deals with physical bodies and actions (the 'Animacy System') and another which deals with mental states (the 'Theory of Mind' or ToM) (e.g., Barrett 2011). The quandary the dead present is the contradiction between the animacy system telling the reader a corpse is dead and the ToM continuing to make inferences about the deceased's needs and beliefs and thus its agency (Bloom 2007; Barrett 2011). This dualism between mind and body 'opens the possibility that people can survive the death of their bodies' (Bloom 2007: 149). Bloom's and Boyer's accounts help explain why the notion of the persistence of human spirits after death 'may well be the most widespread and oldest religious concept' (Barrett 2011: 215). Surely this is the goal Palaeolithic archaeologists should aim for in the elucidation of the emergence of religion.

Archaeologists, however, have been understandably reticent to infer the development of superstitious or religious belief from Palaeolithic archaeology. In order to understand the emergence of such beliefs, however, we do not need to understand their specifics. Identifying the 'function' of 'cave art', for example, tells us more about ourselves than it does 'cave artists' (Bahn and Vertut 1997), and naive and intellectually lazy 'umbrella' interpretations – particularly the recent 'shamanism' fad (e.g., Clottes and Lewis-Williams 1998) – are highly simplistic (Insoll 2011a) and probably account in large part for scepticism about the possibility of interpretation in this field. This should not deter us from identifying general patterns in the archaeological record that can be read to imply the existence of superstitious belief and its origins. Potentially useful examples from the Middle Pleistocene are difficult to interpret. What do the *pierres figures* from Berekhat Ram and Tan-Tan (Goren-Inbar and Peltz 1995; d'Errico and Nowell 2000; Bednarik 2003), or the 'anvils', engraved bones and associated activities at Bilzingsleben (Mania and Mania 2005) – which as Gamble (1999: 171–172) has suggested may represent *foci* for social attachment – imply? At the very least they represent an association of things with bodies and social groups with places respectively and may imply cognitive abilities more advanced than straightforward theory of mind, but this remains speculative. With mortuary activity we are, perhaps, on surer ground, and it is my contention that a demonstrable and repeated association of the dead with a specific place, what I have called an *associative interaction* (Pettitt 2011a), indicates specific meaning was attached to this association. Whether associative interactions necessarily imply belief in the supernatural is open to question, although it does at least provide a point in time on an evolutionary scheme from body-centred mortuary activities, through non-symbolic association of the dead with specific places, to fully symbolic associations. I would argue, then, that associations of the dead and the landscape provide an important step towards fully symbolically mediated belief systems, and thus mark, if not a 'headline change' in hominin evolution, at least a development worthy of several column inches.

An appropriate place to begin a discussion of the origin of mortuary activity is with observed responses to the dead among chimpanzee societies (Pettitt 2011a; Anderson et al. 2010). These may be used as a general comparator for Miocene hominoids and Pliocene hominins. Among chimpanzees one can observe occasional cases of infanticide and cannibalism (e.g., Goodall 1977; Norikoshi 1982; Takahata 1985; Hamai et al. 1992), the curation of dead infants by their mothers for up to 68 days after death (Biro et al. 2010; Matsuzawa 2003), the intellectual and physical investigation of corpses (*morbidity*) and various examples of social theatre in close proximity to corpses which appear to be occasioned by them (e.g., Bygott 1972; Teleki 1973; Goodall 1977; Boesch and Boesch-Achermann 2000; Anderson et al. 2010; Cronin et al. 2011). Elsewhere, I have suggested these activities represent the 'core' (i.e., earliest) mortuary phase which may have been expressed early in hominoid /hominid evolution (Pettitt 2011a). Activities specifically focused on the corpse include smelling and investigation of wounds, what are described as 'inspections' of the body, grooming, pulling the arms, stroking and holding of hands, attempts to open mouths, staring into the face, and dragging over short distances (ibid.). A variety of further activities that seem to reflect social theatre occasioned by the presence of the corpse have also been observed, including male displays, 'play' faces, calls rarely heard in other circumstances, silences, dominant individuals described as 'guarding' corpses and chasing lower-ranked individuals away, and so on. This is perhaps not surprising, as social groups will renegotiate their relative standing in a social group following the removal of an individual.

As primatologists have until recently been understandably interested in only the live chimpanzee, observations of activities around corpses are few and, prior to the 1990s generally anecdotal. Nevertheless, such behaviours are suggestive of the mechanism by which relatively casual morbidity and social

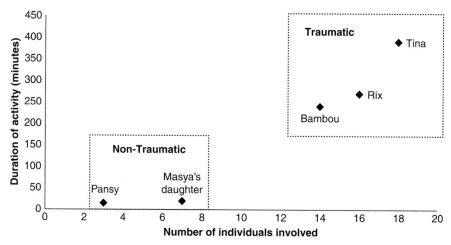

Figure 14.1. Chimpanzee activity around corpses. Duration and number of individuals observed in interaction with the dead among chimpanzees. Data: Rix, Gombe, Tanzania (Teleki 1973); Bambou and Tina, Taï, Ivory Coast (Boesch and Boesch-Achermann 2000); Pansy, Blair Drummond Safari Park, Scotland (Anderson et al. 2010); Masya's daughter, Chimfunshi Wildlife Orphanage, Zambia (Cronin et al. 2011: the infant was observed to be unhealthy from very early in life, thus the observers were not confident that she would survive and did not name her; K. Cronin pers. comm.)

display might be elaborated into more recognisable mortuary behaviour (i.e., behaviours arising from and referring to a corpse). But what conditions might produce such elaboration? Figure 14.1 uses data from the five most detailed published observations of activity around the freshly dead bodies of infant chimpanzees – no data being available for deceased adults – to plot the number of individuals that responded to the presence of the corpse, against the total amount of time corpse focused-activities were observed before the corpse was abandoned. It is apparent that the more individuals 'involved' in these, the longer the group spent doing so. If this pattern holds with future observations, this may suggest that the larger and more complex hominin groups became, the more likely morbidity and corpse-prompted social activity was to evolve in complexity. Thus one might predict that mortuary activity would be one of the social activities under selection to evolve as group size and neocortical size increased (Aiello and Dunbar 1993). The three examples from Figure 14.1 involving the most individuals and time resulted from deaths through sudden physical trauma (Bambou and Rix fell from trees, Tina was ambushed by a leopard); by contrast the two examples with low duration and few participants resulted from the deaths of infants who had been sickly for some time. These deaths, therefore, may have been perhaps 'expected'. This may suggest that the elaboration of behaviours which ultimately become socially determined mortuary rituals may be promoted by sudden and unexpected deaths, and if these occurred in large and socially complex groups, the resulting activities would themselves be relatively complex and under selection for further elaboration. For mobile hunter-gatherers, however, the time which can be spent on morbidity and social theatre to the exclusion of the critical tasks of survival is limited. At some point a critical watershed must have been reached, at which point, I suggest, the natural development would be to leave the dead behind, symbolically, at recognised places in the landscape. Thus through memory and association the face-to-face becomes materialised as place.

FROM FACE-TO-FACE TO PLACE IN NEANDERTHAL MORTUARY ACTIVITY

Dunbar (2003) views the origin of religion in social rather than individual perspective, interpreting brain evolution in terms of intentional states, or levels of cognitive intentionality which increased over the course of hominin evolution from one (*I believe that. . .*) to the normal human limit of four, equating to increasing brain size, group size and grooming time. To Dunbar, a theory of mind, which in modern humans emerges at four to five years, requires level 2 intentionality (*I believe that you believe. . .*); coercing individuals to conform to social norms requires three levels of intention (*I want you to believe that you must behave how we want*), but religion, at least as we know it, requires level four intention (I have to *believe* that *you suppose* that there are supernatural beings *who understand* that *you and I desire* that things happen in a certain way). I have argued elsewhere that the intentional and repeated association of the dead with certain locales requires a mind capable of operating at Dunbar's level 3 intentionality, in this case 1) *I know,* 2) *that we all agree,* 3) *that you must be associated with this place* (Pettitt 2011a, 2011b), and conceivably level 4 intentionality is required if the association is predicated upon supernatural beliefs recognised at a wider group scale.

The repeated burial of multiple individuals at the same site, at least when shown to respect the position of previous interments, and especially if marked out by rocks or cairns, should be an unproblematic indicator of associative interaction between the dead and the landscape. By the early Mid Upper Palaeolithic c. 29 ka uncal BP, certain locales were being used repeatedly to dispose of the dead in artificially created graves, which in combination with attaching rituals among the living, functioned to create social space (Gamble 1999: 405–412). As I shall argue below, the repeated use of certain rockshelters for Neanderthal burial reflects this association by at least c. 75 ka BP, and such associations may also be indicated much earlier by the deliberate placing of corpses in the landscape at the Sima de los Huesos before c. 400 ka BP (Pettitt 2011a). At the Sima, however, the dead are associated with a natural, that is, culturally unmodified place (the single cultural artefact in the Sima, a biface, may represent a degree of cultural modification of this place, although a totally fortuitous reason for its presence cannot be ruled out), an act I have referred to as *funerary caching*. With regard to the importance of such associations, it is irrelevant whether caches simply exploit natural features such as the Sima, modify these in a modest way (e.g., with the *Homo sapiens* burials Skhūl VIII and Qafzeh VIII in Israel) or artificially construct them (in the case of formal burials). Thus, it is possible that the association of the dead with specific locales has a long evolutionary history.

That such associations formed part of the taskscapes of archaic hominins should not be surprising. Meaningful patterning in the quotidian organisation of hominins in the landscape is a well-known characteristic of the Palaeolithic record. Hominin aggregation at recognised locales probably has a very long ancestry in hominin evolution and provided the context for sharing, social negotiation and the division of critical resources (Gamble 1999, 2007; Roebroeks 2001). Archaeologists, however, understandably consider use of the landscape in terms of hominin survivability. However, if Neanderthals were capable of conceptualising the landscape in terms of clustered resource sets and the paths which link them (Gamble and Roebroeks 1999b: 9), then it is possible that they could conceive of the dead in a similar manner, and this understanding can be used as a heuristic for their associations of the dead with specific places. Considerable evidence is available for their organisation of activities in the landscape (e.g., papers in Gamble and Roebroeks 1999a and Conard 2001, 2004). Although the specific reasons for repeated use of certain locales often elude us (Roebroeks and Tuffreau 1999), enough data exist for some broad generalisations of why and how Neanderthals gave importance to certain points in the landscape. These include:

- the importance of certain geographical areas to Neanderthal activities (e.g., Moravian Gate, north Aquitaine basin and Pyrenean foothills: Svoboda 1999; Turq 1999) either purely constrained by resource availability (in which case they might be considered 'local operational areas' – White and Pettitt 2011: 77–82) or given social significance (in which case they might constitute 'territories' potentially recognised and distinguished by differing technotypological traditions and raw material transfers – Gamble 1999: 239–244)
- the repeated use of certain locales probably due to their proximity to water and rich diversity of exploitable resources (papers in Gamble and Roebroeks 1999a; Conard 2001, 2004; Bicho 2004; Walker et al. 2004)
- the repeated use of particular caves and rockshelters for shelter (ibid.) and, on occasion, the physical modification of such sites better provide shelter (e.g., Kolen 1999; Turq 1999: 111; Cabrera et al. 2004; Vaquero et al. 2001, 2004; Foltyn et al. 2004)
- the spatial organisation of activities on campsites, with or without physical modification (e.g., Bonjean and Otte 2004)

- the repeated association of points in the landscape (often of tactical significance) where prey are predictable seasonally and to which Neanderthals repeatedly returned for diverse resources, e.g., in Quercy (Jaubert 1999) or the Jura (Tillet 2001).

While these do not indicate that Neanderthals exercised similar organisational principles with respect to their dead, they do suggest we should not be surprised if they associated certain locales with the dead; if such locales were repeatedly associated with the dead; if mortuary activities involved a degree of physical modification of some locales; and perhaps if such associations varied regionally. With regard to the mortuary sphere, as hunter-gatherers Neanderthals would be familiar with death and decay; body parts of their prey would have surrounded them and fragmentation of lithics and/or of carcasses (perhaps conceptually linked; Pettitt 2007a) provides the context for funerary elaboration of fragmentation of the body. Cutmarks are known on a number of Neanderthal remains and indicate that on occasion they were fragmenting their dead, and while this may sometimes reflect nutritional cannibalism, some examples are difficult to reconcile with any 'prosaic' activities. Frayer et al. (2006: 524) concluded that the cutmarks on the Krapina 3 cranium do not represent cannibalism, nor defleshing, but the repeated cutting/scoring of the deceased's forehead, possibly 'representing some type of symbolic, perimortem manipulation of the deceased'.

It is probably fair to conclude, therefore, that on occasion, some Neanderthal groups processed some of their dead for mortuary reasons, protracting their interaction with the individual body beyond its physical death. In the taskscape, it is the body which provides the conceptual link between the individual and place. For other animals it is sensible to suppose that death provided both reasons for *attraction to* and *avoidance of* certain locales. Clearly Neanderthals were able to recognise (and perhaps deliberately avoid) dangerous places where their own death was a possibility (e.g., places such as caves where carnivores were active: Mussi 1999; Gamble 1986: 309; 1999: 231). By contrast, they could clearly recognise and deliberately frequent places where the *corpses* of suitable prey animals were known to accumulate (e.g., large pachyderms at Lynford, UK; Pagnano d'Asolo, Italy; Lehringen, Germany: Schreve 2006; Mussi 1999). Thus the landscape is imbued with the possibility and expression of death, and if Neanderthals on occasion deliberately interred some of their dead surely their 'paths of view' (Gamble and Roebroeks 1999b: 9–10) must have extended into the funerary realm.

Despite a strong critique (Gargett 1989, 1999), and the fact that some examples previously believed to be strong evidence prove on modern scrutiny to be less clear (e.g., Roc de Marsal; Sandgathe et al. 2011) most specialists agree that there are some convincing examples of simple inhumation among the Neanderthals, and that, though the number of examples is low one can probably assume that some Neanderthal groups buried some of their dead some of the time (Pettitt 2002/1, 2011a: 78–138). For the European Middle Palaeolithic these are all single inhumations, indicating the deliberate modification of a locale to receive the dead; a three-stage process involving a) deliberate excavation of a pit specifically for burial, b) positioning a body within it, and c) covering the body with sediment. In most cases isolated inhumations do not necessarily indicate a specific association of that place with the dead, and as most Neanderthal burials appear to have been in sites which were otherwise used as camps, perhaps such inferences are not justified. However, in the Regourdou 'tomb', an adult Neanderthal was apparently interred in a grave defined by dry stone walling and covered by a large stone slab, beside a cairn covering the skeleton of a bear (discussed in Pettitt 2011a: 112–114). This reflects an obvious modification (and thus association) of the place with a dead Neanderthal and a dead bear, and probably an association between the two. Similarly, even if artefacts found in one or two graves are correctly interpreted as deliberate 'grave goods', while this may indicate some kind of association with the dead (or the individual who deposited them), this need not be specifically symbolic. By contrast, locales where multiple non-contemporaneous but spatially related burials were emplaced may imply a deliberate association of these places with the dead. Elsewhere I have referred to these as *places of multiple burial* to distinguish them formally from larger, later, and spatially discrete 'cemeteries' (2011a). It may well be that places where the fragmentary remains of multiple Neanderthals (e.g., c. 20 at L'Hortus, c. 22 at La Quina, c. 25 at Krapina) are found represent a deliberate association of these places with the dead. Where multiple burials occur, however, such an association seems more secure, and these seem to have appeared by c. 75 ka BP (Table 14.1).

At Shanidar four individuals (Shanidar IV, VI, VII and VIII) at least seem to have been interred very close in time and in very close spatial association, each 'respecting' the position of the others, and others may have been covered with small rock cairns that were distinguishable from rock falls. At La Ferrassie seven individuals – including infants – seem to have been buried in four groups, two of which (burials I and 2 and 5 and 8) were interred close to the shelter's wall: burial I with a stone slab under its head and two flanking it and 5 and 8 apparently associated with several sediment mounds. A third group lay (burials 3, 4/4b) in parallel grave cuttings more centrally and the fourth isolated burial 6 within one of several bowl-shaped pits apparently associated with a limestone block bearing cupules. At both these sites, therefore, one can observe the repeated internment of a number of individuals in deliberately excavated graves, a spatial similarity of the position of these graves, apparent spatial association of 'groups' of interments, and apparent physical modification of the area in close proximity to the burials; and at La Ferrassie stone blocks may in some way have delineated or marked the interments. It is difficult to

TABLE 14.1: *Evidence and possible evidence of mortuary activity among European pre-modern hominins, presented by body or place focus and arranged chronologically. Ages given are in calendrical years unless stated. For inhumation, only sites with multiple burials are included, as with single inhumations one cannot rule out a fortuitous connection with specific places. The Neanderthal remains from Engis are omitted from the list of modified remains, marks on which appear to relate to the post-excavation restoration of the cranial vault rather than modification in antiquity (White and Toth 1989), as is the juvenile mandible from Les Rois which bears some Neanderthal characteristics but which may belong to Homo sapiens (Ramirez-Rozzi et al. 2009).*

Chronology	Body	Place	Body/Place	References
~800–850 ka BP	Gran Dolina, Atapuerca (Spain), TD6 Aurora stratum, *Homo antecessor*: removal of soft tissue on cranial and postcranial remains of several individuals			Bermúdez de Castro et al. 1997, 2008 ; Parés and Pérez-González 1999; Falguères et al. 1999; Jalvo et al. 1999
~400–500 ka BP		Sima de los Huesos, Atapuerca (Spain), *Homo heidelbergensis*: possibly deliberate deposition of at last 28 individuals near shaft. (Cutmarks on teeth appear to pertain to paramasticatory use of the dentition, not to defleshing.)		Arsuaga et al. 1997a, 1997b. Bermúdez de Castro et al. 2004; Lozano-Ruiz et al. 2004; Bischoff et al. 2003
~300–340 ka BP	Castel di Guido, near Rome (Italy), archaic hominin with *H. erectus* and *H. neanderthalensis* features: defleshing of the cranium			Mariani-Costantini et al. 2001

TABLE 14.1: *(continued)*

Chronology	Body	Place	Body/Place	References
~120–140 ka BP	Krapina (Croatia), *Homo neanderthalensis*: defleshing of several individuals including scalping and/or scoring of forehead of Krapina 3			Russell 1987; Rink et al 1995; Frayer et al. 2006; Orscheidt 2008
~100–120 ka BP	Moula Guercy Cave level XV (France), *Homo neanderthalensis*: defleshing and disarticulation of six individuals			Defleur et al. 1999
Probably ~60–75 ka BP			La Ferrassie (France), *Homo neanderthalensis*: deposition of seven individuals in excavated graves/pits, and defleshing of cranium of La Ferrassie 6. Possible use of stone slabs as markers.	Capitan and Peyrony 1912a, b; 1921; Peyrony 1934; Delporte 1976; Heim 1976; Maureille and van Peer 1998
~60–70 ka BP on chronocultural grounds (MIS4)?	Combe Grenal (France), *Homo neanderthalensis*: defleshing			Le Mort 1989
~60–70 ka BP on chronocultural grounds (MIS4)?	Marillac (France), *Homo neanderthalensis*: defleshing			Le Mort 1988
~40–50 ka BP		Shkaft Mazin Shanidar (Iraq), *Homo neanderthalensis*: burial of at least four individuals (possibly more), these four in apparent spatial association		Solecki 1963, 1972; Trinkaus 1983; Cowgill et al. 2007

TABLE 14.1: *(continued)*

Chronology	Body	Place	Body/Place	References
~40–43 ka BP		Sima de las Palomas (Spain), *Homo neanderthalensis*: Deliberate introduction of at least three individuals into cave		Walker et al. 2008, in press
~41–42 ka BP		Feldhoffer Grotte, Neanderthal		
~37–41 ka BP			El Sidrón (Spain), *Homo neanderthalensis*: deposition outside the cave and defleshing and disarticulation of at least eight individuals	Rosas et al. 2006

escape the conclusion that these examples represent the association of these places with the dead; of the dead with each other; and the persistence of these associations over time. To the groups of La Ferrassie and Shanidar, therefore, the dead had not quite departed.

CONCLUSION: THE EVOLUTION OF LANDSCAPES OF THE DEAD

I argue that at least in some Neanderthal groups the dead continued to linger in the imagination, fixed at certain points in the landscape and brought to mind when the groups returned to these locales. This need not imply specifically *symbolic* behaviour, although one cannot rule this out, but at the very least such imaginary constructs must form an important stage on the road to fully symbolic minds. In the wider sense belief in the persistence of the dead and their association with specific places does not necessarily imply religious beliefs; as Barrett (2011) has noted, these probably arose later with the development of a 'metarepresentational ToM', the ability to think about thoughts. It is to my mind no coincidence that funerary caches and graves appear at this time, that is, from ~100 ka BP, as containers such as these (rather than instruments) become more apparent in the archaeological record after 100 ka BP (Gamble 2007, 2010). Prior to this it is possible that mortuary activity required only instruments (hands, the senses, tools for defleshing). Thus, the translocation of mortuary activities from the body to place becomes one from instruments to containers in Gamble's terms. Overall, I suggest the following phases in the development of archaic hominin mortuary activities and the related emergence of associations of the dead with places, which I hope are testable and thus ultimately falsifiable:

- A *core mortuary phase* (Miocene hominoids and Pliocene hominins onwards) defined by variable expression of infanticide and cannibalism of corpses; socially mediated investigation of the corpse ('morbidity'); 'mourning' activity including signs of depression, calls and carrying of corpses as an act of detachment; funerary gatherings comprising social theatre around the corpse and use of corpses socially, e.g., as adjuncts to display. More generally in this phase elements of superstitious thought created in the minds of particularly inventive children may have been exapted for use in pre-existing social rituals, some relating to morbidity and social theatre occasioned by the dead. The conceptual dualism created by the animacy/theory of mind contradiction causes the belief in the persistence of the dead to emerge very early on.
- An *archaic mortuary phase*: (Australopithecine grade hominins and early *Homo* to the origins of *Homo sapiens*) defined by a continuation of prior activities; the developing complexity of social theatre around the corpse as group size and neurological capacities increased; the simple incorporation

of places in the landscape into mortuary activity, that is, through deliberate deposition of corpses into natural features ('funerary caching'). More generally one might predict that as the size and social complexity of hominin groups grew, so did the duration and complexity of mortuary activities. These activities begin to be underpinned by simple, socially mediated belief systems predicated on a theory of mind.

- A *modernising mortuary phase* (Middle Palaeolithic/Middle Stone Age *Homo neanderthalensis* and *Homo sapiens* and possibly European Early Upper Palaeolithic) defined by the continuation of prior activities and a clear association of places in the landscape with the dead; the development of formal burial out of funerary caching (and often an association of the two); the development of places of multiple burial; some use of material culture as adjuncts to burials, for example, rare examples of grave goods, stone markers/covers and ochre. More generally, as the complexity of such face-to-face mortuary activities grew, hominin groups may have come under selection to associate places with the dead, as it became increasingly impractical to spend more time and effort on such activities. Thus, as hominin cognition developed and individuals became able to conceive and communicate more complex models of society and the resource landscape, specific places became associated with the dead.

- A *modern mortuary phase* (European Mid Upper Palaeolithic, possibly from Early Upper Palaeolithic) defined by the continuation of prior activities; a clear association of places in the landscape with the dead and places of multiple burial; the clear use of material culture as adjuncts to burial; elaborated circulation and use of human remains ('relics') and thus commemoration; the elaboration of types of burial (single, double, multiple); new associations with burials, such as fire, symbolism (art); elaborate rules for burial as *containment*; the recognition of the agency of the dead in mortuary ritual; the first signs of continent-scale general practices and regional variations on more widespread themes.

- An *advanced mortuary phase* (Late Upper Palaeolithic/Epipalaeolithic onwards) defined by elements continued from the modern mortuary phase, their spread to new regions (e.g., New World) and increasing regional and cultural variability; the origin of formal cemeteries, that is, recognition of exclusive areas of the dead and the collective representation of death.

I have therefore identified associative interaction with the dead and the landscape with the modernising mortuary phase of the Late Middle and Upper Pleistocene, and specifically with Neanderthals and early, non-European *Homo sapiens*. This is when, for the first time, landscapes of the dead can be identified. If this identification is correct, it provides important archaeological verification of the pre-human religion hypothesis, that is, that religious thought *sensu lato* emerged prior to, or at least not exclusive to, *Homo sapiens*.

CHAPTER 15

ENCODING AND DECODING THE MESSAGE: THE CASE OF THE MID UPPER PALAEOLITHIC FEMALE IMAGERY

MARGHERITA MUSSI

INTRODUCTION

The Gravettian was born in 1938, when Miss Dorothy Garrod published a paper on *The Upper Palaeolithic in the Light of Recent Discovery*. After a discussion of discoveries and theories by Peyrony, Leakey and other archaeologists of the time, she declares that 'Perigordian, like the former Aurignacian, is made to cover too much' (1938: 19). She starts using the name 'Gravettian' for industries with La Font Robert points (Lower Gravettian), and for later industries with backed points (Upper Gravettian). She also underlines at once that a 'close connection' of female statuettes with her Upper Gravettian is 'incontestable', producing a distribution map of Gravettian sites, with a specific symbol for those with figurines. The connection has never since been questioned, even if at the time only a fraction was known of the female imagery available today for investigation.

After Leroi-Gourhan (1965: 66), '*Les unes et les autres (. . .) sont pratiquement interchangeables, aux proportions près*'; that is, they are practically interchangeable, apart from their proportions. However, a degree of variability has been noticed among hundreds of fragmentary or fully preserved images discovered all over Europe, and even beyond the boundaries of the Gravettian world. Notwithstanding an overall *air de famille*, Middle Upper Palaeolithic (MUP) female imagery differs widely not only in size, but also in raw material, technique and typology. Wall engravings, portable engravings, three-dimensional representations, bas-reliefs are all recorded. The female characterisation is the outcome of a detailed representation of primary and/or secondary sexual attributes, or can be just guessed if a putative female symbolism is recognised (Gvozdover 1989a, 1989b; Mussi et al. 2000a). MUP female figures are currently classified among distinct groups and a number of interpretations have been accordingly produced. As summarised by D'Errico et al. (2011, with references), they range from regional style to differences in age or social group membership, physiology, realism and self-portrait, and so on. A different approach was suggested by Gamble (1982) in a paper on *Interaction and Alliance in Palaeolithic*

Society: no attempt was made to elucidate the meaning, which was considered as probably beyond the reach of scholars; full attention was given, instead, to the very fact that a message was conveyed, linking to each other prehistoric human groups. According to Gamble, the capability of encoding and decoding messages was important for a much dispersed population, allowing distant groups to keep in touch with each other. This, in turn, helped them to react to the challenges of a shifting environment.

Neither the 'deciphering' approach of many scholars nor the 'linking' approach of Gamble put into question the fact that any symbol, message or code embedded in the Gravettian female imagery was properly and fully understood by the MUP human groups. In this paper I am not taking this point for granted. Accordingly, I will explore the record, looking for any contradictory evidence pointing to differences in time and space which could be the outcome of some degree of misunderstanding. Examples will be selected and discussed from images and figurines which bear distinct similarities, either in the general shape, or in anatomic details. I will check point-by-point the similarities, to detect subtle changes, if any, during the millennia and in the vast area under scrutiny. The aim is to help develop ideas and hypothesis on the intensity of relationships that MUP human groups were able to establish and maintain, or not, while living in distant parts of a depopulated Europe.

Inevitably, many examples will be taken from a relatively homogeneous group of figurines, the Kostenki-Lespugue group. They have been described elsewhere as sharing a number of characteristics (Mussi et al. 2000a: 112), including a flat upper thorax with minute shoulders; a bulging lower thorax with voluminous pendulous breasts, directly resting on a rounded belly; a straight back, on top of flattish buttocks exhibiting lateral expansion; a marked anus or coccyx; fully and clearly delineated right and left lower limbs. The Kostenki-Lespugue figurines have been discovered from Kostenki on the Don in the East, to Lespugue at the foot of the Pyrenees in the West; and from Zaraysk near Moscow, to the Balzi Rossi and La Marmotta in the Mediterranean (Figure 15.1), making them a suitable sub-sample for any general discussion. However, more specimens, not included in this group, will also be discussed.

There is no general inventory of female statuettes. In the case of sites with many of them, as Kostenki, Avdeevo, Gagarino, each figurine is named as in the relevant literature, namely Abramova (1967), Praslov (1985) and Gvozdover (1995).

The details examined below are the following, in anatomical order from head downwards, followed by whole representation: 1) shape, posture and anatomical details of the head; 2) hair or appendixes of the head; 3) folded arms; 4) anatomical details of the back and fundament; 5) female chimeras.

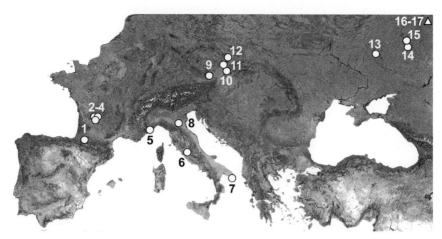

Figure 15.1: Geographic distribution of the female imagery discussed in the text. 1- Lespugue; 2–4 – Cussac, Laussel, Tursac; 5 – Balzi Rossi; 6 – La Marmotta; 7 – Veneri; 8 – Savignano; 9 – Willendorf; 10 – Moravany; 11 – Dolní Věstonice; 12 – Předmostí; 13 – Avdeevo; 14 – Kostenki; 15 – Gagarino; 16–17 – Khotylevo and Zaraysk are both outside the map and north of it.

Shape, posture and anatomical details of the head (Figure 15.2)

In the Kostenki-Lespugue figurines, the profile of the head is rounded, ending with a flat surface. The latter connects the head to a short or even notch-like neck. An ornamented cap or bonnet is sometimes represented. At Kostenki (statuette 3 and statuette 83–2), it is quite clear that the flat surface surrounded by such a garment is the face, portrayed as an inclined facet without any chin: the figurine looks downwards. The forehead is also flat, making an angle with the face. The same posture and outline are found at Gagarino (statuette 1) and Willendorf. At Lespugue, however, the flat facet between head and neck is horizontal, and clearly depicts the throat. The face itself, which is capped by hair, stands upright and displays a definite chin. A face in an upright position and with a distinct chin can similarly be recognised at the Balzi Rossi on the Yellow Venus, and at La Marmotta in central Italy. Statuette 7 of Avdeevo lacks the chin but has a well-defined throat, and the straight face looks forwards.

An intermediate posture is also found at Avdeevo (statuette 76), and at Zaraysk as well: the profile of the head rather suggests a forward-looking face, with a chin and a throat, but the ornamentation of the cap extends from the top of the head, all over the face to the putative chin.

For a human being, it is just impossible to look forwards with a bent neck, and very uncomfortable to bend the neck to the point of making chin and throat totally disappear. In this case, the chin leans on the top of the thorax, and the neck is just a closed fold.

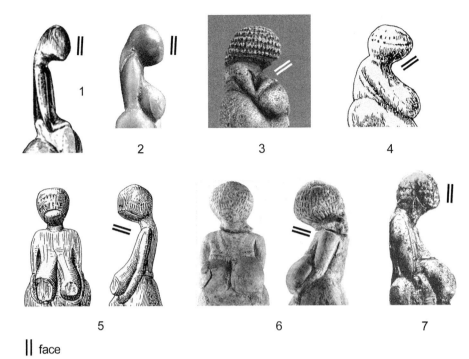

|| face

Figure 15.2: The profile of the head of the Kostenki-Lespugue figurines, at different scales. The arms are also figured. 1 – Lespugue; 2 – Balzi Rossi-Yellow Venus; 3 – Willendorf; 4 – Gagarino statuette 3; 5 – Kostenki statuette 3; 6 – Kostenki statuette 83–2; 7 – Avdeevo statuette 6.

Hair or appendix of the head (Figure 15.3)

Hair is rarely depicted in a detailed way. Locks and bangs appear in a few specimens: Lespugue, the Ochred Lady of the Balzi Rossi and statuette 8 of Mal'ta, surprisingly similar to the previous one (Bolduc et al. 1996). Bangs are also represented on a figurine from Kostenki (Praslov 1985: figure 2), and on statuette 7 of Avdeevo.

A pointed appendix tapering from the back of the head is displayed in a number of cases. At Laussel, on the *Vénus à la corne*, it is often described as hair – for example, as *abondante chevelure* by Delporte (1993a). The same appendix rests on the shoulders of the Yellow Venus, as well as of the Nun of the Balzi Rossi, while at Sireuil only a fragment is preserved. A shorter one is distinctly pictured at Cussac, on the nape of the large female creature incised on the wall. But it is also depicted vertically at Savignano, Grotta delle Veneri and Tursac, producing accordingly elongated conic heads; at Avdeevo (statuette 4) it is a small erect cone on the back of the head; it dips in an intermediate posture on the Lozenge and on the Punchinello of Balzi Rossi. Sometimes it is connected to an apparently decorated cap. At Laussel the pointed shape lies outside the bonnet of the *Femme à la tête quadrillée* and seems to escape from it, while on the

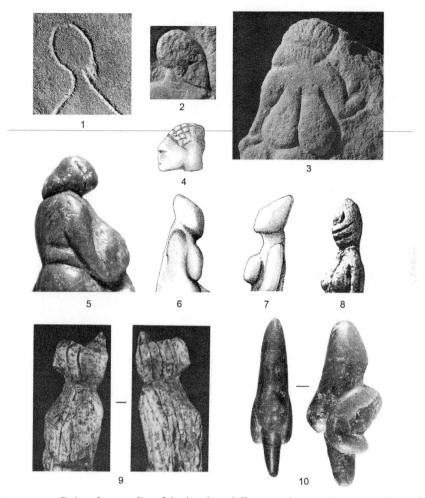

Figure 15.3: Pointed appendix of the head, at different scales: 1 – Cussac; 2 – Laussel-*Vénus à la corne*; 3 – Laussel-*Femme à la tête quadrillée*; 4- Balzi Rossi-*Tête négroide*; 5 – La Marmotta; 6 – Balzi Rossi-*Lozenge*; 7 – Balzi Rossi-Punchinello; 8 – Veneri; 9 – Avdeevo statuette 4; 10 – Tursac.

Negroid Head of Balzi Rossi it is kept inside, producing a pointed profile. At Willendorf it could be suspected that the expansion of the cap on the bent nape of the neck, never found elsewhere, is a limited version of this feature.

Folded arms (Figure 15.4)

Upper limbs are represented in the Kostenki-Lespugue statuettes. At Willendorf, this is highly detailed. The arm is vertical with the elbow resting laterally on the hip. The forearm and hand – folded and more or less at a right angle to the arm – lean on the upper part of the bulging breast. The length of both arm and forearm is correct. A real woman with large breasts could easily stand in the depicted posture.

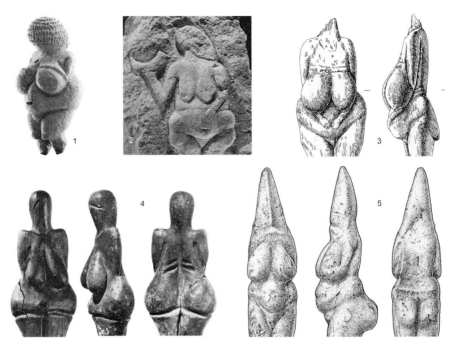

Figure 15.4: The arms, at different scales: 1 – Willendorf; 2 – Laussel-*Vénus à la corne*; 3 – Kostenti statuette 4; 4 – Dolní Věstonice-Black Venus; 5 – Savignano.

A variant is found at Avdeevo (statuette 6), Gagarino (statuette 4), Khotylevo (statuette 3): the arm and elbow are in the usual posture, but the forearm is not folded, with wrist and hand resting on the upper side of the belly. In a real human being, the forearm is significantly longer: when the upper limb extends downwards, it ends with the wrist and hand on the thigh. Accordingly, in the statuettes the forearm is too short and not anatomically correct.

At Laussel, the bas-relief of the *Vénus à la corne* has all the characteristics of a bi-dimensional Kostenki-Lespugue figure, and displays arms of both types: the left one, bent outwards and holding a possible horn, is of realistic length; while the left one, resting on the upper abdomen, is shortened.

In other specimens, distinct arms can be seen from the back, and in a lateral view as well, but in the front view there is no forearm at all, and the upper limb disappears. Examples are Avdeevo (statuette 77–2), Gagarino (statuette 1) and Khotylevo (statuette 1). The same is also true in statuettes of a different typology, as the Black Venus of Dolní Věstonice, the figurine of Moravany, the statuette of Savignano.

Anatomical details of the back and fundament (Figure 15.5)

Leroi-Gourhan (1965: 460) illustrated a series of statuettes from Kostenki, Willendorf and Lespugue, characterised by a progressive enlargement of the small of the back, while the buttocks are unrealistically squeezed. The latter

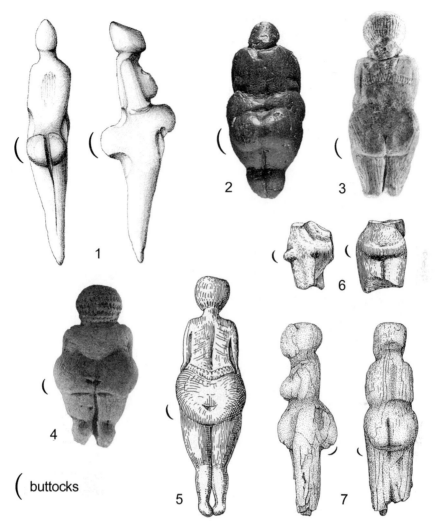

Figure 15.5: Back and fundament, at different scales. Realistic buttocks: 1 – Balzi Rossi-Punchinello. Progressively squeezed buttocks: 2 – La Marmotta; 3 – Kostenki statuette 83–2. Unrealistic buttocks with saddle-like loins: 4 – Willendorf; 5 – Kostenki statuette 3. Unrecognisable buttocks: 6 – Kostenki statuette 7; Balzi Rossi-the Abrachial.

ones eventually nearly disappear, being represented more and more like a fold, or as paired folds, to make room to the expanded, saddle-like loins, with the coccyx ending up in the position of the anus.

The end of this drifting representational process is depicted in a tiny figurine of Kostenki (statuette 7) and in the Abrachial of the Balzi Rossi (Mussi et al. 2000a: 117). In the former one the progressively displaced buttocks are no more than a protruding stripe, at right angle to the thighs. In the Abrachial, the last transformation of the coccyx is a transversal incision which delineates the top of stripe-like buttocks. It is eventually used to start the groove dividing two realistic buttocks, which are then placed on the top of the old, no more recognisable ones.

Female chimeras (Figure 15.6)

Chimeras – that is, beings which are a compound of different species existing separately, or which include non-existing attributes – are known all over the Upper Palaeolithic. They were defined *monsters* or *créatures imaginaires* by Leroi-Gourhan (1983). Primary or secondary sexual attributes sometimes allow them to be identified as female. This is the case of a chimera, first recognised as

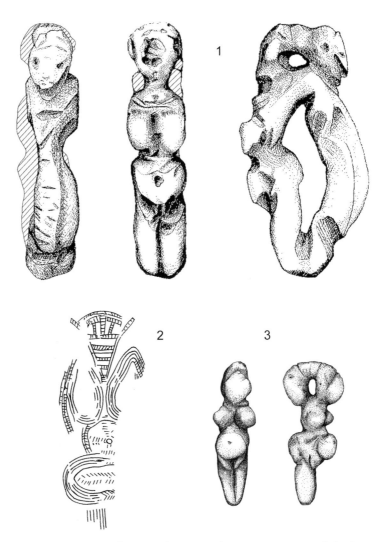

Figure 15.6: Chimeras, at different scales: 1 – Balzi Rossi-Beauty and the Beast; 2 – Balzi Rossi-the Bicephalous; 3 – Předmostí.

engraved on a mammoth tusk of Předmostí, but also discovered at the Balzi Rossi (Mussi 2004). At the Italian site, a steatite carving, which is nicknamed 'Beauty and the Beast', depicts two separate beings: a woman ('Beauty'), with breasts and a vulva, symmetrically opposed to a non-human being ('the Beast'), with a triangular face, little horns, little arms and a serpent-like body. In the Moravian engraving the two creatures are compounded in one: the triangular face with little horns stands on the top of a recognisable female body, and two slim arms are added. In both cases the figures have large oval breasts, and a perfectly circular belly, with the navel exactly in the middle; the face is either destroyed (Balzi Rossi), or made unrecognisable by a superimposed geometric pattern (Předmostí); the head ends, in the upper part, with an arc-shaped element; the lowermost body of the 'Beast' is covered by transverse incisions, while geometric patterns can be seen on the lower part of the Předmostí Venus. In the latter, however, they are added on an unrealistic part of the anatomy, that is, on an unidentifiable oval feature, below the easily recognisable belly. I suggest that the transverse oval is the lower body of the 'Beast', added below the round belly originated by 'Beauty'.

The same extraordinary iconography is displayed by another engraving, also from Předmostí, recently rediscovered and tentatively authenticated by D'Errico et al. (2011), who attributed it to the Gravettian. At the Balzi Rossi there is also another, diminutive double carving: the Bicephalous (27.5 mm; 1.9 g), that is, a female being with a second head on her shoulders, which is triangular and possibly horned. There is not a second body. Because of the tiny size, the head (i.e., a part) stands for the whole, as in a synecdoche.

DISCUSSION

The subtle changes in iconography and patterning described above include well-understood but abridged versions of the same original; lack of comprehension of the model, followed by an attempt of following the rule; innovative reinterpretation of the original. They can be re-arranged in a more or less progressive scale:

1. Arms (Figure 15.4).

Arms progressively shift from folded and realistic to partially extended and unrealistically shortened, to incompletely represented but undoubtedly suggested as existing. The carver and whoever will look at the statuette know the model perfectly well. A rule is apparently followed, as forearm and hands are never depicted on the lower abdomen or thighs. The rendering might be on the verge of abstraction, but the final representation is fully functional.

2. Chimeras (Figure 15.6)

Two distinct beings, including a chimera, are detailed in the round. When they are engraved bi-dimensionally, the elements making each one are combined, and a single creature is produced. The original constituent parts are recognised, and a second, transverse body is added below the round belly. Innovation is the outcome of technical constraint and of a bi-dimensional representation. The original model is carefully followed as much as possible, to the expense of the compounded figure, which is no longer anatomically functional.

3. Small of the back and buttocks (Figure 15.5)

Loins are expanded and buttocks are restricted in size, progressively shifting from realistic to unrealistic, from recognisable to utterly unrecognisable. The original model appears less and less understood, and in the end totally distorted. The traditional, if incomprehensible, pattern is all the same carefully retained, with new anatomical landmarks simply added to the old ones. Realistic buttocks are placed on the top of the disappearing ones, producing a more or less functional back. Innovation occurs, but it is limited.

4. Face bent or upright (Figure 15.2)

Either a bent model without a chin or an upright one with a chin, would have been the archetype. The model is properly reproduced by a carver who understood the original well. When some misunderstanding arises, different solutions are worked out: parallel rows suggestive of a cap, apparently perceived as being of the utmost importance, are applied all over the face, that is, over anatomic landmarks, without much interest for realism; or the face is interpreted/reinterpreted as being in a different and innovative position, which makes it fully functional again.

5. Pointed appendix of the head (Figure 15.3)

The appendix is variously orientated downwards, laterally or upwards. This suggests that a code is followed, each orientation being meaningful and with significance. The model is fully understood and the final representation is functional, accurately transmitting a symbolic message. An alternative is possible if we follow the realistic interpretation of Delporte (1993a) and others. This interpretation would suggest that the raised or skewed appendix is perceived as hair by whoever is looking at the figure and reproducing it. A lock of hair is figured on the shoulders. The original model is misunderstood and the code is lost.

The first case study suggests a full command of the replicated model, while the following ones include degrees of misunderstanding and innovation. The outcome are different scenarios: 1) complete transmission of model and related code in an accurate replica; 2) partial transmission, a recognised lack of comprehension, and an attempt of not breaching any rules; 3) partial transmission, unrecognised lack of comprehension, and unwilling innovation; 4) transmission, unequivocal willingness of innovating and a breach of the code.

CHANGE IN CONTEXT

Varying accuracy in replicas implies different patterns of cultural transmission and a varying behaviour. Starting with radical innovation, this is the case which is easiest to spot, but also the most difficult to put into a firm context. For example, the Petřkovice figurine, in Svoboda's words (2008b: 195) 'in terms of shape (. . .) has no analogy'. Within the Gravettian record, the statuette is also rather late in age. It could well be a case of innovation. However, evidence *ab absentia*, can be falsified at any time by new discoveries.

The opposite, that is, accurate replicas of the same model, are documented at Kostenki I/1 by acephalous, kneeled figurines not discussed in the present paper: Dupuy (2009) identifies 64 such statuettes, most of them roughouts or fragments, corresponding to a well-established chaîne opératoire. As they are all from the same site and layer, this suggests that a homogeneous human group followed strict and well-known rules while replicating the same model. Carvers were in full control of the code and of the transmitted symbolic message.

At the inter-site level, complete transmission and accurate replicas, as well as a degree of misunderstanding and innovation, are both exemplified within the Kostenki-Lespugue group, spreading over some 40° in longitude and 33° in latitude. To account for similarities found at great distances, two non-mutually exclusive hypotheses can be put forward: either the carvers/engravers were travelling and reproducing the model or mobile specimens were transported. There is evidence of 'travelling' figurines, discovered in the open outside any known site, sometimes in regions with scarce or no Gravettian remains. Monpazier, Sireuil, Terme-Pialat, Savignano, Trasimeno and La Marmotta are all part of this specific record of stone statuettes only, as ivory ones cannot be expected to survive in the open. The most conservative hypothesis is that some at least were lost or deposited during a journey.

When misunderstanding is evidenced comparing specimens from distant areas, and related to the same archetype, an obvious explanation is imperfect comprehension, which can arise from the lack of a common language when information is exchanged. The MUP figurative style lasted for a minimum of 5000 years (cf. Svoboda 2008b for an updated but uncalibrated chronology of the figurines). The distribution spreads over more than 3500 x 1000 km. Even assuming, for the sake of simplicity, that the human groups which produced the Gravettian female imagery were originally all speaking the same language – which, of course, is unproven and unlikely (cf. Pagel 2000) – changes must have happened through time within a widely scattered population.

Palaeolithic languages are well beyond the reach of current scientific investigation, and most of the research on early language evolution focuses on the spread of agriculture and on later prehistoric times (e.g., Renfrew 1998;

Diamond and Bellwood 2003; Gray et al. 2011). The analysis of modern languages gives all the same some clues.

Currently there are 75 Bantu and Bantoid languages in central and southern Africa, in an area roughly triangular in shape, with maximum distances in the range of 3500 km. They are believed to mirror the spread of farming across this part of sub-Saharan Africa between c. 3000 BC and AD 500, that is, over 3500 years (Holden 2002). Including the following 1500 years to the present, this dispersion is roughly comparable to the Gravettian extension in time – and in space as well. What Bantu languages have in common is a set of grammatical features and a part of the vocabulary – which does not mean that they are mutually intelligible.

Farming communities, even if small in size, were probably far larger than hunter-gatherer groups. Nettle (1999), using computer simulation, suggests that language change may be faster in small communities, that is, of a few hundred people – which would be rather compatible with a web of Upper Palaeolithic fractioned groups. Pagel et al. (2007), dealing with Indo-European languages, further underlines that infrequently used words evolve at higher rates than frequently used ones – and it is probably reasonable to assume that part or all the aspects related to female imagery and encoded messages were not dealt with every day.

Unless the mechanisms of language transmission at work in the final Upper Pleistocene were totally different from today's, the assembled evidence suggests caution, before taking for granted that all people of the Gravettian world were fluently speaking to each other.

Intermittent contact fosters misunderstanding not only in space, but in time too. Obstacles in comprehension can well have arisen if the imagery was not continuously tended by the same people, or by closely related people. This could have happened if statuettes or other representation were purposefully installed at the site and left behind. For a number of reasons, a long time can elapse before returning to the same general area. The incoming group could have observed any statuette or other figure without having all the requested expertise and knowledge to entirely decode the symbolism and to accurately reproduce it.

Limited circumstantial evidence is available to sort out specimens left on purpose from those just lost or abandoned. In the large open-air sites of central and eastern Europe, many figurines have been discovered in pits, such as at Petřkovice, Avdeevo, Kostenki, Gagarino, Zaraysk (Amirkhanov and Lev 2008; Gvozdover 1995; Praslov 1985; Svoboda 2008b). In a number of cases, the pit was elaborately prepared to keep one or more statuettes, notably at Avdeevo and Kostenki. In western Europe, wall art, discovered in the limestone ranges, is long-lasting by definition. MUP female imagery was identified at Laussel, Pech-Merle, Cussac and Arcy-sur-Cure (Grande Grotte). However, Pech-Merle, Cussac and Grande Grotte are deep cavities: it cannot be proved (or dismissed, at that) that humans came back again after the wall or stalagmite was decorated. Laussel, instead, is a vast rockshelter, with the base of the huge decorated block of *Vénus à la corne* included in a thick Gravettian layer (Roussot 2000). At least one of the decorated *plaquettes*, the *Vénus à la tête quadrillée*, was discovered well within the same layer. Notwithstanding the extremely poor standards of the excavation, there are grounds to believe that during centuries people settled over and again next to the bas-relief. The Red Venus of Weinberg, and the Tursac one, were similarly discovered in the central part of a rockshelter; both were close to the rear wall and rather isolated from other archaeological remains (Zotz 1955; Delporte 1968; Mussi 1997). This possibly did not happen by chance.

Statuettes lying in pits, engraved or carved on walls, or standing in a special part of the rockshelter, all suggest that at least occasionally they had been left behind on purpose. If rediscovered and reproduced after years or generations, reinterpretation could have occurred, willingly or not. In some instances, when an attempt was made to follow rules and reproduce a code which was no longer understood, absurd anatomical characterisation was the outcome.

CONCLUSIONS

After this analysis, innovation was the exception, much more than the rule. Furthermore, it probably stemmed from sheer and unwitting misunderstanding. The chaîne opératoire of the standardised kneeled figurines of Kostenki is mirrored by the rigour in reproducing incomprehensible patterns, ending with the absurd back anatomy displayed by some figurines of Balzi Rossi and Kostenki, or by the engraved chimeras of Předmostí, or by faces covered by cap-like patterns at Avdeevo. In all such cases the artists were abiding by rules which were perceived as mandatory.

Changes obviously happened through time and space because of linguistic difficulties, and/or because of imperfect social transmission of codes and symbols. The latter scenario implies that some individuals had full control of traditional knowledge, while others had a more limited access to it. This social complexity is well in accordance with the articulated way of life suggested for the MUP and namely for the Gravettian (Mussi et al. 2000b). There little doubt, however, that a message was transmitted, even at the cost of great difficulty, and that it mattered much, as originally suggested by Clive Gamble.

CHAPTER 16

CONTEXTUALISING THE FEMALE IMAGE – SYMBOLS FOR COMMON IDEAS AND COMMUNAL IDENTITY IN UPPER PALAEOLITHIC SOCIETIES

SABINE GAUDZINSKI-WINDHEUSER AND OLAF JÖRIS

INTRODUCTION

Past hominin symbolic behaviour is manifest in various media and that which survives in the archaeological material record we today identify as Palaeolithic art. Art can build a bridge between material and non-material culture and often serves as a medium for communicating specific worldviews or cosmologies, thus mirroring the self-perception of past societies. In more recent periods in art history, the social role of a human being and the specific social context is one of the major aspects that determines the way in which humans are depicted (cf. Conkey 1978).

The beginning of the European Upper Palaeolithic (Figure 16.1) witnesses a growth in the visibility of artistic expression both in terms of parietal and portable art. Within the broad range of Palaeolithic art, a large body of anthropomorphic as well as explicit human depictions exists, much of which (to our eyes) depicts females (e.g., Leroi-Gourhan 1968, 1971; Delporte 1979, 1993a, 1993b; Bosinski and Fischer 1980; Bosinski 1982, 1987; Soffer et al. 2000a; Bosinski et al. 2001; Cohen 2003; Guthrie 2005; Svoboda 2007; Valoch and Lázničková-Galetová 2009; Cluzel and Cleyet-Merle 2011). Palaeolithic female figurines have been known since 1864 when the Vénus impudique ('immodest Venus') was discovered at Laugerie Basse in France (e.g., Delporte 1979, 1993a: cf. figure 7.2). Further discoveries followed including several female ivory figurines from the Grotte du Pape at Brassempouy, France, in 1894 (Piette 1895; White 2006), and numerous small figurines of stone, ivory and antler found in the caves of Balzi Rossi, in Italy, between 1883 and 1895 (Bolduc et al. 1996; Mussi et al. 2000a). But it was not until 1908, when the famous Venus of Willendorf (Austria) discovered by Josef Szombathy, Hugo Obermaier and Josef Bayer (Angeli 1989 figure 3.4; Antl-Weiser 2008a, 2008b), that Palaeolithic female depictions and their interpretation significantly changed perceptions of Palaeolithic humans.

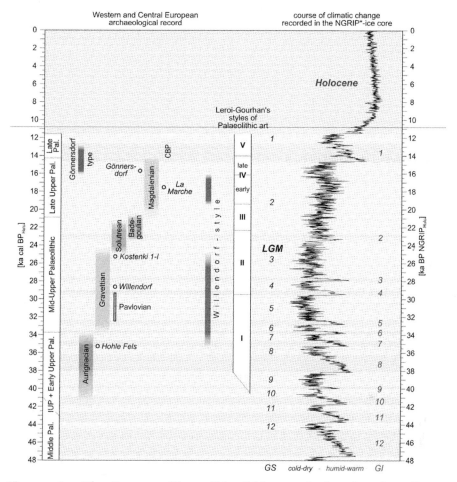

Figure 16.1: The European Upper Palaeolithic record viewed against climate change recorded in the NGRIP-ice core (Andersen et al. 2006, 2007; Svensson et al. 2006 (* -timescale adopted to the Hulu-speleothem chronology of Wang et al. 2001, following Weninger and Jöris 2008). Key-sites and archaeological cultures that have provided female depictions are indicated. Palaeolithic art styles adopted and modified from Leroi-Gourhan 1971. Pal.) Palaeolithic; IUP) Initial Upper Palaeolithic; CBP) Curve-Backed Point industries; LGM) Last Glacial Maximum; GI) Greenland interstadial; GS) Greenland stadial.

Using the term 'Venus' to describe these early discoveries drew comparisons with female nudes in classical art, wrenching the Palaeolithic art objects from their original cosmologic contexts. Subsequently, the name 'Venus' became an umbrella term for Pleistocene anthropomorphic female depictions, and this term implies the entire body of associations which accompany the interpretation of classical art. Surprisingly, this approach has only rarely been challenged, as it was implicitly assumed that past and present human depictions shared similar motivations. Thus, classically derived models for understanding female depictions were seen to be sufficient for understanding those of the Palaeolithic. Consequently, current interpretations often refer to generalising stereotypes (see discussion in e.g., Nelson 1990; White 2006) instead of presenting analyses of individual depictions. Therefore, we virtually lack any sound interpretation of the motivation of their production and their context in society.

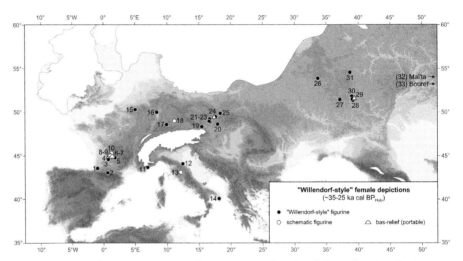

Figure 16.2: The spatio-temporal contexts of Palaeolithic female depictions. 1) 'Willendorf-style' female depictions from the Eurasian Early and Mid Upper Palaeolithic (~35–25 ka cal BP_{Hulu}); 2) Middle Magdalenian 'Willendorf-style' female depictions and Eastern European figurines of comparable age (~19–16 ka cal BP_{Hulu}); 3) 'Gönnersdorf-type' female depictions from the Late Upper Palaeolithic Magdalenian and Curve-Backed Point industries of Western and Central Europe (~16–13 ka cal BP_{Hulu}). Compiled from Bosinski *et al.* 2001; Cluzel and Cleyet-Merle 2011; Delporte 1993a. Note: Maps show European coastlines at average glacial levels of c. -65 m below present day sea level with LGM (maps 1 and 2) and Late Glacial (map 3) ice shields.

Figure 16.2.1: 1) Brassempouy, Grotte du Pape (Landes, France); 2) Lespugne (Haute Garonne, France); 3) Monpazier (Dordogne, France); 4) Termo-Pialat (half-relief; Dordogne, France); 5) Péchialet (Dordogne, France); 6) Sireul (Dordogne, France); 7) Laussel (bas-relief; Dordogne, France); 8) Abri Pataud (bas-relief; Dordogne, France); 9) La Mouthe (bas-relief; Dordogne, France); 10) Tursac, Abri du Facteur (Dordogne, France); 11) Balzi Rossi (Liguria, Italy); 12) Savignano (Bologna, Italy); 13) Trasimeno (Toscany, Italy); 14) Parabita (Lecce, Italy); 15) Trou Magrite (Ardennes, Belgium); 16) Mainz-Linsenberg (Rheinland-Pfalz, Germany); 17) Hohle Fels (Baden-Württermberg, Germany); 18) Mauern (Bavaria, Germany); 19) Willendorf (Lower Austria, Austria); 20) Moravany-Podkovica (Trnava, Slovakia); 21) Pavlov (Moravia, Czech Republic); 22) Dolní Věstoníce (Moravia, Czech Republic); 23) Brno (Moravia, Czech Republic); 24) Předmostí (Moravia, Czech Republic); 25) Petrkovice (Moravia, Czech Republic); 26) Khotylevo II (Russia); 27) Avdeevo (Russia); 28) Kostenki 13 (Russia); 29) Kostenki 1-I (Russia); 30) Gagarino (Russia); 31) Zaraysk (Russia); 32) Mal'ta (Russia); 33) Bouret' (Russia).

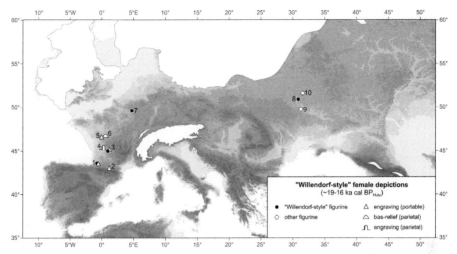

Figure 16.2.2: (*cont.*) 1) Isturitz (Landes, France); 2) Enlène (Ariège), France; 3) Laugerie-Basse (Dordogne, France); 4) Gabillou (Dordogne, France); 5) La Marche (Vienne, France); 6) Angles-sur-l'Anglin (Vienne, France); 7) Farincourt (Haute-Marne, France); 8) Eliseevitchi (Ukraine); 9) Mezhirich (Ukraine); 10) Mezin (Ukraine).

Here we seek to fill this gap, following Gamble (1982), who suggested a connection between stylistic conventions in Mid Upper Palaeolithic artistic depictions and social alliance networks in Pleistocene environments. We consider Palaeolithic female images in their stylistic, spatial and temporal contexts, comparing the Mid Upper Palaeolithic Gravettian with different periods of the Late Upper Palaeolithic record (Figures 16.1–16.2). We conclude that the schematic style characterising Late Magdalenian female depictions (Rosenfeld 1977; Bosinski and Fischer 1980; Bosinski et al. 2001; Bosinski 2011a, 2011b) represents an artistic reflection of changes in the social role of women during a period of rapid range expansion of Late Glacial populations some 16–13,000 years ago (for timescale see Weninger and Jöris 2008; cf. Figure 16.1).

UPPER PALAEOLITHIC HUMAN DEPICTIONS

Male representations are a rarity amongst the large corpus of human representations in Upper Palaeolithic art (Duhard 1996), whilst female-like depictions are the most common subject for Palaeolithic art. Their depictions occur painted on the walls of caves, engraved in stone, sculptured as bas-reliefs or in the form of stone, bone or ivory statuettes (e.g., Leroi-Gourhan 1968; Guthrie 2005). Human depictions of clear female sex occur most frequently in the Eurasian Mid Upper and Late Upper Palaeolithic (Bosinski 1982, 1987, 2011a, 2011b; Delporte 1993a, 1993b; Duhard 1993; Soffer et al. 2000a; Bosinski et al. 2001; Cohen 2003; Svoboda 2007; Valoch and Lázničková-Galetová 2009; Cluzel and Cleyet-Merle 2011). In contrast, most anthropomorphic depictions from the Early Upper Palaeolithic (e.g., Hahn 1988; Neugebauer-Maresch 1989;

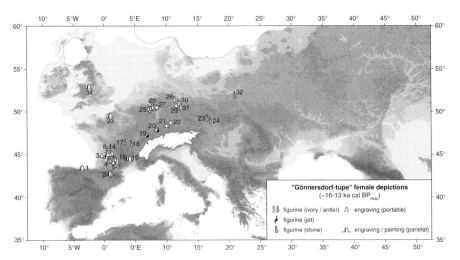

Figure 16.2.3: (*cont.*) 1) Cueva del Linar (Santander, Spain); 2) Gourdan (Haute-Garonne, France); 3) Abri Faustin (Gironde, France); 4) Grotte Courbet (Tarn, France); 5) Fontalès (Tarn-et-Garonne, France); 6) Abri Murat (Lot, France); 7) Grotte Carriot (Lot, France); 8) Les Combarelles (parietal; Dordogne, France); 9)Comarque (parietal; Dordogne, France); 10) Vielmouly II (parietal; Dordogne, France); 11) Rochereil (engraved plaquette; Dordogne, France); 12) Lalinde (engraved plaquette; Dordogne, France); 13) Gare de Couze (engraved parietal; Dordogne, France); 14) Fronsac (parietal; Dordogne, France); 15) Grotte des Deux Ouvertures (Ardèche, France); 16) Grotte du Planchard (Ardèche, France); 17) Enval (Puy-de-Dôme, France); 18) Goutte Roffat (Loire, France); 19) Monruz (Neuchâtel, Switzerland); 20) Petersfels (Baden-Württemberg, Germany); 21) Felsställe (Baden-Württemberg, Germany); 22) Hohlenstein, Ederheim (Bavaria, Germany); 23) Býčí Skála (Moravia, Czech Republic); 24) Pekárna (Moravia, Czech Republic); 25) Andernach-Martinsberg (Rheinland-Pfalz, Germany); 26) Gönnersdorf (Rheinland-Pfalz, Germany); 27) Niederbieber (Rheinland-Pfalz, Germany); 28) Nebra (Sachsen-Anhalt, Germany); 29) Teufelsbrücke, Saalfeld (Thuringia, Germany); 30) Oelknitz (Thuringia, Germany); 31) Bärenkeller, Garsitz (Thuringia, Germany); 32) Wilczyce (Poland); 33) Gouy (Seine-Maritime, France); 34) Church Hole (Nottinghamshire, United Kingdom).

Broglio et al. 2005; Floss and Rouquerol 2007); or from Solutrean/Early Magdalenian contexts are not clearly attributable to sex (Leroi-Gourhan 1971).[1]

With the exception of the Aurignacian Venus of Hohle Fels (Germany) (Conard 2009). Early Upper Palaeolithic anthropomorphic illustrations seem to show humans independent of sex although sex was, however, a frequently displayed topic in this period, as deeply engraved or picked vulvae or phalli amply illustrate (e.g., Leroi-Gourhan 1971; Guthrie 2005; Martin 2007).

UPPER PALAEOLITHIC FEMALE DEPICTIONS

During three specific Palaeolithic periods, there appears to be a strong focus on the depiction of females: (1) the Mid Upper Palaeolithic (Gravettian *sensu lato*) of Eurasia (Figure 16.2.1), (2) the Late Upper Palaeolithic Middle Magdalenian of Western Europe and its Eastern European equivalents (Figure 16.2.2) and (3) the Late Magdalenian and succeeding Curve-Backed Point (CBP) industries of Western and Central Europe (Fig. 16.2.3; cf. Figure 16.1). Distinct stylistic conventions underlying the depictions of these periods allow for a distinction between an older Willendorf-like style (Gravettian *sensu lato* and Middle Magdalenian) and that of the much younger Late Magdalenian/CBP 'Gönnersdorf-type'.

The 'Willendorf-style'

Female depictions from the Mid Upper Palaeolithic are characterised mostly by corpulent female figurines which often display pronounced and sometimes exaggerated sexual attributes (Figure 16.3; Bosinski 1987; Delporte 1993b; Brunn 2007; Verpoorte 2001; Wolf 2010). Aside from a few highly schematic statuettes (Figure 16.3 nos. 21–22), Willendorf-style figurines are striking in their naturalism and display female nakedness in all its splendour: large breasts, wide hips, protruding bellies and buttocks, and bluntly visible genitals with some regional variations. The 'naturalism' which characterises these figurines inevitably results in a high level of 'standardisation' (cf. Verpoorte 2001), epistomised by the Venus of Willendorf which has become the archetype of this particular iconographic style (cf. Gamble 1982; Bosinski 1987).

Most Willendorf-style depictions are carved in stone or ivory as three-dimensional objects and can vary considerably in size from a few centimetres to over 20 cm in height. Only rarely was bone or antler used as raw-material. As three-dimensional sculptures, they function in all perspectives, although their frontal view usually appears most prominent. At Laussel, Abri Pataud, La Mouthe and Termo-Pialat, Willendorf-style bas-reliefs were also carved onto stone blocks spalled from roofs (Figure 16.4), and it may be significant that comparable representations are unknown in parietal art (Delporte 1993a), although a small number of engraved Willendorf-style depictions are known – for example, one from Kostenki 1-I (Efimenko 1958) and the geometrically schematised female engraving from Předmostí (Figure 16.5; Valoch 1969; cf. Marshack 1972; Absolon and Klíma 1977; note that d'Errico et al. 2011 discuss a second engraving).

Willendorf-style depictions almost exclusively occur as singular (i.e., isolated) figurines. With the exception of a statuette named 'The Beauty and the Beast' from Balzi Rossi (Figure 16.3 no. 20; Mussi et al. 2000a) and the bas-relief Personages Opposés from Laussel (Figure 16.4 no. 1; Delporte 1993a), couples or groups of persons are not depicted in Mid Upper Palaeolithic contexts. However, the double statuette no. 6 from Gagarino, which shows two half-complete females still attached at their heads (Figure 16.3 no. 17; Delporte 1993a), provides intriguing evidence that at least some of the figurines were manufactured in series. Together with the fact that some Gravettian

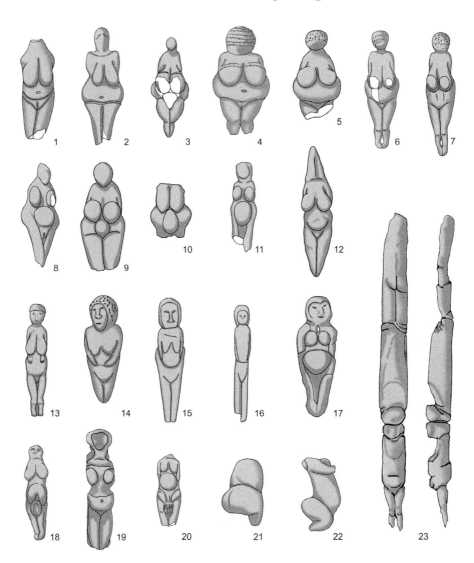

Figure 16.3: Willendorf-style figurines. 1) Moravany-Podkovica; 2) Dolní Věstonice (Venus I); 3) Lespugue; 4) Willendorf (Venus I); 5) Gagarino (statuette no. 12); 6) Kostenki 1-I (statuette no. 3); 7) Avdeevo (statuette no. 77–2); 8) Balzi Rossi (*The Lozenge*); 9) Balzi Rossi (*The Yellow Venus*); 10) Brassempouy (*Manche de Poignard*); 11) Balzi Rossi (*The Abrachial*); 12) Balzi Rossi (*The Janus*); 13) Avdeevo (statuette no. 77–1); 14) Mal'ta (no. 24); 15) Mal'ta (no. 1); 16) Mal'ta (no. 10); 17) Gagarino (statuette no. 6); 18) Monpazier; 19) Balzi Rossi (*The Hermaphrodite*); 20) Balzi Rossi (*The Beauty and the Beast*); 21) Mauern; 22) Sireuil; 23) Savignano. Not to scale.

sites such as the eastern sites of Kostenki 1-I, Avdeevo, Gagarino or Mal'ta have produced series of rather similar figurines, this evidence may suggest that some figurines at least on occasion functioned in groups. At Avdeevo, almost all figurines were found in pits among which some contained two or even three figurines (see Pettitt 2006).

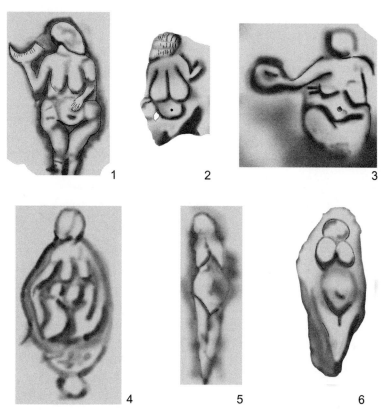

Figure 16.4: Willendorf-style bas-reliefs. 1) Laussel; 2) La Mouthe; 3) Abri Pataud. Not to scale.

With few exceptions (Venus of Monpazier, Kostenki 1-I: statuette no. 3), Willendorf-style depictions depict only rudimentary feet. Where lower legs have been preserved, the base of the figurines can vary considerably and may be conical (pointed), peg-shaped or even flat. Some were clearly prepared for suspension, either with a hole between the lower legs (e.g., Figure 16.3 no. 6) or in the area of the chest/neck (e.g., Figure 16.3 no. 12; cf. Conard 2009). When arms and hands appear, they often rest on breasts or bellies (Figure 16.3 nos. 3–4) or arms are hidden behind the figures' back. Heads are often melon shaped or round and often bend downwards (Taylor 2006). Ornamentation on top of the head is usually interpreted as representing braided hairstyles, caps and headdresses (Figure 16.3 nos. 4–7, 11–16 and 20; Figure 16.6), although in many cases the heads are missing, and it is debatable whether or not this is due to intentional destruction (Guthrie 2005; Verpoorte 2001). In some cases the figurines appear to wear clothes, such as several examples from Mal'ta and Bur'et. Some wear pieces comparable to capes (Balzi Rossi: The Nun; Mussi et al. 2000a), loincloths (Lespugne), shrouds or veils (Brassempouy: Dame à la Capuche), belts (Kostenki 1-I: statuette no. 3) or bras (Kostenki 1-I: statuette

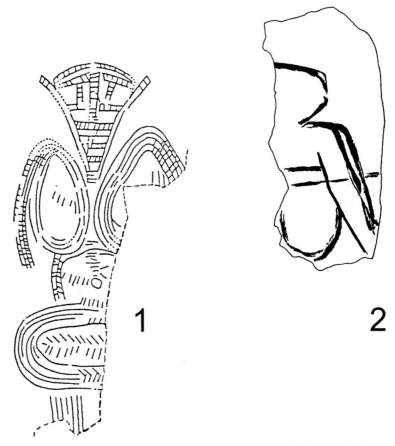

Figure 16.5: Willendorf-style engravings. 1) Kostenki 1-I; 2) Předmostí. Not to scale.

no. 83–2) (Soffer et al. 2000a, 2000b). In addition to these, jewellery, such as necklaces and bracelets, is sometimes given (Kostenki 1-I: statuette no. 2), and at Laussel at least two of the females are depicted carry drinking horns or bugles (Figure 16.4 no. 1; Delporte 1993a).

Most studies of Willendorf-style female figurines published to date assume that the figurines portray female individuals (Delporte 1993a; Brunn 2007; Wolf 2010), although they mostly lack individual faces or facial detail. It seems that females of various age classes are depicted (Rice 1981), in some cases probably pregnant (e.g., Gimbutas 1989).Varied ornamentation of heads and other highly individual attributes (e.g., jewellery) add intriguing detail to these figurines emphasising their individuality. In a few cases, faces are given in great detail, such as Brassempouy (Dame à la Capuche), Balzi Rossi (The Negroid Head), Dolní Věstonice (Venus XV) and Avdeevo (statuette no. 77–1) (Figure 16.6; compiled in Delporte 1993a; Brunn 2007; Wolf 2010), further suggesting that at least some figurines portray particular ('real' or imaginary) individuals (cf. discussion in Verpoorte 2001).

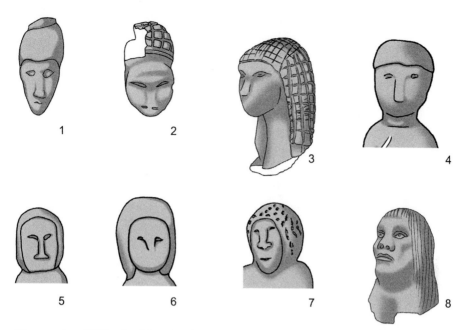

Figure 16.6: Willendorf figurine faces. 1) Dolní Věstonice (Venus III); 2) Balzi Rossi (*The Negroid Head*); 3) Brassempouy (*Dame à la Capuche*); 4) Avdeevo (statuette no. 77–1); 5) Mal'ta (no. 1); 6) Mal'ta (no. 10); 7) Mal'ta (no. 24); 8) Brno. Not to scale.

The earliest figurine of the Willendorf-style derives from the southern German site Hohle Fels (Figure 16.3 nos. 1 and 17; Conard 2009) and dates to the end of the Aurignacien (cf. Figure 16.1; Jöris and Moreau 2010). By the Mid Upper Palaeolithic (Gravettian) it is spread over large parts of Eurasia as far east as Mal'ta and Bur'et in the Baikal region of Siberia (Bosinski 1987; Delporte 1993a; Svoboda 2007).

Some of the basic stylistic elements that characterise the Willendorf-style female figurines, particularly their overall posture, re-occur in the much younger headless statuettes from Eliseevichi in Ukraine (Figure 16.2 nos. 2 and 8), the Mid-Magdalenian of Laugerie Basse (Fig. 16.7 nos. 1–2) and in the impressive, more or less life-sized Middle Magdalenian bas-reliefs of Angles-sur-l'Anglin, France (Figure 16.7 no. 3). They are also well represented in the engraved art of other Middle Magdalenian sites such as Isturitz (the Poursuite Amoureuse), Laugerie-Basse (Femme au Renne) and Gabillou, where females are depicted laying on the ground or crawling (Figure 16.7 nos. 4–6). Most impressive, however, in terms of their naturalism are the numerous engravings of La Marche (Figure 16.7 nos. 7–11; Pales and Tassin de Saint Péreuse 1976; cf. Guthrie 2005). Here, corpulent women, often with large breasts, are depicted in great detail wearing clothes and jewellery (Pales and Tassin de Saint Péreuse 1976). Facial expressions, hairstyle and additional attributes such as bandeaux seem almost to express individuality.

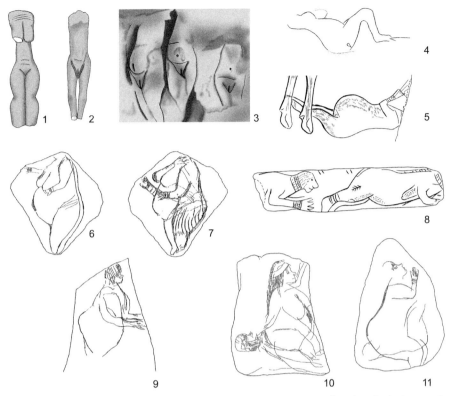

Figure 16.7: Middle Magdalenian and contemporaneous female depictions. 1) Eliseevitchi; 2.6) Laugerie-Basse; 3) Angles-sur-l'Anglin; 4) Gabillou (*La Femme Allongée*); 5) Isturitz; 7–11) La Marche. Not to scale.

The 'Gönnersdorf-type'

Schematic and standardised female depictions are also highly characteristic of the Late Magdalenian and CBP contexts of Central and Western Europe (Figures 16.1a–16.1c). These resemble somewhat a sagittal section through the female body (cf. Rosenfeld 1977; Figures 16.8–16.14) with a strong emphasis on pronounced buttocks, only occasionally showing breasts and generally lacking the head and feet (Bosinski 2011a, 2011b; Bosinski et al. 2001; Cluzel and Cleyet-Merle 2011; Höck 1993; feet are only drawn on Gönnersdorf figure no 73.2: Figure 16.8 no. 6). This iconographic convention has been defined as the 'Gönnersdorf-type' (Bosinski 2007), named after the well-known German Late Magdalenian site, where more than four hundred engravings and sculptured figurines of ivory and schist have been documented (Bosinski et al. 2001; cf. Bosinski and Fischer 1974; Höck 1993). By contrast to the Willendorf-style females, the Gönnersdorf-type lacks individualised traits and instead seems to reference a generic and abbreviated female concept.

Gönnerdorf-type female depictions are known in parietal and portable media. They occur as engravings and sculptures, on ivory, antler and bone

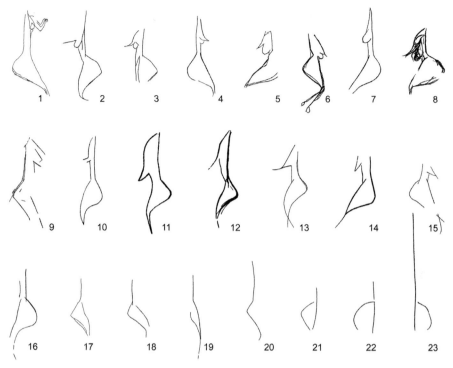

Figure 16.8: Gönnersdorf-type engravings shown at different levels of abstraction. All illustrated examples are from the open-air site of Gönnersdorf (after Boskinski et al. 2001). 1) figure no. 59.1; 2) no. 80.1; 3) no. 206.1; 4) no. 1.1; 5) no. 184.2; 6) no. 73.2; 7) no. 204.2; 8) no. 65.1; 9) no. 65.3; 10) no. 180.2; 11) no. 205A.1; 12) no. 86.1; 13) no. 206.2; 14) no. 203; 15) no. 202.1; 16) no. 43.1; 17) no. 68.5; 18) no. 72.6; 19) no. 72.7; 20) no. 72.5; 21) no. 53.3; 22) no. 213.2. Not to scale.

or various types of stone as well as on cave walls (Bosinski 2011b; Cluzel and Cleyet-Merle 2011). The Gönnersdorf-type figurines (Figure 16.14) are very often highly abstracted and only identifiable as female anthropomorphs when compared to more detailed engravings of less ambiguous nature (cf. Figure 16.8). Even though figurines exist (Höck 1993), they only function in profile, as two-dimensional objects, and are not identifiable in other profiles.

It is usually possible to distinguish between arms and breasts, except in cases where these are indicated by just a few lines. Breasts can be distinguished by their round form (e.g., Figure 16.8 nos. 2–6 and 13–14; Figure 16.9 nos. 1, 5, 10, 13; Figure 16.10 nos. 6–7 and 10; Figure 16.14 nos. 1–4), contrasting with the longitudinal lines which most often denote the arms (Bosinski et al. 2001; cf. Figure 16.8). Only engraved specimens display more details such as (slightly) outstretched arms and fingers (Figure 16.8 nos. 1–11 and 14; Figure 16.9 nos. 2–3, 5, 7–8, 11–13; Figure 16.10 nos. 2, 6–7, 10–11; Figure 16.12 nos. 1–2, 4, 6). Only in very rare cases, such as Gönnersdorf plaquette no. 87 (Figure 16. 11) or in the case of a large ivory sculpture from Andernach-Martinsberg

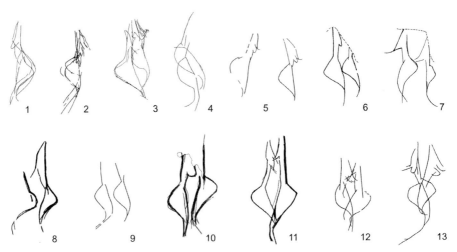

Figure 16.9: Gönnersdorf-type engravings of repeatedly-engraved figures (1–2) or couples of figures in tandem (3–9), opposed to each other (10–12) or back to back (13). All shown examples are from the open-air site of Gönnersdorf (after Bosinski et al. 2001). 1) figure no. 198; 2) no. 75; 3) no. 59; 4) no. 141; 5) no. 67; 6) no. 219; 7) 205A; 8) no. 180; 9) no. 85; 10) no. 176; 11) no. 78; 12) no. 79; 13) no. 80. Not to scale.

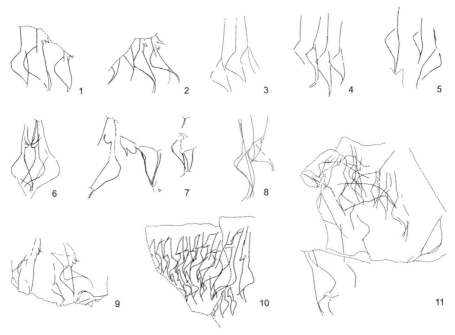

Figure 16.10: Gönnersdorf-type engravings of multiple associated figures ('groups'). All shown examples are from the open-air site of Gönnersdorf (after Bosinski et al. 2001). 1) figure no. 66.1–3; 2) no. 66.4–7; 3) no. 88.8–10; 4) no. 139.2–5; 5) no. 178.4–6; 6) no. 206.1–3; 7) no. 184.1–2.4–5; 8) no. 69.1–4; 9) no. 68b; 10) no. 67b; 11–11a) no. 65. Not to scale.

Figure 16.11: Gönnersdorf-type engravings of four hatched figures in alignment (Photo: Volker Iserhard, Römisch-Germanisches Zentralmuseum; cf. Bosinski et al. 2001: figure no 114, the so called 'Strickvenüsse').

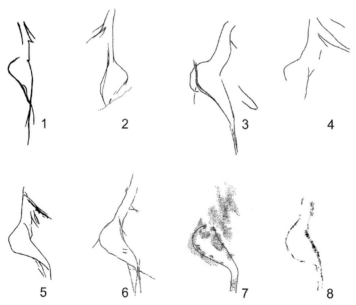

Figure 16.12: Gönnersdorf-type engravings of female depictions (compiled from Bosinski et al. 2001). 1) Andernach, figure no. 8; 2) Andernach, figure no. 7; 3) Abri Murat (engraving on bone); 4) Pestillac (parietal engraving); 5) Grotte Carriot (parietal engraving and painting); 6) Gare de Couze; 8) Grotte du Courbet (engraved plaquette: curated in *London*); 9) Grotte du Planchard (parietal painting). Not to scale.

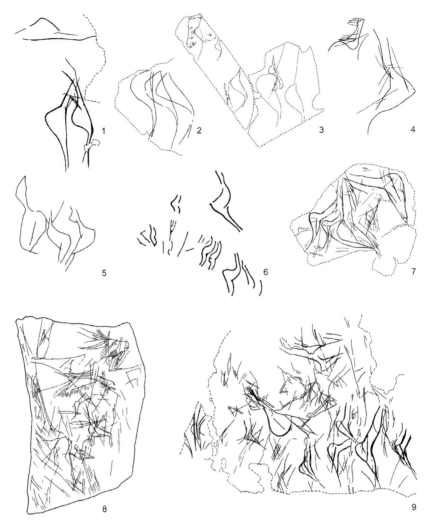

Figure 16.13: Gönnersdorf-type engravings and paintings of groups of figures (compiled from Bosinski et al. 2001). 1) Andernach, figure no. 1; 2) Andernach, figure no. 4; 3) Hohlenstein, Ederheim (engraved plaquette); 4) Fontalès (engraved plaquette); 5) Grotte Carriot (parietal engraving); 6) Combarelles (parietal engraving: *Panneau* 67); 7) Grotte de Fronsac (parietal engraving); 8–9) Lalinde (engraved plaquettes: 8 *Chicago*; 9 *Les Eyzies*). Not to scale.

(Figures 16.14, 16.12; Höck 1993), is the torso decorated with simple geometric design which may be indicative of clothing.

Scenic compositions of multiple representations occur as engravings on cave walls, rocks or plaquettes. Most of these include two figures in tandem (Figure 16.9 nos. 3–9) or facing each other (Figure 16.9 nos. 10–12; Bosinski et al. 2001). More than four figures in a line are only rarely shown (e.g., Figure 16.13 no. 3; Hohlenstein, Ederheim, Germany: Bosinski 1982), although rows of up to seventeen figures have been recorded (Gönnersdorf:

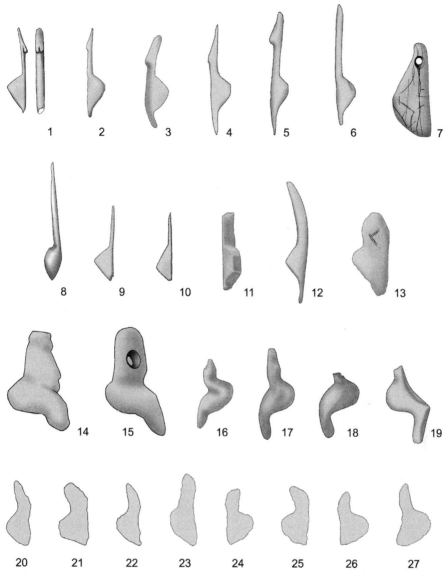

Figure 16.14: Gönnersdorf-type statuettes on different raw materials (compiled, modified and redrawn from Bosinski et al. 2001; Cluzel and Cleyet-Merle 2011; Höck 1993). 1) Gönnersdorf, statuette no. Gö/1; 2–3) Ölknitz; 4–6) Nebra; 7) Goutte Roffat (engraved pebble); 8) Bärenkeller, Garsitz; 9) Gönnersdorf, statuette no. Gö/2; 10) Andernach-Martinsberg, statuette no. An2/10; 11) Petersfels (unfinished); 12) Gönnersdorf, statuette no. Gö/9; 13) Andernach-Martinsberg, statuette no. An2/11; 14) Courbet; 15–17) Petersfels; 18) Monruz; 19) Pekárna; 20–22) Gönnersdorf, statuette nos. Gö/16, Gö/14; 22–27) Wilczyce. Not to scale.

Figure 16.10 no. 11; Bosinski et al. 2001). Also, there exist groups of figures irregularly arranged on large plaquettes (e.g., Gönnersdorf: Figure 16.10 nos. 9–10; Lalinde: Figure 16.14 nos. 8–9). Particularly striking in such scenic depictions are the stylistic elements, such as size and shape, shared by related figures, as well as additional details, such as the presence of arms and/or breasts (Bosinski et al. 2001: Figures 9–11, 13).

Differences occur in how the female illustrations were made. Whereas several of the scenic compositions are rather deeply incised (e.g., Figures 16.9 nos. 8, 10–11; Figure 16.11), single individuals are often indicated by thin lines only.

'Willendorf-style' vs. 'Gönnersdorf-type'

There are clear differences between these two stylistic groups of female depictions. The Willendorf-style can be described as 'exaggerated naturalism', whilst the Gönnersdorf-type is characterised by the schematic reduction of the female profile to an 'abbreviated', relatively standardised form or symbol. Differences also occur in terms of which female body parts are shown or emphasised. Willendorf-style females often display genitals, sometimes exaggerated, as is the case with those of Monpazier and Moravany-Podovica or The Hermaphrodite from Balzi Rossi (Delporte 1993a). Given that the Gönnersdorf-type depictions are in profile this is not possible, and depiction and is therefore restricted to the secondary sexual organs. The makers did not intend to 'complete' the image by adding either heads or feet. This reduction stands in stark contrast to Willendorf-style representations, where head, faces and sometimes feet formed integral parts of the image. On these the head was of special importance, occasionally emphasised by the frequent depiction of facial details and/or hairstyles, perhaps enhanced on occasion: the famous 'Black Venus' (Venus I) of Dolní Vestonice possesses three holes on top of its head, which probably functioned to receive some kind of applied feathers. Another fragmentary head from the same site (Delporte 1993a: figure 133) displays four such holes and in this sense copies the head of the 'Black Venus'.

Body adornments such as jewellery and clothing are of frequent importance in Mid Upper Palaeolithic Willendorf–style figurines. By contrast, clothing or body decoration do not belong to the canon of Gönnersdorf-type females (but see Gönnersdorf plaquettes nos. 87, 51 and 6; Figure 16.11; Bosinski et al. 2001).

Furthermore, the Mid Upper Palaeolithic Willendorf–style depictions were produced in a technically far more skilled and time-demanding manner. They often illustrate great care for detail as regards the carving of heads and faces, hairstyles and jewellery and/or clothing, rendered in a quasi-naturalistic way. By contrast, Gönnersdorf-type depictions lack all of these characteristics. The simple form of the Gönnersdorf-type figurines ensured quick and easy manufacture, as illustrated by numerous experimental reproductions of these figurines (Höck 1993). Engraved depictions of this type are far more numerous than sculptures. Experiments suggest that they can be easily and quickly drawn (Bosinski et al. 2001). However, many scenic representations are deeply engraved suggesting a

TABLE 16.1: *Principal differences between Willendorf-style and Gönnersdorf-type female depictions.*

	Willendorf-style	Gönnersdorf-type
Overall character	Individualised Naturalistic Detailed	Standardised Highly abstract Schematic
What is depicted?	Primary sexual organs (genitals) Heads (often bend down) and frequently faces (occasionally feet)	Secondary sexual characteristics only No heads, no feet
Production	Technically skilled and time consuming	Quickly engraved, easily sculptured
Arrangement	Rarely scenic, if at all!	Frequently in scenes with other Gönnersdorf-type female depictions
Fepictions of males within the periods considered	Fairly frequent	Extremely rarely depicted; if so almost exclusively depicted in groups

higher investment of time. These deep engravings result from repeated carving activity comparable to the production of bas-reliefs. Table 16.1 summarises the general differences between the two stylistic conventions.

FEMALE DEPICTIONS IN CONTEXT

Not only are there stylistic differences between the Willendorf-style and Gönnersdorf-type depictions, but there are differences in their archaeological contexts. Gönnersdorf-type engravings are frequently arranged in scenes with two or more females aligned with or opposed to each other. These and other 'arrangements' of several stereotype depictions of females from Gönnersdorf (Bosinski et al. 2001) or Lalinde (Leroi-Gourhan 1971) have been interpreted as scenes of dancing women (Bosinski 2007; Bosinski et al. 2001). Such depictions of female social interaction are not known from the Mid Upper Palaeolithic. However, two atypical examples (the Personnages Opposés from Laussel: Delporte 1993a; and The Beauty and the Beast doublet from Balzi Rossi: Mussi et al. 2000a) have been suggested as male-female scenic arrangements (e.g., Guthrie 2005).

Further differences relate to the spatial context of the depictions. Throughout the Upper Palaeolithic female depictions are predominantly be found in domestic settings (but see discussion in Pettitt 2006). In Mid Upper Palaeolithic Central and Eastern Europe, they were located in or nearby hearths, pits, activity areas or dwellings (Bosinski and Fischer 1974; Mania 1999; Verpoorte 2001; White 2006; Bosinski 2007, 2011a; Gaudzinski-Windheuser 2013). Gönnersdorf and Andernach are excellent examples to illustrate the general spatial context of Late Magdalenian female depictions in open-air sites. Both sites have a wealth of schist plaquettes, each of which can weigh up to 50 kg. The plaquettes form particular spatial concentrations, which have been interpreted as marking the position of dwellings or other structures. These concentrations represent high-traffic areas within which particular activity zones can be distinguished (Jöris et al. 2011). A remarkable number of plaquettes are engraved, depicting both animals (Bosinski and Fischer 1980; Bosinski 1994, 2008) and females (Bosinski and Fischer 1974; Bosinski 1994; Bosinski et al. 2001). Plaquettes bearing pictures of animals can be found throughout the site (Bosinski 2007, 2008), and only the illustrations of particular species, such as mammoth and birds, are restricted to particular concentrations, while female engravings occur in all but the northernmost concentrations (cf. Terberger 1997).

One major difference between the Late Magdalenian and the older female depictions concerns their appearance in parietal art. The Willendorf-type depictions can be found in rockshelters as bas-reliefs or sculptured on rocks detached from shelter roofs (Delluc and Delluc 1991), but they do not appear in the art of deep caves. Gönnersdorf-type illustrations are found widely and do appear even deep in caves (Bosinski et al. 2001; Bosinski 2011a, 2011b; Cluzel and Cleyet-Merle 2011; cf. Pettitt 2007b).

Interestingly, Palaeolithic female depictions are never directly associated with burials (Wüller 1999; Wolf 2010). The many similarities in site context and design between Mid Upper Palaeolithic burial and female figurines emphasise a certain inter-connection of the two (Pettitt 2006), but only for the site of Dolní Věstonice has it been suggested that the famous sculptured head with a distorted face (albeit of unclear sex), found not far from a female burial, may indeed portray the person buried (Klíma 1995). The large ivory sculpture found within the context of the Mid Upper Palaeolithic Pavlovian male 'ritual deposit' at Brno II is, however, of clear male sex (Makowsky 1892: 82).

There are further differences in the artistic contexts of both styles. The Willendorf-style closely resembles the static manner of the contemporaneous animal depictions with relatively massive bodies and comparably short or reduced extremities (cf. Leroi-Gourhan 1971: 'style I'). In contrast, Late Magdalenian depictions display a dichotomy between those of animals and of humans. Animals are regularly shown as individuals in a hyper-naturalistic and often extremely dynamic manner (cf. Azéma 2008), while female representations appear highly schematised (Leroi-Gourhan 1971; Rosenfeld 1977). Again, the Gönnersdorf engravings illustrate this dichotomy excellently (e.g., Bosinski 1982, 1994, 2007).

Figure 16.15: Males in Late Magdalenian art depicted in unambiguous group activities (modified and redrawn from Leroi-Gourhan 1971). 1) Abri Raymonden, Chancelade (Dordogne, FR); 2) Abri du Châteaux, Les Eyzies (Dordogne, FR). Not to scale.

During the Mid Upper Palaeolithic, but also in the early Late Upper Palaeolithic (Middle Magdalenian), depictions of males occur, albeit in fewer numbers than those of females (Duhard 1996; Guthrie 2005). Male representations are known from Brno (Makowsky 1892) and Laussel (Chasseur: Delporte 1993a), along with a relatively large ivory head from Dolní Vestonice. Several male depictions belonging to the Middle Magdalenian are known from French sites such as Isturitz (Poursuite Amoureuse: Delporte 1993a) and La Marche (Pales and Tassin de Saint Péreuse 1976; Airvaux and Pradel 1984). At the latter site, stylistic differences between the depictions of males and females cannot be identified. Males and females are both rendered in a naturalistic style, often with individual faces; they closely resemble Willendorf-style depictions. A few scenic illustrations of males and females also occur during this period, amongst which the possible copulation scene of the Grande Plaquette from Enlène, France, is the clearest example (Delporte 1993a; Duhard 1996). During the Late Magdalenian, apart from depictions of females, some anthropomorphic engravings are known from sites as Abri Raymonden near Chancelade or from the Abri du Châteaux at Les Eyzies (Figure 16.15; Leroi-Gourhan 1971). Here, slender bodies with faceless heads are shown in a frontal or back view. These depictions are to be distinguished from the profile view which is so characteristic of Late Magdalenian/CBP female depictions. Most of the

anthropomorphs from Raymonden and at least a few of the group of anthropomorphs to be seen on the Les Eyzies engraving seem to carry weapons. They
are interpreted as depicting males (e.g., Guthrie 2005). Late Magdalenian
depictions which show anthropomorphs in a similar style are known, for
example, from La Vache and Gourdan in France (Duhard 1996). Scenic
depictions which show males and females together are absent in the Late
Magdalenian.

INTERPRETATION

Several interpretative schemes for Palaeolithic female depictions have been
suggested (see for example discussions in: Delporte 1993a; Verpoorte 2001;
Pettitt 2006; White 2006). Female depictions have been repeatedly interpreted
as expressions of an underlying ritual system (goddesses: e.g., Abramova 1979),
of sexuality (fertility symbols: e.g., Feustel 1969; Guthrie 2005; Taylor 2006) or
as expressions of the social role of women in Upper Palaeolithic societies (icons
of matriarchy, cf. discussion in Antl-Weiser 2008a; and posture of submission,
in Taylor 2006). Only rarely have they been interpreted in terms of portraits of
individual females (Klíma 1995). Most of these are forwarded on the basis of
the analysis of particular depictions within their specific artistic contexts;
however, one cannot identify a prevalent or more likely interpretation. We
argue that the major differences between Willendorf-style and Gönnersdorf-
type depictions permit a straightforward interpretation at least for the
Gönnersdorf-type depictions, given that they are studied in diachronic perspective and with reference to their cultural contexts. Here we argue that
Gönnersdorf-type depictions must be considered as symbols for the social role
of women in the Late Magdalenian.

Our arguments are as follows:

1. The schematic character of the Gönnersdorf depictions lacks any per-
    sonal traits which would allow us to identify depictions as individuals.
2. Gönnersdorf-type iconography is essentially restricted to the female
    torso. Thus, female sexuality or corporality is clearly not the main
    information intended to be transmitted through these depictions. Due
    to the fact that none of them displays primary sexual organs (in contrast
    to the Willendorf-style figurines, which sometimes do), we refute the
    interpretation that female sexuality should be a major issue here (cf.
    discussion in Feustel 1970, 1971). In contrast, numerous carvings of
    vulvae and phalli in Late Magdalenian parietal art, as well as engraved
    pebbles representing phalli, emphasise the topic of sexuality explicitly
    (see e.g., Feustel 1969, 1971; Bosinski et al. 2001: 346; Martin 2007).
3. Gönnersdorf-type figurines and depictions are quick and easy to pro-
    duce (Höck 1993; Tinnes 1994; Bosinski et al. 2001). The

standardisation points to their highly symbolic character. Symbols are generally meant to convey a complex message quickly in a way that everyone can easily understand. Given that individuals were not depicted and that sexuality was not a key concern of these depictions, it seems highly plausible that the social sphere of females in the Late Magdalenian was encoded in these symbols.

To decipher this social sphere more closely, one must consider the context in which these symbols appear. In engraved art, it appears that female figures are often shown in couples or groups of several females (Figure 16.9 nos. 11 and 13; Bosinski et al. 2001). At Gönnersdorf, many of the individual depictions were repetitively engraved, producing deeper lines increasing their visibility. This has the effect of making the illustration appear similar to a bas-relief. Retracing a symbol over and over again is a process which could be interpreted as the sequential equivalent of a grouping or alignment of several individual symbols. Although the iconographic programme of Gönnersdorf-type depictions is characterised by their extreme schematisation and reduction (Figure 16.8), some figures additionally display arms, hands and fingers. Arms are generally bent forward, often connecting to the figure in front and interpreted in terms of women dancing (Bosinski et al. 2001). Alternatively, these scenes could represent a single figure in motion. Consequently, even depictions of single females possessing arms and even deeply engraved single females may be understood as females as part of a group.

It could be argued that the bonding of females in physical and/or spiritual groups, probably as an integral expression of the 'female sphere', was an important principal component of Late Magdalenian society. This 'female sphere' might express a communal identity in either direct or metaphorical form during this period. The homogeneous design of individual symbols in scenic depictions (Figures 16.9 nos. 3–13; 16.10 nos. 1–5, 7, 11; Figure 16.11; Figure 16.13 nos. 1–3 and 6–9) probably emphasises the idea of a communal identity, which could be communicated over large distances across Europe (Figure 16.2c; cf. Wobst 1977). Pregnancy seems not to have been an issue addressed in Late Magdalenian female depictions, and therefore seems likely that female fertility and motherhood were not primary issues in the definition of the Late Magdalenian 'female sphere'.

In the Late Magdalenian, depictions of men occur only rarely. Males almost exclusively appear in groups with other males, as is evident in the engravings from Raymonden, Les Eyzies, La Vache and Gourdan in France (e.g., Duhard 1996; Guthrie 2005). They appear as silhouettes, often equipped with spears, in concrete situations related to outdoor activities such as hunting, chasing or butchery. The explicit clarity of the depicted group activities contrasts with the coded information provided by the female symbols. Following this line of interpretation, even though groups of men are present in Late Magdalenian art, it seems that this was not a common theme or one that carried coded meaning. This is underlined by the virtual absence of scenic depictions of males and females in the Late Magdalenian, in contrast to some Middle Magdalenian examples (such as the *Grande Plaquette* from Enlène and the *Poursuite Amoureuse* from Isturitz). As the female group symbol codes the 'female sphere' implicitly, the males are depicted un-coded in explicit group activities. Both modes of depiction follow different informational contents which exclude each other (Table 16.2). It is debatable whether these examples can be interpreted as a strict separation of male and female spheres in Late Magdalenian/CBP societies and whether such a separation was of any consequence for the organisation of everyday life routines and/or of its spiritual superstructure.

For the Willendorf-style, a different interpretation seems plausible. Following the interpretation of the Gönnersdorf-type depictions, a series of differences becomes apparent. The overt nakedness of the Willendorf-style figurines, highlighting all facets of the female body, is striking. Many depictions wear garments and jewellery. Posture and clothing are used to emphasise the figurines' primary and secondary sexual attributes. This is very obvious in the Lespugue figurine (Figure 16.3 no. 3), which wears a loincloth that emphasises the woman's buttocks, or by the many figurines whose arms are shown resting on or under the figures' breasts, emphasising their fullness.

Willendorf-style figurines do not depict pre-sexually mature women; instead mature women of all ages are shown. However, a few specimens could be interpreted as pregnant (e.g., Brunn 2007; Wolf 2010). Therefore, fertility does not appear as a key theme in the Mid Upper Palaeolithic iconographic program. Motherhood is not depicted in any form, nor do most figurines represent exaggerated sexual attributes. These facts lead us to conclude that the main information conveyed by Willendorf-style depictions simply concerns female nakedness as a vehicle to emphasise individuality. Thus, it is likely that the females portrayed are individuals, and their individuality is underlined by the frequent depiction of facial traits with the head serving to highlight the individual. This is further illustrated by the plethora of particularly elaborate hairstyles known from these figurines (Figure 16.16 no. 6). The holes in the heads of some specimens suggests the application of additional head gear. Alongside the large degree of variation observed, claims for the standardisation of these figurines (e.g., Bosinski 1987) should be rejected. A simple examination of Kostenki or Mal'ta (Delporte 1993a), where numerous figurines have been found at a single site, demonstrates the high variability of these figurines.

Our interpretation focuses on the notion that individuals as carriers of social functions – individual social agents – are revealed by the Willendorf-style figurines. This leads us to conclude that the basic idea expressed in these figurines concerns the concept of individual females as representations of a common idea. As individuals they may have served as personified symbols of

TABLE 16.2: *The two principal conceptual schemes for Willendorf-style and Gönnersdorf-type female depictions.*

	Willendorf-style	**Gönnersdorf-type**
Carrier of information	Individual, 'real' or imaginary ('personified symbol')	Symbol ('group symbol')
Information coded	Female nakedness	'Female sphere'
Information not contained	Fertility Sexuality Motherhood	Fertility Sexuality Motherhood Individuality
Serving...	Common idea	Communal identity

this common idea (Table 16.2; cf. Wiessner 1983 for the discussion of emblemic vs. assertive style elements).

DISCUSSION

During the Mid Upper Palaeolithic and Middle Magdalenian and in Late Magdalenian/CBP contexts, women were depicted in different ways. Whilst the Willendorf-style represents individuals conveying a common idea, the Gönnersdorf-type can be interpreted to reflect a common idea represented by a symbol (Table 16.2). Do these iconographic differences, however, reflect changes in the social organisation of Upper Palaeolithic societies? The environmental context of the specific periods might help to answer this question. During the Mid Upper Palaeolithic, glaciers and their concomitant periglacial frontiers grew, and populations correspondingly retreated into more southern refugia where they became increasingly residential. By contrast the Late Magdalenian and Late Glacial periods were marked by the rapid retreat of glaciers and the opening of unpopulated and newly accessible landscapes. This period probably witnessed the fastest geographical expansion of populations since the Last Glacial Maximum (Figure 16.1), and in terms of newly colonised pioneer territories, it represents the most dynamic phase of Late Glacial human range expansion into the northerly parts of Europe.

During periods of rapid geographical expansion by populations, careful attention was required in order to maintain the social networks that must have been necessary to connect the 'pioneers' at the front of the expansion to populations which remained in the Magdalenian 'homelands' of south-western Europe. In addition, success in the process of expansion would demand the constant founding and establishment of new social entities and networks to ensure the success of communication over large distances.

It might be assumed that Gönnersdorf-type depictions symbolised the carrier of particular social networks; the 'female sphere'. The spread of such depictions over almost all of Magdalenian Europe indicates that the communication of this symbolic 'female sphere' occurred over this vast area (cf. discussion in Gamble 1982 for the Mid Upper Palaeolithic; Wobst 1974, 1977). It may be, however, that the 'female sphere' had different connotations in particular regions of Europe. Bosinski, for example, points out that in the parietal art of western Europe Gönnersdorf-type depictions are often elements of more complex arrangements that include the illustration of explicit sexual symbols and supernatural creatures (Bosinski et al. 2001: 346). Distinct regional social networks may be reflected in regional styles e.g., in the geographical distribution of Late Magdalenian Gönnersdorf-type ivory and jet figurines (Figure 16.14). Whereas the ivory figurines are to be found at the northern margin of Magdalenian dispersal, figurines made of jet are restricted to sites in southern Central Europe (Figure 16.2c: Petersfels and Monruz). The latter type of figurine is more curved in shape and is similar to an ivory statuette from Pekárna Cave in Moravia.

The success of the rapid and highly dynamic Late Glacial human expansion cannot be envisaged without the establishment of strong, long-distance communication networks (e.g., Gamble 1982). Such networks must have focused intently on the mandatory functioning of individuals within a group to ensure survival. Thus, the individual sphere must have been subordinate for the group and was presumably reflected in the absence of depictions of individuals. A further point underlines our assumption that Gönnersdorf-type depictions were closely connected to the process of expansion and colonisation. Their geographical distribution excludes the Iberian Peninsula, where geographical population expansion seems to have been of subordinate significance (Figure 16.2c).

By contrast, the European Mid Upper Palaeolithic is characterised by the increasing concentration of populations in certain regions as a response to the advancing glaciers and periglacial deserts. 'Human settlement niches' were characterised by different regional traditions, as is evident from the lithic and organic material culture (e.g., Bosinski 1987; cf. Jöris et al. 2010). These regional traditions can be interpreted as the result of a 'cultural diversification' of the rather homogeneous initial substrate of the material culture during the later part of the preceding Aurignacian.

As already stated, the variability of Willendorf-style figurines can be explained in terms of a high degree of individualisation. The latter is also reflected in Mid Upper Palaeolithic burials with their huge variety of grave goods (Pettitt 2011a; Zilhão and Trinkaus 2002) or in the numerous hand prints known from Mid Upper Palaeolithic cave art (e.g., Lorblanchet 1995; Guthrie 2005). The Aurignacian burial from Kostenki 14 (Rogachev 1955; cf. Krause et al. 2010) and the Aurignacian *Venus of Hohle Fels* (Conard 2009) indicate that particular customs regularly expressed during the Mid Upper Palaeolithic were apparently rooted in the Late Aurignacian (cf. Leroi-Gourhan 1971: style I). Given the assumption that these initial customs survived into the early Mid Upper Palaeolithic period of cultural diversification, during which Aurignacian meta-populations split into smaller regional sub-units, the implementation of large meta-regional networks would not have been necessary to explain the geographical spread of this 'common spirit'. The existence of such tele-networks has been repeatedly proposed for the Mid Upper Palaeolithic to explain the extreme geographical distribution of both burials and Willendorf-style figurines (cf. Gamble 1982). Following this interpretation, the Willendorf-style figurines reflected and contributed to securing the communal identity of the group (in terms of an 'emblemic function'; cf. Wiessner 1983).

Against this background, it is most interesting to consider the record between the Mid Upper Palaeolithic and the Late Magdalenian in which we find the social substrate of the succeeding Late Glacial Expansion. The pre-16,000-cal-year-BP-period, especially the Middle Magdalenian, shares characteristics of both Mid Upper Palaeolithic and Late Magdalenian iconographies: one of the key sites in this discussion is the Middle Magdalenian site of La Marche which produced a series of exceptional engravings of women (Pales and Tassin de Saint Péreuse 1976) depicted in 'Willendorf-manner' (Figure 16.7 nos. 7–11). Concerning their general style, the presentation of heads and faces and further details such as clothing, headbands, belts or frequent jewellery, they appear to be reminiscent of the 'Willendorf-style'. Details in the faces of the La Marche depictions apparently confront us with individuals – as was suggested for Mid Upper Palaeolithic Willendorf-style figurines. At La Marche such individual traits also characterise various depictions of men which sometimes resemble caricatures (Airvaux and Pradel 1984). La Marche is not exceptional, however: a famous scene (the *Poursuite Amoureuse*: Figure 16.7 no. 5) of a woman 'followed' by a man found at Isturitz also dates to the Middle Magdalenian. The picture is designed in a manner comparable to the Mid Upper Palaeolithic style in terms of body proportions, facial details and the presence of jewellery (cf. Delporte 1993a). Stylistically, these engravings share more similarities with Mid Upper Palaeolithic figurines than with those of the Late Magdalenian. Contrary to the Mid Upper Palaeolithic, these depictions are frequently embedded in scenic compositions, foreshadowing the context in which human depictions of the subsequent Late Magdalenian occur. Women shown in bas-relief – even at natural size such as on the rear wall of the rockshelter of Angles-sur-l'Anglin (Breuil 1952) or in the slightly younger context of La Magdeleine (Leroi-Gourhan 1971) – were depicted in a public way for many people to see.

The style of female representations has significantly changed through time. By the Late Magdalenian female depictions had lost all the individual traits that constituted the 'Willendorf-style'. It can be assumed that by reduction to a standardised symbolic content during the Late Magdalenian female depictions became increasingly more public as they served as symbols in long-distance communication systems. This 'greater visibility' of female depictions may well have expressed changes in the social role of women during the Late Magdalenian during times of extreme environmental challenges and their influences on population dynamics and group alliance systems.

Note

[1] Only a few anthropomorphic depictions are known from late Mid Upper Palaeolithic, Solutrean or early Late Upper Palaeolithic contexts in southwestern Europe, i.e., ~25–19 ka cal BP_{Hulu} (cf. Fig. 16.1) (Leroi-Gourhan 1971; Guthrie 2005). These include the 'wounded' or speared 'humanoids' known, for example, in Cougnac, Pech-Merle and a few other caves in France (compiled in: Duhard 1996; Guthrie 2005; cf. Bosinski 1987; Floss 2005). In addition to these highly abstract tectiform 'signs' from Cougnac and Le Placard (Lorblanchet 1995) have often been interpreted as stylised representations of females (Guthrie 2005). Finally, it is debatable whether the 'bird-like' or phalliform figurines known from the Eastern European Late Upper Palaeolithic sites of Mezin and Mezhirich (Ukraine) (e.g., Šovkopljas 1965; Bibikov 1981; cf. Leroi-Gourhan 1971; Delporte 1993a), genuinely represent humans, even though many authors have suggested as much (e.g., Šovkopljas 1965; Soffer 1997).

CHAPTER 17

TAKING A GAMBLE: ALTERNATIVE APPROACHES TO THE MESOLITHIC OF WESTERN SCOTLAND

STEVEN MITHEN

INTRODUCTION

Clive Gamble's 1999 *The Palaeolithic Societies of Europe* sought to provide an account of Palaeolithic society rather than of Palaeolithic settlement. To do so, he introduced a suite of new archaeological concepts to complement those of campsites, home bases, caches and so forth. These more familiar terms, primarily associated with Binford's (e.g., 1978a, 1978b, 1980, 1982) ethnographically derived models for hunter-gatherers, have proved valuable for interpreting the Palaeolithic settlement record. Gamble suggested, however, that they have been less useful, even constraining, for the development of an archaeology of Palaeolithic society. For that, he introduced the concepts of locales, rhythms and regions, each of these categories being divided into more specific socially relevant concepts.

> I have further defined locales for archaeological purposes by the unfamiliar terms encounter, gathering and social occasion/place ... I have used these terms rather than the more familiar campsites, home bases, satellite camps or Binford's (1980) distinctions between residential camp, location, caches and field stations. The reason is quite simple. These terms are very useful for investigating settlement. They have been used widely as a set of definitions toward which archaeological analysis aspires. I have used them myself on many occasions. But they are so closely associated with the dichotomous approach to the study of foragers ... [e.g., collector/forager; simple/complex; delayed/immediate return] ... that they have become theory laden. We do not need to abandon them but rather to restrict their use to the analytical approaches that they best serve.
>
> The point about a new vocabulary is its declaration that a new agenda is being explored: in this case a study of Palaeolithic society rather than Palaeolithic settlement ...this shift will only succeed if we change our concepts about society and adjust our terms and methods accordingly.
>
> (Gamble 1999: 96)

That was just over a decade ago and so it is, perhaps, a little too soon to judge the level of Gamble's success. The study of the Palaeolithic period has been theoretically febrile during the last decade, especially with regard to notions of cognitive evolution as exemplified by Gamble's own *From Lucy to Language* project. The study of the Mesolithic in north-west Europe has also become more theoretically driven (e.g., Warren 2005; Waddington and Pedersen 2007; Whittle and Cummings 2007; Finlay et al. 2009) with explicit reference to the need for a greater emphasis on society and symbolism in the Mesolithic. The introduction of new methods such as bone isotope analysis (e.g., Schulting and Richards 2000) and the Bayesian analysis of radiocarbon dates (e.g., Waddington et al. 2007) has been important in terms of extracting further information from what remains a poorly preserved archaeological record. Regrettably, sites with organic preservation, structural remains and 'art' objects remain rare, appearing to inherently constrain the development of both a settlement and a social archaeology of the Mesolithic.

The constraint on developing an archaeology of Mesolithic society may, however, derive as much from the conceptual framework and vocabulary we adopt as from the data we have to work with – just as Gamble (1999) was arguing for the Palaeolithic. As such, and as a tribute to Clive Gamble's contribution to Palaeolithic archaeology, I will explore whether the conceptual framework he formulated for an archaeology of Palaeolithic society, might also be applied to the Mesolithic. To do so, I will use the Mesolithic of western Scotland (Figure 17.1) as a case study and explore its archaeology via the concepts of locales, rhythms and regions.

Some might consider this to be rather premature because a Binfordian-like settlement approach has yet to be developed for the Mesolithic of western Scotland: one can hardly declare such an approach inadequate before it has even been attempted. But as Gamble made clear (1999: 96), he was not recommending the abandonment of terms such as home-bases, satellite camps and caches but simply restricting them to the analytical approaches they best served. Consequently, prior to turning to a Gamble-inspired archaeology of Mesolithic society, I will begin to explore a Binfordian-like settlement approach to the Mesolithic of western Scotland. This will also enable some critical reflections about their similarities, differences and relative utility. Exploring that Mesolithic settlement approach is itself a tribute to Clive Gamble, who has himself demonstrated how Binford's ethnoarchaeological studies are of considerable value for interpreting the Palaeolithic archaeological record. Indeed, while it is easy to acknowledge the new insights and approaches that have pervaded Gamble's relatively recent work, we should not forget the originality of that he undertook in the late 1970s and 1980s which did indeed focus on the development of a settlement archaeology for the Palaeolithic (e.g., Gamble 1979, 1983, 1986).

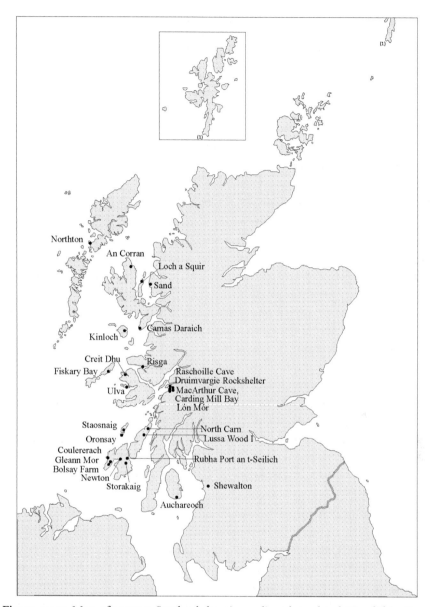

Figure 17.1: Map of western Scotland showing radiocarbon-dated Mesolithic sites

THE MESOLITHIC OF WESTERN SCOTLAND

Extending c. 350 km from the southern tip of the Isle of Arran in the south to the Butt of Lewis in the North, covering the Inner and Outer Hebrides and the adjacent mainland, western Scotland is one of the most intensively studied regions for Mesolithic archaeology in Britain (Figure 17.1). Paul Mellars' (1987) excavations of the shell middens on Oronsay during the 1970s, notably Cnoc Coig, marked the start of the modern period of

Mesolithic research in western Scotland, following a long history reaching back to the late nineteenth century. In the 1970s, the Oronsay middens were associated with those in caves around Oban to form the 'Obanian culture'. Mellars' research had an explicit concern with the human ecology of Mesolithic hunter-gatherers, recovering a wide range of artefactual and palaeoenvironmental material and dating the middens to the fifth millennium BC. Notable amongst the artefacts were bevel-ended bone implements, often referred to as limpet hammers, while microlithic technology, otherwise diagnostic of the Mesolithic period, was absent. Mellars' ecological approach marked a shift from a predominant concern with culture history, although debates about the reality or otherwise of the 'Obanian culture' continued well into the 1990s (e.g., Bonsall 1996).

The 1970s was also the period that John Mercer was undertaking fieldwork on Jura, finding a suite of sites that lacked organic preservation but had large numbers of microliths. Most notable are his excavations at Glenbatrick (Mercer 1974), Lussa Wood (Mercer 1980) and Glengarrisdale (Mercer and Searight 1986). The artefact typology and small number of dates from Jura suggested that those sites were chronologically earlier than the Oronsay middens, although rising sea level may have destroyed an earlier phase of midden activity. The claim that seasonality evidence from otoliths recovered from the Oronsay middens suggested all-year round occupation of the island (Mellars and Wilkinson 1980) led to Mithen's search on the adjacent islands of Islay and Colonsay for Mesolithic sites contemporary with those on Oronsay, within his 'Southern Hebrides Mesolithic Project' between 1987 and 1995 (Mithen 2000b). This project discovered and excavated a suite of sites including Gleann Mor, Bolsay, Coulererach and Aoradh on Islay, and Staosnaig on Colonsay – all of which were chronologically earlier than the Oronsay middens (Mithen 2000c) with activity predominantly in the seventh millennium BC. This was also the period during which Clive Bonsall undertook excavations in Ulva Cave and Tony Pollard on Risga, both excavating microlithic-rich assemblages (Bonsall et al. 1991, 1992; Pollard et al. 1996; Pollard 2000). Caroline Wickham-Jones and colleagues then undertook the 'First Settlers project' around the Inner Sound of Skye, finding a large number of sites but few which could be confidently dated to the Mesolithic period (Hardy and Wickham-Jones 2009). Of most importance was the discovery and excavation of Sand, having a microlithic chipped stone assemblage and shell midden deposits dating to the sixth and seventh millennia BC.

In 1993, rescue excavations were undertaken at the collapsed rockshelter site of An Corran, recovering a remarkably well preserved collection of fauna and organic artefacts, some of which is certainly dated to the Mesolithic period (Saville et al. 2012). Most recently, Mithen undertook a second phase of fieldwork in the Hebrides between 2004 and 2011 on Tiree, Coll and north-west Mull. The most notable new site discoveries are Creit Dubh, Mull,

(Mithen and Wicks 2011a) and Fiskary, Coll, (Mithen et al. 2007; Mithen and Wicks 2008), both of which have been placed into their palaeoenvironmental context by further work on vegetation history (Wicks 2012). Mithen and Pirie also began an ongoing project to catalogue, analyse and publish the chipped stone artefacts from Mellars' Oronsay excavations (Pirie et al. 2006) and Pollard's Risga excavation. Most recently, two new Mesolithic sites have been discovered on Islay, Rubha Port an-t Seilich and Storakaig (Mithen and Wicks 2011b). Both have preserved animal fauna and microlith-rich assemblages but are of quite different dates, with seventh and eighth millennium BC activity at Rubha Port an-t Seilich, while that at Storakaig occurs during the fifth millennium BC, having a chronological overlap with activity on Oronsay.

Arising from this all-too briefly summarised fieldwork since 1970 is an archaeological record that has Creit Dubh, Isle of Mull, as its earliest dated settlement at 9040±40 14C BP (8430–8230 cal BC) (Mithen and Wicks 2011a), followed by Kinloch on Isle of Rum with an earliest date of 8590±95 14C BP (7950–7480 cal BC; Wickham-Jones 1990). Then there are at least 32 dated Mesolithic sites, defined by possessing either microlithic technology or 'Obanian' bevelled ended bone artefacts before the appearance of pottery, sheep/goat and chambered cairns at c. 3800 BC, marking the start of the Neolithic (Ashmore 2004). Supplementing these 32 radiocarbon dated sites is a large number of undated artefact scatters characterised by a microlithic technology which most likely fall into the Mesolithic period along with scatters lacking in diagnostic artefacts that could feasibly be Mesolithic.

This Mesolithic archaeological record is placed into its palaeoenvironmental context by an extensive amount of palynological research and that concerning sea-level change – both having particularly complex histories in western Scotland (Ballantyne and Dawson 1997; Edwards and Whittington 1997). The on-going construction of a Bayesian chronological model for the Mesolithic of western Scotland (Wicks and Mithen, in preparation) suggests a phase of pioneering colonisation between 8500 and 7000 cal BC, an intensification of activity between 7000 and 6000 cal BC and then a marked reduction in activity until 3800 cal BC, when Mesolithic sites disappear and are replaced by those of the Neolithic. It remains unclear whether the Neolithic transition arose from a population replacement, the adoption of Neolithic lifestyles by the indigenous hunter-gatherers, or a combination of both processes.

AN ARCHAEOLOGY OF MESOLITHIC SETTLEMENT

From this field research of the last four decades, a relatively rich Mesolithic archaeological and palaeoenvironmental record has now been recovered from western Scotland. This is ripe for a regional synthesis using the Binfordian-derived settlement-system approach that employs the terminology of campsites, home bases, satellite camps and so forth. With the available data one can be reasonably confident that different types of activities occurred at different localities which are most likely elements of a continually evolving regional settlement system: groups would have travelled in small boats from island to island, and from island to mainland; they would have travelled by foot to different locations within single landmasses, responding to both predictable and unpredictable social and ecological factors. A few examples will show the potential for developing this settlement archaeology approach.

Hunting, plant gathering and fishing camps

Bolsay on Islay (Mithen, Lake and Finlay 2000a, 2000b) is located at an inland location, one used by modern-day hunters stalking and shooting deer. It has a spatially extensive and dense scatter of chipped stone artefacts within which the retouched forms are dominated by microliths and more particularly by scalene triangles (Finlay et al. 2000; Figure 17.2). In addition to this Mesolithic component, fragments of Neolithic ground stone axes and beaker pottery were recovered from the site, indicating a complex and long-term palimpsest of activity. Of the ten radiocarbon dates, three can be confidently associated with the microlithic artefacts alone which indicate Mesolithic activities in the late sixth millennium and early seventh millennium BC.

With the presence of only a small number of features and no detectable spatial patterning in the artefact distribution the site appears to derive from multiple short-term events. In light of the high frequency of microliths, some

Figure 17.2: Excavation at Bolsay, Islay, 1992, an inland Mesolithic site at the base of Benin Tart a'Mhill and most probably a Mesolithic hunting camp for large game. Photo by the author.

Figure 17.3: Storakaig, Islay, excavation 2012 showing the occupation horizon containing fragments of animal bone. Photo by the author.

of which have impact fractures (Finlayson and Mithen 2000), and the site's location at a modern-day hunting location, Bolsay is reasonably interpreted as a frequently visited short-term hunting camp. It would appear to be a site where tools were made for hunting deer and wild boar and where carcasses were butchered. Although no fauna has survived, deer and wild boar bones have now being recovered from Storakaig, Islay (Figure 17.3), which has similarities with regard to its topographic location and chipped stone artefact assemblage (Mithen and Wicks 2011b).

In contrast to Bolsay, the site of Staosnaig on Colonsay appears to be largely dedicated to the harvesting and processing of wild plant foods especially hazelnuts (Mithen and Finlay 2000a; Mithen et al. 2001). This is located within a sheltered bay on the east coast of the island and has numerous pits, with one being particularly large (four metre diameter) and containing a dense assemblage of chipped stone, charred hazelnut shell fragments and plant remains of apple and lesser celandine (Figure 17.4). Of fifteen AMS radiocarbon dates from the site, eight derived from this large feature one of which indicated Neolithic activity. But all other dates pointed to recurrent activity at the site throughout the seventh millennium BC, with continuing visits to the site in the late sixth and early fifth millennia BC.

It is unlikely that deer or wild boar were ever present on Colonsay, it being too far from neighbouring landmasses for them to have colonised in the early postglacial. The chipped stone artefacts manufactured at Staosnaig could have

Figure 17.4: Large pit at Staosnaig, Colonsay, excavated 1990, containing a dense accumulation of charred hazelnut shell, chipped stone and coarse stone artefacts. Photo by the author.

been made for hunting otter, for fowling and for fishing. Alternatively they might have been used as plant processing equipment. Interestingly, the microlith forms at Staosnaig are quite different from those from Bolsay, containing a higher frequency of backed bladelets and lower frequencies of scalene triangles (Finlay et al. 2000). A dedicated plant processing site appears the most reasonable interpretation in light of the quantity of plant remains recovered from large features. These are likely to have been the waste from intensive hazelnut roasting, with the shells possibly being used for fuel, perhaps for smoking fish.

A third type of specialist activity site is represented by Fiskary Bay on the Isle of Coll (Mithen et al. 2007; Mithen and Wicks 2008). Here we find a chipped stone assemblage associated with fragments of charred hazelnut shell, wood charcoal and fish bones. The six AMS radiocarbon dates from Fiskary indicate activity within the early eighth millennium and seventh millennium BC. Just like Bolsay and Staosnaig, it was a repeatedly visited site, appearing to be part of a regional settlement-subsistence system.

The Fiskary fish bones come from a variety of in-shore species, including whiting, haddock, hake and pollock. These are the type of fish likely to be caught within a fish trap and so it is significant that the topography of the bay is ideally suited to trapping fish with an especially narrow entrance (Figure 17.5). Indeed, a *cairidh* – a low wall that is exposed at low tide – was built across this entrance to form a fish trap in the nineteenth century (or perhaps earlier) and still partially survives. It is reasonable to assume that a similar structure would have been built in the Mesolithic enabling the small in-shore fish to be either

Figure 17.5: Fiskary Bay, Isle of Coll, at low tide in 2007. The Mesolithic site is located at the poly-tunnel, with the nineteenth-century *cairidh* visible at the entrance to the bay. Photo by the author.

netted or speared within the enclosed low tide water of the bay. The quantity of charred hazelnuts suggests that these were also used as a source of food, but no animal bones or mollusc shells have been recovered. As such, Fiskary Bay is most reasonably interpreted as a fishing camp, complementing the hunting camp of Bolsay and plant processing site of Staosnaig on Islay – although these were not necessarily elements of the same subsistence-settlement system.

Raw material acquisition and coastal foraging sites

Coulererach, located on the west coast of Islay, provides a fourth type of site – one dedicated to raw material acquisition and the initial stages of tool manufacture (Mithen and Finlay 2000b). Being deeply buried below peat, this site has only been sampled by test-pitting and trial trenching, providing a single AMS date that indicates activity with the early part of the seventh millennium BC. Coulererach is adjacent to one of the most flint-rich beaches of western Scotland, located on the Atlantic-exposed west coast of Islay. This is a setting that would not have been conducive to domestic activities. The artefact assemblage is dominated by the primary stages of core preparation – split pebbles and primary flakes (Finlayson et al. 2000; Figure 17.6). The cores are especially large compared with those found elsewhere on Islay. These artefacts and site location suggest that the collecting, sorting and initial preparation of flint cores was the primary activity at Coulererach. This is also indicated

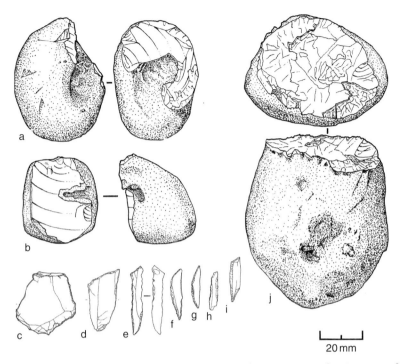

Figure 17.6: Stone artefacts from Coulererach, showing a predominance of the primary stages of lithic reduction

by the presence of technically poorly worked flint pebbles implying the presence of novice knappers, perhaps children; artefacts requiring considerable knapping skill were also present suggesting experienced knappers for the novices to observe. It seems most likely that partially worked cores were taken from Coulererach to other locations, the site acting as a specialist raw material acquisition site with a Mesolithic subsistence-settlement system.

A fifth element of the Mesolithic settlement system is the coastal foraging site. Shell middens are not only found on Oronsay but also within caves around Oban, at Risga, Ulva, Sand and An Corran. The middens date throughout the duration of the Mesolithic period, indicating that coastal foraging was a persistent element of the evolving settlement pattern. Cnoc Coig on Oronsay (Mellars 1987), dating to the fifth millennium BC, and Sand on the Applecross Peninsular, dating to the sixth and seventh millennium BC (Hardy and Wickham-Jones 2009) have been studied in most detail and show striking similarities. The faunal remains at both sites indicate generalised coastal foraging from a mix of shellfish and crustaceans, and the exploitation of fish, sea birds and sea mammals. The bones of terrestrial game – deer and boar – are present at Oronsay but seem most likely to relate to artefact manufacture, the bones having been brought there from other islands. Equivalent but different craft activities are present at Sand involving cutting shells and using pigments.

Elusive base camps

All of the sites considered so far appear to be locations of specialised activity where one might expect a task group from a hunter-gatherer community to be based for a short period, while other members are active elsewhere. The potential base-camps for such a settlement system have remained rather more elusive in the archaeological record. The most likely candidate is Kinloch on Rum where a large number of features were located (Wickham-Jones 1990), with dates indicating activity in the eighth and seventh millennia BC. Creit Dubh on Mull, which had activity in at least the ninth and seventh millennia, is also a possibility for a base-camp. This is in an especially sheltered location at the head of Loch a'Chumhainn on the north-west coast of Mull, which would have been an especially rich foraging and fishing locality. It appears to have a similar range of features as at Kinloch, although excavation has so far been limited (Mithen and Wicks 2011a; Figure 17.7).

It should be apparent from these brief interpretive summaries that a Binfordian-like settlement approach to the archaeology of the Mesolithic in western Scotland is not only feasible but is essential as a means to interpret the data acquired from fieldwork undertaken during the last four decades. The use of terms such as base camps, specialist task sites, settlement-systems have enormous potential for understanding this critical period of prehistory in

Figure 17.7: 2010 excavation at Creit Dhu, Isle of Mull, showing exposure of features. Photo by the author.

the far north-west of Britain. This is not however, the only interpretative approach. As Gamble (1999) has argued, this approach and vocabulary may actually be constraining us from developing an archaeology of society. So can the alternative terminology that he introduced in 1999 to facilitate this for the Palaeolithic of Europe, also help for the Mesolithic of western Scotland?

AN ARCHAEOLOGY OF MESOLITHIC SOCIETY?

Locales, rhythms and regions

Gamble (1999) proposed an alternative set of concepts to those of base-camp, satellite camp, settlement-system and so forth, suggesting that a new vocabulary might facilitate investigating Palaeolithic society. His starting point is the individual rather than the group, adopting what he describes as a 'bottom up' approach that envisages the individual playing an active role in performing society and its structures into existence (Gamble 1999: 32–33). Having established this focus, Gamble proposes three analytical levels for the interpretation of the archaeological record – locales, rhythms and regions.

Locales are where interactions took place, either between a person and his or her environment or between persons; when residues are left behind such locales are referred to as 'gatherings'. When objects such as structures or rock art are used to structure such interactions, Gamble refers to such gatherings as 'social occasions'. At both locales and gatherings individuals send information to others, either via their body – words, frowns, gestures – or disembodied in material culture which extends their contacts with other when they themselves are not present. Gamble also notes that social occasions can occur in the absence of cultural objectswhen the locale is invested with associations and meanings or has natural features that structure social interactions, such as caves. Gamble refers to such locales as 'places'.

With regard to region, Gamble renamed his previous term 'local hominid network' as 'landscape of habit'. Each person has his or her own landscape of habit, most likely ranging between a radius of 40 km and 100 km on the basis of ethnographic analogies and Palaeolithic raw material movements. This is the region in which individuals engage with the physical environment and other people: 'a continuous process involving interaction between individuals where negotiation is achieved through display, gesticulation, grooming, language, performance, sign and symbol. In other words, the routinization of life' (Gamble 1999: 87). The 'social landscape' is the sum total of all of the landscapes of habit, constituting a substantially more extensive region.

According to Gamble, locales are connected by the rhythms of the human body: walking, treading, digesting, sleeping and making. All of these produce temporality in human behaviour and many are habitual actions, occurring without us giving them much thought. The chaîne opératoire provides the classic description of a rhythm, one that fuses together social and technical activity. Gamble regrets that this notion has become almost solely associated with lithic reduction, implying that it should be applied to all types of human rhythms. That most stressed by Gamble is simply walking:

> The starting point is the individual and his/her movement through their environment. This involves ambulatory perception along paths and tracks ... as they move they perceive affordances, or use values, along the track they walk. Where their path intersects with another we can describe a locale or node where such perceptual interaction takes place. The encounter may involve an animal running across the hunter's path or another person coming into view. These encounters will also involve plants and raw materials such as timber or stone.
>
> (Gamble 1999: 68–69)

Overlaps with a Binfordian and evolutionary-ecological approach

Before exploring how these concepts might be utilised in the interpretation of the Mesolithic record of western Scotland, it is important to note two key areas of overlap with the Binfordian-like settlement approach.

First, Gamble's emphasis on the body matches that of Binford's when seeking to explain the spatial patterning of artefacts and features within a hunter-gatherer campsite, exemplified by his study of the Mask site (Binford 1978a). Both stress how the size of the human body and its sensory faculties impose environmental limits on the spatial scale of inter-personal interaction at a gathering location. Binford's view is perhaps more mechanistic – how far people can reach and hear – while Gamble's emphasis is on perceiving the character of each person's performance, including their subtle gestures and momentary expressions.

A second area of overlap is when Gamble (1999: 76) refers to the temporality of social activity: 'what is important is the persistence of gatherings and social occasions, their recurrence in space and time. Are they attached to particular locales or are they moveable feasts around the landscape? How often do they occur: weekly, yearly or every generation?' Answering these questions effectively amounts to adopting a Binfordian-like settlement approach: identifying what specific activities took place at each site and hence which might be task-specific locations and which residential camps; identifying which sites were used on single occasions and which were repeatedly used, either for the same of for different activities; seeking to understand why specific activities were undertaken at particular sites by the by reference to the immediate environment, such as opportunities for fishing, hunting big game and so forth.

It should also be noted that Gamble's emphasis on the individual and encounters has critical similarities with standard evolutionary ecological approaches to both animal and human foraging behaviour (Mithen 1993b). My own computer simulations of Mesolithic foraging behaviour were ultimately based around the encounters of individual hunters with the signs of prey animals leading to decisions about whether or not to attempt to track and kill the animal (Mithen 1990). Gamble characterises these encounters as affordances and places greater emphasis on the recurrent use of known pathways and tracks through the landscape.

Tracks and pathways, on land and sea in Mesolithic western Scotland

For the Mesolithic of western Scotland we need to extend Gamble's focus on ambulatory perception along paths and tracks to include movement across water in boats, most probably small groups rather than lone individuals. The majority of Mesolithic sites in western Scotland are on islands or along the deeply indented coastline of the mainland. Travel by either dug-out canoe or more probably animal skin boats would have been essential and may have dominated their perception of their world.

Rather than thinking about landscape archaeology, we ought to be trying to formulate a seascape archaeology (Hardy and Wickham-Jones 2002). Tracks and pathways across and around the islands would, of course, have been used, and I have already referred to the inland sites of Bolsay and Storakaig likely to have been used for hunting. But many of these tracks would have been to and from locations where boats were moored. Some of the most important 'tracks' would have been those across open water when travelling between islands. We ought to be able to outline more clearly where those sea-tracks may have been: by using our knowledge of currents, tides and seasonal changes; by drawing on historical records of crofters moving cattle by boats between islands and visiting sea-bird colonies (e.g., Macfarlane 2012: 117–138); and by our knowledge of modern-day canoeing and kayaking.

I suspect that one 'well-worn' Mesolithic sea-track would have been between Fiskary Bay on the south-east coast of Coll and the estuary of Loch a'Chumhainn on the north-west coast of Mull (Figure 17.8). The direct measure between these two locations is 22 km, but one might suspect that currents and tides would have made the travelled distance longer. Mesolithic sites are known at both locations, there being at least four with microlithic artefacts around the estuary on Mull (Kildowie, Penmore, Croig Field and Creit Dubh; Figure 17.9). This was a traditional crossing for crofters bringing their cattle in boats from Coll to Mull, to then follow the drover's road across the island before crossing the sea again to the mainland.

The Fiskary Bay-Loch a'Chumhainn sea-track would have crossed open water; so too would have any route to Oronsay or Colonsay. Whether coming from the west coast of Jura or the north coast of Islay, this would have been a direct distance of about 10 km and may have posed a considerable challenge. Even if some individuals were residing on Oronsay throughout the year, as Mellars and Wilkinson (1980) suppose, one should assume that other individuals were crossing reasonably frequently. The radiocarbon

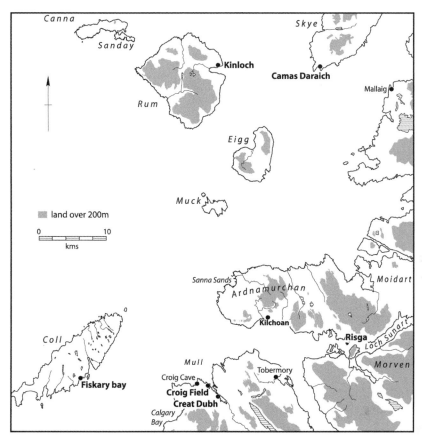

Figure 17.8: Small Isles, Coll, north-west Mull, Sleat of Skye and Ardnamurchan, showing location of Mesolithic sites and suggesting the presence of sea-tracks between them. Base map data ©Crown Copyright/database right 2009. An Ordnance Survey/EDINA supplied service.

dates from Staosnaig, Colonsay, indicate multiple visits during the seventh millennium BC, suggesting there was a well-worn sea-track to the island.

A third likely sea-track is that directly between the southern-tip of the Sleat of Skye, where the site of Camas Daraich (Wickham-Jones and Hardy 2004) is located to Loch Scresort, Rum, which has the Kinloch site positioned on its northern side (Figure 17.8). Indeed, in light of the distribution of blood stone coming from its single source on the west coast of Rum (Clarke and Griffiths 1990), one might suggest a number of sea tracks between the group of islands known as the Small Isles – Rum, Muck, Eigg and Canna (Figure 17.8). However sophisticated their boats, it is not unreasonable to assume that such sea crossings, and especially those crossing open water away from the protection of the land, were periods of especially heightened emotional state for Mesolithic seafarers. They faced the danger of the crossing and the uncertainty of what would be found at their destination. Would the hazelnuts in the

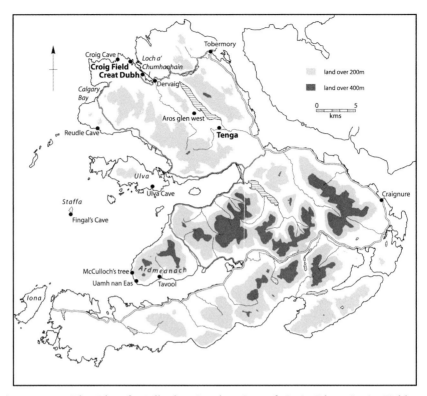

Figure 17.9: The Isle of Mull, showing location of Creit Dhu, Croig Field and suggesting route-way to Tenga along the Aros Glen. Base map data © Crown Copyright/database right 2009. An Ordnance Survey/EDINA supplied service.

woodland around Staosnaig will be ripe for harvest? Who else would have arrived at Kinloch to participate in a social occasion? Will the weather hold?

Just as the specific geography of the west coast suggests which sea-tracks may have been regularly taken, so too does the topography of the landscape with regard to land-tracks and pathways. The presence of long estuaries which almost cut islands in half and severely indent the mainland coast, along with steep inland cliffs and deep valleys, constrain the route-ways which are likely to have been undertaken on foot. It is not unreasonable to suggest, for instance, that the route from the sites of Creit Dubh to the inland site of Tenga on Mull would have followed the Aros Glen (Figure 17.9) and that the route from Gleann Mor to Bolsay on Islay would have followed around the edge of Loch a'Bhogaidh (Figure 17.10), both of these being the least-effort routes defined by local topography. Gamble's assertion that the image foragers have of the world is linked to an itinerary, and not to concentric surface area as proposed by site catchment analysis, appears appropriate for the Mesolithic of western Scotland.

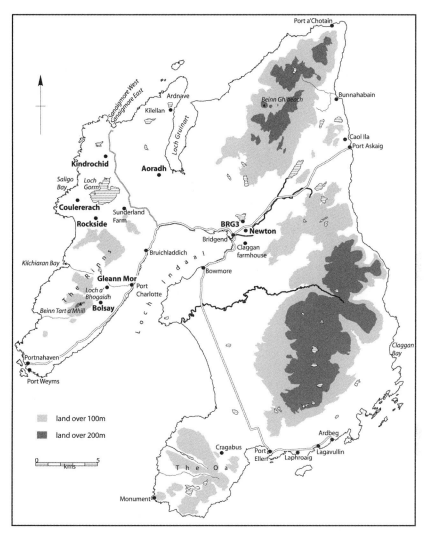

Figure 17.10: Islay, showing location of Mesolithic sites and probable route-way between Gleann Mor and Bolsay around the edge of Loch a' Bhogaidh. Base map data ©Crown Copyright/database right 2009. An Ordnance Survey/EDINA supplied service.

As I have previously suggested (Mithen 2004), the present-day experience of walking across the islands must share some of the Mesolithic experience, not only in terms of choosing the least-effort route-ways, but also in terms of the views gained across the land- and seascapes from particular vantage points, along with some of the sounds and smells. The one key difference is, of course, the extent of tree cover. Much of the Mesolithic landscape is likely to have been covered in mixed oak woodland, which can be difficult to pass through unless one is following a previously followed track, perhaps made by deer or even wild boar if one is in the Mesolithic. Hazel thicket, likely to have been

Figure 17.11: Woodland of Collie Mhor on the east coast of Colonsay. Photo by the author.

especially widespread, can be especially impenetrable. Even when the actual density of tree cover may have been sparse, such as on the more exposed Western Isles and on Tiree and Coll, the type of dwarf birch scrub that is likely to have existed can be extremely difficult to walk through. Fortunately, patches of woodland similar to that of the Mesolithic do survive in western Scotland. A visit to Collie Mhor on the east coast of Colonsay (Figure 17.11) is especially useful if one wants to recreate what walking in the Mesolithic may have been like – and to experience the painful struggle when not following an existing path through woodland (e.g., Mithen 2011: 110–111).

Affordances, encounters and gathering

Gamble describes how, as individuals move, they have a constant stream of 'encounters'. These might be with an animal running across the path, another person coming into view or the sight of useful raw materials – beach pebbles, shed antler, a stand of hazel. Such encounters might be audible – bird calls, thunder, human voices – or of smell, such as that of wild garlic. We can, of course, have a sea-track equivalent: the sight of a shoal of fish, a beached whale, a gathering storm; or the sound of an otter calling. The traveller's assessment of the affordance, or potential use value, will lead to a decision about what action to undertake. As noted above, although couched in a different terminology, this is effectively the same approach as used in decision-making foraging models, in which use value is weighed up in terms of costs, benefits and risks (e.g., Mithen 1990).

Such an approach is appropriate for the Mesolithic in western Scotland during which individuals would have always been operating in states of uncertainty. Although there may have been some degree of predictability about where and when particular resources would have been available – hazelnuts to harvest from known patches of woodland on Coll and Colonsay in the autumn, bird eggs to collect from the sea-bird colonies on the cliffs of Skye in the spring – a high degree of opportunism in the acquisition of resource would have been required. Again, a sense of this can be appreciated by one's own encounters and affordances. Although the specific topography of the coastline of Oronsay may be different today from that when the midden of Cnoc Coig accumulated, the specific make-up of the modern-day beach is unlikely to be significantly different from that along which the Mesolithic individuals had collected limpets, periwinkles and other resources (Figure 17.12). Such activity is undertaken by walking, looking, listening, experiencing a constant stream of encounters, evaluating their affordances and then either collecting the observed resource or passing on. One can do the same today (Mithen 2004, 2011).

For western Scotland, one of the key affordances to be encountered on a beach would have been flint beach pebbles (Marshall 2000a). This was the principal source of stone for tool making throughout the region, although a range of other raw materials were also used, especially in the more northerly areas. Pebbles might have been collected during the course of generalised coastal foraging or as a specifically directed activity. At Coulererach, one might think of the coastline and its vicinity as providing the particular affordance or raw material procurement. Even with this, however, there is uncertainty: beaches can be unexpectedly covered in thick seaweed after storms or even a blanket of snow. On some occasions flint pebbles appear abundant, on others scarce (Marshall 2000b).

The affordances of locating a cluster of limpets, a pebble of flint, or a patch of ripe hazelnuts concern static resources; another type of affordance referred to by Gamble is the sign of animals to hunt, either of the beast itself or tracks. Here, information from gamekeepers who stalk red deer in the highlands today should be extremely useful for thinking about similar activity in the Mesolithic. It is unfortunate that this has not been explored. One would, of course, have to be extremely cautious not only because the loss of vegetation will have changed the patterns of animal behaviour but also because today's deer are restricted in their movement by deer fences. Whereas today we tend to think of finding deer in the hills, their 'natural' location, and where they would have been located in the Mesolithic was in woodlands, around estuaries and along the coast.

It is reasonable to assume that Mesolithic hunters would have had an extensive understanding of animal behaviour and were able to position

Figure 17.12: The east coast of Oronsay, looking towards the midden of Cnoc Coig. Photo by the author.

themselves to gain the maximum encounters and affordances. This would not necessary have involved walking: several Mesolithic sites, such as Aoradh (Mithen, Woodman et al. 2000) and Storakaig (Mithen and Wicks 2011b), provide extensive views across the landscape, which one assumes was the intent of those who gathered at the sites (Figure 17.13). Viewshed analysis suggests this may have been characteristic of Mesolithic sites (Lake et al. 1998). Nevertheless, some events with very significant affordances would have been highly unpredictable as to where and when they occurred, notably the beaching of whales and other large sea mammals – as occurred at Saligo Bay, Islay in 1993.

Gamble describes encounters as 'information sound bites' which do not result in a residue which will survive. Some encounters are likely to result in action, such as the testing of a flint pebble found on a beach in order to assess its quality before deciding whether or not to carry it away. While this might require no more than inspecting its surface for flaws or gently striking it to listen to the resonance, it might involve splitting the pebble, which certainly would leave a residue of discarded flakes which has the possibility of surviving, although it would perhaps be unlikely to ever be found by an archaeologist. Similarly, encounters with static food resources may result in residues that could feasibly survive, such as discarded mollusc or hazelnut shells or even a small fireplace made by a lone individual. Again, it is not so much the lack of a residue surviving but the extreme unlikelihood of it ever being found and identified which is critical.

Figure 17.13: The Mesolithic site of Storakaig (2012), marked by the poly-tunnel below the peaks of the Paps of Jura. The site is located at the head of a valley providing extensive views for watching game, birds and the weather. Photo by the author.

Gamble suggests the use of the term 'gathering' for a locale at which the quantity of the residue left behind is such that it will endure. The term itself implies locales where more than one person is present. Gamble refers to gatherings being of short duration and differentiates them from social occasions, which he defines as locales where there is a 'context for performance which is established by objects disembodied from the body' (Gamble 1999: 75).

The term 'gathering' for a locale involving more than one individual and which leaves a sufficient quantity of residue for it to endure is an attractive way of thinking about Mesolithic sites in western Scotland. This avoids the prioritisation of one particular form of subsistence activity as happens in the settlement approach, such as in 'fishing camp' or 'hunting camp', which may have been the least important form of activity underway. It also provides a term rather better than 'artefact scatter' to refer to those sites which have nothing more than scatters of artefacts and are effectively ignored in settlement models. There are many of these in western Scotland, such as those located during field surveys on Islay (Mithen, Finlayson et al. 2000).

The term *gathering*, or a locale of multiple successive gatherings, also appears useful for thinking about the larger Mesolithic sites that appear to be palimpsests from repeated events which cannot be archaeologically distinguished. The site of Fiskary Bay, Coll, for instance, has six radiocarbon dates indicating several visits were made to the site during the seventh millennium. Whether all of these had involved fishing activity is unclear because the separate chronological events cannot be differentiated from the palimpsest of remains. Consequently, to describe the site as a 'fishing camp' fails to recognise the complexity – and poor resolution – of the archaeological record. The same applies to many, perhaps all, of the larger Mesolithic sites, notably Kinloch, Sand, Bolsay and Rubha Port an-t Seilich: the radiocarbon determinations of these suggest multiple occupation events, each of which may have had a different type of activity. This was, of course, recognised by Binford (1982) in his settlement approach when he explained how specific sites would be used for different purposes at different times of the year. But his sophisticated understanding in this respect is often forgotten when prehistoric settlement systems are proposed.

Gatherings, social occasions and places

The distinction that Gamble makes between gatherings and social occasions, the latter being locales where social interaction is mediated by disembodied material culture, is difficult to utilise for the Mesolithic of western Scotland. I assume that Gamble is primarily referring to architectural structures. Traces of these are rare in Mesolithic western Scotland, and when they do exist are usually relatively small or amorphous pits, post-holes and stakeholes, the interpretation of which is fraught with difficulties. Moreover, the extent of excavation at many sites is quite limited in extent and so the absence of features may reflect sampling rather than reality. Stoasnaig is a good example (Mithen and Finlay 2000a). Three years of field-walking, test-pitting and trial trenching had failed to locate any substantial features at this site. When these were eventually detected they were shown to have been located in the areas between each test-pit and just beyond the extent of each trial trench – a sequence of near misses. To this we must add the likelihood that the construction of windbreaks or shelters may often leave no archaeological residue. As such, it is difficult to distinguish between which locales may have been mere gatherings and which social occasions.

The significance of using material culture to structure social interaction, transforming a mere gathering locale into a social occasion and transmitting information even when one is absent in person, might help to explain the creation of the Oronsay shell middens. These are most likely to have derived from multiple short-term visits, with shell and bone waste from each visit being dumped onto an existing midden (Figure 17.14). Why do that? Why not just discard the waste from each visit separately, letting it get washed away by the tide? Having visited Oronsay on several occasions, I can see no reason why coastal foraging would have been preferred at a midden location than anywhere else on the coastline, other than for the

Figure 17.14: Cnoc Sligeach, Oronsay. A prominent mound of shells and other debris accumulated around exposed frag on the east coast of Oronsay. Photo by the author.

pre-existence of a midden itself. As such, the middens appear to have been deliberately created as a built environment providing a means to structure social activity – to create a social occasion. This may have been simply to define a meeting place or perhaps to structure activity concerning the dead (Pollard 1996) or with regard to symbolic associations with the natural landscape (Cummings 2003).

Gamble's caveat that social occasions may have also occurred at locales without a built environment but which were invested with meaning provides further complications. For the European Palaeolithic Gamble cites the example of caves as being such locales, which he terms as 'places'. This may have also been the case in the Mesolithic of western Scotland. It is difficult, for instance, to visit Ulva Cave on the Isle of Mull with its impressive seascape vista and not to imagine that it was invested with special significance where gatherings of particular social and emotional significance would have occurred. There is nothing, however, in the archaeology from the cave which distinguishes it from other locations. An Corran at Staffin Bay, Isle of Skye (Figure 17.15) also provides that same subjective impression. The cave itself no longer exists but was positioned at a spectacular coastal location. In this case, there is a further reason why the site may have had special significance – the cave is immediately adjacent to a seam of baked mudstone (Saville et al. 2012).

Figure 17.15: View across Staffin Bay from An Corran, Skye. Photo by the author.

It is conceivable that locations other than caves may have been invested with special significance. One must suspect that the topographic features of western Scotland had been embedded into stories by the Mesolithic settlers, perhaps into creation myths. This region has a number of especially striking natural forms: the Scurr of the Isle of Eigg, Fingal's Cave of the Isle of Staffa, the Old Man of Storr and crags at Quiran on Isle of Skye (Figure 17.16), the Paps of the Isle of Jura (Figure 17.13). All of these and many other features have a rich suite of stories associated with them today, and we must assume the same was the case in Mesolithic times. Indeed, I wonder whether the vast accumulation of chipped stone artefacts and debitage at Bolsay, Islay, is because this site is located at the foot of Benin Tart a 'Mhill, the most prominent hill on the Rinns of Islay and hence possibly a special place for social occasions.

Landscapes of habit and the social landscape

Gamble uses the term 'landscape of habit' to refer to the region 'traversed by the individual and all those with whom he or she interacts, [which] forms a spatial network of interacting paths' (Gamble 1999: 87). This is the wider spatial network for the negotiation and reproduction of social life that occurs at locales. Gamble suggests that the distance of raw material movements from their source can be used to measure the spatial extent of such a landscape

Figure 17.16: The crags at Quiran, Isle of Skye. Photo by the author.

of habit. This could certainly be explored within western Scotland in light of a several distinctive materials from discrete sources, including bloodstone from the west coast of Isle of Rum (Clarke and Griffiths 1990), baked mudstone from Staffin Bay, Isle of Skye, and pitchstone from the Isle of Arran. Although we currently lack an up-to-date analysis of their distribution, my impression is that these are not moving more than 30 km from their source. That seems unrealistically small as a measure of the landscape of habit. The dilemma we face is that stone is heavy to carry and is widely available throughout the study region, especially as flint or quartz. Hence during the course of any one single itinerary there may be a switch from using raw material carried from a source to those locally available. That said, it is certainly time for a detailed study of raw material movements in western Scotland.

We can gain some impression of the landscape of habit by considering the spatial dimensions of the chaîne opératoire of stone tool manufacture, another of Gamble's rhythms. Gamble is attracted to Nathan Schlanger's concept of this as the 'inter-play between the fixed and flexible'. That certainly appears appropriate for the working of flint beach pebbles because each pebble provides unique opportunities and challenges, these varying in size, morphology, granularity and presence or otherwise of flaws of various types – as one soon appreciates from experimental knapping (Mithen, Marshall et al. 2000). Although often characterised as no more than a platform core technology producing bladelets for microlith manufacture, Mesolithic technology from western Scotland was far more diverse with a variety of core forms and reduction methods. This partly reflects the range of raw materials that were used – flint, quartz, quartzite, mudstone, chalcedony, jasper – although there has yet to be a formal analysis of how reduction methods varied by raw material type. Nevertheless, bladelet production and the manufacture of microliths were pervasive occupations through the region and period of study and consequently there must have been a constant interplay between the fixed cultural template of a process and end product, and flexibility of how those are achieved.

By tracing the different stages of tool manufacture across the landscape we may gain some impression of the landscape of habit. I have already referred to Coulererach as a locale where flint pebbles were tested and initial stages of reduction undertaken. At Bolsay, c. 5 km from the flint-rich west coast of Islay, there is a relatively low frequency of primary flakes, suggesting that partially worked cores had been brought to the site – this being possible to recognise by having a template for the frequencies of different flake types within a complete debitage sequence (Mithen and Finlayson 2000). Fiskary Bay on Coll also appears to have a low frequency of initial manufacture stages represented within its assemblage (Pirie pers. comm.). Although flint pebbles have been found on the island, these are scarce and Mesolithic foragers most likely had to bring their flint to the island, apparently carrying partially prepared cores.

The diversity of raw materials present on sites may also inform us about the landscape of habit. On-going analysis of raw materials within the chipped stone assemblages from Risga and Oronsay indicate a striking difference. Both of these are small islands with shell middens, but on Oronsay only local raw materials are present – small flint and quartz pebbles – while on Risga there is a much greater diversity (Pirie pers. comm.). This may reflect their geographical positions: Risga, located in the middle of Loch Sunart is more easily envisaged as being 'on the way' to other locales on the mainland and hence at the interaction of multiple itineraries; in contrast, Oronsay provides less options for further travel.

If I understand Gamble correctly, he uses the term 'social landscape' to be the sum total of the landscapes of habit, these being connected by the movement of objects rather than people. At a minimum, and on the known basis of mobility and exchange patterns of historically documented hunter-gatherers, this must surely cover the whole of western Scotland. A key question is whether this had also extended to Northern Ireland. We know from the recovery of stone axes in western Scotland made from stone from Antrim that there had been movement between Northern Ireland and Scotland in the Neolithic. There seems no reason to think that such contact has not also occurred in the Mesolithic as the distance by boat is no more than 22 km from the Mull of Kintyre and 44 km from the Rhinns of Islay.

CONCLUSION: ARCHAEOLOGIES OF SETTLEMENT AND SOCIETY

While I am absolutely confident that within this short article I have been quite unable to do justice to Gamble's conceptual scheme for an archaeology of society, neither this nor the Binford-inspired archaeology of settlement approach appear as wholly satisfactory for interpreting the archaeological record of the Mesolithic in western Scotland. The settlement approach veers towards creating a rather too static impression of Mesolithic life, with fixed activities in fixed places. It struggles to capture the dynamism, uncertainty and continual flux that must have been a key element of Mesolithic lifestyles. The site of Fiskary Bay on Coll may have been a location where in-shore fishing occurred, but by defining it as a 'fishing camp' we immediately relegate any other activities that may have occurred at that locale; nor do we have any means to discuss how that location came to be a fishing camp on multiple occasions during the seventh millennium BC nor why it became no longer visited. Gamble's archaeology of society provides us with a better sense of dynamic change, but struggles to engage with the type of archaeological remains we have to deal with in the Mesolithic. We can describe Fiskary Bay as a locale where individuals encountered certain affordances resulting in an intensity of activity that left sufficient residues for archaeologists to find; we may also debate whether this locale should be defined as a gathering, a social occasion or a place. Ultimately, however, we are frustrated by our lack of sufficient knowledge about the site – large, open-area excavation is required here and elsewhere – and not engaging with the most striking archaeological evidence – fish bones. Fiskary Bay was a locality where fishing took place, and so it seems almost perverse to resist calling it a fishing camp.

While neither approach seems perfect, they both have a great deal to offer. Our knowledge of the Mesolithic archaeological record of western Scotland has increased substantially during the last two decades. We now have a sufficient number of well-dated sites with varying types of archaeological remains to enable substantive interpretations of the Mesolithic lifestyle. Both settlement and society archaeological approaches need to be undertaken – and my ideal is that there should be some fusion between the two with a focus on individual decision making (Mithen 1990, 1993b). Whatever approach one chooses to adopt, Clive Gamble's (1999) approach to the European Palaeolithic has a considerable amount to offer the Mesolithic of western Scotland.

REFERENCES

Abramova Z. A. 1967. 'Palaeolithic art in the U.S.S.R.', *Arctic Anthopology* IV: 1–177

Abramova, Z. A. 1979. 'Les correlations entre l'art et la faune dans le Paléolithique de la Plaine Russe', in Bandi, H. G., Huber, W., Sauter, M. R. and Sitte, B. (eds.) *La contribution de la zoologie et de l'ethologie à l'interprétation de l'art des peuples chasseurs préhistoriques*. Fribourg: Editions Universitaires, pp. 333–343

Absolon, K. and Klíma, B. 1977. *Předmostí. Ein Mammutjägerplatz in Mähren*. Praha: Fontes Archaeologiae Moraviae VIII

Ackerman, R. E. 2007. 'The miocroblade complexes of Alaska and Yukon: Early interior and coastal adaptations', in Kuzmin, Y. V., Keates, S. G. and Shen, C. (eds.) *Origin and Spread of Microblade Technology in north-eastern Asia and North America*. Simon Fraser University, Barnaby, BC.: Archaeology Press, pp. 147–170

Adam E. 2007. Looking out for the Gravettian in Greece. *Paléo* 19: 145–158.

Agusti, J., Blain, H.-A., Cuenca-Bescós, G. and Bailon, S. 2009. 'Climate forcing of the first hominid dispersal in Western Europe', *Journal of Human Evolution* 57: 815–821

Agusti, J., Blain, H.-A., Furió, M., De Marfá, R. and Santos-Cubedo, A. 2010. 'The early Pleistocene small vertebrate succession from the Orcé region (Guadix-Baza Basin, SE Spain) and its bearing on the first human occupation of Europe', *Quaternary International* 223–224: 162–169

Aiello, L. C. and Dunbar, R. I. M. 1993. 'Neocortex size, group size, and the evolution of language', *Current Anthropology* 34(2): 184–193

Aiello, L. C. and Key, C. 2002. 'Energetic consequences of being a *Homo erectus* female', *American Journal of Human Biology* 14: 551–565

Aiello, L. C. and Wheeler, P. 1995. 'The expensive tissue hypothesis: the brain and the digestive system in human and primate evolution', *Current Anthropology* 36: 199–221

Aiello, L. C. and Wheeler, P. 2003. 'Neanderthal thermoregulation and the glacial climate', in van Andel, T. and Davies, W. (eds.) *Neanderthals and Modern Humans in the European Landscape during the Last Glaciation: Archaeological Results of the Stage 3 Project*. Cambridge: Cambridge University Press, pp. 147–166

Airvaux, J. and Pradel, L. 1984. 'Gravure d'une tête humaine de face dans le Magdalénien III de la Marche, commune de Lussac-les-Châteaux (Vienne)', *Bulletin de la Société Préhistorique Française* 81(7): 214–215

Albert, R.E. 2010. 'Hearths and plant uses during the Upper Palaeolithic At Klissoura Cave 1 (Greece): The Results from phytolith analyses', *Eurasian Prehistory* 7(2): 71–85

Alcock, S. E. and Cherry, J. F. 2004. 'Introduction', in Alcock, S. E. and Cherry, J. F. (eds.) *Side by side survey: Comparative Regional Studies in the Mediterranean Word*. Oxford, Oxbow Books, pp. 1–9

Alden Smith, E., Gurven, M. and Borgerhoff Mulder, M. 2011. 'Anthropology: it can be interdisciplinary', *Nature* 471: 448

Alperson-Afil, N. 2008. 'Continual fire-making by Hominins at Gesher Benot Ya'aqov, Israel', *Quaternary Science Reviews* 27: 1733–1739

Altmann, S. A. 1967. 'The structure of primate social communication', in Altmann, S. A. (ed.) *Social Communication among Primates*. Chicago: University of Chicago Press, pp. 325–362

Amaral, L. Q. 1996. 'Loss of body hair, bipedality and thermoregulation. Comments on recent papers in the Journal of Human Evolution', *Journal of Human Evolution* 30: 357–366

Ambrose, S. H. 2001. 'Paleolithic Technology and Human Evolution', *Science* 291: 1748–1753

Ambrose, S. H. 2010. 'Coevolution of composite-tool technology, constructive memory and language: implications for the evolution of modern human behavior', *Current Anthropology* 51/S1, *Working memory: beyond language and symbolism*, Wenner-Gren Symposium Supplement 1: S135–138.

Amici, F., Aureli, F. and Call, J. 2008. 'Fission-fusion dynamics, behavioral flexibility, and inhibitory control in primates', *Current Biology* 18: 1415–1419

Amici, F., Aureli, F. and Call, J. 2010. 'Monkeys and apes: Are their cognitive skills really so different?' *American Journal of Physical Anthropology* 143: 188–197

Amici, F., Call, J. and Aureli, F. 2009. 'Variation in withholding of information in three monkey species', *Proceedings of the Royal Society B – Biological Sciences* 276: 3311–3318

Amirkhanov H. and Lev S. 2008. 'New finds of art objects from the Upper Palaeolithic site of Zaraysk, Russia', *Antiquity* 82: 862–870

Ammerman, A.J., Efstratiou, N. and Adam, E. 1999. 'First evidence for the Palaeolithic in Aegean Thrace', in Bailey, G. N., Adam, E., Panagopoulou, E., Perlès, C. and Zachos, K. (eds.) *The Palaeolithic of Greece and Adjacent Areas. Proceedings of the ICOPAG Conference, Ioannina (September 1994)*. British School at Athens Studies 3. Athens: British School at Athens, pp. 293–302

Andersen, K. K., Bigler, M., Clausen, H. B., Dahl-Jensen, D., Johnsen, S. J., Rasmussen, S. O., Seierstad, I., Steffensen, J. P., Svensson, A., Vinther, B. M., Davies, S. M., Muscheler, R., Parrenin, F. and Röthlisberger, R. 2007. 'A 60,000 Year Greenland Stratigraphic Ice Core Chronology', *Climate of the Past Discussions* 3: 1235–1260

Andersen, K. K., Svensson, A., Johnsen, S. J., Rasmussen, S. O., Bigler, M., Röthlisberger, R., Ruth, U., Siggaard-Andersen, M.-L., Steffensen, J. P., Dahl-Jensen, D., Vinther, B. M. and Claussen, H. B. 2006. 'The Greenland Ice Core Chronology 2005, 15–42 kyr. Part 1: Constructing the Time Scale'. *Quaternary Science Reviews* 25: 3246–3257

Anderson, J. R. (ed.) 1981. *Cognitive Skills and Their Acquisition*. Hillsdale, New Jersey: Erlbaum

Anderson, J. R., Gillies, A. and Lock, L. C. 2010. 'Panthanatology', *Current Biology* 20: R348–351

Anderson-Gerfaud, P. 1990. 'Aspects of behaviour in the Middle Palaeolithic: functional analysis of stone tools from southwest France', in Mellars, P. (ed.) *The Emergence of Modern Humans: An Archaeological Perspective*. Edinburgh: Edinburgh University Press, pp. 89–418

Angeli, W. 1989. *Die Venus von Willendorf*. Wien: Edition Wien.

Antl-Weiser, W. 2008a. *Die Frau von W. Die Venus von Willendorf, ihre Zeit und die Geschichte(n) um ihre Auffindung*. Veröffentlichungen der Prähistorischen Abteilung 1. Wien: Naturhistorisches Museum, Wien.

Antl-Weiser, W. 2008b. 'The Anthropomorphic Figurines from Willendorf'. *Wissenschaftliche Mitteilungen aus dem Niederösterreichischen Landesmuseum* 19: 19–30

Antoine, P., Auguste, P., Bahain, J.-J., Chaussé, C., Falguères, C., Ghaleb, B., Limondin-Lozouet, N., Locht, J.-L. and Voinchet, P. 2010. 'Chronostratigraphy and palaeoenvironments of Acheulean occupations in northern France (Somme, Seine and Yonne valleys)', *Quaternary International* 223–224: 456–461

Antoine P., Limondin-Lozouet N., Auguste P., Locht J.-L., Galheb B., Reyss J.-L., Escudé E., Carbonel P., Mercier N., Bahain J.-J., Falguères, C. and Voinchet, P. 2006. 'Le tuf de Caours (Somme, France): mise en évidence d'une séquence eemienne et d'un site paléolithique associé', *Quaternaire* 17(4): 281–320

Anton, M. and Turner, A. 2000. *The Big Cats and their Fossil Relatives*. New York: Columbia University Press

Apel, J. 2001. *Daggers, Knowledge and Power: The Social Aspects of Flint Dagger Technology in Scandinavia, 2350–1500 cal BC*. Uppsala: Coast-to-Coast Books

Apel, J. 2008. 'Knowledge, know-how and raw material – The production of late neolithic flint daggers in Scandinavia', *Journal of Archaeological Method and Theory* 15: 91–111

Arhem, K. 1989. 'Maasai food symbolism: The cultural connotations of milk, meat and blood in the pastoral Maasai diet', *Anthropos* 84(1–3): 1–23

Arsuaga, J. L., Martínez, I., Gracia, A., Carretero, J. M., Lorenzo, C. and García, N. 1997a. 'Sima de los Huesos (Sierra de Atapuerca, Spain), the site', *Journal of Human Evolution* 3: 109–127

Arsuaga, J. L., Martínez, I., García, A. and Lorenzo, C. 1997b. 'The Sima de los Huesos crania (Sierra de Atapuerca, Spain). A comparative study', *Journal of Human Evolution* 33(2/3): 219–281

Arzarello, M., Marcolini, F., Pavia, G., Pavia, M., Petronio, C., Petrucci, M., Rook, L. and Sardella, R. 2007. 'Evidence of earliest human occurrence in Europe: the site of Pirro Nord (southern Italy)', *Naturwissenschaften* 94: 107–112

Ashmore, P. 2004. 'A date list (to October 2002) for early foragers in Scotland', in Saville, A. (ed.) *Mesolithic Scotland and Its Neighbours*. Edinburgh: Society of Antiquaries of Scotland

Ashton, N. 2001. 'One step beyond. Flint shortage above the Goring Gap: the example of Wolvertcote', in Milliken, S. and Cook, J. (ed.) *A Very Remote Period Indeed: papers on the Palaeolithic Presented to Derek Roe*. Oxford: Oxbow Books, pp. 199–206

Ashton N. 2002. 'Absence of Humans in Britain during the last interglacial (oxygen isotope stage 5e)', in Tuffreau, A. and Roebroeks, W. W (eds.) *Le Dernier Interglaciaire et les occupations humaines du Paléolithique moyen*. Lille:

CERP/Université des Sciences et Technologies de Lille, pp. 93–103

Ashton, N. M., Bowen, D. Q., Holman, J. A., Hunt, C. O., Irving, B. G., Kemp, R. A., Lewis, S. G., McNabb, J., Parfitt, S. and Seddon, M. B. 1994. 'Excavations at the Lower Palaeolithic site at East Farm, Barnham, Suffolk 1989–92', *Journal of the Geological Society of London* 151: 599–605

Ashton, N. M, Cook, J., Lewis, S. G. and Rose, J. (eds.) 1992. *High Lodge: Excavations by G. de G. Sieveking 1962–68 and J. Cook 1988*. London: British Museum Press, London

Ashton, N. and Hosfield, R. 2009. 'Mapping the human record in the British early Palaeolithic: evidence from the Solent River system', *Journal of Quaternary Science* 25: 737–753

Ashton, N. M. and Hosfield, R. T. 2010. 'Mapping the human record in the British early Palaeolithic: evidence from the Solent River system', *Journal of Quaternary Science* 25: 737–753

Ashton, N. and Lewis, S. 2002. 'Deserted Britain: Declining Populations in the British Late Middle Pleistocene', *Antiquity* 76: 388–396

Ashton, N. M. and Lewis, S. G. 2005. 'Maidscross Hill, Lakenheath', *Proceedings of the Suffolk Institute of Archaeology and Natural History* XLI (part 1): 122–123

Ashton, N. M. and Lewis, S. G. 2012. 'The environmental contexts of early human occupation of northwest Europe: The Lower Palaeolithic record', *Quaternary International* 271: 50–64

Ashton, N., Lewis, S. and Hosfield, R. 2011. 'Mapping the human record: population change during the later Middle Pleistocene', in Ashton, N., Lewis, S. and Stringer, C. (eds.) *The Ancient Human Occupation of Britain*. Amsterdam: Elsevier, pp. 39–52

Ashton, N. M., Lewis, S. G. and Parfitt, S. 1998. *Excavations at the Lower Palaeolithic site at East Farm, Barnham, Suffolk 1989–94*. London: British Museum Press

Ashton, N., Lewis, S., Parfitt, S., Candy, I., Keen, D., Kemp, R., Penckman, K., Thomas, G., Whittaker, J. and White, M. J. 2005. 'Excavations at the

Lower Palaeolithic site at Elveden, Suffolk, UK', *Proceedings of the Prehistoric Society* 71: 1–61

Ashton, N. M., Lewis, S. G., Parfitt, S. A., Penkman, K. E. H. and Coope, G. R. 2008. 'New evidence for complex climate change in MIS 11 from Hoxne, UK', *Quaternary Science Reviews* 27: 652–668

Ashton, N. M., Lewis, S. G., Parfitt, S. A., White, M., 2006. 'Riparian landscapes and human habitat preferences during the Hoxnian (MIS 11) Interglacial', *Journal of Quaternary Science* 21: 497–505

Ashton, N. M., Lewis, S. G. and Stringer, C. B. (eds.) 2011. *The Ancient Human Occupation of Britain*. Amsterdam: Elsevier.

Ashton, N. M. and McNabb, J. 1994. 'Bifaces in perspective', in Ashton, N. M. and David, A. (eds.) *Stories in Stones*. London: Lithic Studies Society Occasional Paper 4, pp. 182–191

Ashton, N., McNabb, J., Irving, B., Lewis, S. and Parfitt, S. 1994. 'Contemporaneity of Clactonian and Acheulean flint industries at Barnham, Suffolk', *Antiquity* 68: 585–589

Ashton, N., Parfitt, S. A., Lewis, S. G., Coope, G. R. and Larkin, N. 2008. 'Happisburgh Site 1 (TG388307)', in Candy, I., Lee, J. R. and Harrison, A. M. (eds.) *The Quaternary of Northern East Anglia, Field Guide*. London: Quaternary Research Association, pp. 151–156

Atran, S. 2002. *In Gods We Trust. The Evolutionary Landscape of Religion*. Oxford: Oxford University Press

Atran, S. and Norenzayan, A. 2004. 'Religion's evolutionary landscape: counterintuition, commitment, compassion, communion', *Behavioural and Brain Sciences* 27: 713–770

Aubry, T., Bradley, B., Almeida, M., Bertrand, W., Neves, J., Pelegrin, J., Lenoir, M. and Tiffagom, M. 2008. 'Solutrean Laurel Leaf Production at Maitreux: an experimental approach guided by techno-economic analysis', *World Archaeology* 40(1): 48–66

Aureli, F., Schaffner, C. M., Boesch, C., Bearder, S. K., Call, J., Chapman, C. A., Connor, R. Di Fiore, A., Dunbar, R. I. M., Henzi, S. P., Holekamp, K., Korstjens, A. H., Layton, R., Lee, P., Lehmann, J., Manson, J. H., Ramos-Fernandez, G., Strier, K. B. and Van Schaik, C. P. 2008. 'Fission-fusion dynamics: new research frameworks', *Current Anthropology* 49: 627–654

Azéma, M. 2008. 'Representation of movement in the Upper Palaeolithic: An ethological approach to the interpretation of parietal art', *Anthropozoologica* 43: 117–154

Baddeley, A. 2003. 'Working memory: Looking back and looking forward', *Nature Reviews (Neuroscience)* 4: 829–839

Baddeley, A. 2007. *Working Memory, Thought and Action*. Oxford: Oxford University Press

Baddeley, A. and Hitch, G. 1974. 'Working memory', in Bower, G. H. (ed.) *The Psychology of Learning and Motivation: Advances in Research and Theory (Vol. 8)*. New York: Academic Press, pp. 47–89

Bae, K. 2010. 'Origins and patterns of Upper Palaeolithic in the Korean peninsula and movement of modern humans in East Asia', *Quaternary International* 211(1–2): 103–112

Bahn, P. and Vertut, J. 1997. *Journey through the Ice Age*. London: Weidenfeld and Nicolson

Bailey, G. 1997. 'Klithi: A synthesis', in Bailey, G. (ed.) *Klithi: Palaeolithic settlement and Quaternary landscapes in northwest Greece. Volume 2: Klithi in its local and regional setting*. Cambridge: McDonald Institute Monographs, pp. 655–677

Bailey, G. and Gamble C. 1990. 'The Balkans at 18,000 BP: the view from Epirus', in Gamble, C. S. and Soffer, O. (eds.) *The World at 18,000 BP*. London: Unwin-Hyman, pp. 148–167

Bailey, G. N., Cadbury, T., Galanidou, N. and Kotjabopoulou, E. 1997. 'Rockshelters and open-air sites: Survey strategies and regional site distributions', in Bailey, G. N. (ed.) *Klithi: Palaeolithic settlement and Quaternary landscapes in northwest Greece. Vol.2: Klithi in its local and regional setting*. Cambridge: McDonald Institute Monographs, pp. 441–457

Bailey R. C., Head G., Jenike M., Owen B., Rechtman R. and Zechenter E. 1989.

'Hunting and gathering in tropical rain forest: Is it possible?' *American Anthropologist* 91(1): 59–82

Bakels C. C. in press. 'A reconstruction of the vegetation in and around the Neumark-Nord 2 basin, based on a pollen diagram from the key section HP7 supplemented by section HP10', in Gaudzinski-Windheuser, S. and Roebroeks, W. (eds.) *Multidisciplinary Studies of the Middle Palaeolithic Record from Neumark-Nord (Germany) Volume I.* Halle: LDASA.

Ballantyne, C. K. and Dawson, A. G. 1997. 'Geomorphology and landscape change', in Edwards, K. J. and Ralston, I. (eds.) *Scotland after the Ice Age*. Edinburgh: Edinburgh University Press, pp. 23–44

Bamforth, D. B. and Finlay, N. 2008. 'Introduction: archaeological approaches to lithic production skill and craft learning', *Journal of Archaeological Method and Theory* 15: 1–27

Barbieri, M. 2010. 'On the origin of language: A bridge between biolinguistics and biosemiotics', *Biosemiotics* 3: 201–223

Bard, E., Hamelin, B., Arnold, M., Montaggioni, L., Cabioch, G., Faure, G. and Rougerie, F. 1996. 'Deglacial sea-level record from Tahiti corals and the timing of global meltwater discharge', *Nature* 382: 18

Bard, E., Antonioli, F., Roestek, F., Silenzi, S. and Schrag, D. 2000. 'The penultimate glaciation as viewed from geochemical data measured in submerged speleothem from Italy', *EOS* 81(19): Supplement S79

Barham, L. 2002. 'Systematic pigment use in the Middle Pleistocene of south central Africa', *Current Anthropology* 43: 181–190

Barham, L. 2010. 'A technological fix for Dunbar's Dilemma?' in Dunbar, R., Gamble, C. and Gowlett, J. (eds.) *Social Brain, Distributed Mind*. Oxford: Oxford University Press/The British Academy, pp. 371–394

Barnard, A. 1999. 'Modern hunter-gatherers and early symbolic culture', in Dunbar, R., Knight, C. and Power, C. (eds.) *The Evolution of Culture.*

An Interdisciplinary View. New Brunswick, New Jersey: Rutgers University Press, pp. 50–70

Barrett, J. L. 2010. 'The relative unnaturalness of atheism: On why Geertz and Markusson are both right and wrong', *Religion* 40(3): 169–172

Barrett, J. L. 2011. 'Metarepresentation, Homo religious and Homo symbolicus', in Henshilwood, C. S. and d'Errico, F. (eds.) *Homo Symbolicus. The Dawn of Language, Imagination and Spirituality.* Amsterdam: John Benjamins, pp. 205–224

Barrett, L., Henzi, P. and Dunbar, R. 2003. 'Primate cognition: from 'what now?' to 'what if?'' *Trends in Cognitive Sciences* 7: 494–497

Barrett, L., Henzi, P. and Rendall, D. 2007. 'Social brains, simple minds: does social complexity really require cognitive complexity?' *Philosophical Transactions of the Royal Society B – Biological Sciences* 362: 561–575

Barton, L., Brantingham, P. J. and Ji, D. 2007. 'Late Pleistocene climate change and Palaeolithic cultural evolution in northern China: Implications from the Last Glacial Maximum', in Madsen, D. B., Chen, F. H. and Gao, X. (eds.) *Late Quaternary Climate Change and Human Adaptation in Arid China*. Oxford: Elsevier, pp. 105–128

Bar-Yosef, O. and Belfer-Cohen, A. 2013. 'Following road signs of human dispersals across Eurasia', *Quaternary International* 283: 30–43

Bar-Yosef, B. and Kuhn, S. 1999. 'The big deal about blades: laminar technologies and human evolution', *American Anthropologist* 101: 322–338

Bar-Yosef, O. and Wang, Y. 2012. 'Palaeolithic Archaeology in China', *Annual Review of Anthropology* 41: 319–335

Bar-Yosef, O. and Zilhão, J. (eds.) 2006. *Towards a Definition of the Aurignacian*. Lisboa: Instituto Português de Arqueologia

Basell, L. S. 2008. 'Middle Stone Age (MSA) site distributions in eastern Africa and their relationship to Quaternary environmental change, refugia and the evolution of *Homo sapiens*', *Quaternary Science Reviews* 27: 2484–2498

Bates, M. R., Parfitt, S.A. and Roberts, M. B. 1997. 'The chronology, palaeogeography and archaeological significance of the marine Quaternary record of the West Sussex Coastal Plain, Southern England, UK', *Quaternary Science Reviews* 16: 1227–1252

Bavelier, D., Green, S. and Dye, M. W. 2010. 'Children, wired: For better and for worse', *Neuron* 9: 692–701

Beck, M., Gaupp, R., Kamradt, I., Liebermann, C. and Pasda, C. 2007. 'Bilzingsleben site formation processes: geoarchaeological investigations of a Middle Pleistocene deposit: preliminary results of the 2003–2005 excavations', *Archäologisches Korrespondenzblatt* 37: 1–18

Bednarik, R. 2003. 'A figurine from the African Acheulian', *Current Anthropology* 44(3): 405–412

Belfer-Cohen, A. and Grosman, L. 2007. 'Tools or Cores? Carinated artifacts in Levantine Late Upper Palaeolithic assemblages and why does it matter', in McPherron, S. P. (ed.) *Tools versus Cores? Alternative Approaches to Stone Tool Analysis*. Newcastle: Cambridge Scholars Publishing, pp. 143–163

Benjafield, J. 1976. 'The "golden rectangle": Some new data', *American Journal of Psychology* 89: 737–743

Benjafield, J. and Davis, C. 1978. 'The Golden Section and the structure of connotation', *Journal of Aesthetics and Art Criticism* 36: 423–427

Benazzi, S., Douka, K., Fornai, C., Bauer, C.C., Kullmer, O., Svoboda, J., Pap, I., Mallegni, F., Bayle, P., Coquerelle, M., Condemi, S., Ronchitelli, A., Harvati, K. and Weber, G.W. 2011. 'Early dispersal of modern humans in Europe and implications for Neanderthal behaviour', *Nature* 479: 525–528

Bennett, J. 2010. *Vibrant Matter. A Political Ecology of Things*. Durham and London: Duke University Press

Bermúdez de Castro, J. M., Arsuaga, J. L., Carbonell, E., Rosas, A., Martínez, I. and Mosquera, M. 1997. 'A hominid from the Lower Pleistocene of Atapuerca, Spain: possible ancestor to Neanderthals and modern humans', *Science* 276: 1392–1395

Bermúdez de Castro, J. M., Martinón-Torres, M., Carbonell, E., Sarmiènto, S., Rosas, A., Van der Made, J. And Lozano, M. 2004. 'The Atapuerca sites and their contribution to the knowledge of human evolution in Europe', *Evolutionary Anthropology* 13: 25–41

Bermúdez de Castro, J. M., Pérez-González, Martinón-Torres, M., Gómez-Roblez, A., Rosell, J., Prado, L., Sarmiento, S. and Carbonell, E. 2008. 'A new early Pleistocene hominin mandible from Atapuerca-TD6, Spain', *Journal of Human Evolution* 55: 729–735

Bettinger, R. L., Barton, L., Richerson, P. J., Boyd, R., Hui, W. and Won, C. 2007. 'The transition to agriculture in north-western China', in Madsen, D. B., Chen, F. H. and Gao, X. (eds.) *Late Quaternary Climate Change and Human Adaptation in Arid China*. Oxford: Elsevier, pp. 83–101

Bettencourt, L., Lobo, J., Helbing, D., Kühnert, C., West, G. B. 2007. 'Growth, innovation, scaling and the pace of life in cities', *Proceedings of the National Academy of Sciences (USA)*, 104 (17): 7301–7306

Bettinger, R. L., Barton, L. and Morgan, C. 2010. 'The origins of food production in north China: A different kind of agricultural revolution', *Evolutionary Anthropology* 19: 9–21

Bibikov, S. N. 1981. *Drevnejschij musikalnij kompleks is kostej mamonta*. Kiev: Isdatel'stvo 'Naukova Dumka'.

Bicho, N. 2004. 'The Middle Paleolithic occupation of southern Portugal', in Conard, N. (ed.) *Settlement Dynamics of the Middle Paleolithic and Middle Stone Age Volume II*. Tübingen: Kerns, pp. 513–531

Binford, L. R. 1978a. 'Dimensional analysis of behavior and site structure: learning from an Eskimo hunting stand', *American Antiquity* 43: 330–361

Binford, L. R. 1978b. *Nunamiut Ethnoarchaeology*. New York: Academic Press

Binford, L. R. 1979. 'Organisation and formation processes: looking at curated technologies', *Journal of Anthropological Research* 35: 255–273

Binford, L. R. 1980. 'Willow smoke and dogs' tails: Hunter-gatherer settlement systems and archaeological site formation', *American Antiquity*, 45(1): 4–20

Binford, L. R. 1981. *Bones: Ancient Men and Modern Myths*. New York: Academic Press.

Binford, L. R. 1982. 'The archaeology of place', *Journal of Anthropological Archaeology* 1: 5–31

Binford, L. R. 1984. *Faunal Remains from Klasies River Mouth*. New York: Academic Press.

Binford, L. R. 1985. 'Human ancestors: Changing views of their behavior', *Journal of Anthropological Archaeology* 4: 292–327

Binford, L. R. 1989. 'Isolating the transition to cultural adaptations: An organisational approach', in Trinkaus, E. (ed.) *The Emergence of Modern Humans: biocultural adaptations in the later Pleistocene*. Cambridge: Cambridge University Press, pp. 18–41

Binford, L. R. 2001. *Constructing Frames of Reference: An Analytical Method for Archaeological Theory Building Using Hunter-gatherer and Environmental Data Sets*. Berkeley, C. A.: University of California Press

Bird-David, N. 1990. 'The giving environment: Another perspective on the economic systems of gatherer-hunters', *Current Anthropology* 31(2): 189–196

Bird-David, N. 1992. 'Beyond "The hunting and gathering mode of subsistence": Culture-sensitive observations on the Nayaka and other modern hunter-gatherers', *Man (N.S.)* 27: 19–44

Bird-David, N. 1993. 'Tribal metaphorization of human-nature relatedness: A comparative analysis', in Milton, K. (ed.) *Environmentalism. The View from Anthropology*. London: Routledge, pp. 112–125

Bird-David, N. 1999. 'Animism revisited. Personhood, environment and relational epistemology', *Current Anthropology* 40 (Supplement February 1999): S67–S91

Birdsell, J. B. 1958. 'On population structure in generalized hunting and collecting populations', *Evolution* 12: 189–205

Birdsell, J. B. 1968. 'Some predictions for the Pleistocene based on equilibrium systems among recent hunter-gatherers', in Lee, R. and DeVore, I. (eds.) *Man the Hunter*. Chicago: Aldine, pp. 229–240

Biro, D., Humle, T., Koops, K., Sousa, C., Hayashi, M., and Matsuzawa, T. 2010. 'Chimpanzee mothers at Bossou, Guinea carry the mummified remains of their dead infants', *Current Biology* 20(8): R351–R352

Bischoff, J. L., Shamp, D. D., Aramburu, A., Arsuaga, J. L., Carbonell, E. and Bermudez de Castro, J. M. 2003. 'The Sima de los Huesos hominids date to beyond U/Th equilibrium (>350Kyr) and perhaps to 400–500 kyr: new radiometric dates', *Journal of Archaeological Science* 30: 275–280

Bishop, W. W. 1972. 'Stratigraphic succession 'versus' calibration in East Africa', in Bishop, W. W. and Miller, J. A. (eds.) *Calibration of Hominoid Evolution*. Edinburgh: Scottish Academic Press, pp. 219–246

Bishop, W. W. 1978. 'Geological framework of the Kilombe Acheulian Site, Kenya', in Bishop, W. W. (ed.) *Geological Background to Fossil Man*. Edinburgh: Scottish Academic Press, pp. 329–336

Blain, H.-A., Bailon, S. and Cuenca-Bescós, G. 2008. 'The Early-Middle Pleistocene palaeoenvironmental change based on the squamate reptile and amphibian proxies at the Gran Dolina site, Atapuerca, Spain', *Palaeogeography, Palaeoclimatology, Palaeoecology* 261: 177–192

Blain, H.-A., Bailon, S., Cuenca-Bescós, G., Arsuaga, J. L., Bermúdez de Castro, J. M. and Carbonell, E. 2009. 'Long-term climate record inferred from Early-Middle Pleistocene amphibian and squamate reptile assemblages at the Gran Dolina cave, Atapuerca, Spain', *Journal of Human Evolution* 56: 55–65

Blasco R. 2006. *Estrategias de subsistencia de los homínidos del nivel XII de la Cova del Bolomor (La Valldigna, Valencia)*. Tarragona: Universitat Rovira i Virgili.

Blasco R. 2008. 'Human consumption of tortoises at Level IV of Bolomor Cave (Valencia, Spain)', *Journal of Archaeological Science* 35(10): 2839–2848

Blasco R. and Fernández Peris J. 2009. 'Middle Pleistocene bird consumption at Level XI of Bolomor Cave (Valencia Spain)', *Journal of Archaeological Science* 36 (10): 2213–2223

Bleed, P. 1986. 'The optimal design of hunting weapons: Maintainability or reliability', *American Antiquity* 51: 737–747

Bleed, P. 2001. 'Trees or chains, links or branches: conceptual alternatives for consideration of stone tool production and other sequential activities', *Journal of Archaeological Method and Theory* 8: 101–127

Bleed, P. 2002. 'Cheap, regular, and reliable: implications of design variation in Late Pleistocene Japanese microblade technology', in Elston, R. G. and Kuhn, S. L. (eds.) *Thinking Small: Global Perspectives on Microlithization*. Sante Fe: American Anthropological Association, pp. 95–102

Bleed, P. 2008. 'Skill matters', *Journal of Archaeological Method and Theory* 15: 154–166

Bloch, M. 2009. 'Why religion is nothing special but is central', in Renfrew, C., Frith, C. and Malafouris, L. 2009. *The Sapient Mind: Archaeology Meets Neuroscience*. Oxford: Oxford University Press: 187–197

Blome, M. W., Cohen, A. S., Tryon, C. A., Brooks, A. S. and Russell, J. 2012. 'The environmental context for the origins of modern human diversity: A synthesis of regional variability in African climate 150,000–30,000 years ago', *Journal of Human Evolution* 62: 563–592

Bloom, H. S. (ed.) 1985. *Developing Talent in Young People*. New York: Ballantine Books

Bloom, P. 2007. 'Religion is natural', *Developmental Science* 10(1): 147–151

Blumenschine, R. J., Masao, F. T., Tactikos, J. C. and Ebert, J. I. 2008. 'Effects of distance from stone source on landscape-scale variation in Oldowan artifact assemblages in the Paleo-Olduvai Basin, Tanzania', *Journal of Archaeological Science* 35: 76–86

Blurton-Jones, N. and Marlowe, F. W. 2002. 'Selection for Delayed Maturity: Does it take 20 years to learn to hunt and gather?' *Human Nature* 13: 199–238

Bocherens H., Billiou D., Mariotti A., Patou-Mathis M., Otte M., Bonjean D. and Toussaint M. 1999. 'Palaeoenvironmental and palaeodietary implications of isotopic biogeochemistry of last Interglacial Neanderthal and mammal bones in Scladina Cave (Belgium)', *Journal of Archaeological Science* 26: 599–607

Boëda, E., Connan, J. and Muhesan, S. 1998. 'Bitumen as hafting material on Middle Paleolithic artefacts from the El Kowm Basin, Syria', in Akazawa, T., Aoki, K. and Bar-Yosef, O. (eds.) *Neanderthals and Modern Humans in Western Asia*. New York: Plenum Press, pp. 181–204

Boëda, E., Connan, J., Dessort, D., Muhesen, S., Mercier, N., Valladas, H. and Tisnérat, N. 1996. 'Bitumen as a hafting material on Middle Palaeolithic artefacts', *Nature* 380: 336–338

Boëda, E., Geneste, J.M., Griggo, C., Mercier, N., Muhesen, S. Reyss, J. L., Taha, A. and Valladas, H. 1999. 'A Levallois point embedded in the vertebra of a wild ass (*Equus africanus*): hafting, projectiles and Mousterian hunting weapons', *Antiquity* 73: 394–402

Boesch, C. and Boesch, H. 1984. 'Mental map in wild chimpanzees (*Pan troglodytes verus*): An analysis of hammer transports for nut cracking', *Primates* 25: 160–170

Boesch, C. and Boesch-Achermann, H. 2000. *The Chimpanzees of the Taï Forest: Behavioural Ecology and Evolution*. Oxford: University Press

Boismier, W. A., Gamble, C. S. and Coward, F. (eds.) 2012. *Neanderthals among mammoths: excavations at Lynford Quarry, Norfolk UK*. Swindon: English Heritage Monographs

Bolduc P., Cinq-Mars J. and Mussi M. 1996. 'Les figurines des Balzi Rossi (Italie): une collection perdue et retrouvée', *Bulletin Société Préhistorique de l'Ariège* 51: 15–53

Bonjean, D. and Otte, M. 2004. 'Une organisation fonctionelle de l'espace d'habitat. Le cas de La Grotte Scladina (Sclayn, Belgique)', in Conard, N. (ed.) *Settlement Dynamics of the Middle Paleolithic and Middle Stone Age Volume II*. Tübingen: Kerns, pp. 261–271

Bonsall, C. 1996. 'The "Obanian Problem": coastal adaptation in the Mesolithic of western Scotland', in Pollard, T. and Morrison, A. (eds.) *The Early Prehistory of Scotland*. Edinburgh: Edinburgh University Press, pp. 183–197

Bonsall, C., Sutherland, D. and Lawson, T. 1991. 'Excavations in Ulva Cave, western Scotland 1987: a preliminary report', *Mesolithic Miscellany* 12(2): 18–23

Bonsall, C., Sutherland, D., Lawson, T. and Russell, N. 1992. 'Excavations in Ulva Cave, western Scotland 1989: a preliminary report', *Mesolithic Miscellany* 13(1): 7–13

Bordes, F. 1961. 'Mousterian cultures in France', *Science* 134: 803–810

Boreham, S. and Gibbard P. L. 1995. 'Middle Pleistocene Hoxnian Stage interglacial deposits at Hitchin, Hertfordshire, England', *Proceedings of the Geologists' Association* 106: 259–270

Boroditsky, L. 2000. 'Metaphoric structuring: understanding time through spatial metaphors', *Cognition* 75: 1–28

Bosinski, G. 1982. *Die Kunst der Eiszeit in Deutschland und der Schweiz*. Kataloge vor- und frühgeschichtlicher Altertümer 20. Bonn: Rudolf Habelt

Boselie, F. 1984. 'The aesthetic attractivity of the Golden Section', *Psychological Research* 45: 367–375

Bosinski, G. 1987. 'Die große Zeit der Eiszeitjäger. Europa zwischen 40.000 und 10.000 v. Chr', *Jahrbuch des Römisch-Germanischen Zentralmuseums* 34: 3–139

Bosinski, G. 1994. 'Die Gravierungen des Magdalénien-Fundplatzes Andernach-Martinsberg', *Jahrbuch des Römisch-Germanischen Zentralmuseums* 41: 19–58

Bosinski, G. 1995. 'The earliest occupation of Europe: Western central Europe', in Roebroeks, W. and van Kolfschoten, T. (eds.) *The Earliest Occupation of Europe*. Leiden: University of Leiden, pp. 103–128

Bosinski, G. 2007. *Gönnersdorf und Andernach-Martinsberg. Späteiszeitliche Siedlungplätze am Mittelrhein*. Archäologie an Mittelrhein und Mosel 19. Koblenz: Direktion Archäologie, Aussenstelle Koblenz

Bosinski, G. 2008. *Tierdarstellungen von Gönnersdorf. Nachträge zu Mammut und Pferd sowie die übrigen Tierdarstellungen*. Der Magdalénien-Fundplatz Gönnersdorf 9. Mainz: Verlag des Römisch-Germanischen Zentralmuseums.

Bosinski, G. 2011a. 'Les figurations féminines de la fin des temps glaciaires', in Cluzel, J.-P. and Cleyet-Merle, J.-J. (eds.) *Mille et une femmes de la fin des temps glaciaires*. Paris: Grand Palais, pp. 49–67

Bosinski, G. (ed.) 2011b. *Femmes sans tête. Une icône culturelle dans l'Europe de la fin de l'ère glaciaire*. Paris: Errance

Bosinski, G., d'Errico, F. and Schiller, P. 2001. *Die gravierten Frauendarstellungen von Gönnersdorf*. Der Magdalénien-Fundplatz Gönnersdorf 8. Stuttgart: Franz Steiner

Bosinski, G. and Fischer, G. 1974. *Die Menschendarstellungen von Gönnersdorf. Ausgrabung 1968*. Der Magdalénien-Fundplatz Gönnersdorf 1. Wiesbaden: Franz Steiner

Bosinski, G. and Fischer, G. 1980. *Mammut- und Pferdedarstellungen von Gönnersdorf*. Der Magdalénien-Fundplatz Gönnersdorf 5. Wiesbaden: Franz Steiner

Bougard, E. 2011. 'Les ceramiques gravettiennes de Moravie. Derniers apports des recherche actuelles', *L'Anthropologie* 115: 465–504

Bousman, C. B. 1993. 'Hunter-gatherer adaptations, economic risk and tool design', *Lithic Technology* 18: 59–86

Bowman B. M. J. S. 1998. 'The impact of Aboriginal landscape burning on the Australian biota', *New Phytologist* 140: 385–410

Boyer, P. 2008. 'Religion: bound to believe?' *Nature* 455: 1038–1039

Brain, C. K. and Sillen, A. 1988. 'Evidence from the Swartkrans Cave for the earliest use of fire', *Nature* 336: 464–466

Brantingham, P. J. 2006. 'Measuring forager mobility', *Current Anthropology* 47: 435–459

Brantingham, J. P. and Gao, X. 2006. 'Peopling of the northern Tibetan Plateau', *World Archaeology* 38(3): 387–414

Brantingham, P. J., Krivoshapkin, A. I., Zinzeng, L. and Tserendagva, Y. 2001. 'The initial Upper Palaeolithic in

Northeast Asia', *Current Anthropology* 42(5): 735–747

Brantingham, P. J., Kuhn, S. L. and Kerry, K. W. 2004. 'On the difficulty of the Middle-Upper Palaeolithic transitions', in Brantingham, P. J., Kuhn, S. L. and Kerry, K. W. (eds.) *The Early Upper Palaeolithic beyond Western Europe.* Berkeley: University of California Press, pp. 1–13

Braun, D. R., Plummer, T., Ferraro, J. V., Ditchfield, P. and Bishop, L. C. 2009. 'Raw material quality and Oldowan hominin toolstone preferences: evidence from Kanjera South, Kenya', *Journal of Archaeological Science* 36: 1605–1614

Breuil, H. 1952. *Quatre cents siècles d'art pariétal. Les cavernes ornées de l'âge du renne.* Montignac: Fernand Windels

Bridgland, D. R. 1994. *Quaternary of the Thames.* London: Chapman and Hall

Bridgland, D. 1996. 'Quaternary river terrace deposits as a framework for the Lower Palaeolithic record', in Gamble, C. and Lawson, A. (eds.) *The English Palaeolithic Reviewed.* Wessex: Trust for Wessex Archaeology, pp. 24–39

Bridgland, D. R., Antoine, P., Limondin-Lozouet, N., Santisteban, J. I., Westaway, R. and White, M. J. 2006. 'The Palaeolithic occupation of Europe as revealed by evidence from the rivers: data from IGCP 449', *Journal of Quaternary Science* 21: 437–455

Bridgland, D., Gibbard, P. and Preece, R. 1990. 'The geology and significance of the interglacial sediments at Little Oakley, Essex', *Philosophical Transactions of the Royal Society of London. B – Biological Sciences* 328: 307

Bridgland, D. R., Lewis, S. G. and Wymer, J. J. 1995. 'Middle Pleistocene stratigraphy and archaeology around Mildenhall and Icklingham, Suffolk: report on the Geologists' Association Field Meeting, 27th June 1992', *Proceedings of the Geologists' Association* 106: 57–69

Bril, B., Rein, R., Nonaka, T., Wenban-Smith, F. and Dietrich, G. 2010. 'The role of expertise in tool use: Skill differences in functional action adaptations to task constraints', *Journal of Experimental Psychology: Human perception and Performance* 36(4): 825–839

Bril, B., Smaers, J., Steele, J., Rein, R., Nonaka, T., Dietrich, G., Biryukova, E. Hirata, S. and Roux, V. 2012. 'Functional mastery of percussive technology in nut-cracking and stone flaking actions: Experimental comparison and implications for the evolution of the human brain', *Philosophical Transactions of the Royal Society B: Biological Sciences* 367(1585): 59–74

Brink, J. S., Herries, A. I. R., Moggi-Cecchi, J., Gowlett, J. A. J., Bousman, C. B., Hancox, J., Grün, R., Eisenmann, V., Adams, J. and Rossouw, L. 2012. 'First hominine remains from a 1.07–0.99 Ma hyaena accumulation at Cornelia-Uitzoek, Free State Province, South Africa', *Journal of Human Evolution* 63: 527–535

Brody, H. 1982, *Maps and Dreams.* New York: Pantheon Books

Broglio, A., Cremaschi, M., Peresani, M., de Stefani, M., Bertola, S., Gurioli, S., Marini, D. and Anastasio, G. 2005. 'Le Pietre dipinte dell'aurignaziano', in Broglio, A. and Dalmeri, G. (eds.) *Pitture Paleolitiche nelle prealpi venete. Grotta di Fumane e Riparo Dalmeri.* Verona: Museo Civico di storia naturale di Verona, pp. 38–63

Brown, K. S., Marean, C. W., Herries, A. I. R., Jacobs, Z., Tribolo, C., Braun, D., Roberts, D. L., Meyer, M. C. and Bernatchez, J. 2009. 'Fire as an engineering tool of early modern humans', *Science* 325: 859–862

Brown, K. S., Marean, C. W., Jacobs, Z., Schoville, B. J., Oestemo, S., Fisher, E. C., Bernatchez, J., Karkanas, P. and Matthews, T. 2012. 'An early and enduring advanced technology originating 71,000 years ago in South Africa', *Nature* 491(7425): 590–593

Brown, P., Sutikna, T., Moorwood, M. J., Soejono, R. P., Jatmiko, Wayhu Saptomo, E. and Due, R. A. 2004. 'A new small-bodied hominin from the Late Pleistocene of Flores, Indonesia', *Nature* 431: 1055–1061

Brunn, S. 2007. *Untersuchungen zu einer neuen Venusstatuette vom mittel-jungpaläolithischen*

Fundplatz Dolni Vestonice (Mähren). Johannes-Gutenberg Universität Mainz: unpublished MA thesis

Burkart, J. M., Hrdy, S. B. and Van Schaik, C. P. 2009. 'Cooperative breeding and human cognitive evolution' *Evolutionary Anthropology* 18: 175–186

Busschers, F., Van Balen, R., Cohen, K., Kasse, C., Weerts, H., Wallinga, J. and Bunnik, F. 2008. 'Response of the Rhine-Meuse fluvial system to Saalian ice-sheet synamics', *Boreas* 37: 377–398

Bygott, J. D. 1972. 'Cannibalism among wild chimpanzees', *Nature* 238: 410–411

Byrne, R. W. and Corp, N. 2004. 'Neocortex size predicts deception rate in primates', *Proceedings of the Royal Society B – Biological Sciences* 271: 1693–1699

Cabrera, V., Pike-Tay, A. And Bernaldo de Quiros, F. 2004. 'Trends in Middle Paleolithic settlement in Cantabrian Spain: the Late Mousterian at Castillo Cave', in Conard, N. (ed.) *Settlement Dynamics of the Middle Paleolithic and Middle Stone Age Volume II.* Tübingen: Kerns: 437–460

Call, J. 2001. 'Chimpanzee social cognition', *Trends in Cognitive Sciences* 5: 388–393

Callon, M. 1986. 'Some elements of a sociology of translation: Domestication of the scallops and the fishermen of Saint Brieuc Bay', in Law, J. (ed.) *Power, Action and Belief: A New Sociology of Knowledge?* Sociological Review Monograph 32. London: Routledge and Kegan Paul, pp. 196–233

Callon, M. and Caliskan, K. 2005. 'New and old directions in the anthropology of markets', paper presented at the *Conference on New Directions in the Anthropology of Markets*, New York University April 5, 2005

Candy, I, Rose, J. and Lee, J. R. 2006. 'A seasonally 'dry' interglacial climate in Eastern England during the early Middle Pleistocene: Palaeopedology and stable isotopic evidence from Pakefield, UK', *Boreas* 35: 255–265

Candy, I. and Schreve, D. 2007. 'Land–sea correlation of Middle Pleistocene temperate sub-stages using high-precision uranium-series dating of tufa deposits from Southern England', *Quaternary Science Reviews* 26: 1223–1235

Capitan, L. and Peyrony, D. 1912a. 'Station préhistorique de La Ferrassie, commune de Savignac-du-Bugue (Dordogne)', *Revue Anthropologique* 22: 29–50

Capitan, L. and Peyrony, D. 1912b. 'Trois nouveaux squelettes humains fossiles', *Revue Anthropologique* 22: 439–442

Capitan, L. and Peyrony, D. 1921. 'Nouvelles foilles à La Ferrassie (Dordogne)', *Association Française pour l'Avancement des Sciences.* Strasbourg 1920: 540–542

Carbonell, E., Bermúdez de Castro, J., Arsuaga, J. L., Díez, J.C., Rosas, A., Cuenca-Bescós, G., Sala, R., Mosquera, M. and Rodríguez, X. P. 1995. 'Lower Pleistocene hominids and artefacts from Atapuerca-TD6 (Spain)', *Science* 269: 826–829

Carbonell, E., Bermúdez de Castro, J., Parés, J., Pérez-González, A., Cuenca-Bescós, G., Ollé, A., Mosquera, M., Huguet, R., van der Made, J., Rosas, A., Sala, R., Vallverdú, J., García, N., Granger, D. E., Martinón-Torres, M., Rodríguez, X. P. Stock, G. M., Vergès, J. M., Allué, E., Burjachs, F., Cáceres, I., Canals, A., Benito, A., Díez, C., Lozano, M., Mateos, A., Navazo, M., Rodríguez, J., Rosell, J. and Arsuaga, J. L. 2008. 'The first hominin of Europe', *Nature* 452: 465–469

Cârciumaru M., Ion, R. M. Niţu, E. C. Stefânescu, R. 2012. 'New evidence of adhesive as hafting material on Middle and Upper Palaeolithic artefacts from Gura Cheii-Râşnov Cave (Romania)', *Journal of Archaeological Science* 39 (7): 1942–1950

Carruthers, P. and Chamberlain, A. (eds.) 2000. *Evolution and the human mind: Modularity. Language and meta-cognition.* Cambridge: Cambridge University Press

Casasanto, D. and Boroditsky, L. 2008. 'Time in the mind: Using space to think about time'. *Cognition* 106: 579–593

Catt, J., Hubbard, R. N. L. B. and Sampson, C. G. 1978. 'Summary and Conclusions', in Sampson, C. G. (ed.) *Paleocology and Archaeology of an Acheulean Site at Caddington, England.* Dallas: Southern Methodist University, pp. 139–149

Chapais, B. 2008. *Primeval Kinship: How Pair Bonding Gave Birth to Human Society*. Cambridge: Harvard University Press

Chapman, C. A., Wrangham, R. W. and Chapman, L. J. 1995. 'Ecological constraints on group size: An analysis of spider monkey and chimpanzee subgroups', *Behavioral Ecology and Sociobiology* 36: 59–70

Chapman, J. 2000. *Fragmentation in Archaeology: People, Places and Broken Objects in the Prehistory of South-Eastern Europe*. London: Routledge

Chapman, J. and Gaydarska, B. 2007. *Parts and Wholes: Fragmentation in prehistoric context*. Oxford: Oxbow Books

Charness, N., Krampe, R. and Mayer, U. 1996. 'The role of practice and coaching in entrepreneurial skill domains: an international comparison of life-span chess skill acquisition', in Ericcson, K. A. (ed.) *The Road to Excellence: The Acquisition of Expert Performance in the Arts and Sciences, Sports and Games*. New Jersey: Lawrence Erlbaum Associates, pp. 51–80.

Charnov, E. L. and Berrigan, D. 1993. 'Why do female primates have such long lifespans and so few babies', *Evolutionary Anthropology* 1: 191–194

Chase, P. G. 1991. 'Symbols and Paleolithic artifacts: Style, standardization, and the imposition of arbitrary form', *Journal of Anthropological Archaeology* 10: 193–214

Chatwin, B. 1987 *The Songlines*. New York: Penguin Books

Chen, C. 1984. 'The Microlithic in China', *Journal of Anthropological Archaeology* 3: 79–115

Chavaillon, J., Chavaillon, N. and Hours F. 1969. 'Industries Paléolithiques de l'Elide II-region du Kastron', *Bullétin de Correspondance Hellenique* 92: 97–151

Cheledonio, G. 2001. 'Manufatti litici su Ciottolo da Milos (isile Cicladi) Pegaso', *Rivista di Cultura Mediterranea* 1: 117–144

Chen, C. 2007. 'Techno-typological comparison of microblade cores from East Asia and North America', in Kuzmin, Y. V., Keates, S. G. and Shen, C. (eds.) *Origin and Spread of Microblade Technology in Northern Asia and North America*.

Simon Fraser University, Burnaby, B.C.: Archaeology Press, pp. 7–38

Chen, C. and Wang, X.-Q. 1989. 'Upper Palaeolithic microblade industries in north China and their relationships with northeast Asia and North America', *Arctic Anthropology* 26(2): 127–156

Chen, Q.-J., Wang, C.-X., Fang, Q. and Zhao, H.-L. 2006. 'Palaeolithic artifacts from Shirengou site, Helong county, Yanbian city', *Acta Anthropologica Sinica* 25(2): 106–114

Chen, S. 2004. *Adaptive changes of Prehistoric hunter-gatherers during the Pleistocene-Holocene transition in China*. Southern Methodist University: Unpublished Thesis

Cheney, D. L. and Seyfarth, R. M. 1990. *How Monkeys See the World*. Chicago: University of Chicago Press

Cherry, J. 1982. 'A preliminary definition of site distribution on Melos', in Renfrew, C. and Wagstaff, M. (eds.) *An Island Polity: the archaeology of exploitation in Melos*. Cambridge: Cambridge University Press, pp. 10–23

Chi, M. T. H. 2006. 'Two approaches to the study of experts' characteristics', in Ericcson, K. A., Charness, N., Feltovich, P. J. and Hoffman, R. R. (eds.) *The Cambridge Handbook of Expertise and Expert Performance*. Cambridge: Cambridge University Press, pp. 21–30

Chi, M. T. H., Farr, M.J. and Glaser, R. (eds.) 1988. *The Nature of Expertise*. Hillsdale, New Jersey: Erlbaum

Chu, W. 2009. 'A functional approach to Paleolithic open-air habitation structures', *World Archaeology* 41: 348–362

Clark, A. 2008. *Supersizing the Mind*. Oxford: Oxford University Press

Clark, A. and Chalmers, D. 1998. 'The extended mind (Active externalism)', *Analysis* 58: 7–19

Clark J. D. 1980. 'The Plio-Pleistocene environmental and cultural sequence at Gadeb, northern Bale, Ethiopia', in Leakey, R. E. and Ogot, B. A. (eds.) *Proceedings of the 7th Panafrican Congress of Prehistory and Quaternary Studies*. Nairobi: TILLMIAP, pp. 189–193

Clark, J. D. (ed.) 2001. *Kalambo Falls Prehistoric Site: Volume III*. Cambridge: Cambridge University Press

Clark, J. S., Merkt, J. and Muller, H. 1989. 'Post-Glacial fire, vegetation, and human history on the Northern alpine forelands, South-Western Germany', *Journal of Ecology* 77: 897–925

Clarke, A. and Griffiths, D. 1990. 'The use of bloodstone as a raw material for flaked stone tools in the west of Scotland', in Wickham-Jones, C. (ed.) *Rhum: Mesolithic and Later Sites at Kinloch 1984–86.* Edinburgh: Society of Antiquaries of Scotland 7, pp. 149–156

Clayton, N. S., Bussey, T. J. and Dickinson, A. 2003. 'Can animals recall the past and plan for the future?' *Nature Reviews Neuroscience* 4: 685–691

Clayton, N. S. and Dickinson, A. 1998. 'Episodic-like memory during cache recovery by scrub jays', *Nature* 395: 272–274

Cleveringa P., Meijer T., van Leeuwen R. J. W., de Wolf F., Pouwer R., Lissenberg T. and Burger A. W. 2000. 'The Eemian type locality at Amersfoort in the central Netherlands: redeployment of old and new data', *Geologie en Mijnbouw/ Netherlands Journal of Geosciences* 79(2/3): 197–216

Clottes, J. (ed.). 2003. *Return to Chauvet Cave: Excavating the Birthplace of Art. The First Full Report.* London: Thames & Hudson

Clottes, J. and Lewis-Williams, D. 1998. *The Shamans of Prehistory. Trance and Magic in the Painted Caves.* New York: Abrams

Cluzel, J.-P. and Cleyet-Merle, J.-J. (eds.) 2011. *Mille et une femmes de la fin des temps glaciaires.* Paris: Grand Palais

Cohen, C. 2003. *La femme des origines. Images de la femme dans la Préhistoire occidentale.* Paris and Berlin: Herscher

Cohen, K., MacDonald, K, Joordens, J. C. A., Roebroeks, W. and Gibbard, P. 2012. 'Earliest occupation of north-western Europe: a coastal perspective', *Quaternary International* 271: 70–83

Cole, J. N. 2011. *Hominin cognitive and behavioural complexity in the Pleistocene: Assessment through identity, intentionality and visual display.* University of Southampton: Unpublished Ph.D. Thesis

Cole, J. N. 2012. 'The Identity Model: a method to access visual display within the Palaeolithic', *Human Origins* 1: 24–40

Cole, J. N. 2014. 'Hominin language development: a new method of archaeological assessment', *Biosemiotics* DOI: 10.1007/s12304-014-9198-8.

Coles B. J. 2006. *Beavers in Britain's Past.* Oxford: Oxbow Books

Conard, N. (ed.) 2001. *Settlement Dynamics of the Middle Paleolithic and Middle Stone Age.* Tübingen: Kerns

Conard, N. J. 2003. 'Paleolithic ivory sculptures from southwestern Germany and the origins of figurative art', *Nature* 426: 830–832

Conard, N. (ed.) 2004. *Settlement Dynamics of the Middle Paleolithic and Middle Stone Age Volume II.* Tübingen: Kerns

Conard, N. J. 2008. 'Die Neugrabungen am Vogelherd', in Conard, N. J. and Seidl, E. (eds.) *Das Mammut vom Vogelherd: Tübinger Funde der ältesten erhaltenen Kunstwerke.* Tübingen: Museum der Universität Tübingen, pp. 34–43

Conard, N. J. 2009. 'A female figurine from the basal Aurignacian of Hohle Fels Cave in southwestern Germany', *Nature* 459: 248–252

Conard, N. J., Malina, M. and Verrept, T. 2009. 'Weitere Belege für eiszeitliche Kunst und Musik aus den Nachgrabungen 2008 am Vogelherd bei Niederstotzingen-Stetten ob Lontal, Kreis Heidenheim', *Archäologische Ausgrabungen in Baden-Württemberg* 2008: 21–24

Conkey, M. W. 1978. 'Style and information in cultural evolution. Toward a predictive model for the Paleolithic', in Redman, C. L., Langhorne, W., Berman, M., Versaggi, N., Connolly, W. 2011. *A World of Becoming.* Durham and London: Duke University Press

Conway, B., McNabb, J. and Ashton, N. (eds.) 1996. *Excavations at Barnfield Pit, Swanscombe, 1968–1972.* London: British Museum

Cook, J. 1999. 'Description and analysis of the flint finds from Westbury Cave', in Andrews, P., Cook, J. and Jacobi, R. M. 1998. 'Observations on the artefacts from the Breccia at Kent's Cavern', in Ashton, N. M., Healy, F. and Pettitt, P. (eds.) *Stone Age Archaeology.* Oxbow

Monograph 102; Lithic Studies Society Occasional Paper 6. Oxford: Oxbow, pp. 77–89

Coolidge, F.L. and Wynn, T. 2005. 'Working memory, its executive functions, and the emergence of modern thinking', *Cambridge Archaeological Journal* 15: 5–26

Coolidge, F.L. and Wynn, T. 2007. 'The working memory account of Neandertal cognition: How phonological storage capacity may be related to recursion and the pragmatics of modern speech', *Journal of Human Evolution* 52: 707–710

Coope, G. R. 2006. 'Insect faunas associated with Palaeolithic industries from five sites of pre-Anglian age in central England', *Quaternary Science Reviews* 25: 1738–1754

Cordain, L., Miller, J. B., Eaton, S. B., Mann, N., Holt, S. H. A. and Speth, J. D. 2000. 'Plant-animal subsistence ratios and macronutrient energy estimations in world-wide hunter-gatherer diets', *The American Journal of Clinical Nutrition* 71: 682–692

Coss, R. G., McCowan, B. and Ramakrishnan, U. 2007. 'Threat-related acoustical differences in alarm calls by wild Bonnet Macaques (*Macaca radiata*) elicited by python and leopard models', *Ethology* 113: 352–367

Cowan, N. 2000. 'The magical number 4 in short-term memory: A reconsideration of mental storage capacity', *Behavioral and Brain Sciences* 24: 87–185

Cowan, N. 2005. *Working Memory Capacity*. New York: Psychology Press

Coward, F. and Gamble, C. 2008. 'Big brains, small worlds: material culture and the evolution of the mind', *Philosophical Transactions of the Royal Society series B – Biological Sciences* 363: 1969–1979

Coward, F. and Grove, M. 2011. 'Beyond the tools: social innovation and hominin evolution', *PaleoAnthropology* 2011: 111–129

Cowgill, L. W., Trinkaus, E. and Zeder, M. A. 2007. 'Shanidar 10: A Middle Palaeolithic lower distal limb from Shanidar Cave, Iraqi Kurdistan', *Journal of Human Evolution* 53: 213–223

Coyle, D. 2011. *The Talent Code: Greatness isn't Born it's Grown*. London: Arrow

Cranshaw, S. 1983. *Handaxes and Cleavers: Selected English Acheulean Industries*. Oxford: British Archaeological Reports British Series 113

Crockford, C., Wittig, R. M., Mundry, R. and Zuberbühler, K. 2012. 'Wild chimpanzees inform ignorant hroup members of danger', *Current Biology* 22: 142–146

Curtin, E. and Wanswer, J. (eds.) *Social Archaeology: Beyond Subsistence and Dating*. New York: Academic Press, pp. 61–85

Crompton, R. H. and Gowlett, J. A. J. 1993. 'Allometry and multidimensional form in Acheulean bifaces from Kilombe, Kenya', *Journal of Human Evolution* 25: 175–199

Cronin, K. A., van Leeuwen, E. J. C., Chitalu Mulenga, I. and Bodamer, M. D. 2011. 'Behavioral response of a chimpanzee mother toward her dead infant', *American Journal of Primatology* 73: 415–421

Cubuk, G. A. 1976. 'Erste Altpaläolitische funde in Griechland bei nea Skala, Kephallinia Ionische Inseln', in K. Valoch (ed.) *Les prémiers industries de l'Europe*. Coll. III. Nizza: UISPP Coll. III, pp. 152–177

Cummings, V. 2003. 'Mesolithic worldviews of the landscape in western Britain', in Larson, L. (eds.) *Mesolithic on the Move: papers presented at the sixth international conference on the Mesolithic in Europe, Stockholm 2000*. Oxford: Oxbow Books, pp. 74–81

Currant, A. and Stringer, C. (ed.) *Westbury Cave: The Natural History Museum Excavations*. Bristol: Western Academic and Specialist Press, pp. 212–261

Cutler, K. B., Edwards, R. L., Taylor, F. W., Cheng, H., Adkins, J., Gallup, C. D., Cutler, P. M., Burr, G. S. and Bloom, A. L. 2003. 'Rapid sea level fall and deep-ocean temperature change since the last interglacial period', *Earth and Planetary Science Letters* 206: 253–271

Dagley, P., Mussett, A. E. and Palmer, H. C. 1978. 'Preliminary observations on the palaeomagnetic stratigraphy of the area west of Lake Baringo, Kenya', in Bishop, W. W. (ed.) *Geological Background to Fossil Man*. Edinburgh: Scottish Academic Press, pp. 225–236

Dakaris, S., Higgs, E. and Hey R. 1964. 'The climate, environments and industries of Stone Age: Part I'. *Proceedings of the Prehistoric Society* XXX: 199–244

Daniau A.-L., d'Errico F. and Sánchez Goñi M. F. 2010. 'Testing the hypothesis of fire use for ecosystem management by Neanderthal and Upper Palaeolithic Modern Human populations', *PLoS ONE* 5(2), e9157

Darlas, A. 1999. 'Palaeolithic research in Western Achaia', in Bailey, G. N., Adam, E., Panagopoulou, E., Perlès, C. and Zachos, K. (eds.) *The Palaeolithic of Greece and Adjacent Areas. Proceedings of the ICOPAG Conference, Ioannina (September 1994)*. British School at Athens Studies 3. Athens: British School at Athens, pp. 303–310

Darlas, A. 2007. 'Le Moustérien de Grèce à la lumière des récentes recherches', *L'anthropologie* 111: 346–366

Darlas, A. and de Lumley, H. 1999. 'Paleolithic research in Kalamakia Cave, Areopolis, Peloponnesse', in Bailey, G. N., Adam, E., Panagopoulou, E., Perlès, C. and Zachos, K. (eds.) *The Palaeolithic of Greece and Adjacent Areas. Proceedings of the ICOPAG Conference, Ioannina (September 1994)*. British School at Athens Studies 3. Athens: British School at Athens, pp. 293–302

Darlas, A., Karkanas, P., Palli, O. and Papadea, A. 2007. 'Paleolithic excavation in the Korissia lagoon', in Arvanitou-Metallinou, G. (ed.) *Prehistoric Corfu and its adjacent areas: Problems-perspectives. Proceedings of the conference dedicated to A. Sordinas, Corfu, 17 December 2004*. Corfu: Ministry of Culture, pp. 77–84

Darlas, A. and Psathi, E. 2008. 'Le Paléolithique supérieur dans la peninsule du Mani (Peloponnese, Greece)', in Darlas, A. and Mihailovic, D. (ed.) *The Palaeolithic of the Balkans. Session C33. Proceedings of the XV World Congress (Lisbon, 4–9 September 2006)*. BAR British

International Series 1819. Oxford: Archaeopress, pp. 51–59

Davidson, I. and Noble, W. 1989. 'The archaeology of perception: Traces of depiction and language', *Current Anthropology* 30: 125–155

Deacon, T. 1997. *The Symbolic Species: The co-evolution of language and the brain*. New York/London: W. W. Norton & Company

Deaner, R. O., van Schaik, C. P. and Johnson, V. 2006. 'Do some taxa have better domain-general cognition than others? A meta-analysis of nonhuman primate studies', *Evolutionary Psychology* 4: 149–196

Defleur, A. 1993. *Les sépultures moustériennes*. Paris: CNRS Editions

Defleur, A., White, T., Valensi, P., Slimak, L. and Crégut-Bonnoure, E. 1999. 'Neanderthal cannibalism at Moula-Guercy, Ardèche, France', *Science* 286: 128–131

De Landa, M. 1997. *A Thousand Years of Nonlinear History*. New York: Swerve Editions

Deleuze, G. 1989. *Cinema 2: the Time Image*. Trans. Tomlinson, H. and Galeta, R. Minneapolis: University of Minneapolis Press

Deleuze, G. and Guattari, F. 1987. *A Thousand Plateaus: Capitalism and Schizophrenia*. Trans. Massumi, B. Minneapolis: University of Minneapolis Press

Delluc, B. and Delluc, G. 1991. *L'art pariétal archaique en Aquitaine. XXVIIIe supplément à Gallia Préhistoire*. Paris: Éditions du Centre National de la Recherche Scientifique

Delporte H. 1968. 'L'Abri du Facteur à Tursac (Dordogne) – I : Etude générale', *Gallia Préhistoire* XI: 1–121

Delporte, H. 1976. 'Les sépultures moustériennes de La Ferrassie', in Vandermeersch, B. (ed.) *Les Sépultures Néanderthaliennes*. Nice: Union Internationale des Sciences Préhistoriques et Protohistoriques IXe Congrès, pp. 8–11

Delporte, H. 1979. *L'image de la femme dans l'art préhistorique*. Paris: Picard

Delporte, H. 1993a. *L'image de la femme dans l'art préhistorique*. Paris: Picard

Delporte, H. 1993b. 'Gravettian female figurines: A regional survey', in Knecht, H., Pike-Tay, A. and White, R. (eds.) *Before Lascaux. The Complex Record of the Early Upper Palaeolithic.* Boca Raton: CRC Press, pp. 243–257

Delson, E. 1974. 'Preliminary review of cercopithecid distribution in the circum-Mediterranean region', *Mémoires du Bureau des Recherches Géologiques et Minières (France)* 78: 131–135

Delson, E. 1980. 'Fossil macaques, phyletic relationships and a scenario of deployment', in Lindburg, D. G. (ed.) *The Macaques: Studies in Ecology, Behavior and Evolution.* New York: Van Nostrand, pp. 10–30

Dennell, R. 2009. *The Palaeolithic Settlement of Asia.* Cambridge: Cambridge University Press

Dennell, R. 2010. 'Out of Africa I: current problems and future prospects', in Fleagle, J.G., Shea, J.J., Grine, F.E., Baden, A.L. and R.E Leaky (eds.), *Out of Africa I.* Springer, Dordrecht, pp. 247–273

Dennell, R. W., Martinón-Torres, M. and Bermúdez de Castro, J. M. 2010. 'Out of Asia: The initial colonisation of Europe in the Early and Middle Pleistocene', *Quaternary International* 223–224: 439

Dennell, R. W., Martinón-Torres, M. and Bermúdez de Castro, J. M. 2011. 'Hominin variability, climatic instability and population demography in Middle Pleistocene Europe', *Quaternary Science Reviews* 30(11): 1511–1524.

Dennell, R. W. and Roebroeks, W. 1996. 'The earliest colonisation of Europe: the short chronology revisited', *Antiquity* 70: 535–542

Derevianko, A. P. 2009. *Middle to Upper Palaeolithic transition and formation of Homo sapiens sapiens in Eastern, Central and Northern Asia.* Novosibirsk: Institute of Archaeology and Ethnography Press

Derevianko, A. P. 2011. *The Upper Palaeolithic in Africa and Eurasia and the Origin of Anatomically Modern Humans.* Novosibirsk: Institute of Archaeology and Ethnography, Russian Academy of Sciences, Siberian Branch

d'Errico, F. 2003. 'The invisible frontier: a multiple species model for the origin of behavioural modernity', *Evolutionary Anthropology* 12: 188–202

d'Errico, F., Henshilwood, C., Lawson, G., Vanhaeren, M., Tillier, A.-M., Soressi, M., Bresson, F., Maureille, B., Nowell, A., Lakarra, J., Backwell, L. and Julien, M. 2003. 'Archaeological evidence for the emergence of language, symbolism, and music – an alternative multidisciplinary perspective', *Journal of World Prehistory* 17(1): 1–70

d'Errico, F., Henshilwood, C., Vanhaeren, M. and van Niekerk, K. 2005. '*Nassarius kraussianus* shell beads from Blombos Cave: Evidence for symbolic behaviour in the Middle Stone Age', *Journal of Human Evolution* 48: 3–24

d'Errico, F. and Nowell, A. 2000. 'A new look at the Berekhat Ram figurine: implications for the origins of symbolism', *Cambridge Archaeological Journal* 10(1): 123–167

d'Errico F., Lázničková-Galetová M. and Caldwell D. 2011. 'Identification of a possible engraved Venus from Předmostí, Czech Republic', *Journal of Archaeological Science* 38: 672–685

de Ruiter, J., Weston, G. and Lyon, S. M. 2011. 'Dunbar's Number: Group size and brain physiology in humans re-examined', *American Anthropologist* 113: 557–568

Descola, P. 1994. *In the Society of Nature: a Native Ecology in Amazonia.* Cambridge: Cambridge University Press

Despriée, J., Voinchet, P., Tissoux, H., Moncel, M.-H., Arzarello, M., Robin, S., Bahain, J.-J., Falguères, C., Courcimault, G., Dépont, J., Gageonnet, R., Marquer, L., Messager, E., Abdessadok, S. and Puaud, S. 2010. 'Lower and middle Pleistocene human settlements in the Middle Loire River Basin, Centre Region, France', *Quaternary International* 223–224: 345–359

De Veer, M. W. and Van Den Bos, R. 1999. 'A critical review of methodology and interpretation of mirror self-recognition research in nonhuman primates', *Animal Behaviour* 58: 459–468

Diamond J. and Bellwood P. 2003. 'Farmers and their languages: the first expansions', *Science* 300: 597–603

Dickson, D. B. 1990. *The Dawn of Belief. Religion in the Upper Paleolithic of Southwestern Europe*. Tucson: University of Arizona

Douka, K., Perlès, C., Valladas, H., Vanhaeren, M. and Hedges, R. E. M. 2011. 'Franchthi Cave revisited: The Age of the Aurignacian in south-eastern Europe', *Antiquity* 85: 1131–1150

Douka, K., Bergman, C.A., Hedges, R.E.M., Wesselingh, F.P. and Higham, T. F.G. 2013. 'Chronology of Ksar Akil (Lebanon) and implications for the colonization of Europe by Anatomically Modern Humans', *PLOS ONE*, 8(9): 1–10

Dowson, T. A. and Porr, M. 2001. 'Special objects – special creatures. Shamanistic imagery and the Aurignacian art of Southwest Germany', in Price, N. (ed.) *The Archaeology of Shamanism*. London and New York: Routledge, pp. 165–177

Duerr, H. P. 1984. *Sedna, oder, Die Liebe zum Leben*. Frankfurt am Main: Suhrkamp

Duhard, J-P. 1993. *Réalisme de l'image féminin paléolithique*. Paris: Éditions du Centre National de la Recherche Scientifique

Duhard, J-P. 1996. *Réalisme de l'image masculine paléolithique*. Grenoble: Jérôme Million

Dunbar, R. I. M. 1992. 'Neocortex size as a constraint on group size in primates', *Journal of Human Evolution* 20: 469–493

Dunbar, R. I. M. 1993. 'Coevolution of neocortical size, group size and language in humans', *Behavioral and Brain Sciences* 16: 681–694

Dunbar, R. I. M. 1998a. 'The Social Brain Hypothesis', *Evolutionary Anthropology* 6: 178–190

Dunbar, R. I. M. 1998b. 'Theory of mind and the evolution of language', in Hurford, J. R., Studdert-Kennedy, M. and Knight, C. (eds.) *Approaches to the Evolution of Language*. Cambridge: Cambridge University Press, pp. 92–110

Dunbar, R. I. M. 2003. 'The social brain: mind, language, and society in evolutionary perspective', *Annual Review of Anthropology* 32: 163–181

Dunbar, R. I. M. 2004. *The Human Story: A new history of mankind's evolution*. London: Faber and Faber

Dunbar, R. I. M. 2007. 'The social brain and the cultural explosion of the human revolution', in Mellars, P., Boyle, K., Bar-Yosef, O. and Stringer, C. (eds.) *Rethinking the human revolution*. Cambridge: McDonald Institute Monographs, pp. 91–98

Dunbar, R. I. M. 2009. 'Why only humans have language', in Knight, C. and Botha, R. (eds.) *The Prehistory of Language*. Oxford: Oxford University Press, pp. 12–35

Dunbar, R. I. M. and Shultz, S. 2007. 'Evolution in the social brain', *Science* 317: 1344–1347

Dupuy D. 2009. 'Les sculptures mobilières du site gravettien Kostenki 1-I. De l'analyse technique à l'identification des figures', *Bulletin de la Société Préhistorique Ariège-Pyrénées* 44: 127–137

Dusseldorp G. L. 2009. *A View to a Kill: Investigating Middle Palaeolithic subsistence using an Optimal Foraging perspective*. Leiden: Leiden University Press

Dutton, A., Antonioli, F. and Bard, E. 2009a. 'A new chronology of sea level highstand for the penultimate interglacial', *Nature Geoscience* 17(2): 66–68.

Dutton, A., Bard, E., Antonioli, F., Esat, T. M., Lambeck, K. and McCulloch, M. T. 2009b. 'The phasing and amplitude of climate and sea level during the penultimate interglacial', *Nature Geoscience* 2(5): 355–359

Edwards, K. J. and Whittington 1997. 'Vegetation change', in Edwards, K. J. and Ralston, I. (eds.) *Scotland after the Ice Age*. Edinburgh: Edinburgh University Press, pp. 63–82

Efimenko, P. P. 1958. *Kostenki I*. Moskow and Leningrad: Akademia Nauk

Efstratiou, N., Biagi, P., Elefanti, P., Karkanas, P. and Ntinou, M. 2006. 'Prehistoric exploitation of Grevena highland zones: hunters and herders along the Pindus chain of western Macedonia (Greece)', *World Archaeology* 38(3): 415–435

Efstratiou, N. and Kiriakou, D. 2011. 'Following the traces of the last hunter-gatherers of east Mediterranean', *Anaskamma* 5: 53–74

Einwögerer, T., Friesinger, H., Händel, M., Neugebauer-Maresch, C., Simon, U. and Teschler-Nicola, M. 2006. 'Upper Paleolithic infant burials', *Nature* 444: 285

Eissman L. 2002. 'Quaternary geology of the eastern Germany (Saxony, Saxon-Anhalt, South Brandenburg, Thüringia), type area of the Elsterian and Saalian Stages in Europe', *Quaternary Science Reviews* 21: 1275–1346

Elefanti, P., Panagopoulou, E. and Karkanas, P. 2008. 'The transition from the Middle to the Upper Palaeolithic in the southern Balkans: the evidence from the Lakonis Cave, Greece', *European Prehistory* 5: 85–95

Elefanti, P. Marshall, G. and Gamble C. S. 2010. 'The Prehistoric Stones of Greece: a resource of archaeological surveys and sites', *Antiquity project gallery*. [Available at: 84(322)/antiquity.ac.uk/projgall/elefanti323]

Elefanti, P. Marshall, G. and Gamble C. forthcoming. Surveying the Greek Palaeolithic and Mesolithic landscape: "*The Prehistoric Stones of Greece*" Research Programme.

Eliot, T. S. 1974. *Collected Poems 1909–1962*. London: Faber and Faber

Elston, R. G. and Brantingham, P. J. 2002. 'Microlithic Technology in Northern Asia: a risk-minimizing strategy of the Late Palaeolithic and Early Holocene', *Archaeological Papers of the American Anthropological Association* 12: 103–116

Elston, R. G., Emery, N. J. and Clayton, N. S. 2001. 'Effects of experience and social context on prospective caching strategies by scrub jays', *Nature* 414: 443–446

Elston, R. G., Dong, G. and Zhang, D. 2011. 'Late Pleistocene intensification technologies in northern China', *Quaternary International* 242: 401–415

Elston, R. G. and S. L. Kuhn (eds.) 2002. *Thinking Small: Global Perspectives on Microlithization*. Washington, D.C.: American Anthropological Association, pp. 103–116

Endicott, P., Ho, S. and Stringer, C. 2010. 'Using genetic evidence to evaluate four Palaeoanthropological hypotheses for the timing of Neanderthal and modern human origins', *Journal of Human Evolution* 59: 87–95

Ephorate of Palaeoanthropology and Speleology of Northern Greece (EPSNG). *Internal report of the proceedings of the archaeological work carried out by the Ephorate between 2000–2010*

Ericsson, K. A. 1996. 'The Acquisition of expert performance: An introduction to some of the issues', in Ericsson, K. A. (ed.) *The Road to Excellence: The Acquisition of Expert Performance in the Arts and Sciences, Sports and Games*. New Jersey: Lawrence Erlbaum Associates, pp. 1–50

Ericsson, K. A. 2006a. 'An Introduction to The Cambridge Handbook of Expertise and Expert Performance: Its development, organisation and content', in Ericsson, K. A., Charness, N., Feltovich, P. J. and Hoffman, R. R. (eds.) *The Cambridge Handbook of Expertise and Expert Performance*. Cambridge: Cambridge University Press, pp. 3–19

Ericsson, K. A. 2006b. 'The influence of experience and deliberate practice on the development of superior expert performance', in Ericsson, K. A., Charness, N., Feltovich, P. J. and Hoffman, R. R. (eds.) *The Cambridge Handbook of Expertise and Expert Performance*. Cambridge: Cambridge University Press, pp. 683–703

Ericsson, K. A. and Charness, N. 1994. 'Expert performance: Its structure and acquisition', *American Psychologist* 49(8): 725–747

Ericsson, K. A. and Charness, N. 1995. 'Abilities: Evidence for talent or characteristics acquired through engagement in relevant activities?' *American Psychologist* 49: 803–804

Ericsson, K. A., Charness, N., Feltovich, P. J. and Hoffman, R. R. (eds.) 2006. *The Cambridge Handbook of Expertise and Expert Performance*. Cambridge: Cambridge University Press

Ericsson, K. A. and Kintsch, W. 1995. 'Long term working memory', *Psychological Review* 102: 211–245

Ericsson, K. A., Krampe, R.T. and Tesch-Römer, C. 1993. 'The role of deliberate practice in the acquisition of expert performance', *Psychological Review* 100(3): 363–406

Ericsson, K. A., Roring, R. W. and Nandagopal, K. 2007. 'Giftedness and evidence for reproducibly superior performance: an account based on the expert performance framework'. *High Ability Studies* 18(1): 3–56

Ericsson, K. A. and Smith, J., (eds.) 1991. *Toward a General Theory of Expertise: Prospects and Limits.* Cambridge: Cambridge University Press

Erin, M. I., Greenspan, A. and Sampson, C. G. 2008. 'Are Upper Paleolithic blade cores more productive than Middle Paleolithic discoidal cores? A replication experiment', *Journal of Human Evolution* 55(6): 952–961

Evans, J. 1872. *Ancient Stone Implements, Weapons and Ornaments of Great Britain.* London: Longmans and Co.

Evans, J. 1897. *The Ancient Stone Implements, Weapons and Ornaments of Great Britain.* London: Longmans and Co.

Evetts, J., Mieg, H. A. and Felt, U. 2006. Professionalisation, scientific expertise and elitism: A sociological perspective, in Ericsson, K. A., Charness, N., Feltovich, P. J. and Hoffman, R. R. (eds.) *The Cambridge Handbook of Expertise and Expert Performance.* Cambridge: Cambridge University Press, pp. 105–123

Facorellis, Y., Damiata, B.N., Vardala-Teodorou, E., Ntinou, M. and Southon, J. 2010. 'AMS radiocarbon dating of the Mesolithic site Maroulas on Kythnos and calculation of the regional marine reservoir effect', in Sampson, A., Kaczanowska, M. and Kozłowski, J.K. (eds.) *The prehistory of the island of Kythnos (Cyclades, Greece) and the Mesolithic settlement at Maroulas.* Kraków: The Polish Academy of Arts and Sciences. The University of the Aegean, pp. 127–135

Facorellis, Y., Karkanas, P., Higham, T., Brock, F., Ntinou, M. and Kyparissi-Apostolika, N. 2013. 'Interpreting radiocarbon dates from the paleolithic layers of Theopetra Cave in Thessaly, Greece', in Jull, A. J. T. and Hatté, C. (eds.) *Proceedings of the 21st International Radiocarbon Conference. RADIOCARBON,* 55(2–3): 1432–1442

Falguères, C., Bahain, J.-J., Yokoyama, Y., Arsuaga, J. L., Bermúdez de Castro, J. M., Bischoff, J. L. and Dolo, J.-M. 1999. 'Earliest humans in Europe: the age of TD6 Gran Dolina, Atapuerca, Spain', *Journal of Human Evolution* 37: 343–352

Falk, D. 1990. 'Brain evolution in Homo: The "radiator" theory', *Behavioural and Brain Sciences* 13: 333–381

Fay, N., Garrod, S. and Carletta, J. 2000. 'Group discussion as interactive dialogue or as serial monologue: The influence of group size', *Psychological Science* 11(6): 481–486

Fay, N., Garrod, S. and Roberts, L. 2008. 'The fitness and functionality of culturally evolved communication systems', *Philosophical Transactions of the Royal Society of London B – Biological Sciences* 363: 3553–3561

Fay, N., Garrod, S., Roberts, L. and Swoboda, N. 2010. 'The interactive evolution of human communication systems', *Cognitive Science* 34(3): 351–386

Féblot-Augustins, J. 1997. *La Circulation des matieres premieres au Paleolithique.* Liege: ERAUL 75.

Fensom, D. S. 1981. 'The golden section and human evolution', *Leonardo* 14: 232–233

Ferguson, J. 2008. 'The when, where and how of novices in craft production', *Journal of Archaeological Method and Theory* 15: 51–67

Fernandes, P., Raynal, J.-P. and Moncel, M.-H. 2008. 'Middle Palaeolithic raw material gathering territories and human mobility in the southern Massif Central, France: First results from a petro-archaeo logical study on flint', *Journal of Archaeological Science* 35: 2357–2370

Fernández-Jalvo, Y., Carlos Diez, J., Cáceres, I. and Rosell, J. 1999. 'Human cannibalism in the Early Pleistocene of Europe (Gran Dolina, Sierra de Atapuerca, Burgos, Spain)', *Journal of Human Evolution* 37: 591–622

Feustel, R. 1969. 'Eiszeitliche Sexualdarstellungen und ihre Deutung. Wissenschaftliche Zeitschrift der

Humbolt-Universität zu Berlin', *Math.-Nat. Reihe* XVIII: 857–862

Feustel, R. 1970. 'Statuettes Féminines Paléolithiques de la République Démocratique Allemande', *Bulletin de la Société Préhistorique Française* 67 : 12–16

Feustel, R. 1971. 'Sexuologische Reflexionen über jungpaläolithische Objekte', *Alt-Thüringen* 11: 7–46

Field, M. 2012. 'The first British record of *Actinidia faveolata* C. Reid and E. M. Reid (Actinidiaceae family)', *Quaternary International* 271: 64–69

Finlay, N., Finlayson, B. and Mithen, S. J. 2000. 'The secondary technology: its character and inter-site variability', in Mithen, S. J. (ed.) *Hunter-gatherer Landscape Archaeology: The Southern Hebrides Mesolithic Project*. Cambridge: McDonald Institute for Archaeological Research, pp. 571–588

Finlay, N., McCarten, S., Milner, N. and Wickham-Jones, C. (eds.) 2009. *From Bann Flakes to Bushmills: Papers in Honour of Professor Peter Woodman*. Oxford: Oxbow Books

Finlayson, C., Brown, K., Blasco, R., Rosell, J. and Negro, J. J. 2012. 'Birds of a feather: Neanderthal exploitation of raptors and corvids', *PLoS ONE* 7(9): e45927

Finlayson, B., Finlay, N. and Mithen, S. J. 2000. 'The primary technology: its character and inter-site variability', in Mithen, S. J. (ed.) *Hunter-gatherer Landscape Archaeology: The Southern Hebrides Mesolithic Project*. Cambridge: McDonald Institute for Archaeological Research, pp. 533–570

Finlayson, B. and Mithen, S. J. 2000. 'The morphology and microwear of microliths from Bolsay Farm and Gleann Mor: A comparative study', in S. J. Mithen (ed.) *Hunter-gatherer Landscape Archaeology: The Southern Hebrides Mesolithic Project*. Cambridge: McDonald Institute for Archaeological Research, pp. 589–593

Finsinger W., Tinner W., Van der Knaap, W.O. and Amman B. 2006. 'The expansion of hazel (*Corylus avellana L.*) in the southern Alps: a key for understanding its early Holocene history in Europe?' *Quaternary Science Reviews* 25: 612–631

Flenniken, J. J. 1987. 'The Palaeolithic Dyuktai pressure blade technique of Siberia', *Arctic Anthropology*, 24(2): 117–132

Floss, H. 2005. 'Die Kunst der Eiszeit in Europa', in Schürle, W. and Conard, N. J. (eds.) *Zwei Weltalter. Eiszeitkunst und die Bildwelt Willi Baumeisters. Galerie 40tausend Jahre Kunst, Urgeschichtliches Museum Blaubeuren.* Alb und Donau, Kunst und Kultur 43. Ostfildern: Hatje Cantz, pp. 8–69

Floss, H. 2007. 'Die Kleinkunst des Aurignacien auf der Schwäbischen Alb und ihre Stellung in der paläolithischen Kunst', in Floss, H. and Rouquerol, N. (eds.) *Les chemins de l'art Aurignacien en Europe – Das Aurignacien und die Anfänge der Kunst in Europa. Aurignac.* Aurignac: Éditions Musée-forum Aurignac, pp. 295–316

Floss, H. and Rouquerol, N. (eds.) 2007. *Les chemins de l'Art aurignacien en Europe/ Das Aurignacien und die Anfänge der Kunst in Europa. Colloque international/Internationale Fachtagung Aurignac 2005.* Aurignac: Éditions Musée-forum Aurignac

Foley, R. and Gamble, C. S. 2009. 'The ecology of social transitions in human evolution', *Philosophical Transactions of the Royal Society B – Biological Sciences* 364: 3267–3279

Foltyn, E., Foltyn, E. M. and Kozłwski, J. 2004. 'Early Middle Paleolithic habitation structures from Rozumice Site C (Upper Silesia, Poland)', in Conard, N. (ed.) *Settlement Dynamics of the Middle Paleolithic and Middle Stone Age Volume II.* Tübingen: Kerns, pp. 165–184

Formicola, V. 2007. 'From the Sunghir children to the Romito Dwarf: Aspects of the Upper Paleolithic funerary landscape', *Current Anthropology* 48(3): 446–453

Forsén, J., Forsén, B. and Lavento, M. 2003. 'The Asea Valley survey: Catalogue of sites', in Forsén J. and Forsén B. (eds.) *The Asea Valley survey. An Arcadian Mountain Valley from the Palaeolitic period until modern times.* Stockholm, Acta Instituti Atheniensis Regni Sueciae, Series in 4°, LI, pp. 77–126

Frayer, D. W., Orscheidt, J., Cook, J., Russell, M. D. and Radovčić, J. 2006. 'Krapina 3: cut marks and ritual behaviour?' *Periodicum Biologorum* 108: 519–524

Frere, J. 1800. 'Account of flint weapons discovered at Hoxne in Suffolk', *Archaeologia* 13: 204–205

Funnell, B. M. 1995. 'Global sea-level and the (pen-)insularity of late Cenozoic Britain', in Preece, R. C. (ed.) *Island Britain: A Quaternary perspective*. London: Geological Society Special Publication 96, pp. 3–13

Funnell, B. M. 1996. 'Plio-Pleistocene palaeogeography of the southern North Sea Basin (3.75–0.60 Ma)'. *Quaternary Science Reviews* 15: 391–405

Gabunia, L., Vekua, A. and Lordkipanidze, D. 2000. 'The environmental contexts of early human occupation of Georgia (Transcaucasia)', *Journal of Human Evolution* 38: 785–802

Gagné, F. 2004. 'Transforming gifts into talents: the DMGT as a developmental theory', *High Ability Studies* 15(2): 119–147

Galanidou, N. 1997. 'Lithic refitting and site structure at Kastritsa', in G. Bailey (ed.) *Klithi: Palaeolithic settlement and Quaternary landscapes in northwest Greece. Vol.2: Klithi in its local and regional setting*. Cambridge: McDonald Institute Monographs, pp. 497–520

Galanidou, N. 2003. 'Reassessing the Greek Mesolithic: the pertinence of the Markovits collection', in Galanidou, N. and Perlès, C. (eds.) *The Greek Mesolithic. Problems and perspectives*. London: British School at Athens, pp. 99–112

Galanidou, N., Cole, J., Iliopoulos, G. and McNabb, J. 2013. 'East meets West: the Middle Pleistocene site of Rodafnidia on Lesvos, Greece', *Antiquity project gallery*. [Available at: 87(336)/antiquity.ac.uk/projgall//galanidou336].

Galinier, J., Becquelin, A. M., Bordin, G., Fontaine, L., Fourmaux, F., Roullet Ponce, J., Salzarulo, P., Simonnot, P., Therrien, M. and Zilli, I. 2010. 'Anthropology of the Night. Cross-disciplinary investigations', *Current Anthropology* 51(6): 819–845

Gallup, C. D., Edwards, R. L. and Johnson, R. G. 1994. 'The timing of high-sea levels over the past 200,000 years', *Science* 263: 796–800

Gamble, C. 1979. 'Hunting strategies in the central European Palaeolithic', *Proceedings of the Prehistoric Society* 45: 35–52

Gamble, C. 1980. 'Information exchange in the Palaeolithic', *Nature* 283: 522–523

Gamble, C. S. 1982. 'Interaction and alliance in Palaeolithic society', *Man* 17: 92–107

Gamble, C. 1983. 'Culture and society in the Upper Palaeolithic of Europe', in Bailey, G. N. (ed.) *Hunter-gatherer Economy in Prehistory*. Cambridge: Cambridge University Press, pp. 201–211

Gamble, C. 1985. 'Hunter-gatherers and the origins of states', in Hall, J. (ed.) *The State in History*. Oxford: Basil Blackwell, pp. 22–47

Gamble, C. S. 1986. *The Palaeolithic Settlement of Europe*. Cambridge: Cambridge University Press

Gamble C. S. 1987. 'Man the Shoveller: Alternative Models for Middle Pleistocene Colonization and Occupation in Northern Latitudes', in Soffer, O. (ed.) *The Pleistocene Old World Regional Perspectives*. New York: Plenum Press, pp. 81–98

Gamble, C. S. 1991. 'The social context for European Paleolithic art', *Proceedings of the Prehistoric Society* 57(1): 3–16

Gamble, C. S. 1992a. 'Comment on Roebroeks, W, Conard, N. J. and van Kolfschoten, T. Dense forests, cold steppes and the Paleolithic settlement of northern Europe', *Current Anthropology* 33: 569–571

Gamble, C. S. 1992b. 'Uttermost ends of the Earth', *Antiquity* 66: 710–783

Gamble, C. S. 1993. 'Exchange, foraging, and local hominid networks', in Scarre, C. and Healy, F. (eds.) *Trade and Exchange in Prehistoric Europe*. Oxford: Oxbow Books, pp. 35–44

Gamble, C. S. 1995. 'The earliest occupation of Europe: the environmental background', in Roebroeks, W. and van Kolfschoten, T. (eds.) *The Earliest Occupation of Europe*. Leiden: University of Leiden, pp. 279–295

Gamble, C. S. 1996a. 'Making tracks: Hominid networks and the evolution of the social landscape', in Steele, J. and Shennan, S. (eds.) *The Archaeology of Human Ancestry: Power, Sex, and Tradition*. London: Routledge, pp. 253–277

Gamble, C. S. 1996b. 'Hominid behaviour in the Middle Pleistocene: An English perspective', in Gamble, C. and Lawson, A. (eds.) *The English Palaeolithic Reviewed*. Salisbury: Trust for Wessex Archaeology

Gamble, C. S. 1997. 'The animal bones from Klithi', in Bailey, G. (ed.) *Klithi: Palaeolithic settlement and Quaternary landscapes in northwest Greece. Volume 1: Excavation and intra-site analysis at Klithi*. Cambridge: McDonald Institute of Archaeological Research Monograph, pp. 207–244

Gamble, C. S. 1998a. 'Palaeolithic society and the release from proximity: a network approach to intimate relations', *World Archaeology* 29(3): 426–47

Gamble, C. S. 1998b. 'Handaxes and Palaeolithic individuals', in Ashton, N., Healy, F. and Pettitt, P. (eds.) *Stone Age Archaeology: Essays in honour of John Wymer*. Oxbow Monograph 102; Lithic Studies Society Occasional Paper 6. Oxford: Oxbow Books, pp. 105–109

Gamble, C. S. 1999. *The Palaeolithic Societies of Europe*. Cambridge: Cambridge University Press

Gamble, C. S. 2007. *Origins and Revolutions: Human identity in earliest prehistory*. Cambridge: Cambridge University Press

Gamble, C. S. 2009. 'Human display and dispersal: A Britain in the Middle and Upper Pleistocene', *Evolutionary Anthropology* 18: 144–156

Gamble, C. S. 2010. 'Technologies of separation and the evolution of social extension', in Dunbar, R., Gamble, C. and Gowlett, J. (eds.) *Social Brain, Distributed Mind*. Oxford: Oxford University Press/The British Academy, pp. 17–42

Gamble, C. S. and Gittins, E. 2004. 'Social archaeology and origins research: A Paleolithic perspective', in Meskell, L. and Preucel, R. W. (eds.) *A Companion to Social Archaeology*. Malden, MA.: Blackwell, pp. 96–118

Gamble, C. S., Gowlett, J. and Dunbar, R. 2011. 'The social brain and the shape of the Palaeolithic', *Cambridge Archaeological Journal* 21: 115–135

Gamble, C. S. and Kruszynski, R. 2009. 'John Evans, Joseph Prestwich and the stone that shattered the time barrier', *Antiquity* 83: 461–475

Gamble, C. S. and Marshall, G. 2001. 'The shape of handaxes, the structure of the Acheulian world', in Milliken, S. and Cook, J. (eds.) *A Very Remote Period Indeed: Papers on the Palaeolithic presented to Derek Roe*. Oxford: Oxbow Books, pp. 19–27.

Gamble, C. S. and Porr, M. 2005a. 'From empty spaces to lived lives: Exploring the individual in the Palaeolithic', in Gamble, C. S. and Porr, M. (eds.) *The Hominid Individual in Context: Archaeological Investigations of Lower and Middle Palaeolithic Landscapes, Locales and Artefacts*. London and New York: Routledge, pp. 1–12

Gamble, C. S. and Porr, M. (eds.) 2005b. *The hominid individual in context: archaeological investigations of Lower and Middle Palaeolithic Landscapes, Locales and Artefacts*. London and New York: Routledge

Gamble, C. S. and Roebroeks W. (eds.) 1999a. *The Middle Palaeolithic Occupation of Europe*. Leiden: University of Leiden

Gamble, C. S. and Roebroeks, W. 1999b. 'The Middle Palaeolithic: a point of inflection', in Roebroeks, W. and Gamble, C. (eds.) *The Middle Palaeolithic Occupation of Europe*. Leiden: University of Leiden, pp. 3–21

Gamble, C. S. and Steele, J. 1999. 'Hominid ranging patterns and dietary strategies', in Ulrich, H. (ed.) *Hominid Evolution: Lifestyles and Survival Strategies*. Gelsenkirchen: Editions Archaea, pp. 396–409

Gammage B. 2008. 'Plain facts: Tasmania under Aboriginal management', *Landscape Research* 33: 241–254

Gardner, H. 1995. 'Why would anyone become an expert?' *American Psychologist* 49: 802–803

Gargett, R. H. 1989. 'Grave shortcomings: the evidence for Neanderthal burial', *Current Anthropology* 30: 157–190

Gargett, R. H. 1999. 'Middle Palaeolithic burial is not a dead issue: the view from Qafzeh, Saint-Cézaire, Kebara, Amud and Dederiyeh', *Journal of Human Evolution* 37: 27–90

Garrod D. A. E. 1938. 'The Upper Palaeolithic in the light of recent discovery', *Proceedings of the Prehistoric Society* IV: 1–25

Gaudzinski-Windheuser, S. 2013. *Raumnutzungsmuster des späten Jungplaäolithikums in Oelknitz (Thüringen)*. Mainz: Verlag des Römisch-Germanischen Zentralmuseums

Gaudzinski-Windheuser, S. and Niven, L. 2009. 'Hominin subsistence patterns During the Middle and Late Paleolithic in Northwestern Europe', in Hublin, J.-J. and Richards, M. P. (eds.) *The Evolution of Hominin Diets: Integrating Approaches to the Study of Palaeolithic Subsistence*. Leipzig: Springer, pp. 99–111

Gaudzinski-Windheuser, S. and Roebroeks, W. 2011. 'On Neanderthal subsistence in last interglacial forested environments in Northern Europe', in Conrad, N. J. and Richter, J. (eds.) *Neanderthal Lifeways, Subsistence and Technology*. Netherlands: Springer, pp. 61–71

Geneste, J. 1988a. 'Systèmes d'approvisionnement en matières premieres au Paléolithique moyen et au Paléolithique superieur en Aquitaine', in Kozlowski, J. K. (ed.) *L'Homme de Neandertal, vol.8: La Mutation*. Liège: ERAUL 35, pp. 61–70

Geneste, J. 1998b. 'Les industries de la Grotte Vaufrey: technologie du débitage, économie et circulation de la matière premiere lithique', in Rigaud, J.-P. (ed.) *La Grotte Vaufrey a Cenac et Saint-Julien (Dordogne): Paléoenvironments, Chronologie et Activités Humaines*. Paris: Mémoires de la Société Préhistorique Française 19, pp. 441–518

Geneste, J.-M. and Plisson, H. 1990. 'Technologie Fonctionelle des Pointes a Cran Solutrennes: l'Apport des Nouvelles Donnees de la Grotte de Combe-Sauniere', in Kozlowski, J. K. (ed.) *Feuilles de Pierre*. Leiden: ERAUL 42, pp. 293–320

Geribas, N., Mosquera, M. and Verges, J. M. 2010. 'What novice knappers have to learn to become expert stone toolmakers', *Journal of Archaeological Science* 37: 2857–2870

Germonpré, M. and Hämäläinen, R. 2007. 'Fossil bear bones in the Belgian Upper Paleolithic: the possibility of a proto bear-ceremonialism', *Arctic Anthropology* 44(2): 1–30

Gershon, I. 2011. 'Neoliberal agency', *Current Anthropology* 52(4): 537–555

Gibbard, P. L. 1988. 'The history of the great northwestern European rivers during the past three milion years', *Philosophical Transactions of the Royal Society of London B – Biological Sciences* 318: 559–602

Gibbard, P. L. 1995. 'Palaeogeographic evolution of the Lower Thames', in Bridgland, D. R., Allen, P. A. and Haggart, B. A. (eds.) *The Quaternary of the lower reaches of the Thames, Field Guide*. London: Quaternary Research Association, pp. 5–34

Gibbard, P. L. 2007. 'Palaeogeography: Europe cut adrift', *Nature* 448: 259–60

Gibbard, P. L., Pasanen, A. H., West, R. G., Lunkka, J. P., Boreham, S., Cohen, K. M. and Rolfe, C. 2009. 'Late Middle Pleistocene glaciation in East Anglia, England', *Boreas* 38: 504–528

Gibert, L., Scott, G. and Ferràndez-Cañadell, C. 2006. 'Evaluation of the Olduvaui subchron in the Orcé ravine (SE Spain). Implications for Plio-Pleistocene mammal biostratigraphy and the age of the Orcé archaeological sites', *Quaternary Science Reviews* 25: 507–525

Gibson, J. J. 1979. *The Ecological Approach to Visual Perception*. Boston: Houghton Mifflin

Gibson, K. R. 1986. 'Cognition, brain size and the extraction of embedded food resources', in Else, J. and Lee, P. (eds.) *Primate Ontogeny, Cognition and Social Behaviour*. Cambridge: Cambridge University Press, pp. 93–104

Gibson, K. R. 1993. 'Tool use, language and social behaviour in relation to information processing capabilities', in Gibson, K. R. and Ingold, T. (eds.) *Tools, Language and Cognition in Human Evolution*. Cambridge: Cambridge University Press, pp. 251–279

Gilligan, I. 2010. 'The prehistoric development of clothing: Archaeological implications of a thermal model', *Journal of Archaeological Method and Theory* 17(1): 15–80

Gimbutas, M. 1989: *The Language of the Goddess*. London: Thames and Hudson

Gladwell, M. 2008. *Outliers: the story of success*. London: Penguin

Glass, B. 1966. 'Evolution of hairlessness in man', *Science* 152: 294

Glover J. 1836. *A Catalogue of Sixty Eight Pictures*. London: A. Snell

Goebel, T. 1999. 'Pleistocene human colonisation of Siberia and peopling of the Americas: an ecological approach', *Evolutionary Anthropology* 8: 208–227

Goebel, T. 2002. 'The "microblade adaptation" and recolonization of Siberia during the Late Upper Pleistocene', in Elston, R. G. and Kuhn, S. L. (eds.) *Thinking Small: Global Perspectives on Microlithization*. Washington D.C.: American Anthropological Association, pp. 117–131

Goebel, T., Waters, M. R. and Dikova, M. 2003. 'The archaeology of Ushki Lake, Kamchatka, and the Pleistocene Peopling of the Americas', *Science* 301: 501–505

Goldman-Neuman, T. and Hovers, E. 2009. 'Methodological considerations in the study of Oldowan raw material selectivity: Insights from A.L. 894 (Hadar, Ethiopia)', in Hovers, E. and Braun, D. R. (eds.) *Interdisciplinary Approaches to the Oldowan*. Dordrecht: Springer, pp. 71–84

Gomez, J. C. 2005. 'Species comparative studies and cognitive development', *Trends in Cognitive Sciences* 9: 118–125

Goodall, J. 1977. 'Infant killing and cannibalism in free-living chimpanzees', *Folia Primatologica* 28: 259–282

Goren-Inbar, N. and Peltz, S. 1995. 'Additional comments on the Berekhat Ram figurine', *Rock Art Research* 12(2): 131–132

Gosden, C. 1994. *Social Being and Time*. Oxford: Blackwell

Gosden, C. 2008. 'Social ontologies', *Philosophical Transactions of the Royal Society B – Biological Sciences* 363: 2003–2010

Gosden, C. and Marshall, Y. 1999. 'The cultural biography of objects', *World Archaeology* 31(2): 169–178

Gowlett, J. A. J. 1978. 'Kilombe – an Acheulian site complex in Kenya', in Bishop, W. W. (ed.) *Geological Background to Fossil Man*. Edinburgh: Scottish Academic Press, pp. 337–360

Gowlett, J. A. J. 1980. 'Acheulean sites in the Central Rift Valley, Kenya', in Leakey, R. E. and Ogot, B. A. (eds.) *Proceedings of the 8th Panafrican Congress of Prehistory and Quaternary Studies, Nairobi, 1977*. Nairobi: TILLMIAP, pp. 213–217

Gowlett, J. A. J. 1982. 'Procedure and form in a Lower Palaeolithic industry: stoneworking at Kilombe, Kenya', *Studia Praehistorica Belgica* 2: 101–109

Gowlett, J. A. J. 1984. 'Mental abilities of early man: a look at some hard evidence', in Foley, R. A. (ed.) *Hominid Evolution and Community Ecology*. London: Academic Press, pp. 167–192

Gowlett, J. A. J. 1988. 'A case of developed Oldowan in the Acheulean?' *World Archaeology* 20(1): 13–26

Gowlett, J. A. J. 1991. 'Kilombe – Review of an Acheulean site complex', in Clark, J. D. (ed.) *Approaches to Understanding Early Hominid life-ways in the African Savanna*. Bonn: GMBH, Römisch – Germanisches Zentralmuseum Forschungsinstitut für Vor- und Frühgeschichte in Verbindung, Monographien Band 19, pp. 129–136

Gowlett, J. A. J. 1993. 'Le site Acheuléen de Kilombe: stratigraphie, géochronologie, habitat et industrie lithique', *L'Anthropologie* 97(1): 69–84

Gowlett, J. A. J. 1996. 'Mental abilities of early Homo: elements of constraint and choice in rule systems', in Mellars, P. and Gibson, K. (eds.) *Modelling the Early Human Mind*. Cambridge: McDonald Institute for Archaeological Research, pp. 191–215

Gowlett, J. A. J. 2005. 'Seeking the Palaeolithic individual in East Africa and

Europe during the Lower-Middle Pleistocene', in Gamble, C. S. and Porr, M. (eds.) *The Hominid Individual in Context: Archaeological investigations of Lower and Middle Palaeolithic landscapes, locales and artefacts*. London: Routledge, pp. 50–67

Gowlett, J. A. J. 2006. 'The elements of design form in Acheulian bifaces: modes, modalities, rules and language', in Goren-Inbar, N. and Sharon, G. (eds.) *Axe Age: Acheulian Tool-making from Quarry to Discoid*. London: Equinox, pp. 203–221

Gowlett, J. A. J. 2009. 'Artefacts of apes, humans and others: towards comparative assessment', *Journal of Human Evolution* 57: 401–410

Gowlett, J. A. J. 2011. 'The vital sense of proportion', *Paleoanthropology* 2011: 174–187

Gowlett, J. A. J. 2012. 'Shared intention in early artefacts: an exploration of deep structure and implications for communication and language', in Reynolds, S. C. and Gallagher, A. (eds.) *African Genesis: Perspectives on Hominin Evolution*. Cambridge: Cambridge University Press, pp. 506–530

Gowlett, J. and Carter, P. 1997. 'The basal Mousterian of Asprochaliko rockshelter, Louros valley', in G. Bailey (ed.) *Klithi: Palaeolithic settlement and Quaternary landscapes in northwest Greece. Vol.2: Klithi in its local and regional setting*. Cambridge, McDonald Institute Monographs, pp. 441–457

Gowlett, J. A. J. and Crompton, R. H. 1994. 'Kariandusi: Acheulean morphology and the question of allometry', *The African Archaeological Review* 12: 3–42

Gowlett, J. A. J., Crompton, R. H. and Yu, L. 2001. 'Allometric comparisons between Acheulean and Sangoan large cutting tools at Kalambo Falls', in Clark, J. D. (ed.) *Kalambo Falls Prehistoric Site: Volume III*. Cambridge: Cambridge University Press: 612–619

Gowlett, J. A. J., Harris, J. W. K., Walton, D. and Wood, B. A. 1981. 'Early archaeological sites, hominid remains and traces of fire from Chesowanja, Kenya', *Nature* 294: 125–129

Gowlett, J., Hedges, R. and Housley, R. 1997. 'Klithi: the AMS Radiocarbon Dating program for the site and its environs', in Bailey, G. (ed.) *Klithi: Palaeolithic settlement and Quaternary landscapes in northwest Greece. Vol.1: Klithi in its local and regional setting*. Cambridge: McDonald Institute Monographs, pp. 25–40

Gray R. D., Atkinson Q. D. and Greenhill S. J. 2011. 'Language evolution and human history: what a difference a date makes', *Philosophical Transactions of the Royal Society B – Biological Sciences* 366: 1090–1100

Green, C. P., Gibbard, P. L. and Bishop, B. J. 2004. 'Stoke Newington: geoarchaeology of the Palaeolithic "floor"', *Proceedings of the Geologists' Association* 115: 193–208

Grove, M. 2009. 'Hunter-gatherer movement patterns: Causes and constraints', *Journal of Anthropological Archaeology* 28: 222–233

Grove, M. 2010a. 'Logistical mobility reduces subsistence risk in hunting economies', *Journal of Archaeological Science* 37: 1913–1921

Grove, M. 2010b. 'Stone circles and the structure of Bronze Age society', *Journal of Archaeological Science* 37: 2612–2621

Grove, M. 2010c. 'The archaeology of group size', in Dunbar, R., Gamble, C. and Gowlett, J. (eds.) *Social Brain, Distributed Mind*. Oxford: Oxford University Press/The British Academy, pp. 391–411

Grove, M. 2011. 'An archaeological signature of multi-level social systems: The case of the Irish Bronze Age', *Journal of Anthropological Archaeology* 30: 44–61

Grove, M. and F. Coward. 2008. 'From individual neurons to social brains', *Cambridge Archaeological Journal* 18: 387–400

Grove, M., Pearce, E. and Dunbar, R. I. M. 2012. 'Fission-fusion and the evolution of hominin social systems', *Journal of Human Evolution* 62: 191–200

Grün, R. 1996. 'A re-analysis of electron spin resonance dating results associated with the Petralona hominid', *Journal of Human Evolution* 30: 227–241

Grünberg, J. M. 2002. 'Middle Palaeolithic birch-bark pitch', *Antiquity* 76: 15–16

Gupta, S., Collier, J. S., Palmer-Felgate, A. and Potter, G. 2007. 'Catastrophic flooding origin of the shelf valley systems of the English Channel', *Nature* 448: 342–345

Gurven, M. and Kaplan, H. S. 2006. 'Determinants of time allocation across the lifespan', *Human Nature* 17(1): 1–49

Gurven, M. and Kaplan, H. S. 2007. 'Longevity amongst Hunter-gatherers: a cross-cultural examination', *Population and Development Review* 33(2): 321–365

Gurven, M., Kaplan, H. and Gutierrez, M. 2006. 'How long does it take to become a proficient hunter? Implications for the evolution of extended development and long life span', *Journal of Human Evolution* 51: 454–470

Guthrie R. D. 1990. *Frozen Fauna of the Mammoth Steppe: the story of Blue Babe.* Chicago: Chicago University Press

Guthrie, R. D. 2005. *The Nature of Paleolithic Art.* Chicago and London: University of Chicago Press

Gvozdover M. 1989a. 'Ornamental decoration on artifacts of the Kostenki Culture', *Soviet Anthropology and Archeology* 27: 8–31

Gvozdover M. 1989b. 'The typology of female figurines of the Kostenki Paleolithic culture', *Soviet Anthropology and Archeology* 27: 32–94

Gvozdover, M. 1995. *The Art of the Mammoth Hunters: The Finds from Avdeevo.* Oxford: Oxbow Books

Hahn, J. 1986. *Kraft und Aggression. Die Botschaft der Eiszeitkunst im Aurignacien?* Tübingen: Archaeologica Venatoria

Hahn, J. 1988. *Die Geißenklösterle-Höhle im Achtal bei Blaubeuren I. Fundhorizontbildung und Besiedlung im Mittelpaläolithikum und im Aurignacien.* Forschungen und Berichte zu Vor- und Frühgeschichte in Baden-Württemberg 26. Stuttgart: Konrad Theiss

Haidle, M. 2010. 'Working memory capacity and the evolution of modern cognitive capacities – implications from animal and early human tool use', *Current Anthropology* 51/S1. *Working memory: beyond language and symbolism,* Wenner-Gren Symposium Supplement 1: S149–S166

Hallos, J. 2005. '"15 minutes of fame": Exploring the temporal dimension of Middle Pleistocene lithic technology', *Journal of Human Evolution* 49: 155–179

Hamai, M., Nishida, T., Takasaki, H. and Turner, L. A. 1992. 'New records of within-group infanticide and cannibalism in wild chimpanzees', *Primates* 33(2): 151–162

Hamilton, M. J., Milne, B. T., Walker, R. S., Burger, O. and Brown, J. H. 2007. 'The complex structure of hunter-gatherer social networks', *Proceedings of the Royal Society, London* 274B: 2195–2202

Hardy, B. L., Kaye, M., Marks, A. E. and Monigal, K. 2001. 'Stone tool functions at the Palaeolithic sites of Starosele and Buran Kaya III, Crimea: Behavioural implications', *Proceedings of the National Academy of Sciences* 98: 10972–10977

Hardy B. L. and Moncel M.-H. 2011. 'Neanderthal use of fish, mammals, birds, starchy plants and wood 125–250,000 years ago', *PLoS ONE* 6(8), e23768

Hardy, K. V. 2007. 'Food for thought: starch in Mesolithic diet', *Mesolithic Miscellany* 18.2: 2–11

Hardy, K. and Wickham-Jones, C. 2002. 'Scotland's First Settlers: the Mesolithic seascape of the Inner Sound, Skye and its contribution to the early prehistory of Scotland', *Antiquity* 76: 825–833

Hardy, K. and Wickham-Jones, C. R. 2009. 'Scotland's First Settlers: Mesolithic and later sites around the Inner Sound, Scotland: the work of the Scotland's First Settlers Project 1998–2004', *Scottish Archaeological Internet Reports* 31: http://www.sair.org.uk/sair31 (accessed 3rd March 2011)

Harvati, K. 2009. 'Petralona: link between Africa and Europe?' in Schepartz, L., Bourbou, C. and Fox, S. (eds.) *New Directions in the Skeletal Biology of Greece.* Occasional Wiener Laboratory Series. ASCSA, Athens: ASCSA, pp. 31–49

Harvati, K., Panagopoulou, E., Karkanas, P., Athanassiou, A. and Frost, S. R. 2008. Preliminary results of the Aliakmon Paleolithic/Paleoanthropological survey, Greece, 2004–2005, in Darlas, A. and Mihailović, D. (eds.) *The Palaeolithic of the Balkans. Proceedings of the XV World Congress of the IUPPS (Lisbon, 4–9 September 2006)*: BAR 1819. Oxford: Archaeopress, pp. 15–20.

Harvati, K., Panagopoulou, E. and Runnels, C. 2009. 'The Paleoanthropology of Greece', *Evolutionary Anthropology* 18: 131–143

Harvati, K., Hublin, J.-J. and Gunz, P. 2010. 'Evolution of middle-late Pleistocene human cranio-facial form: a 3-d approach', *Journal of Human Evolution* 59(5): 445–464

Harvati, K., Stringer, C. and Karkanas, P. 2011. 'Multivariate analysis and classification of the Apidima 2 cranium from Mani, Southern Greece', *Journal of Human Evolution* 60: 246–250

Harvati, K., Darlas, A., Bailey, S.E., Rein, T.R., El Zaatari, S., Fiorenza, L., Kullmer, O. and Psathi, E. 2013. 'New Neanderthal remains from Mani peninsula, Southern Greece: The Kalamakia Middle Paleolithic cave site', *Journal of Human Evolution* 64: 486–499

Hawkes, K., Altman, J., Beckerman, S., Grinker, R. R., Harpending, H., Jeske, R. T., Peterson, N., Smith, E. A., Wenzel, G. W. and Yellen, J. E. 1993. 'Why Hunter-gatherers work: An ancient version of the problem of public goods', *Current Anthropology* 34(4): 341–361

Hawkes, K. and Bliege-Bird, R. 2002. 'Showing off, handicap signalling and the evolution of men's work', *Evolutionary Anthropology* 11(2): 58–67

Hawkes, K., O'Connell, J. F. and Blurton-Jones, N. 1997. 'Hadza women's time allocation, offspring provisioning, and the evolution of long post-menopausal lifespans', *Current Anthropology* 38: 551–577

Hawkes, K. O'Connell, J. F., Blurton-Jones, N., Alvarez, H. and Charnov, E. L. 1998. 'Grandmothering, menopause and the evolution of the human life histories', *Proceedings of the National Academy of Sciences* 95: 1336–1339

Hawkes, K., O'Connell, J. F. and Coxworth, J. E. 2010. 'Family provisioning

is not the only reason men hunt: a comment on gurven and hill', *Current Anthropology* 51(2): 259–264

Haynes, G. 1991. *Mammoths, Mastodonts & Elephants. Biology, Behaviour and the Fossil Record*. Cambridge: Cambridge University Press

Haynes, G. 2006. 'Mammoth landscapes: Good country for hunter-gatherers', *Quaternary International* 142–143: 20–29

Heim J.-L. 1976. *Les Hommes Fossiles de La Ferrassie*. I. Paris: Masson, pp. 3–8

Henneberg, M. 1998. 'Evolution of the human brain: is bigger better?' *Clinical and Experimental Pharmacology and Physiology* 25: 745–749

Henry A. G., Brooks A. S. and Piperno, D. R. 2011. 'Microfossils in calculus demonstrate consumption of plants and cooked foods in Neanderthal diets (Shanidar III, Iraq; Spy I and II, Belgium)', *Proceedings of the National Academy of Sciences* 108(2): 486–491

Henshilwood, C. S. and d'Errico, F. (eds.) 2011. *Homo Symbolicus. The Dawn of Language, Imagination and Spirituality*. Amsterdam: John Benjamins

Henshilwood, C. and Marean, C. 2003. 'The origin of modern human behaviour: critique of the models and their test implications', *Current Anthropology* 44(5): 627–651

Herries, A. I. R., Davies, S., Brink, J., Curnoe, D., Warr, G., Hill, M., Rucina, S., Onjala, I. and Gowlett, J. A. J. 2011. 'New explorations and magnetobiostratigraphical analysis of the Kilombe Acheulian locality, Central Rift, Kenya', *Paleoanthropology* 2011: A16

Heyes, C. M. 1998. 'Theory of mind in nonhuman primates', *Behavioural and Brain Sciences* 21: 101–148

Hijmans, R. J., Cameron, S. E., Parra, J. L., Jones, P. G. and Jarvis, A. 2005. 'Very high resolution interpolated climate surfaces for global land areas', *International Journal of Climatology* 25: 1965–1978

Hill, R. A. and Dunbar, R. I. M. 2003. 'Social network size in humans', *Human Nature – an Interdisciplinary Biosocial Perspective* 14: 53–72

Hinds, P. J. 1999. 'The curse of expertise: The effects of expertise and debiasing methods on predictions of novice performance', *Journal of Experimental Psychology* 5(2): 205–221

Höck, C. 1993. 'Die Frauendarstellungen des Magdalénien von Gönnersdorf und Andernach', *Jahrbuch des Römisch-Germanischen Zentralmuseums* 40: 253–316.

Hockett B. 2011. 'The consequences of Middle Paleolithic diets on pregnant Neanderthal women', *Quaternary International* 264: 78–82

Hockett, C. F. 1960. 'Logical considerations in the study of animal communication', in Lanyon, W. E. and Tavolga, W. N. (eds.) *Animal Sounds and Communication*. Washington, D.C.: American Institute of Biological Sciences, pp. 392–430

Hockett, C. F. 1963. 'The problem of universals in language', in Greenberg, J. H. (ed.) *Universals of Language*. Cambridge, MA: M.I.T. Press, pp. 1–22

Hockett, C. F. and Altmann, S. A. 1968. 'A note on design features', in Sebeok, T. A. (ed.) *Animal Communication*. Bloomington: Indiana University Press, pp. 61–72

Hodder, I. 1990. *The Domestication of Europe*. Oxford: Blackwell

Hodgson, D. 2009. 'Evolution of the visual cortex and the emergence of symmetry in the Acheulean techno-complex', *Comptes Rendus Palevol* 8: 93–97

Holden C. J. 2002. 'Bantu language trees reflect the spread of farming across sub-Saharan Africa: a maximum-parsimony analysis', *Proceedings of the Royal Society London B – Biological Sciences* 269: 793–799

Holman, J.A. 1999. 'Herpetofauna', in Roberts, M. B. and Parfitt, S. A. (eds.) *Boxgrove. A Middle Pleistocene Hominid Site at Eartham Quarry, Boxgrove, West Sussex.* London: English Heritage, pp. 181–187

Holmes, J. A., Atkinson, T., Darbyshire, D. P. F., Horne, D. J., Joordens, J., Roberts, M. B., Sinka, K.J. and Whittaker, J. E. 2010. 'Middle Pleistocene climate and hydrological environment at the Boxgrove hominin site (West Sussex, UK) from ostracod records', *Quaternary Science Reviews* 29: 1515–1527

Holst D. 2010. 'Hazelnut economy of early Holocene hunters-gatherers: a case study from Mesolithic Duvensee, northern Germany', *Journal of Archaeological Science* 37(11): 2871–2880

Hopkinson, T. and White, M. J. 2005. 'The Acheulean and the handaxe: structure and agency in the Palaeolithic', in Gamble, C. S. and Porr, M. (eds.) *The Hominid Individual in Context: Archaeological investigations of Lower and Middle Palaeolithic landscapes, locales and artefacts.* London and New York: Routledge, pp. 13–28

Hosfield, R. 1999. *The Palaeolithic of the Hampshire Basin: A Regional Model of Hominid Behaviour during the Middle Pleistocene.* Oxford: Archaeopress. British Archaeological Reports British Series 286

Hosfield, R. 2011. 'The British Lower Palaeolithic of the early Middle Pleistocene'. *Quaternary Science Reviews* 30: 1486–1510

Howe, M. J. A. 1996. 'The childhoods and early lives of geniuses: Combining psychological and biographical evidence', in Ericsson, K. A. (ed.) *The Road to Excellence: The Acquisition of Expert Performance in the Arts and Sciences, Sports and Games.* New Jersey: Lawrence Erlbaum Associates, pp. 255–270

Howe, M. J. A., Davidson, J. W. and Sloboda, J. 1998. 'Innate talents: Reality or myth?' *Behavioural and Brain Sciences* 21: 399–442

Hublin J.-J. and Roebroeks W. 2009. 'Ebb and flow or regional extinctions? On the character of Neanderthal occupation of northern environments', *Comptes Rendues Palevol* 8(5): 503–509

Hunt, C. O. 1992. Pollen and algal microfossils from the High Lodge clayey-silts, in Ashton, N. M., Cook, J., Lewis, S. G. and Rose, J. (eds.) *High Lodge: Excavations by G. de G. Sieveking 1962–68 and J. Cook 1988*: 109–115. London: British Museum Press

Hunt, E. 2006. 'Expertise, Talent and Social Encouragement', in Ericsson, K. A., Charness, N., Feltovich, P. J. and Hoffman, R. R. (eds.) *The Cambridge Handbook of Expertise and Expert*

Performance. Cambridge: Cambridge University Press, pp. 31–38

Huntington, R. and Metcalf, P. 1979. *Celebrations of Death: the Anthropology of Mortuary Ritual.* Cambridge: University Press

Huxtable, J. Gowlet, J. A. J., Bailey, G. N., Carter, P. L. and Papaconstantinou, V. 1992. 'Thermoluminescence dates and a new analysis of the Early Mousterian from Asprochaliko', *Current Anthropology* 33(1): 109–114

Ikawa-Smith, F. 2007. 'In search of the origins of microblades and microblade technology', in Kuzmin, Y. V., Keates, S. G. and Shen, C. (eds.) *Origin and Spread of Microblade Technology in Northern Asia and North America.* Simon Fraser University Burnaby, B.C.: Archaeology Press, pp. 189–198

Ingold, T. 1992. 'Culture and the perception of the environment', in Croll, E. and Parkin, D. (eds.) *Bush Base – Forest Farm: Culture, Environment, and Development.* London: Routledge, pp. 39–56

Ingold, T. 1993. 'The temporality of the landscape', *World Archaeology* 25(2): 24–174

Ingold, T. 2000. *The Perception of the Environment: essays in livelihood, dwelling and skills.* London: Routledge

Ingold, T. 2001. 'From the transmission of representations to the education of attention', in Whitehouse, H. (ed.) *The Debated Mind: Evolutionary Psychology versus Ethnography.* Oxford: Berg, pp. 113–153

Ingold, T. 2007. 'Materials against materiality', *Archaeological Dialogues* 14: 1–16

Ingold, T. 2011. *Being Alive. Essays on Movement, Knowledge and Description.* London and New York: Routledge

Ingold, T. 2012. 'Toward an ecology of materials', *Annual Review of Anthropology* 41: 427–442

Inizan, M.-L. 1991. 'Le débitage par pression: des choix culturels', in Perlès, C. 25 *Ans d'Études Technologiques en Préhistoire. Bilan et perspectives. XI Rencontres Internationales d'Archéologie et d'Histoire d'Antibes.* Ville d'Antibes: Éditions APDCA, pp. 367–378

Inizan, M.-L. 2002. 'Tailler des Roches par Pression: Emergence d'une technique, etapes de sa diffusion dans le monde', in Guilaine, J. (ed.) *Materiaux, Productions,*

Circulations du Neolithique a l'Age du Bronze. Paris: Éditions Errance, pp. 33–46

Inizan, M.-L. and Lechevallier, M. 1994. 'L'adaption du débitage laminaire par pression au Proche-Orient', in Gebel, H. G. and Kozlowski, S. K. (eds.) *Neolithic Chipped Stone Industries of the Fertile Crescent: Proceedings of the First Workshop on PPN Chipped Lithic Industries.* Berlin: Ex Oriente, pp. 23–32

Inizan, M.-L., Lechevallier, M. and Plumet, P. 1992. 'A technological marker of the penetration into North America: pressure microblade debitage, its origin in the Palaeolithic of North Asia and its diffusion', *Materials Research Society Symposium Proceedings* 267: 661–681

Insoll, T. 2004. *Archaeology, Ritual, Religion.* Abingdon: Routledge

Insoll, T. 2011a. 'Ancestor cults', in Insoll, T. (ed.) *The Oxford Handbook of the Archaeology of Ritual and Religion.* Oxford: Oxford University Press, pp. 1043–1058

Insoll, T. 2011b. 'Animism and totemism', in Insoll, T. (ed.) *The Oxford Handbook of the Archaeology of Ritual and Religion.* Oxford: Oxford University Press, pp. 1004–1016

Institute of Archaeology of the Academy of Social Sciences and the Shaanxi Institute of Archaeology. 2007. 'The Palaeolithic site of Longwangchan Yichuan county, Shaanxi', *Archaeology* 7: 579–584 (in Chinese)

Iovita, R. and McPherron, S. P. 2011. 'The handaxe reloaded: A morphometric reassessment of Acheulian and Middle Paleolithic handaxes', *Journal of Human Evolution* 61: 61–74

Isaac, G. Ll. 1972. 'Chronology and tempo of cultural change during the Pleistecene', in Bishop, W. W. and Miller, J. (eds.) *Calibration in Hominid Evolution.* Edinburgh: Scottish Academic Press, pp. 381–430

Isaac, G. Ll. 1977. *Olorgesailie: Archaeological Studies of a Middle Pleistocene Lake Basin in Kenya.* Chicago: University of Chicago Press

Isaac, G. Ll. 1978. 'The food-sharing behaviour of proto-human hominids', *Scientific American* 238: 90–108

Isaac, G. Ll. 1983. 'Bones in contention: competing explanations for the juxtaposition of Early Pleistocene arte-facts and faunal remains', in Clutton-Brock, J. and Grigson, C. (eds.) *Animals and Archaeology: Hunters and Their Prey*. Oxford: British Archaeology Reports International Series 163, pp. 3–19

Isaac, G. Ll. 1997. *Koobi Fora Research Project, Volume 5: Plio-Pleistocene Archaeology*. Oxford: Clarendon Press

Jaubert, J. 1999. 'The Middle Palaeolithic of Quercy (Southwest France): palaeoenvironment and human settlements', in Roebroeks, W. and Gamble, C. (eds.) *The Middle Palaeolithic Occupation of Europe*. Leiden: University of Leiden, pp. 93–106

Jennett, K. D. 2008. *Female Figurines of the Upper Paleolithic*. Honors, Texas State University

Jennings, D. J. 1971. *Geology of the Molo area*. Nairobi: Ministry of Natural Resources, Geological Survey of Kenya report 86

Jochim, M. A. 1983. 'Palaeolithic cave art in ecological perspective', in Bailey, G. (ed.) *Hunter-gatherer Economy in Prehistory*. Cambridge: Cambridge University Press, pp. 212–219

Johnson, S. R. and McBrearty, S. 2010. '500,000 year-old blades from the Kapthurin Formation, Kenya', *Journal of Human Evolution* 58: 193–200

Johnson-Laird, P. 1983. *Mental Models*. Cambridge: Cambridge University Press

Jones R. 1969. 'Fire-stick farming', *Australian Natural History* 16: 224

Jones, W. B. 1975. *The geology of the Londiani area of the Kenya Rift Valley*. UCL: Unpublished Ph.D. Thesis

Jones, W. B. 1985. 'Discussion on the geological evolution of the trachyte caldera volcano Menegai, Kenya Rift Valley', *Journal of the Geological Society, London* 142: 711–712

Jones, W. B. and Lippard, S. J. 1979. 'New age determinations and geology of the Kenya Rift-Kavirondo Rift junction, West Kenya', *Journal of the Geological Society, London* 136: 693–704

Jöris, O. and Moreau, L. 2010. 'Vom Ende des Aurignacien. Zur chronologischen Stellung des Freilandfundplatzes Breitenbach im Kontext des Frühen und Mittleren Jungpaläolithikums in Mitteleuropa', *Archäologisches Korrespondenzblatt* 40: 1–20

Jöris, O., Neugebauer-Maresch, C., Weninger, B. and Street, M. 2010. 'The radiocarbon chronology of the Aurignacian to Mid-Upper Palaeolithic Transition along the Upper and Middle Danube', in Neugebauer-Maresch, C. and Owen, L. R. (eds.) *New Aspects of the Central and Eastern European Upper Palaeolithic – Methods, Chronology, Technology and Subsistence. Symposium by the Prehistoric Commission of the Austrian Academy of Sciences: Vienna, November 9–11, 2005*. Mitteilungen der Prähistorischen Kommission 72. Wien: Akademie der Wissenschaften, pp. 101–137

Jöris, O., Street, M. And Turner, E. 2011. 'Spatial Analysis at the Magdalenian Site of Gönnersdorf (Central Rhineland, Germany) – an Introduction', in Gaudzinski-Windheuser, S., Jöris, O., Sensburg, M., Street, M. and Turner, E. (eds.) *Site-internal Spatial Organization of Hunter-gatherer Societies: Case Studies from the European Palaeolithic and Mesolithic*. Mainz: Verlag des Römisch-Germanischen Zentralmuseums, pp. 53–80

Kaczanowska, M., Kozłowski, J. K. and Sobczyk, K. 2010. 'Upper Palaeolithic human occupations and material culture at Klissoura Cave 1', *Eurasian Prehistory* 7 (2): 133–285

Karkanas P. 2001. 'Site formation processes in Theopetra cave: a record of climatic change during the Late Pleistocene and Early Holocene in Thessaly, Greece', *Geoarchaeology* 16(4): 373–399

Karkanas, P. 2010. 'Geology, stratigraphy, and site formation processes of the Upper Palaeolitic and later sequence in Klissoura cave 1', *Eurasian Prehistory* 7(2): 15–35

Kopaka, K. and Matzanas, C. 2009. 'Palaeolithic industries from the island of Gavdos, near neighbour to Crete in Greece', *Antiquity Project Gallery* 83, 321 [Available at: http://antiquity.ac.uk/projgall/kopaka321].

Kahlke, R.-D. 1994. *Die Entstehungsgeschichte des oberpleistozänen Mammuthus-Coelodonta-Faunenkomplexes in Eurasien*

(Großsäuger). Frankfurt am Main: Walde-mar Kramer

Kahlke, R.-D., Garćia, N., Kostopoulos, D. S., Lacombat, F., Lister, A. M., Mazza, P. P. A., Spassov, N. and Titov, V. V. 2011. 'Western Palaearctic palaeoenvironmental conditions during the Early and early Middle Pleistocene inferred from large mammal commu-nities, and implications for hominin dis-persal in Europe', *Quaternary Science Reviews* 30: 1368–1395

Kajiwara, H. 2008. 'Microlithization in Eurasia: a brief review on the micro-blade reduction technology and its sig-nificance as a behavioral threshold of modern humans', *Bulletin of Tohoku Fukushi University* 32: 207–234

Kaplan, H. S., Lancaster, K., Bock, J. A. and Johnson, S. E. 2000. 'A theory of human life history evolution: Diet, intelligence and longevity', *Evolutionary Anthropology* 9: 156–183

Kaplan, H. S. and Robson, A. J. 2002. 'The emergence of humans: the coevo-lution of intelligence and longevity with intergenerational transfers', *Proceedings of the National Academy of Sciences* 99(1): 10221–10226

Kappeler, P. M. and van Schaik, C. P. 2002. 'Evolution of primate social systems', *International Journal of Primat-ology* 23: 707–740

Kato, S. and Tsurumaru, T. 1980. *Sekki no Kisochishiki [fundamentals of lithic analysis]*. Tokyo: Kashiwa Shobo.

Keates, S. G. 2007. 'Microblade technology in Siberia and neighbouring regions: An overview', in Kuzmin, Y. V., Keates, S. G. and Shen, C. (eds.) *Origin and Spread of Microblade Technology in Northern Asia and North America*. Simon Fraser University, Burnaby, B.C.: Archaeology Press, pp. 125–146

Keeley, L. H. 1984. 'Hafting and retooling: Effects on the archaeological record', *American Antiquity* 47(4): 798–809

Keen, D. H. 1995. 'Raised beaches and sea-levels in the English Channel in the Middle and Late Pleistocene: problems of interpretation and implications for the isolation of the British Isles', in Preece, R. C. (ed.) *Island Britain:*

A Quaternary Perspective. London: Geo-logical Society Special Publication 96

Keen, D. H., Hardaker, T. and Lang, A. T. O. 2006. 'A Lower Palaeolithic industry from the Cromerian (MIS 13) Baginton Formation of Waverley Wood and Wood Farm Pits, Bubbenhall, Warwickshire, UK', *Journal of Quaternary Science* 21: 457–470

Kelly, R. L. 1983. 'Hunter-gatherer mobility strategies', *Journal of Anthropo-logical Research* 39: 277–306

Kelly, R. L. 1995. *The Foraging Spectrum: Diversity in Hunter-gatherer Lifeways*. Washington, DC: Smithsonian Institu-tion Press

Kelly, K. 2009. *Technology or the Evolution of Evolution. The Technium.* Available at: http://www.kk.org/thetechnium/arch-ives/2009/01/technology_or_t.php. [Accessed 19/10/11.

Kelly, R. L. and Todd, L. C. 1988. 'Coming into the country: early paleoindian hunting and mobility', *American Antiquity* 53: 231–244

Kennard, A. S. 1944. 'The Crayford Brick-earths', *Proceedings of Geologists Associ-ation* 55: 121–169

Kerney, M. P. 1971. 'Interglacial deposits at Barnfield Pit, Swanscombe and their molluscan fauna', *Journal of the Geological Society of London* 127: 69–86

Killick, D. 2004. 'Social constructionist approaches to the study of technology', *World Archaeology* 36: 571–578

Klein, R. 1999. *The Human Career: Human Biological and Cultural Origins*. Chicago: Chicago University Press

Kleindienst, M. R. 1961. 'Variability within the late Acheulean assemblage in eastern Africa', *South African Archaeo-logical Bulletin* 16(62): 35–52

Kleindienst, M. R. 1962. 'Components of the East African Acheulian assemblage: an analytic approach', in Mortelmans, C. and Nenquin, J. (eds.) *Actes du IVe Congres panafricain de Préhistoire et de l'étude du Quaternaire*. Belgium: Tervu-ren, pp. 81–105

Klíma, B. 1995. *Dolní Vestonice II. Ein Mammutjägerrastplatz und seine Bestattun-gen. Dolní Vestonice Studies* 3. ERAUL 73. Liège: ERAUL

Knoblich, G. and Sebanz, N. 2008. 'Evolving intentions for social interaction: From entrainment to joint action', *Philosophical Transactions of the Royal Society of London B – Biological Sciences* 363: 2021–2031

Kobayashi, T. 1970. 'Microblade industries in the Japanese Archipelago', *Arctic Anthropology* 7: 38–58

Kohn, M. and Mithen, S. 1999. 'Handaxes: products of sexual selection?' *Antiquity* 73: 518–526

Koii, H., Johnston, P., Lambeck, K., Smither, C. and Molendijk, R. 1998. 'Geological causes of recent (~100 yr) vertical land movement in the Netherlands', *Tectonophysics* 299: 297–316

Kolen, J. 1999. 'Hominids without homes: on the nature of Middle Palaeolithic settlement in Europe', in Roebroeks, W. and Gamble, C. S. (eds.) *The Middle Palaeolithic Occupation of Europe*. Leiden: Leiden University Press, pp. 139–175

Koller, J., Brauner, U. and Dietrich M. 2001. 'High-tech in the Middle Palaeolithic: Neanderthal manufactured pitch identified', *European Journal of Archaeology* 4(3): 385–397

Kopp, R. E., Simons, F. J., Mitrovica, J. X., Maloof, A. C. and Oppenheimer, M. 2009. 'Probabilistic assessment of sea level during the last interglacial stage', *Nature* 462: 863–867

Kotjabopoulou, E. 2001. *Patterned fragments and fragments of patterns: Upper Palaeolithic rockshelter faunas from Epirus north western Greece*. University of Cambridge: Unpublished Ph.D. dissertation.

Kotjabopoulou, E. and Adam, E. 2004. 'People, mobility and ornaments in Upper Palaeolithic Epirus, NW Greece', in M. Otte (ed.) *La Spiritualité. Colloque International de Liége (2003)*. Liége: ERAUL 106, pp. 37–53

Koukouli-Chrisanthaki, C. and Weisgerber, G. 1996. 'A Palaeolithic ochre mine on Thassos', *Archaiologia and Technes* 60: 82–89

Kourtessi-Philippaki, G. 1986. *Le Paleolithique de la Grèce continentale. Etat de la question et perspectives de récherche*. Paris: Publications de la Sorbonne.

Koumouzelis M., Ginter B., Kozłowski J. K., Pawlikowski M., Bar-Yosef O., Albert M., Zajac, M. L., Stworzewicz, E., Wojtal P., Lipecki P., Tomek T., Bocheński Z.M.and Pazdur A. 2001. 'The Early Upper Paleolithic in Greece: The Excavations in Klisoura Cave', *Journal of Archaeological Science* 28: 515–539

Koumouzelis M., Kozłowski J. K. and Kaczanowska M. 2004. 'End of the Paleolithic in the Argolid (Greece): Excavation in Cave 4 and Cave 7 in the Klisoura Gorge', *Eurasian Prehistory* 2(2): 33–56

Krause, J., Briggs, A., Kircher, M., Maricic, T., Zwyns, N., Derevianko, A. and Pääbo, S. 2010. 'A complete mtDNA genome of an Early Modern Human from Kostenki, Russia', *Current Biology* 20: 231–236

Kudo, H. and Dunbar, R. I. M. 2001. 'Neocortex size and social network size in primates', *Animal Behaviour* 62: 711–722

Kuhn, S. L. (eds.) YEAR *Thinking Small: Global Perspectives on Microlithization*. Washington D.C.: American Anthropological Association, pp. 103–116

Kuhn, S.L, Pigati, J., Karkanas, P., Koumouzelis, M., Kozłowski, J., Ntinou, M. and Stiner, M. C. 2010. 'Radiocarbon dating results for the early Upper Paleolithic of Klissoura Cave 1', *Eurasian Prehistory* 7(2): 37–46

Kuhn, S. and Stiner, M. 2006. 'What's a mother to do? A hypothesis about the division of labor and modern human origins', *Current Anthropology* 47(6): 953–980

Kuhn, S. and Stiner, M. 2007. 'Palaeolithic Ornaments: Implications for cognition, demography and identity', *Diogenes* 214: 40–48

Kuijper W. J. In Press. 'Investigation of inorganic, botanical and zoological remains of an exposure of Last Interglacial (Eemian) sediments at Neumark – Nord 2 (Germany)', in Gaudzinski-Windheuser, S. and Roebroeks, W. (eds.) *Multidisciplinary Studies of the Middle Palaeolithic Record from Neumark-Nord (Germany) Volume I*. Halle: LDASA.

Kukla, G. and Cílek, V. 1996. 'Plio-Pleistocene megacycles: record of climate and tectonics', *Palaeogeography, Palaeoclimatology, Palaeoecology* 120: 171–194

Kull, K. 2009. 'Vegetative, animal, and cultural semiosis: The semiotic thresholds', *Cognitive Semiotics* 4: 8–27

Kuman, K. 2001. 'An Acheulean factory site with prepared core technology near Taung, South Africa', *South African Archaeological Bulletin* 56: 8–22

Kummer, H. 1971. *Primate Societies: Group Techniques of Ecological Adaptation.* Chicago: Aldine

Kuper, A. and Marks, J. 2011. 'Anthropologists unite!' *Nature* 470: 166–168

Kuzmin, Y. V., Keates, S. G. and Shen, C. (eds.) 2007. *Origin and Spread of Microblade Technology in Northern Asia and North America.* Simon Fraser University Burnaby, B.C.: Archaeology Press, pp. 189–198

Kuzmin, Y. V. 2007. 'Geoarchaeological aspects of the origin and spread of microblade technology in northern and central Asia', in Kuzmin, Y. V., Keates, S. G. and Shen, C. (eds.) *Origin and Spread of Microblade Technology in Northern Asia and North America.* Simon Fraser University Burnaby, B.C.: Archaeology Press, pp. 115–124

Kuzmin, Y. V., Keates, S. G. and Shen, C. (eds.) 2007. *Origin and spread of microblade technology in Northeastern Asia and North America.* Simon Fraser University, Burnaby, B.C.: Archaeology Press

Kyparissi-Apostolika, N. 2000. 'The excavations in Theopetra Cave 1987–1998', in Kyparissi-Apostolika, N. (ed.) *Theopetra Cave. Twelve years of excavation and research 1987–1998. Proceedings of the International Conference, Trikala (6–7 November 1998).* Athens: Ministry of Culture, pp. 17–36

Lachièze-Rey, M. 2003. *Au-delà de l'espace et du temps.* Paris: Le Pommier

Lagarde, J., Amorese, D., Font, M., Laville, E. and Dugu, O. 2003. 'The structural evolution of the English Channel area', *Journal of Quaternary Science* 18: 201–213

Lake, M. W., Woodman, P. E. and Mithen, S. J. 1998. 'Tailoring GIS software for archaeological applications: an example concerning viewshed analysis', *Journal of Archaeological Science* 25: 27–38

Lakoff, G. and Johnson, M. 1999. *Philosophy in the Flesh: the Embodied Mind and its Challenge to Western Thought.* New York: Basic Books

Laland K. N., Odling-Smee J. and Feldman M. W. 2000. 'Niche construction, biological evolution, and cultural change', *Behavioural and Brain Sciences* 23(1): 131–175

Lane, D., Pumain, D., van der Leeuw, S. and West, G. (eds.) *Complexity Perspectives in Innovation and Social Change.* Berlin: Springer Verlag

Lang, J., Winsemann, J., Steinmetz, D., Polom, U., Pollok, L., Böhner, U., Serangeli, J., Brandes, C., Hampel, A. and Winghart, S. 2012. 'The Pleistocene of Schöningen, Germany: a complex tunnel valley fill revealed from 3D subsurface modelling and shear wave seismics', *Quaternary Science Reviews* 39: 86–105

Langley, M., Clarkson, C. and Ulm, S. 2008. 'Behavioural complexity in Eurasian Neanderthal populations: A chronological examination of the archaeological evidence', *Cambridge Archaeological Journal* 18(3): 289–307

Laskaris, N., Sampson, A., Mavridis, F. and Liritzis, I. 2011. 'Late Pleistocene/Early Holocene seafaring in the Aegean: new obsidian hydration dates with the SIMS-SS method', *Journal of Arcaeological Science* 38: 2475–2479

Latour, B. 2005. *Re-assembling the Social: An Introduction to Actor Network Theory.* Oxford: Oxford University Press

Laurat T. and Brühl E. 2006. 'Zum Stand der archäologischen Untersuchungen im Tagebau Neumark-Nord, Ldkr. Merseberg-Querfurt (Sachsen-Anhalt) – Vorbericht zu den Ausgrabungen 2003–2005', *Jahresschrift für Mitteldeutsche Vorgeschichte* 90: 9–69

Law, J. 1992. 'Notes on the theory of the actor-network: Ordering, strategy and heterogeneity', *Systems Practice* 5: 379–393

Lea, D. W., Martin, P. A., Pak, D. K. and Spero, H. J. 2002. 'Reconstructing a 350 ky history of sealevel using planktonic Mg/Ca and oxygen isotope records from a Cocos Ridge core', *Quaternary Science Reviews* 21: 283–293

Leaf, M. and D. Read. 2012. *The Conceptual Foundation of Human Society and Thought: Anthropology on a New Plane.* Lanham, MD.: Lexington Press

Leakey, M. D. 1971. *Olduvai Gorge, Volume 3: Excavations in Beds I and II, 1960–1963.* Cambridge: Cambridge University Press

Leakey, M. D. 1975. 'Cultural patterns in the Olduvai sequence', in Butzer, K. W. and Isaac, G. Ll. (eds.) *After the Australopithecines.* The Hague: Mouton, pp. 477–494

Leat, P. T. 1984. 'Geological evolution of the trachyte caldera volcano Menengai, Kenya Rift Valley', *Journal of the Geological Society, London* 141: 1057–1069

Lee, R. 1968. 'What hunters do for a living, or how to make out on scarce resources', in Lee, R. and DeVore, I. (eds.) *Man the Hunter.* Chicago: Aldine, pp. 30–48

Lee, R. and DeVore, I. (eds.) 1968. *Man the Hunter.* Chicago: Aldine

Lee, J. R., Rose, J., Hamblin, R. J. O. and Moorlock, B. S. P. 2004. 'Dating the earliest lowland glaciation of eastern England: the pre-Anglian early Middle Pleistocene Happisburgh Glaciation', *Quaternary Science Reviews* 23: 1551–1566

Lee, J. R., Rose, J., Riding, B. S. P., Hamblin, R. J. O. and Moorlock, B. S. P. 2008. 'Happisburgh cliffs (TG380312): glacial lithostratigraphy, till provenance and ice-marginal deposits', in Candy, I., Lee, J. R. and Harrison, A. M. (eds.) *The Quaternary of Northern East Anglia.* Cambridge: Quaternary Research Association, pp. 137–150

Lefevre, D., Raynal, J. P., Vernet, G., Kieffer, G. and Piperno, M. 2010. 'Tephrostratigraphy and the age of ancient Southern Italian Acheulean settlements: the sites of Loreto and Nielsen, Notarchirico (Venosa, Basilicata, Italy)', *Quaternary International* 223–224: 360–368

Lehmann, J., Lee, P. C. and Dunbar, R. I. M. 2014. 'Unravelling the evolutionary function of communities', in Dunbar, R. I. M., Gamble, C. and Gowlett, J. A. J. (eds.) *The Lucy Project: The Benchmark Papers.* Oxford: Oxford University Press, pp. 245–276

Liebenberg, L. 1990. *The Art of Tracking: the Origin of Science.* London, David Philip

Milliken, S. 1998. 'The ghost of Childe and the question of craft specialisation in the Palaeolithic', in Milliken, S. and Vidale, M. (eds.) *Craft Specialization: Operational Sequences and Beyond.* Oxford: Archaeopress, British Archaeological Reports International Series 720, pp. 1–8

Leigh, S. R. 1996. 'Evolution of human growth spurts', *American Journal of Physical Anthropology* 97: 455–474

Leigh, S. R. 2002. 'The evolution of human growth', *Evolutionary Anthropology* 10: 223–236

Leigh, S. R. 2004. 'Brain growth, life history and cognition in primate and human evolution', *American Journal of Primatology* 62: 139–164

Leigh, S. R. and Park, P. B. 1998. 'Evolution of human growth prolongation', *American Journal of Physical Anthropology* 107: 331–350

Le Mort, F. 1988. 'Le décharnement du cadavre chez le Néanderthaliens: quelques examples', in Otte, M. (ed.) *L. Homme de Néanderthal* vol 5 *La Pensée.* Liège: ERAUL 32, pp. 43–55

Le Mort, F. 1989. 'Traces de décharnement sur les ossements néandertaliens de Combe-Grenal (Dordogne)', *Bulletin de la Société Préhistorique Française* 86: 79–97

Leroi-Gourhan, A. 1957. *Prehistoric Man.* New York: Philosophical Library

Leroi-Gourhan A. 1965. *Préhistoire de l'art occidental.* Paris: Mazenod

Leroi-Gourhan, A. 1968. *The Art of Prehistoric Man in Western Europe.* London: Thames & Hudson

Leroi-Gourhan, A. 1971. *Préhistoire de l'art occidental.* Paris: Éditions d'Art Lucien Mazenod

Leroi-Gourhan, A. 1982. *The Dawn of European Art: An Introduction to Palaeolithic Cave Painting.* Cambridge: Cambridge University Press

Leroi-Gourhan, A. 1983. 'Les entités imaginaires. Esquisse d'une recherche sur les monstres pariétaux paléolithiques', in *Homenaje al Prof. Martin Almagro Bash,* vol. I. Madrid: Ministero de Cultura, pp. 251–263

Leroy, S. A. G., Arpe, K. and Mikolaje-wicz, U. 2011. 'Vegetation context and climatic limits of the Early Pleistocene hominin dispersal in Europe', *Quaternary Science Reviews* 30: 1448–1463

Lewis, S. G. 1992. 'High Lodge – stratigraphy and depositional environments', in Ashton, N. M., Cook, J., Lewis, S. G. and Rose, J. (eds.) *High Lodge: Excavations by G. de G. Sieveking 1962–68 and J. Cook 1988*. London: British Museum Press, pp. 51–85

Lewis, S. G., Ashton, N. and Jacobi, R. 2011. 'Testing human presence during the Last Interglacial (MIS5e): a review of the British evidence', in Ashton, N., Lewis, S. G. and Stringer, C. (eds.) *The Ancient Human Occupation of Britain*. Amsterdam: Elsevier, pp. 125–164

Lewis-Williams, J. D. and Dowson, T. A. 1988. 'The signs of all times: Entoptic phenomena in Upper Palaeolithic art', *Current Anthropology* 29(2): 201–245

Lichtenfeld, L. L. 2005. *Our Shared Kingdom at Risk: Human – Lion Relationships in the 21st Century*. Yale University: Unpublished Ph.D. Thesis

Lieberman, D. E. and Shea, J. J. 1994. 'Behavioral differences between archaic and modern humans in the Levantine Mousterian', *American Anthropologist* 96: 300–332

Lieberman, P. 1984. *The Biology and Evolution of Language*. Cambridge, MA: Harvard University Press

Lindenfors, P. 2005. 'Neocortex evolution in primates: the "social brain" is for females', *Biology Letters* 1: 407–410

Lister, A. and Bahn, P. G. 2007. *Mammoths: Giants of the Ice Age*. Berkeley: University of California Press

Liu, Z.-Z. 1991. 'Shiye Zhijie Dazhi Jishu de Yanjiu (A study on the technique of blade detachment)', *Shiqian Yanjiu* 1: 225–244

Lombard, M., 2005. 'Evidence of hunting and hafting during the Middle Stone Age at Sibudu Cave, KwaZulu-Natal: A multi-analytical approach', *Journal of Human Evolution* 48: 279–300

Lombard, M. 2006. 'Direct evidence for the use of ochre in the hafting technology of Middle Stone Age tools from Sibudu Cave, KwaZulu-Natal', *South African Humanities* 18: 57–67

Lombard, M. 2011. 'Quartz-tipped arrows older than 60 ka: further use-trace evidence from Sibudu, KwaZulu-Natal, South Africa', *Journal of Archaeological Science* 38: 1918–1830

Lombard, M., Haidle, M. 2012. 'Thinking a bow-and-arrow set: Cognitive implications of Middle Stone Age bow and stone-tipped arrow technology', *Cambridge Archaeological Journal* 22(2): 237–264

Lombard, M. and Phillipson, L. 2010. 'Indications of bow and stone-tipped arrow use 64,000 years ago in KwaZulu-Natal, South Africa', *Antiquity* 84(325): 635–648

Lorblanchet, M. 1995. *Les grottes ornées de la Préhistoire – nouveau regards*. Paris: Errance

Lowe, J., Barton, N., Blockley, S., Ramsey, C. B., Cullen, V. L., Davies, W. and Tzedakis, P. C. 2012. 'Volcanic ash layers illuminate the resilience of Neanderthals and early modern humans to natural hazards', *Proceedings of the National Academy of Sciences* 109(34): 13532–13537

Lozano-Ruiz, M., Bermúdez de Castro, J. M., Martinón-Torres, M. and Sarmiento, S. 2004. 'Cutmarks of fossil human anterior teeth of the Sima de los Huesos site (Atapuerca, Spain)', *Journal of Archaeological Science* 31: 1127–1135

Lu, L.-D. T. 1998. 'The microblade tradition in China: Regional chronologies and significance in the transition to Neolithic', *Asian Perspectives* 37(1): 84–112

Lu, L.-D. T. 2010. 'Early pottery in south China', *Asian Perspectives* 49(1): 1–44

Lubbock, J. 1865. *Pre-Historic Times, As Illustrated by Ancient Remains, and the Manners and Customs of Modern Savages*. London: Williams & Norgate

Lucquin, A., March, R. J. and Cassen, S. 2007. 'Analysis of adhering organic residues of two "coupes-à-socles" from the Neolithic funerary site "La Hougue

Bie" in Jersey: evidences of birch bark tar utilization', *Journal of Archaeological Science* 34: 704–710

de Lumley, H. 1969. 'A Paleolithic camp at Nice', *Scientific American* 220: 42–50

Lundberg, J. and McFarlane, D. A. 2007. 'Pleistocene depositional history in a periglacial terrane: A 500ka record from Kents Cavern, Devon, United Kingdom', *Geosphere* 3: 199–219

Lycett, S. J. 2008. 'Acheulean variation and selection: does handaxe symmetry fit neutral expectations?' *Journal of Archaeological Science* 35: 2640–2648

Lycett, S.J. and Gowlett, J. A. J. 2008. 'On questions surrounding the Acheulean "tradition"', *World Archaeology* 40 (3): 295–315

Lycett, S. J. and von Cramon-Taubadel, N. 2008. 'Acheulean variability and hominin dispersals: a model-bound approach', *Journal of Archaeological Science* 35: 553–562

MacDonald, K., Martinón-Torres, M., Dennell, R. W., Bermúdez de Castro, J.-M. 2012. 'Discontinuity in the record for hominin occupation in southwestern Europe: implications for occupation of middle latitudes of Europe', *Quaternary International* 271: 84–97

Macfarlane, R. 2012. *The Old Ways*. London: Hamish Hamilton

Machin, A., Hosfield, R. T. and Mithen, S. J. 2007. 'Why are some handaxes symmetrical? Testing the influence of handaxe morphology on butchery effectiveness', *Journal of Archaeological Science* 34(6): 883–893

Machin, A. and Mithen, S. 2004. 'Reply to McNabb et al. 2004. The large cutting tools from the South African Acheulean and the questions of social traditions', *Current Anthropology* 45: 653–677

Madsen, D. B., Ma, H., Brantingham, J. P., Gao, X., Rhode, D., Zhang, H. and Olsen, J. W. 2006. 'The Late Upper Palaeolithic occupation of the northern Tibetan Plateau margin', *Journal of Archaeological Science* 33: 1433–1444

Magne, M. and Fedje, D. 2007. 'The spread of microblade technology in northwestern North America', in Kuzmin, Y. V., Keates, S. G. and Shen, C.

(eds.) *Origin and Spread of Microblade Technology in northeastern Asia and North America*. Simon Fraser University, Barnaby, B.C.: Archaeology Press, pp. 171–188

Major Archaeological Discoveries in 2005. 2006. *Further important achievements from the 2005 excavation at the Donghulin site, Beijign*. Beijing: Wenwu Press, pp. 608

Makowsky, A. 1892. 'Der diluviale Mensch im Löss von Brünn', *Mitteilungen der Anthropologischen Gesellschaft in Wien* XXII: 73–84

Malafouris, L. 2008. 'Beads for a plastic mind: the 'Blind Man's Stick' (BMS) Hypothesis and the active nature of material culture', *Cambridge Archaeological Journal* 18: 401–414

Malafouris, L. 2010. 'The brain-artefact interface (BAI): A challenge for archaeology and cultural neuroscience', *Social Cognitive and Affective Neuroscience* 5 (2–3), 264–273

Malafouris, L. 2012. 'Prosthetic gestures: How the tool shapes the mind. (Open Peer Commentary)', *Behavioral and Brain Sciences* 35(4), 28–29

Mania, D. 1995. 'The earliest occupation of Europe: the Elbe-Saale region (Germany)', in Roebroeks, W. and Gamble, C. S. (eds.) *The Middle Palaeolithic Occupation of Europe*. Leiden: Leiden University Press, pp. 85–101

Mania, D. 1999. *Nebra – eine jungpaläolithische Freilandstation im Saale-Unstrut-Gebiet. Veröffentlichungen des Landesamtes für Archäologie Sachsen-Anhalt* 54. Halle, Saale: Landesamtes für Archäologie Sachsen-Anhalt

Mania, D. and Mania, U. 2005. 'The natural and socio-cultural environment of *Homo erectus* at Bilzingsleben, Germany', in Gamble, C. and Porr, M. (eds.) *The Hominid Individual in Context*. London: Routledge, pp. 98–114

Mania D. and Mania U. 2008. 'La stratigraphie et le Paléolithique du complexe saalien dans la région de la Saale et de l'Elbe', *L'Anthropologie* 112: 15–47

Mania D., Thomae M., Litt T. and Weber T. 1990. 'Neumark – Gröbern: Beiträge zur Jagd des mittelpaläolithischen Menschen', *Veröffentlichungen des*

Landesmuseum für Vorgeschichte in Halle 43: 1–319

Mania, D. and Toepfer, V. 1973. *Königsaue: Gliederung, Oekologie und mittelpaläolithische Funde der Letzten Eiszeit.* Berlin: VEB Deutscher

Marcus, J. and Flannery, K. 1996. *Zapotec Civilization: How Urban Society Evolved in Mexico's Oaxaca Valley.* London: Thames and Hudson

Margulis, L. 1998. *The Symbiotic Planet. A New Look at Evolution.* London: Phoenix Books

Mariani-Costantini, R., Ottini, L., Caramiello, S., Palmirotta, R., Mallegni, F., Rossi, A., Frati, L. and Capasso, L. 2001. 'Taphonomy of the fossil hominid bones from the Acheulian site of Castel di Guido near Rome, Italy', *Journal of Human Evolution* 41: 211–225

Marshack, A. 1972. *The Roots of Civilization.* New York: McGraw-Hill

Marshall, G. 2000a. 'The distribution of beach pebble flint in western Scotland with reference to raw material use during the Mesolithic', in Mithen, S. J. (ed.) *Hunter-gatherer Landscape Archaeology: The Southern Hebrides Mesolithic Project.* Cambridge: McDonald Institute for archaeological research, pp. 75–78

Marshall, G. 2000b. 'The distribution and character of beach pebble flint in on Islay as a source for Mesolithic chipped stone artefact production', in Mithen, S. J. (ed.) *Hunter-gatherer Landscape Archaeology: The Southern Hebrides Mesolithic Project.* Cambridge: McDonald Institute for archaeological research, pp. 79–90

Martin, Y. 2007. 'The engravings of Gouy: France's northernmost decorated cave', in Pettitt, P., Bahn, P., Munoz, F. J. and Ripoll, S. (eds.) *Palaeolithic Cave Art: Art at Creswell Crags in European Context.* Oxford: Oxford University Press, pp. 140–193

Martinez-Navarro, B., Turq, A., Agusti, J. and Oms, O. 1997. 'Fuente-Nueva 3 (Orcé, Granada, Spain) and the first human occupation of Europe', *Journal of Human Evolution* 33: 615–620

Maschenko, E. N., Gablina, S. S., Tesakov, A. S. and Simakova, A. N. 2006. 'The Sevsk woolly mammoth (*Mammuthus primigenius*) site in Russia: Taphonomic, biological and behavioral interpretations', *Quaternary International* 142–143: 147–165

Mason S. L. R. 2000. 'Fire and Mesolithic subsistence – managing oaks for acorns in northwest Europe?' *Palaeogeography, Palaeoclimatology, Palaeoecology* 164(1–4): 139–150

Matsuzawa, T. (2003) *Jokro: the Death of An Infant Chimpanzee (DVD film with associated leaflet).* Kyoto: Primate Research Insititute

Maureille, B. and van Peer, P. 1998. 'Une donné peu connue sur la sépulture du premier adulte de La Ferrassie (Savignac-de-Miremont, Dordogne)', *Paléo* 10: 291–301

Mays, A. J. 2011. 'Safety culture – revealing the complexity', Paper presented at the Eighth International Conference on Complex Systems (ICCS 2011), Boston Marriott, Quincy, MA., June 26–July 1

Mazza, P., Martini F., Sala B., Magi M., Colombini M. P., Giachi G., Landucci F., Lemorini C., Modugno F. and Ribechini, E. 2006. 'A new Palaeolithic discovery: tar-hafted stone tools in a European Mid-Pleistocene bone-bearing bed', *Journal of Archaeological Science* 33: 1310–1318

Mazza P. P. A., Martini F., Sala B., Magi M., Colombini M. P., Giachi G., Landucci F., Lemorini C., Modugno F. and Ribechini E. 2006. 'A new Palaeolithic discovery: tar-hafted stone tools in a European Mid-Pleistocene bone-bearing bed', *Journal of Archaeological Science* 33: 1310–1318

McBrearty, S. 1999. 'The archaeology of the Kapthurin formation', in Andrews, P. and Banham, P. (eds.) *Late Cenozoic Environments and Hominid Evolution: A tribute to Bill Bishop.* London: Geological Society, pp. 143–156

McBrearty, S. and Brooks, A. 2000. 'The revolution that wasn't: a new interpretation of the origin of modern human behaviour', *Journal of Human Evolution* 39(5): 453–563

McBrearty, S. 2012. 'Palaeoanthropology: Sharpening the mind', *Nature* 491(7425): 531–532

McCall, G. J. H. 1964. 'Kilombe caldera, Kenya', *Proceedings of the Geologists' Association* 75: 563–572

McManus, C. 1980. 'The aesthetics of simple figures', *British Journal of Psychology* 71: 505–524

McNabb, J. 1992. *The Clactonian: British Lower Palaeolithic flint technology in biface and non-biface assemblages.* University of London: Unpublished Ph.D. Thesis

McNabb, J. 1996. 'More from the cutting edge: Further discoveries of Clactonian bifaces', *Antiquity* 70: 428–436

McNabb, J. 2001. 'The shape of things to come: A speculative essay on the role of the Victoria West phenomenon at Canteen Koppie, during the South African Earlier Stone Age', in Milliken, S. and Cook, J. (eds.) *A Very Remote Period Indeed: Papers on the Palaeolithic Presented to Derek Roe.* Oxford: Oxbow Books, pp. 37–46

McNabb, J. 2007. *The British Lower Palaeolithic: Stones in Contention.* London: Routledge

McNabb, J. 2013. 'Pole to Pole: Archaeology and adaptation in the Middle Pleistocene at opposite ends of the Acheulean World', *Oxford Journal of Archaeology* 32(2): 123–146

McNabb, J. and Beaumont, P. 2011. *A Report on the Archaeological Assemblages from Excavations by Peter Beaumont at Canteen Koppie, Northern Cape, South Africa.* University of Southampton Series in Archaeology 4. Oxford: Archaeopress

McNabb, J., Binyon, F. and Hazelwood, L. 2004. 'The large cutting tools from the South African Acheulean and the questions of social traditions', *Current Anthropology* 45: 653–677

McNabb, J. and Sinclair, A. 2009. *The Cave of Hearths: Makapan Middle Pleistocene Research Project: Field research by Anthony Sinclair and Patrick Quinney, 1996–2001.* University of Southampton Series in Archaeology 1. Oxford: Archaeopress

McPhail, R. I. 1999. 'Sediment micromorphology', in Roberts, M. B. and Parfitt, S. A. (eds.) *Boxgrove. A Middle Pleistocene Hominid Site at Eartham Quarry, Boxgrove, West Sussex.* London: English Heritage, pp. 118–149

McPherron, S. P. 1994. *A Reduction Model for Variability in Acheulian Biface Morphology.* University of Pennsylvania: Unpublished Ph.D. Thesis

McPherron, S. 1996. 'A Re-examination of British Biface Data', *Lithics* 16: 47–63

McPherron, S. P. 2000. 'Handaxes as a measure of the mental capabilities of early hominids', *Journal of Archaeological Science* 27: 655–663

Mehlman, M. 1991. 'Context for the emergence of Modern man in eastern Africa: some new Tanzanian evidence', in Clark, J. D. (ed.) *Approaches to Understanding Early Hominid life-ways in the African Savanna.* Bonn: GMBH, Römisch – Germanisches Zentralmuseum Forschungsinstitut für Vor- und Frühgeschichte in Verbindung Monographien Band 19, pp. 177–196

Meijer, T. and Preece, R. C. 1995. 'Malacological evidence relating to the insularity of the British Isles during the Quaternary', in Preece, R. C. (eds.) *Island Britain: a Quaternary perspective.* London: Geological Society Special Publication 96, pp. 89–110

Mellars, P. 1987. *Excavations on Oronsay: Prehistoric human economy on a small island.* Edinburgh, Edinburgh University Press

Mellars, P. 1989. 'Major issues in the emergence of modern humans', *Current Anthropology* 30: 349–385

Mellars, P. 1991. 'Cognitive changes and the emergence of modern humans in Europe', *Cambridge Archaeological Journal* (1): 63–76

Mellars, P. 1995. *The Neanderthal Legacy: An Archaeological Perspective from Western Europe.* Princeton: Princeton University Press

Mellars, P. 2011. 'The earliest modern humans in Europe', *Nature* 479, 483–484

Mellars, P. A. and Wilkinson, M. R. 1980. 'Fish otoliths as indicators of seasonality in prehistoric shell middens: the evidence from Oronsay (Inner Hebrides)', *Proceedings of the Prehistoric Society* 46: 19–44

Menke B. and Tynni R. 1984. 'Das Eeminterglazial und das Weichselfrühglazial von Rederstall/Dittmarschen und ihre Bedeutung für die mitteleuropäische

Jungpleistozängliederung', *Geologisches Jahrbuch* A76: 3

Mercer, J. 1974. 'Glenbatrick Waterhole, a microlithic site on the Isle of Jura', *Proceedings of the Society of Antiquaries of Scotland* 105: 9–32

Mercer, J. 1980. 'Lussa Wood I: the late glacial and early post-glacial occupation of Jura', *Proceedings of the Society of Antiquaries of Scotland* 110: 1–31

Mercer, J. and Searight, S. 1986. 'Glengarrisdale: confirmation of Jura's third microlithic phase', *Proceedings of the Society of Antiquaries of Scotland* 116: 41–55

Merrick, H. V. and Brown, F. H. 1984. 'Obsidian sources and patterns of source utilisation in Kenya and northern Tanzania: some initial findings', *African Archaeological Review* 2: 129–152

Messager, E., Lebreton, V., Marquer, L., Russo-Ermolli, E., Orain, R., Renault-Miskovsky, J., Lordkipanidze, D., Despriée Peretto, C. and Arzarello, M. 2011. 'Palaeoenvironments of early hominins in temperate and Mediterranean Eurasia: new palaeobotanical data from Palaeolithic key-sites and synchronous natural sequences', *Quaternary Science Reviews* 30: 1439–1447

Mitchell, J. and Westaway, R. 1999. 'Chronology of Neogene and Quaternary uplift and magmatism in the Caucasus: constraints from K–Ar dating of volcanism in Armenia', *Tectonophysics* 304, 157–186

Michels, J. W., Tsong, I. S. T. and Nelson, C. M. 1983. 'Obsidian dating and East African archaeology', *Science* 219: 361–366

Miller, A. and Barton, C. M. 2008. 'Exploring the land: a comparison of land-use patterns in the Middle and Upper Palaeolithic of the western Mediterranean', *Journal of Archaeological Science* 35: 1427–1437

Miller, G. A. 1956. 'The magical number seven, plus or minus two: Some limits on our capacity for processing information', *Psychological Review* 63: 81–97

Milojcic, V., Boessneck, J., Jung, D. and Schneider, H. 1965. *Palaeolithikum um Larissa in Thessalien*. Bonn: Rudolf Habelt Verlag.

Milton, K. 1981. 'Diversity of plant foods in tropical forests as a stimulus to mental development in primates', *American Anthropologist* 83: 534–548

Mithen, S. J. 1990. *Thoughtful Foragers: A Study of Prehistoric Decision Making*. Cambridge: Cambridge University Press

Mithen, S. 1991. 'Ecological interpretations of Palaeolithic art', *Proceedings of the Prehistoric Society* 57(1): 103–114

Mithen, S. 1993a. 'Technology and society during the Middle Pleistocene: hominid group size, social learning and industrial variability', *Cambridge Archaeological Journal* 3: 1–18

Mithen, S. J. 1993b. 'Individuals, groups and the Palaeolithic record: A reply to Clark', *Proceedings of the Prehistoric Society* 59: 393–398

Mithen, S. 1996. *The Prehistory of the Mind*. London: Thames and Hudson

Mithen, S. J. 2000a. 'Mind, brain, and material culture: An archaeological perspective', in Carruthers, P. and Chamberlain, A. (eds.) *Evolution and the Human Mind*. Cambridge: Cambridge University Press, pp. 207–217

Mithen, S. J (ed.) 2000b. *Hunter-gatherer Landscape Archaeology: The Southern Hebrides Project 1988–98*. Cambridge: McDonald Institute for Archaeological Research (2 volumes).

Mithen, S. J. 2000c. 'Mesolithic sedentism on Oronsay? New evidence from radiocarbon dates from adjacent islands', *Antiquity* 74: 28–304

Mithen, S. J. 2004. 'The Mesolithic experience in Scotland', in Saville, A. (ed.) *Mesolithic Scotland: The Early Holocene Prehistory of Scotland and its European Context*. Edinburgh: Society of Antiquaries of Scotland, pp. 243–260

Mithen, S. J. 2011. *To The Islands. . .* Uig: Two Ravens Press

Mithen, S. J. and Finlay, N. 2000a. 'Staosnaig, Colonsay: excavations 1989–1995', in Mithen, S. J. (ed.) *Hunter-gatherer Landscape Archaeology: The Southern Hebrides Mesolithic Project*. Cambridge: McDonald Institute for Archaeological Research, pp. 359–441

Mithen, S. J. and Finlay, N. 2000b. 'Coulererach, Islay: test-pit survey and trial excavation', in Mithen, S. J. (ed.) *Hunter-gatherer Landscape Archaeology: The Southern Hebrides Mesolithic Project.* Cambridge: McDonald Institute for Archaeological Research, pp. 217–229

Mithen, S. J. and Finlayson, B. 2000. 'Variability in assemblage composition: comparisons with an experimentally produced debitage template', in Mithen, S. (ed.) *Hunter-gatherer Landscape Archaeology: The Southern Hebrides Mesolithic Project.* Cambridge: McDonald Institute for Archaeological Research, pp. 547–552

Mithen, S. J., Finlay, N., Carruthers, W., Carter, P. and Ashmore, P. 2001. 'Plant use in the Mesolithic: The case of Staosnaig', *Journal of Archaeological Science* 28: 223–234

Mithen, S. J., Finlayson, B., Mathews, M. and Woodman, P. E. 2000. 'The Islay survey', in Mithen, S. J. (ed.) *Hunter-gatherer Landscape Archaeology: The Southern Hebrides Mesolithic Project.* Cambridge: McDonald Institute for Archaeological Research, pp. 153–186

Mithen, S. J., Lake, M. and Finlay, N. 2000a. 'Bolsay Farm, Islay: test-pit survey and trial excavation', in Mithen, S. J. (ed.) *Hunter-gatherer Landscape Archaeology: The Southern Hebrides Mesolithic Project.* Cambridge: McDonald Institute for Archaeological Research, pp. 259–290

Mithen, S. J., Lake, M. and Finlay, N. 2000b. 'Bolsay Farm, Islay: area excavation', in Mithen, S. J. (ed.) *Hunter-gatherer Landscape Archaeology: The Southern Hebrides Mesolithic Project.* Cambridge: McDonald Institute for Archaeological Research, pp. 291–330

Mithen, S. J., Marshall, G., Dopel, B. and Lake, M. 2000. 'The experimental knapping of flint beach pebbles', in Mithen, S. J. (ed.) *Hunter-gatherer Landscape Archaeology: The Southern Hebrides Mesolithic Project.* Cambridge: McDonald Institute for Archaeological Research, pp. 529–540

Mithen, S. J. and Wicks, K. 2008. 'Inner Hebrides Archaeological Project – Fiskary Bay', *Discovery and Excavation in Scotland* 9: 36

Mithen, S. J. and Wicks, K. 2011a. 'Inner Hebrides Mesolithic Project (IHMP) – Creit Dhu, Isle of Mull', *Discovery and Excavation in Scotland* 11: 45

Mithen, S. J. and Wicks, K. 2011b. 'Inner Hebrides Mesolithic Project (IHMP) – Storakaig and Rubha Port an t-Seilich, Islay', *Discovery and Excavation in Scotland* 11: 42

Mithen, S.J., Wicks, K. and Hill, J. 2007. 'Fiskary Bay: A Mesolithic fishing camp on Coll', *Scottish Archaeology News* 55: 14–15

Mithen, S. J., Woodman, P. E., Finlay, N. and Finlayson, B. 2000. 'Aoradh: test-pit survey and trial excavation', in Mithen, S. J. (ed.) *Hunter-gatherer Landscape Archaeology: The Southern Hebrides Mesolithic Project.* Cambridge: McDonald Institute for Archaeological Research, pp. 231–240

Modugno, F., Ribechini, E. and Colombini, M. P. 2006. 'Chemical study of triterpenoid resinous materials in archaeological findings by means of direct exposure electron ionisation mass spectrometry and gas chromatography/mass spectrometry', *Rapid Communications in Mass Spectrometry* 20(1): 1787–1800

Molyneaux, B. L. and Vitebsky, P. 2000. *Sacred Earth, Sacred Stones: Spiritual Sites and Landscapes, Ancient Alignments, Earth Energy.* London: Duncan Baird Publishers

Monnier, G. F. 2006. 'Testing retouched flake tool standardisation during the Middle Palaeolithic: Patterns and implications', in Hovers, E. and Kuhn, S. L. (eds.) *Transitions before the transition: evolution and stability in the Middle Palaeolithic and Middle Stone Age.* New York: Springer, pp. 57–83

Mooney S. D., Harrison S. P., Bartlein P. J., Daniau A.-L., Stevenson J., Brownlie K. C., Buckman S., Cupper M., Luly J., Black M., Colhoun, E., D'Costa, D., Dodson, J., Haberle, S., Hope, G. S., Kershaw, P., Kenyon, C., McKenzie, M. and Williams, N. 2011. 'Late Quaternary fire regimes of Australasia', *Quaternary Science Reviews* 30(1–2): 28–46

Morlan, R. E. 1967. 'The Preceramic Period of Hokkaido: an outline', *Arctic Anthropology* 4(1): 164–220

Morlan, R. E. 1970. 'Wedge-shaped core technology in northern North America', *Arctic Anthropology* 4(1): 17–37

Moroni, A., Boscato, P. and Ronchitelli, A. 2013. 'What roots for the Uluzzian? Modern behaviour in Central-Southern Italy and hypotheses on AMH dispersal routes', *Quaternary International* 316: 27–44

Mortensen, P. 2008. 'Lower to Middle Palaeolithic artefacts from Loutró on the south coast of Crete', *Antiquity Project Gallery* 82: 317 [Available at: http://antiquity.ac.uk/projgall/mortensen 317].

Mowaljarlai, D. and Malnic, J. 1993. *Yorro Yorro – Everything Standing up Alive. Spirit of the Kimberley*. Broome: Magabala Books Aboriginal Corporation

Mulcahy, N. J. and Call, J. 2006. 'Apes save tools for future use', *Science* 312: 1038–1040

Murdock, G. P. 1949. *Social Structure*. New York: MacMillan

Murdock, G. P. 1969. *Ethnographic Atlas*. Pittsburgh: University of Pittsburgh Press

Mussi M. 1997. 'Die Rote von Mauern: la "Dame rouge" de Mauern revisitée', *Bulletin de la Société Préhistorique de l'Ariège* LII: 45–60

Mussi, M. 1999. 'The Neanderthals in Italy: a tale of many caves', in Roebroeks, W. and Gamble, C. (eds.) *The Middle Palaeolithic Occupation of Europe*. Leiden: University of Leiden, pp. 49–80

Mussi M. 2004. 'East and South of the Alps: the MUP funerary and artistic record of Italy and Moravia compared', in Svoboda, J. A. and Sedláčková, L. (eds.) *The Gravettian Along the Danube. Proceedings of the Mikulov Conference, 20–21 November 2002*. The Dolní Věstonice Studies 11. Brno: Archeologický ústav AV ČR pp. 252–269

Mussi M., Cinq-Mars J. and Bolduc P. 2000a. 'Echoes from the Mammoth Steppe: the case of the Balzi Rossi', in Roebroeks, W., Mussi, M., Svoboda, J. and Fennema, K. (eds.) *Hunters of the Golden Age: the Mid Upper Palaeolithic of Eurasia (30.000–20.000 bp)*. Leiden: Leiden University Press, pp. 105–124

Mussi M., Roebroeks W. and Svoboda J. 2000b. Hunters of the Golden Age: An introduction', in Roebroeks, W., Mussi, M., Svoboda, J. and Fennema, K. (eds.) *Hunters of the Golden Age: the Mid Upper Palaeolithic of Eurasia (30.000–20.000 bp)*. Leiden: Leiden University Press, pp. 2–11

Mussi, M. and Villa, P. 2008. 'Single carcass of *Mammuthus primigenius* with lithic artifacts in the Upper Pleistocene of northern Italy', *Journal of Archaeological Science* 35: 2606–2613

Muttoni, G., Scardia, G. and Kent, D.V. 2010. 'Human migration into Europe during the late Early Pleistocene climate transition', *Palaeogeography, Palaeoclimatology, Palaeoecology* 296: 79–93

Nakazawa, Y., Izuho, M., Takakura, J. and S. Yamada, S. 2005. 'Toward understanding the technological variability in microblade assemblages in Hakkaido, Japan', *Asian Perspectives* 44 (2): 276–292

Nelson, N. C. 1937. 'Notes on cultural relations between Asia and America', *American Antiquity* 2: 267–272

Nelson, S. M. 1990. 'Diversity of the Upper Palaeolithic "Venus" Figurines and Archaeological Mythology', in Nelson, S. M. and Kehoe, A. B. (eds.) *Powers of Observation: Alternative Views in Archaeology*. Archaeological Papers of the American Anthropological Association 2. Washington DC: American Anthropological Association, pp. 11–22

Nettle D. 1999. 'Is the rate of linguistic change constant?' *Lingua* 108: 119–136

Neugebauer-Maresch, C. 1989. 'Zum Neufund einer weiblichen Statuette bei den Rettungsgrabungen an der Aurignacien-Station Stratzing/Krems-Rehberg. Niederösterreich', *Germania* 67: 551–559

Newell, R. R. and Constandse-Westerman, T. S. 1986. 'Testing an ethnographic analogue of Mesolithic social structure and the archaeological resolution on Mesolithic ethnic groups and breeding populations', *Proceedings of the Koninklijke Nederlandse Akademie van Kunsten en Wetenschappen* 89: 243–310

Ngara, C. and Portah, M. 2004. 'Shona culture of Zimbabwe's views of giftedness', *High Ability Studies* 15(2): 189–209

Ngara, C. and Portah, M. 2007. 'Ndebele culture of Zimbabwe's views of giftedness', *High Ability Studies* 18(2): 191–208

Nielsen, M. and Dissanayake, C. 2004. 'Pretend play, mirror self-recognition and imitation: a longitudinal investigation through the second year', *Infant Behaviour and Development* 27: 342–365

Ningxia [Ningxia Kaogu Yanjiusuo]. 2003. *Shuidonggou: The report of 1980 excavation*. Beijing: Science Press (in Chinese).

Niven, L. 2007. 'From carcass to cave: Large mammal exploitation during the Aurignacian at Vogelherd, Germany', *Journal of Human Evolution* 53, 362–382

Niven, L. 2008. *The Palaeolithic Occupation of Vogelherd Cave: Implications for the Subsistence behaviour of Late Neanderthals and Early Modern Humans*. Tübingen: Kerns Verlag

Nonaka, T., Bril, B. and Rein, R. 2010. 'How do stone knappers predict and control the outcome of flaking? Implications for understanding early stone tool technology', *Journal of Human Evolution* 59(2): 155–167

Norikoshi, K. 1982. 'One observed case of cannibalism among wild chimpanzees of the Mahale Mountains', *Primates* 23(1): 66–74

Norman, D. A. 1988. *The Psychology of Everyday Things*. New York: Basic Books

Nowell, A. and White, M. J. 2010. 'Growing up in the Middle Pleistocene: Life history strategies and their relationship to Acheulian industries', in Nowell, A. and Davidson, I. (eds.) *Stone Tools and the Evolution of Human Cognition*. Colorado: University of Colorado Press, pp. 67–82

Ntinou M. and Kyparissi-Apostolika N. 2008. 'The Pleistocene–Holocene charcoal record from Theopetra Cave, Thessaly, Greece: Implications for vegetation, climate and human use', in Damblon, F. and Court-Picon, M. (eds.) *Programme and Abstracts, 4th International Meeting of Anthracology, Brussels, 8–13 September 2008*. Brussels: Royal Belgian Institute of Natural Sciences, p. 105

Ntinou, M. 2010. 'Wood charcoal Analysis at Klissoura Cave 1 (Prosymna, Peloponnese): The Upper Palaeolithic vegetation', *Eurasian Prehistory* 7(2): 47–69

O'Connell, J. F., Hawkes, K. and Blurton Jones, N. G. 1999. 'Grandmothering and the evolution of *Homo erectus*', *Journal of Human Evolution* 36: 461–485

Olausson, D. 2008. 'Does practice make perfect? Craft expertise as a factor in aggrandizer strategies', *Journal of Archaeological Method and Theory* 15: 28–50

Ollé, A., Mosquera, M., Rodríguez, X. P., de Lombera-Hermida, A., García-Antón, M. D., García-Medrano, P., Peña, L., Menéndez, L., Navazo, M., Terradillos, M., Bargalló, A., Márquez, B., Sala, R. and Carbonell, E. 2013. 'The Early and Middle Pleistocene technological record from Sierra de Atapuerca (Burgos, Spain)', *Quaternary International* 295: 138–167

Oms, O., Parés, J. M., Martínez-Navarro, B., Agustí, J., Toro, I., Martínez-Fernández, G. and Turq, A. 2000. 'Early human occupation of western Europe: paleomagnetic dates for two palaeolithic sites in Spain', *Proceedings of the Natural Academy of Science of the United States of America* 97: 10666–10670

Origgi, G. and Sperber, D. 2000. 'Evolution, communication and the proper function of language', in Carruthers, P. and Chamberlain, A. (eds.) *Evolution and the human mind: Modularity, language and meta-cognition*. Cambridge: Cambridge University Press, pp. 140–169

Orschiedt, J. 2008. 'Der fall Krapina – neue ergebnisse zur frage von kannibalismus beim Neanderthaler', *Quartär* 55: 63–81

Osvath, M. and Osvath, H. 2008. 'Chimpanzee (*Pan troglodytes*) and orangutan (*Pongo abelii*) forethought: self-control and pre-experience in the face of future tool use', *Animal Cognition* 11: 661–674

Ottoni, E. B. and Izar, P. 2008. 'Capuchin monkey tool use: Overview and implications', *Evolutionary Anthropology* 17: 171–178

Pagel M. 2000. 'The history, rate and pattern of world linguistic evolution', in Knight, C., Studdert-Kennedy, M. and Hurford, J. (eds.) *The Evolutionary*

Emergence of Language. Cambridge: Cambridge University Press, pp. 391–416

Pagel M., Atkinson Q. D. and Meade A. 2007. 'Frequency of word-use predicts rates of lexical evolution throughout Indo-European history', *Nature* 449: 717–720

Pales, L. and Tassin de Saint Péreuse, M. 1976. *Les gravures de La Marche. II: Les Humains*. Paris: Éd. Ophrys

Palmer, F. 2007. 'Die Entstehung von Birkenpech in einer Feuerstelle unter paläolithischen Bedingungen', *Mitteilungen der Gesellschaft für Urgeschichte* 16: 75–83

Panagopoulou, E., Karkanas, P., Kotjabopoulou, E., Tsartsidou, G., Harvati, K. and Ntinou, M. 2002–2004. 'Late Pleistocene archaeological and fossil human evidence from Lakonis cave, Southern Greece', *Journal of Field Archeology* 2: 323–349

Pantukhina, I. 2007. 'The role of raw material in microblade technology at three Late Palaeolithic sites, Russian far east', *Indo-Pacific Prehistory Association Bulletin* 27: 144–153

Papagianni, D. 2009. 'Mediterranean southeastern Europe in the Late Middle and Early Upper Palaeolithic: modern human route to Europe or Neanderthal refugium?', in. Camps, M. and Szmidt, C. (eds.) *The Mediterranean from 50,000 to 25,000: Turning points and new directions*. Oxbow Books, Oxford, pp. 115–136

Parés, J. M. and Pérez-González, A. 1999. 'Magnetochronology and stratigraphy at Gran Dolina section, Atapuerca (Burgos, Spain)', *Journal of Human Evolution* 37: 325–342

Parfitt, S. 1998. 'Pleistocene vertebrates faunas of the West Sussex Coastal Plain: their environment and palaeoenvironmental significance', in Murton, J. B., Whiteman, C. A., Bates, M. R., Bridgland, D., Long, A. J., Roberts, M. B. and Waller, M. P. (eds.) *The Quaternary of Kent & Sussex: Field Guide*. London: Quaternary Research Association, pp. 121–135

Parfitt, S. A. 1999. 'Mammalia', in Roberts, M. B. and Parfitt, S. A. (eds.) *Boxgrove. A Middle Pleistocene Hominid Site at Eartham Quarry, Boxgrove, West Sussex*. London: English Heritage, pp. 197–290

Parfitt, S. A. 2008. 'Pakefield cliffs: archaeology and palaeoenvironment of the Cromer Forest-bed Formation', in Candy, I., Lee, J. R. and Harrison, A. M. (eds.) *The Quaternary of Northern East Anglia*. Cambridge: Quaternary Research Association, pp. 130–136

Parfitt, S. A., Ashton, N. M., Lewis, S. G., Abel, R. L., Coope, G. R., Field, M. H., Gale, R., Hoare, P. G., Larkin, N. R., Lewis, M. D., Karloukovski, V., Maher, B. A., Peglar, S. M., Preece, R. C., Whittaker, J. E. and Stringer, C. B. 2010. 'Early Pleistocene human occupation at the edge of the boreal zone in northwest Europe', *Nature* 466: 229–233

Parfitt, S. A., Barendregt, R. W., Breda, M., Candy, I., Collins, M. J., Coope, R. G., Durbidge, P., Field, M. H., Lee, J. R., Lister, A. M., Mutch, R., Penkman, K. E. H., Preece, R. C., Rose, J., Stringer, C. B., Symmons, R., Whittaker, J. E., Wymer, J. J. and Stuart, A. J. 2005. 'The earliest record of human activity in northern Europe', *Nature* 438: 1008–1012

Parker, S. T. and Gibson, K. R. 1977. 'Object manipulation, tool use and sensorimotor intelligence as feeding adaptations in cebus monkeys and great apes', *Journal of Human Evolution* 6: 623–641

Patzek, T. and Tainter, J. A. 2011. *Drilling Down: The Gulf Oil Debacle and Our Energy Dilemma*. New York: Springer

Pawlik, A. 2004. 'Identification of hafting traces and residues by scanning electron microscopes and energy-dispersive analysis of X-rays', in Walker, E. A., Wenban-Smith, F. and Healy, F. (eds.) *Lithics in Action: Papers from the Conference Lithic Studies in the Year 2000*. Oxford: Oxbow Books, pp. 172–183

Pawlik, A. and Thissen, J. 2011a. 'Hafted armatures and multi-component tool design at the Micoquian site of Inden-Altdorf, Germany', *Journal of Archaeological Science* 38: 1699–1708

Pawlik, A. and Thissen, J. 2011b. 'The "Palaeolithic prospection in the Inde Valley" Project', *Quaternary Science Journal* 60(1): 66–77

Pei, S., Gao, X., Wang, H., Kuman, K., Bae, C. J., Chen, F., Guan, Y., Zhang, Y., Zhang, X., Peirce, C. S. 1906. 'The basis of pragmaticism', in Hartshorne, C. and Weiss, P. (eds.) *The collected papers of Charles Sanders Peirce Vol I – VI*. Cambridge: Harvard University Press, pp. 1931–1935

Peng, F. and Li, X. 2012. 'The Shuidonggou site complex: new excavations and implications for the earliest Late Palaeolithic in North China', *Journal of Archaeological Science* 39: 3610–3626

Peresani, M., Fiore, I., Gala, M., Romandini, M. and Tagliacozzo, A. 2011. 'Late Neandertals and the intentional removal of feathers as evidenced from bird bone taphonomy at Fumane Cave 44 ky B.P. Italy', *Proceedings of the National Academy of Sciences* 108(10): 3888–3893

Perlès C. 1999. 'Long-term perspectives on the occupation of the Franchthi cave: continuity and discontinuity', in. Bailey, G. N., Adam, E., Panagopoulou, E., Perlès, C. and Zachos, K. (eds.) *The Palaeolithic of Greece and Adjacent Areas. Proceedings of the ICOPAG Conference, Ioannina (September 1994)*. British School at Athens Studies 3. London: British School at Athens, pp. 311–318

Perreault, C. and Brantingham, P. J. 2011. 'Mobility-driven cultural transmission along the forager-collector continuum', *Journal of Anthropological Archaeology* 30: 62–68

Pettitt, P. 2002. 'The Neanderthal dead: Exploring mortuary variability in Middle Palaeolithic Eurasia', *Before Farming* 1(4): 1–19

Pettitt, P. B. 2002/1. 'The Neanderthal dead: exploring mortuary variability in Middle Palaeolithic Eurasia', *Before Farming* 1(1): 1–26

Pettitt, P. B. 2006. 'The living dead and the dead living: Burials, figurines and social performance in the European Mid Upper Palaeolithic', in Knüsel, C. and Gowland, R. (eds.) *The Social Archaeology of Funerary Remains*. Oxford: Oxbow Books, pp. 292–308

Pettitt, P. B. 2007a. 'The ghosts of the Palaeolithic: individual agency and behavioural change in perspective (review article)', *Antiquity* 81: 1083–1085

Pettitt, P. B. 2007b. 'Cultural context and form of some of the Creswell images: An interpretative model', in Pettitt, P., Bahn, P., Munoz, F. J. and Ripoll, S. (eds.) *Palaeolithic Cave Art: Art at Creswell Crags in European Context*. Oxford: Oxford University Press, pp. 112–139

Pettitt, P. B. 2008. 'The British Upper Palaeolithic', in Pollard, J. (ed.) *Prehistoric Britain*. London: Blackwell Studies in Global Archaeology, pp. 18–57

Pettitt, P. 2011a. *The Palaeolithic Origins of Human Burial*. London and New York: Routledge

Pettitt, P. B. 2011b. 'The living as symbols, the dead as symbols. Problematising the scale and pace of hominin symbolic evolution', in Henshilwood, C. S. and d'Errico, F. (eds.) *Homo Symbolicus. The Dawn of Language, Imagination and Spirituality*. Amsterdam: John Benjamins, pp. 141–161

Pettitt, P. B. 2011c. 'Religion and ritual in the Lower and Middle Palaeolithic', in Insoll, T. and Maclean, R. (eds.) *The Oxford Handbook of the Archaeology of Ritual and Religion*. Oxford: University Press, pp. 329–343

Pettitt, P. B. and White, M. J. 2012. *The British Palaeolithic: Hominin societies at the edge of the Pleistocene World*. London: Routledge

Peyrony, D. 1934. 'La Ferrassie: Moustérien. Périgordien. Aurignacien. *Préhistoire* 3: 1–92

Ramirez Rozzi, F. V., d'Errico, F., Vanhaeren, M., Grootes, P. M., Kerautret, B. and Dujardin, V. 2009. 'Cut-marked human remains bearing Neanderthal features and modern human remains associated with the Aurignacian at Les Rois', *Journal of Anthropological Sciences* 87, pp. 153–185

Piaget, J. 1952. *The Origins of Intelligence in Children*. New York: International University Press

Piette, E. 1895. 'La station de Brassempouy et les statuettes humaines de l période glyptique', *Anthropologie* 6: 129–151

Pigeot, N. 1987a. 'Elements d'un modele d'habitation Magdalenienne (Etiolles)',

Bulletin de la Société Préhistorique Française 84(10–12): 358–363

Pigeot, N. 1987b. 'Magdaléniens d'Etiolles: Economie et débitage et organisation sociale (L'Unite d'Habitation U5)'. *Supplément à Gallia Préhistoire XXV*, pp. 9–157.

Pigeot, N. 1990. 'Technical and social actors: Flintknapping specialists at Magdalenian Etiollles', *Archaeological Review from Cambridge* 9(1): 126–141

Pigeot, N. 1991. 'Reflexions sur l'histoire technique de l'homme: De l'évolution cognitive à l'évolution culturelle', *Paléo* 3: 167–200

Piprani, J. 2011. 'Material culture, behavior, and identity: The human body as experiential nexus', *Time and Mind: The Journal of Archaeology, Consciousness and Culture* 4(3): 325–336

Pirie, A., Mellars, P. A. and Mithen, S. J. 2006. 'Cnoc Coig: a Mesolithic shell midden assemblage', *Lithics* 27: 4–11

Pleurdeau, D. 2006. 'Human technical behavior in the African Middle Stone Age: the lithic assemblage of Porc-Epic Cave (Dire Dawa, Ethiopia)', *African Archaeological Review* 22: 177–197

Plotnik, J. M., de Waal, F. B. M. and Reiss, D. 2006. 'Self-recognition in an Asian Elephant', *Proceedings of the National Academy of Sciences* 103: 17053–17057

Plug, C. 1980. 'The golden section hypothesis', *American Journal of Psychology* 93: 467–487

Pollard, T. 1996. 'Time and tide: Coastal environments, cosmology and ritual practice in early prehistoric Scotland', in Pollard, T. and Morrison, A. (eds.) *The Early Prehistory of Scotland*. Edinburgh: Edinburgh University Press, pp. 198–210

Pollard, T. 2000. 'Risga and the Mesolithic occupation of Scottish Islands', in Young, R. (ed.) *Mesolithic Lifeways: Current Research from Britain and Ireland*. Leicester: University of Leicester, pp. 143–152

Pollard, T., Atkinson, J. and Banks, I. 1996. 'It is the technical side of the work which is my stumbling block: a shell midden site on Risga reconsidered', in Pollard, T. and Morrison, A. (eds.)

The Early Prehistory of Scotland. Edinburgh: Edinburgh University Press, pp. 165–182

Pope, M. 2004. 'Behavioural implications of biface discard: assemblage variability and land-use at the Middle Pleistocene site of Boxgrove', in Walker, E., Wenban-Smith, F. and Healy, F. (eds.) *Lithics in Action*. Oxford: Oxbow Books, Lithics Studies Society Occasional Paper 8: pp. 38–47

Pope, M. and Roberts, M. B. 2005. 'Individuals and artefact scatters at Boxgrove', in Gamble, C. S. and Porr, M. (eds.) *The Hominid Individual in Context*. Abingdon: Routledge, pp. 81–97

Pope, M., Roberts, M. B., Maxted, A. and Jones, P. 2009. 'The Valdoe: archaeology of a locality within the Boxgrove palaeolandscape, West Sussex', *Proceedings of the Prehistoric Society* 75: 239–263

Pope, M., Russel, K. and Watson, K. 2006. 'Biface form and structured behaviour in the Acheulean', *Lithics* 27: 44–57

Porr, M. 2001. 'Between Nyae Nyae and Anaktuvuk – Some remarks on the use of anthropology in Palaeolithic archaeology', *Ethnographisch-Archäologische Zeitschrift* 42: 159–173

Porr, M. 2002. *Reflections of Human Beings. The Aurignacian Art of Central Europe*. University of Southampton: Unpublished Ph.D. Thesis

Porr, M. 2005. 'The making of the biface and the making of the individual', in Gamble, C. S. and Porr, M. (eds.) *The Hominid Individual in Context. Archaeological Investigations of Lower and Middle Palaeolithic Landscapes, Locales and Artefacts*. Abingdon: Routledge, pp. 68–80

Porr, M. 2010a. 'The Hohle Fels "Venus": Some remarks on animals, humans and metaphorical relationships in Early Upper Palaeolithic art', *Rock Art Research* 27(2): 147–159

Porr, M. 2010b. 'Identifying behavioural modernity: Lessons from Sahul', *Bulletin of the Indo-Pacific Prehistory Association* 30: 28–34

Porr, M. 2010c. 'Palaeolithic art as cultural memory. A case study of the Aurignacian art of Southwest Germany', *Cambridge Archaeological Journal* 20(1): 87–108

Porr, M. 2011. 'One step forward, two steps back: The issue of "behavioral modernity" again: A comment on Shea', *Current Anthropology* 52(4): 581–582

Porr, M. and Bell, H. R. 2012. '"Rock-art", "animism" and two-way thinking: Towards a complementary epistemology in the understanding of material culture and 'rock-art' of hunting and gathering people', *Journal of Archaeological Method and Theory* 19: 161–205

Potts, R. 1983. 'Foraging for faunal resources by Early Hominids at Olduvai Gorge, Tanzania', in Clutton-Brock, J. and Grigson, C. (eds.) *Animals and Archaeology 1: Hunters and their prey.* Oxford: British Archaeological Reports International Series 163, pp. 51–62

Potts, R. 1988. *Early Hominid Activities at Olduvai.* New York: Aldine de Gruyter

Potts, R. 2004. 'Paleoenvironmental basis of cognitive evolution in great apes', *American Journal of Primatology* 62: 209–228

Potts, R., Behrensmeyer, A. K. and Ditchfield, P. 1999. 'Paleolandscape variation and Early Pleistocene hominid activities: Members 1 and 7, Olorgesailie Formation, Kenya', *Journal of Human Evolution* 37: 747–788

Povinelli, D. J., Gallup, G. G., Eddy, T. J., Bierschwale, D. T., Engstrom, M. C., Perilloux, H. K. and Toxopeus, I. B. 1997. 'Chimpanzees recognize themselves in mirrors', *Animal Behaviour* 53: 1083–1088

Praslov N. 1985. 'L'art du Paléolithique supérieur à l'Est de l'Europe', *L'Anthropologie* 89: 181–192

Praslov, N. D. 1993. 'Eine neue Frauenstatuette aus Kalkstein von Kostenki I (Don, Russland)', *Archäologisches Korrespondenzblatt* 23: 165–173

Preece, R. 1990. 'The molluscan fauna of the Middle Pleistocene interglacial deposits at Little Oakley, Essex, and its environmental and stratigraphical implications', *Philosophical Transactions of the Royal Society of London B – Biological Sciences* 328: 387

Preece, R. C. (ed.) 1995. *Island Britain: A Quaternary perspective.* London: Geological Society Special Publication 96

Preece, R. C., Gowlett, J. A. J., Parfitt, S. A., Bridgland, D. R. and Lewis, S. G. 2006. 'Humans in the Hoxnian: habitat, context and fire use at Beeches Pit, West Stow, Suffolk, UK', *Journal of Quaternary Science* 21: 485–496

Preece, R. C. and Parfitt, S. A. 2012. 'The Early and early Middle Pleistocene context of human occupation and lowland glaciation in Britain and northern Europe', *Quaternary International* 271: 6–28

Preece R. C., Parfitt S. A., Bridgland D. R., Lewis S. G., Rowe P. J., Atkinson T. C., Candy I., Debenham N. C., Penkman K. E. H., Rhodes E. J. Schwenninger, J.-L., Griffths, H. I., Whittaker, J. E. and Gleed-Owen, C. 2007. 'Terrestrial environments during MIS 11: evidence from the Palaeolithic site at West Stow, Suffolk, UK', *Quaternary Science Reviews* 26: 1236–1300

Preece, R. C., Parfitt, S. A., Coope, G. R., Penkman, K. E. H., Ponel, P. and Whittaker, J. E. 2009. 'Biostratigraphic and aminostratigraphic constraints on the age of the Middle Pleistocene glacial succession in North Norfolk, UK', *Journal of Quaternary Science* 24: 557–580

Premack, D. and Woodruff, G. 1978. 'Does the chimpanzee have a theory of mind?' *The Behavioural and Brain Science* 4: 515–526

Price, T. D. 2000, *Europe's First Farmers.* Cambridge: Cambridge University Press

Qu, T., Bar-Yosef, O., Wang, Y. and Wu, X. 2013. 'The Chinese Upper Palaeolithic: Geography, chronology and typo-technology', *Journal of Archaeological Research* 15(1): 1–73

Pyne S. J. 1982. *Fire in America: A Cultural History of Wildland and Rural Fire.* Princeton, NJ: Princeton University Press

Ragir, S. and Brooks, P. J. 2012. 'The key to cultural innovation lies in the group dynamic rather than in the individual mind. (Open Peer Commentary)', *Behavioral and Brain Sciences* 35(4): 237–238

Randsborg, K. 2002. *Kephallénia. Archaeology and History. The Ancient Greek Sites.* Kobenhavn: Blackwell/Munksgaard

Read, D. 1987. 'Foraging society organisation: A simple model of a complex transition', *European Journal of Operational Research* 30: 230–236

Read, D. 1990. 'The utility of mathematical constructs in building archaeological theory', in Voorips, A. (ed.) *Mathematics and Information Science in Archaeology: A Flexible Framework*. Bonn: Helos, pp. 29–60

Read, D. 1998. 'Kinship based demographic simulation of societal processes', *Journal of Artificial Societies and Social Simulation* 1(1): http://jasss.soc.surrey.ac.uk/1/1/1.html

Read, D. 2001. 'What is kinship?' in Feinberg, R. and Ottenheimer, M. (eds.) *The Cultural Analysis of Kinship: The Legacy of David Schneider and Its Implications for Anthropological Relativism*. Urbana: University of Illinois Press, pp. 78–117

Read, D. 2007. 'Kinship theory: A paradigm shift'. *Ethnology* 46: 329–364

Read, D. 2008. 'Working memory: A cognitive limit to non-human primate recursive thinking prior to hominid evolution', *Evolutionary Psychology* 6: 603–643

Read, D. 2010a. 'Agent-based and multi-agent simulations: Coming of age or in search of an identity?' *Computational and Mathematical Organisation Theory* 16: 329–347

Read, D. 2010b. 'From experiential-based to relational-based forms of social organisation: A major transition in the evolution of Homo sapiens', in Dunbar, R. I. M., Gamble, C. and Gowlett, J. (eds.) *Social Brain, Distributed Mind*. Oxford: Oxford University Press, pp. 190–230

Read, D. 2012. *How Culture Makes Us Human: Primate Social Evolution and the Formation of Human Societies*. Walnut Creek, CA: Left Coast Press

Read, D., Lane, D. and van der Leeuw, S. E. 2009. 'The innovation innovation', in Lane, D. Pumain, D., van der Leeuw, S. and West, G. (eds.) *Complexity Perspectives in Innovation and Social Change*. Berlin: Springer Verlag, pp. 43–84

Read, D. and LeBlanc, S. 2003. 'Population growth, carrying capacity, and conflict', *Current Anthropology* 44: 59–85

Read, D. and van der Leeuw, S. E. 2008. 'Biology is only part of the story...' *Philosophical Transactions of the Royal Society B – Biological Sciences* 363(1499): 1959–1968

Reader, S. M. and Laland, K. N. 2002. 'Social intelligence, innovation, and enhanced brain size in primates', *Proceedings of the National Academy of Sciences* 99: 4436–4441

Regert, M., Vacher, S., Moulherat, C. and Decavallas, O. 2003. 'Adhesive production and pottery function during the Iron Age at the site of Grand Aunay (Sarthe, France)', *Archaeometry* 45(1): 101–120

Reich, D., Green, R. E., Kircher, M., Krause, J., Patterson, N., Durand, E. Y., Viola, B., Briggs, A. W., Stenzel, U., Johnson, P. L. F., Tomislav Maricic, T., Good, J. M. M.-B., T., Alkan, C., Fu, Q., Mallick, S., Li, H., Meyer, M., Eichler, E. E., Stoneking, M., Richards, M., Talamo, S., Shunkov, M., Derevianko, A. P., Hublin, J.-J., Kelso, J., Slatkin, M. and Pääbo, S. 2010. 'Genetic history of an archaic hominin group from Denisova Cave in Siberia', *Nature* 468: 1053–1060

Reisch, L. 1976. 'Beobachtungen an Vogelknochen aus der Spätplaistozen der Höhle von Kephalari', *Archaologische Korespondezblatt* 6: 261–265

Reiss, D. and Marino, L. 2001. 'Mirror self-recognition in the bottlenose dolphin: A case of cognitive convergence', *Proceedings of the National Academy of Sciences of the United States of America* 98: 5937–5942

Rendu, W., Costamagno, S., Meignen, L. and Soulier, M.-C. 2012. 'Monospecific faunal spectra in Mousterian contexts: Implications for social behavior', *Quaternary International* 247(9): 50–58

Renfrew, C. 1972. *The Emergence of Civilisation: The Cyclades and the Aegean in the Third Millenium* BC. London: Methuen and Co Ltd.

Renfrew C. 1998. *Archaeology and Language. The puzzle of Indo-European origin*. London: Pimlico

Renfrew, C. 2004. 'Towards a theory of material engagement', in Demarrais, E.,

Gosden, C. and Renfrew, C. (eds.) *Rethinking Materiality*. Cambridge: McDonald Archaeological Insititute, pp. 23–32

Renfrew, C., Frith, C. and Malafouris, L. (eds.) 2009. *The Sapient Mind: Archaeology Meets Neuroscience*. Oxford: Oxford University Press

Reynolds, P. C. 1993. 'The complementation theory of language and tool use', in Gibson, K. R. and Ingold, T. (eds.) *Tools, Language and Cognition in Human Evolution*. Cambridge: Cambridge University Press, pp. 407–428

Rice, P. C. 1981. 'Prehistoric Venuses: Symbols of motherhood or womanhood?' *Journal of Anthropological Research* 37: 402–414

Rice, P. M. 1999. 'On the origins of pottery', *Journal of Archaeological Method and Theory* 6(1): 1–54

Richards, M. P. 2007. 'Diet shift at the Middle/Upper Palaeolithic Transition in Europe? The stable isotope evidence', in Roebroeks, W. (ed.) *Guts and Brains: An Integrative Approach to the Hominin Record*. Leiden: Leiden University Press, pp. 223–234

Richards, M., Harvati, K., Grimes, V., Smith, C., Smith, T., Hublin, J.-J., Karkanas, P. and Panagopoulou, E. 2008. 'Strontium isotope evidence of Neanderthal mobility at the site of Lakonis, Greece using laser-ablation PIMMS', *Journal of Archaeological Science* 35: 1251–1256

Richards, M. P., Pettitt, P. B., Stiner, M. and Trinkaus, E. 2001. 'Stable isotope evidence for increasing dietary breadth in the European mid-Upper Paleolithic', *Proceedings of the National Academy of Sciences* 98(11): 6528–6532

Richman, H. B. and Gobet, F. 1996. 'Perceptual and memory processes in the acquisition of expert performance: the EPAM Model', in Ericcson, K. A. (ed.) *The Road to Excellence: The Acquisition of Expert Performance in the Arts and Sciences, Sports and Games*. New Jersey: Lawrence Erlbaum Associates, pp. 167–187

Riek, G. 1934. *Die Eiszeitjägerstation am Vogelherd im Lonetal. Erster Band: Die Kulturen*. Tübingen: Akademische Verlagsbuchhandlung Franz F. Heine

Rink, W. J., Schwarcz, H. P., Smith, F. H. and Radovčić, J. 1995. 'ESR ages for Krapina hominids', *Nature* 378: 24

Roberts, M. B. and Parfitt, S. A. 1999a. *Boxgrove. A Middle Pleistocene Hominid Site at Eartham Quarry, Boxgrove, West Sussex*. London: English Heritage

Roberts, M. B. and Parfitt, S. A. 1999b. 'Biostratigraphy and summary', in Roberts, M. B. and Parfitt, S. A. (eds.) *Boxgrove. A Middle Pleistocene Hominid Site at Eartham Quarry, Boxgrove, West Sussex*. London: English Heritage, pp. 303–307

Roberts, M. B. 1999. 'Flintwork from other contexts', in Roberts, M. B. and Parfitt, S. (eds.) *Boxgrove. A Middle Pleistocene Hominid Site at Eartham Quarry, Boxgrove, West Sussex*. London: English Heritage, pp. 378–384

Roberts, M. B. and Parfitt, S. A. (eds.) 1999. *Boxgrove: A Middle Palaeolithic Pleistocene Hominid Site at Eartham Quarry, Boxgrove, West Sussex*. London: English Heritage

Roberts, M. B., Stringer, C. B. and Parfitt, S. A. 1994. 'A hominid tibia from Middle Pleistocene deposits at Boxgrove, UK', *Nature* 369: 311–313

Roberts, S. G. B. 2010. 'Constraints on social networks', in Dunbar, R. Gamble, C. and Gowlett, J. (eds.) *Social Brain, Distributed Mind*. Oxford: Oxford University Press/The British Academy, pp. 115–134

Robson, A. J. and Kaplan, H. S. 2003. 'The Evolution of human life expectancy and intelligence in hunter-gatherer economies'. *The American Economic Review* 93(1): 150–169

Robson, A. J. and Kaplan, H. S. 2006. 'Viewpoint: the economics of hunter gatherer societies and the evolution of human intelligence'. *Canadian Journal of Economics* 39(2): 375–398

Rodríguez, J., Burjachs, F., Cuenca-Bescós, G., García, N., Van der Made, J., Pérez González, A., Blain, H. A., Expósito, I., López-García, J. M., García Antón, M., Allué, E., Cáceres, I., Huguet, R., Mosquera, M., Ollé, A.,

Rosell, J., Parés, J. M., Rodríguez, X. P., Díez, C., Rofes, J., Sala, R., Saladié, P., Vallverdú, J., Bennasar, M. L., Blasco, R., Bermúdez de Castro, J. M. and Carbonell, E. 2011. 'One million years of cultural evolution in a stable environment at Atapuerca (Burgos, Spain)', *Quaternary Science Reviews* 30: 1396–1412

Rodseth, L., Wrangham, R. W., Harrigan, A. M. and Smuts, B. B. 1991. 'The human community as a primate society', *Current Anthropology* 32: 221–254

Roe, D. A. 1968a. 'British Lower and Middle Palaeolithic handaxe groups', *Proceedings of the Prehistoric Society* 34: 1–82

Roe, D. A. 1968b. 'A Gazetteer of British Lower and Middle Palaeolithic Sites', *Council for British Archaeology* 8: 355

Roe, D. 1981. *The Lower and Middle Palaeolithic Periods in Britain*. London: Routledge and Kean Paul

Roe, D. 2001. 'The Kalambo Falls large cutting tools: a comparative metrical and statistical analysis', in Clark, J. D. (ed.) *Kalambo Falls Prehistoric Site: Volume III*. Cambridge: Cambridge University Press, pp. 492–599

Roe, H. M., Coope, G. R., Devoy, R. J., Harrison, C. J., Penkman, K. E., Preece, R. C. and Schreve, D. C. 2009. 'Differentiation of MIS 9 and MIS 11 in the continental record: vegetational, faunal, aminostratigraphic and sea-level evidence from coastal sites in Essex, UK', *Quaternary Science Reviews* 28: 2342–2373

Roebroeks, W. 2006. 'The human colonisation of Europe: where are we?' *Journal of Quaternary Science* 21: 425–436

Roebroeks, W., Connard, N. J. and van Kolfschoten, T. 1992. 'Dense forests, cold steppes, and the Palaeolithic settlement of Northern Europe', *Current Anthropology* 33: 551–586

Roebroeks, W., Hublin, J.-J. and MacDonald, K. 2011. 'Continuities and discontinuities in Neanderthal presence: a closer look at northwestern Europe', in Ashton, N., Lewis, S. and Stringer, C. (eds.) *The Ancient Human Occupation of Britain*. Amsterdam: Elsevier, pp. 113–123.

Roebroeks, W. 2001. 'Hominid behaviour and the earliest occupation of Europe: an exploration', *Journal of Human Evolution* 41(5): 437–461

Roebroeks, W. 2005. 'Archaeology: Life on the Costa del Cromer', *Nature* 438: 921–922

Roebroeks, W. 2006. 'The human colonisation of Europe. Where are we?' *Journal of Quaternary Science* 21: 425–435

Roebroeks W. 2007. 'Building blocks from an old brickyard', *Quaternary Science Reviews* 26: 1194–1196

Roebroeks W., Conard N. J. and van Kolfschoten T. 1992. 'Dense forests, cold steppes and the Palaeolithic settlement of Northern Europe', *Current Anthropology* 33(5): 551–586

Roebroeks W., Hublin J.-J. and MacDonald K. 2011. 'Continuities and discontinuities in Neanderthal presence: A closer look at Northwestern Europe', in Ashton, N. M., Lewis, S. G. and Stringer, C. B. (eds.) *The Ancient Human Occupation of Britain*. Amsterdam: Elsevier, pp. 113–123

Roebroeks, W., Mussi, M., Svoboda, J. and Fennema, K. (eds.) 1999. *Hunters of the Golden Age. The Mid-Upper Palaeolithic of Eurasia 30,000–20,000 BP*. Leiden: Leiden University Press

Roebroeks, W. and Tuffreau, A. 1999. 'Palaeoenvironment and settlement patterns of the Northwest European Middle Palaeolithic', in Roebroeks, W. and Gamble, C. (eds.) *The Middle Palaeolithic Occupation of Europe*. Leiden: University of Leiden, pp. 121–138

Roebroeks, W. and van Kolfschoten, T. (eds.) 1995. *The Earliest Occupation of Europe*. Leiden: University of Leiden

Roebroeks W. and Verpoorte A. 2009. 'A "language-free" explanation for differences between the European Middle and Upper Paleolithic Record', in Botha, R. and Knight, C. (eds.) *The Cradle of Language*. New York: Oxford University Press, pp. 150–166

Roebroeks, W. and Villa, P. 2011a. 'On the earliest evidence for habitual use of fire in Europe', *Proceedings of the National Academy of Sciences* 108(13): 5209–5214 and supporting materials

Roebroeks W. and Villa P. 2011b. 'Reply to Sandgathe et al.: Neanderthal use of fire', *Proceedings of the National Academy of Sciences* 108(29): E299

Rogachev, A.N. 1955. 'Pogrebenie drevnekamennogo veka na stoyanke Kostenki XIV (Markina Gora)', *Sovetskaya Etnografiya* 1955: 29–38

Rolland N. 2004. 'Was the emergence of home bases and domestic fire a punctuated event? A review of the Middle Pleistocene record in Eurasia', *Asian Perspectives* 43(2): 248–280

Rondoyanni, T., Mettos, A. and Georgiou, C. 1995. 'Geological-morphological observations in the greater Oitilo-Diros area, Mani', *Acta Anthropologika* 1: 93–102

Ronen, A. (ed.) 1982. *The Transition from the Lower to Middle Palaeolithic and the Origins of Modern Man*. Oxford: British Archaeological Reports International Series 151.

Rosas, A., Martínez-Maza, C., Bastira, M., García-Tabernero, A., Lalueza-Fox, C., Huguete, R., Ortiz, J. E., Julià, R., Soler, V., de Torres, T., Martínez, E., Cañaveras, J. C., Sánchez-Moral, S., Cuezva, S., Lario, J., Santamaría, D., de la Rasilla, M. and Fortea, J. 2006. 'Paleobiology and comparative morphology of a late Neanderthal sample from El Sidrón, Asturias, Spain', *Proceedings of the National Academy of Sciences (USA)* 103(51): 19266–19271

Rose, S. 2005. *Lifelines. Life beyond the Gene*. London: Vintage

Rosenfeld, A. 1977. 'Profile figures: Schematisation of the human figure in the Magdalenian culture of Europe', in Ucko, P. J. (ed.) *Form in Indigenous Art*. London: Duckworth, pp. 90–109

Rossano, M. J. 2010a. 'Making friends, making tools, and making symbols', *Current Anthropology* 51/S1. *Working memory: beyond language and symbolism*, Wenner-Gren Symposium Supplement 1: S89–98

Rossano, M. J. 2010b. *Supernatural Selection: How Religion Evolved*. Oxford: Oxford University Press

Rots, V. 2002. '*Hafting traces on flint tools: possibilities and limitations of macro- and microscopic approaches*'. Katholieke Universiteit, Leuven: Unpublished Ph.D. Thesis

Rots, V. 2003. 'Towards an understanding of Hafting: the macro- and microscopic evidence', *Antiquity* 77(298): 805–815

Rots, V. 2013. 'Insights into early Middle Palaeolithic tool use and hafting in Western Europe. The functional analysis of level IIa of the early Middle Palaeolithic site of Biache-Saint-Vaast (France)', *Journal of Archaeological Science* 40(1): 497–506

Rots, V. and Williamson, B. S. 2004. 'Microwear and residue analyses in perspective: the contribution of ethnoarchaeological evidence', *Journal of Archaeological Science* 31: 1287–1299

Rots, V. and Van Peer, P. 2006. 'Early evidence of complexity in lithic economy: core-axe production, hafting and use at Late Middle Pleistocene site 8-B-11, Sai Island (Sudan)', *Journal of Archaeological Science* 33: 360–371

Roussot A. 2000. *La Vénus à la corne et Laussel*. Paris: Editions du Sud Ouest

Roux, V., Bril, B. and Dietrich, G. 1995. 'Skills and learning difficulties involved in stone tool technology', *World Archaeology* 27(1): 63–87

Runnels, C. 1996. 'The Palaeolitic and Mesolithic remains', in Wells, B. and Runnels, C. (eds.) *The Berbati-Limnes archaeological survey 1988–1990*. Stockholm, Acta Instituti Atheniensis Regni Sueciae, Series in 4°, XLIV, pp. 23–35

Runnels, C., Andreou, S., Kotsakis, K. and van Andel T. H. Unpublished report. 'Early prehistoric finds from the Langadas regional survey (Macedonia, Northern Greece)'.

Runnels, C., Karimali, E. and Cullen, B. 2003. 'Early Upper Palaeolithic Spilaion: An artifact-rich surface site', in Wiseman, J. and Zachos, K. (eds.) *Landscape archaeology in Southern Epirus, Greece I*. Hesperia Supplement 32. Princeton: The American School of Classical Studies at Athens, pp. 135–156

Runnels, C., Muzafer Korkuti, M., Galaty, M. L., Timpson, M. E., Sharon R. Stocker, S. R., Davis, J. L., Bejko, L. and Muçaj, S. 2009. 'Early prehistoric landscape and landuse in the Fier region of Albania'. *Journal of Mediterranean Archaeology* 22(2): 151–182

Runnels, C. and Özdoğan, M. 2001. 'The Palaeolithic of the Bosporus region,

NW Turkey', *Journey of Field Archaeology* 28(1–2): 69–92

Runnels, C. and van Andel, T. H. 1993. 'The Lower and Middle Palaeolithic of Thessaly, Greece', *Journal of Field Archaeology* 20(3): 299–317

Runnels, C. and van Andel, T. H. 2003. 'The Early Stone Age of the nomos of Preveza: Landscape and settlement', in J. Wiseman and K. Zachos (eds.) *Landscape archaeology in Southern Epirus, Greece I.* Hesperia Supplement 32. Princeton: The American School of Classical Studies at Athens, pp. 47–133

Rupert, R. 2009. *Cognitive Systems and the Extended Mind.* Oxford: Oxford University Press

Russell, M. 1987. 'Mortuary practice at the Krapina Neanderthal site', *American Journal of Physical Anthropology* 72: 381–397

Sahlins, M. 2011. 'What kinship is (part one)', *Journal of the Royal Anthropological Institute* 17: 2–19

Sampson, A., Kaczanowska, M. and Kozłowski, J. K. 2010. *The prehistory of the island of Kythnos (Cyclades, Greece) and the Mesolithic settlement at Maroulas.* Kraków: The Polish Academy of Arts and Sciences. The University of the Aegean.

Sandgathe, D., Dibble, H. L., Goldberg, P. and McPherron, S. 2011. 'The Roc de Marsal Neanderthal child: a reassessment of its status as a deliberate burial', *Journal of Human Evolution* 61: 243–253

Sandgathe D. M., Dibble H. L., Goldberg P., McPherron S. P., Turq A., Niven L. and Hodgkins J. 2011. 'Timing of the appearance of habitual fire use', *Proceedings of the National Academy of Sciences* 108 (29): E298

Sandgathe, D. M. and Hayden, B. 2003. 'Did Neanderthals eat inner bark?' *Antiquity* 77: 709–718

Sano, K. 2007. 'Emergence and mobility of microblade industries in the Japanese Islands', in Kuzmin, Y. V., Keates, S. G. and Shen, C. (eds.) *Origin and Spread of Microblade Technology in Northeastern Asia and North America.* Simon Fraser University, Burnaby, B.C: Archaeology Press, pp. 79–90

Saragusti, I., Sharon, I., Katzenelson, O. and Avnir, D. 1998. 'Quantitative analysis of the symmetry of artefacts. Lower Paleolithic handaxes', *Journal of Archaeological Science* 25: 817–825

Sartwell, C. 2003. 'Aesthetics of the everyday', in Levinson, J. (ed.) *The Oxford Handbook of Aesthetics.* Oxford: Oxford University Press, pp. 763–776

Sato, H. and Tsutsumi, T. 2007. 'The Japanese microblade industries: Technology, raw material procurement, and adaptations', in Kuzmin, Y. V., Keates, S. G. and Shen, C. (eds.) *Origin and Spread of Microblade Technology in Northeastern Asia and North America.* Simon Fraser University, Burnaby, B.C: Archaeology Press, pp. 53–78

Saville, A., Hardy, K., Miket, R. and Ballin, T. B. 2012. 'An Corran, Staffin, Skye: A rockshelter with Mesolithic and later occupation', *Scottish Archaeological Internet Reports* 51: http://www.sair.org.uk/SAIR_51 (accessed 26 January 2011)

Sayles, J. S. and Mulrennan, M. E. 2010. 'Securing a future: Cree hunters' resistance and flexibility to environmental changes, Wemindji, James Bay', *Ecology and Society* 15: 22

School of Archaeology and Museology of Peking University and Zhengzhou Municipal Institute of Archaeology. 2011. 'The preliminary results of the excavations of the Lijiagou site, Xinmi City', *Kao Gu (Archaeology)* 4: 1–13 (in Chinese)

Schick, K. D. 1987. 'Modeling the formation of Early Stone Age artifact concentrations', *Journal of Human Evolution* 16: 789–807

Schreier, A. L. and Grove, M. 2010. 'Ranging patterns of hamadryas baboons: random walk analyses', *Animal Behaviour* 80: 75–87

Schreier, A. L. and Swedell, L. 2009. 'The fourth level of social structure in a multilevel society: Ecological and social functions of clans in Hamadryas baboons', *American Journal of Primatology* 71: 948–955

Schreve, D. 1997. *Mammalian biostratigraphy of the later Middle Pleistocene in Britain.* University of London: Unpublished Ph.D. Thesis

Schreve, D. C. 2001a. 'Differentiation of the British late Middle Pleistocene interglacials: the evidence from mammalian biostratigraphy', *Quaternary Science Reviews* 20: 1693–1705

Schreve, D. C. 2001b. 'Mammalian evidence from Middle Pleistocene fluvial sequences for complex environmental change at the oxygen isotope substage level', *Quaternary International* 79: 65–74

Schreve, D. C. 2006. 'The taphonomy of a Middle Devensian (MIS3) vertebrate assemblage from Lynford, Norfolk, UK, and its implications for Middle Palaeolithic subsistence strategies', *Journal of Quaternary Science* 21(5): 543–556

Schreve, D. C., Bridgland, D. R., Allen, P., Blackford, J. J., Gleed-Owen, C. P., Griffiths, H. I., Keen, D. H. and White, M. J. 2002. 'Sedimentology, palaeontology and archaeology of late Middle Pleistocene River Thames terrace deposits at Purfleet, Essex, UK', *Quaternary Science Reviews* 21: 1423–1464

Schulting, R. J. and Richards, M. P. 2000. 'The use of stable isotopes in studies of subsistence and seasonality in the British Mesolithic', in Young, R. (ed.) *Mesolithic Lifeways: Current Research in Britain and Ireland*. Leicester: Leicester University Department of Archaeology, pp. 55–65

Scott, B. 2010. *Becoming Neanderthals: The Earlier British Middle Palaeolithic*. Oxford: Oxbow Books

Scott, G. R., Gibert, L. and Gibert, J. 2007. 'Magnetostratigraphy of the Orce region (Baza Basin), SE Spain: new chronologies for Early Pleistocene faunas and hominid occupation sites', *Quaternary Science Reviews* 26: 415–435

Semaw, S., Renne, P., Harris, J. W. K., Feibel, C. S., Bernor, R. L., Fesseha, N. and Mowbray, K. 1997. '2.5-million-year-old stone tools from Gona, Ethiopia', *Nature* 385: 333–336

Seong, C. 1998. 'Microblade technology in and adjacent north-east Asia', *Asian Perspectives* 37: 245–278

Seong, C. 2007. 'Late Pleistocene microlithic assemblages in Korea', in Kuzmin, Y.V., Keates, S. G. and Shen, C. (eds.) *Origin and Spread of Microblade Technology in Northeastern Asia and North America*. Simon Fraser University, Burnaby, B.C: Archaeology Press, pp. 103–114

Sennett, R. 1998. *The Corrosion of Character: the Personal Consequences of Work in the New Capitalism*. London: Norton

Sennett, R. 2009. *The Craftsman*. London: Penguin

Serikov, I. B. and Serikova, A. I. 2005. 'The mammoth in the myths, ethnography, and archeology of Northern Eurasia', *Anthropology & Archeology of Eurasia* 43(4): 8–18

Shackleton, N. J. 1987. 'Oxygen isotopes, ice volumes and sea-level', *Quaternary Science Reviews* 6: 183–190

Shackleton, N. J. 2000. 'The 100,000-year Ice-Age cycle identified to lag temperature, carbon dioxide and orbital eccentricity', *Science* 289: 1897–1902

Shackleton N. J., Berger, A and Peltier, W. R. 1991. 'An alternative astronomical calibration of the lower Pleistocene timescale based on ODP Site 677', *Transactions of the Royal Society of Edinburgh* 81: 252–261

Shapiro, L. 2011. *Embodied Cognition*. New York: Routledge

Sharon, G. 2007. *Acheulian Large Flake Industries: Technology, Chronology, and Significance*. Oxford: Archaeopress. British Archaeological Reports International Series 1701

Shaw, C., Davis, T., Trinkhaus, E. and Stock, J. 2013. 'Humeral biomechanics and habitual behavior: Is the humeral rigidity of Neandertals and Upper Palaeolithic moderns unique?' Paper presented at the 2013 European Society for Study of Human Evolution conference, Vienna, 20–22 September 2013

Shea, J. J. 1988. 'Spear points from the Middle Paleolithic of the Levant', *Journal of Field Archaeology* 15: 441–450

Shea, J. J. 2006. 'The origins of lithic projectile point technology: evidence from Africa, the Levant and Europe', *Journal of Archaeological Science* 33: 823–846

Shelley, P. H. 1990. 'Variation in lithic assemblages: an experiment', *Journal of Field Archaeology* 17(2): 187–193

Shen, C. 2007. 'Re-evaluation of micro-blade industries and the Fenghuangling cultural complex in Shandong Penisular, Northern China', in Kuzmin, Y. V., Keates, S. G. and Shen, C. (eds.) *Origin and Spread of Microblade Technology in Northeastern Asia and North America.* Simon Fraser University, Burnaby, B.C: Archaeology Press, pp. 39–52

Shepard, P. (1998). A post-historic primitivism, in J. Gowdy (ed.) *Limited Wants, Unlimited Means. A Reader on Hunter-gatherer Economics and the Environment.* Washington, D.C.: Island Press, pp. 281–325

Shi, J. and Song, Y. 2010. 'Shanxi Jixian Shizitan yizhi dijiu didian fajue jianbao (Preliminary report of excavation at Locality 9 of the Shizitan site cluster in Jixian, Shanxi)', *Kaogu* 10: 7–17 (in Chinese).

Shizitan Archaeology Team. 2002. 'The excavation of the Palaeolithic site, Shizitan (Loc. S14), Ji county, Shanxi province', *Archaeology (Tiayuan)* 4: 1–28 (in Chinese)

Shitzan Archaeology Team. 2010. 'The excavation report at Shizitan, Loc. 9, Ji County, Shanxi Province', *Kao Gu (Archaeology)* 10: 7–17 (in Chinese)

Shotton, F. W., Keen, D. H., Coope, G. R., Currant, A. P., Gibbard, P. L., Aalto, M., Pelgar, S. M. and Robinson, J. E. 1993. 'The Middle Pleistocene deposits of Waverly Wood pit, Warwickshire, England', *Journal of Quaternary Science* 8: 293–325

Siddall, M., Rohling, E. J., Almogi-Labin, A., Hemleben, C., Meischner, D., Schmelzer, I. and Smeed, D. A. 2003. 'Sea level fluctuations during the last glacial cycle', *Nature* 423: 853–858

Sier M. J., Roebroecks W., Bakels C. C., Dekkers M. J., Bruhl E., De Loecker D., Gaudzinski-Windheuser S., Hesse N., Jagich A., Kindler L., Kuijper, W. J., Laurat, T., Mücher, H. J., Penkman, K., Richter, D. And van Hinsbergen, J. J. 2010. 'Direct terrestrial-marine correlation demonstrates surprisingly late onset of the last interglacial in Central and Northwestern Europe', *Quaternary Research* 75(1): 213–218

Sigg, H. and Stolba, A. 1981. 'Home range and daily march in a hamadryas baboon troop', *Folia Primatologica* 36: 40–75

Simmons, I. G. and Innes, J. B. 1987. 'Mid-Holocene adaptations and Later Mesolithic forest disturbance in northern England', *Journal of Archaeological Science* 14: 385–403

Simonton, D. K. 1996. 'Creative expertise: A life-span developmental perspective', in Ericsson, K. A. (ed.) *The Road to Excellence: The Acquisition of Expert Performance in the Arts and Sciences, Sports and Games.* New Jersey: Lawrence Erlbaum Associates, pp. 227–253

Sinclair, A. 2000. 'Constellations of knowledge: Human Agency and Material Affordance in Lithic Technology', in Dobres, M.-A. and Robb, J. E. (ed.) *Agency in Archaeology.* London, Routledge, pp. 196–212

Singer, R., Wymer, J. J., Gladfelter, B. G. and Wolff, R. 1973. 'Excavations of the Clactonian industry at the Golf Course, Clacton-on Sea, Essex', *Proceedings of the Prehistoric Society* 39: 6–74

Sirocko, F., Seelos, K., Schaber, K., Rein, B., Dreher, F., Diehl, M., Lehne, R., Jäger, K., Krbetschek, M. and Degering, D. 'A late Eemian aridity pulse in central Europe during the last glacial inception', *Nature* 436: 833–836

Sloboda, J. A. 1996. 'The acquisition of musical performance expertise: Deconstructing the "talent" account of individual differences in musical expressivity', in Ericcson, K. A. (ed.) *The Road to Excellence: The Acquisition of Expert Performance in the Arts and Sciences, Sports and Games.* New Jersey: Lawrence Erlbaum Associates, pp. 107–126

Smagas, A. 2007. *Human presence in prehistoric habitation in Sithonia.* Aristotle University of Thessaloniki: Unpublished Ph. D. dissertation, volumes 1 and 2

Smith, A. G. 1970. 'The influence of Mesolithic and Neolithic man on British vegetation: a discussion', in Walker, D. and West, R. G. (eds.) *Studies in the Vegetational History of the British Isles.* Cambridge: Cambridge University Press, pp. 81–96

Smith, A. J. 1985. 'A catastrophic origin for the palaeovalley system of the eastern English Channel', *Marine Geology* 64: 65–75

Smith, A. J. 1989. 'The English Channel – by geological design or accident?' *Proceedings of the Geologists' Association* 100: 325–337

Smith, P. E. L. 1966. *Le Solutreen en France*. Bordeaux: Imprimeries Delmas.

Smith, P. E. L. 1973. 'Some thoughts on variations among certain Solutrean artefacts', in Ripoll Perello, E. (ed.) *Estudios Dedicados al Prof. Dr Luis Pericot*. Barcelona: Diputación Provincial, pp. 67–75

Snodgrass, J. J. and Leonard, W. R. 2009. 'Neandertal energetics revisited', *PaleoAnthropology* 2009: 220–237

de Sonneville-Bordes, D. and Perrot, J. 1953. 'Essai d'adaptation des méthodes statistiques au Paléolithique supérieur: Premiers résultats', *Bulletin de la Société Préhistorique Française* 50: 323–333

Soffer, O. 1985. *The Upper Paleolithic of the Central Russian Plain*. Orlando: Academic Press

Soffer, O. 1989. 'Storage, sedentism and the Eurasian Palaeolithic record', *Antiquity* 63: 719–732

Soffer, O. 1997. 'The mutability of Upper Paleolithic art in Central and Eastern Europe: Patterning and significance', in Conkey, M., Soffer, O., Stratmann, D. and Jablonski, N. (eds.) *Beyond Art: Pleistocene Image and Symbol*. San Francisco: California Academy of Sciences/ University of California Press, pp. 239–262

Soffer, O., Adovasio, J. M. and Hyland, D. C. 2000a 'The "Venus" figurines: Textiles, basketry, gender and status in the Upper Paleolthic', *Current Anthropology* 41: 511–536

Soffer, O., Adovasio, J. M. and Hyland, D. C. 2000b. 'The well-dressed "Venus": Women's wear ca. 27,000 BP', *Archaeology, Ethnology and Anthropology of Eurasia* 1: 37–47

Soffer, O., Adovasio, J., Illingworth, J., Amirkhanov, H., Praslov, N. and Street, M. 2000. 'Palaeolithic perishables made permanent', *Antiquity* 74: 812–821

Solecki, R.S.1963. 'Prehistory in Shanidar Valley, northern Iraq', *Science* 139: 179–193

Sordinas, A. 1969. 'Investigations of the prehistory of Corfu during 1964–1966', *Balkan Studies* 10: 393–424

Sorensen, M. V. and Leonard, W. R. 2001. 'Neandertal energetic and foraging efficiency', *Journal of Human Evolution* 40: 483–495

Šovkopljas I. G. 1965. *Mezinskaja stojanka*. Kiev: Isdatel'stvo 'Naukova Dumka'

Speth, J. D. 2004. 'Hunting pressure, subsistence intensification, and demographic change in the Levantine late Middle Palaeolithic', in Goren-Inbar, N. and Speth, J. D. (eds.) *Human Paleoecology in the Levantine Corridor*. Oxford: Oxbow Books, pp. 149–166

Speth, J. D. and Clark, J. L. 2006. 'Hunting and overhunting in the Levantine Late Middle Palaeolithic', *Before Farming* 2006/3

Speth, J. D., Newlander, K., White, A. A., Lemke, A. K. and Anderson, L. E., 2010. 'Early Paleoindian big-game hunting in North America: Provisioning or Politics?' *Quaternary International* XXX: 1–29

Starkes, J. L. and Allard, F. (eds.) 1993. *Cognitive Issues in Motor Expertise*. Amsterdam: North Holland

Starkes, J. L. and Ericsson, K. A. (eds.) 2003. *Expert Performance in Sport: Recent Advances in Research on Sport Expertise*. Champaign, Illinois: Human Kinetics

Starkovich, B. M. 2012. 'Intensification of small game resources at Klissoura Cave 1 (Peloponnese, Greece) from the Middle Paleolithic to Mesolithic', *Quaternary International* 264: 17–31

Steegmann, A. T., Cerny, F. J. and Holliday, T. W. 2002. 'Neandertal cold adaptation: physiological and energetic factors', *American Journal of Human Biology* 14: 566–583

Sternberg, R. 2003. 'WICS as a model of Giftedness', *High Ability Studies* 14(2): 109–137

Sterelny, K. 2011. 'From hominins to humans: how sapiens became behaviourally modern', *Philosophical Transactions of the Royal Society of London B – Biological Sciences* 366(1566): 809–822

Stiner, M. C., Kozłowski, J., Kuhn, S. L., Karkanas, P. and Koumouzelis, M. 2010. 'Klissoura Cave 1 and the Upper Paleolithic of Southern Greece', *Eurasian Prehistory* 7(2): 309–321

Stiner, M. C. and Munro, N. D. 2011. 'On the evolution of diet and landscape during the Upper Paleolithic through Mesolithic at Franchthi Cave (Peloponnese, Greece)', *Journal of Human Evolution* 60(5): 618–636

Stiner M. C., Munro N. D. and Surovell T. A. 2000. 'The tortoise and the hare. Small-game use, the broad-spectrum revolution, and Paleolithic demography', *Current Anthropology* 41(1): 39–73

Stout, D. 2002. 'Skill and cognition in stone tool production: An ethnographic case study from Irian Jaya', *Current Anthropology* 43(5): 693–722

Stout, D. and Chaminade, T. 2009. 'Making tools and making sense: complex, intentional behaviour in human evolution', *Cambridge Archaeological Journal* 19: 85–96

Stout, D. and Chaminade, T. 2012. 'Stone tools, language and the brain in human evolution', *Philosophical Transactions of the Royal Society B – Biological Sciences* 367: 75–87

Stout, D., Toth, N., Schick, K. and Chaminade, T. 2008. 'Neural correlates of Early Stone Age toolmaking: technology, language and cognition in human evolution', *Philosophical Transactions of the Royal Society of London B – Biological Sciences* 363: 1939–1949

Strasser, T. F., Panagopoulou, E., Runnels, C., Murray, P. M., Thompson, N., Karkanas, P., McCoy, F. W. and Wegmann, K. W. 2010. 'Stone Age seafaring in the Mediterranean. Evidence from the Plakias Region for Lower Palaeolithic and Mesolithic habitation of Crete', *Hesperia* 55: 782–802

Strasser, T. F., Runnels, C., Wegmann, K., Panagopoulou, E., McCoy, F., DiGregorio, C., Karkanas, P. and Thompson, N. 2011. 'Dating Lower Palaeolithic sites in south-western Crete, Greece', *Journal of Quaternary Science* 26: 553–560

Straus, L. G. 1986. 'Late Würm adaptive systems in Cantabrian Spain: The case of Eastern Asturias', *Journal of Anthropological Archaeology* 5: 330–368

Straus, L. 1987. 'Review of *The Palaeolithic Settlement of Europe*', *American Journal of Archaeology* 91: 617–618

Stringer, C. B. 2005. *Homo britannicus*. London: Allen Lane

Stringer, C. 2011a. *The Origin of Our Species*. London: Allen Lane

Stringer, C. B. 2011b. 'The changing landscapes of the earliest occupation of Britain and Europe', in Ashton, N. M., Lewis, S. G. and Stringer, C. B. (eds.) *The Ancient Human Occupation of Britain*. Amsterdam: Elsevier, pp. 1–10

Stringer, C. B. 2012. 'The staus of *Homo heidelbergensis* (Schoetensack 1908)', *Evolutionary Anthropology* 21: 101–107

Stringer C. B. and Gamble C. 1993. *In Search of the Neanderthals: Solving the Puzzle of Human Origins*. London/New York: Thames and Hudson

Stringer, C. and Hublin, J.-J. 1999. 'New age estimates for the Swanscombe hominid, and their significance for human evolution', *Journal of Human Evolution* 37: 873–877

Stuart, A. J. 1992. 'The High Lodge mammalian fauna', in Ashton, N. M., Cook, J., Lewis, S. G. and Rose, J. (eds.) *High Lodge: Excavations by G. de G. Sieveking 1962–68 and J. Cook 1988*. London: British Museum Press, pp. 120–123

Suddendorf, T., Addis, D. R. and Corballis, M. C. 2009. 'Mental time travel and the shaping of the human mind'. *Philosophical Transactions of the Royal Society B – Biological Sciences* 364: 1317–1324

Suddendorf, T. and Corballis, M. C. 1997. 'Mental time travel and the evolution of the human mind', *Genetic Social and General Psychology Monographs* 123: 33–167

Suddendorf, T. and Corballis, M. C. 2007. 'Mental time travel across the disciplines: The future looks bright', *Behavioral and Brain Sciences* 30: 335–351

Svensson, A., Andersen, K. K., Bigler, M., Clausen, H. B., Dahl-Jensen, D., Davies, S. M., Johnsen, S. J., Muscheler, R., Rasmussen, S. O., Röthlisberger, R., Steffensen, J. P., Vinther, B. M. 2006. 'The Greenland Ice Core Chronology 2005, 15–42 kyr. Part 2: Comparison to other records', *Quaternary Science Reviews* 35: 3258–3267

Svoboda, J. 1999. 'Environment and Middle Palaeolithic adaptations in eastern Central Europe', in Roebroeks, W. and Gamble, C. (eds.) *The Middle Palaeolithic Occupation of Europe*. Leiden: University of Leiden, pp. 80–92

Svoboda, J. A. 2007. 'Upper Palaeolithic anthropomorphic images of Northern Eurasia', in Renfrew, C. and Morley, I. (eds.) *Image and Imagination*. Cambridge: McDonald Institute Monographs, pp. 57–68

Svoboda, J. 2008a. 'Upper Paleolithic burial area at Předmostí: Ritual and taphonomy', *Journal of Human Evolution* 54: 15–33

Svoboda J. 2008b. 'Upper Paleolithic female figurines of Northern Eurasia', in Svoboda, J. (ed.) *Petřkovice – On Shouldered Points and Female Figurines*. Brno: Academy of Sciences of the Czech Republic, Institute of Archaeology at Brno, pp. 193–223

Swedell, L., Hailemeskel, G. and Schreier, A. 2008. 'Composition and seasonality of diet in wild hamadryas baboons: Preliminary findings from Filoha', *Folia Primatologica* 79: 476–490

Syed, M. 2011. *Bounce: The myth of talent and the power of practice*. London: Fourth Estate

Tactikos, J. C. 2003. 'A re-evaluation of Paleolithic stone tool cutting edge production rates and their implications', in Maloney, N. and Shott, M. J. (eds.) *Lithic Analysis at the Millennium*. London: Institute of Archaeology, UCL, pp. 151–162

Tainter, J. A. 1988. *The Collapse of Complex Societies*. Cambridge: Cambridge University Press

Takahata, Y. 1985. 'Adult male chimpanzees kill and eat a male newborn infant: newly observed intragroup infanticide and cannibalism at Mahale national park, Tanzania', *Folia Primatologica* 44, pp. 161–170

Tang, C. 2000. 'The Upper Palaeolithic of North China: The Xiachuan culture', *Journal of East Asian Archaeology* 2: 37–49

Tattersall, I. 1998. *Becoming Human. Evolution and Human Uniqueness*. New York: Harcourt Brace

Taylor, T. 2006. 'Why the Venus of Willendorf has no face', *Archäologie Österreichs* 17: 26–29

Teleki, G. 1973. 'Group response to the accidental death of a chimpanzee in Gombe National Park, Tanzania', *Folia Primatologia* 20: 81–94

Tennie, C. and Over, H. 2012. 'Cultural intelligence is key to explaining human tool use. (Open Peer Commentary)', *Behavioral and Brain Sciences* 35(4): 243–242

Le Tensorer, J. M. 2006. 'Les cultures acheuléennes et la question de l'emergence de la pensée symbolique chez Homo erectus à partir des données relatives à la forme symétrique et harmonique des bifaces', *Comptes Rendues Palevol* 5(1–2): 127–135

Terberger, T. 1997. *Die Siedlungsbefunde des Magdalénien-Fundplatzes Gönnersdorf. Konzentration III und IV*. Der Magdalénien-Fundplatzes Gönnersdorf 6. Stuttgart: Franz Steiner

Thieme, H. 1999. 'Lower Palaeolithic throwing spears and other wooden implements from Scöningen, Germany', in Ullrich, H. (ed.) *Hominid Evolution: Lifestyles and Strategies*. Edition Archaea, Gelsenkirchen/Schwelm, pp. 383–395

Thieme, H. 2005. 'The Lower Palaeolithic art of hunting. The case of Schöningen 13 II-4, Lower Saxony, Germany', in Gamble, C. and Porr, M. (eds.) *The Hominid Individual in Context: Archaeological investigations of Lower and Middle Palaeolithic landscapes, artefacts and locales*. London: Routledge, pp. 115–132

Thompson, E. P. 1967. 'Time, work-discipline, and industrial capitalism', *Past and Present* 38: 56–97

Thompson, M. E., Kahlenberg, S. M., Gilby, I. C. and Wrangham, R. W. 2007. 'Core area quality is associated with variance in reproductive success among female chimpanzees at Kibale National Park', *Animal Behaviour* 73: 501–512

Thompson, W. G. and Goldstein, S. L. 2005. 'Open-system coral ages reveal persistent suborbital sea-level cycles', *Science* 308: 401–404

Tillet, T. 2001. 'Le Paléolithique Moyen dans les Alpes et le Jura: exploitation de milieu de contraintes d'altitude', in Conard, N. (ed.) *Settlement Dynamics of the Middle Paleolithic and Middle Stone Age*. Tübingen: Kerns, pp. 421–446

Tinner W. and Lotter A. F. 2001, 'Central European vegetation response to abrupt climate change at 8.2 ka', *Geology* 29: 551–554

Tinnes, J. 1994. *Die Geweih-, Elfenbein- und Knochenartefakte der Magdalénienfundplätze Gönnersdorf und Andernach*. University of Cologne: Unpublished Ph.D. thesis

Tixier, J. 1963. *Typologie de l'Epipaléolithique du Maghreb*. Paris: C. R. A. P. E. 2.

Toepfer V. 1958. 'Steingeräte und Palökologie der mittelpleistozänen Fundstelle Rabutz bei Halle (Saale)', *Jahresschrift für Mitteldeutsche Vorgeschichte* 41/42: 140–177

Tomasello, M. and Call, J. 1997. *Primate Social Cognition*. Oxford: Oxford University Press

Tomasello, M. and Call, J. 2008. 'Does the chimpanzee have a theory of mind? 30 years later', *Trends in Cognitive Sciences* 12: 187–192

Tong, Z. 1979. 'On microlithic cultures in north and north-east China', *Kaogu Xuebao* 4: 403–422

Torrence, R. 1983. 'Time budgeting and hunter-gatherer technology', in Bailey, G. N. (ed.) *Hunter-gatherer Economy in Prehistory: A European Perspective*. Cambridge: Cambridge University Press, pp. 11–22

Torrence, R. 1986. *Production and Exchange of Stone Tools: Prehistoric Obsidian in the Aegean*. Cambridge: Cambridge University Press

Torrence, R. 1989. 'Re-tooling: towards a behavioural theory of stone tools', in Torrence, R. (ed.) *Time, Energy and Stone Tools*. Cambridge: Cambridge University Press, pp. 57–66

Toucanne, S., Zaragosi, S., Bourillet, J. F., Cremer, M., Eynaud, F., Van Vliet-Lanoë, B., Penaud, A., Fontanier, C., Turon, J. L., Cortijo, E. and Gibbard, P. L. 2009. 'Timing of massive "Fleuve Manche" discharges over the last 350kyr: insights into the European ice-sheet oscillations and the European drainage network from MIS 10 to 2', *Quaternary Science Reviews* 28: 1238–1256

Tourloukis, V. and Karkanas, P. 2012. 'The Middle Pleistocene archaeological record of Greece and the role of the Aegean in hominin dispersals: new data and interpretations', *Quaternary Science Review* 43: 1–15

Trauth, M. H., Maslin, M. A. and Deino, A. 2005. 'Late Cenozoic moisture history of East Africa', *Science* 309: 2051–2053

Trinkaus, E. 1983. *The Shanidar Neanderthals*. New York: Academic Press

Trinkaus, E. 1995. 'Neanderthal mortality patterns', *Journal of Archaeological Science* 22: 121–142

Trinkaus, E. 2010. 'Late Pleistocene adult mortality patterns and modern human establishment', *Proceedings of the National Academy of Sciences* 108(4): 1267–1271

Trinkaus, E. and Svoboda, J. (eds.) 2006. *Early Modern Humans in Central Europe: The Pavlovian People of Southern Moravia*. Oxford: Oxford University Press

Tryon, C. A. 2006. '"Early" Middle Stone Age lithic technology of the Kapthurin Formation (Kenya)', *Current Anthropology* 47: 367–375

Tryon, C. A. and McBrearty, S. 2002. 'Tephrostratigraphy and the Acheulian to Middle Stone Age transition in the Kapthurin Formation, Kenya', *Journal of Human Evolution* 42: 211–235

Tryon, C. A. and McBrearty, S. 2006. 'Tephrostratigraphy of the Bedded Tuff Member (Kapthurin Formation, Kenya) and the nature of archaeological change in the later middle Pleistocene', *Quaternary Research* 65: 492–507

Tsartsidou, G., Karkanas, P., Marsall, G. and Kyparissi-Apostolika, N. 2014. 'Palaeoenviromental reconstruction and flora exploitation at the Palaeolithic cave of Theopetra, central Greece: the evidence from phytolith analysis'. *Archaeological and Anthropological Sciences*, 1–17. DOI: 10.1007/s12520-014-0183-6

Tuffreau, A., Lamotte, A. and Marcy, J.-L. 1997. 'Land-use and site function in Acheulean complexes of the Somme Valley', *World Archaeology* 29: 225–241

Tulving, E. 1983. *Elements of Episodic Memory*. Oxford: Clarendon Press

Tulving, E. 2002. 'Episodic memory: From mind to brain'. *Annual Review of Psychology* 53: 1–25

Turner C. 2000. 'The Eemian interglacial in the North European plain and adjacent areas', *Geologie en Mijnbouw – Netherlands Journal of Geosciences* 79(2/3): 217–231

Turner, E. 2000a. *Miesenheim I. Excavations at a Lower Palaeolithic Site in the Central Rhineland of Germany*. Mainz: Verlag des Romisch-Germanischen Zentralmuseums

Turner, E. 2000b. 'Summary', in Turner, E. (ed.) *Miesenheim I. Excavations at a Lower Palaeolithic Site in the Central Rhineland of Germany*. Mainz: Verlag des Romisch-Germanischen Zentralmuseums, pp. 138–146

Turq, A. 1999. 'Reflections on the Middle Palaeolithic of the Aquitaine Basin', in Roebroeks, W. and Gamble, C. (eds.) *The Middle Palaeolithic Occupation of Europe*. Leiden: University of Leiden, pp. 107–120

Tzedakis, P. C., Frogley, M. R., Lawson, I. T. Preece, R. C. Cacho, I. and de Abreu, L. 2004. 'Ecological thresholds and patterns of millennia scale climate variability: The response of vegetation in Greece during the last glacial period', *Geological Society of America* 32(2): 109–112

Underhill, D. 2007. 'Subjectivity inherent in by-eye symmetry judgements and the large cutting tools at the Cave of Hearths, Limpopo Province, South Africa', *Papers from the Institute of Archaeology* 18: 1–12

Valladas, H., Mercier, N. Froget, L., Joron, J. J., Reyss, J. L. Karkanas, P., Panagopoulou, E. and Kyparissi-Apostolika N. 2007. 'TL age-estimates for the Middle Palaeolithic layers at Theopetra cave (Greece)', *Quaternary Geochronology* 2: 303–308

Valoch, K. 1969. 'Darstellungen von Mensch und Tier in Předmostí in Mähren', *IPEK* 1966–69: 1–9

Valoch, K. and Láznička-Galetová, M. (eds.) 2009. *Nejstarší umění střední Evropy. [The Oldest Art of Central Europe]. První mezinárodí výstava originálu paleolitického umění. [The First International Exhibition of Original Art from the Palaeolithic]*. Brno: Moravské zemské muzeum.

van Andel, T. H. 2002. 'The climate and landscape of the middle part of the Weichselian Glaciation in Europe', *Quaternary Research* 57(1): 2–8

van Andel, T. H., Davies, W. and Weninger, B. 2003. 'The human presence in Europe during the Last Glacial Period I: Human migration and the changing climate', in van Andel, T. H. and Davies, W. (eds.) *Neanderthals and modern humans in the European landscape during the last glaciation*. Cambridge: McDonald Institute Monographs, pp. 31–56

van der Leeuw, S. E. 1982. 'How objective can we become? Some reflections on the nature of the relationship between the archaeologist, his data and his interpretations', in Renfrew, A. C., Rowlands, M. J. and Segraves, B. A. (eds.) *Theory and Explanation in Archaeology*. New York: Academic Press, pp. 431–457

van der Leeuw, S. E. 2000. 'Making tools from stone and clay', in Anderson, A. and Murray, T. (eds.) *Australian Archaeologist: Collected papers in Honour of Jim Allen*. Coombs, Australia: Coombs Academic Publishing, pp. 69–88

van der Leeuw, S. E. 2007. 'Information processing and its role in the rise of the European world system', in Constanza, R., Graumlich, L. J. and Steffen, W. (eds.) *Sustainability or Collapse?* Dahlem Workshop Reports. Cambridge: MIT Press, pp. 213–241

van der Leeuw, S. E. 2010. 'The archaeology of innovation: Lessons for our times', in Moss, F. and Machover, T. (eds.) *Innovation: Perspectives for the 21st Century*. Madrid: BBVA, pp. 33–53

van der Leeuw, S. E. 2012. 'Global systems dynamics and policy: Lessons from the distant past', *Complexity Economics* 1: 33–60

van der Leeuw, S., Lane, D. and Read, D. 2009. 'The long-term evolution of social organisation', in Lane, D. Pumain, D., van der Leeuw, S. and West, G. (eds.) *Complexity Perspectives on Innovation and Social Change*. Berlin: Springer Verlag, pp. 85–116

Vanhaeren, M. and d'Errico, F. 2006. 'Aurignacian ethno-linguistic geography of Europe revealed by personal ornaments', *Journal of Archaeological Science* 33(8): 1105–1128

Vanhaeren, M. and d'Errico, F. 2007. 'La parure aurignacienne reflet d'unités ethno-culturelles', in Floss, H. and Rouquerol, N. (eds.) *Les chemins de l'art Aurignacien en Europe – Das Aurignacien und die Anfänge der Kunst in Europa*. Aurignac: Éditions Musée-forum Aurignac, pp. 233–248

van Leeuwen R. J. W., Beets D. J., Bosch J. H. A., Burger A. W., Cleveringa P., van Harten D., Herngreen G. F. F., Krug R. W., Langereis C. G., Meijer T. Pouwer, R. and de Wolf, H. 2000. 'Stratigraphy and integrated facies analysis of the Saalian and Eemian sediments in the Amsterdam Terminal borehole, the Netherlands', *Geologie en Mijnbouw – Netherlands Journal of Geosciences* 79: 161–198

van Schaik, C. P. and Pradham, G. R. 2003. 'A model for tool-use traditions in primates: implications for the coevolution of culture and cog', *Journal of Human Evolution* 44: 645–664

Van Zeist W, 1970. Betrekkingen tussen palynologie en vegetatiekunde. In Venema, H.J., Doing, H. and Zonneveld, I. S. (eds.) *Vegetatiekunde als synthetische wetenschap*. Wageningen: Proceedings Symposium LandbouwHogeschool Wageningen, pp. 127–140

Vaquero, M., Chacón, G., Fernández, C., Martínez, K. and Rando, J. M. 2001. 'Intrasite spatial patterning and transport in the Abric Romaní Middle Palaeolithic site (Capellades, Barcelona, Spain)', in Conard, N. (ed.) *Settlement Dynamics of the Middle Paleolithic and Middle Stone Age*. Tübingen: Kerns, pp. 573–595

Vaquero, M., Rando, J. M. and Chacón, G. 2004. 'Neanderthal spatial behaviour and social structure: hearth-related assemblages from the Abric Romaní Middle Paleolithic site', in Conard, N. (ed.) *Settlement Dynamics of the Middle Paleolithic and Middle Stone Age Volume II*. Tübingen: Kerns, pp. 367–392

Vaughan, C. D. 2001. 'A million years of style and function: regional and temporal variation in Acheulean handaxes', in Hurt, T. D. and Rakita, G. F. M. (eds.) *Style and Function: Conceptual Issues in Evolutionary Archaeology*. Westport, CT.: Bergin and Garvey, pp. 141–163

Veil, S. and Plisson, H. 1990. *The elephant kill-site of Lehringen near Verden on Aller, Lower Saxony (Germany)*. Unpublished manuscript in possession of S. Veil, Niedersächsisches Landesmuseum, Hanover, Germany.

Verpoorte, A. 2001. *Places of Art, Traces of Fire. A contextual approach to Anthropomorphic Figurines in the Pavlovian (Central Europe, 29–24 kyr BP)*. Archaeological Studies Leiden University 8. Leiden: Leiden University Press

Verpoorte, A. 2009. 'Limiting factors on early modern human dispersals: The human biogeography of late Pleniglacial Europe', *Quaternary International* 201: 77–85

Villa, P. 1982. 'Conjoinable pieces and site formation processes', *American Antiquity* 47: 276–290

Villa, P., Boscato, P., Ranaldo, F. and Ronchitelli, A. 2009. 'Stone tools for the hunt: points with impact scars from a Middle Palaeolithic site in southern Italy', *Journal of Archaeological Science* 36: 850–859

Villa, P., Soriano, S., Teyssandier, N. and Wurz, S. 2010. 'The Howiesons Poort and MSA III at Klasies River main site, Cave 1A', *Journal of Archaeological Science* 37: 630–655

Viveiros de Castro, E. 1998. 'Cosmological Deixis and Amerindian Perspectivism', *Journal of the Royal Anthropological Institute* 4: 469–488

Voormolen, B. 2008a *Ancient Hunters, Modern Butchers. Schöningen 13II-4, a kill-butchery site dating from the northwest European Lower Palaeolithic*. University of Leiden: Unpublished Ph.D. thesis

Voormolen B. 2008a. 'Ancient hunters, modern butchers. Schöningen 13II-4, a kill-butchery site dating from the Northwest European Lower Palaeolithic', *Journal of Taphonomy* 6(2): 71–247

Vrba, E. S. 1988. 'Late Pliocene climatic events and hominid evolution', in

Grine, F. E. (ed.) *Evolutionary History of the 'Robust' Australopithecines*. New York: Aldine de Gruyter, pp. 405–426

Waddington, C., Bailey, G., Bayliss, A. and Milner, N. 2007. 'Howick in its North Sea context', in Waddington, C. (ed.) *Mesolithic Settlement in the North Sea Basin*. Oxford: Oxbow Books, pp. 203–224

Waddington, C. and Pedersen, K. (eds.) 2007. *Mesolithic Studies in the North Sea Basin and Beyond*. Oxford: Oxbow Books

Wadley, L. 2001. 'What is cultural modernity? A general view and a South African perspective from Rose Cottage Cave', *Cambridge Archaeological Journal* 11(2): 201–221

Wadley, L. 2010. 'Compound adhesive manufacture as a proxy for complex cognition in the Middle Stone Age', *Current Anthropology* 51/S1, *Working memory: beyond language and symbolism*, Wenner-Gren Symposium Supplement 1: S111–S120

Wadley, L., Hodgskiss, T. and Grant, M. 2009. 'Implications for complex cognition from the hafting of tools with compound adhesives in the Middle Stone Age, South Africa', *Proceedings of the National Academy of Sciences* 106(24), 9590–9594

Wadley, L., Williamson, B. and Lombard, M. 2004. 'Ochre in hafting Middle Stone Age southern Africa: a practical role', *Antiquity* 78: 661–675

Waelbroeck, C., Labeyrie, L., Michel, E., Duplessy, J. C., McManus, J. F., Lambeck, K., Balbon, E. and Labracherie, M. 2002. 'Sea-level and deep water temperature changes derived from benthic foraminifera isotopic records', *Quaternary Science Reviews* 21: 295–305

Wagner, G. A., Krbetschek, M., Degering, D., Bahain, J.-J., Shao, Q, Falguères, C., Voinchet, P., Dolo, J. M., Garcia, T, and Rightmire, G. P. 2010. 'Radiometric dating of the type-site for *Homo heidelbergensis* at Mauer, Germany', *Proceedings of the National Academy of Sciences* 107: 19726–19730

Walker, M. J., Gibert, J., López, M. V., Lombardi, A. V., Pérez-Pérez, A., Zapata, J., Ortega, J., Higham, T., Pike, A., Schwenninger, J.-L., Zilhão, J. and Trinkaus, E. 2008. 'Late Neanderthals in southeastern Iberia: Sima de las Palomas del Cabezo Gordo, Murcia, Spain', *Proceedings of the National Academy of Sciences (USA)* 105: 20631–20636

Walker, M. J., Gobert Clols, J., Eastham, A., Rodríguez Estrella, T., Carríon García, J. S., Yll, E. I., Legaz López, A., López Jiménez, A., López Martínez, M. and Romero Sánchez, G. 2004. 'Neanderthals and their landscapes: Middle Palaeolithic land use in the Segura Basin and adjacent areas of southeastern Spain', in Conard, N. (ed.) *Settlement Dynamics of the Middle Paleolithic and Middle Stone Age Volume II*. Tübingen: Kerns, pp. 461–511

Walker, M., Johnsen, S., Rasmussen, S.O., Popp, T. Steffensen, J-P., Gibbard, P., Hoek, W., Lowe, J., Andrews, J., Björck, S., Cwynar, L.C., Hugen, K., Kershaw, P., Kromer, B., Litt, t., Lowe, D.J., Nakagawa, T., Newnham, R. and Schwander, J. 2009. 'Formal definition and dating of the GSSP (Global Stratotype Section and Point) for the base of the Holocene using the Greenland NGRIP ice core, and selected auxiliary records', *Journal of Quaternary Science* 24: 3–17

Walker, M. J., López, M. V., Ortega-Rodigánez, J., Haber-Uriarte, M., López-Jiménez, A., Aviles-Fernández, A., Polo-Camacho, J. L., Campillo-Boj, M., García-Torres, J., Carrión García, J. S., San Nicolás-del Toro, M. and Rodríguez-Estrella, T. 2012. 'The excavation of buried articulated Neanderthal skeletons at Sima de las Palomas (Murcia, SE Spain)'. *Quaternary International* 258: 7–21

Wang, J., Wang, X. and J. Chen, J. 1978. 'Xiachuan Culture: the survey report of Xiachuan sites, Shanxi province', *Journal of Archaeology* 50(3): 259–288 (in Chinese)

Wang X.-K, Wei, J., Chen, Q.-J., Tang, Z.-W. and Wang C.-X. 2010. 'A preliminary study of the excavation of the Jinsitai cave site', *Acta Anthropologica Sininica* 29: 15–32

Wang, Y. 2005. *The Roots of Pleistocene Hominids and Cultures in China*. Beijing: Science Press (in Chinese).

Wang, Y. J., Cheng, H., Edwards, R. L., An, Z. S., Wu, J. Y., Shen, C. and Dorale, J. A. 2001. 'A high-resolution absolute-dated late Pleistocene monsoon record from Hulu Cave, China', *Science* 294: 2345–2348

Warren, G, 2005. *Mesolithic Lives in Scotland*. London: The History Press.

Warren, S. H. 1923. 'The *Elephas-antiquus* bed of Clacton-on-Sea (Essex) and its flora and fauna', *Quarterly Journal of the Geological Society of London* 79: 606–636

Washburn, S. 1982. 'Fifty years of studies on human evolution', *Bulletin of the American Academy of Arts and Sciences* 35: 25–39

Washburn, S. L. and Devore, I. 1961. 'Social behaviour of baboons and early man', in Washburn, S. L. (ed.) *Social Life of Early Man*. Viking Fund Publications in Anthropology, 31. Chicago: University of Chicago Press, pp. 91–105

Weber, C.A. 1920. 'Der Aufbau, die Flora und das Alter des Tonlagers von Rabutz', *Veröffentlichungen des Provinzialmuseums zu Halle Band I, Heft IV*: 1–40

Wehrberger, K. and Reinhardt, B. (eds.) 1994. *Der Löwenmensch. Tier und Mensch in der Kunst der Eiszeit*. Sigmaringen: Thorbecke

Wendorf, F. and Schild, R. 1974. *A Middle Stone Age sequence from the Central Rift Valley, Ethiopia*. Warsaw: Institute for History and Material Culture, Polish National Academy.

Wengrow, D. 2008. 'Prehistories of commodity branding', *Current Anthropology* 49(1): 7–34

Weninger, B. and Jöris, O. 2008. 'A ¹⁴C Age Calibration Curve for the Last 60ka: the Greenland-Hulu U/Th Timescale and its impact on understanding the Middle to Upper Paleolithic Transition in Western Eurasia', in Adler, D. S. and Jöris, O. (eds.) 'Setting the record straight: Toward a systematic chronological understanding of the Middle to Upper Paleolithic Boundary in Eurasia', *Journal of Human Evolution* 55: 772–781

West, F. H. (ed.) 1996. *American Beginnings*. Chicago: University of Chicago Press

Wenban-Smith, F. 2004. 'Handaxe typology and Lower Palaeolithic cultural development: ficrons, cleavers and two giant handaxes from Cuxton', *Lithics* 25: 11–21

Wenban-Smith, F. F. 2007. 'The Palaeolithic archaeology of Kent', in Williams, J. H. (ed.) *The Archaeology of Kent to AD 800*. Woodbridge: The Boydell Press, pp. 25–64

Wenban-Smith, F. F., Gamble, C. S. and Apsimon, A. 2000. 'The Lower Palaeolithic site at Red Barns, Porchester, Hampshire: bifacial technology, raw material quality, and the organisation of archaic behaviour', *Proceedings of the Prehistoric Society* 66: 209–255

Westaway, R. 2009a. 'Quaternary vertical crustal motion and drainage evolution in East Anglia and adjoining parts of southern England: chronology of the Ingham River terrace deposits', *Boreas* 38: 261–284

Westaway, R. 2009b. 'Calibration of decomposition of serine to alaline in *Bithynia opercula* as a quantitative dating technique for Middle and Late Pleistocene sites in Britain', *Quaternary Geochronology* 4: 241–259

Westaway, R. 2011. 'A re-evaluation of the timing of the earliest reported human occupation of Britain: The age of the sediments at Happisburgh, eastern England', *Proceedings of Geologists' Association* 122: 383–396

Westley, F., Olsson, P., Folke, C., Homer-Dixon, Th., Vredenburg, H., Loorbach, D., Thompson, J., Nilsson, M., Lambin, E., Sendzimir, J., Banarjee, B., Galaz, V. and van der Leeuw, S. E. 2011. 'Tipping towards sustainability: Emerging pathways of transformation', *Ambio* 40(7): 762–780

Whallon, R. 2006. 'Social networks and information: Non-"utilitarian" mobility among hunter-gatherers', *Journal of Anthropological Archaeology* 25: 259–270

Wheeler, P.E. 1984. The evolution of bipedality and loss of functional body hair in hominids. *Journal of Human Evolution* 13: 91–98.

Wheeler, P. E. 1991. 'The thermoregulatory advantages of hominid bipedalism in open equatorial environments: the contribution of increased convective heat loss and cutaneous evaporative cooling', *Journal of Human Evolution* 21: 107–115

Wheeler, P. E. 1992. 'The influence of the loss of functional body hair on the water budgets of early hominids', *Journal of Human Evolution* 23: 379–388

White, L. 1959. *The Evolution of Culture*. New York: McGraw-Hill

White, M. and Ashton, N. 2003. 'Lower Palaeolithic core technology and the origins of the Levallois method in northwestern Europe', *Current Anthropology* 44: 598–609

White, M. J. 1998a. 'On the significance of Acheulean biface variability in Southern Britain', *Proceedings of the Prehistoric Society* 64: 15–44

White, M. J. 1998b. 'Twisted Ovate Bifaces in the British Lower Palaeolithic: Some observations and implications', in Ashton, N., Healy, F. and Pettitt, P. (eds.) *Stone Age Archaeology: Essays in honour of John Wymer*. Oxford: Oxbow Monograph 102, Lithic Studies Society Occasional Paper 6, pp. 98–104

White, M. J. 1996. *Biface variability and human behaviour: A case study from southeast England*. University of Cambridge: Unpublished Ph.D. Thesis

White, M. 1997. 'The earlier Palaeolithic occupation of the Chilterns (southern England): re-assessing the sites of Worthington G. Smith', *Antiquity* 71: 912–931

White, M. J. 1998a. 'Twisted ovate bifaces in the British Lower Palaeolithic: some observations and Implications', in Ashton, N. M., Healy, F. and Pettitt, P. B. (eds.) *Stone Age Archaeology: Essays in Honour of John Wymer*. Oxford: Oxbow Books, Lithic Studies Occasional Paper 6, pp. 98–104

White, M. J. 1998b. 'On the significance of Acheulean biface variability in Southern Britain'. *Proceedings of the Prehistoric Society* 64: 15–44

White, M. J. 2000a. 'The Clactonian Question: On the interpretation of core-and-flake assemblages in the British Lower Palaeolithic', *Journal of World Prehistory* 14: 1–63

White, M. J. 2000b. 'Review of Westbury Cave: The Natural History Museum Excavations 1976–1984', in Andrews, P., Cook, J., Currant, A. and Stringer, C. (eds.) 1999. Bristol: WASP. *Proceedings University of Bristol Speleological Society* 22: 115–117

White, M. J. 2006a. 'Things to do in Doggerland when you're dead: surviving OIS3 at the northwestern fringe of Middle Palaeolithic Europe', *World Archaeology* 38: 547–575

White, M. J. 2006b. 'Axeing Cleavers: reflections on broad-tipped large cutting tools in the British Lower and Middle Palaeolithic', in Goren-Inbar, N. and Sharon, G. (eds.) *Axe Age: Acheulean Toolmaking from Quarry to Discard*. Jerusalem: Equinox

White, M. J. and Ashton, N. M. 2003. 'Lower Palaeolithic core technology and the origins of the Levallois method in NW Europe', *Current Anthropology* 44: 598–609

White, M. J., Bridgland, D. R., Ashton, N., McNabb, J. and Berger, M. 1995. 'Wansunt Pit, Dartford Heath (TQ 513737)', in Bridgland, D. R., Allen, P. and Haggart, B. A. (eds.) *The Quaternary of the Lower Reaches of the Thames: Field Guide*. London: Quaternary Research Association, pp. 117–128

White, M. J. and Pettitt, P. P. 1995. 'Technology of early Palaeolithic western Europe: innovation, variability and a unified framework', *Lithics* 16: 27–40

White, M. J. and Pettitt, P. B. 2011. 'The British Late Middle Palaeolithic: an interpretative synthesis of Neanderthal occupation at the northwestern edge of the Pleistocene world', *Journal of World Prehistory* 24(1): 25–97

White, M. J. and Plunkett, S. J. 2004. *Miss Layard Excavates: A Palaeolithic site at Foxhall Road, Ipswich, 1903–1905*. Liverpool: Western Academic & Specialist Press

White, M. J. and Schreve, D. C. 2000. 'Island Britain – Peninsula Britain: Palaeogeography, colonization, and the Lower Palaeolithic settlement of the British Isles', *Proceedings of the Prehistoric Society* 66: 1–28

White, M., Scott, R. and Ashton, N. 2006. 'The Early Middle Palaeolithic in Britain: archaeology, settlement history and human behaviour', *Journal of Quaternary Science* 21: 525–542

White, M. J., Scott, B. and Ashton, N. M. 2011. 'The emergence, diversity and significance of Mode 3 (Prepared Core) Technologies', in Ashton, N., Lewis, S. and Stringer, C. (eds.) *The Ancient Human Occupation of Britain*. Amsterdam: Elsevier, pp. 53–68

White, R. 2006. 'The women of Brassempouy: A century of research and interpretation', *Journal of Archaeological Method and Theory* 13: 251–304

White, T. D. and Toth, N. 1989. 'Engis: preparation damage, not ancient cutmarks', *American Journal of Physical Anthropology* 78: 361–367

Whiten, A. 1996. 'Imitation, pretense, and mindreading: Secondary representation in comparative primatology and developmental psychology?' in Russon, A. E., Bard, K. A. and Taylor Parker, S. (eds.) *Reaching into Thought: The minds of the great apes*. Cambridge: Cambridge University Press, pp. 300–324

Whittle, A. and Cummings, V. (eds.) 2007. *Going Over: The Mesolithic-Neolithic Transition in North-West Europe*. Proceedings of the British Academy 44. Oxford: Oxford University Press

Wickham-Jones, C. R. 1990. *Rhum: Mesolithic and later sites at Kinloch: excavations 1984–1986*. Edinburgh, Society of Antiquaries of Scotland Monograph Series

Wickham-Jones, C. R. and Hardy, K. 2004. 'Camas Daraich: a Mesolithic site at the Point of Sleat, Skye', *Scottish Archaeological Internet Reports* 12: http://www.sair.org.uk/SAIR12 (accessed 26 January 2011).

Wicks, K. 2012. *Vegetation History, Climate Change and Human Impact during Prehistory: An Island Perspective from Tiree, Coll and NW Mull, Inner Hebrides, western Scotland*. University of Reading: Unpublished Ph.D. Thesis

Wiessner, P. 1983. 'Style and social information in Kalahari San Projectilc Points', *American Antiquity* 48: 253–276

Williams, J. P. and Andrefsky, W. 2011. 'Débitage variability among multiple flint knappers', *Journal of Archaeological Science* 38: 865–872

Winner, E. 1996. 'The rage to master: The decisive role of talent in the visual arts', in Ericsson, K. A. (ed.) *The Road to Excellence: The Acquisition of Expert Performance in the Arts and Sciences, Sports and Games*. New Jersey: Lawrence Erlbaum Associates, pp. 271–301

Wobst, H. M. 1974. 'Boundary conditions for Palaeolithic social systems: a simulation approach', *American Antiquity* 39: 147–178

Wobst, H. M. 1977. 'Stylistic behaviour and information exchange', in Cleland, C. E. (ed.) *For the Editor: Research Essays in Honor of James B. Griffin*. Anthropological Papers 61. Ann Arbor: University of Michigan Press

Wolf, S. 2010. Eine neue Venusstatuette vom jungpaläolithischen Fundplatz Dolni Vestonice (Mähren). *Jahrbuch des Römisch-Germanischen Zentralmuseums* 55, 1–40.

Wragg Sykes, R.M. 2012. 'Neanderthals 2.0? Evidence for expanded social networks, ethnic diversity and encultured landscapes in the Late Middle Palaeolithic', in Ruebens, K., Byno, R. and Romanowska, I. (eds.) *Unravelling the Palaeolithic: Ten years of research at the Centre for Archaeology of Human Origins Symposium, 28–29 January 2011, Conference Proceedings*. Southampton: University of Southampton Archaeology Monograph Series

Wu, X., Zhang, C., Goldberg, P., Cohen, D., Yan, P., Arpin, T. and Bar-Yosef, O. 2012. 'Early pottery 20,000 years ago in Xianrendong, China', *Science* 336: 1696–1700

Wüller, B. 1999: *Die Ganzkörperbestattungen des Magdalénien. Universitätsforschungen zur prähistorischen Archäologie* 57. Bonn: Habelt.

Wymer, J. J. 1968. *The Lower Palaeolithic of Britain: as represented by the Thames Valley*. London: John Baker.

Wymer, J. J. 1985. *Palaeolithic Sites of East Anglia*. Norwich: Geo Books

Wymer, J. J. 1988. 'Palaeolithic archaeology and the British Quaternary sequence', *Quaternary Science Reviews* 7: 79–98

Wymer, J. J. 1996. *Regions 7 (Thames) and 10 (Warwickshire Avon). English Rivers Palaeolithic Project Report*. Salisbury: Wessex Archaeology

Wymer, J. J. 1999. *The Lower Palaeolithic Occupation of Britain*. Salisbury: Wessex Archaeology and English Heritage

Wynn T. 2002. 'Archaeology and cognitive evolution', *Behavioral and Brain Sciences* 25: 389–438

Wynn, T. 1979. 'The intelligence of later Acheulean hominids', *Man* 14: 371–391

Wynn, T. 1981. 'The intelligence of Oldowan hominids', *Journal of Human Evolution* 10: 529–541

Wynn, T. 1985. 'Piaget, stone tools and the evolution of human intelligence', *World Archaeology* 17: 32–43

Wynn, T. 1991. 'Tools, grammar and the archaeology of cognition', *Cambridge Archaeological Journal* 1: 191–206

Wynn, T. 1993. 'Layers of thinking in tool behaviour', in Gibson, K. R. and Ingold, T. (eds.) *Tools, Language and Cognition in Human Evolution*. Cambridge: Cambridge University Press, pp. 389–406

Wynn, T. 1995. 'Handaxe enigmas', *World Archaeology* 27: 10–23

Wynn, T. 2004. 'Comments on McNabb et al. 2004. The large cutting tools from the South African Acheulean and the question of social traditions', *Current Anthropology* 45: 653–677

Wynn, T. 2009. 'Hafted spears and the archaeology of mind', *Proceedings of the National Academy of Sciences* 106(24): 9544–9545

Wynn, T. and Coolidge, F. L. 2004. 'The expert Neandertal mind', *Journal of Human Evolution* 46: 467–487

Wynn, T. and Coolidge, F. L. 2010. 'Beyond symbolism and language. An Introduction to Supplement 1', *Working Memory. Current Anthropology* 51/S1, *Working memory: beyond language and symbolism*, Wenner-Gren Symposium Supplement 1: S5–S16

Wynn, T. and Tierson, F. 1990. 'Regional comparison of the shapes of later Acheulean handaxes', *American Anthropologist* 92: 73–84

Xie, F., Li, J. and Liu, L. 2006. *The Palaeolithic of the Nihewan Basin*. Hebei: Huashan Culture Press

Yellen, J. 1977. *Archaeological Approaches to the Present: Models for Reconstructing the Past*. New York: Academic Press

Yi, S. and G. Clark. 1985. 'The "Duktai culture" and new world origins', *Current Anthropology* 26: 1–20

Zagwijn W. H. 1961. 'Vegetation, climate and radiocarbon datings in the late Pleistocene of the Netherlands: Part I. Eemian and Early Weichselian', *Mededelingen van de Geologische Stichting Nieuwe Serie* 14: 15–45

Zagwijn W. H. 1989. 'Vegetation and climate during the warmer intervals in the Late Pleistocene of Western and Central Europe', *Quaternary International* 3–4: 57–67

Zhao, C., Wang, T., Wu, X., Liu, M., Yuan, X., Yu, J. and Gu, J. 2006. 'Donghulin, Zhuannian, Nanzhuangtou, and Yujiagou sites', in Institute of Archaeology [CASS] (ed.) *Prehistoric Archaeology of South China and south-east Asia (Collected papers of an international academic workshop, celebrating 30 years for the excavations of Zengpiyan cave)*. Beijing: Wen wu chu ban she, pp. 116–127

Zhao, H.-L. 2011. 'An experimental study of flaking microblades', *Acta Anthropologica Sinica* 30(1): 22–31

Zhang, J.-F., Wang, X.-Q., Qiu, W.-L., Shelach, G., Hu, G., Fu, X., Zhuang, M.-G. and Zhou, L.-P. 2011. 'The Palaeolithic site of Longwanchan in the middle Yellow River, China: Chronology, Paleoenvironment and implications', *Journal of Archaeological Science* 38 (7): 1537–1550

Zhang, X., Shen, C., Gao, X., Chen, F. and Wang, C. 2010. 'Use-wear evidence confirms the earliest hafted chipped-stone adzes of Upper Palaeolithic in northern China', *Chinese Science Bulletin* 55: 229–236

Zhou, W. X., Sornette, D., Hill, R. A. and Dunbar, R. I. M. 2005. 'Discrete hierarchical organization of social group sizes', *Proceedings of the Royal Society B – Biological Sciences* 272: 439–444

Zilhão, J. 2006. 'Neandertals and Moderns mixed and it matters', *Evolutionary Anthropology* 15: 183–195

Zilhão, J. 2007. 'The emergence of ornaments and art: an Archaeological prespective on the origins of "behavioural modernity"', *Journal of Archaeological Research* 15: 1–54

Zilhão, J., Angelucci, D., Badal-García, E., d'Errico, F., Daniel, F., Dayet, L., Douka, K., Higham, T., Martínez-Sánchez, M., Montes-Bernárdez, R., Murcia-Mascarós, S., Pérez-Sirvent, C., Roldán-García, C., Vanhaeren, M., Villaverde, V., Wood, R. and Zapata, J. 2010. 'Symbolic use of marine shells and mineral pigments by Iberian Neandertals', *Proceedings of the National Academy of Sciences* 107(3): 1023–1028

Zilhão, J. and d'Errico, F. (eds.) 2003. *The Chronology of the Aurignacian and of the Transitional Technocomplexes*. Lisboa: Instituto Português de Arqueologia

Zilhão, J. and Trinkaus, E. (eds.) 2002. *Portrait of the Artist as a Child. The Gravettian Human Skeleton from the Abrigo do Lagar Velho and its Archaeological Context*. Trabalhos de Arqueologia 22. Lisboa: Instituto Português de Arqueologia.

Zotz L. 1955. *Das Paläolithikum in den Weinberghöhlen bei Mauern*. Berlin: Quartär-Bibliothek 2

Zvelebil, M. 1986. *Hunters in Transition: Mesolithic Societies of Temperate Eurasia and Their Transition to Farming*. Cambridge: Cambridge University Press

INDEX